LAKE O'HARA

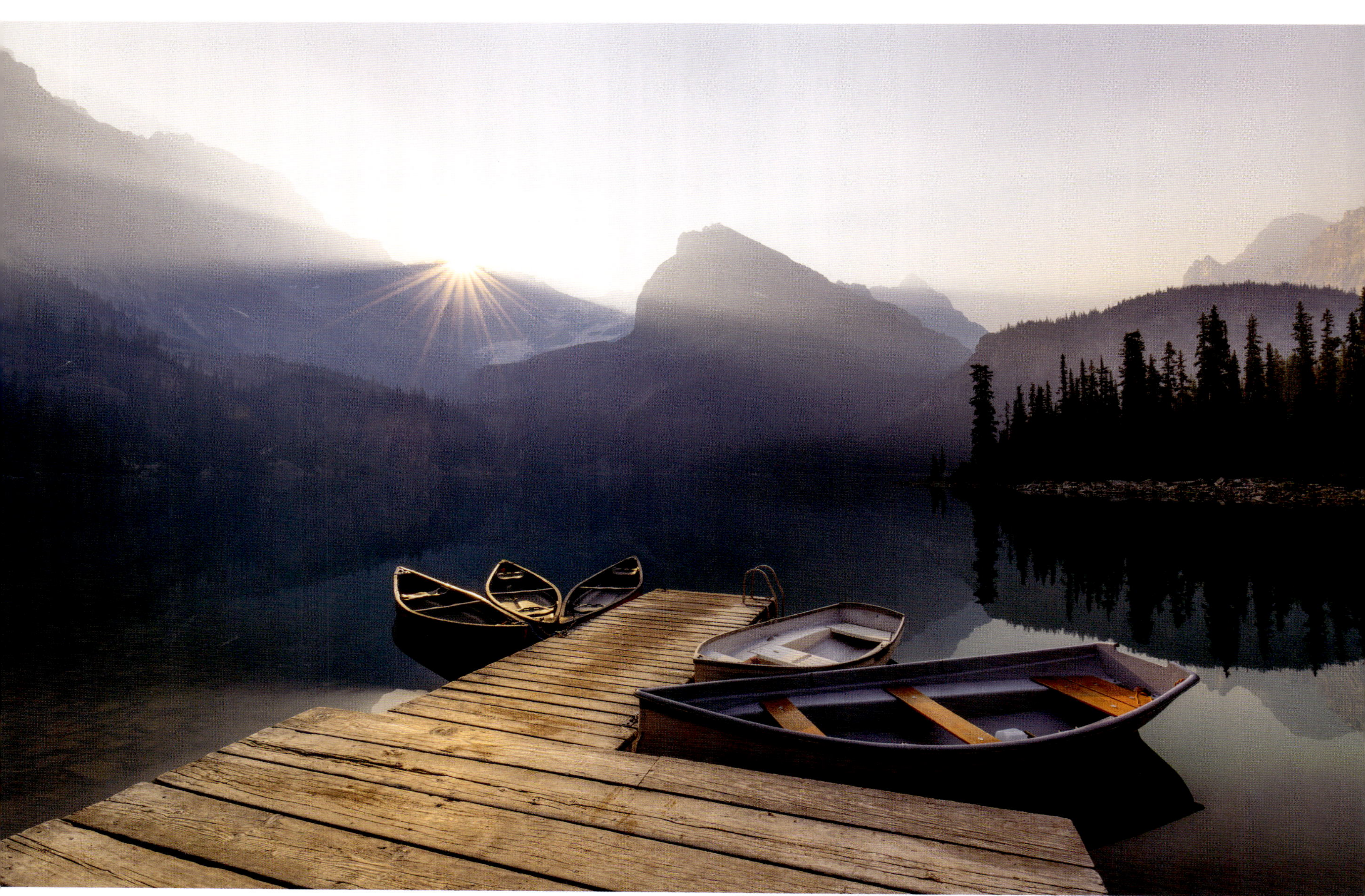

Lake O'Hara

SECLUDED JEWEL OF THE CANADIAN ROCKIES

TEXT AND PHOTOGRAPHY BY SCOTT FORSYTH

ESSAY BY MARC ST-ONGE

RMB

For information on purchasing bulk quantities of this book, or to obtain media excerpts or invite the author to speak at an event, please visit rmbooks.com and select the "Contact" tab.

RMB | Rocky Mountain Books Ltd.
rmbooks.com
@rm_books
facebook.com/rmbooks

Cataloguing data available from Library and Archives Canada
ISBN 9781771605946 (softcover)

Frontispiece: Sunburst over Mount Lefroy (2021). Gunwales of canoes light up with the rising sunburst over Mount Lefroy. A scene through the decades.

Printed and bound in China

We would like to take this opportunity to acknowledge the Traditional Territories upon which we live and work. In Calgary, Alberta, we acknowledge the Niitsítapi (Blackfoot) and the people of the Treaty 7 region in Southern Alberta, which includes the Siksika, the Piikuni, the Kainai, the Tsuut'ina, and the Stoney Nakoda First Nations, including Chiniki, Bearpaw, and Wesley First Nations. The City of Calgary is also home to Métis Nation of Alberta, Region III. In Victoria, British Columbia, we acknowledge the Traditional Territories of the Lkwungen (Esquimalt and Songhees), Malahat, Pacheedaht, Scia'new, T'Sou-ke, and W̱SÁNEĆ (Pauquachin, Tsartlip, Tsawout, Tseycum) Peoples.

We acknowledge the financial support of the Government of Canada through the Canada Book Fund and the Canada Council for the Arts, and of the province of British Columbia through the British Columbia Arts Council and the Book Publishing Tax Credit.

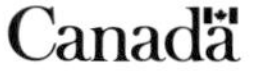
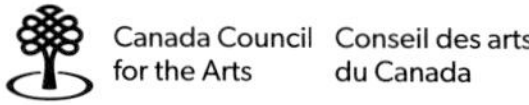
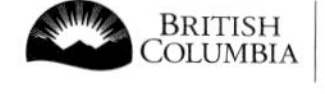
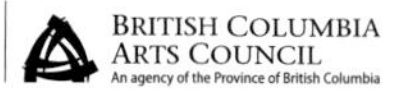

CONTENTS

To my spouse, Rossana Arcega, and our daughter, Maia Forsyth,
who accompanied me throughout the years of visits to Lake O'Hara,
waiting patiently as I stopped to take these photographs.

I am eternally grateful for your love and encouragement.
I hope that together we may have many more visits to come,
along with other members of our family and friends.

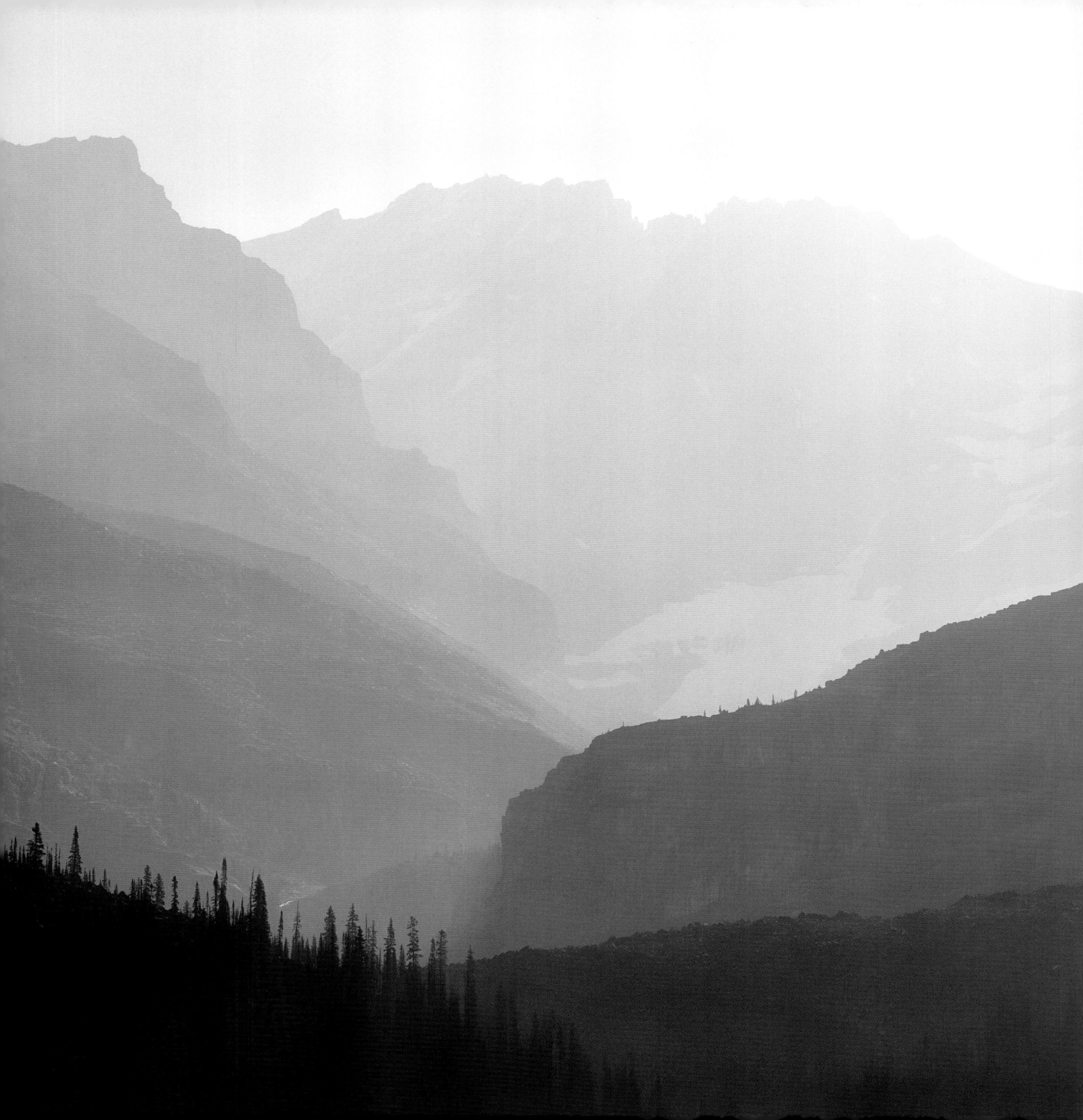

Acknowledgements

I am very grateful for the visionary support of Rocky Mountain Books publisher Don Gorman and his entire talented team, including Kirsten Craven and Chyla Cardinal, for championing nonfiction photography books and enabling them to exist in an ever-shifting business climate. Canada is a better place for it, with the dynamic and thoughtful publications RMB produces.

When I first contacted Lake O'Hara Lodge in 2006 to make a reservation, I had meticulously planned out the summer moon cycles so as to coordinate my stay with dark-sky opportunities. I could hear the smile in Alison Millar's voice on the other end of the lodge phone line as she explained there was a reservation wait list and all she could do was record my request. Fortunately, there was an opening at the beginning of the next season, and thus started my annual tradition of returning there each year. Over the years, lodge co-owners and operators Bruce and Alison Millar and I became friends, and it felt like coming home each and every season. I am very appreciative for their hospitality. Likewise I came to know Lonnie Wake, who worked at the lodge for many years and has become the next generation of operators, along with her spouse Jonny, to carry on the tradition. I'm very grateful to Lonnie for the opportunity to continue our annual visits, which enabled the completion of this book.

Yukness Ledges (2021)
Summer wildfire smoke is becoming a regular occurrence in the west, and here it provided cascading silhouettes with the foreground relief of Yukness Ledges along which the Lake O'Hara Alpine Circuit winds.

For many years I had the privilege of working as a photographer and Zodiac driver for Adventure Canada on trips through the Northwest Passage each autumn. The trips would be three weeks in duration, sometimes more, and given the remoteness involved, saying goodbye to family was always difficult. Our trips to Lake O'Hara became a way of spending quality time together, without cell phones and the internet. During these Arctic passage trips, I had the opportunity to meet fascinating staff members, including artists, scientists, and explorers, who were part of the resource team. This is how I came to meet Marc St-Onge, an inspiring geologist and equally remarkable person. For 37 years he served as officer and project leader for the Geological Survey of Canada, and has received numerous awards for his work. Marc and his colleagues are credited with finding what is perhaps considered the Holy Grail of geology – the oldest rocks on Earth – in the Coppermine River area in the Canadian Arctic. It is such a privilege to have Marc's geological story of Lake O'Hara included in the book. Far exceeding any reasonable expectation, he also created custom-drawn figures to illustrate how the broader principles behind the interaction of the Pacific Ocean with North America translates into the specific rock formations in the Lake O'Hara region. His contribution significantly elevates the content of the book, and I am very grateful!

Bruce Millar introduced me to the Lake O'Hara Lodge backcountry winter guide, and to mountaineer James Blench. James, in turn, taught me the basics of rope and harness rock climbing and guided me to the top of Wiwaxy Peaks for a panoramic view of the Lake O'Hara region.

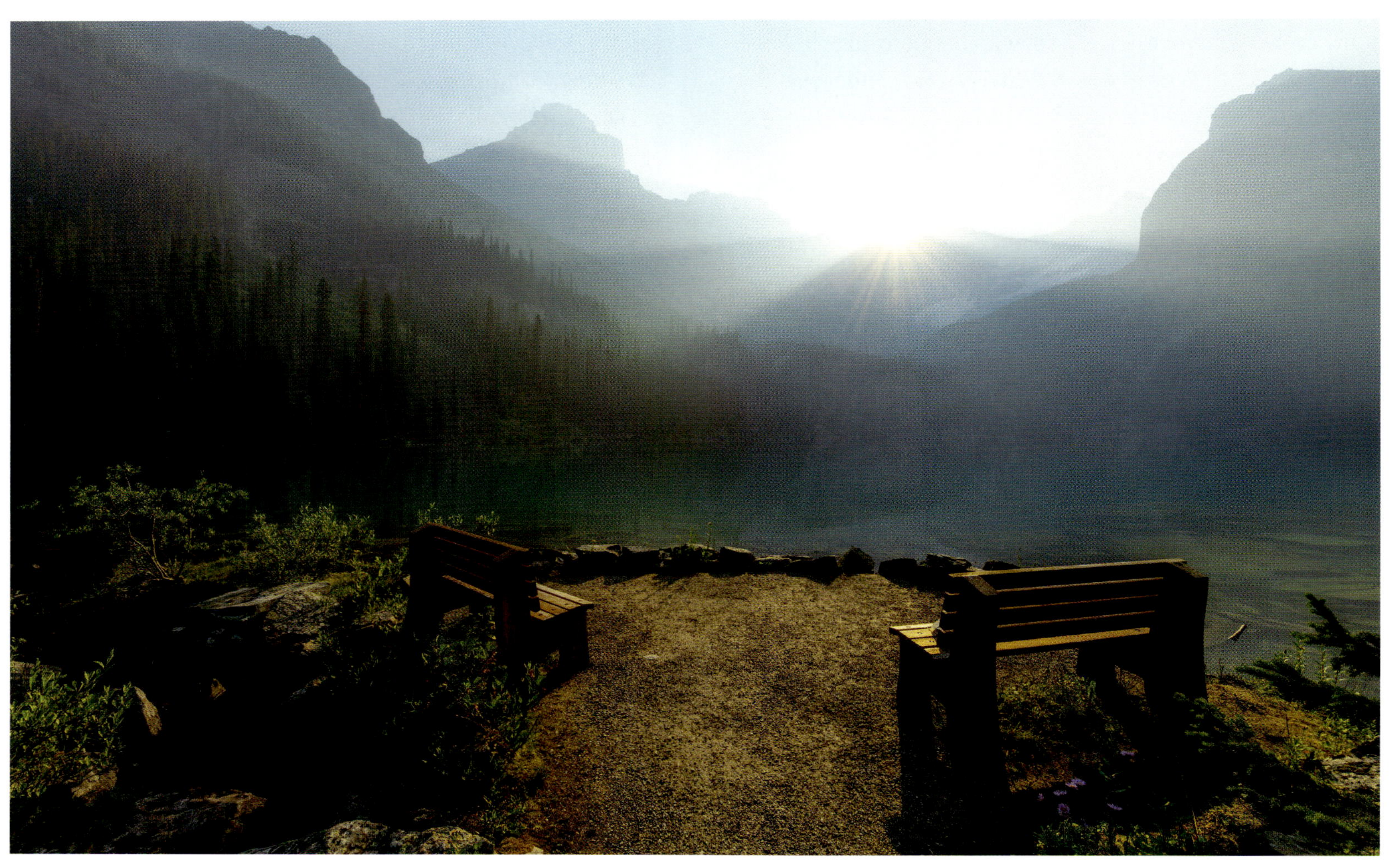

Contemplation (2021)
Out of reach of cell service, it's possible to sit on these benches and simply be present in an ephemeral scene of shifting light.

James was a very patient teacher and also, as often seems to happen with those around me, ended up helping me carry some of my camera gear back down the mountain. I blame it on my new hiking boots, which were too tight, but thank you very much, James, for an incredible experience!

I also wish to express gratitude to Adam Brash, spouse of my co-worker Shannon Brash, who happens to be related to Walter Feuz. Walter was the Swiss guide who was the caretaker at Lake O'Hara Lodge during the Second World War, when the lodge was closed to the public. Adam lent me Walter's original Eastman Kodak No. 2 Folding Autographic Brownie. It looked to be in excellent condition, but it was missing the front lens, so I was unable to take pictures with it—something for a future time. I did, however, bring it with me and took pictures through its viewfinder to record what Walter likely saw all those years ago.

Obtaining access to Lake O'Hara is a challenge. I've not been fortunate enough to win the day-use shuttle bus lottery for the last two seasons, and even the mountaineer guiding bus spaces were unavailable to James Blench and me this past season. Thanks very much to my former family medicine physician partner, Matthew Ferrao, who invited me to accompany him on his reservation to Lake O'Hara Lodge in August 2024. Without this opportunity, the book wouldn't have been complete, as I was able to capture the entire section on Linda Lake and Cathedral Prospect during this trip.

Finally, I'm very grateful to my family members who accompanied me on trips in recent years. My sister-in-law Hannah Arcega, and her partner, Rob Anderson, were patient models as I added them into compositions for scale. My stepson, Timothy Albinati, assisted me on the hike to Odaray Grandview Prospect, where I seemed to struggle with the weight of my 14-kg camera backpack. Those darned hiking boots that were too tight, again!

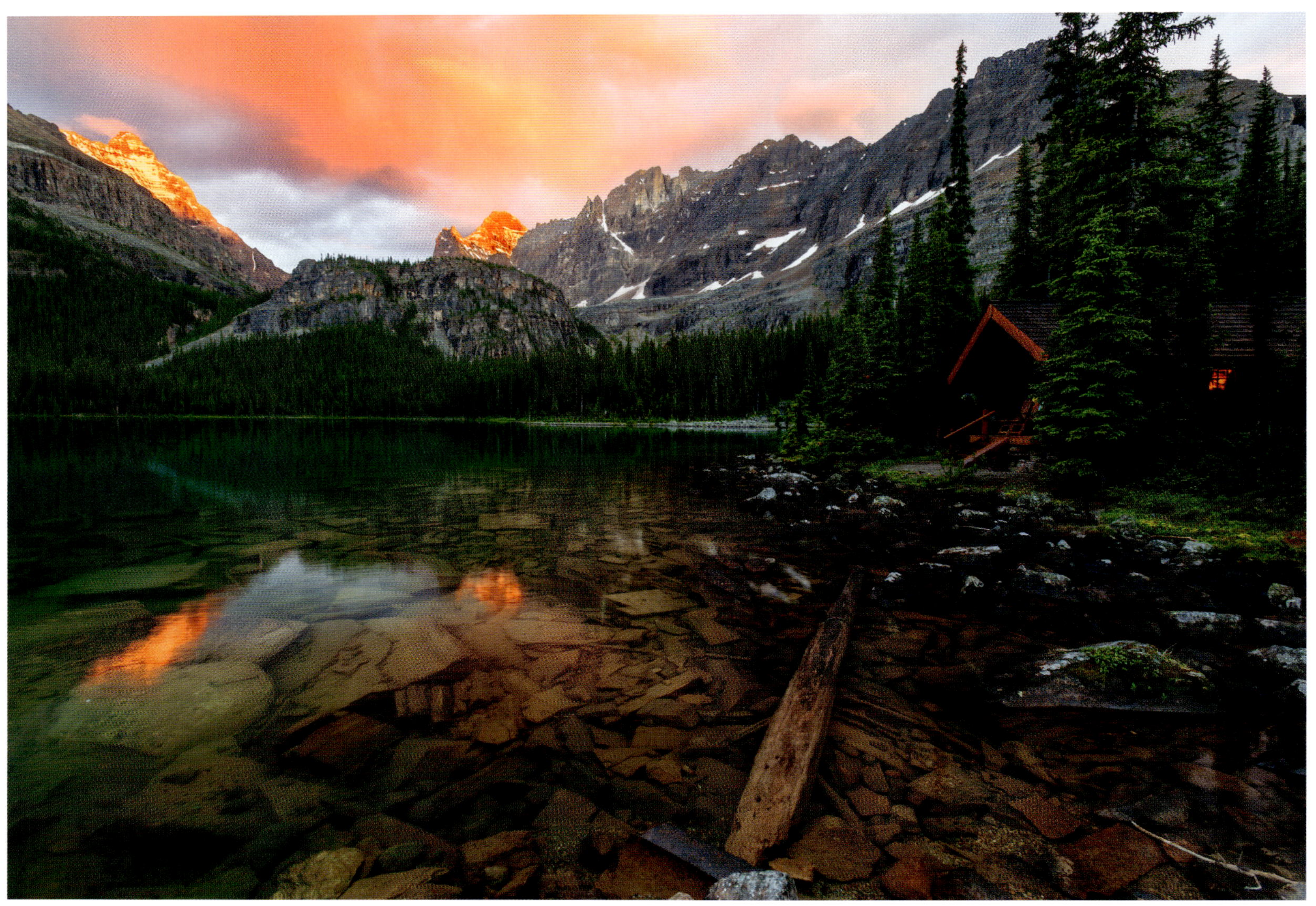

Alpine Glow (2007)
Sunset changes by the second during the final moments of the
day as the tips of Mount Biddle and Hungabee Mountain glow
against the alpine evening sky.

Introduction

ORIGINS

Lake O'Hara is one of the world's most beautiful backcountry Rocky Mountain hiking destinations. Only a short drive from the well-known Lake Louise, and just across the border from Alberta in Yoho National Park, in British Columbia, it is far less known even to residents of Calgary, the nearest city. Seclusion is part of its appeal, and this is the result of a purposeful effort by Parks Canada to carefully control access to this region in order to preserve the fragile and unique alpine environment for generations to come.

For those fortunate enough to stand upon the shoreline of Lake O'Hara, the effect of its beauty, combined with the sound of a distant waterfall and the scent of pine, is profound. Suddenly, all human-made architectural accomplishments seem a little smaller in the face of this ancient creation by forces hard to imagine. Later in the book, Marc St-Onge elucidates this mysterious process for us through his custom-created figures and text, explaining Lake O'Hara's geological origins and present-day state.

The origin story of Lake O'Hara is intricately tied to the existence of the Pacific Ocean and its interaction with western North America. As our geological knowledge expands through Marc's story, we begin to see 500-million-year-old ocean floor sediments thrust so high into the sky that they touch the clouds. This was the result of tectonic forces created by the opening of the Atlantic Ocean 180 million years ago, pushing North America over the subducting Pacific Ocean crust. This intense mountain-building period 180 million–66 million years ago stacked rock layers of differing periods into the complex, thrust-fault-laden wedges seen today as the rugged mountain peaks surrounding Lake O'Hara.

Tectonic forces drove the ancient rocks into the sky, while ice erosion sculpted them into their present-day form. The high-altitude mountain peaks caused the rising, moist Pacific Ocean air to condense into snow that compacted into ice. Glaciers formed over the tallest peaks, while the ice flowed outward following topography and meeting other ice flows, merging and expanding until the most recent climax of 17,000 years ago. At that time, the resulting Cordilleran Ice Sheet was 900 km wide and 2000–3000 m in elevation. The rapid climate warming of the Holocene (<11,700 years ago) marked the end of the glacial cycle. As the ice melted away, it left behind the cirques (e.g., Lake Oesa, Opabin Lake), mountain valleys (e.g., Cataract Brook), and glacial troughs or U-shaped valleys we see today. It is an immense construction process spanning hundreds of millions of years. As we take in the stunning scenery of Lake O'Hara, with a better understanding of how it came to be, it is truly humbling and inspiring.

INDIGENOUS PEOPLES

The Ktunaxa and Secwépemc nations inhabited the area around present-day Yoho National Park for thousands of years, including the Lake O'Hara region. It is thought the highland areas and trails around Lake O'Hara were part of their travel routes and sacred landscapes. It is quite likely there were many names and stories about the Lake O'Hara region, but due to the impacts of colonization on traditional oral history these names and stories remain underrepresented in today's historical accounts. Prior to the formation of Yoho (Cree for "awe") National Park, the Ktunaxa used the area, especially Kicking Horse Pass, to cross the Rockies for bison hunting on the eastern side of the mountains.

THE CANADIAN PACIFIC RAILWAY

The Canadian Pacific Railway's (CPR's) transcontinental line was completed in 1885, and in 1886 the Yoho and Glacier national parks were created on the same day, making them the second and third national parks in the country, after the creation of Banff National Park. The creation of these parks contributed to the interruption of Indigenous use of the lands, and today Parks Canada is working with local Indigenous Peoples to address issues relating to their rightful access to this region.

The surveyor James J. McArthur was the first European to describe Lake McArthur and Lake O'Hara, the former being named after him. Lake O'Hara is named after Lieutenant-Colonel Robert O'Hara, a surveyor who is said to have first learned of the lake from McArthur, visiting it in 1889. The lake was formally named in 1894 by Samuel Evans Stokes Allen, a Philadelphia alpinist. It was common practice at this time for mountains and lakes to be named after the government and CPR surveyors documenting them. However, these surveyors often relied on the assistance of Indigenous guides and would sometimes incorporate their guides' names for locations such as Wiwaxy Peaks, Yukness and Odaray mountains, Lake Oesa, and Opabin Lake.

Lake O'Hara became part of the CPR's edge-of-the-wilds camps marketed to adventurous tourists interested in something more backcountry than the luxurious Banff Springs and Chateau Lake Louise hotels. In 1906, the Alpine Club of Canada (ACC) was founded to develop hiking routes and mountaineering. In the alpine meadows, where there were a series of sleeping cabins, the CPR Swiss Guides constructed Wiwaxy Lodge in 1912, the oldest structure still in the region. It was a horse camp, and as its popularity grew, the CPR completed construction of the present-day Lake O'Hara Lodge in 1926 on the peninsula. The following winter, the 11 log cabins in the alpine meadows were drawn by horse to their current place along the peninsula shoreline.

In the early days of the railway, the CPR issued special passes to encourage painters and other artists to experience the natural beauty of the O'Hara region and help promote it through their artistic creations. Among such painters was one of the original Group of Seven, Lawren Harris, who told his colleague J.E.H. MacDonald about this natural wonder. MacDonald visited the region in 1924 and fell under its spell, returning annually for the next seven years, resulting in a prodigious number of sketches and paintings of the region.

PARKS CANADA

Today, the Lake O'Hara region is managed by Parks Canada, which carefully limits the number of visitors to the area during its June–October season through its own highly popular campsite and the Elizabeth Parker Hut (EP Hut) operated by the ACC. Visitors arrive to the region by Parks Canada's day-use shuttle bus, which requires reservations allotted through an annual lottery. They are transported from the parking lot up an 11-km road to Le Relais Day Shelter near the shoreline of Lake O'Hara. Lake O'Hara Lodge and the Lake O'Hara Trails Club operate the day shelter, which provides updated information on the extensive network of hiking trails.

MAKING THIS BOOK

Everyone who visits Lake O'Hara wishes to return. I first came to the region in 2007, in June when the trails and lakes were still covered in snow and ice, and then in early October that same year when the snowcapped mountains were reflected in the open water of Lake O'Hara. Like so many before me, I too fell under O'Hara's spell. I have returned with my family every year but two over the past 18 years, and the two missed seasons were due to the COVID-19 pandemic. This book is a collection of photographs taken over this time span from 2007 to 2025, starting with my very first digital camera (Nikon D200) and ending with my current mirrorless Nikon Z series cameras and lenses. Looking back, I am surprised by the quality of the 2007 images, showing that, ultimately, it's not the camera but rather the subject that is most important.

The book follows Gem Trek's *Lake O'Hara Map and Trail Guide* spellings for place and trail route names and hiking divisions. Each section touches upon elements relating to the pictures taken and also items of natural and historical relevance, in the hope that if you hike here, you can pre-visualize the sights you will encounter. Given the restrictions on visitors to this region, it is also my desire to share its visual wonder with those who may never have the opportunity to visit. No photograph can ever substitute for the experience of being in a location, but hopefully this book helps stir the imagination.

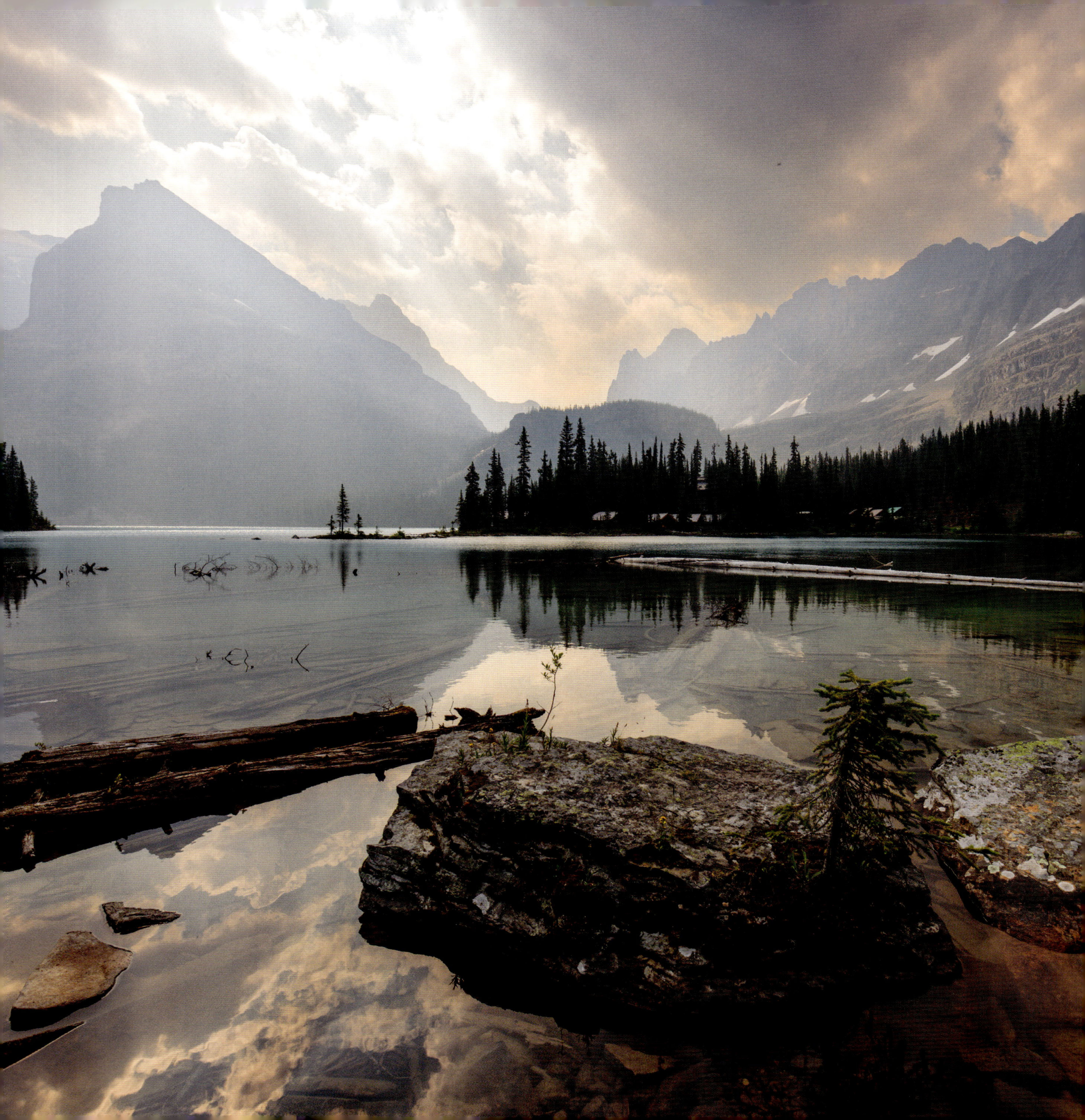

PART ONE

Lakeshore Trail

Lakeshore Trail, also referred to as Lake O'Hara Circuit, is a 3-km loop following the shoreline of Lake O'Hara. The elevation gain is negligible and the route is often utilized for access to the trailheads of the grand hikes to Lake Oesa, Opabin Lake, and the alpine circuit trails. However, the lakeshore trail is a worthy destination in its own right, offering some of the most beautiful vantage points in all of the Lake O'Hara region. The symmetrical reflections of the surrounding mountains create surreal compositions. No special photography equipment required here; a stroll around the lake with a cell phone camera will garner calendar-worthy pictures. It often requires getting up early or lingering after sunset to catch the lake's surface free of ripples from the sun-generated breezes. When calm descends on the lake, the resulting scene literally stops people in their tracks.

One recent July, the smoke of forest fires lingered lightly in the area for a few days. I recall using a smoke-coloured filter with a film camera in my early days of photography. Paradoxically, the undesirable condition of atmospheric smoke actually turned out to create some of my favourite Lake O'Hara photographs. The morning sun rays reflected in the lake could be fully appreciated due to their interaction with atmospheric particles. No smoke lens required.

Early Start (2021)
From left to right, Mount Schäffer, Mount Biddle, Opabin Plateau, and Yukness Mountain provide an alpine backdrop along Lake O'Hara Lakeshore Trail.

Adding to the unparalleled natural scenic beauty of Lake O'Hara is the gentle background sound of running water from Seven Veils Falls. The effect of this visual beauty, combined with the soothing sound and scent of pine, washes over visitors, displacing the noise of daily urban experience with a peace that is medicinal. Sometimes a lone rowboat will drift by on the distant horizon, or a red canoe will glide through the scene as a reminder of scale, while also providing evidence that what we see actually exists. It's like watching somebody step out of a calendar cover before your very eyes.

Lakeshore Trail is also often referred to as the Adeline Link Circuit, and there is a commemorative plaque along the trail. The conditions that led to the dust bowl of the 1930s, associated with increased Pacific Northwest forest fires choking the skies of the American Glacier National Park, led a Chicago couple, George (Tommy) K.K. Link and his spouse Adeline, to visit Lake O'Hara in 1928. Like most who happen upon this lake, they were captivated by it and returned every season for the next 14 years. In September, guests at Lake O'Hara Lodge often stayed only for a night, with the exception of the Group of Seven painter J.E.H. MacDonald and his painting companions and guides, Peter and Catharine Whyte. This group of extended-stay guests, including the Links, became a cohesive society, sharing a common appreciation for intellectual subjects, combined with humour, love of poetry, and a predisposition for vigorous activity. MacDonald introduced the Links to

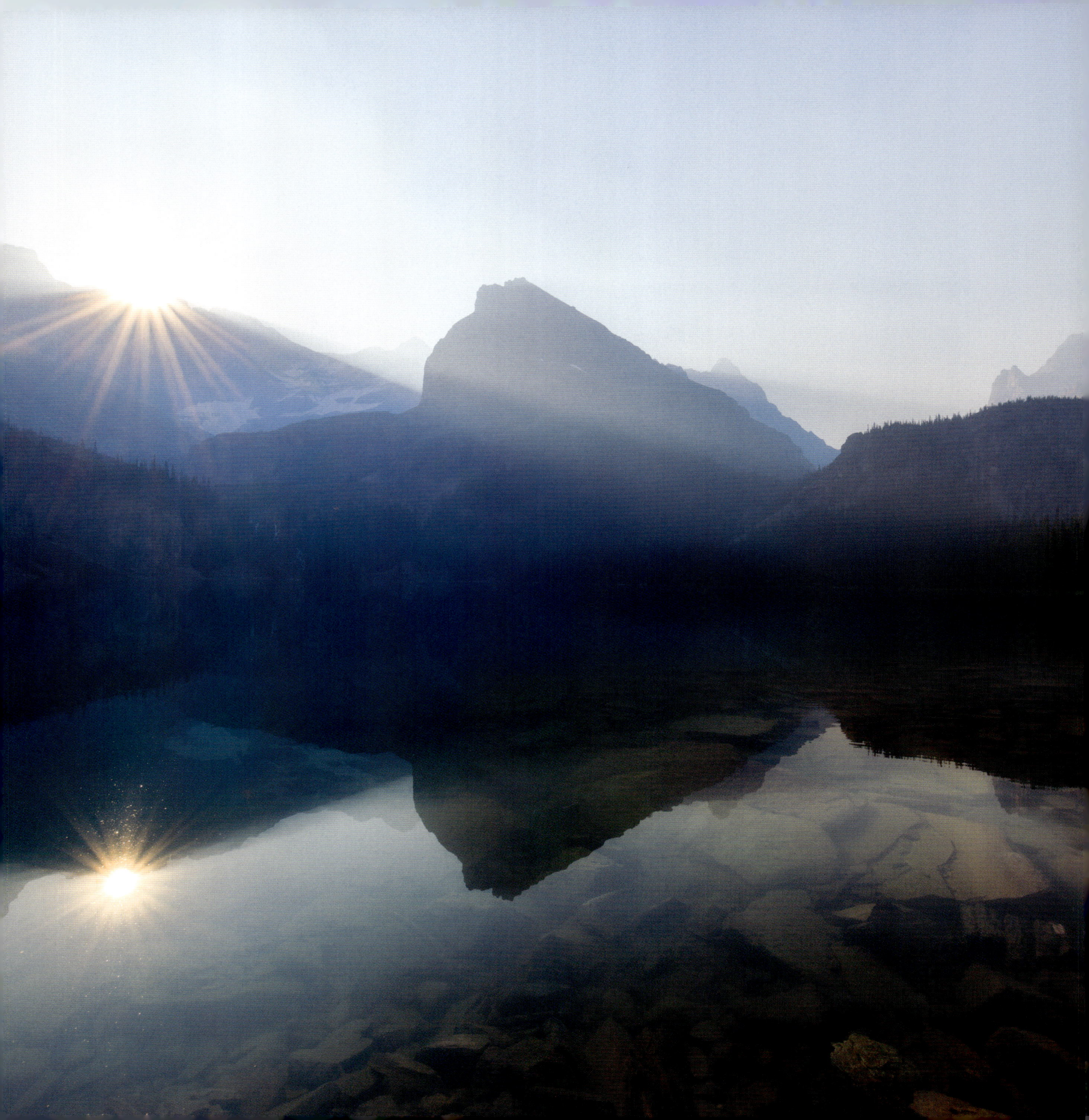

his favourite sketching sites as he expanded their knowledge of the area. In September 1930, after a morning of sketching on the Opabin Plateau, MacDonald conducted a ceremony, uttering secret sacred words and pronouncing the five of them in the group to be members of the "Opabin Shale-Splitters." Each of them then split a slab of shale to commemorate the event. A few days later, the group accompanied MacDonald to Lake Oesa, where he sketched an early snowfall, the subject of his last great large-format painting before his untimely death in 1932 at the age of 59.

During the Second World War, the CPR closed both its large hotels (Banff Springs and Chateau Lake Louise) and its smaller resorts such as Lake O'Hara Lodge. Walter Feuz was the caretaker of the lodge during those summers and the Links were allowed to visit. Adeline was a scientist, teacher, and committee chairwoman for the American Association of University Women, in addition to being an accomplished pianist and trail companion who would cook for the group as the chef de cuisine.

The lakeshore trail was not yet a loop at this time. Reasonable access to Lake Oesa Trail required rowing across Lake O'Hara, and Tommy and Adeline would often peruse the shoreline, scouting for a future trail route that wouldn't need to rise more than 152 m. In 1942, through their exploring and scrambling, they identified a possible path that required fracturing a vertical, blade-like cliff rock. The following year, in 1943, the crew went to work on the proposed circuit, Adeline joining them in the mornings and spending the afternoons in the kitchen preparing the evening meals. It took the crew (Tommy and Adeline Link, Walter and Ronnie Feuz, and Carson Simpson) a month of arduous labour to complete the circuit, and Adeline was the first person to walk around it. They named it "Wiwaxy Trail," and Adeline and Tommy returned to Chicago a few days later. Sadly, less than two weeks after that, Adeline suffered a stroke that would end her life in November 1943 at the age of 51.

In 1944, Tommy returned to Lake O'Hara, where he strewed her ashes in accordance with her wishes on a special rock they had shared. In late August 1946, three years after her departure, the surviving members of the trail crew stood at the dedication point and held a ceremony proclaiming the lakeshore trail to be the Adeline Link Circuit in her honour. A storm had been raging for three days, leaving a blanket of fresh snow over the forests, while the morning mist slowly rose off the lake as occasional breaks in the clouds revealed the surrounding mountain peaks. This is one of the most beautiful times of the year at Lake O'Hara, and must have befitted this event. A leisurely reflective stroll around the Adeline Link Circuit is well worth the time.

Natural Smoke Filter (2021)
Morning sun rises above distant Mount Lefroy through the lingering smoke of July wildfires.

Overleaf **Morning** (2021)
Surreal view for a morning coffee on Lake O'Hara Lodge's lakeshore cabin porch. This was the same vista seen by Group of Seven painter J.E.H. MacDonald in the 1920s.

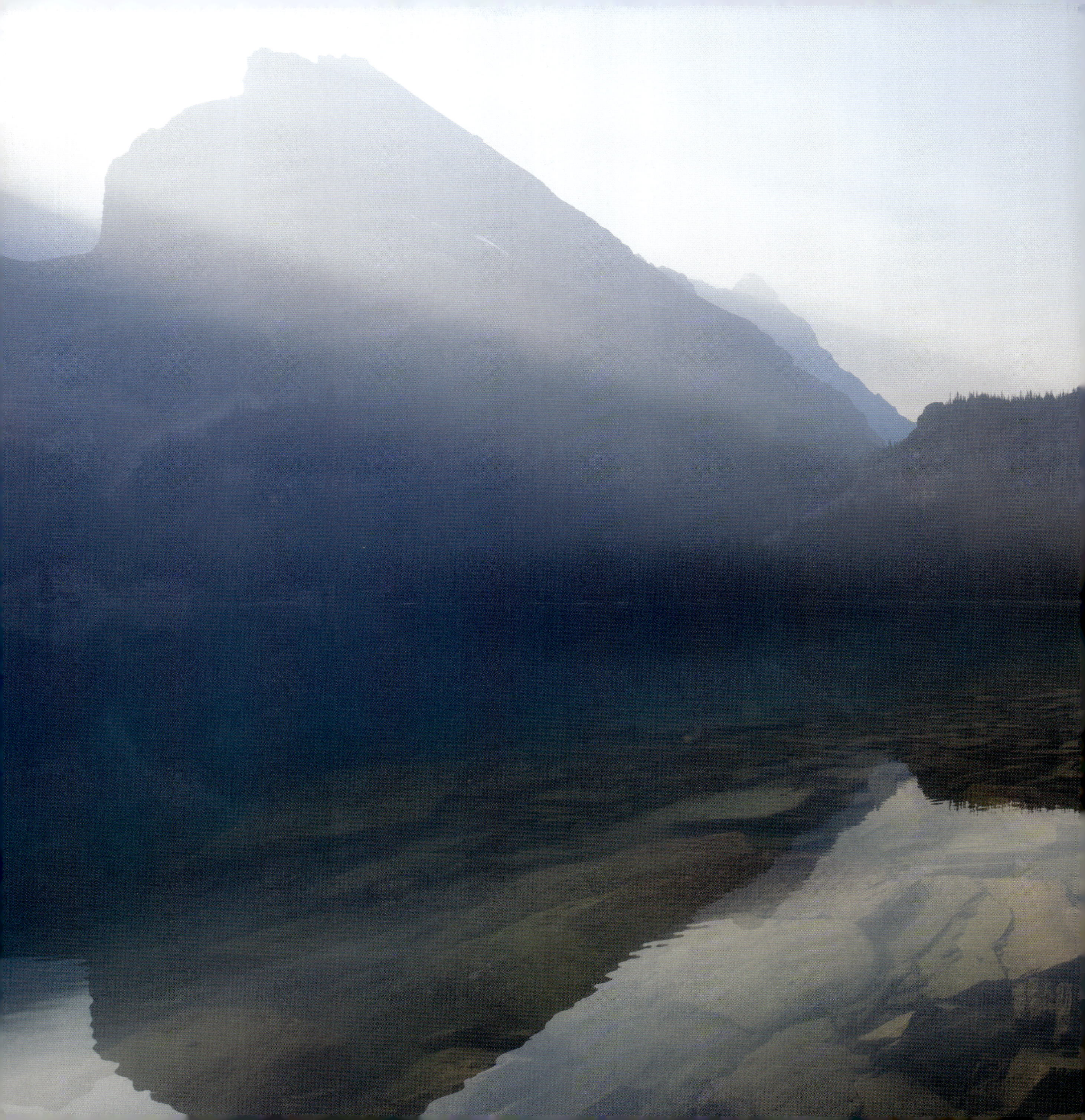

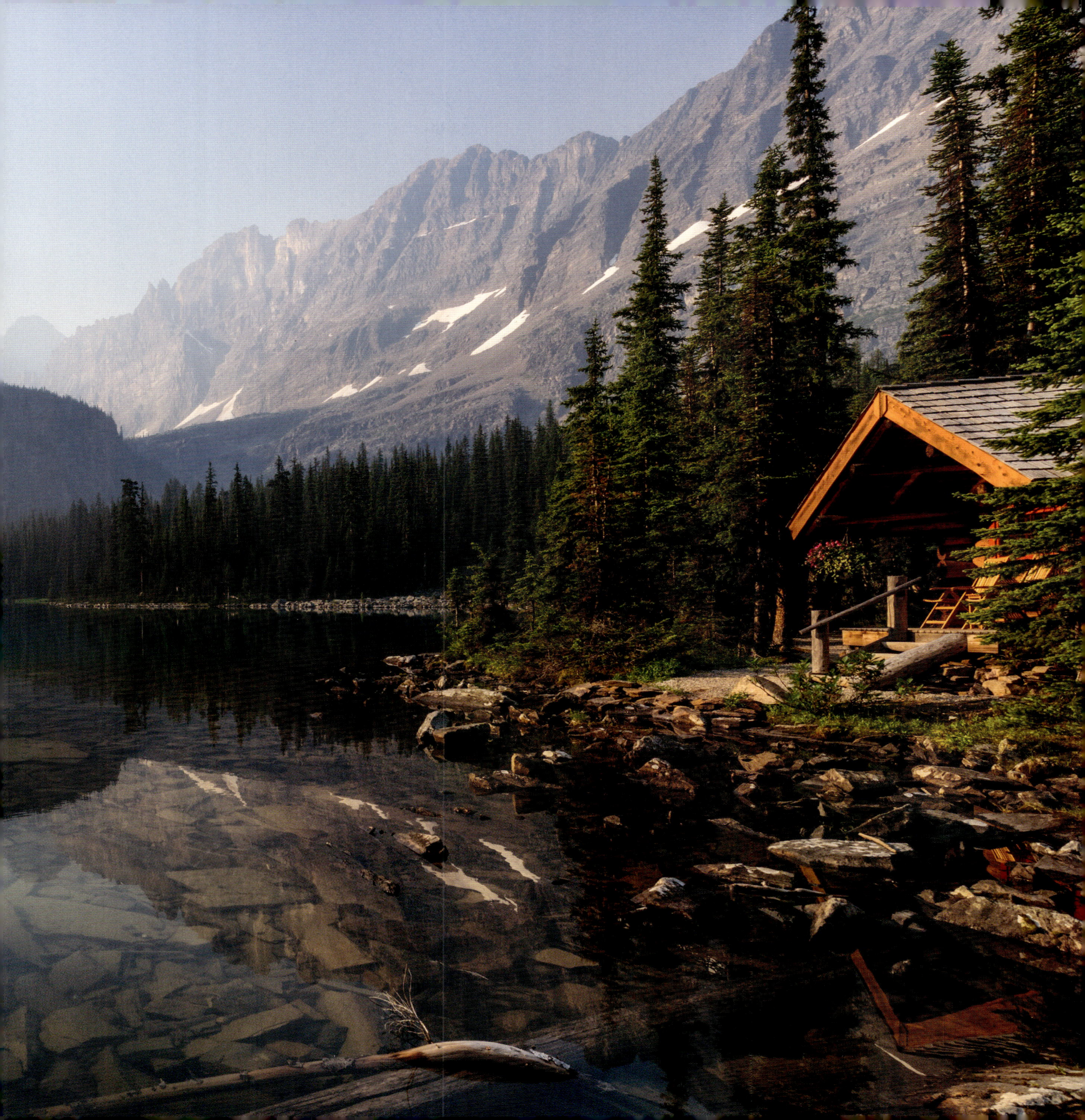

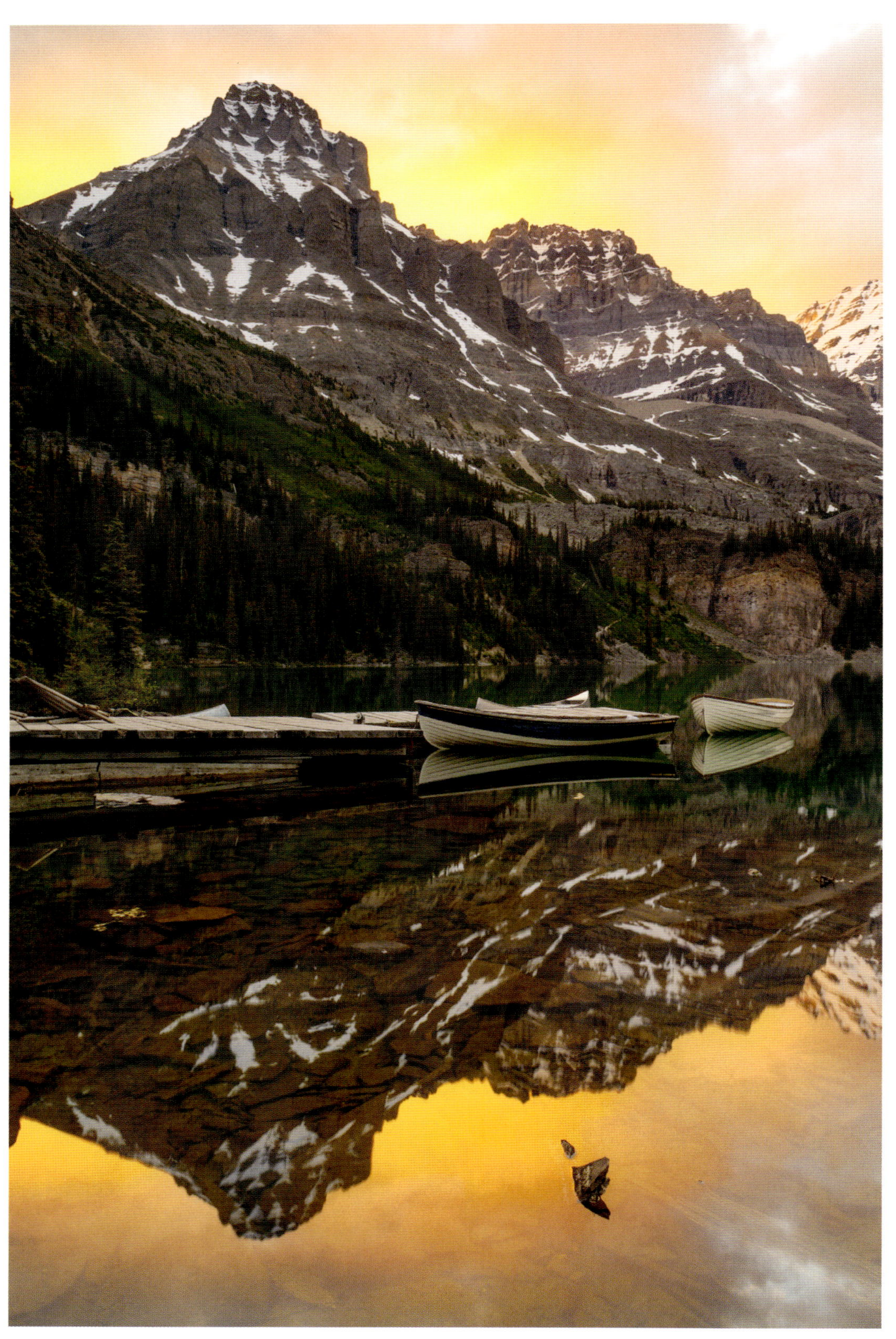

Early Rising's Reward (2007)
As the temperature increases with the rising sun, so do the winds. A 5:00 a.m. outing captured the stillness of this reflection on Lake O'Hara.

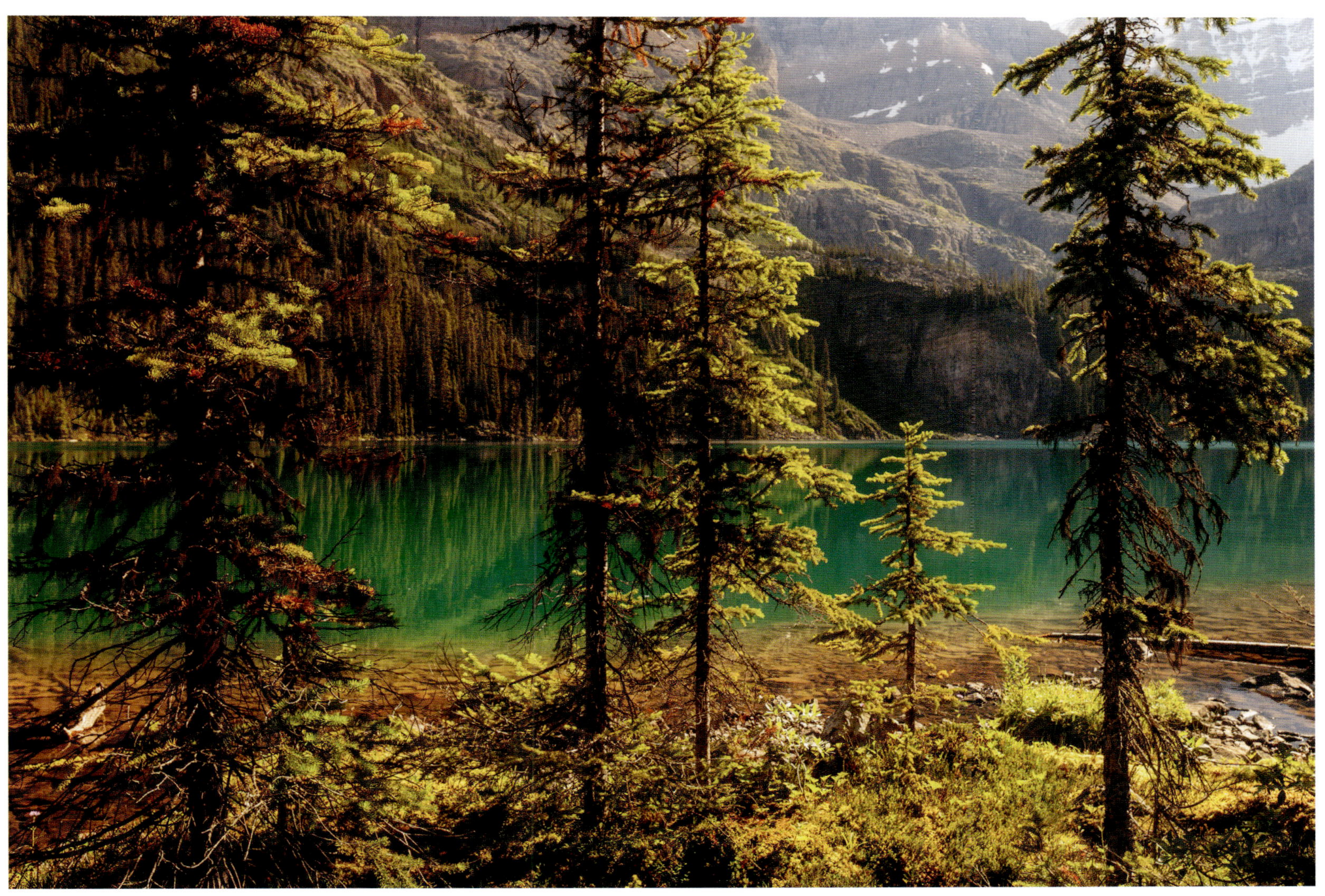

Afternoon Light (2007)
Rock flour glacial sediment in Lake O'Hara provides an
ever-changing emerald hue throughout the relatively short
summer season.

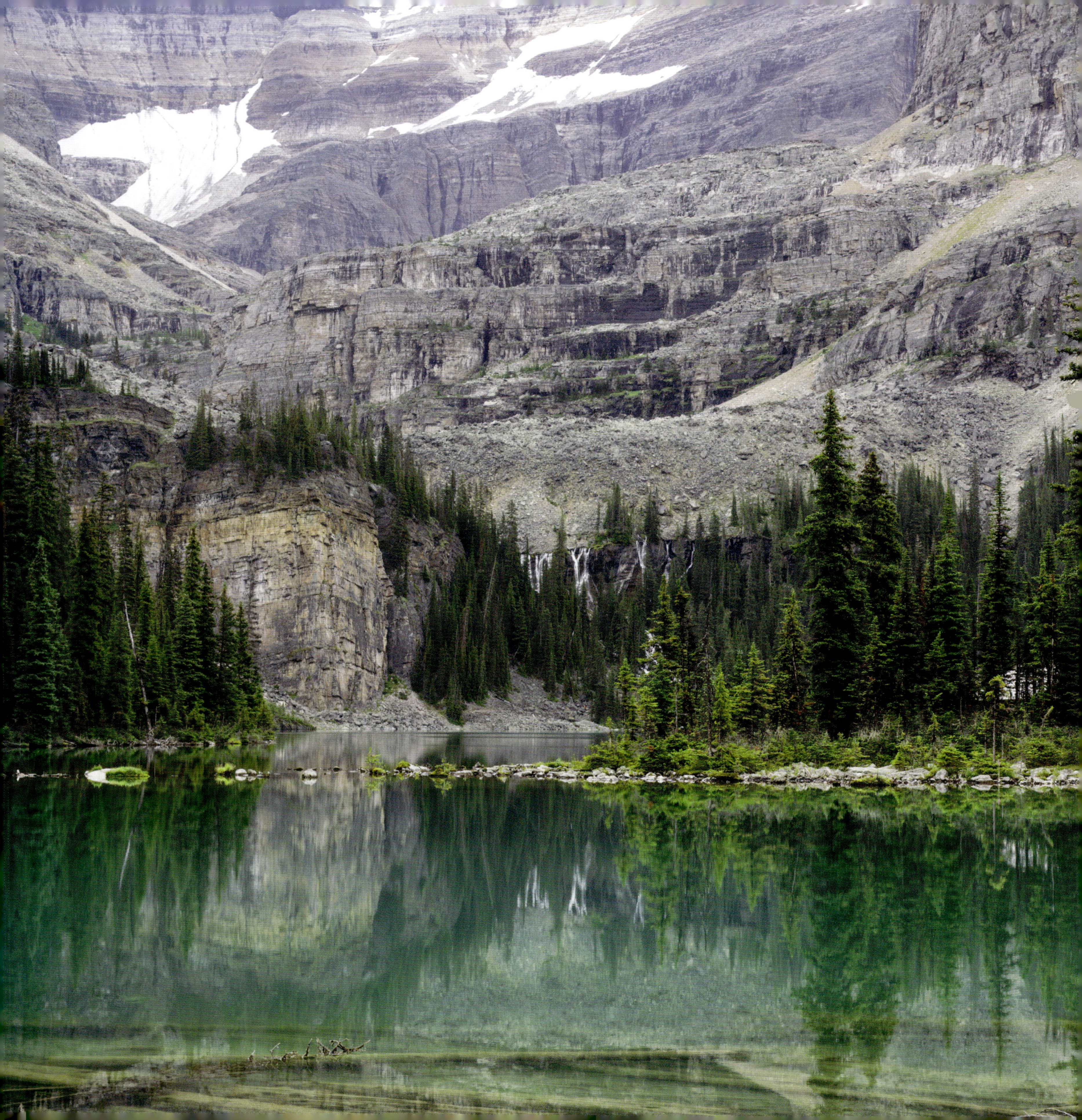

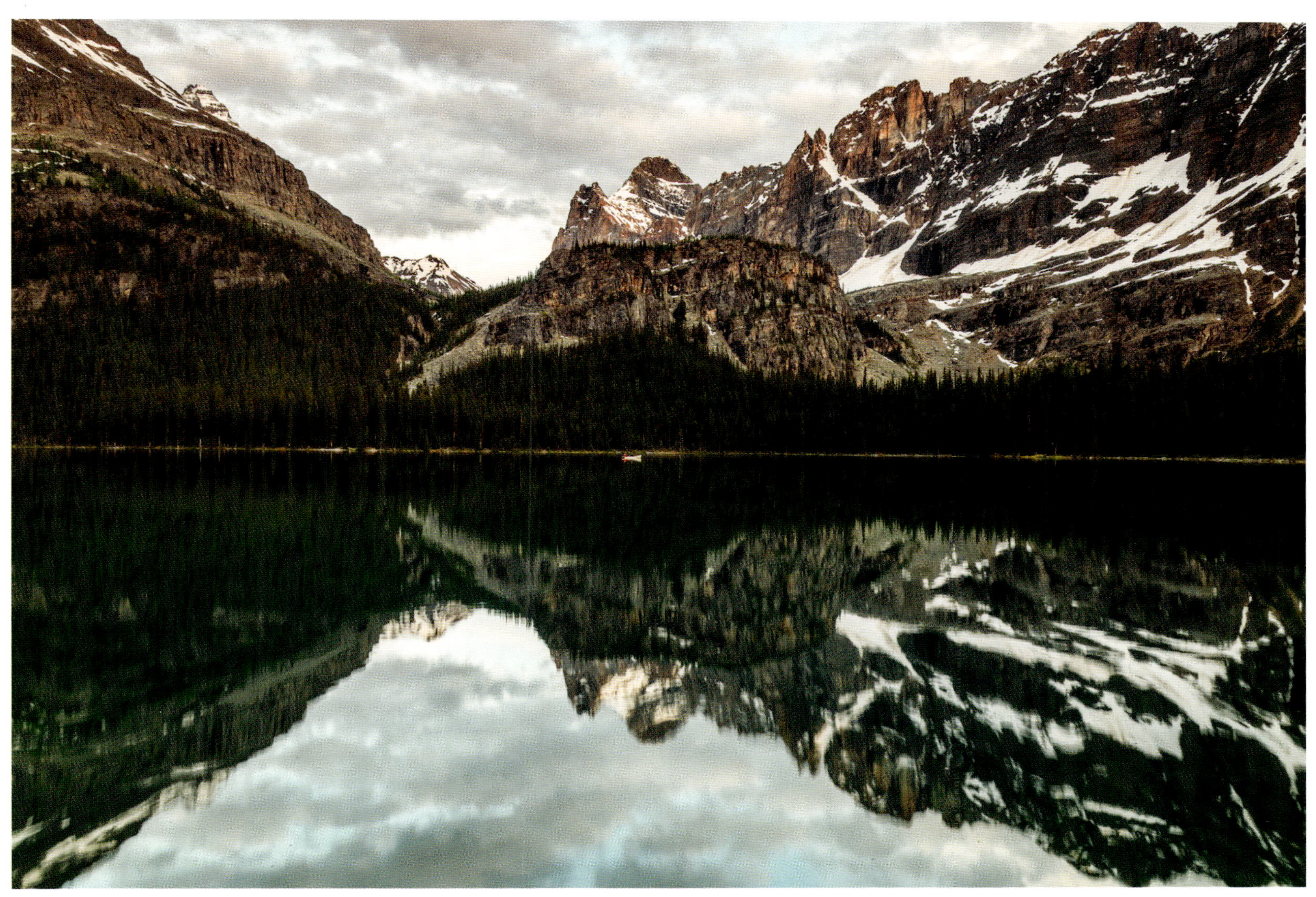

Solitary Row (2007)
A morning row in a Lake O Hara Lodge boat. Parks Canada carefully restricts access to this backcountry region to protect its delicate alpine environment and prevent overcrowding.

Seven Veils Falls Refection (2024)
The quiet of Lake O'Hara, encapsulated by towering rock walls, is punctuated only by the distant soft sound of Seven Veils Falls.

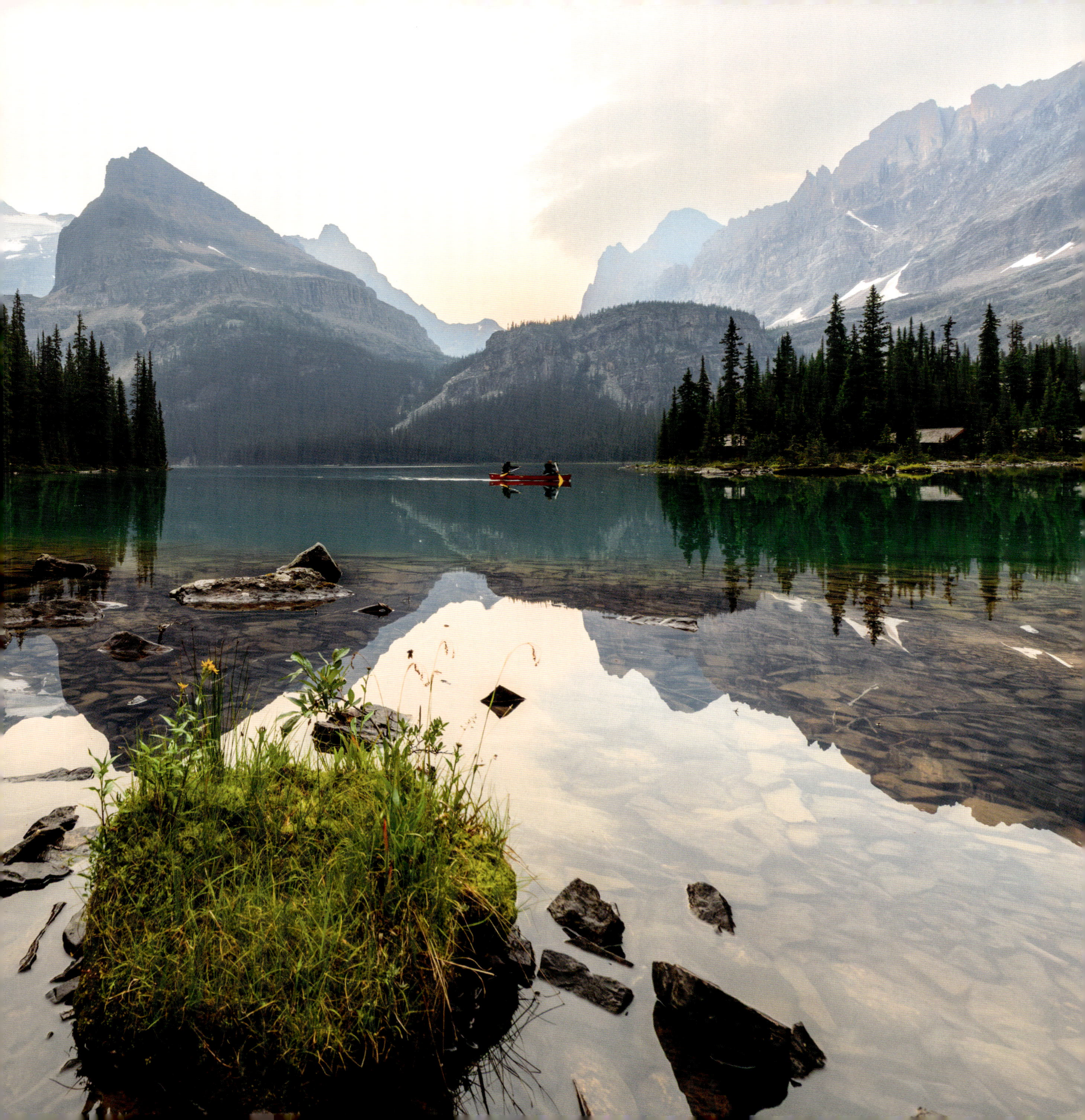

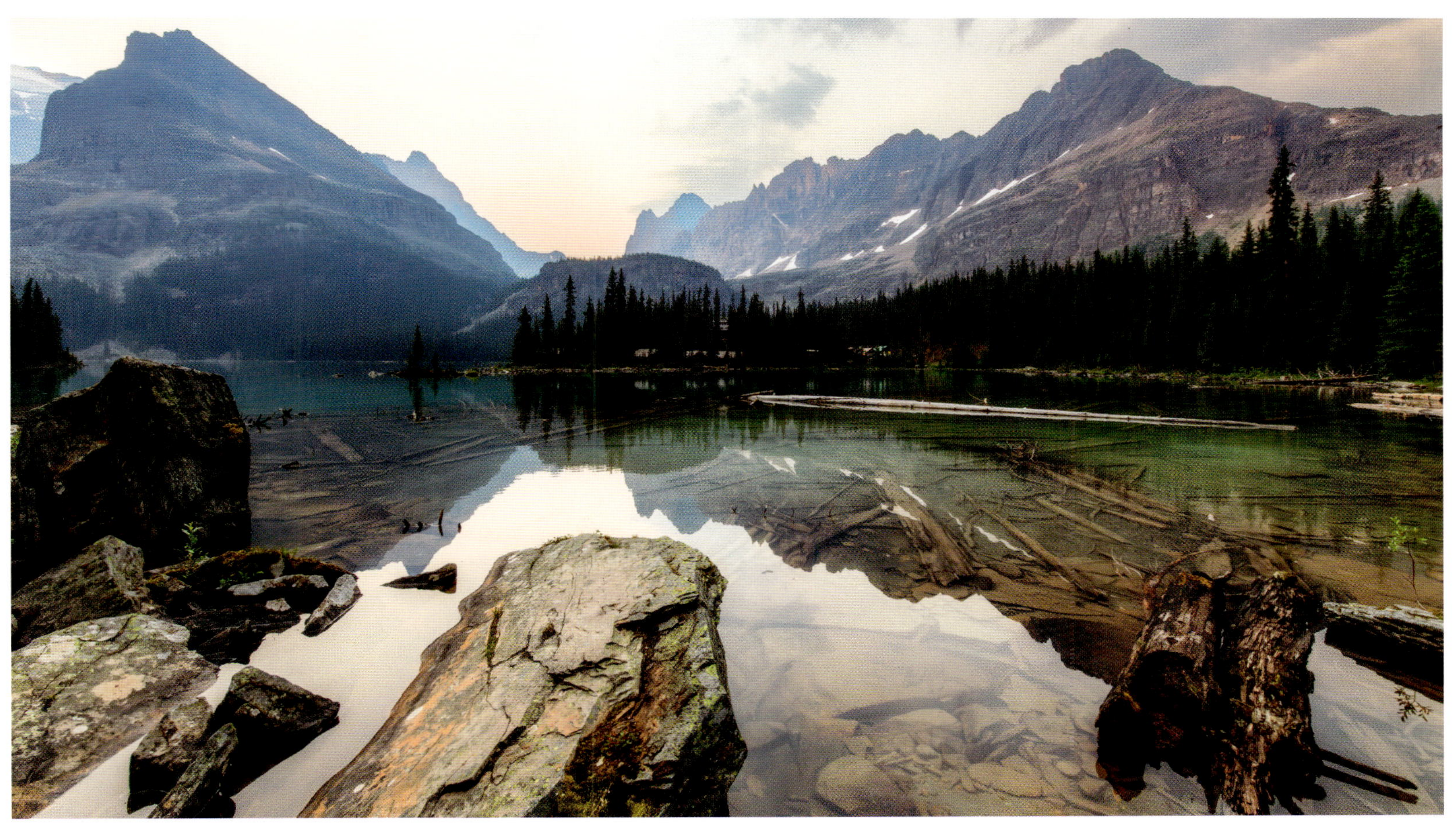

Submerged Leading Lines (2021)
Fallen trees submerged in Lake O'Hara shoals lead our eyes to
Lake O'Hara Lodge's cabins.

Morning Paddle (2021)
Paddlers glide through still reflections on Lake O'Hara.

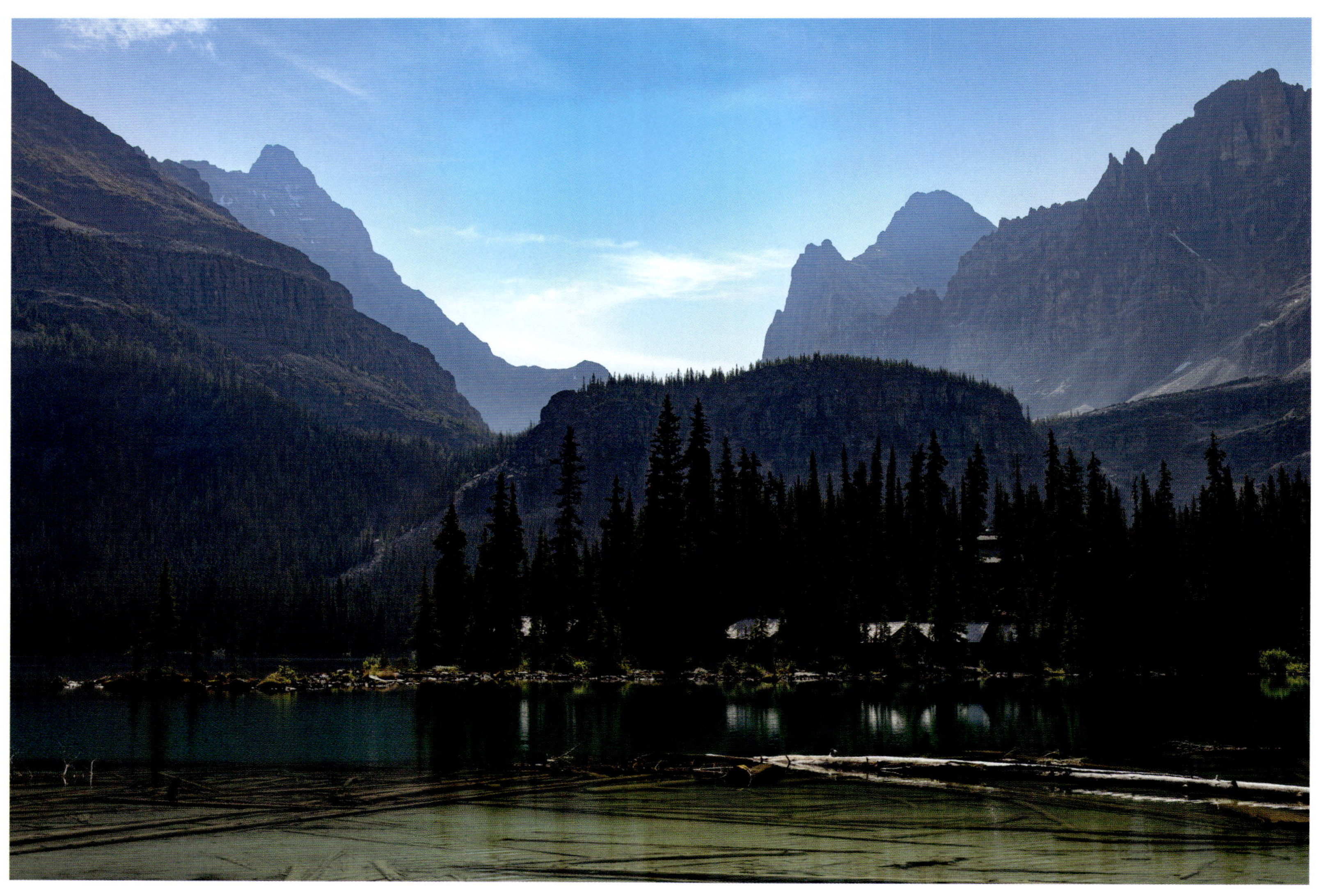

Secluded Gem (2025)
Encapsulated by towering rock walls, such as Hungabee Mountain and Mount Biddle in the distance, Lake O'Hara is an ideally secluded gem in the Canadian Rockies.

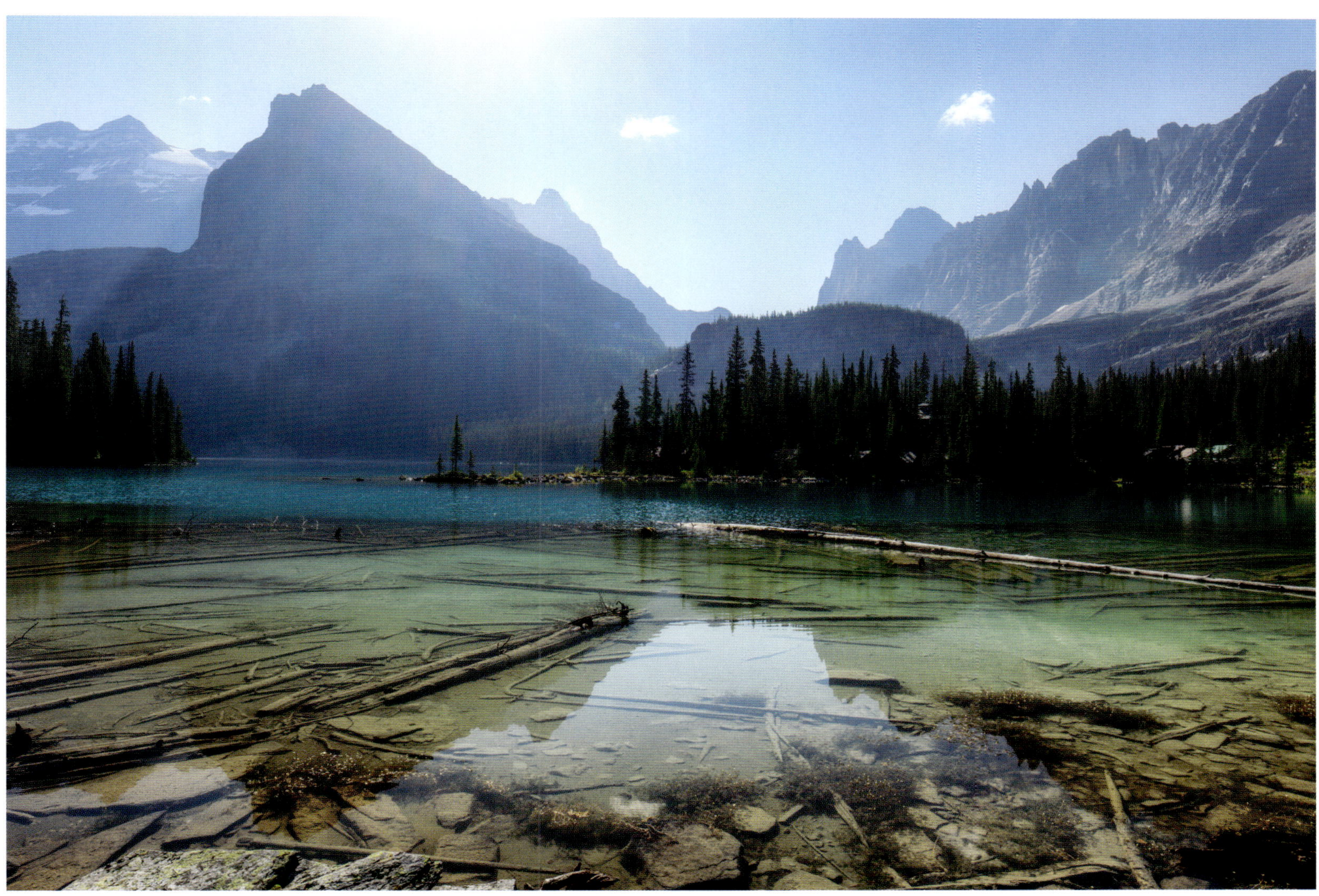

Natural Distraction (2025)
The abundant beautiful views along Lake O'Hara Alpine Circuit
often lead to distraction, causing delays while on the way to
any number of trailhead routes that depart from the circuit.

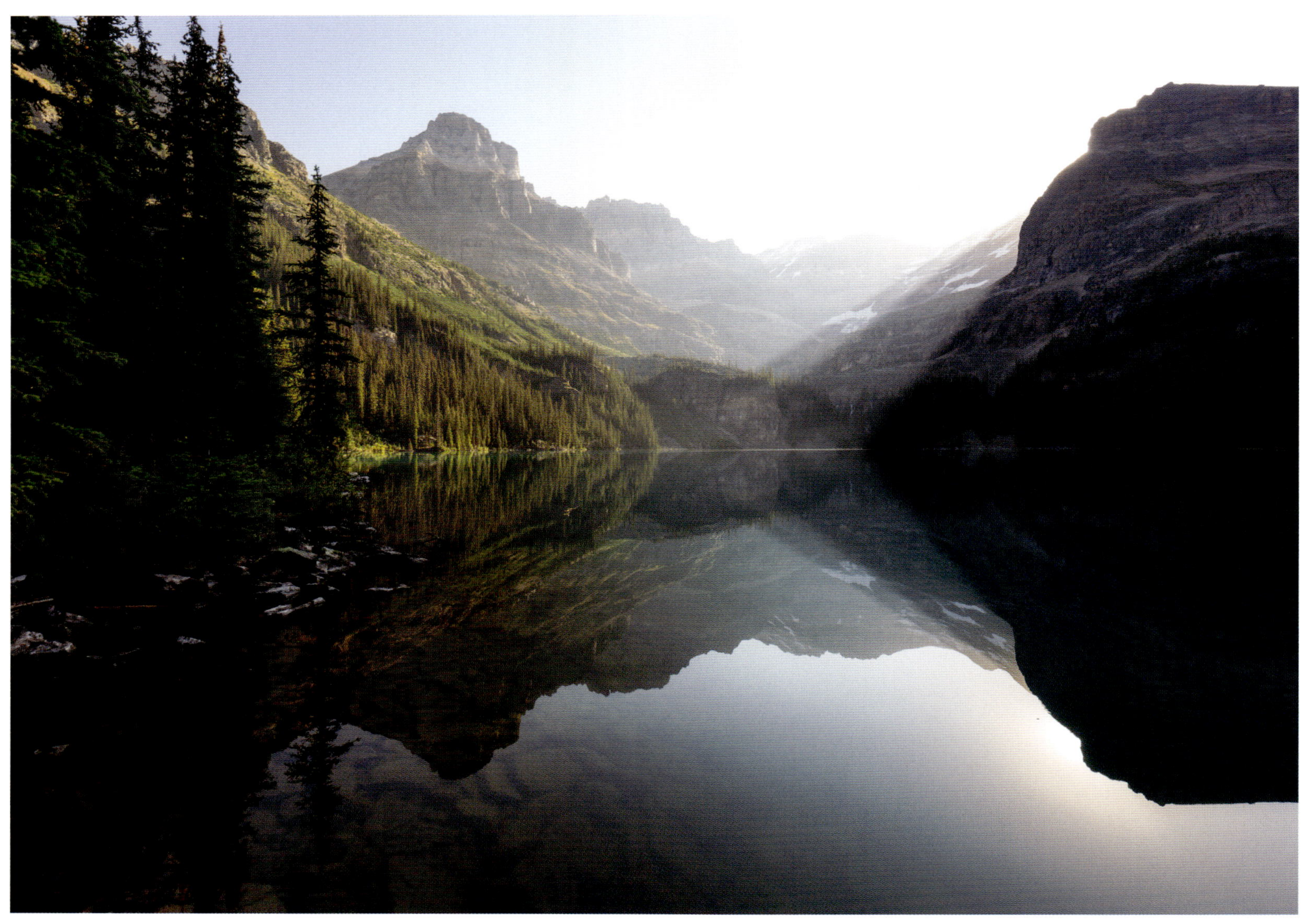

Layers of Line (2025)
Sunrays combine with moisture in the morning air to create virtual geometric shapes from the shadows of Yukness Mountain.

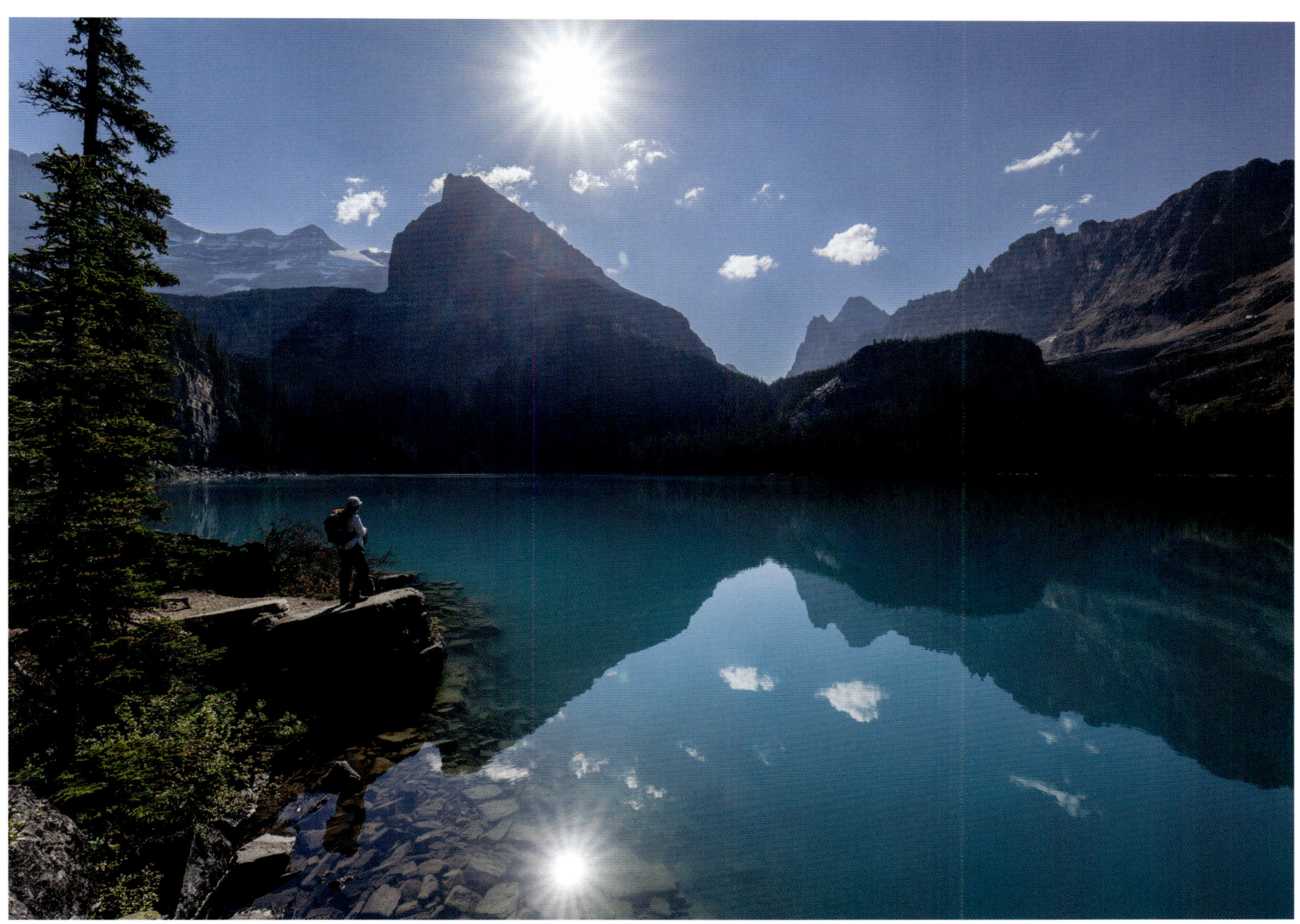

Autumn Blues (2025)
A morning hiker (Rossana Arcega) peers out over the perfectly
still reflection atop the cerulean water of Lake O'Hara, thick
with autumn glacier sediment.

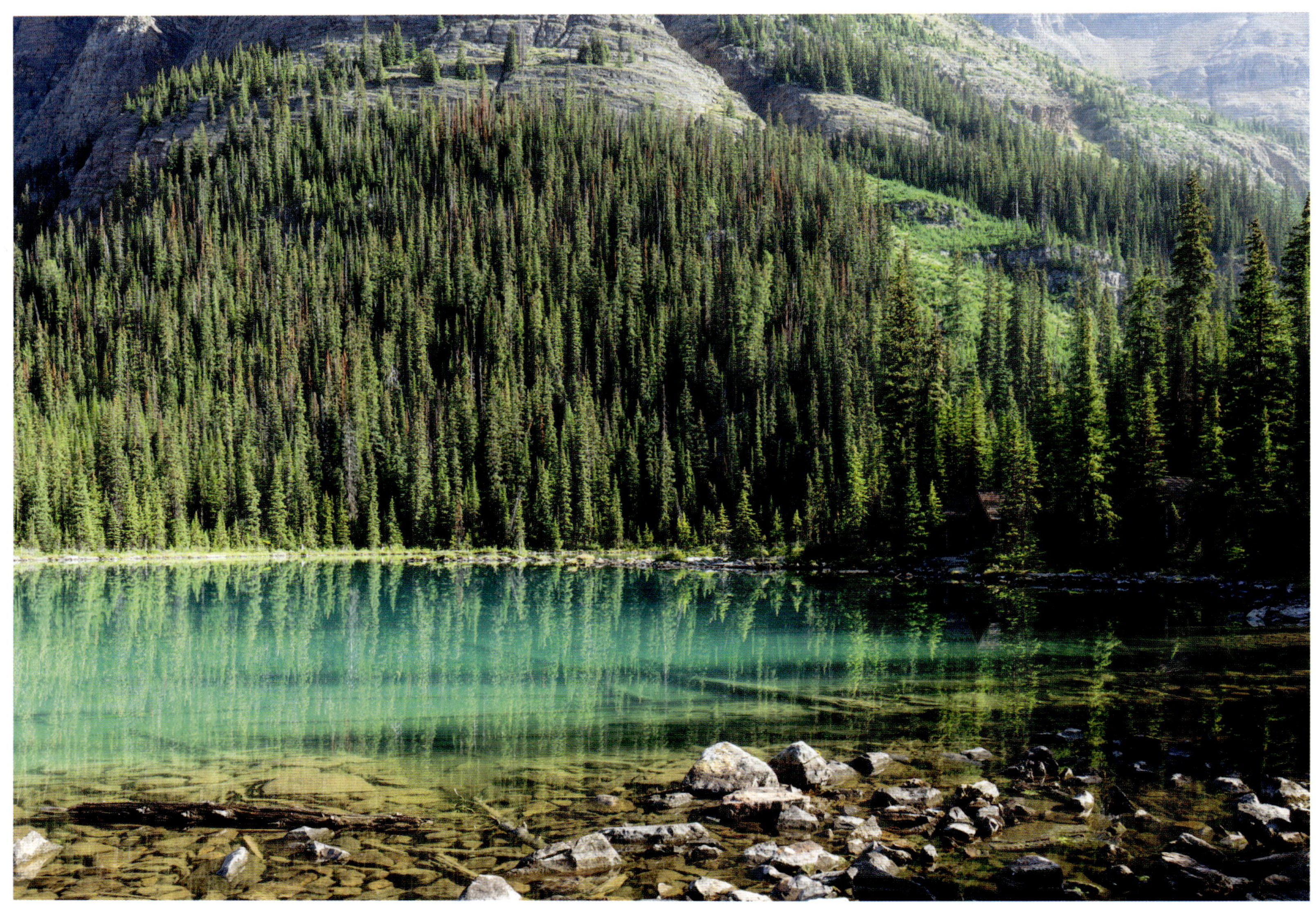

Tranquility (2025)
The first sight of Lake O'Hara from the bus ride up from the Parks Canada parking lot is this tranquil bay that leads to the lake's outlet.

Enjoying the View (2025)
Resting on the still surface of Lake O'Hara as daylight slips into darkness, this group of ducks takes a break from feeding, as if to enjoy the view.

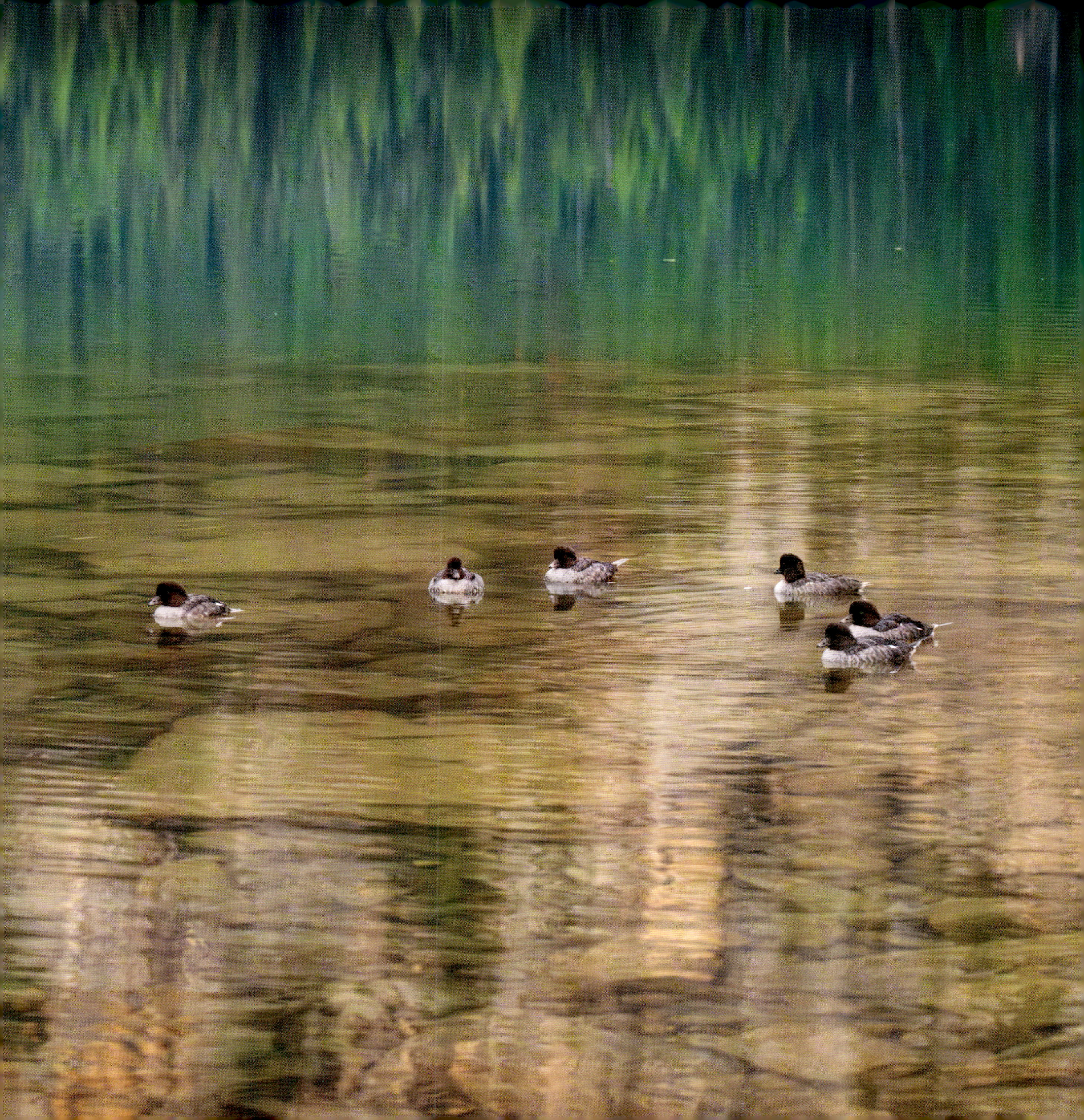

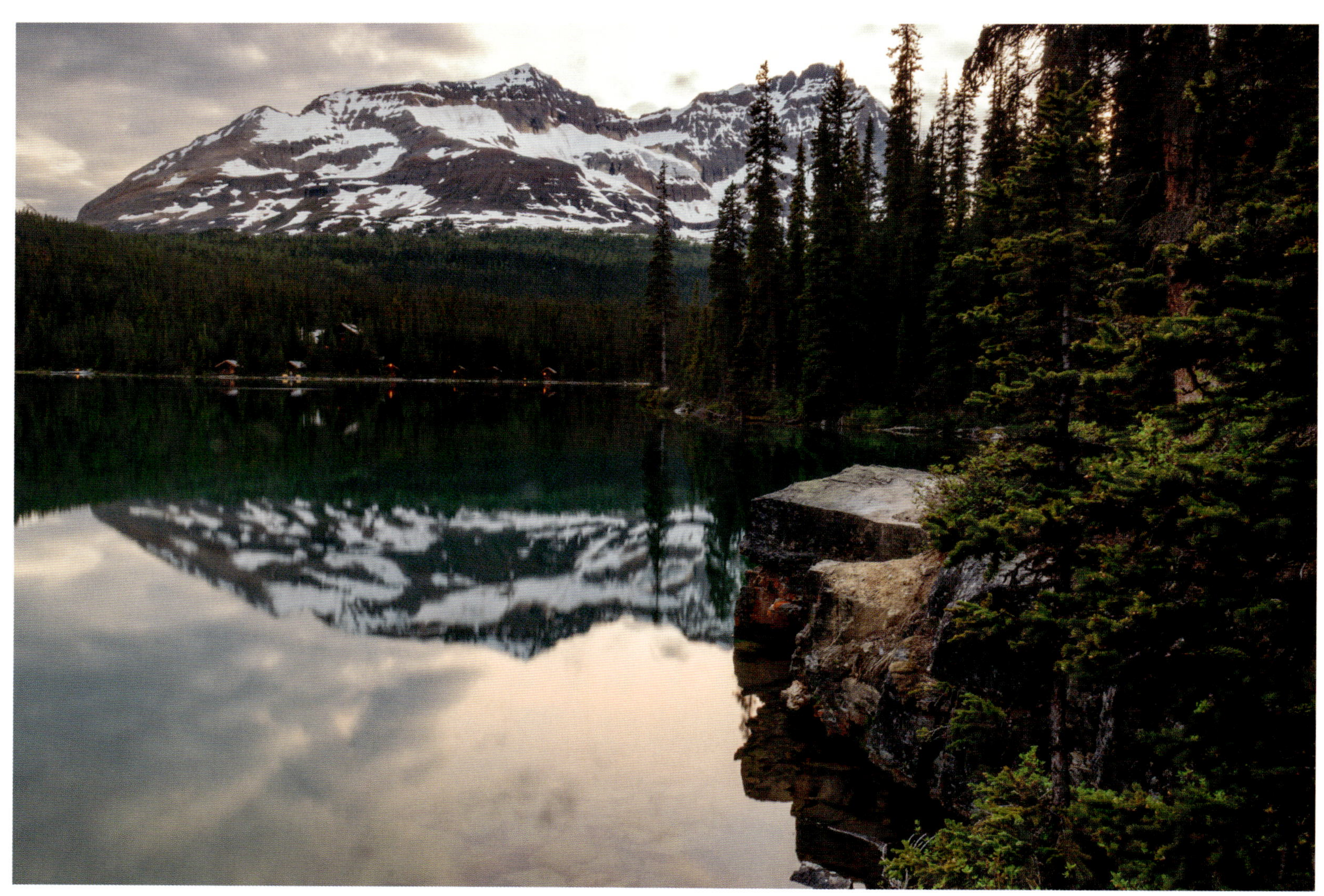

Lakeshore Cabins Aglow (2007)
Very few trees stood near Lake O'Hara Lodge's lakeshore cabins when they were relocated to the peninsula in 1928. Today
they are nearly camouflaged by the dense surrounding forest.

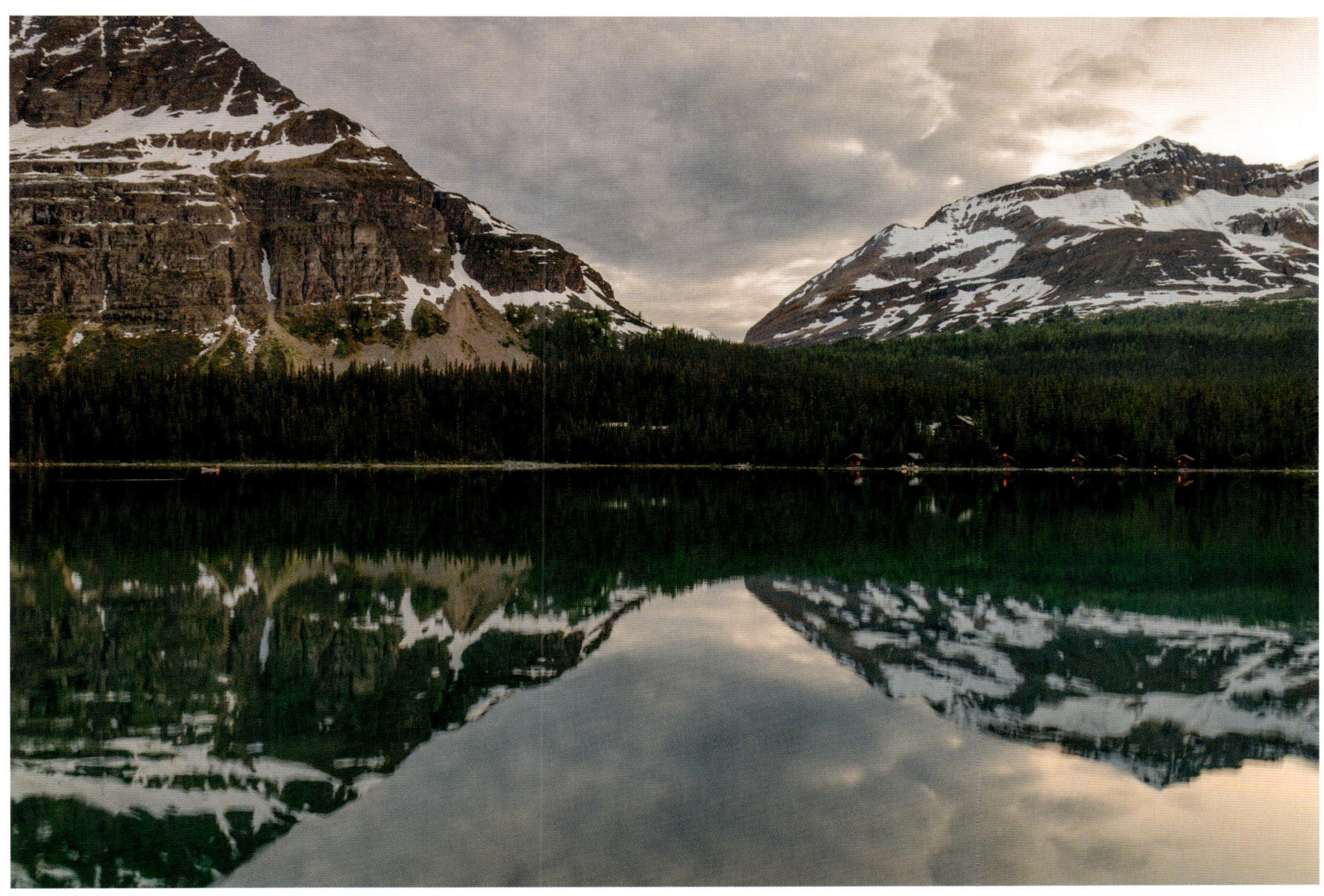

Evening Still (2007)
Lake O'Hara Lodge's lakeshore cabins begin to glow as evening approaches. Mount Schäffer and Odaray Mountain are
reflected in the lake.

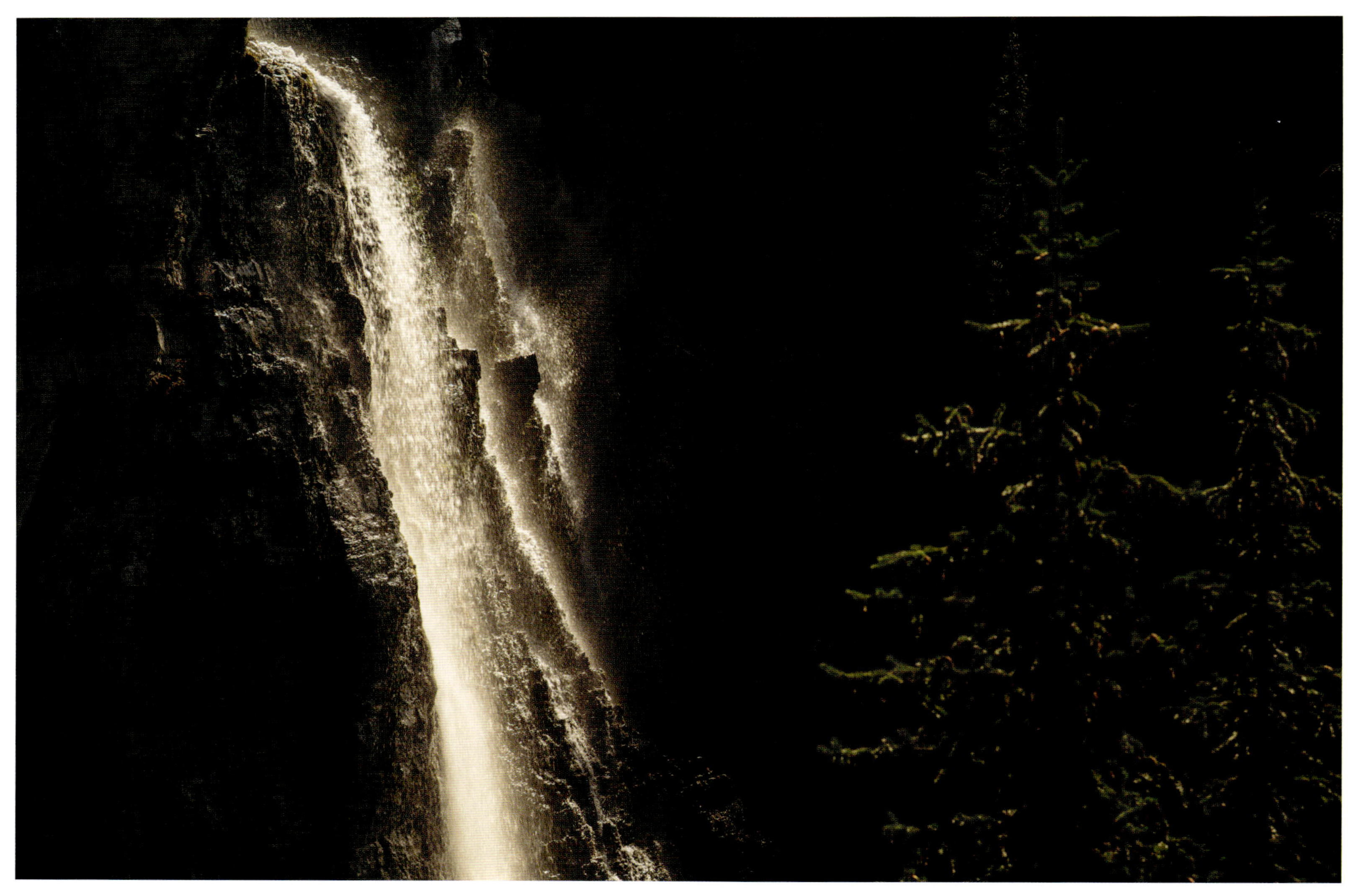

Falling (2025)
Midday sunlight backlights the cascading water of Seven Veils
Falls as it peeks through alpine forest tree tops.

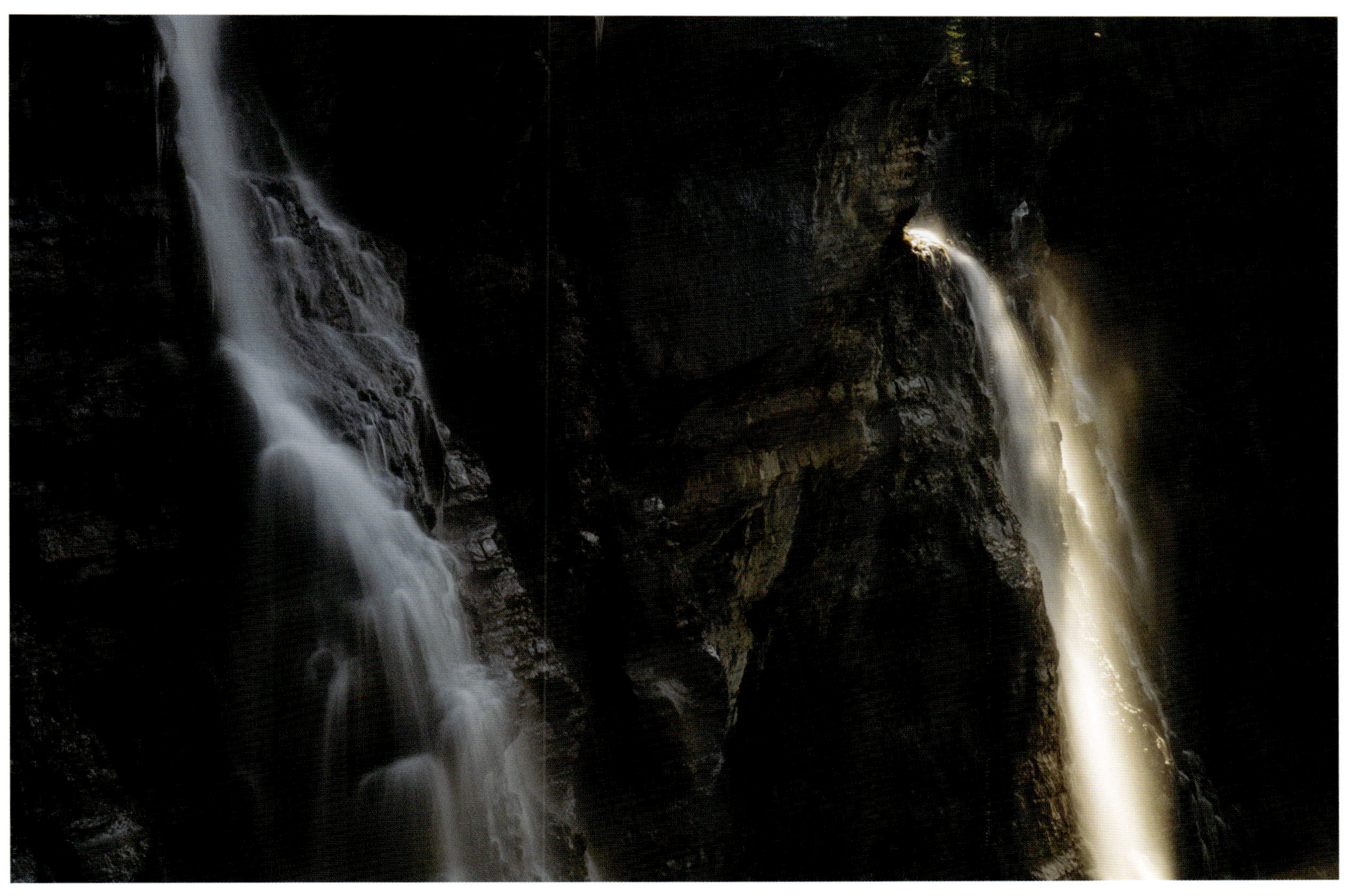

Fluid Veils (2025)
Strands of water streaming over the rocky precipice create the
phenomenon that is Seven Veils Falls.

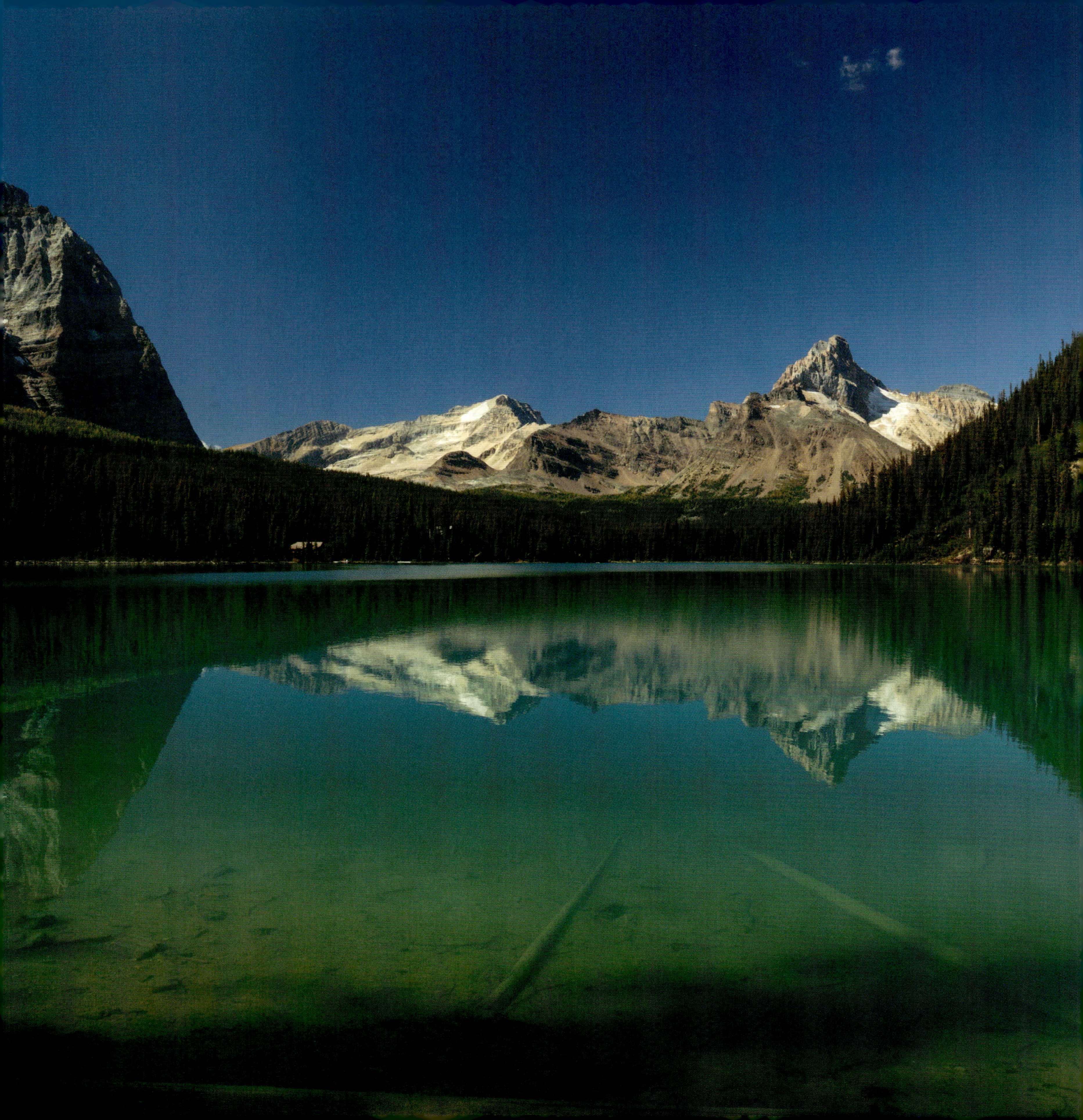

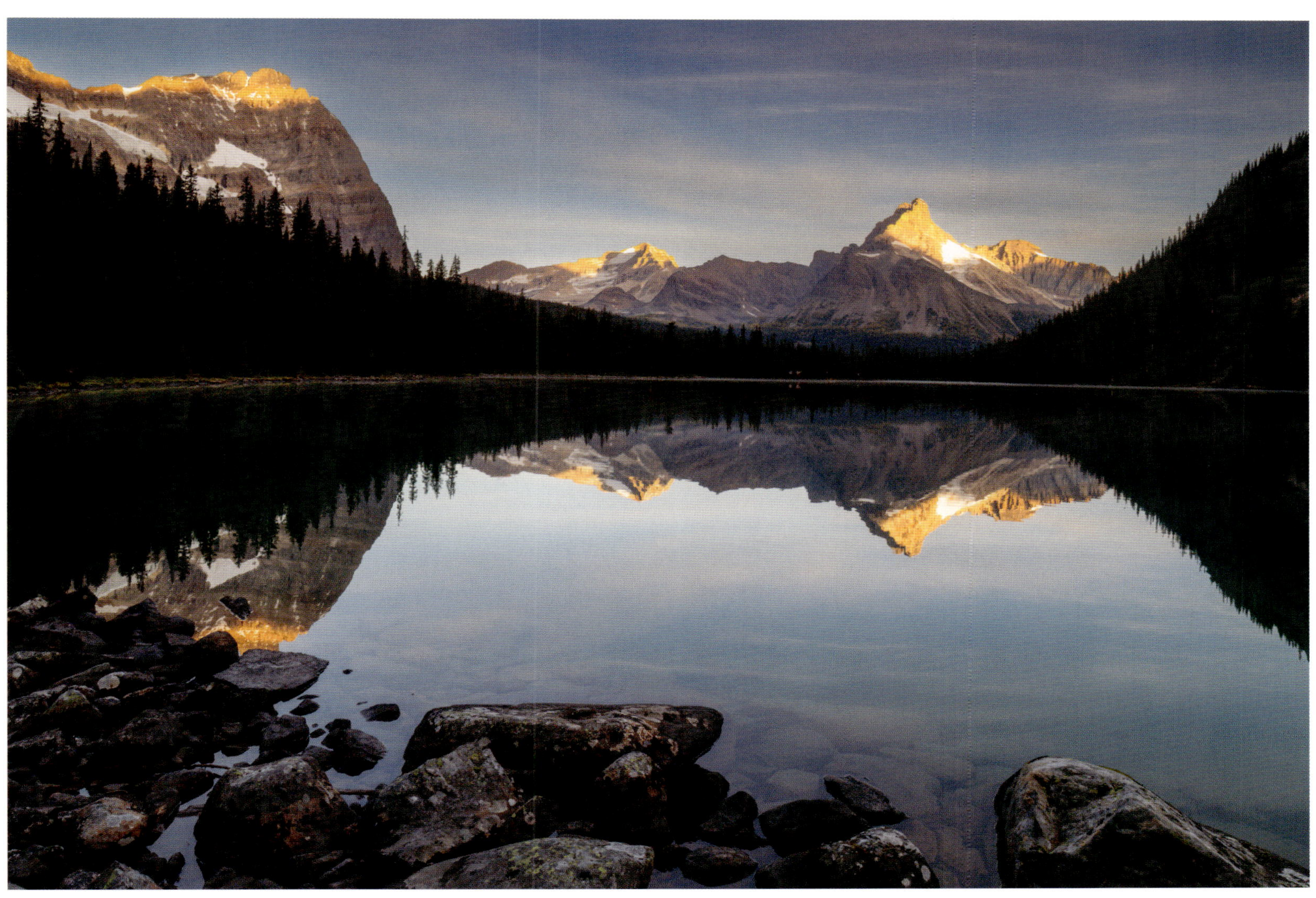

Golden Tips (2012)
The first light of day illuminates the tips of Cathedral Mountain and Odaray Mountain as it works its way toward their bases and onto Lake O'Hara.

Emerald Jewel (2013)
Lake O'Hara's "moods" change throughout the day and the seasons. By early autumn, the glacial meltwaters rich in rock flour sediments transform it into an emerald jewel.

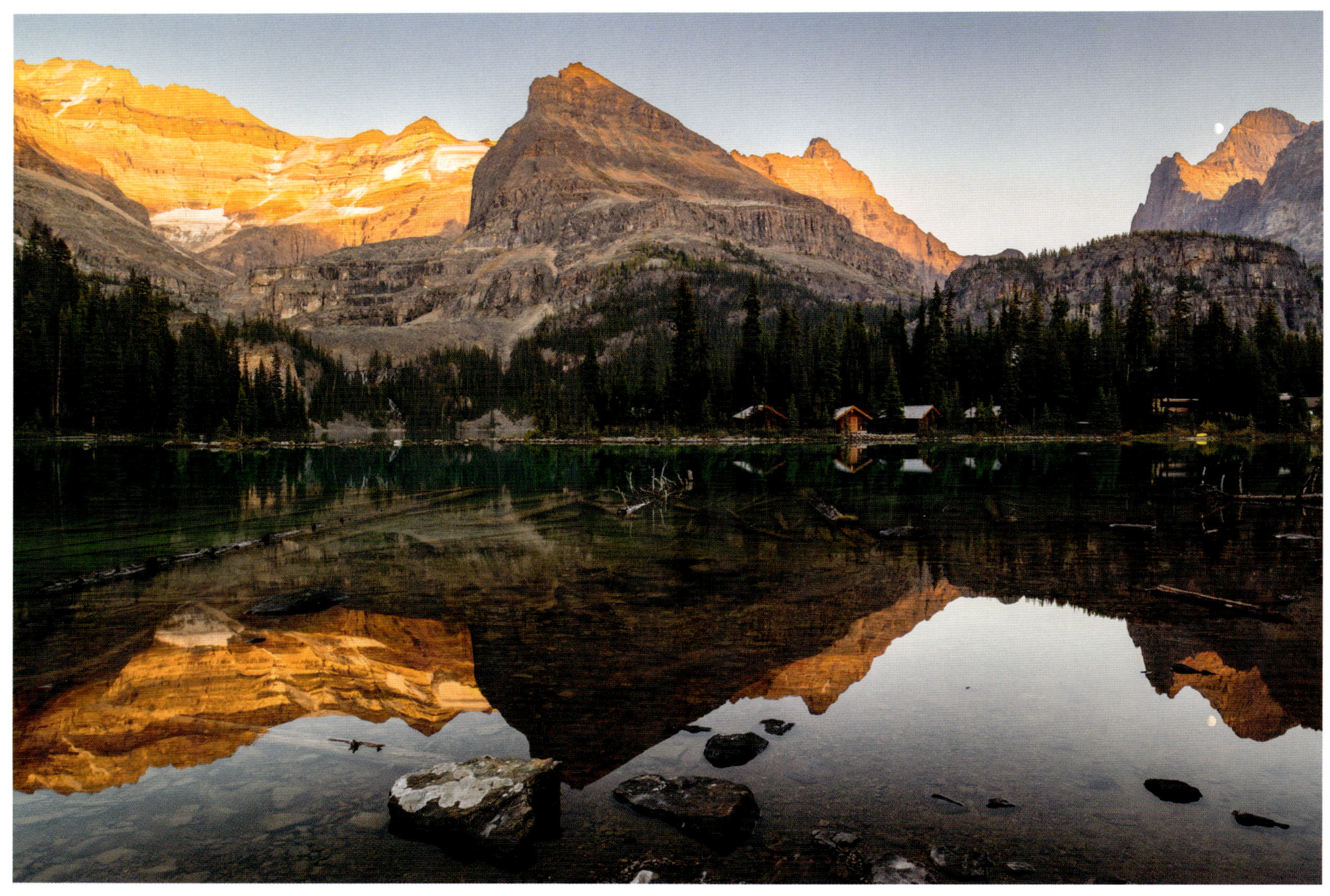

Light Theatre (2013)
Nature's light theatre, free to all who are able to stop and witness. Open daily.

Evening Reflection (2013)
Lake O'Hara Lodge's lakeshore cabins along the peninsula immersed between golden-hour Mount Lefroy and its reflection in the lake.

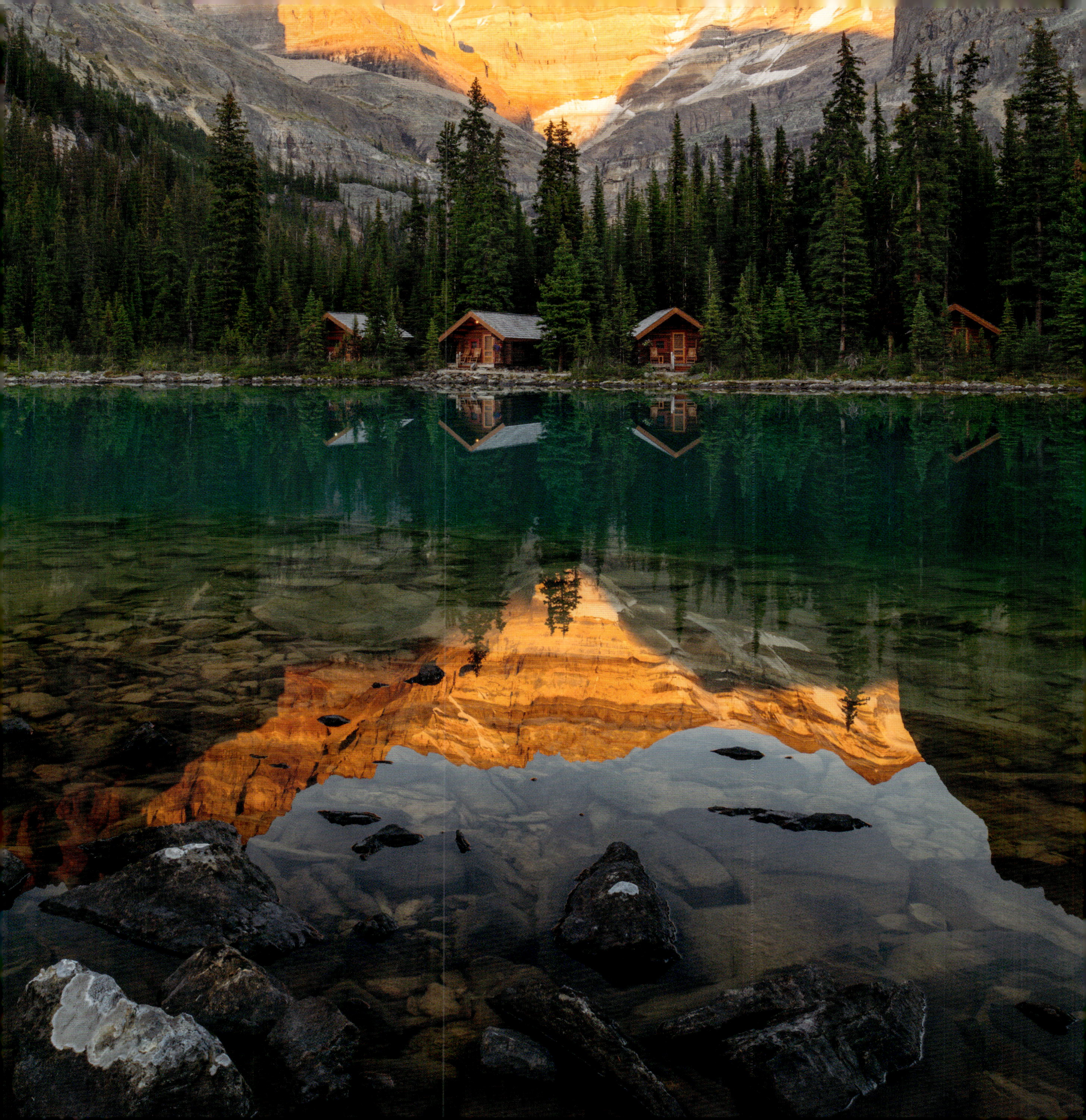

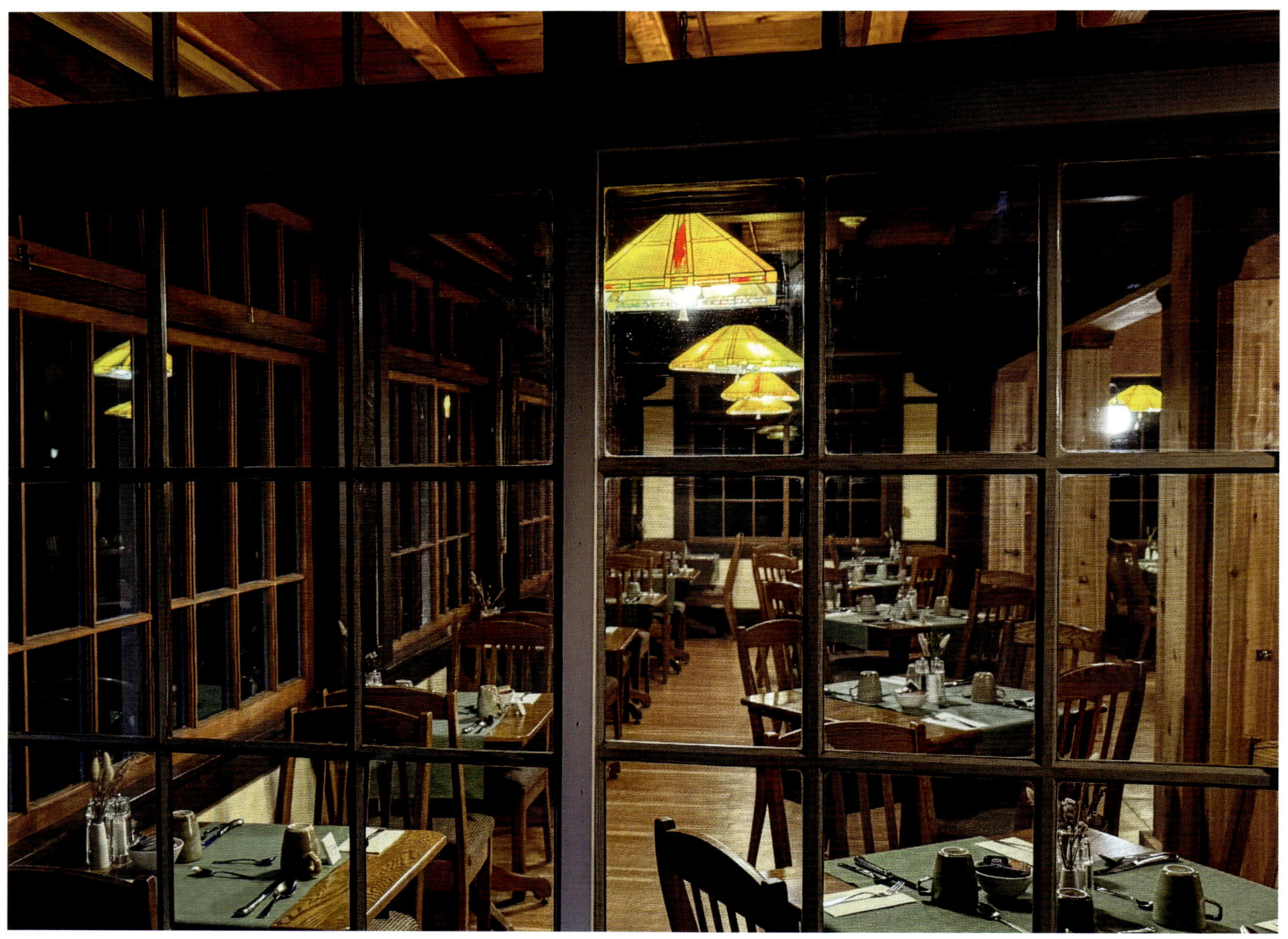

Preparation (2024)
Peering into the dining room at the breakfast tables set in preparation for the next day. The lodge remained without electricity, using oil lamps and wood stoves, until the 1960s.

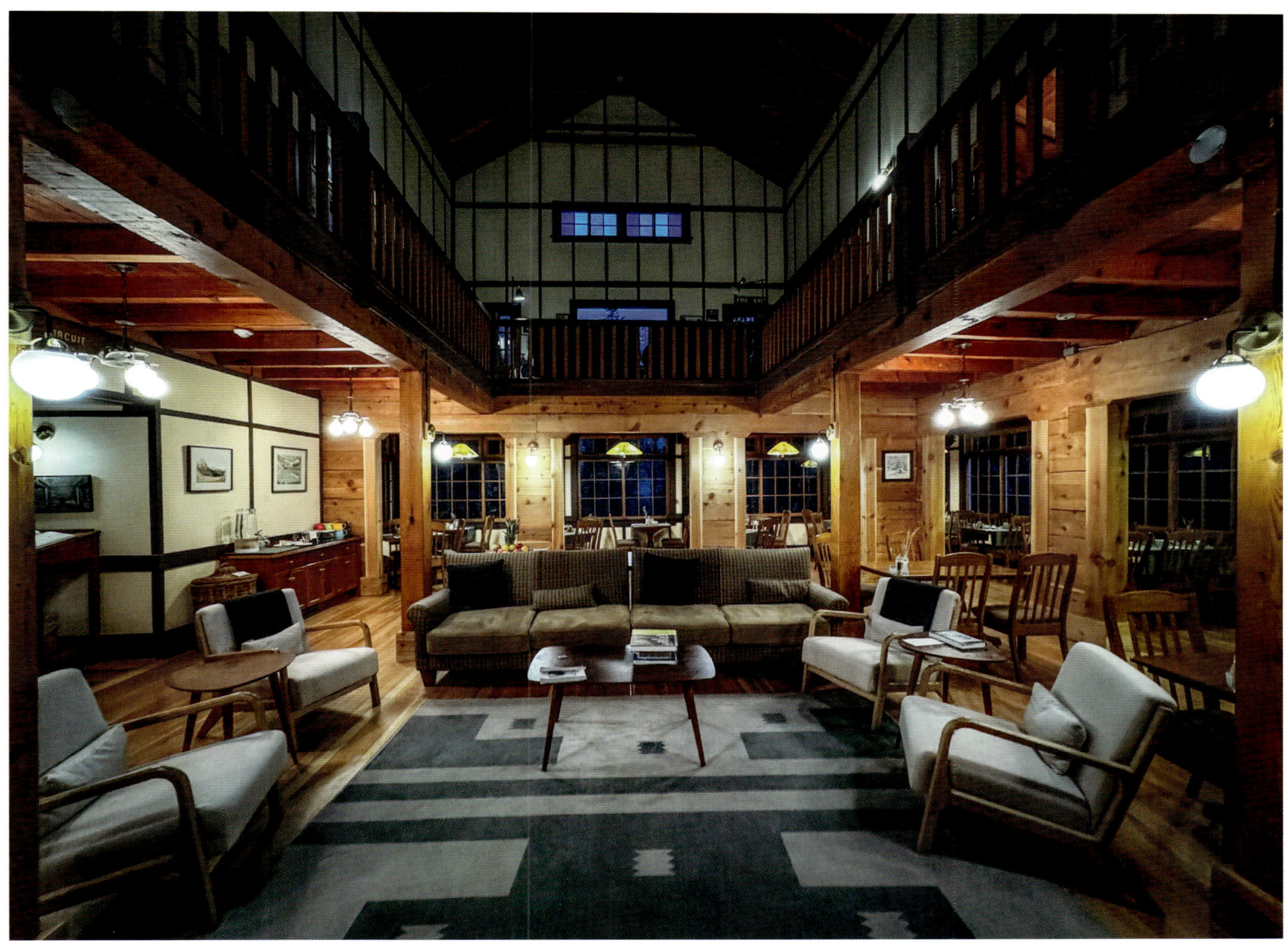

Conversations in Time (2024)
Tales of the day's hiking adventures blend with stories from
around the world in this meeting space intended to foster
discussion.

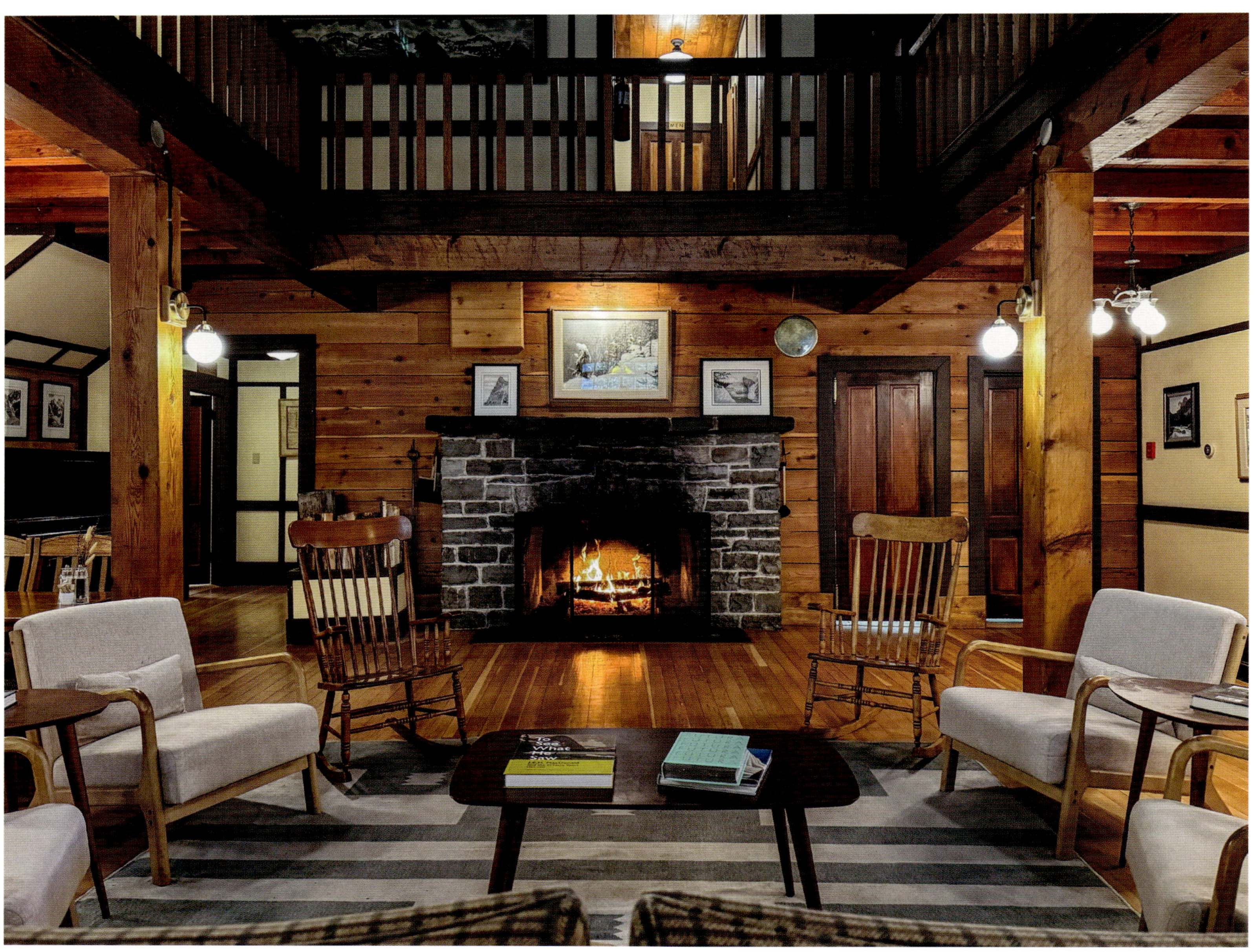

Fireside Tales (2024)
This hearth has warmed many souls over its 100 years of existence In recognition of its historical and architectural signifi-
cance, Lake O'Hara Lodge is designated a Federal Heritage
Building.

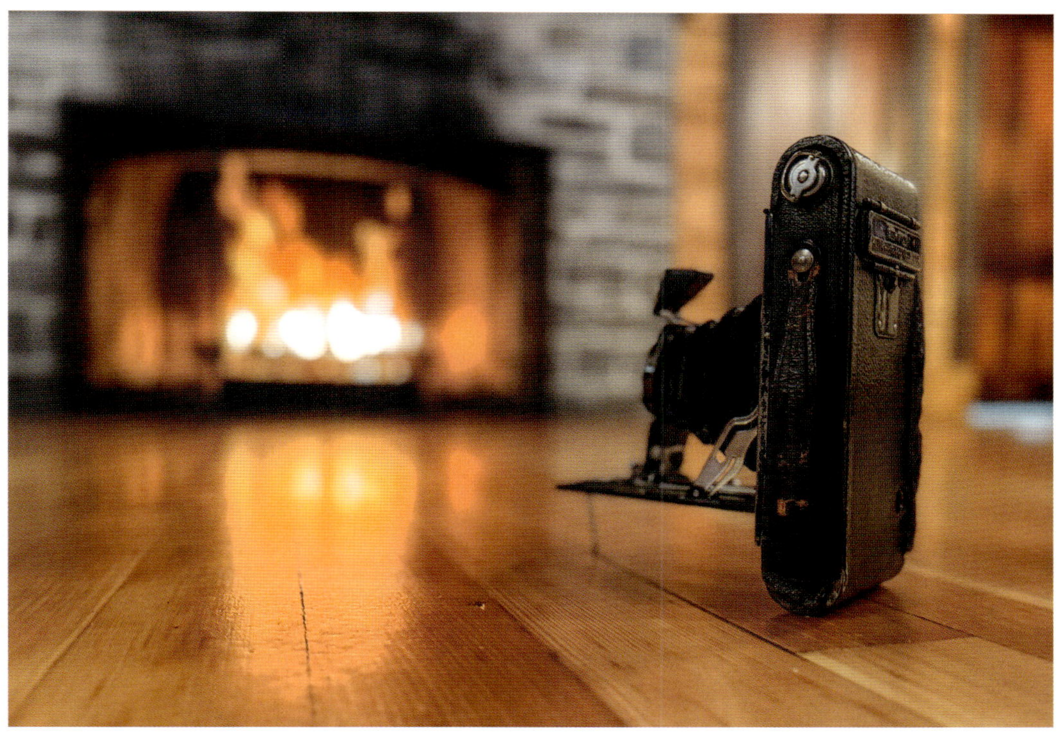

Photographing Time (2024)
Many historic photographs of the Lake O'Hara region were taken by Walter Feuz with this very camera. The Eastman Kodak No. 2 Folding Autographic Brownie (1916–1932) made the formerly obscure art of photography affordable and accessible to amateurs.

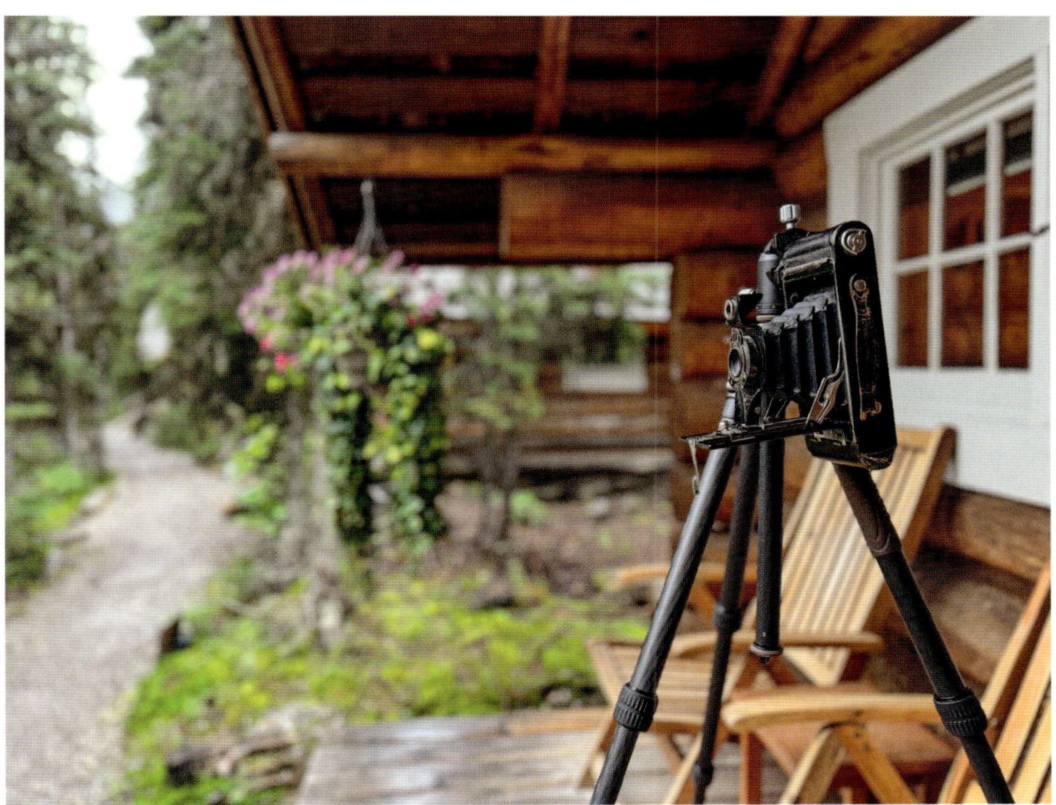

Historic Vantage (2024)
Due to wartime travel restrictions, fuel rationing, and labour shortages, the CPR suspended Lake O'Hara Lodge's operations during the Second World War. Walter Feuz tended to the lodge during this time, improving trails and taking photographs.

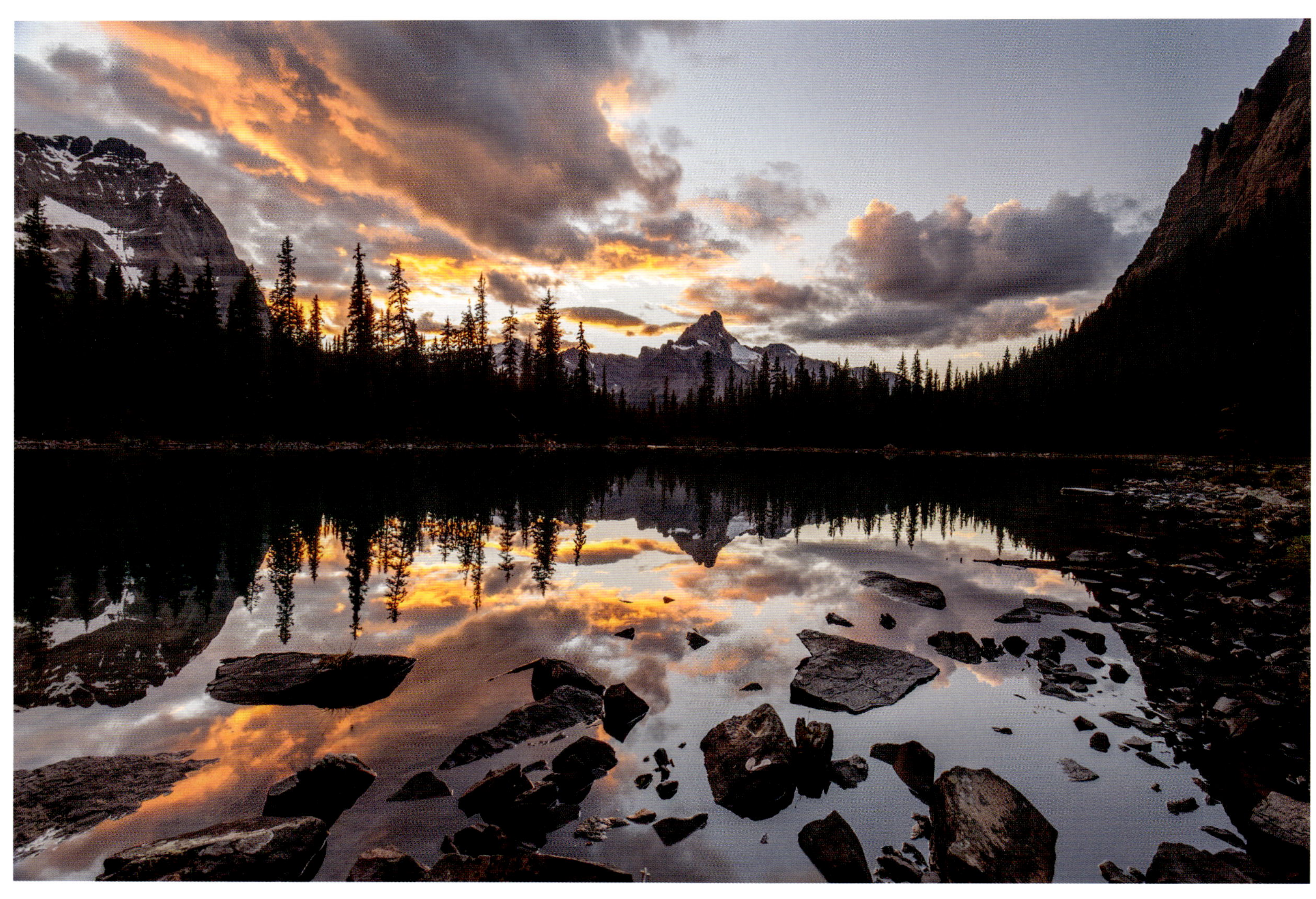

Day's End (2007)
Evening sunset reflections on the western section of Lake O'Hara.

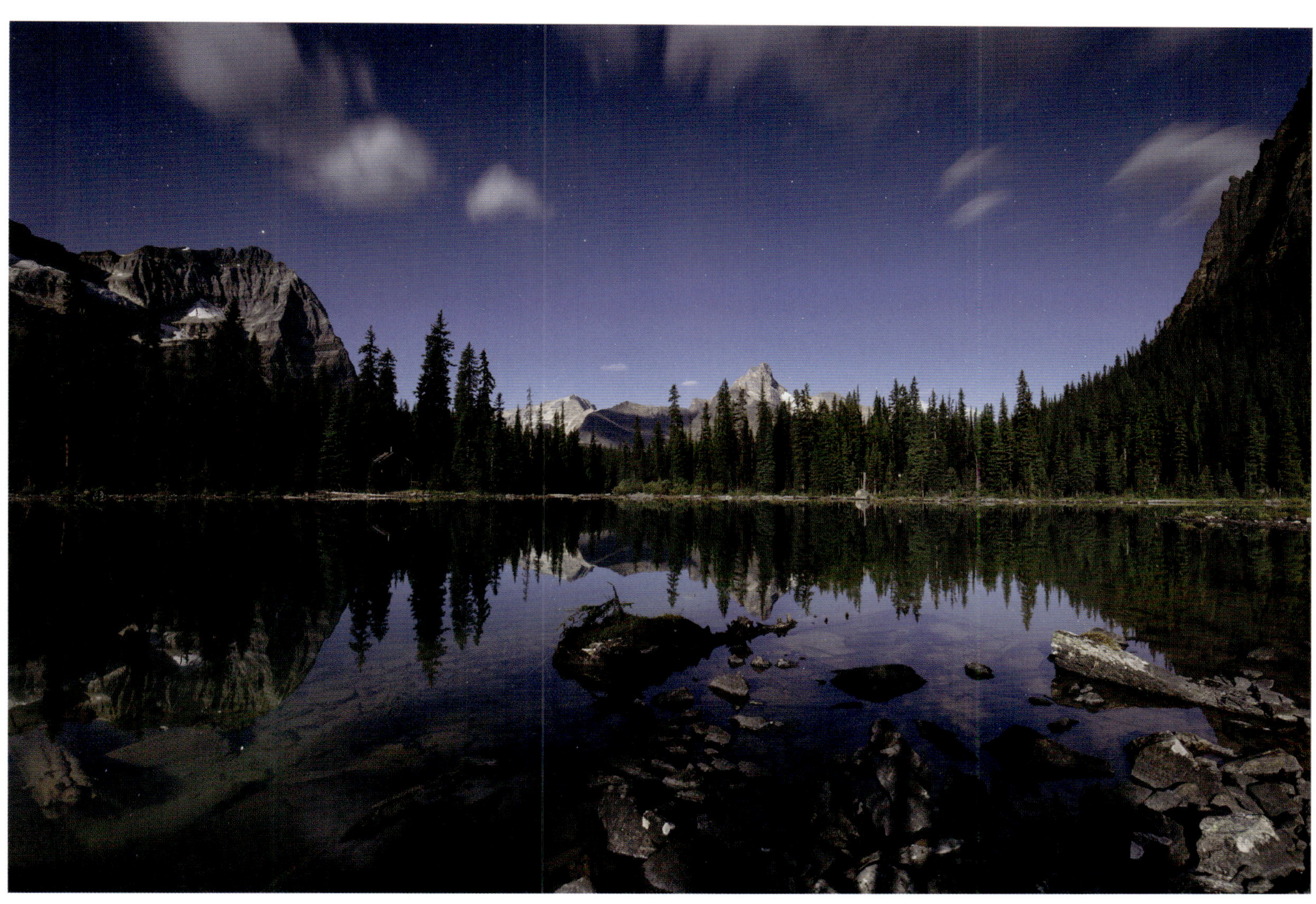

Blue Hour (2017)
Stars appear as night approaches over the western end of
Lake O'Hara.

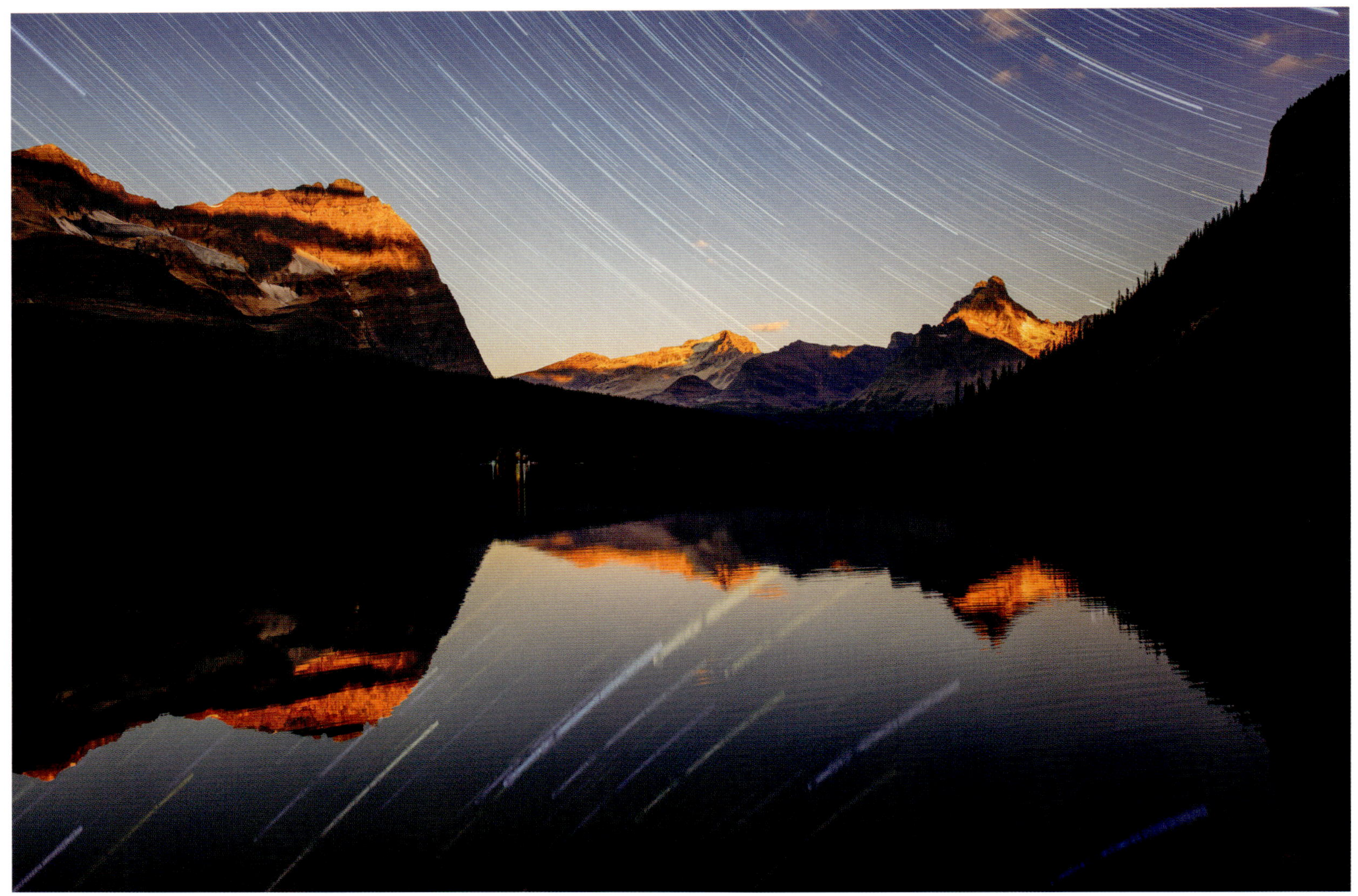

Star Time (2013)
Stars leave light trails across the sky over a seven-hour period until daybreak lights the peaks of Odaray and Cathedral mountains reflecting into the mirror of Lake O'Hara.

Circle of Time (2012)
A three-hour time-lapse exposure centred on the northern hemisphere's North Star, Polaris. Star trails over Mount Huber.

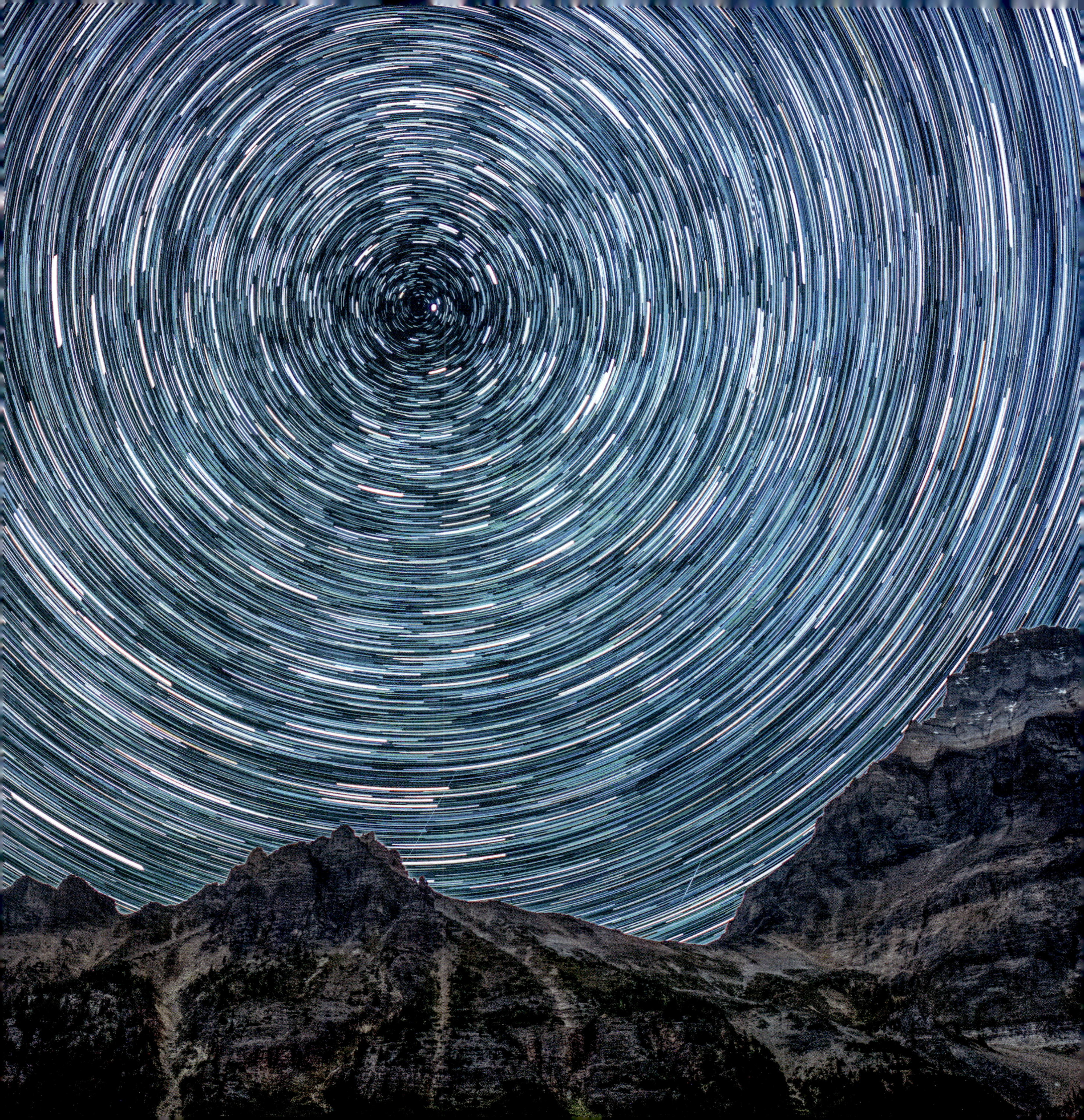

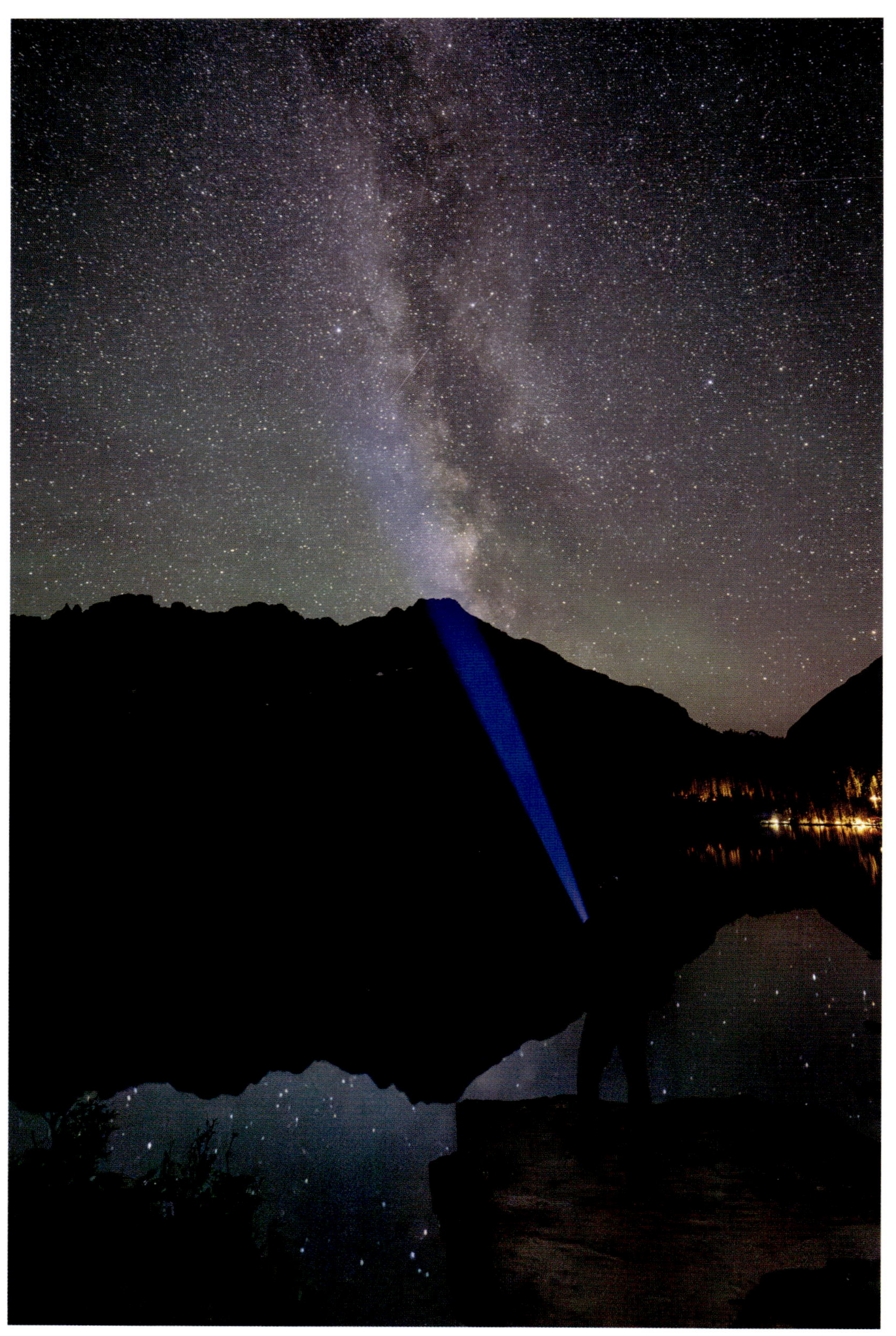

Dark Sky Splendour (2025)
Taking a moment to participate in the imagery of the night sky. The glow of Lake O'Hara Lodge's dwellings defines the distant shoreline.

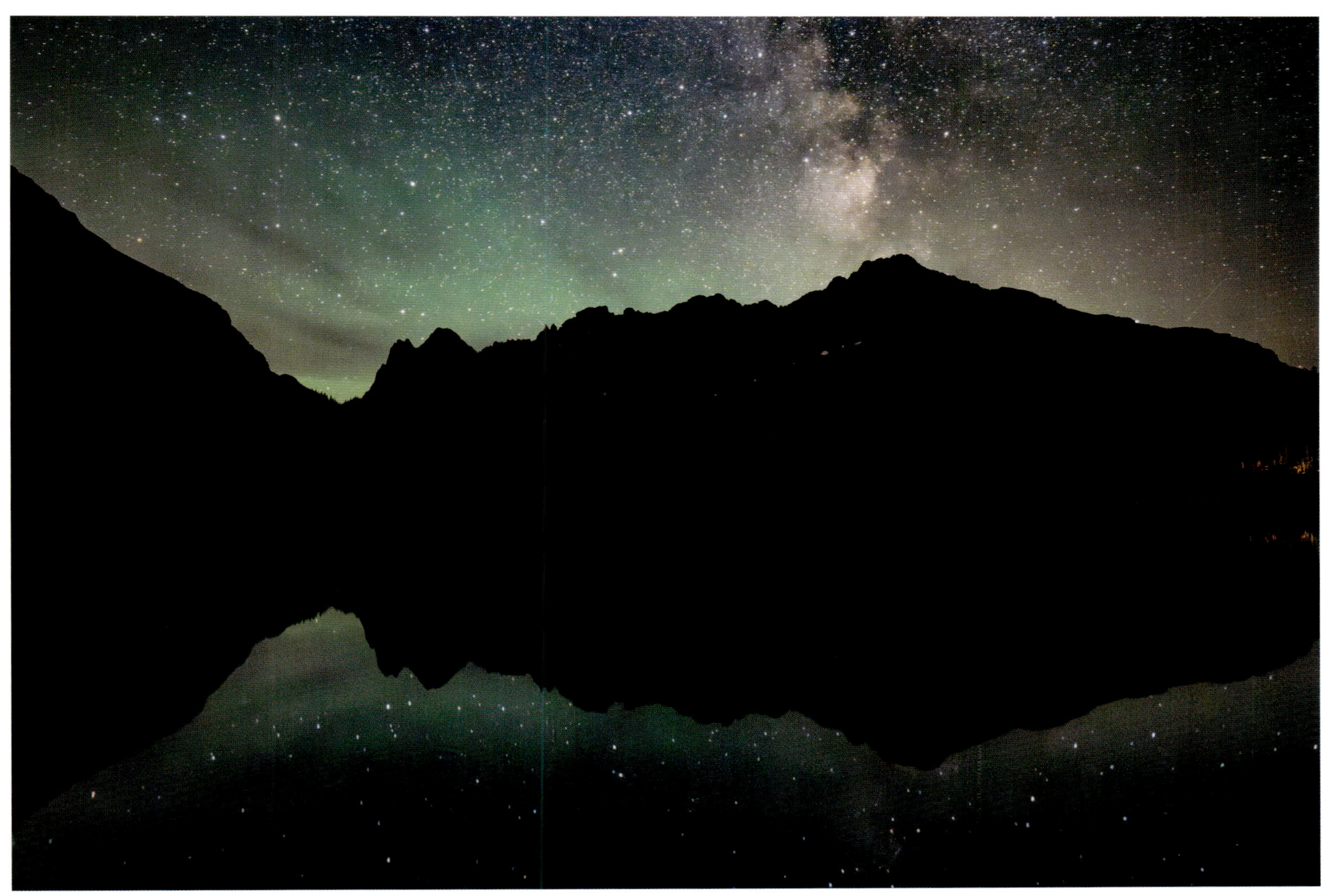

Galaxy Reflection (2025)
The Milky Way and strands of aurora borealis illuminate the
night sky above Mount Schäffer and Schäffer Ridge.

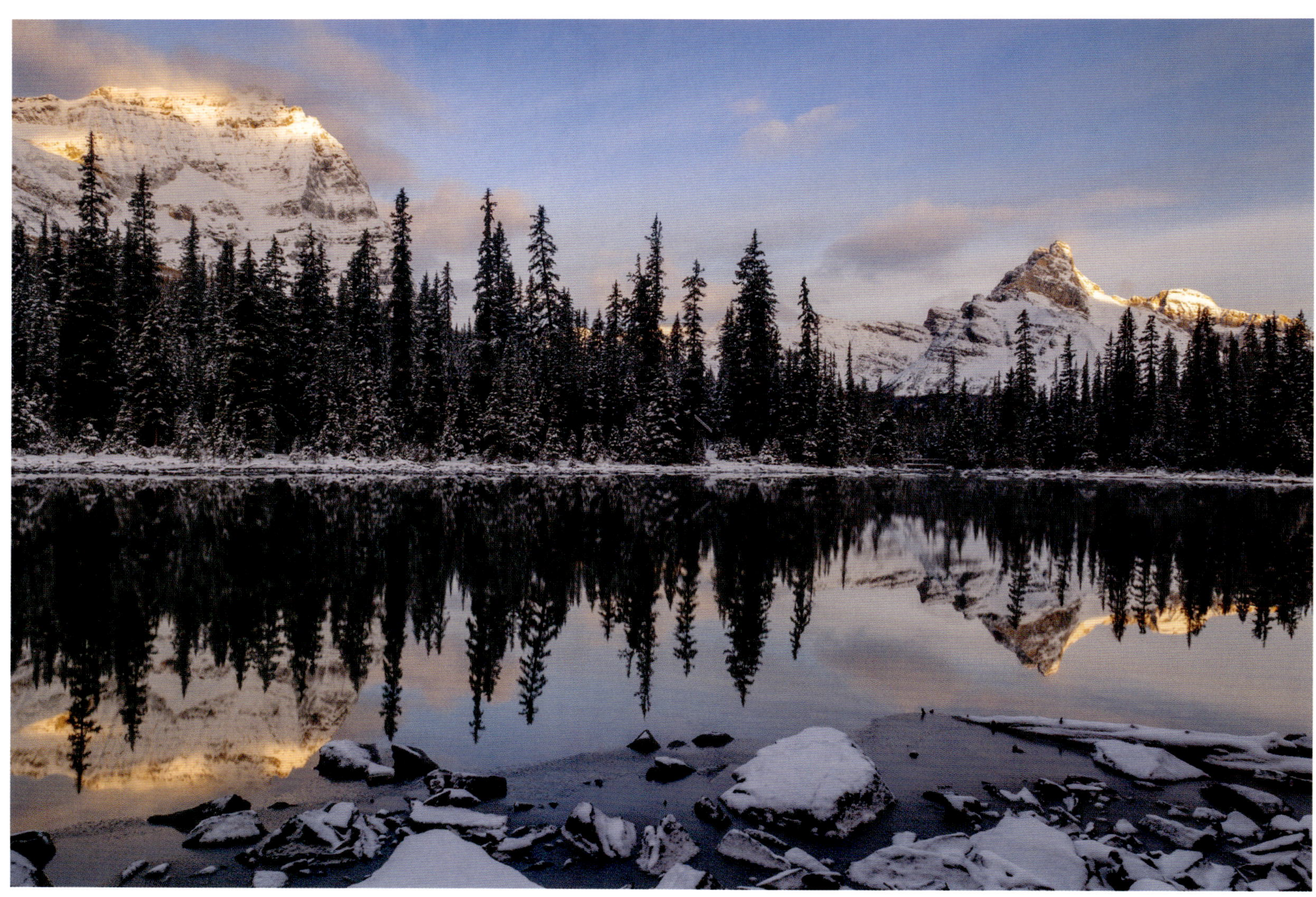

Autumn Morning (2007)
Morning sun illuminates the snowy peaks of Odaray Mountain
and Cathedral Mountain, their symmetry reflected in the surface of the cooling water of Lake O'Hara.

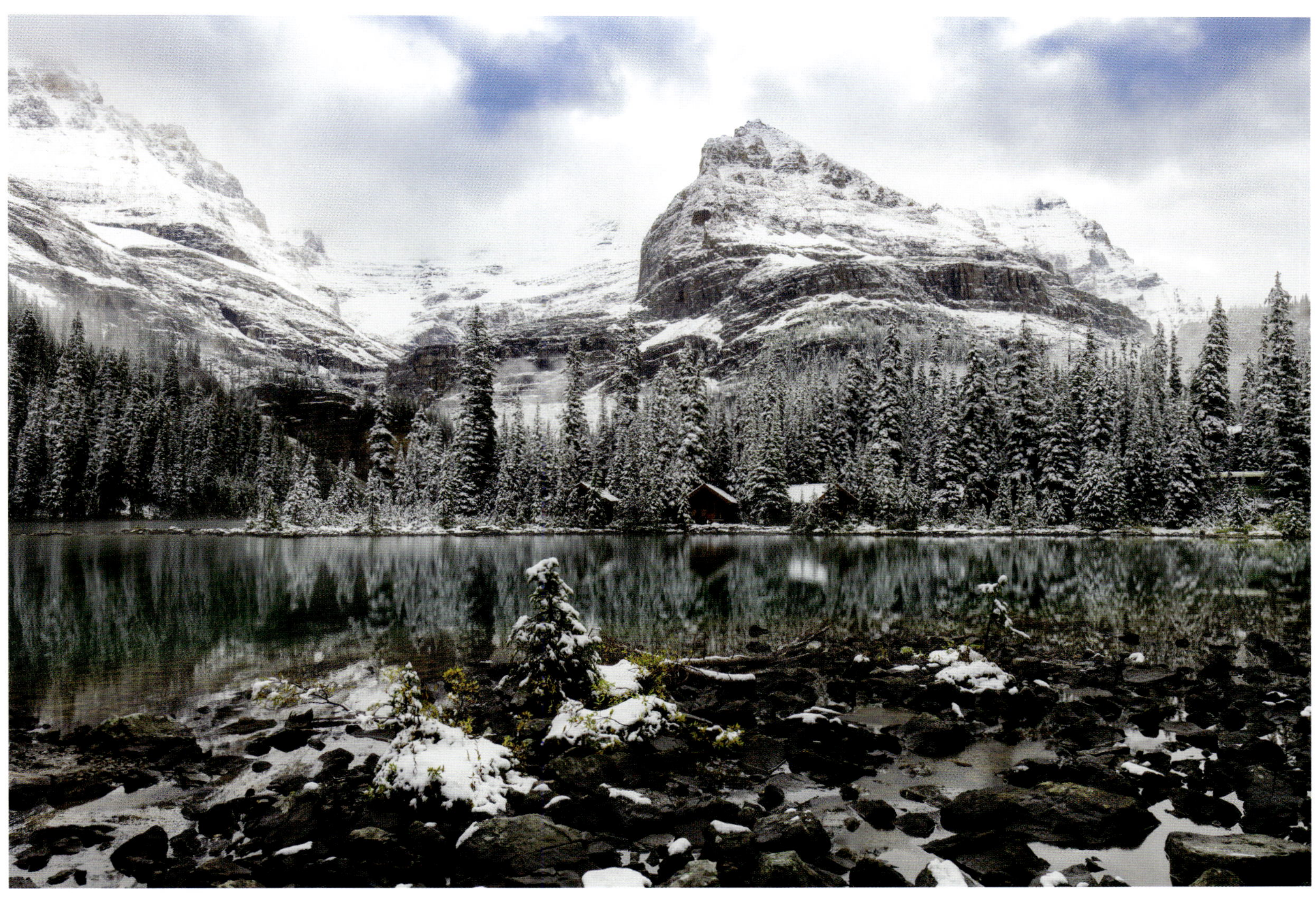

Autumn Emerald (2018)
Autumn snowfall juxtaposed against the open water highlights
the late-season emerald hue of the lake.

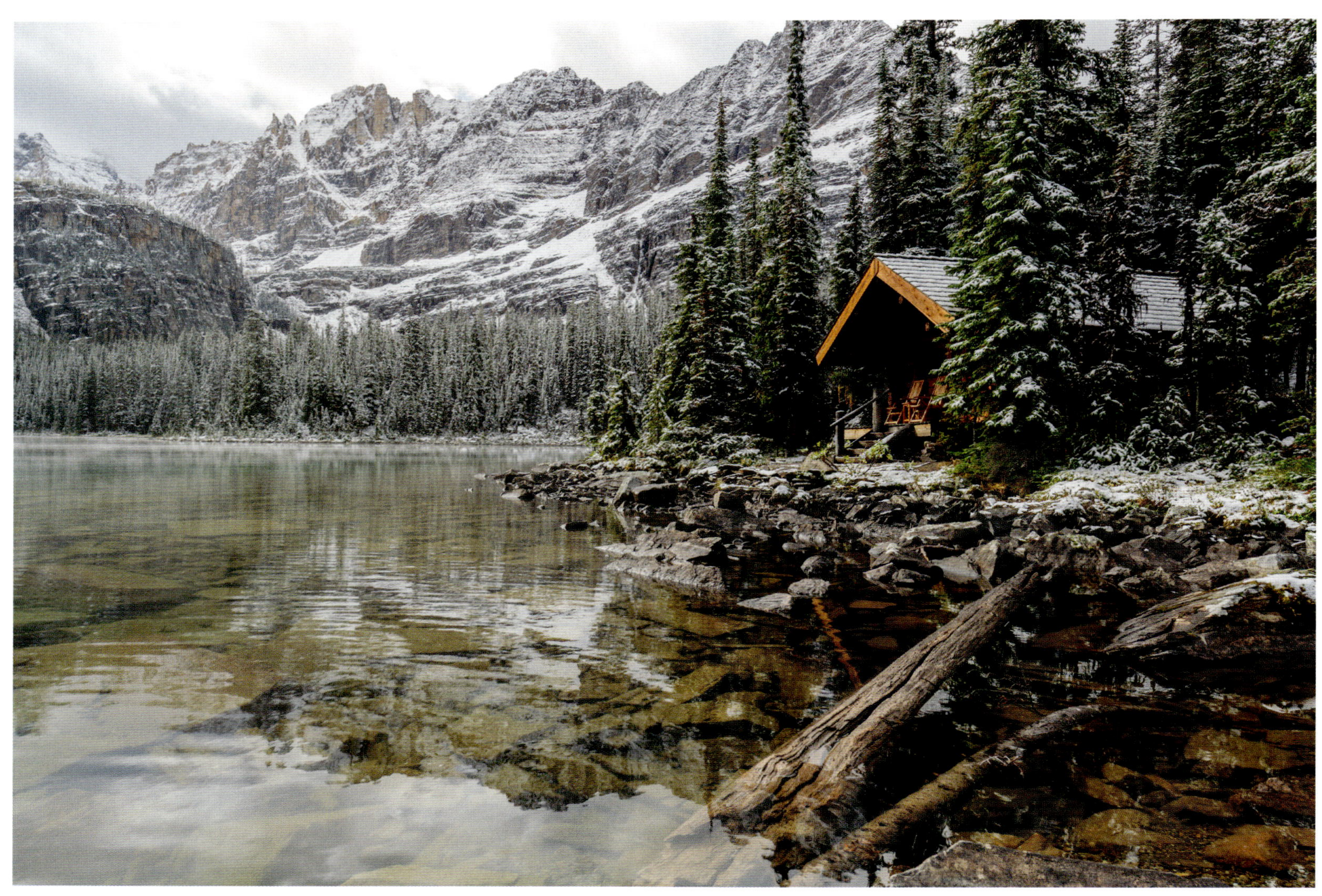

Autumn's Nod (2018)
Warm mist rising from the cooling water of Lake O'Hara on a
September morning. Soon the lodge and its lakeshore cabins
will be closed to the public until June.

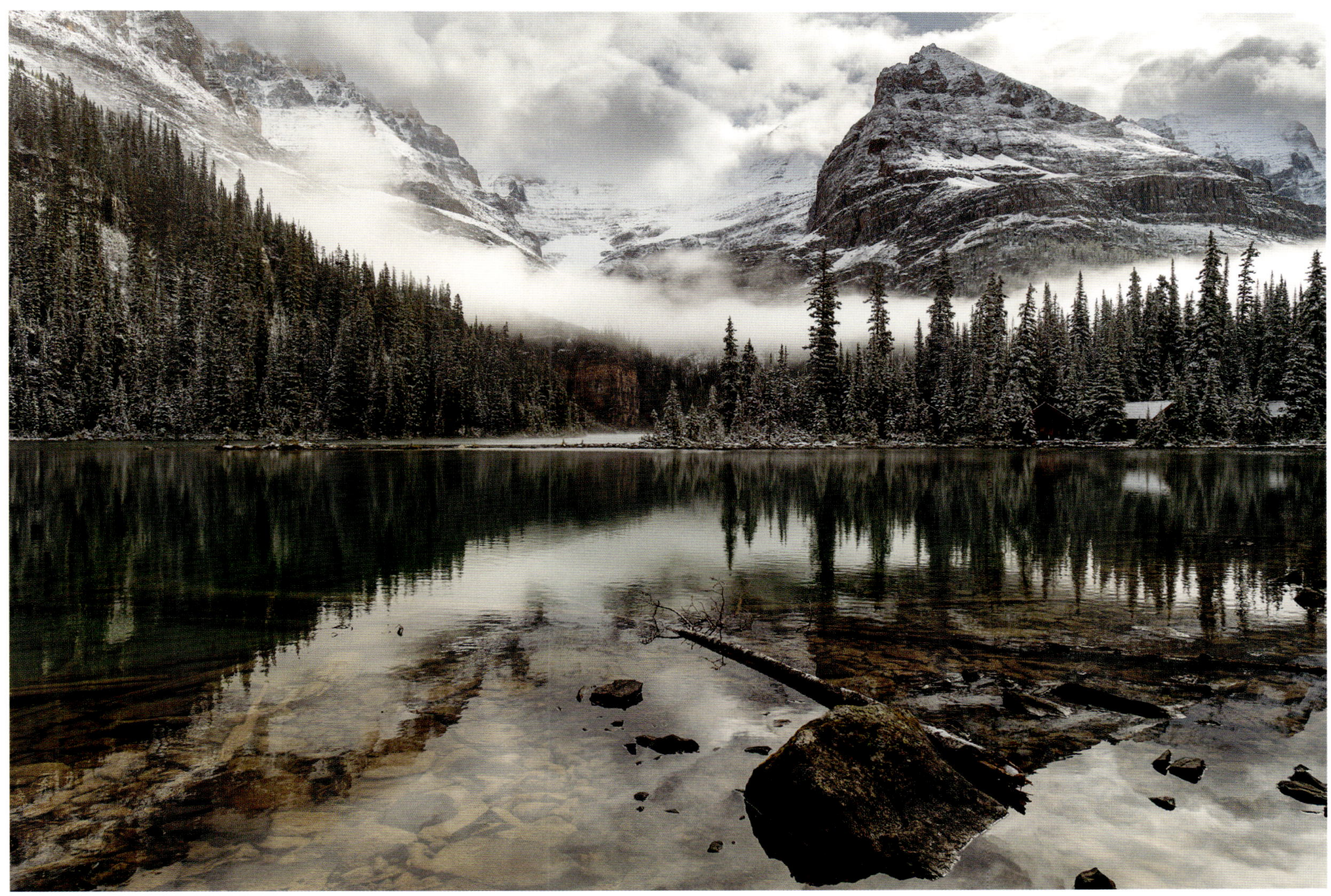

Morning Fog Rising (2018)
The changing of seasons creates some of the most beautiful
transitory scenes as morning fog lifts slowly from the lake and
lingers over the treeline.

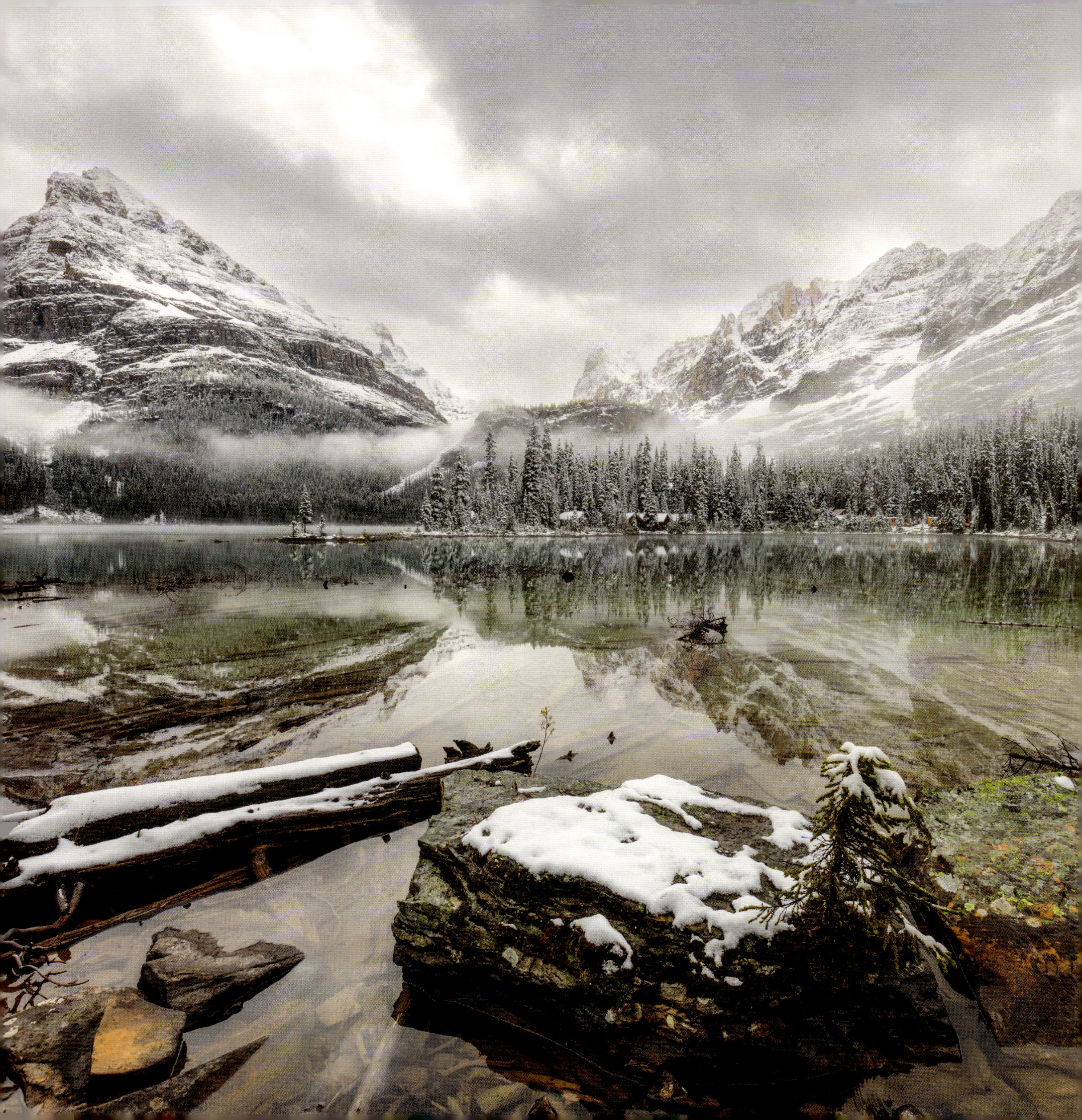

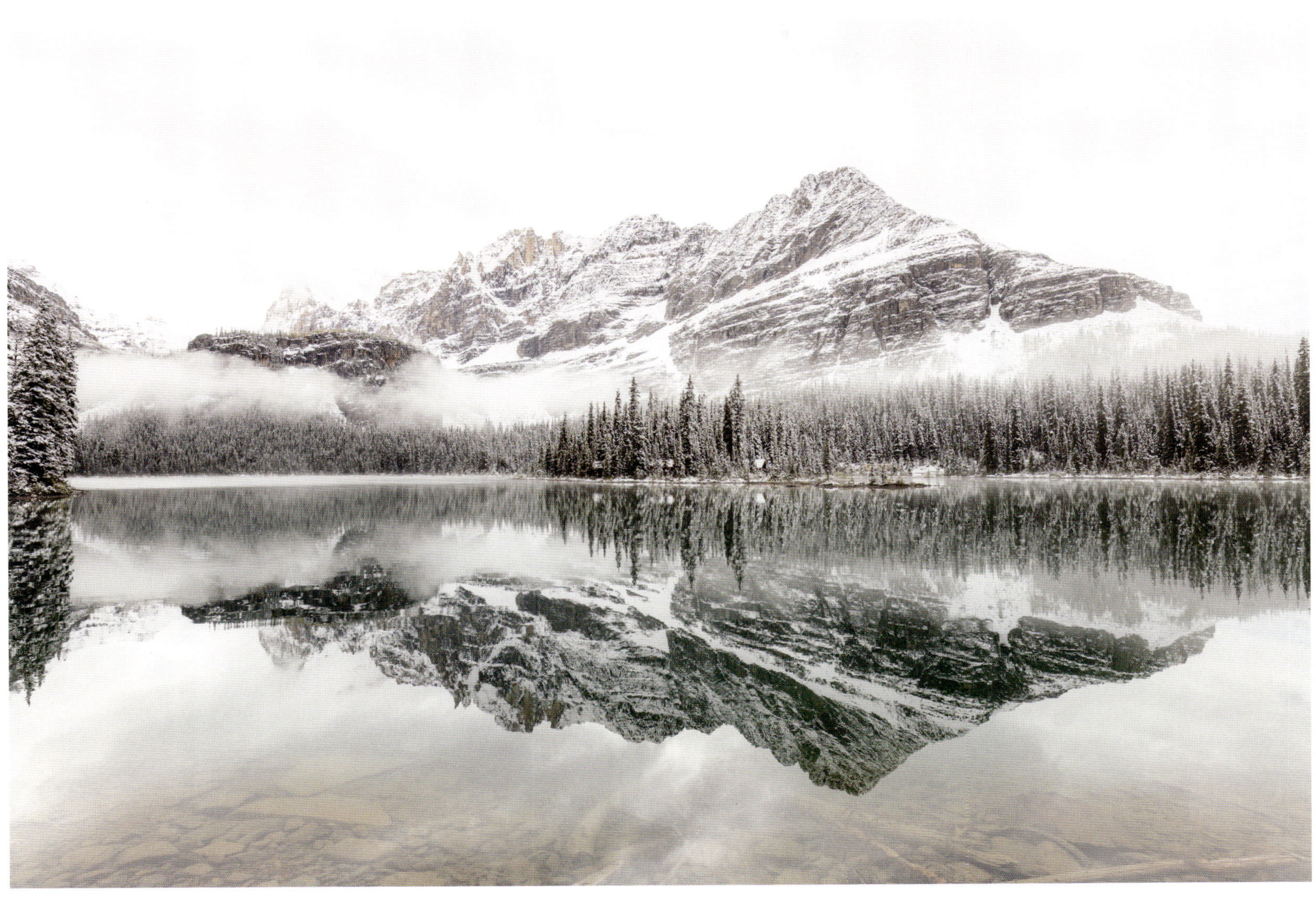

Reflection on Hue (2018)
A mirror reflection of Mount Schäffer and Schäffer Ridge altered only by Lake O'Hara's glacier-formed sedimentary hue.

Adeline's View (2018)
The same sights take on entirely new faces as the seasons change. Historically referred to as the Adeline Link Circuit after Adeline (Schäffer) Link, who, with her spouse, Alfred Link, was integral to the creation and maintenance of this lakeshore connector trail.

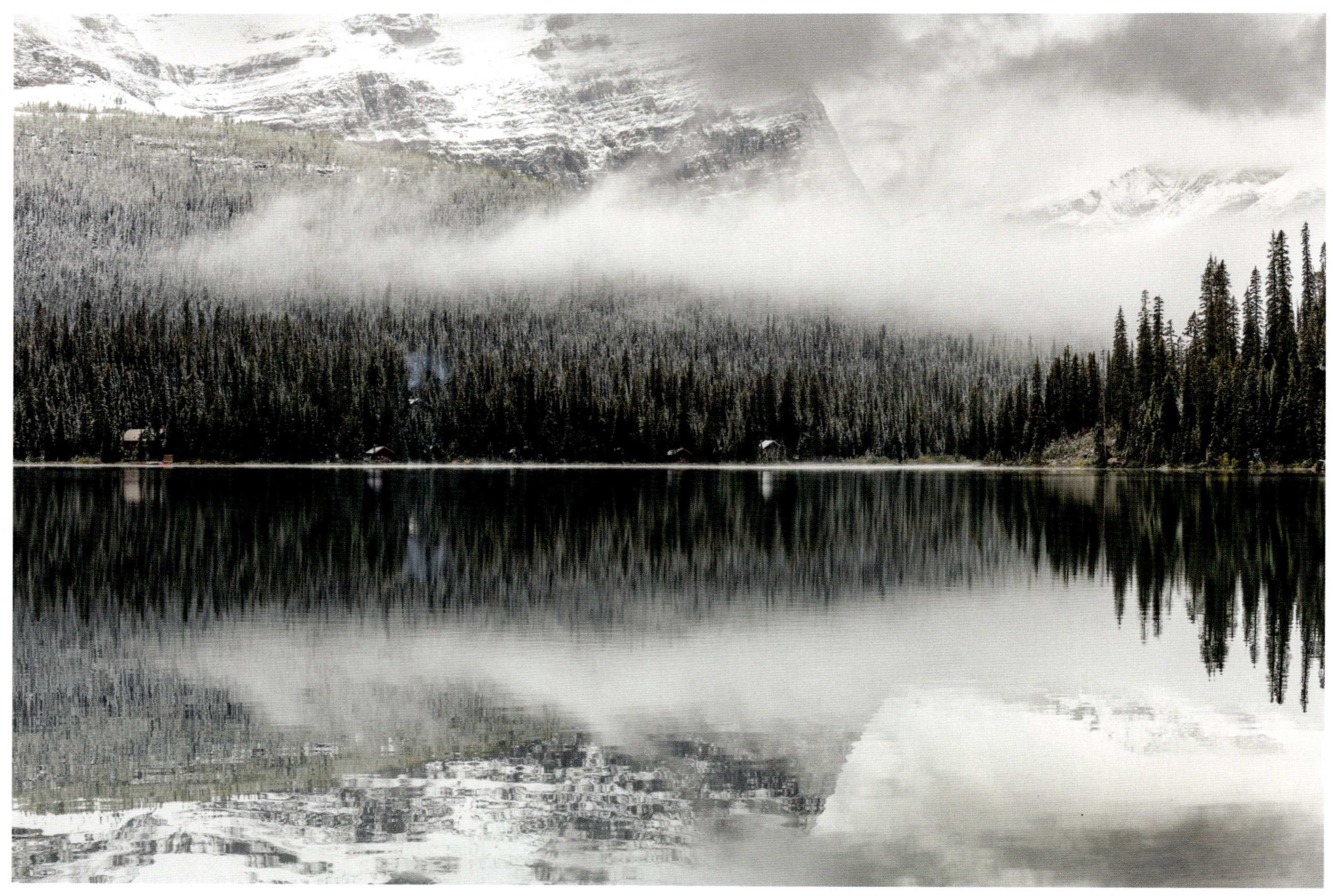

Smoke Signal (2018)
Visible only by the smoke from its fireplace, the shelter of Lake O'Hara Lodge is hidden away within the spruce, fir, and larch forests of the Lake O'Hara region.

Century Shelter (2018)
Very few trees surrounded these lakeside cabins when they were first relocated here from the alpine meadows area a century ago.

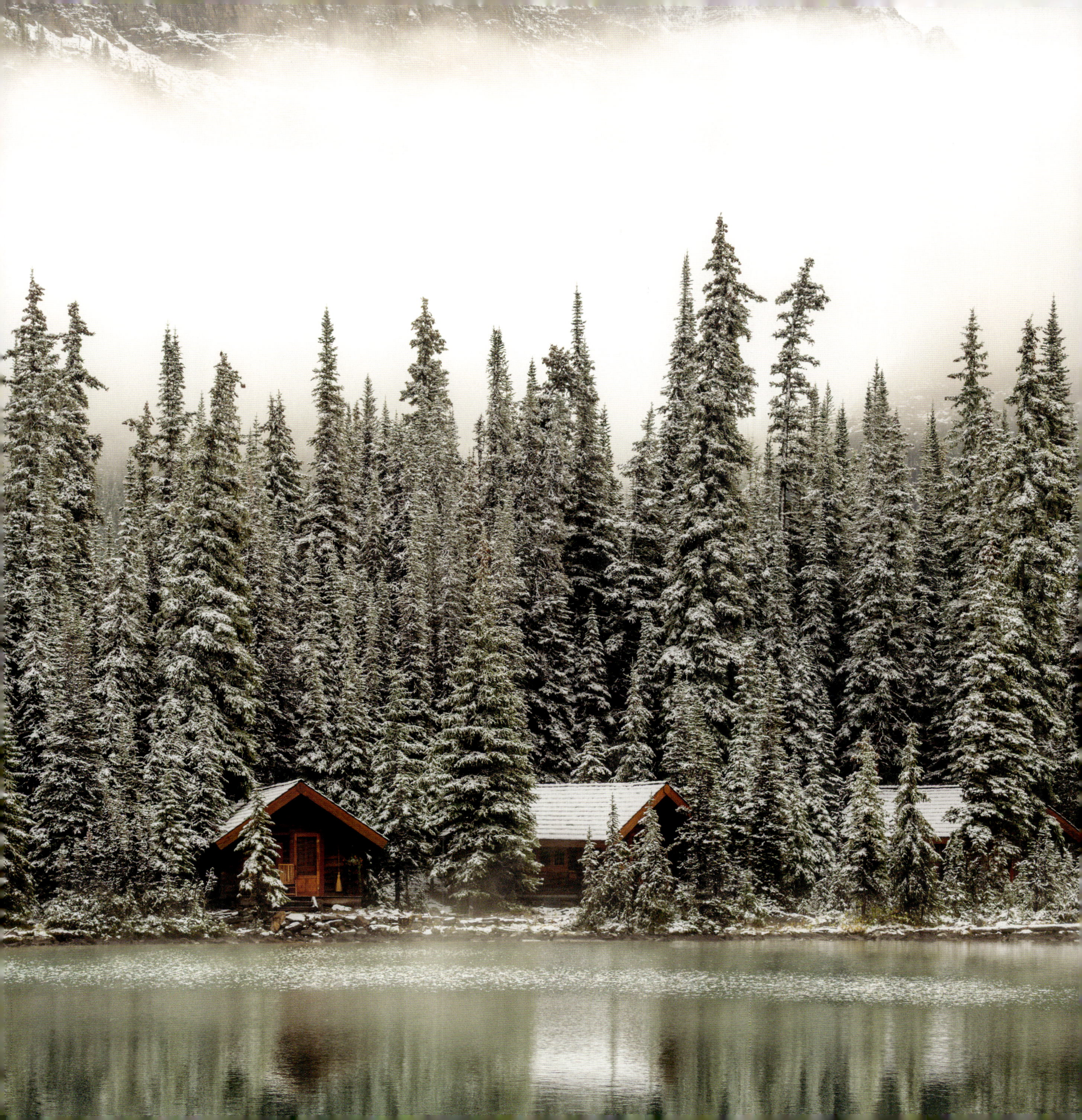

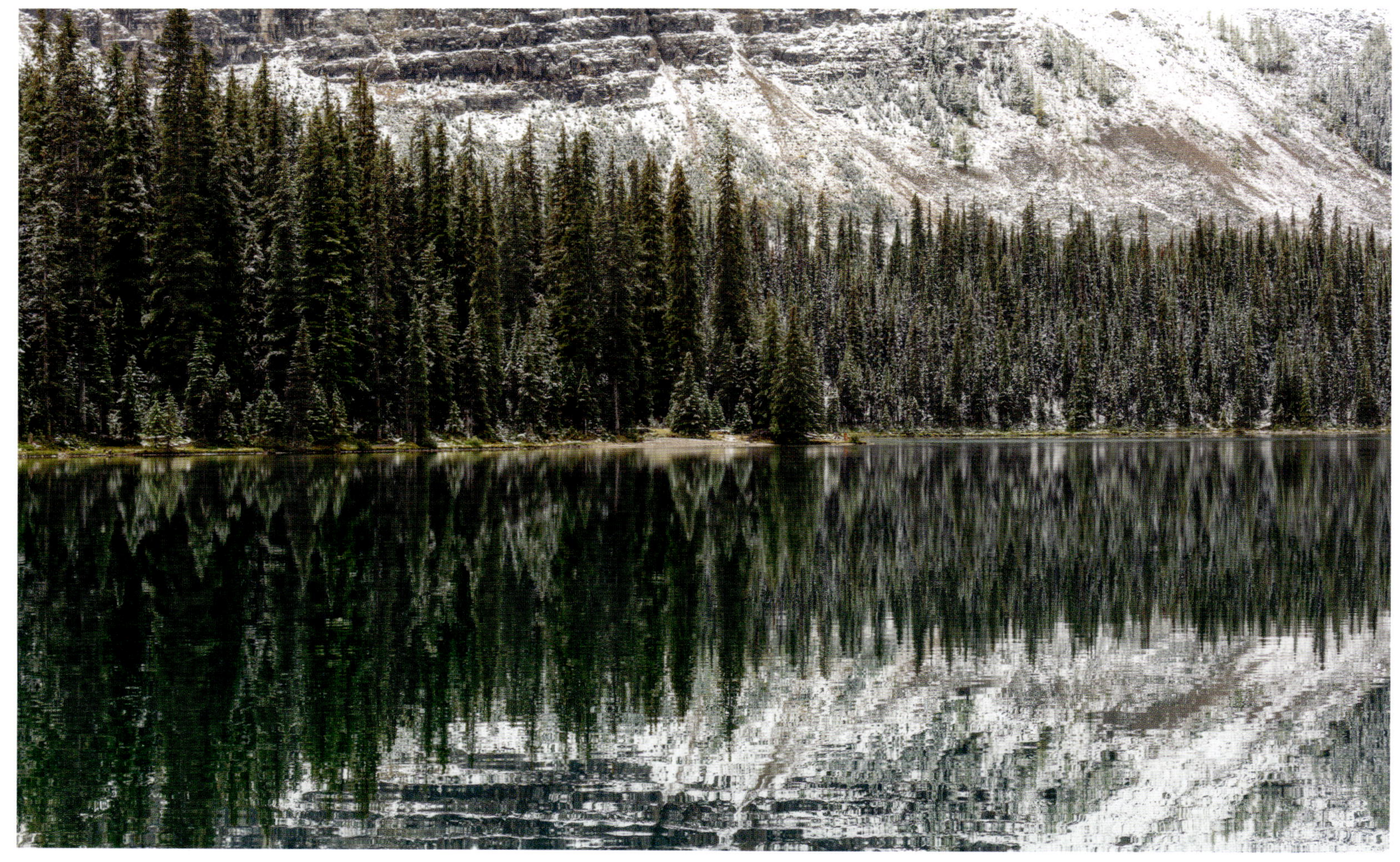

Lakeside Trail (2018)
It's a world of "rock" for sky at the lakeside-trail level circum-
navigating Lake O'Hara.

Mirror, Mirror (2018)
Mirror reflection of the forest – mountain transition on the surface of Lake O'Hara.

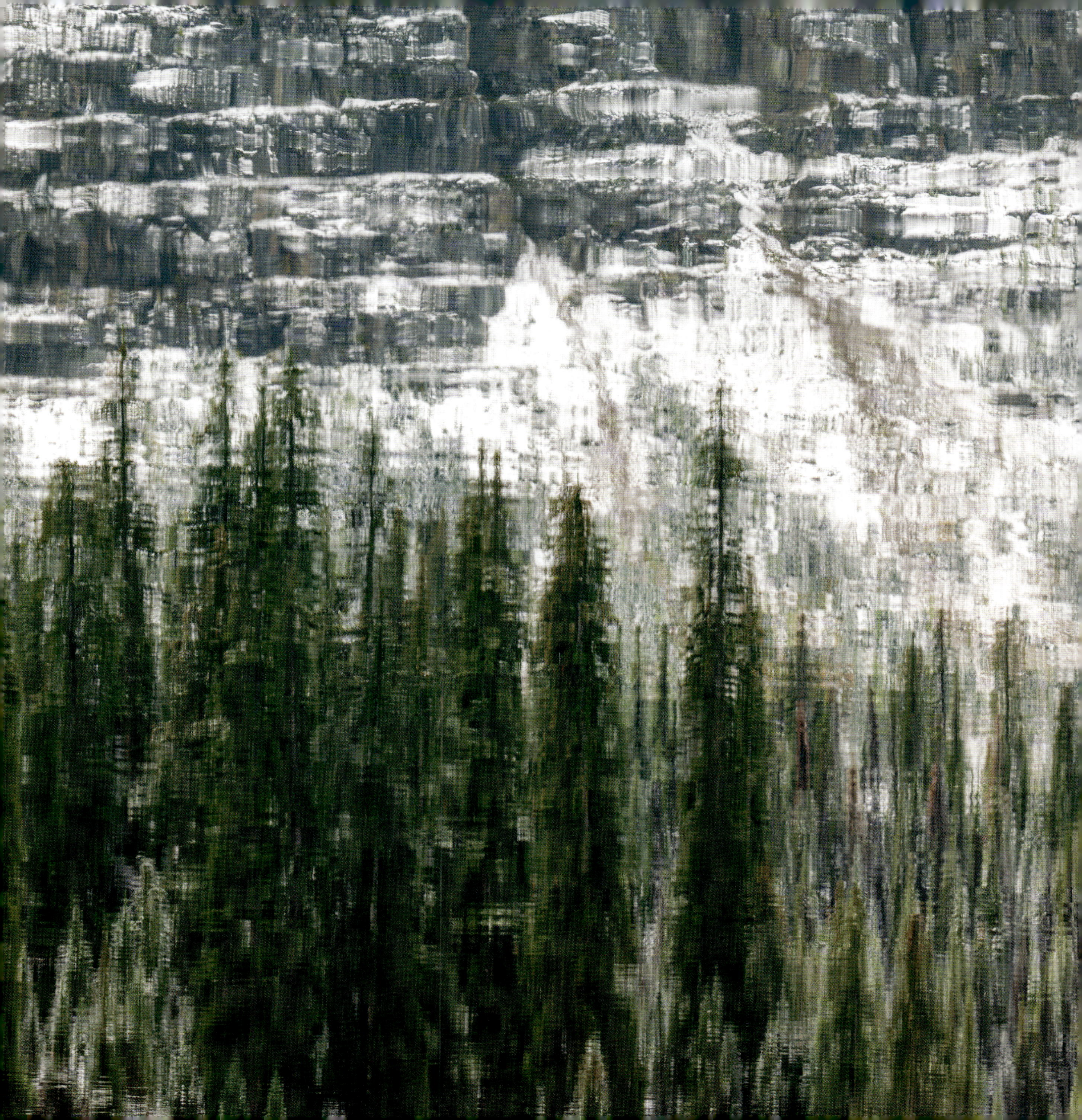

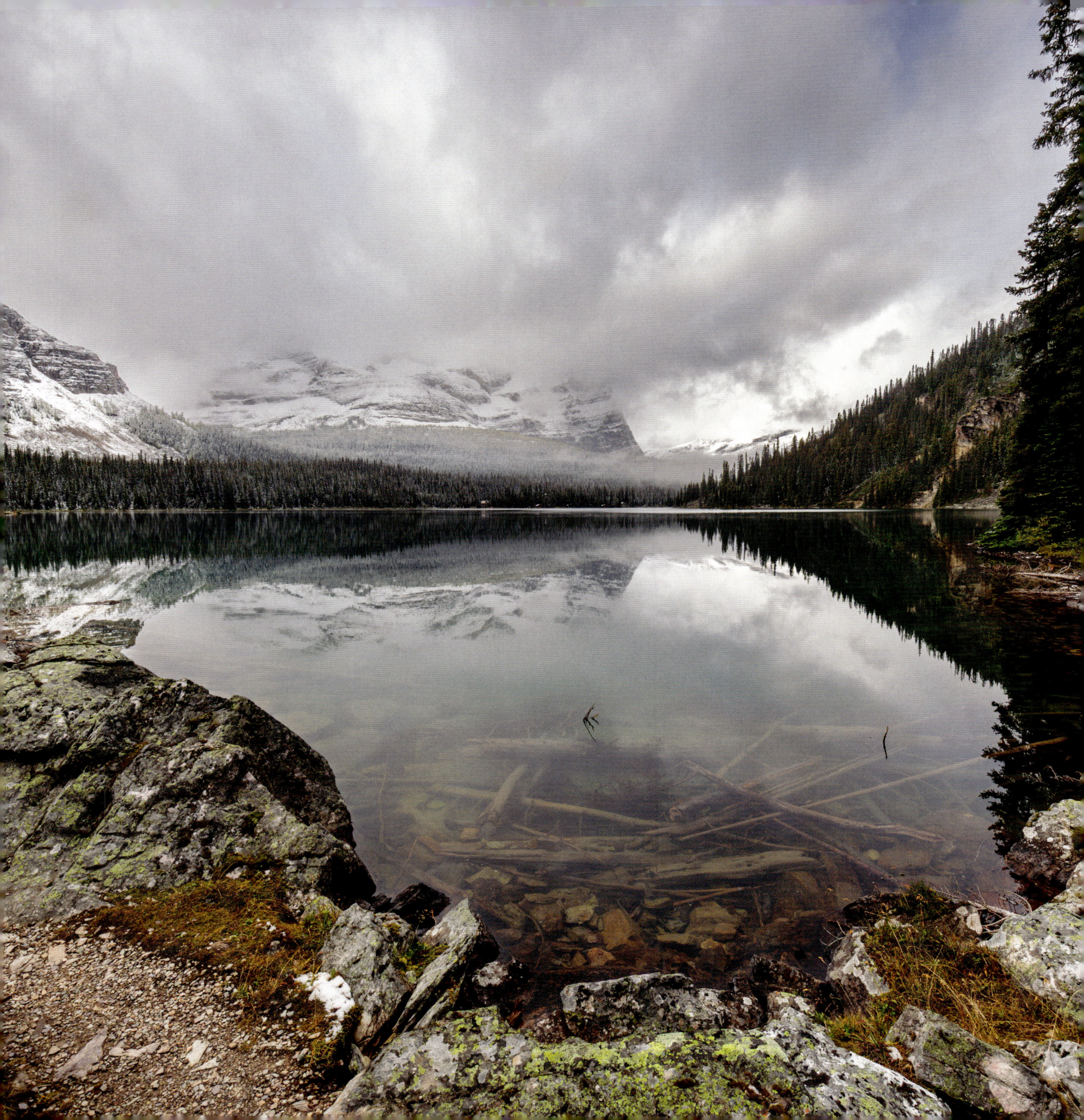

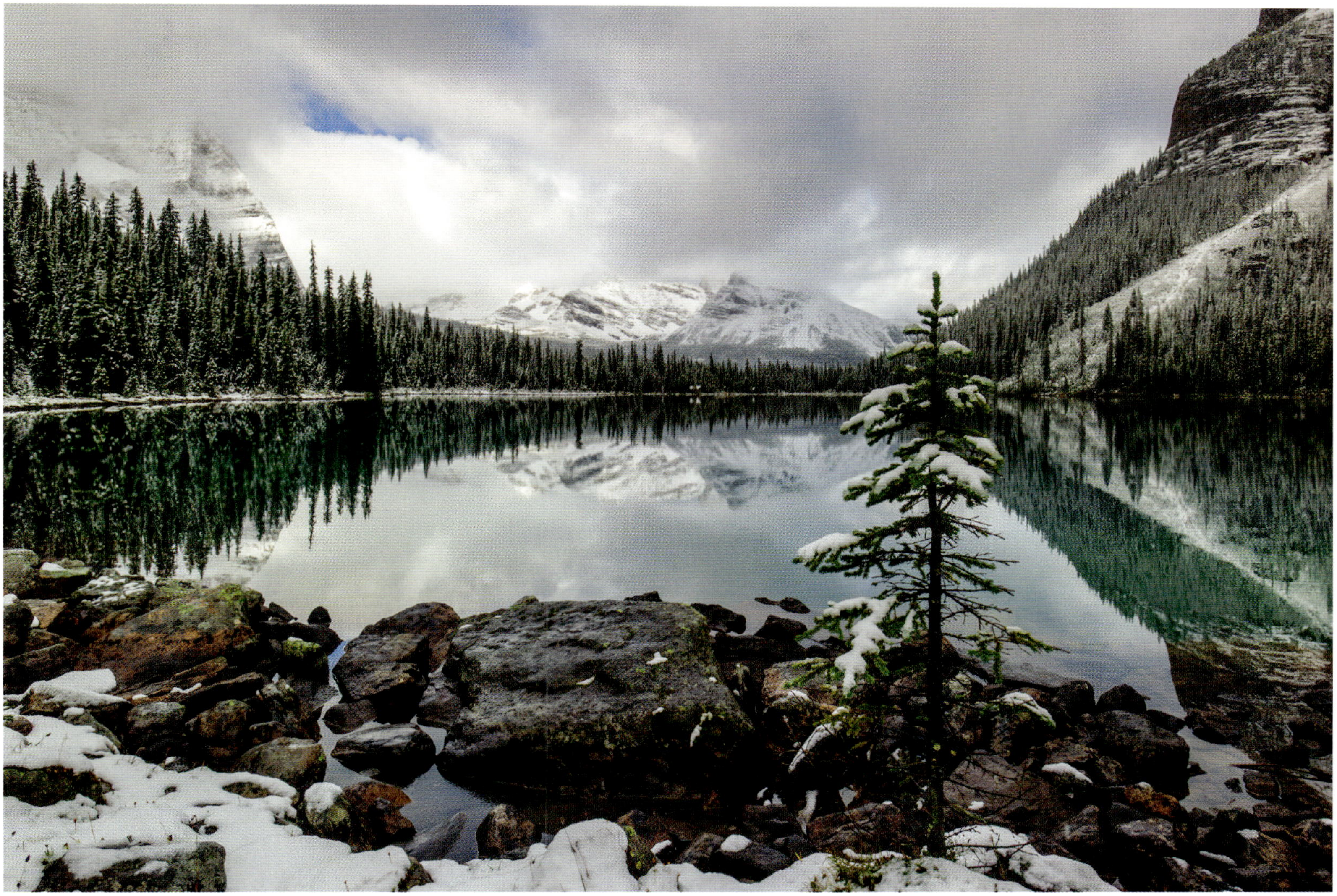

Winter's Approach (2011)
Fresh snowfall on the mountains surrounding Lake O'Hara creates an artistic aesthetic.

Distant Shore (2018)
Lake O'Hara Lodge and its cabins are barely visible on the distant shore of Lake O'Hara, embedded in the backdrop of Odaray Mountain.

Overleaf **Emerald Reflections Envelop the Distant Lodge** (2016)
Open water and the early snowfalls of September make wonderful vistas along the shore ine of Lake O'Hara.

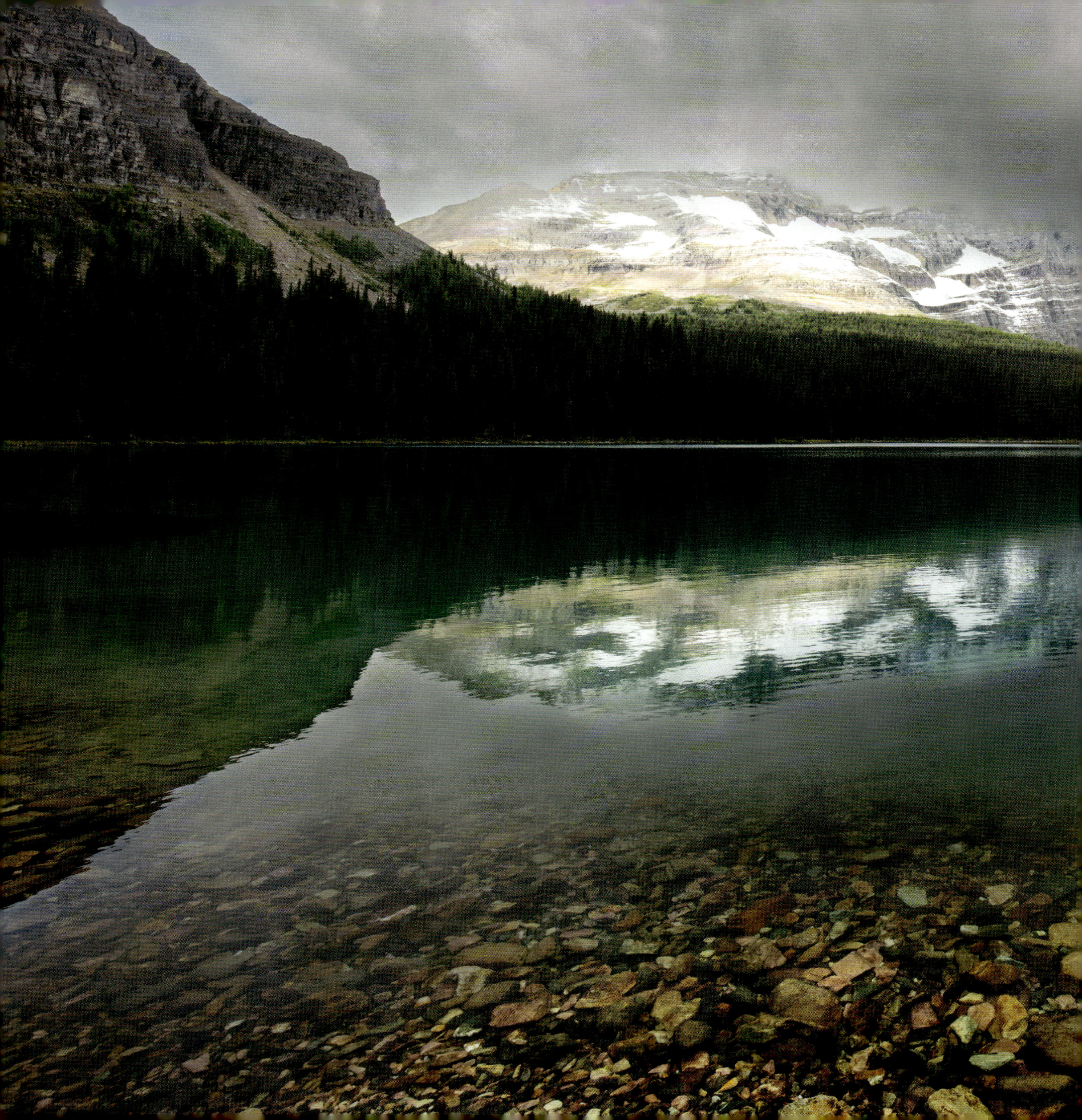

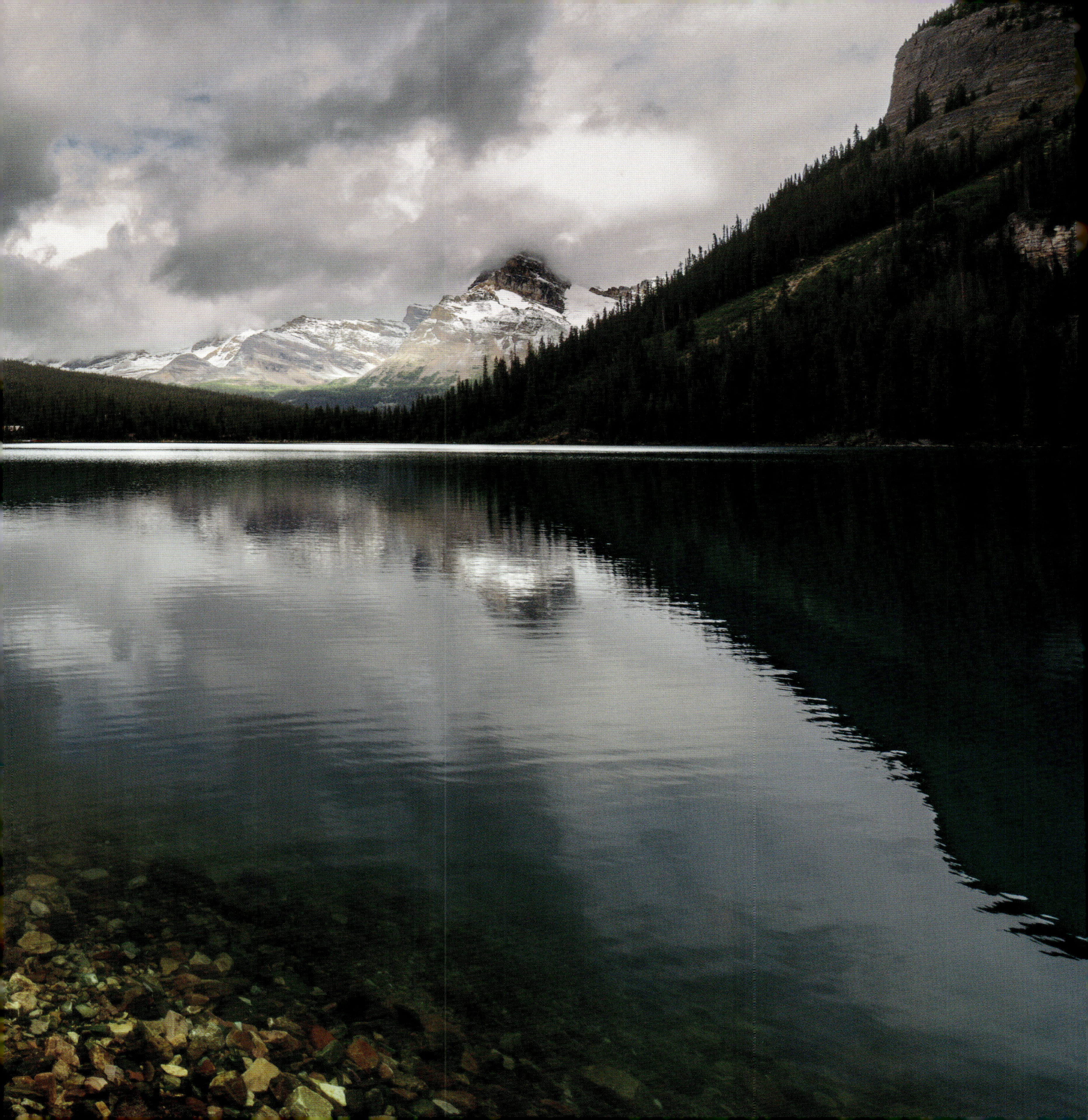

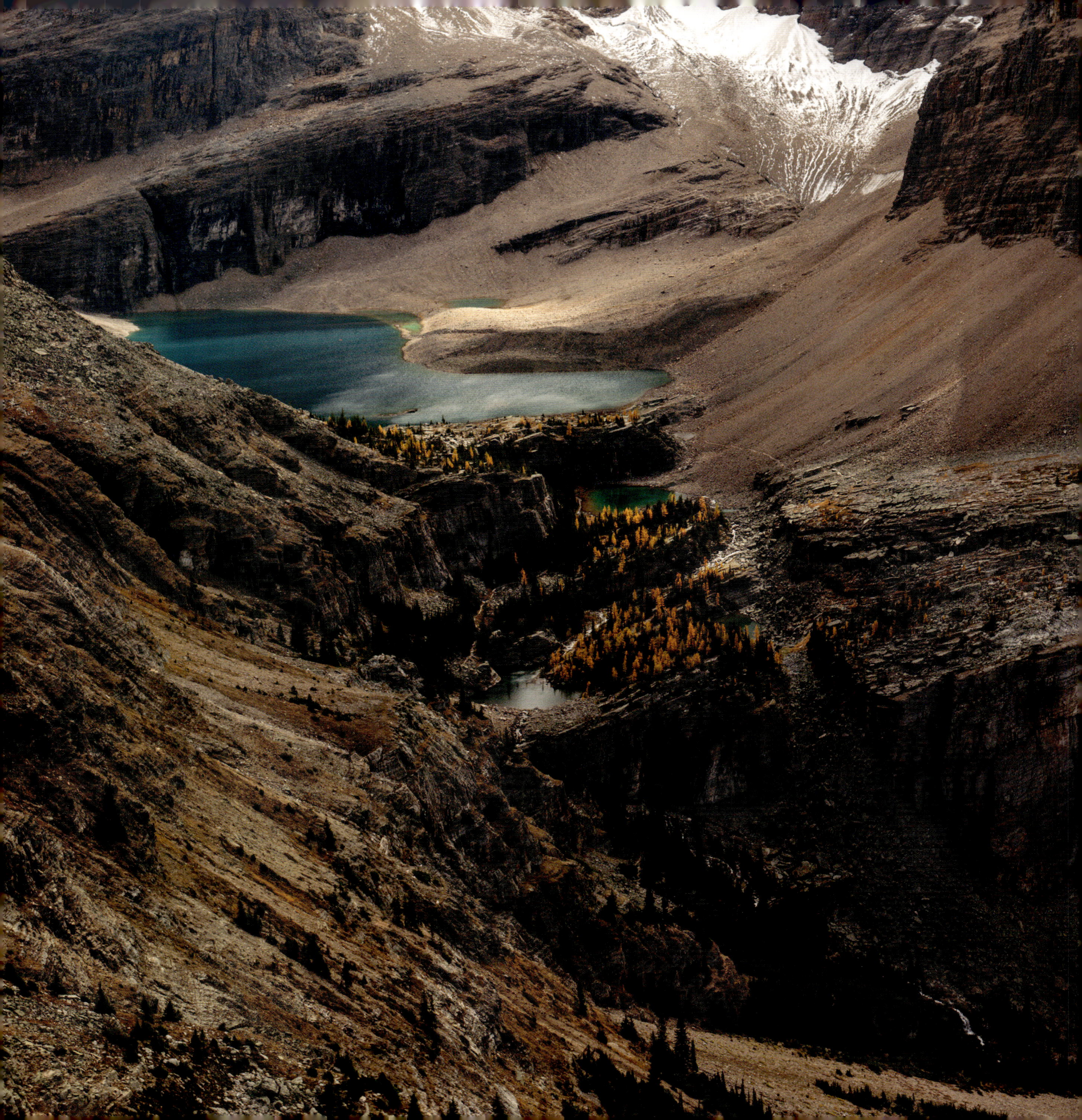

PART TWO

Lake Oesa

Regarding Lake Oesa Trail, the Gem Trek *Lake O'Hara Map and Trail Guide* states, "If you have time to do only one hike at Lake O'Hara, this is it." There is no better illustration of the saying "the journey is as compelling as the destination" than this 3.2-km trail hike up the 245-m gain in elevation to Lake Oesa.

An exquisite construction of heavy stone steps guides hikers along the route. Lake Oesa Trail is particularly indebted to the immortal legacy of Lawrence Grassi, an Italian immigrant who came to Canada in 1912 and settled in Canmore, where he worked as a coal miner. Notwithstanding the physical demands of his occupation, he spent his free time exploring the mountains, becoming an accomplished mountaineer and trail builder. Despite his short stature, his strength was legendary. A story still circulates today about the time he carried an entire stove up to a campsite after two younger men had given up on the task. Described as a self-contained man, he lived humbly in a simple cabin, and never married or returned to Italy. This generosity of labour to create trails so that others could follow was the way he expressed his emotions. The ACC erected a plaque in his honour in 1970 along a portion of switchbacks and stone steps on the Lake Oesa Trail to commemorate his contribution.

Alpine Cascade (2021)
View of Lake Oesa, Lefroy Lake, and Victoria Lake. Gem Trek's *Lake O'Hara Map and Trail Guide* states, "If you have time for only one hike at Lake O'Hara, this is it."

Humans are not the only ones to appreciate his trails. Hoary marmots are often seen scurrying across these stone trails, and on sunny days they like to sprawl on the warm rocks to thermoregulate. Referred to as "whistle pigs" for their loud piercing warning calls to caution others of an approaching predator, they are related to the same genus as groundhogs, but are a separate species that lives at much higher elevations. Summer is a critical time for marmots, as they hibernate for 7–8 months of the year in burrows below boulders and stones, living off their fat reserves while their heart rates often drop to as low as 3–4 beats per minute.

The Lake Oesa region is composed of sediments from 500-million-year-old shallow tropical seas, which, through the forces of plate tectonics, were thrust-faulted high into the sky. The older Cambrian limestone formations were pushed over younger strata during the mountain-building period approximately 180–66 million years ago. Subsequent glacial erosion left behind the glacial tarn of Lake Oesa resting in a cirque basin surrounded by steep mountain walls. The U-shaped valley contains a cascade of lakes, such as Victoria Lake and Lefroy Lake, that distract the hiker with their beauty on the journey to Lake Oesa, making this the must-do hike of the Lake O'Hara region.

The stunning geological features of Lake Oesa made this a favourite location for the painter J.E.H MacDonald, who availed himself of the CPR's artist's rail pass from 1924 to 1926. Having become enchanted by Lake O'Hara, he used his own resources to return here every summer up to and including 1930. He first stayed in the alpine-meadows cabins of the Lake O'Hara Bungalow Camp, until in 1926 when he stayed in the newly built Lake O'Hara Lodge. In his remaining visits he stayed in a lakeshore cabin. All of this and much more is richly described in the book *To See What He Saw: J.E.H. MacDonald and the O'Hara Years 1924–1932*, by Stanley Munn and Patricia Cucman. As an artist, MacDonald worked for himself "to present honestly and reverently the outward aspect and inward feeling of the landscape."[1] I have long been an admirer of the Group of Seven painters and their stylized depictions of the Canadian landscape, so it was wonderful to discover that during the first year I stayed at Lake O'Hara Lodge, in 2007, I was in the very room J.E.H. MacDonald had stayed in 83 years prior.

MacDonald would typically complete two sketches each day, and spanning the seven years he painted here it is estimated he created as many as 105 paintings. Over that time the weather was inhospitable enough to force him to stay indoors for only 15 days. Several of the trails in existence today were not present at that time. He would often traverse Lake O'Hara by boat to start the trek up to Lake Oesa. The effect of the natural beauty of this region was so influential on MacDonald that he would often be thinking about it long after his stays as he created large-format canvas paintings from his onsite sketches in his Toronto studio. His affection particularly for Lake Oesa is evident by the subject matter of his last large-canvas painting – an early snowfall on the lake – before his untimely death in 1932.

1 Stanley Munn and Patricia Cucman, *To See What He Saw: J.E.H. MacDonald and the O'Hara Years 1924–1932* (Figure 1 Publishing, 2024), 14.

Italian Stairway (2021)
The incredible trail engineering of Lawrence Grassi along the Lake Oesa Trail.

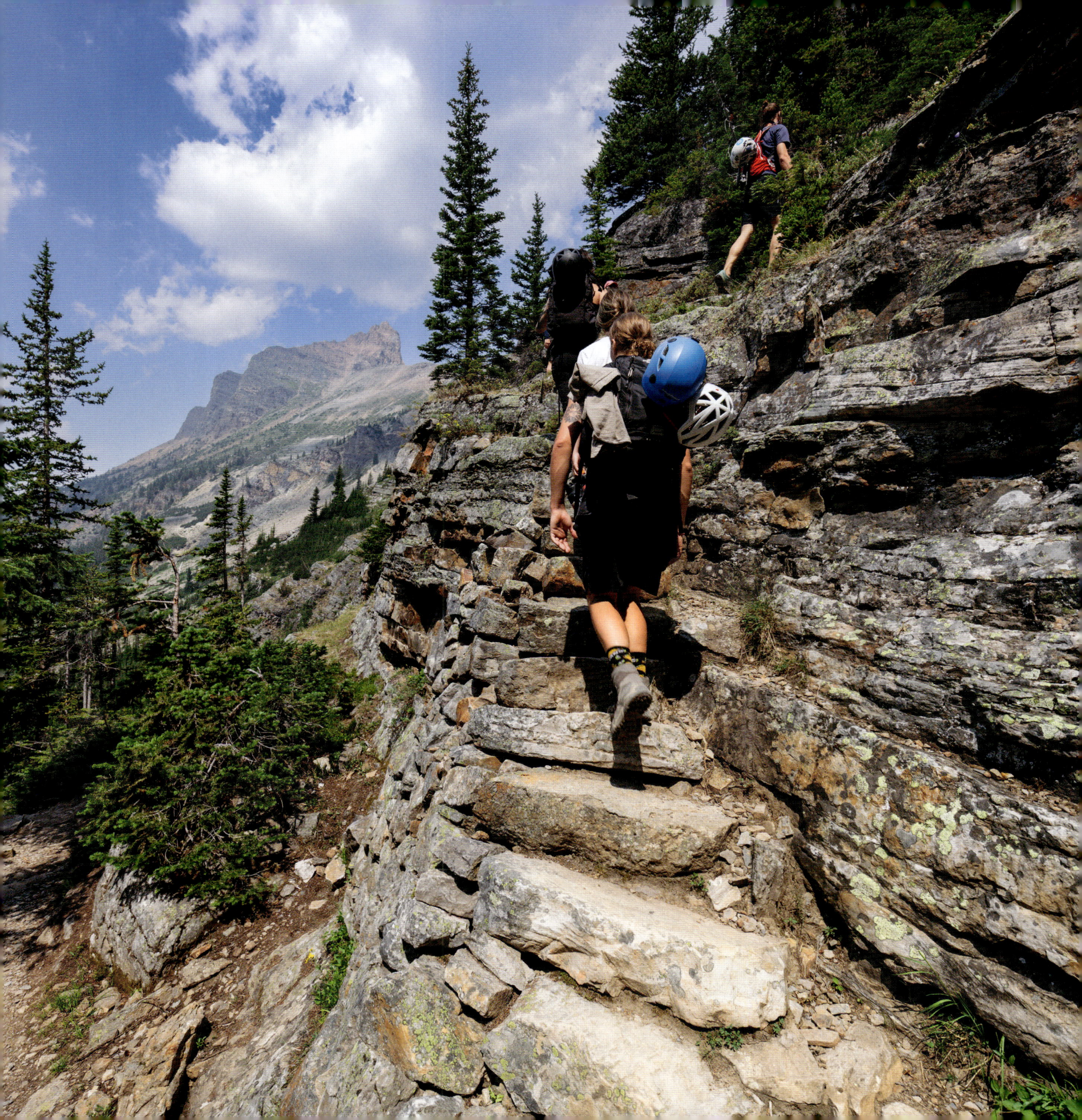

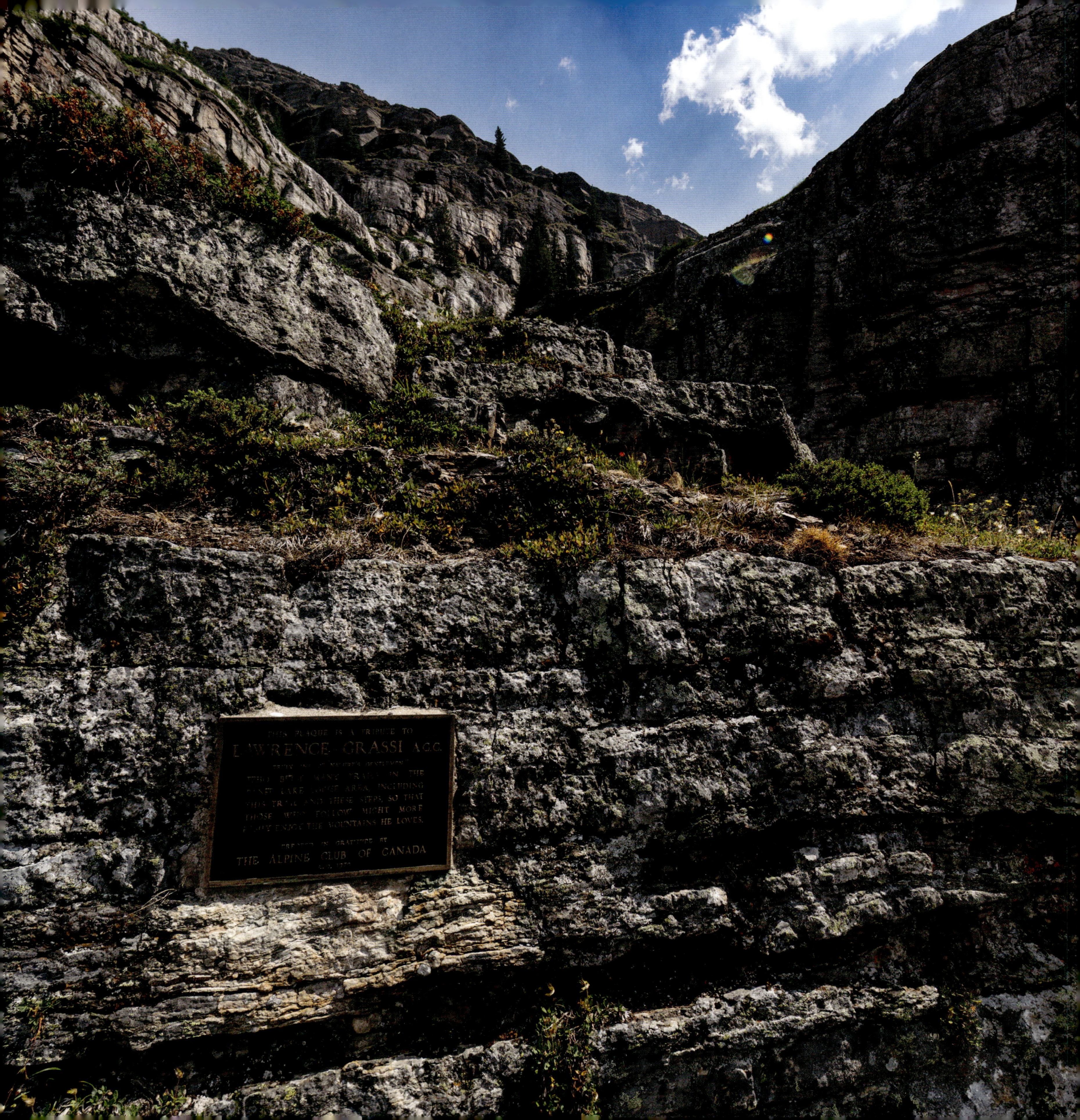
THIS PLAQUE IS A TRIBUTE TO
LAWRENCE GRASSI A.C.C.
TRULY ONE OF NATURE'S GENTLEMEN
WHO BUILT MANY TRAILS IN THE
BANFF LAKE LOUISE AREA, INCLUDING
THIS TRAIL AND THESE STEPS, SO THAT
THOSE WHO FOLLOW MIGHT MORE
FULLY ENJOY THE MOUNTAINS HE LOVES.
ERECTED IN GRATITUDE BY
THE ALPINE CLUB OF CANADA
A.D. 1979

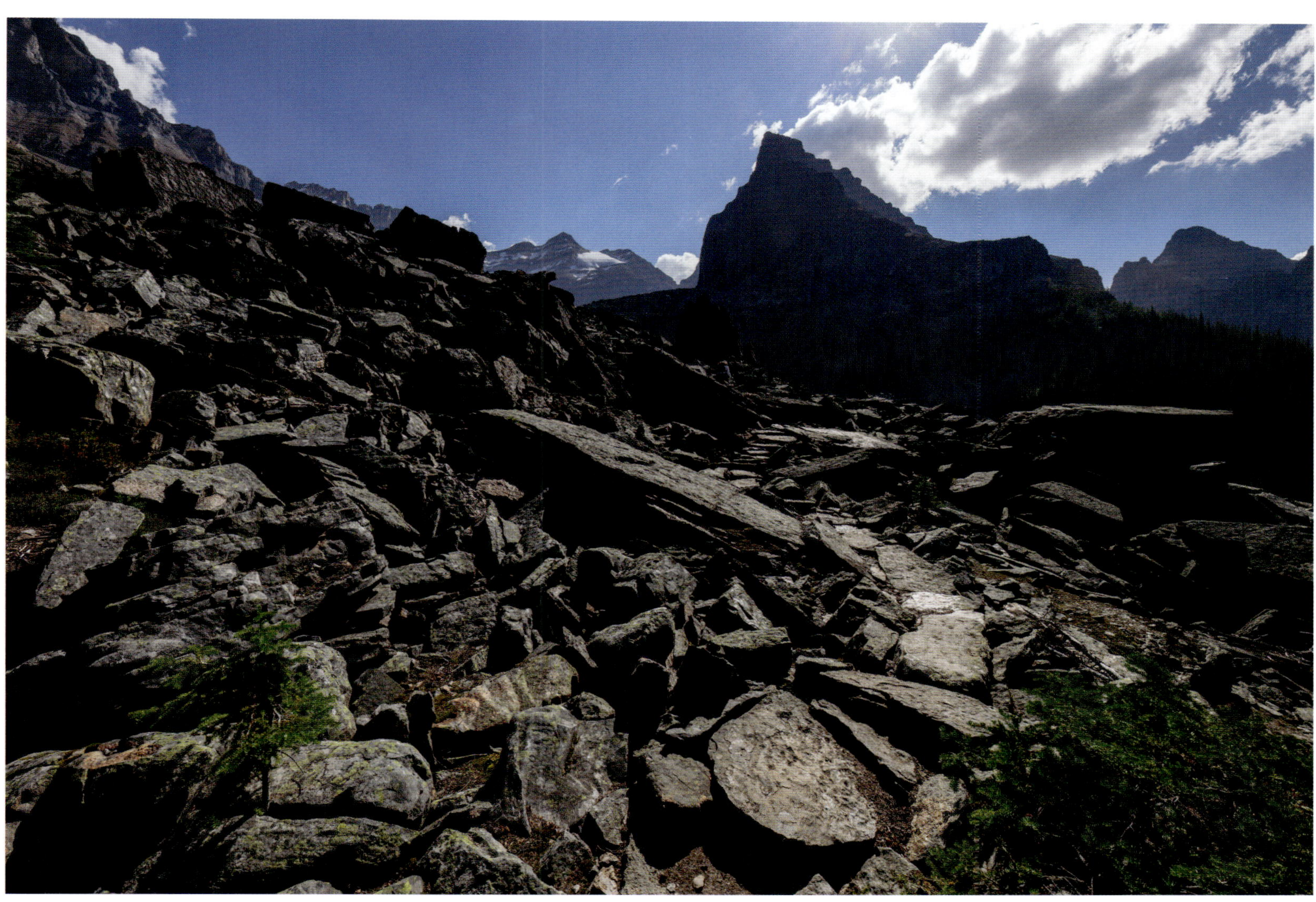

Giant's Stride (2025)
Large slabs of stone, like strides of a giant, lead the route up to Lake Oesa. The marvel of this physical feat of labour by Lawrence Grassi is palpable in every step along the way.

Gratitude (2021)
The Alpine Club of Canada's tribute to Lawrence Grassi along the trail he constructed for those of us fortunate enough to follow.

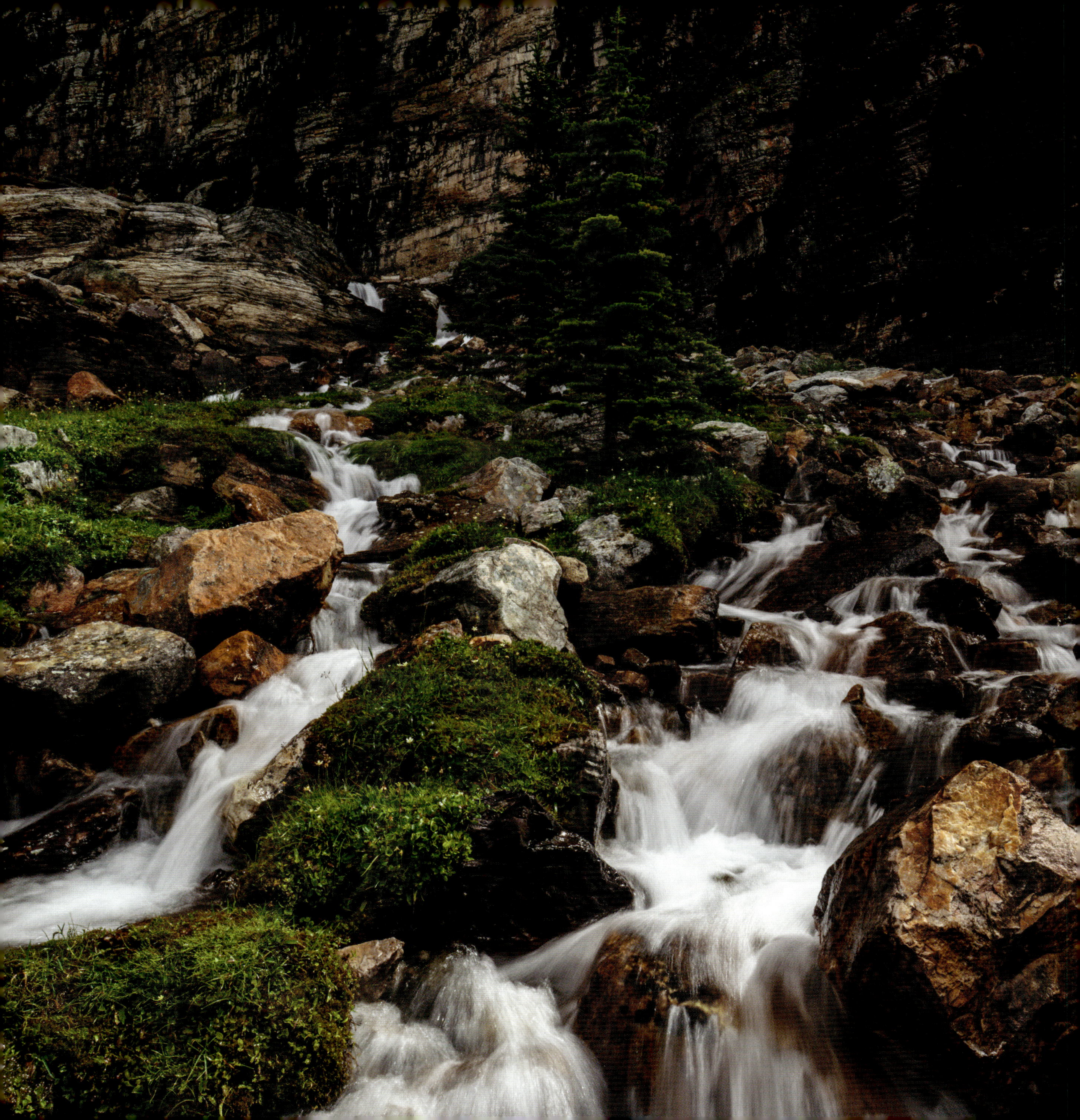

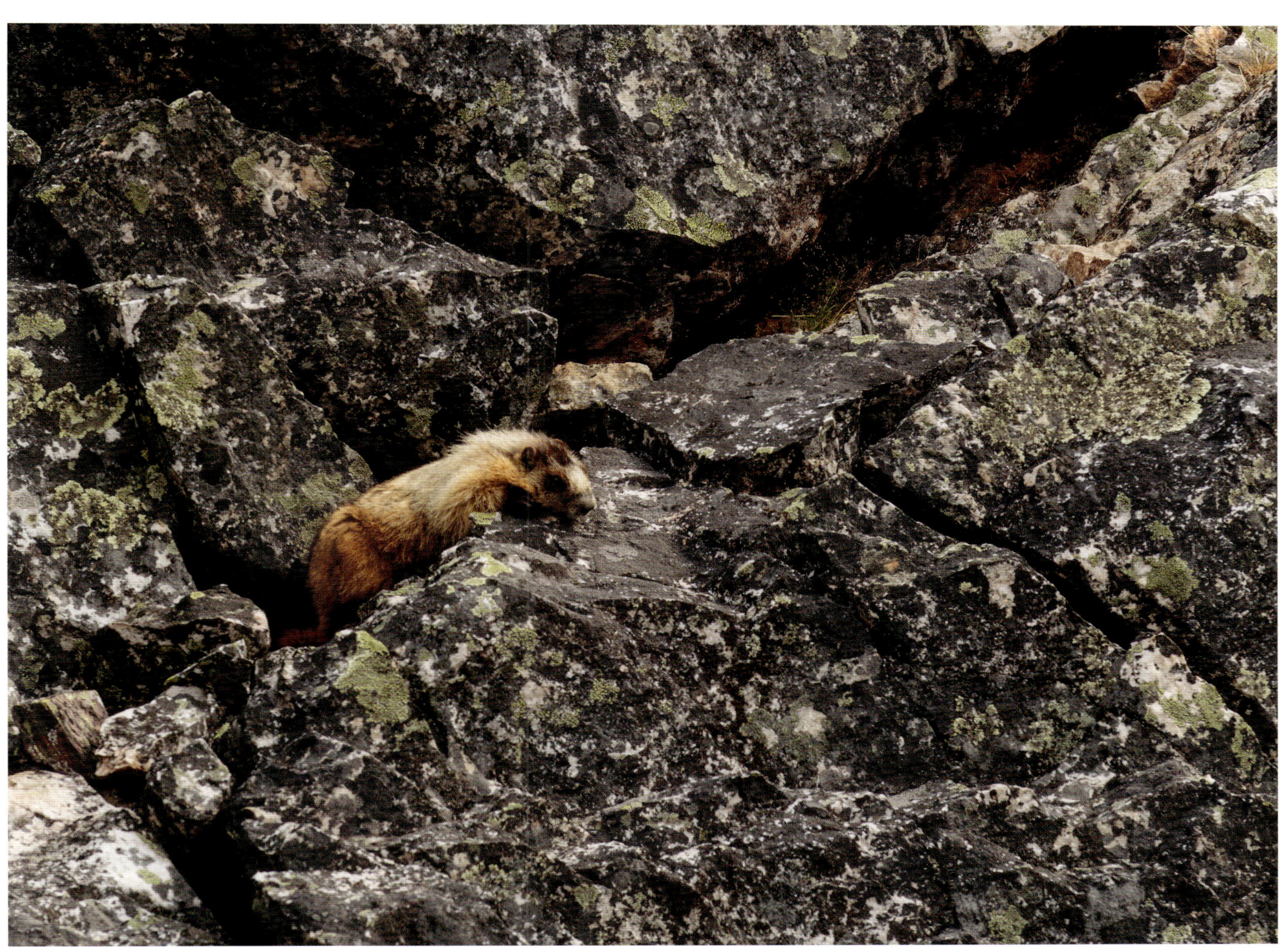

On the Rocks (2021)
Hoary marmots are within the same genus as groundhogs, but they're a separate species living at much higher elevations. On sunny days, they lie on the rocks to absorb the heat.

Resting Place (2014)
A wonderful, humid resting place along the hike to Lake Oesa.
This is also a favourite location for the resident hoary marmots.

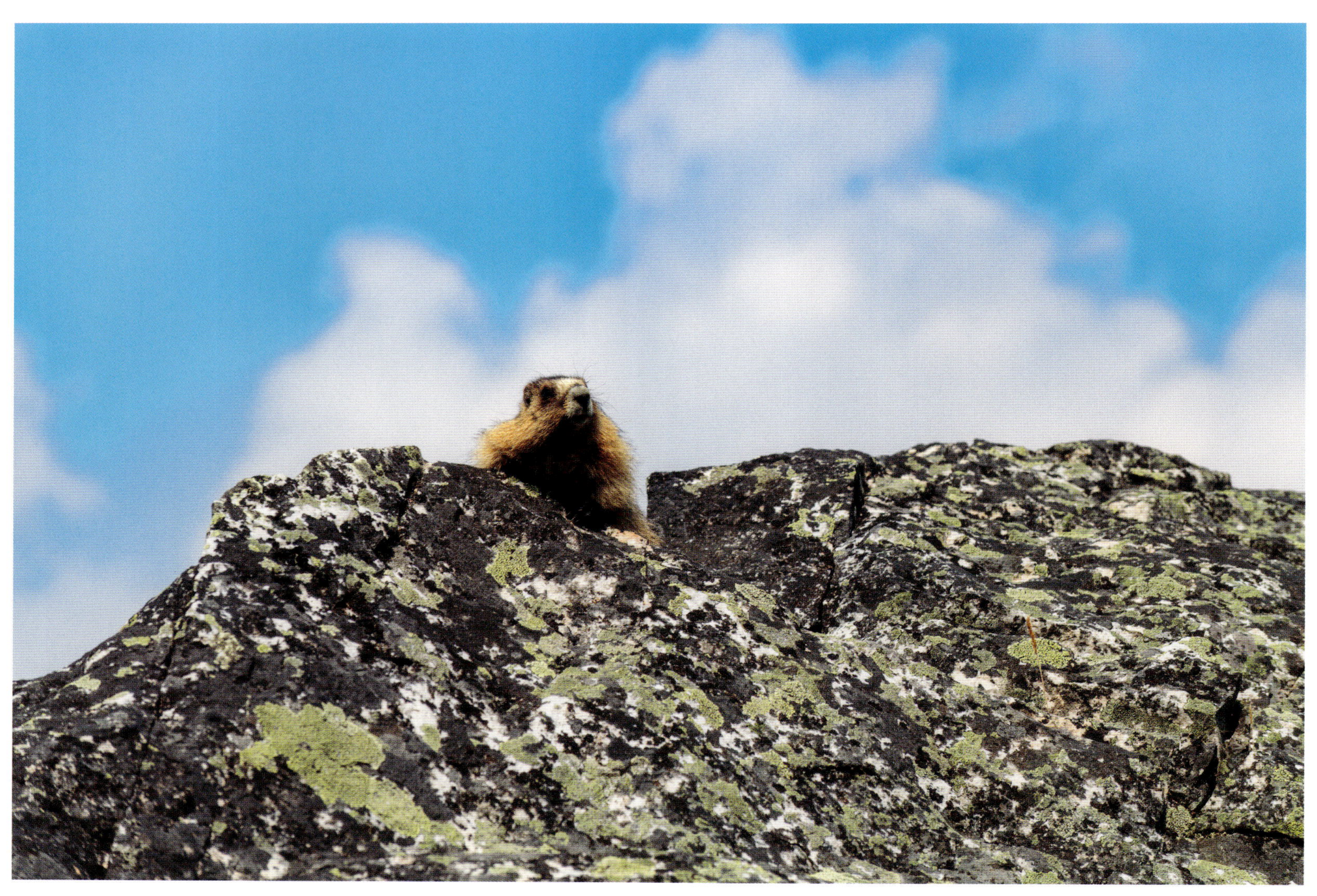

Somebody's Watching You (2021)
Whether or not we see them, they most certainly see us.
Marmots are nicknamed "whistle pigs" for their sharp warning
calls.

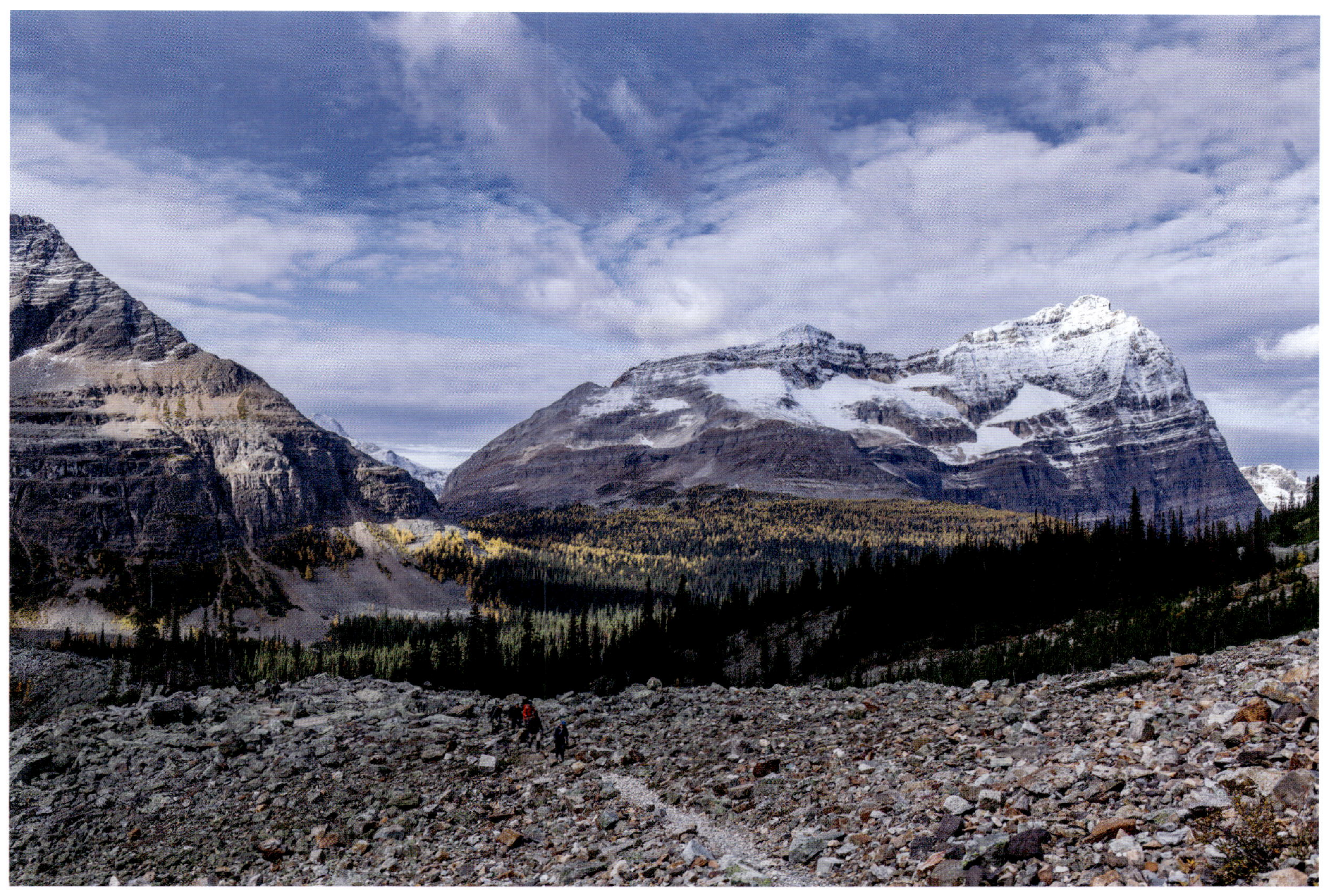

Levelled Off (2021)
Hikers making their way along the rock debris of Mount Huber
on their way toward Victoria Falls.

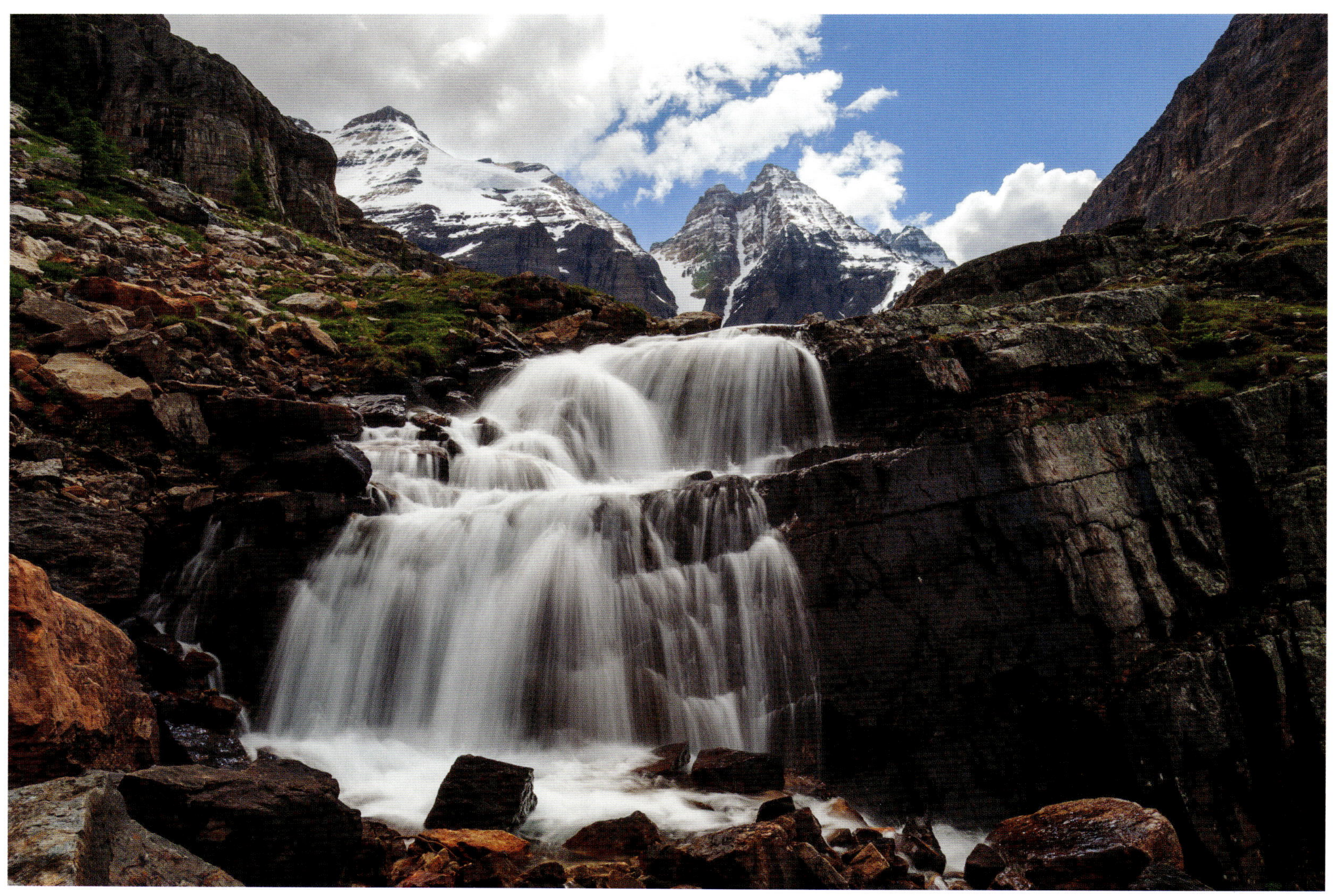

Victoria Falls (2007)
The freshly melted glacier water of Lake Oesa cascades over
the first of many falls on its path to Lake O'Hara 200 m below.

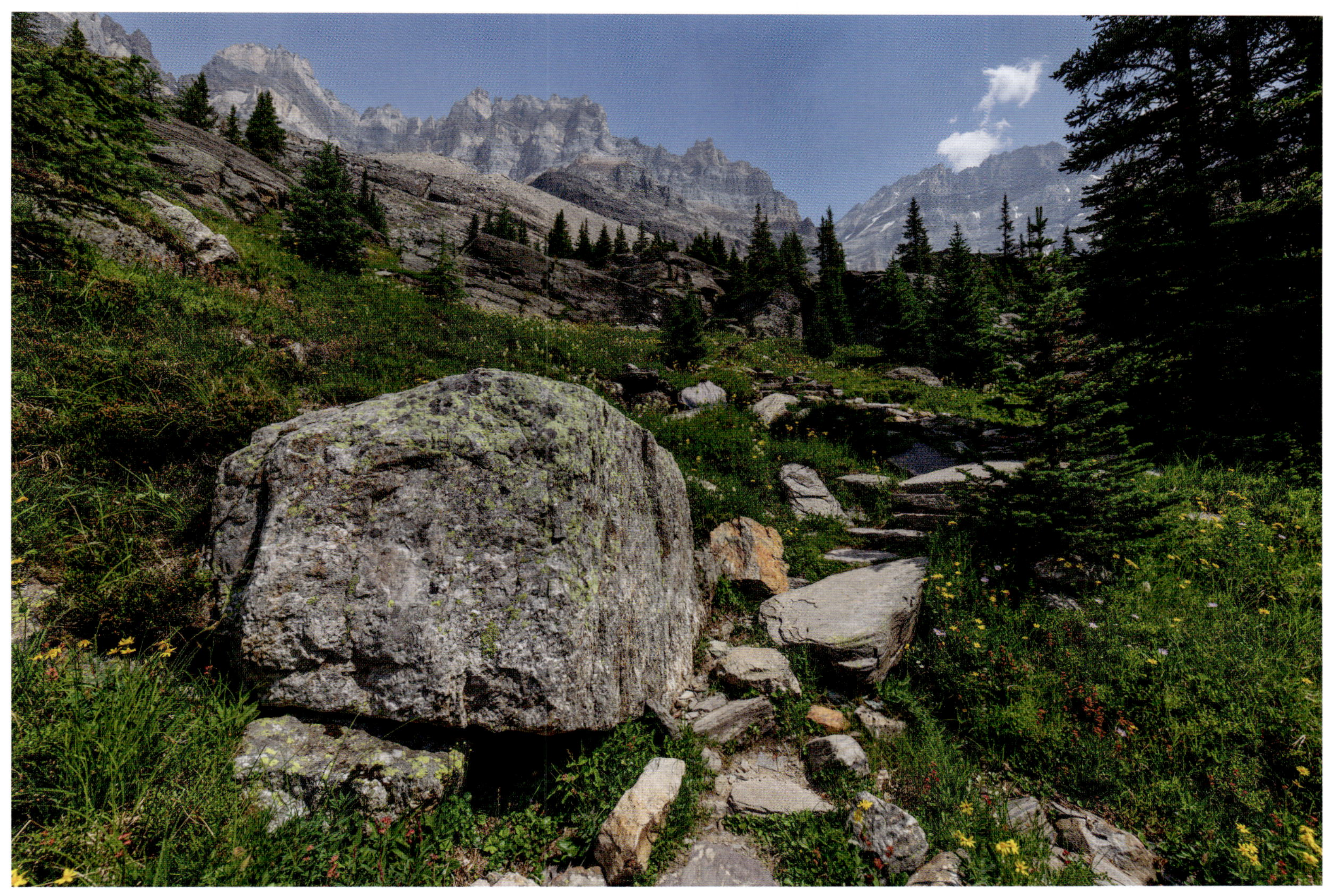

Alpine Meadow Pathway (2021)
Giant stone steps from the labour of Lawrence Grassi lead the
way to Lake Oesa.

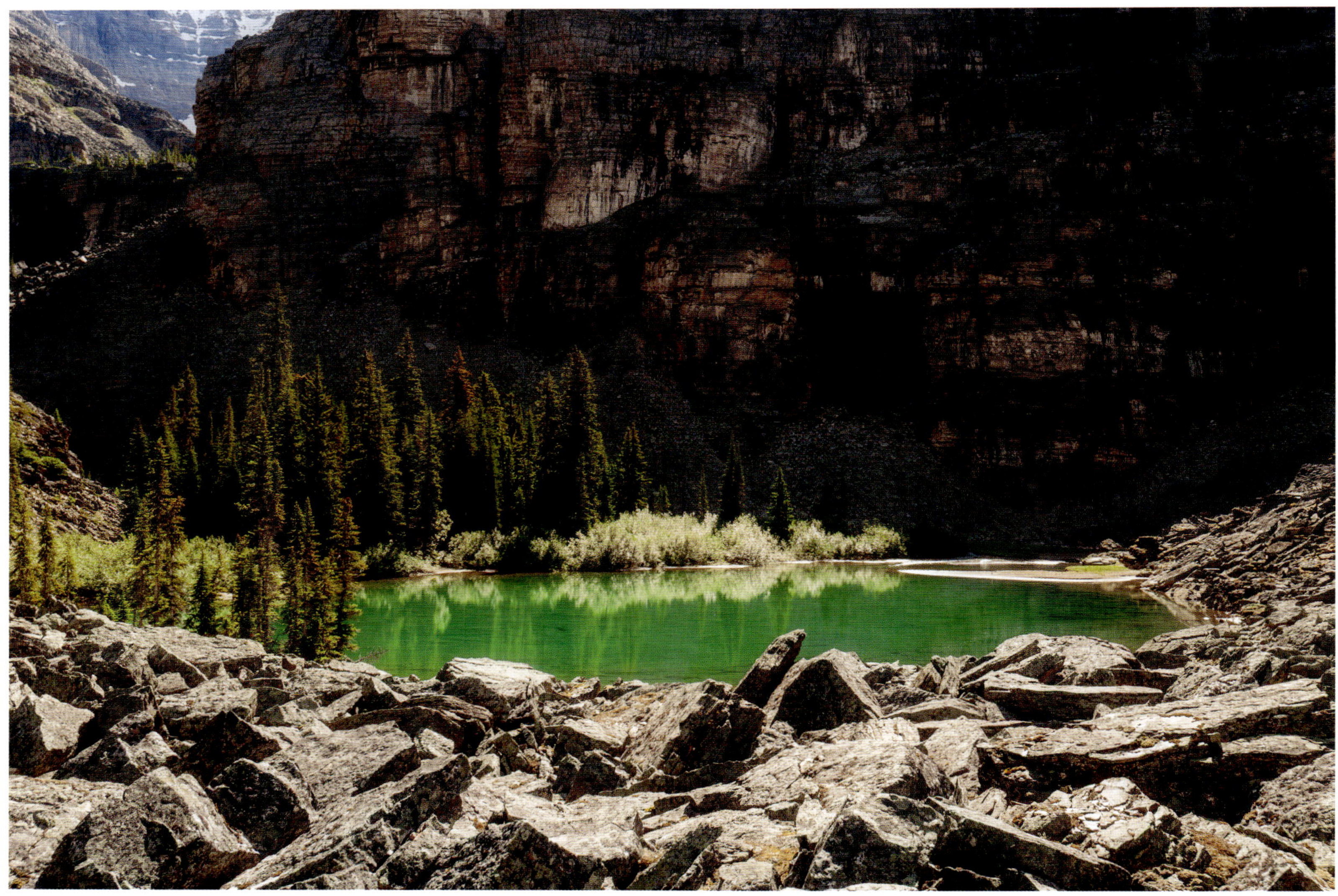

Yukness Lake (2007)
The first of a series of stunning lakes on the hike to Lake Oesa. Yukness Lake lies under the towering Yukness Mountain Ledge.

Natural Palette (2025)
Late summer glacial silt sediments contribute to the milky blue colour of the water of Victoria Lake.

Overleaf **Nature's Work of Art** (2016)
When the daytime winds calm down, shallow, protected Victoria Lake is one of the most picturesque along the journey to Lake Oesa.

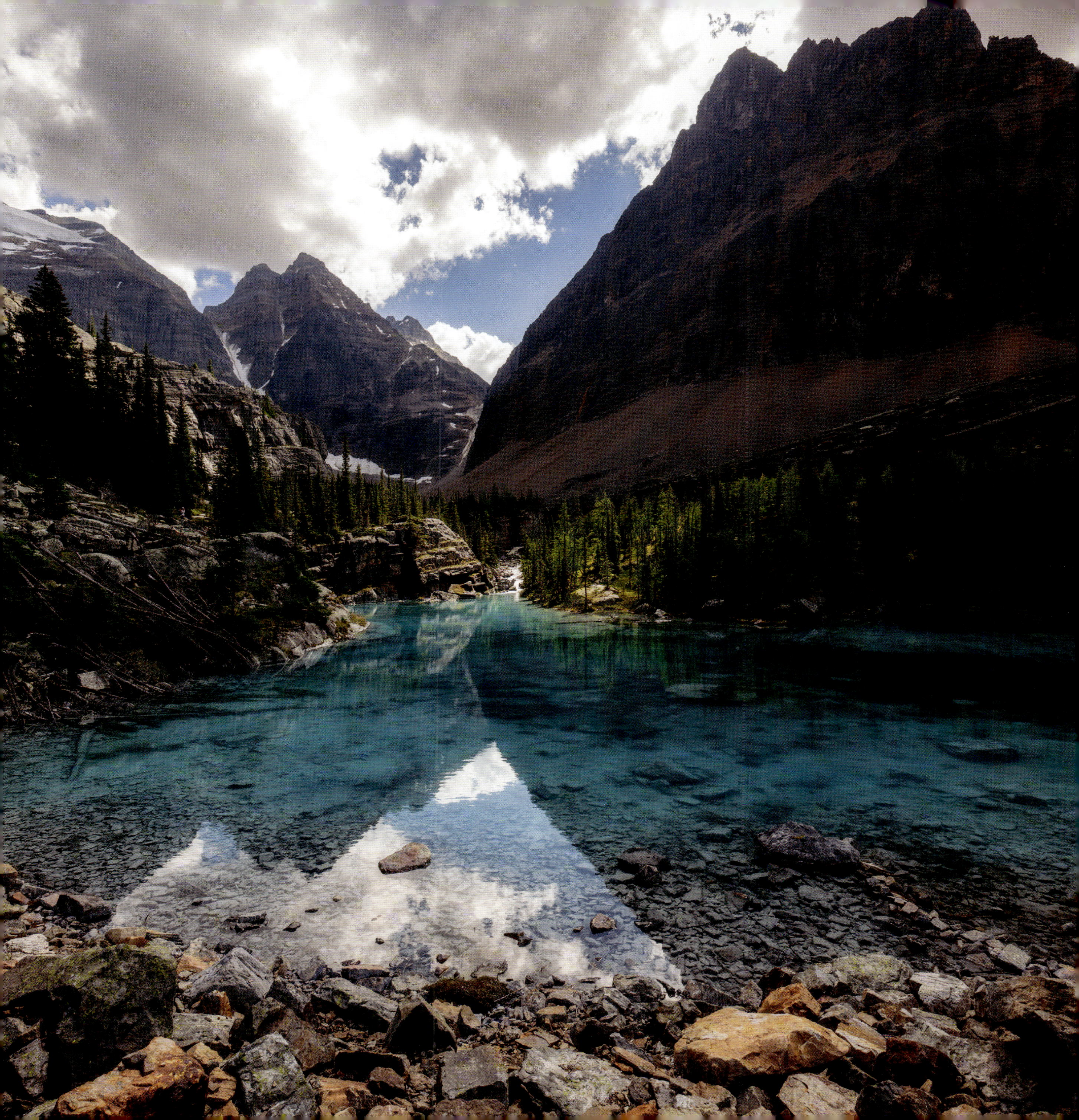

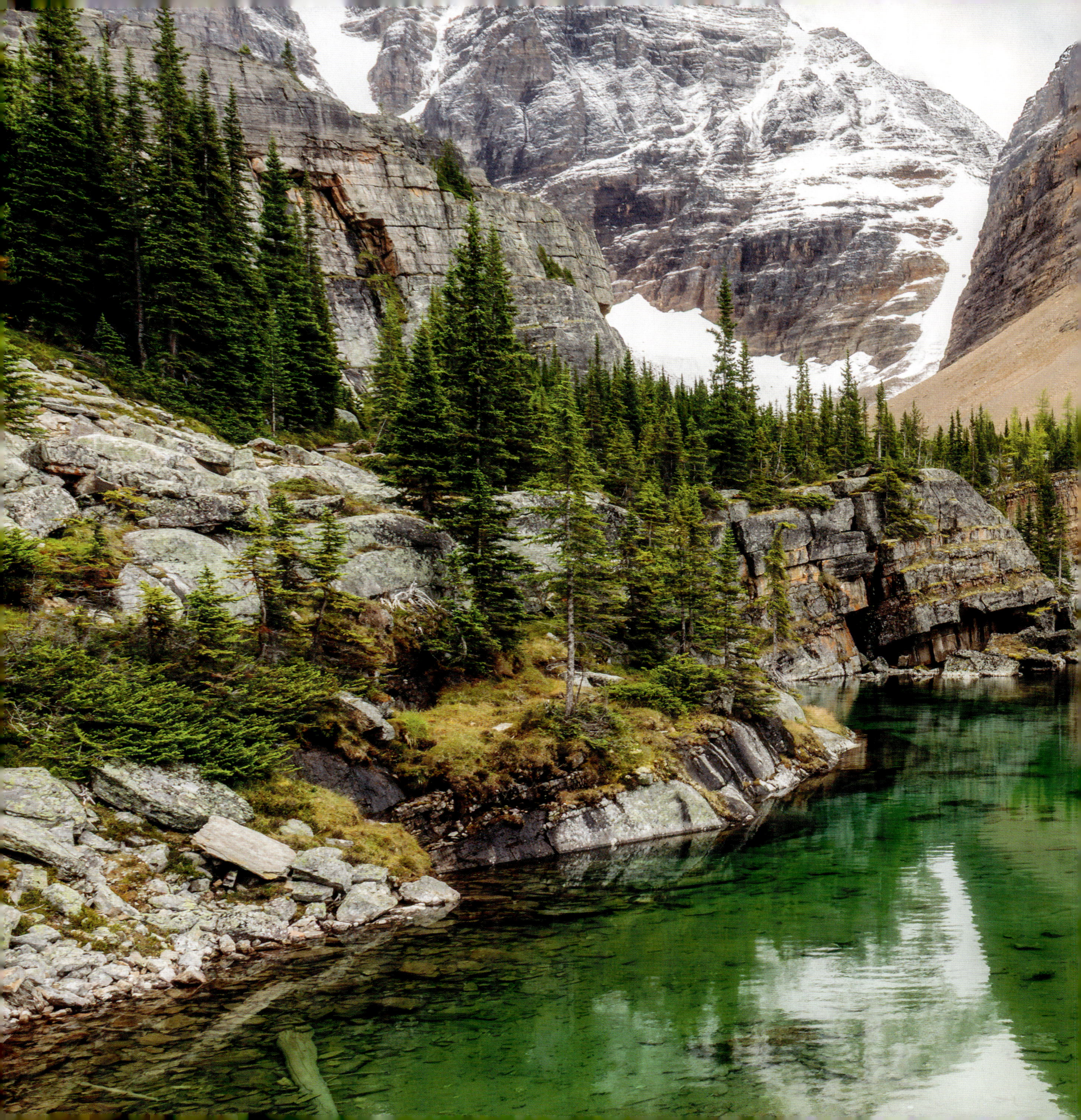

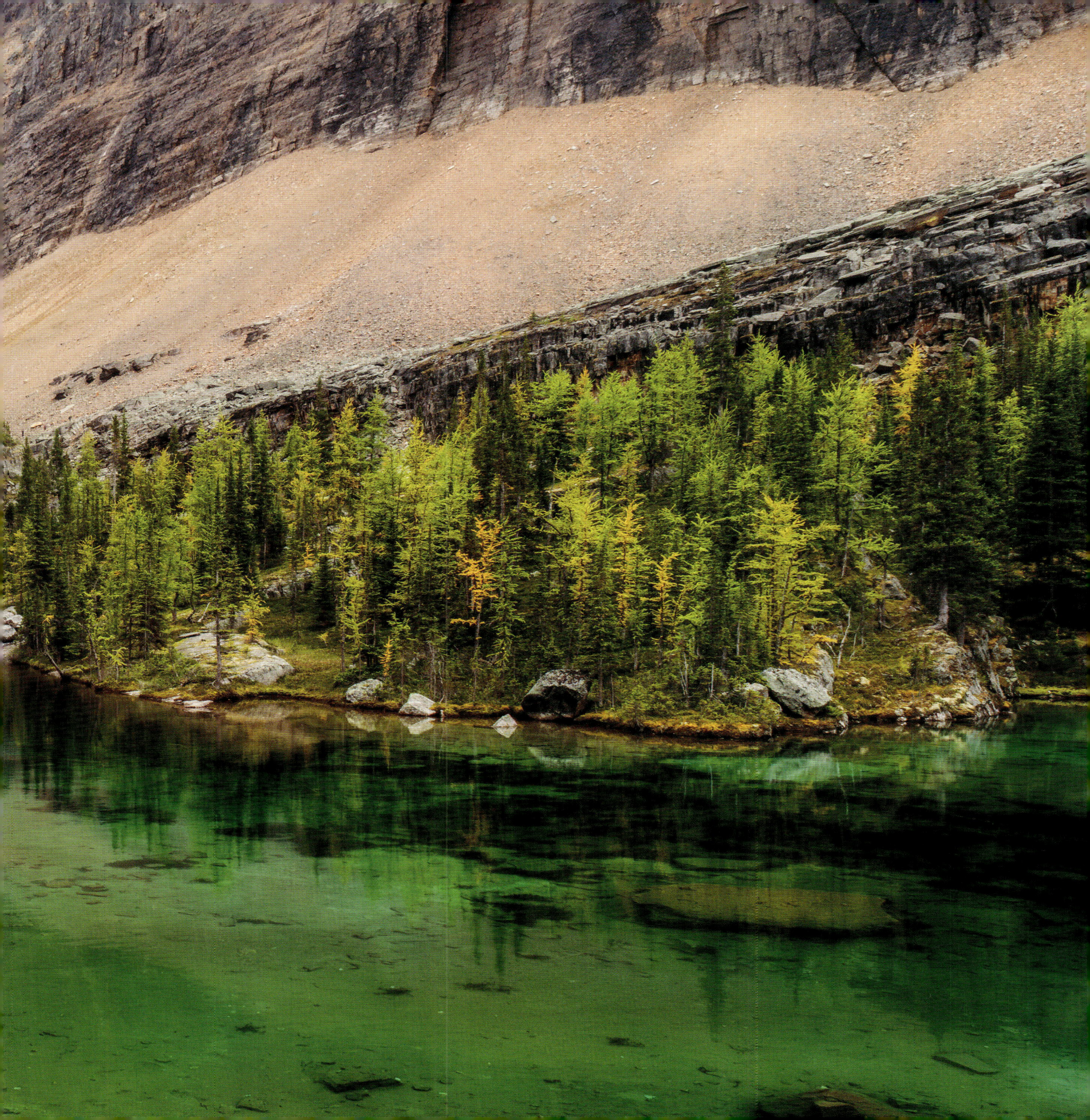

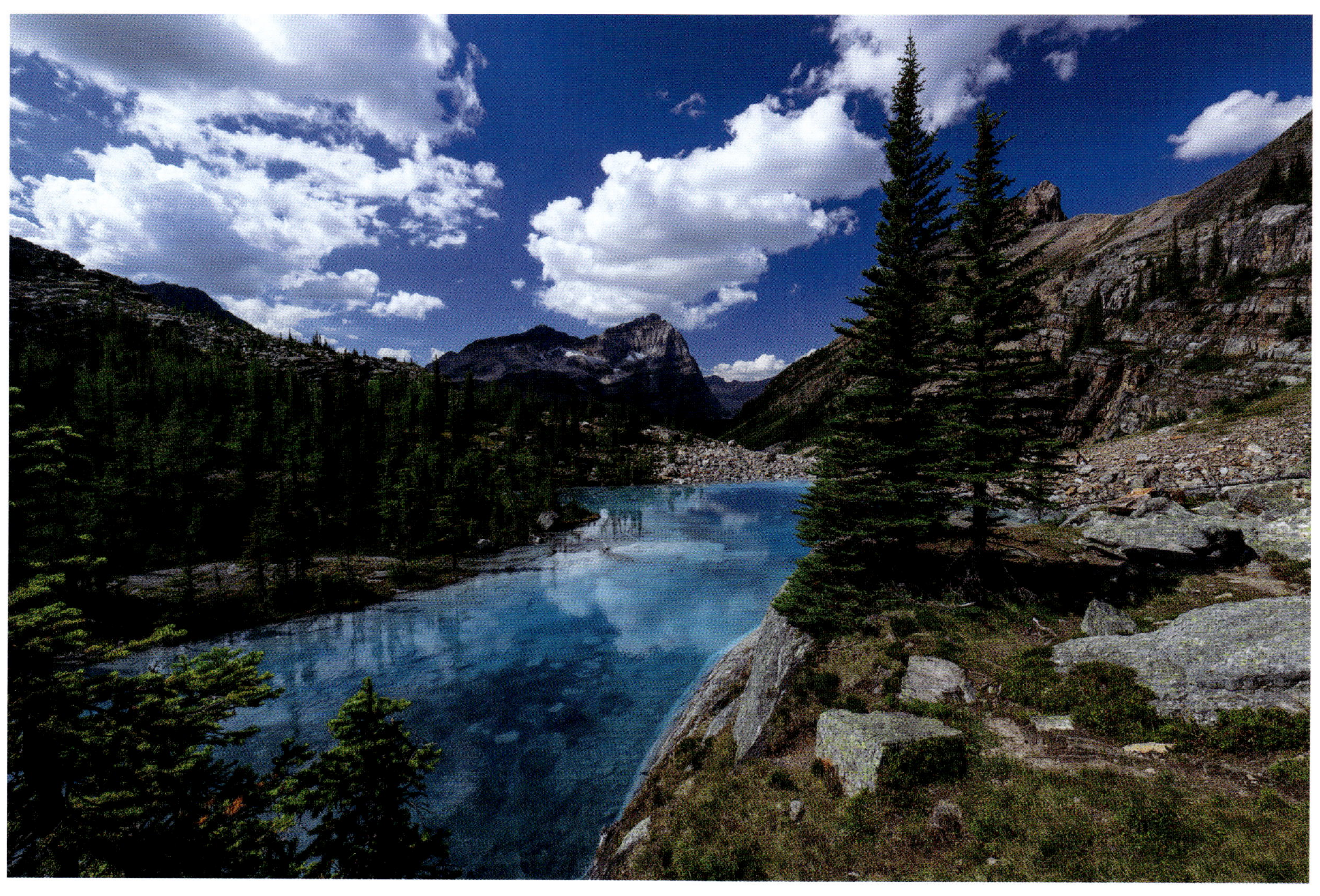

Blue Sky Lake (2025)
The still water of Victoria Lake mirrors the blue sky above, as
seen from the southeast shore.

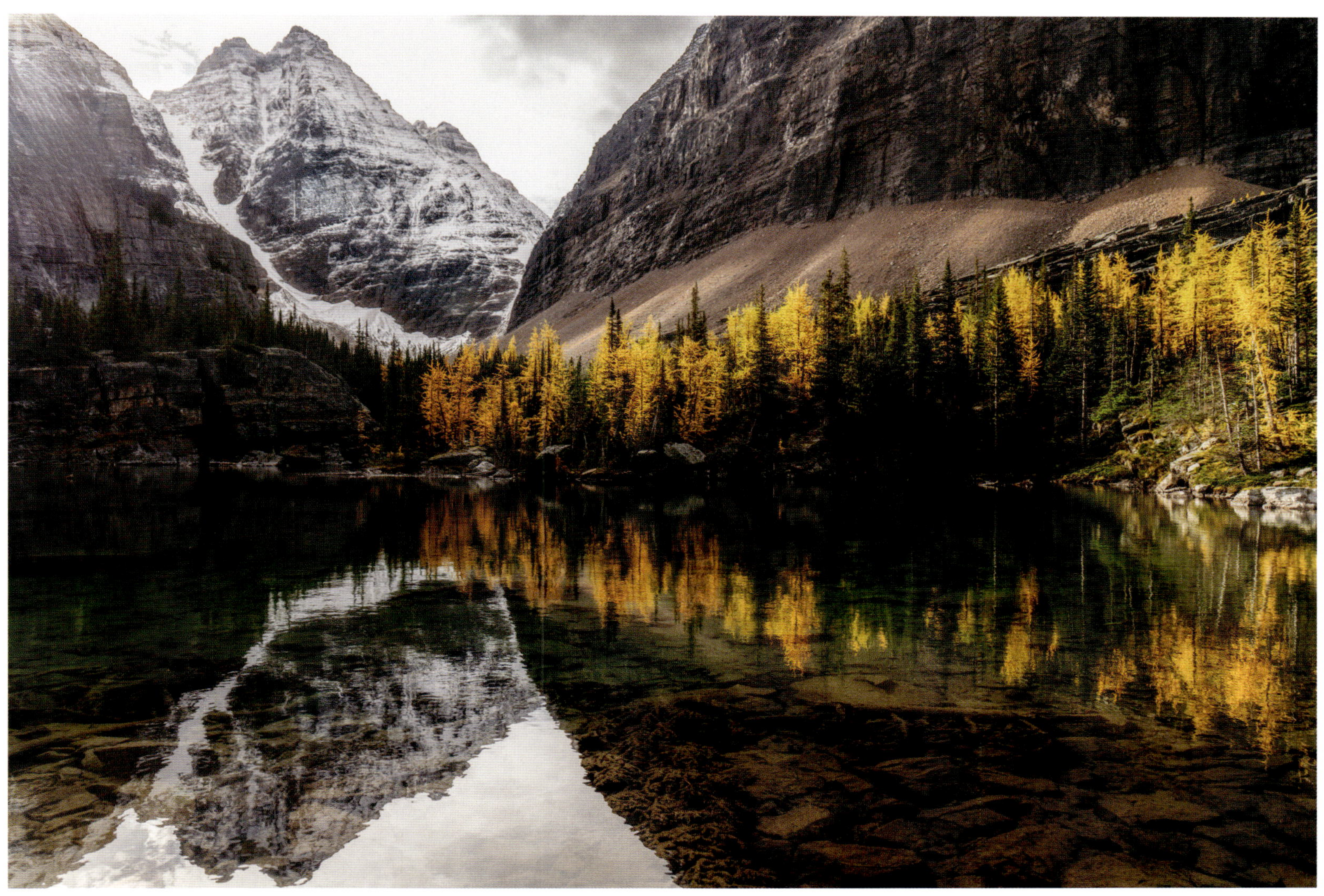

Autumn Gold (2021)
Autumn larch trees turn golden before dropping their needles, creating a mid-September window for these beautiful
reflections.

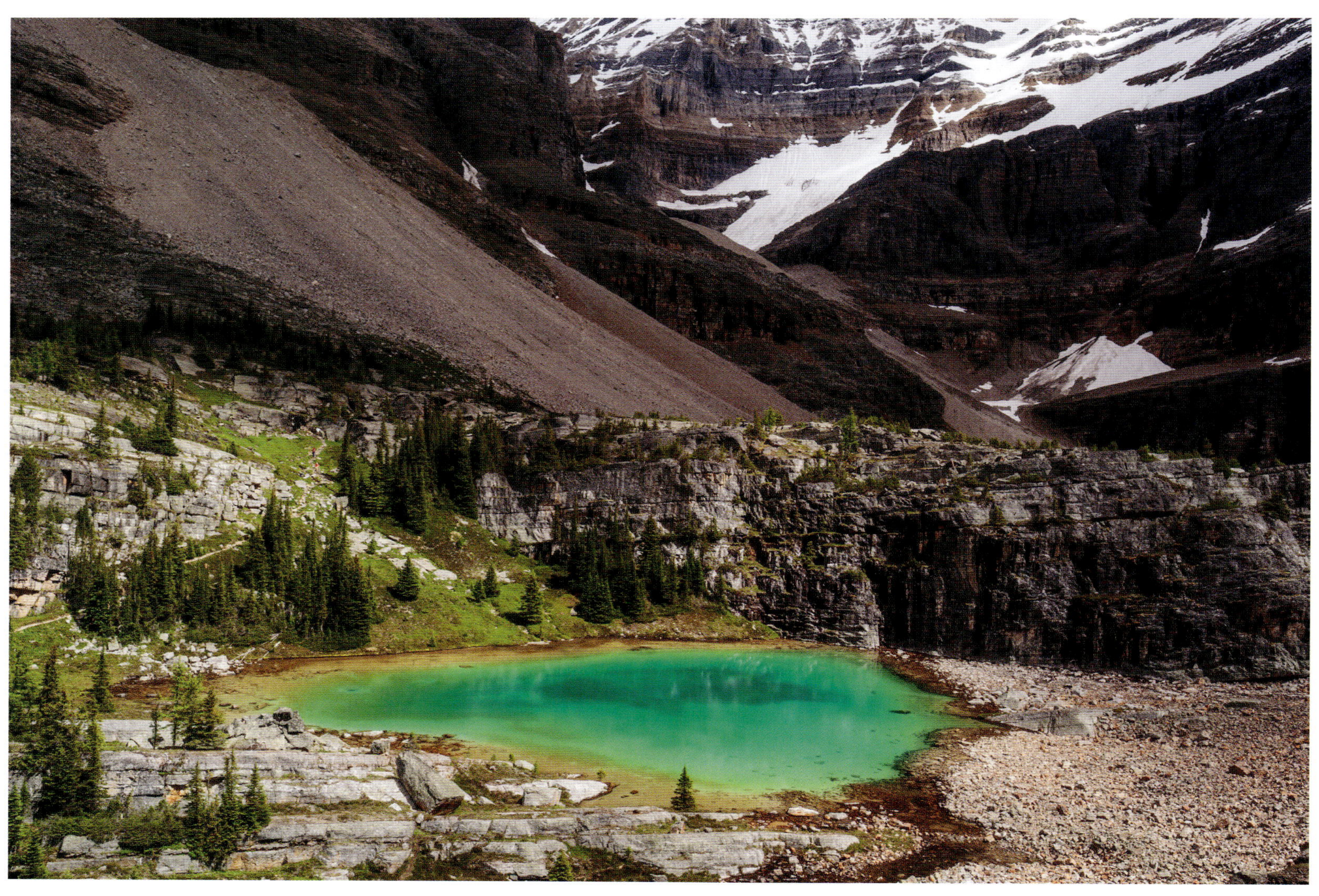

Primal Hues (2007)
The last major photographic distraction on the way to Lake Oesa, Lefroy Lake rests at the foot of Yukness Mountain's scree.

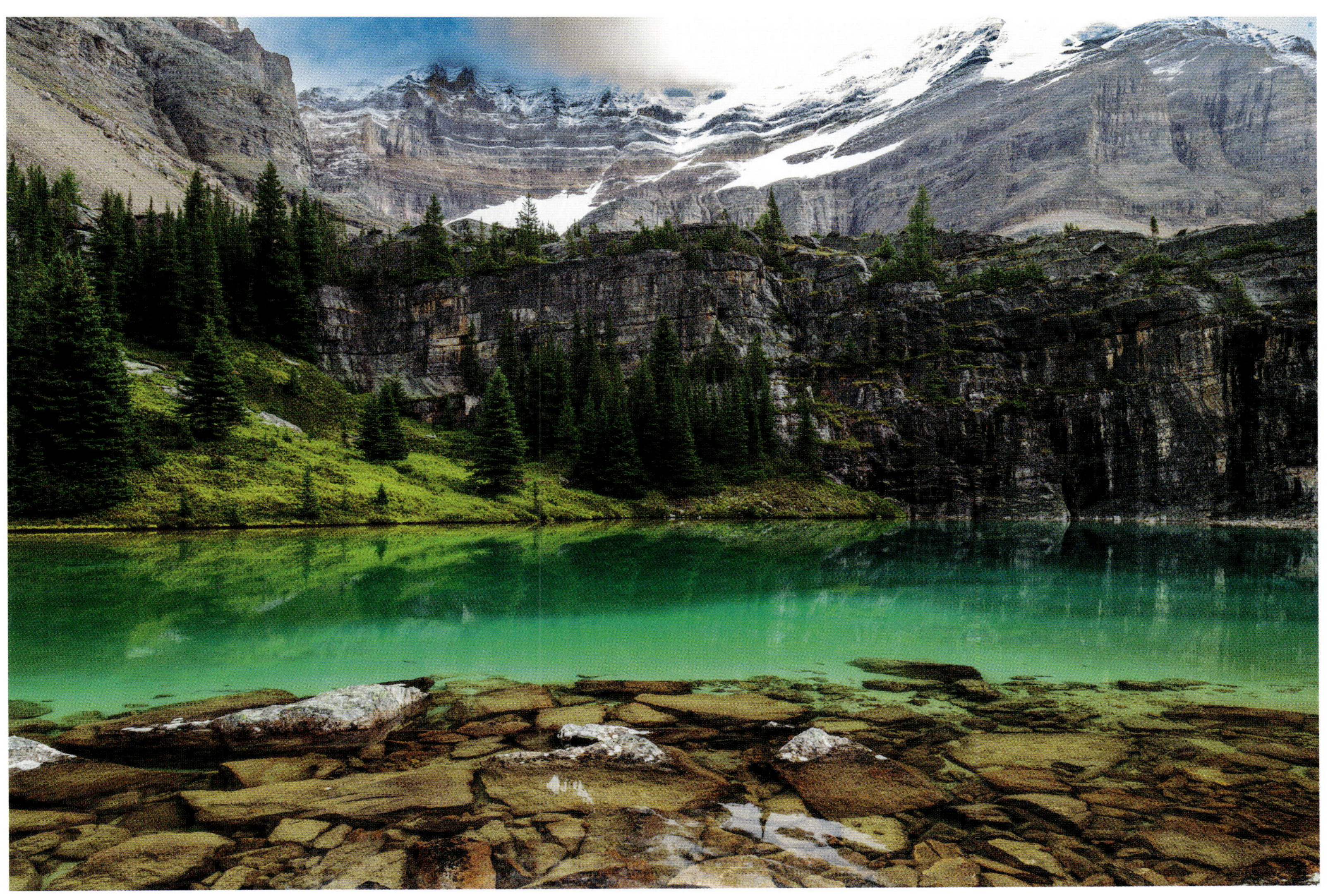

Pristine (2014)
The lucency of the glacial meltwater of Lefroy Lake creates a
transparent lens over the foreground of submerged rocks.

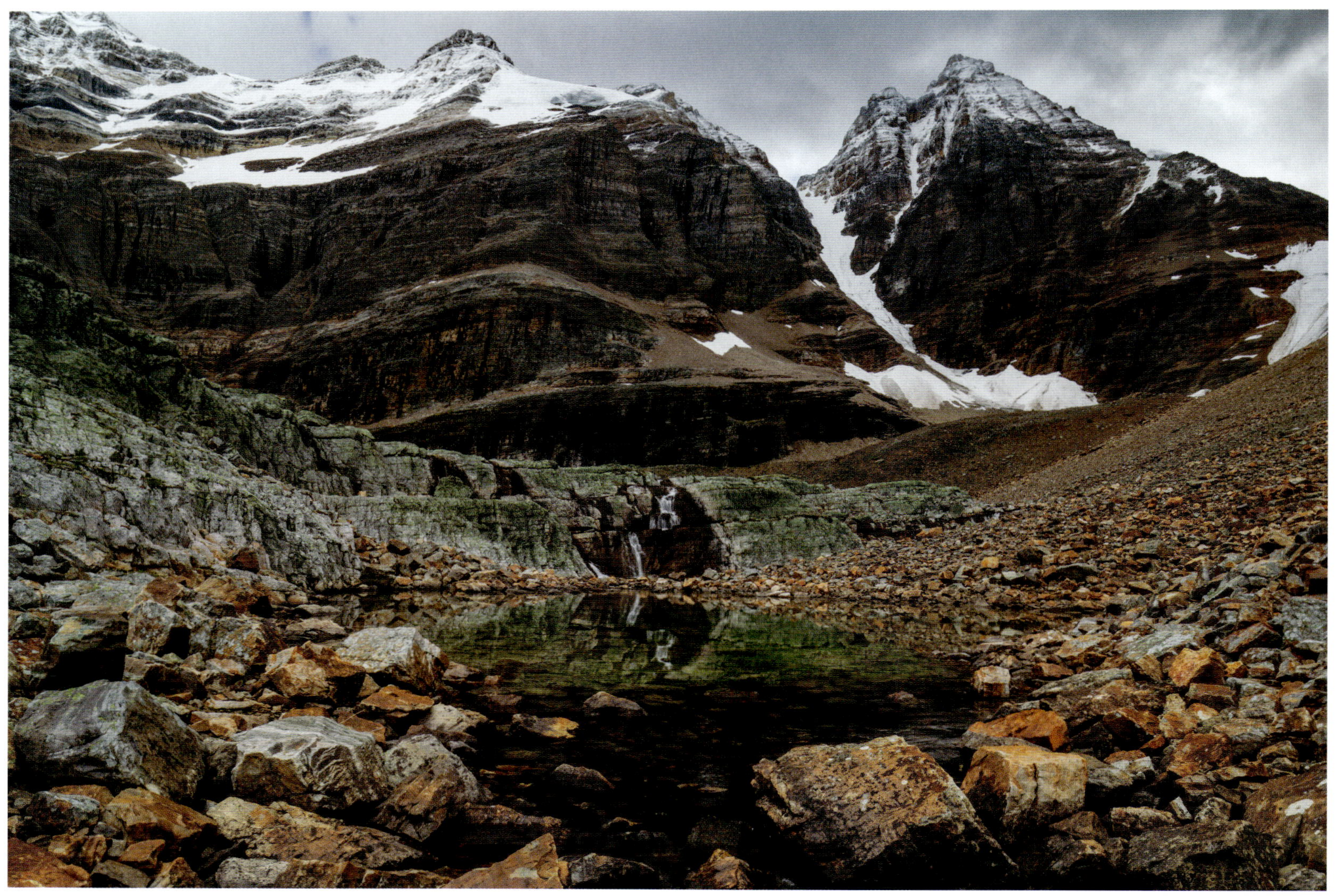

Lake Oesa Outlet (2014)
Lake Oesa's outlet appears just before the destination comes into view.

Natural Treasure (2021)
A hiker in the distance (Timothy Albinati) takes in the rewarding vista of Lake Oesa after a two-hour hike up from Lake O'Hara.

Overleaf **Lake Oesa Shoal** (2021)
Lake Oesa's shoreline shoals provide scenic areas to explore and photograph.

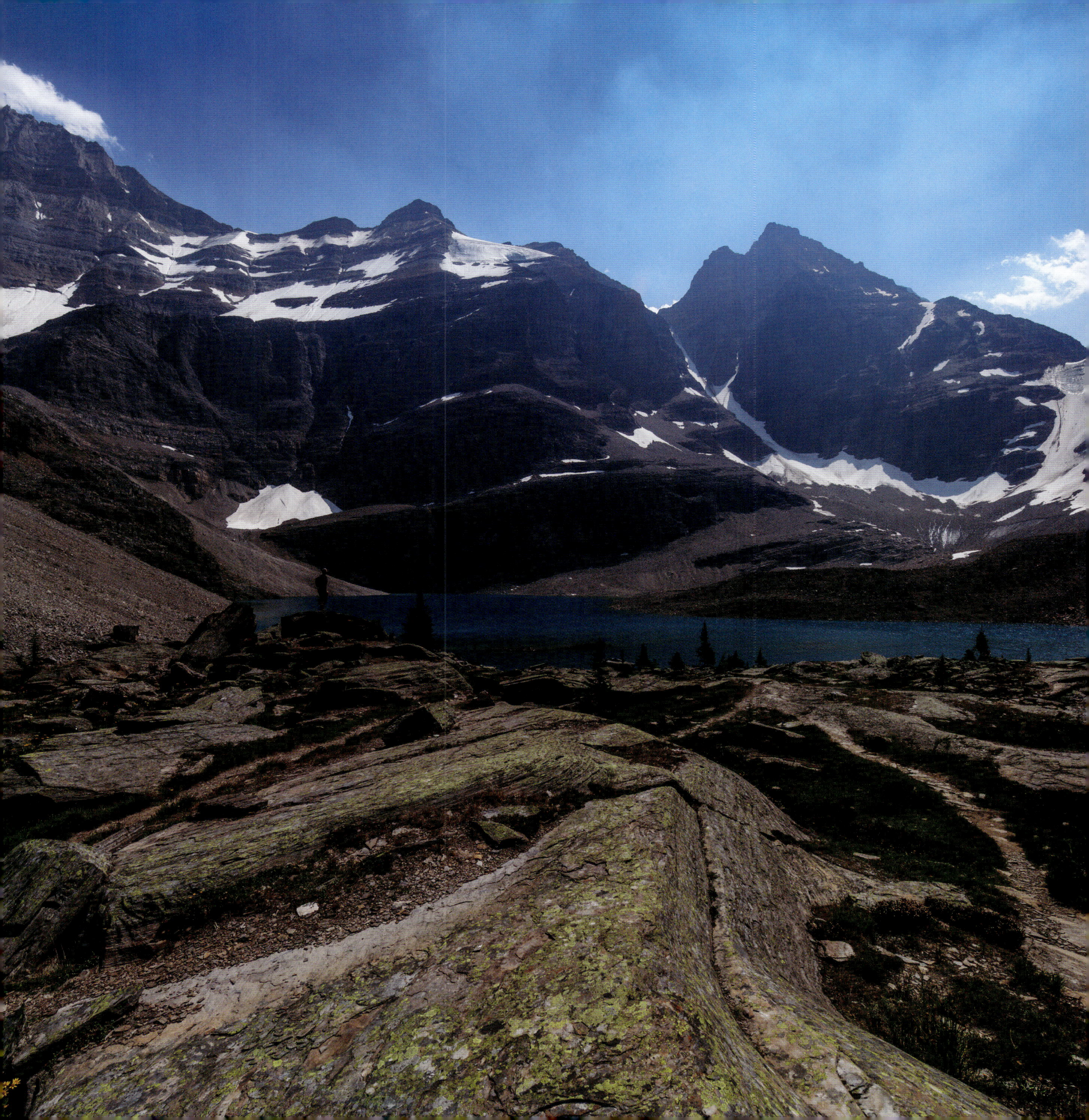

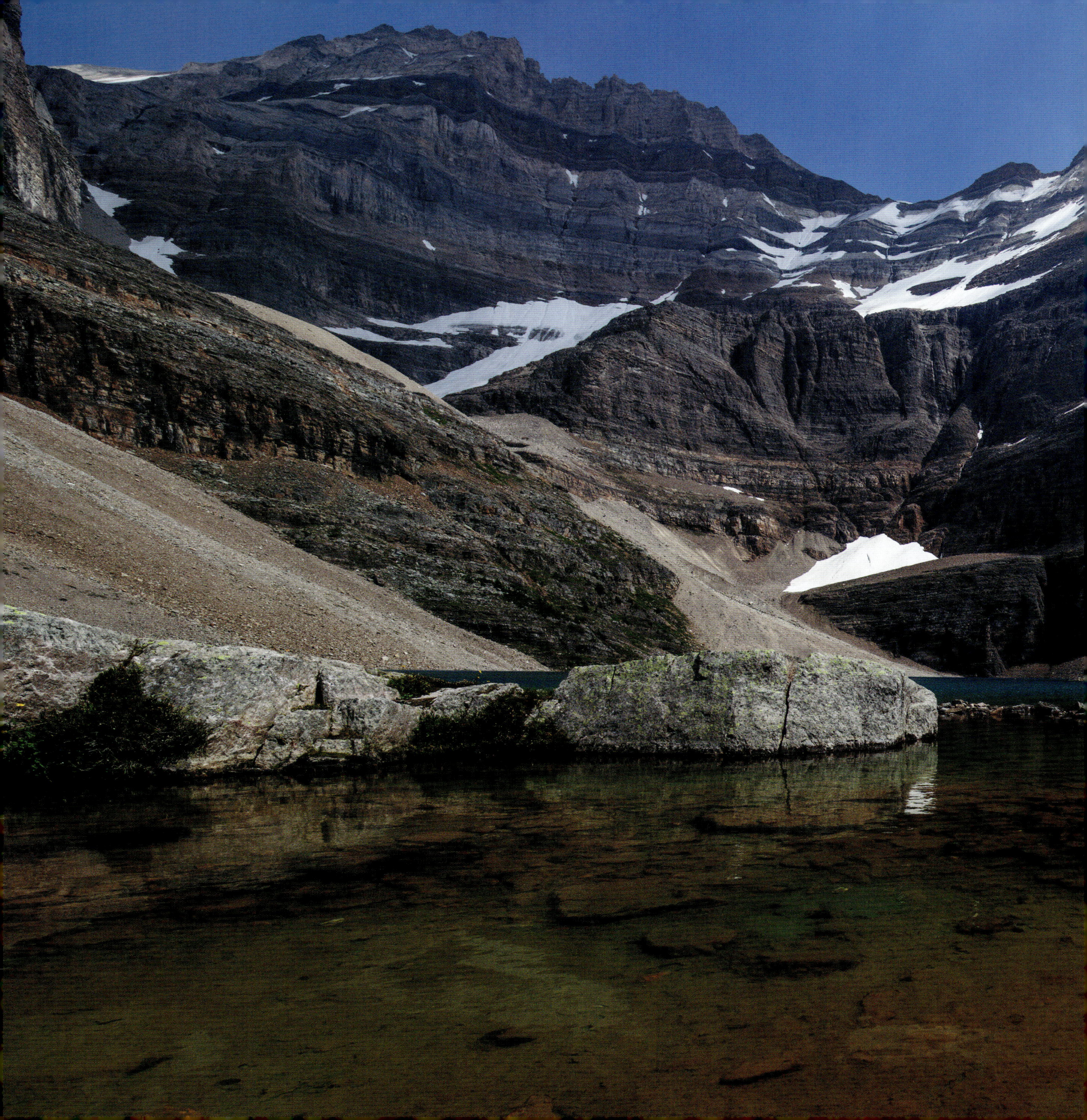

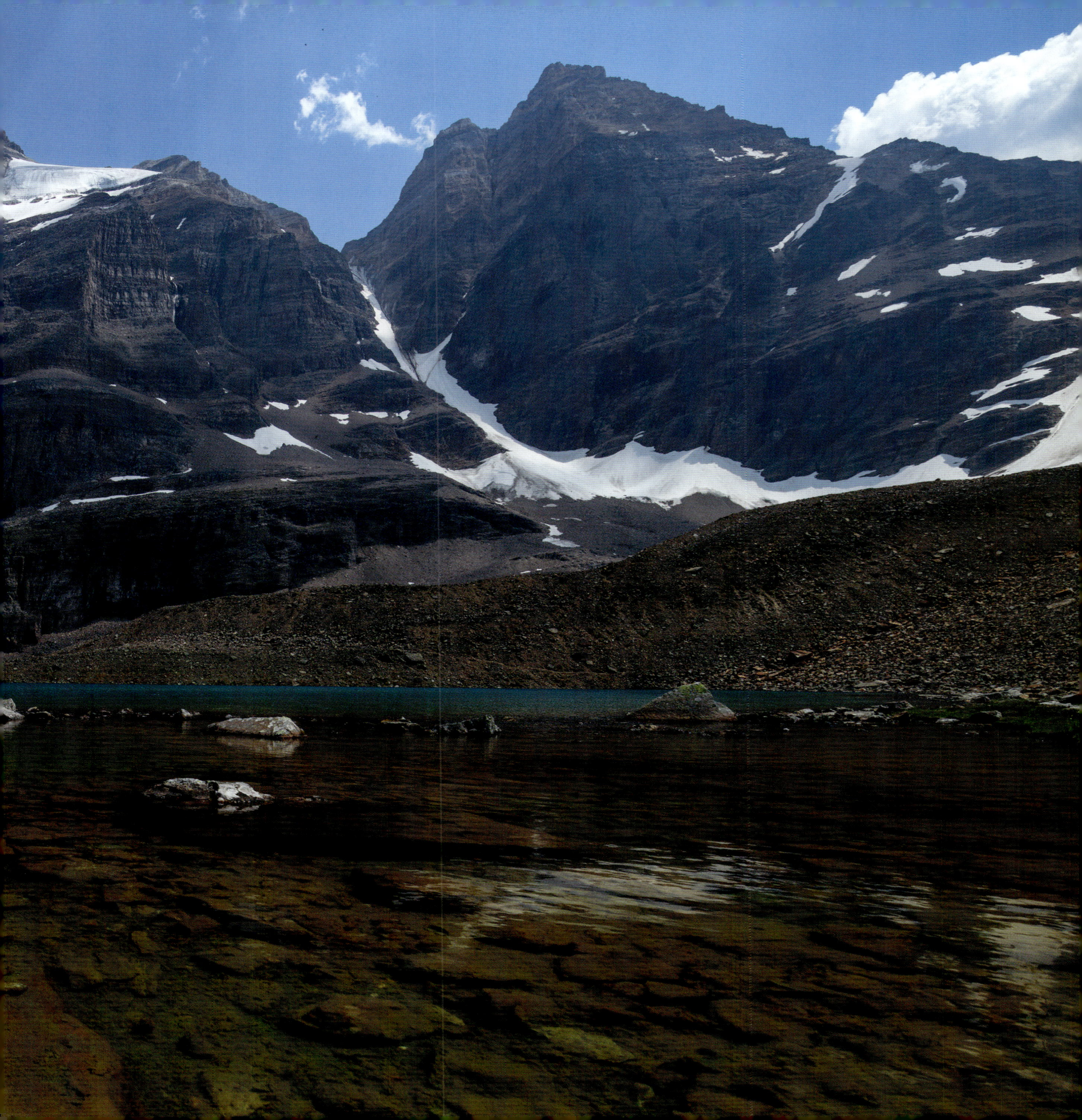

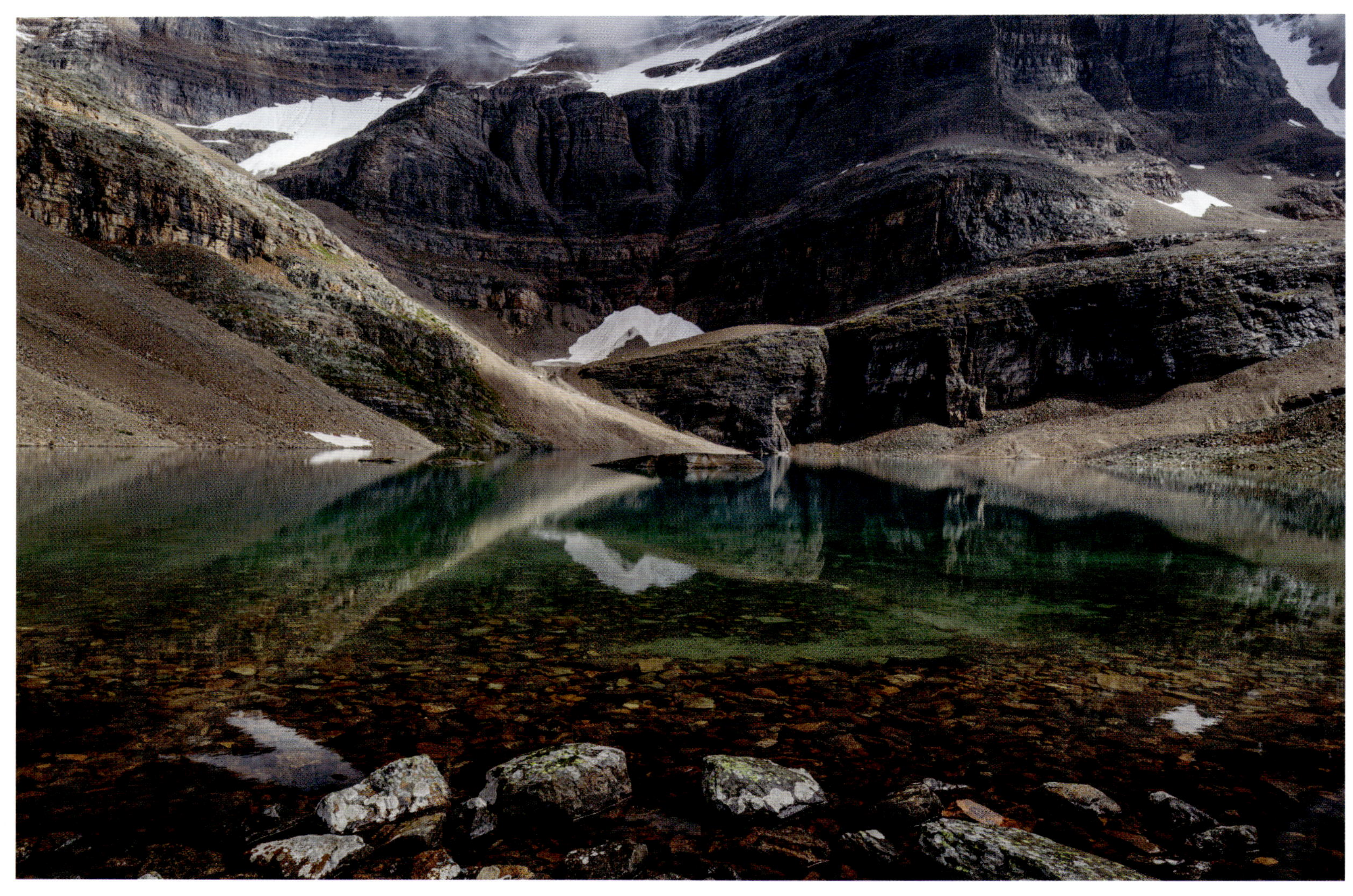

Geometric Aesthetic (2014)
Lake Oesa's geometrical patterns make it stand out from all of
the other nearby lakes, as impressive as they are.

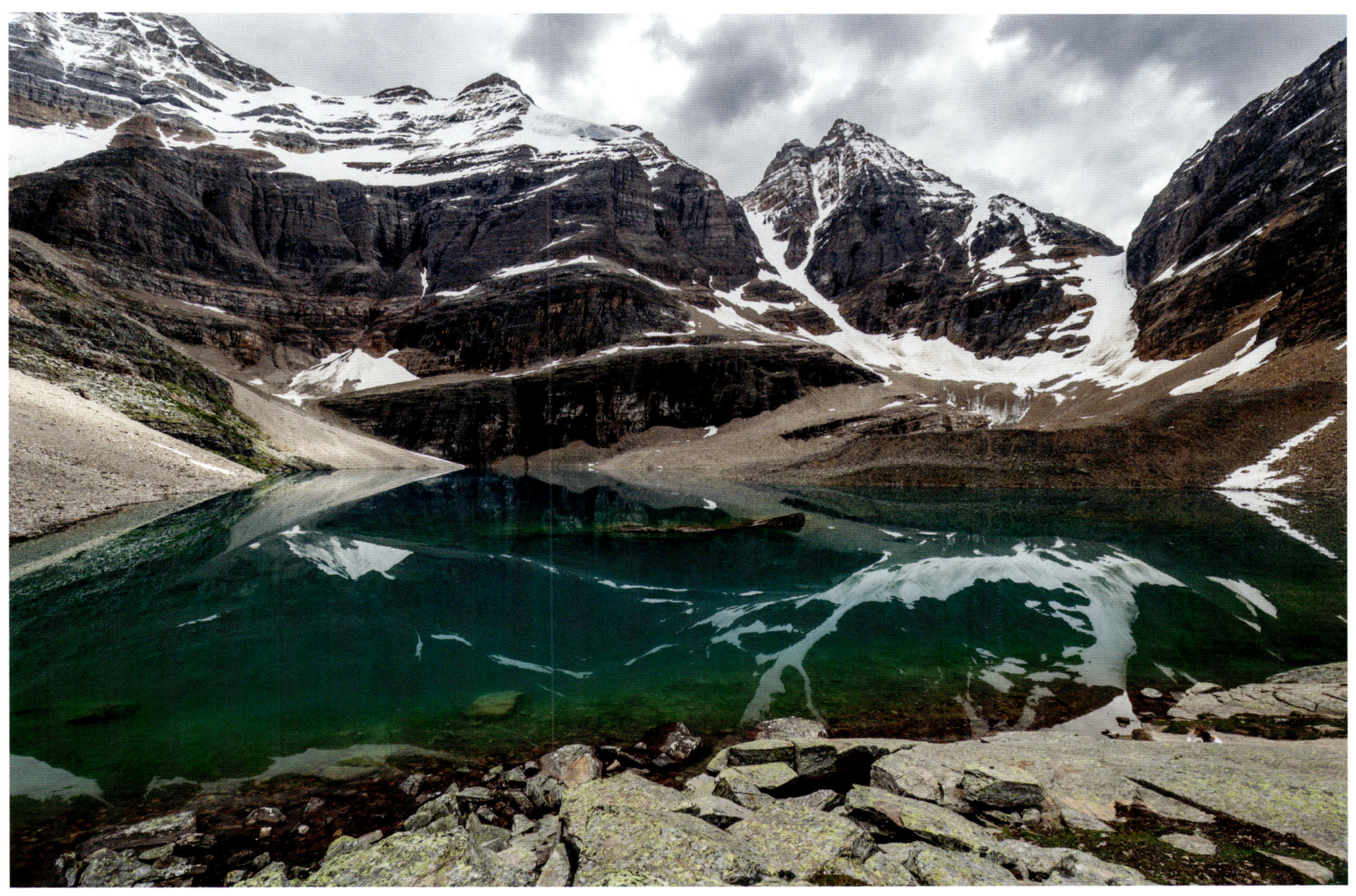

Immortal Landscape (2007)
An early snowfall over Lake Oesa was the subject of artist
J.E.H. MacDonald's last large-format painting, completed just
before his death in 1932.

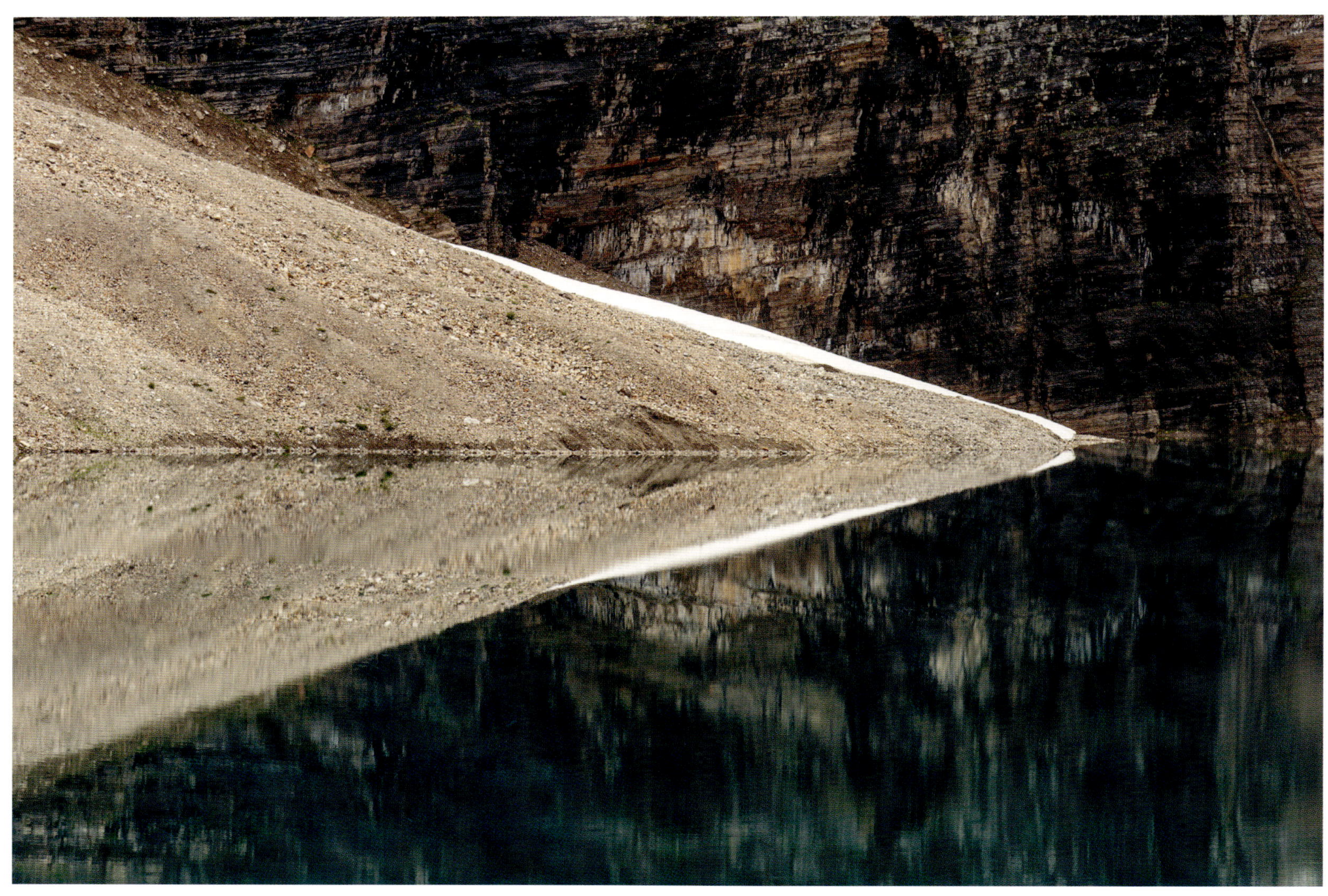

Natural Symmetry (2007)
The rock flour sediment suspended in the glacial and snowmelt
waters of Lake Oesa transforms the terrestrial reflections into
turquoise hues.

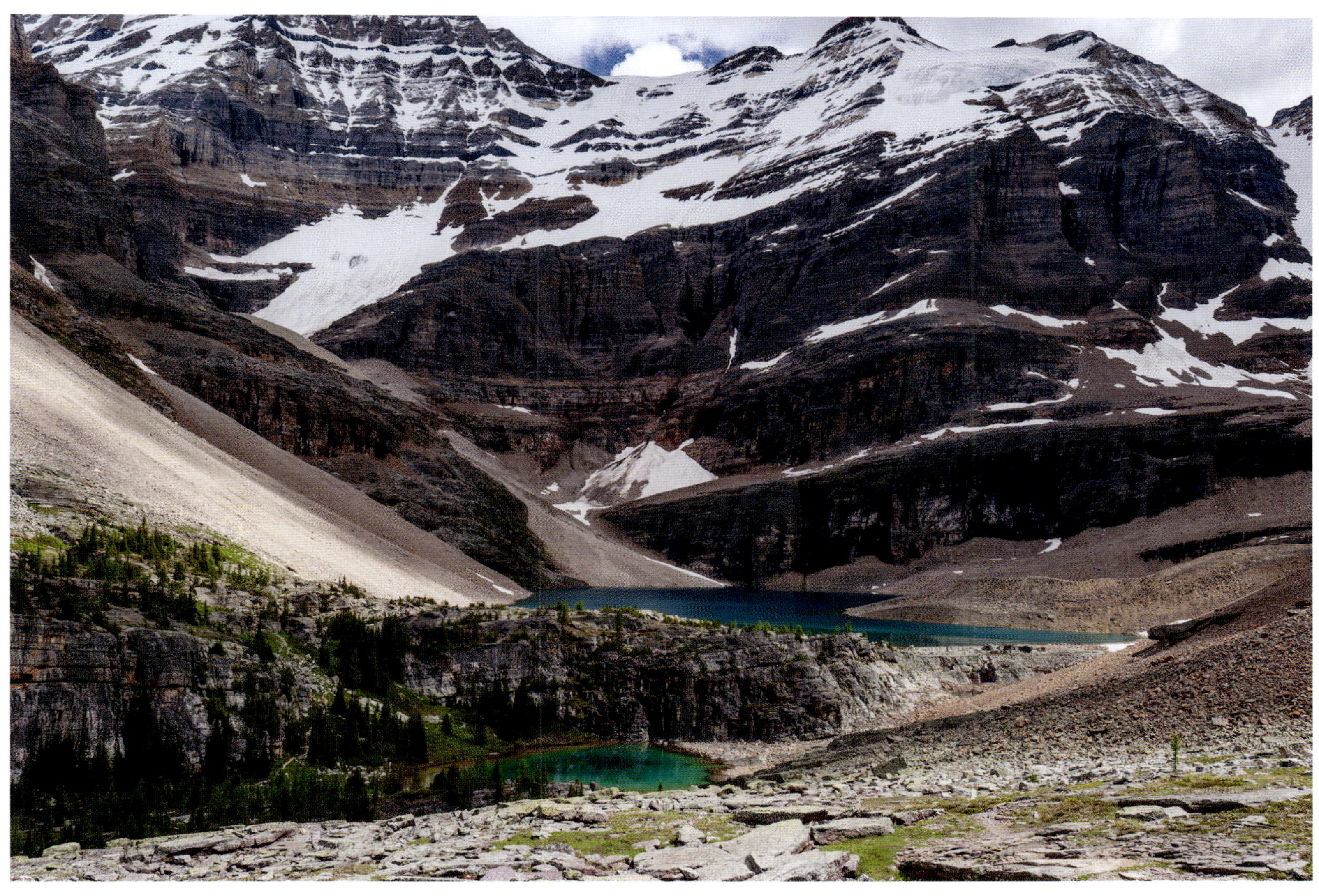

Looking Back (2007)
Lake Oesa and Lefroy Lake come into view together from
Yukness Ledges Alpine Route along the Lake O'Hara Alpine
Circuit.

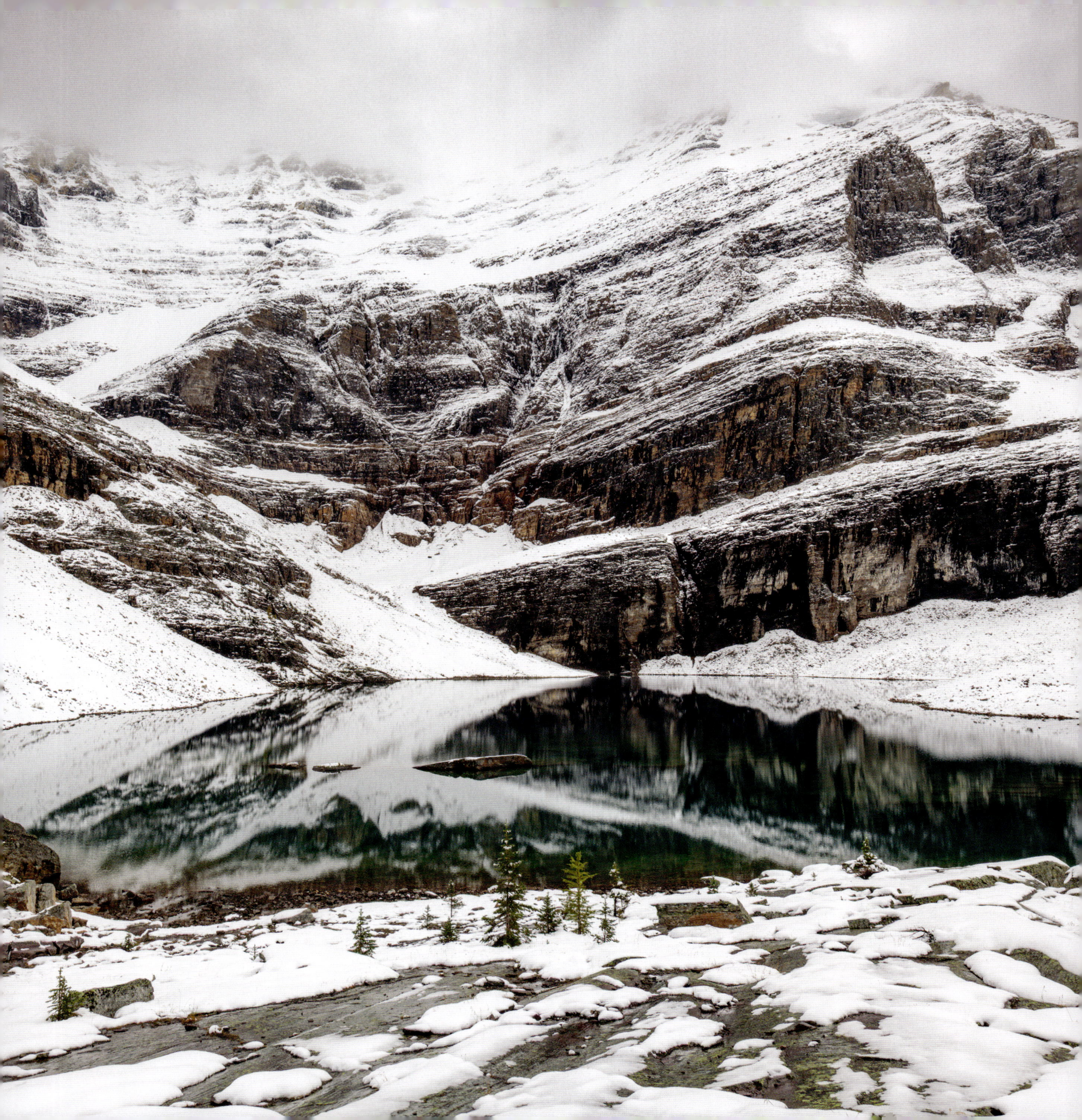

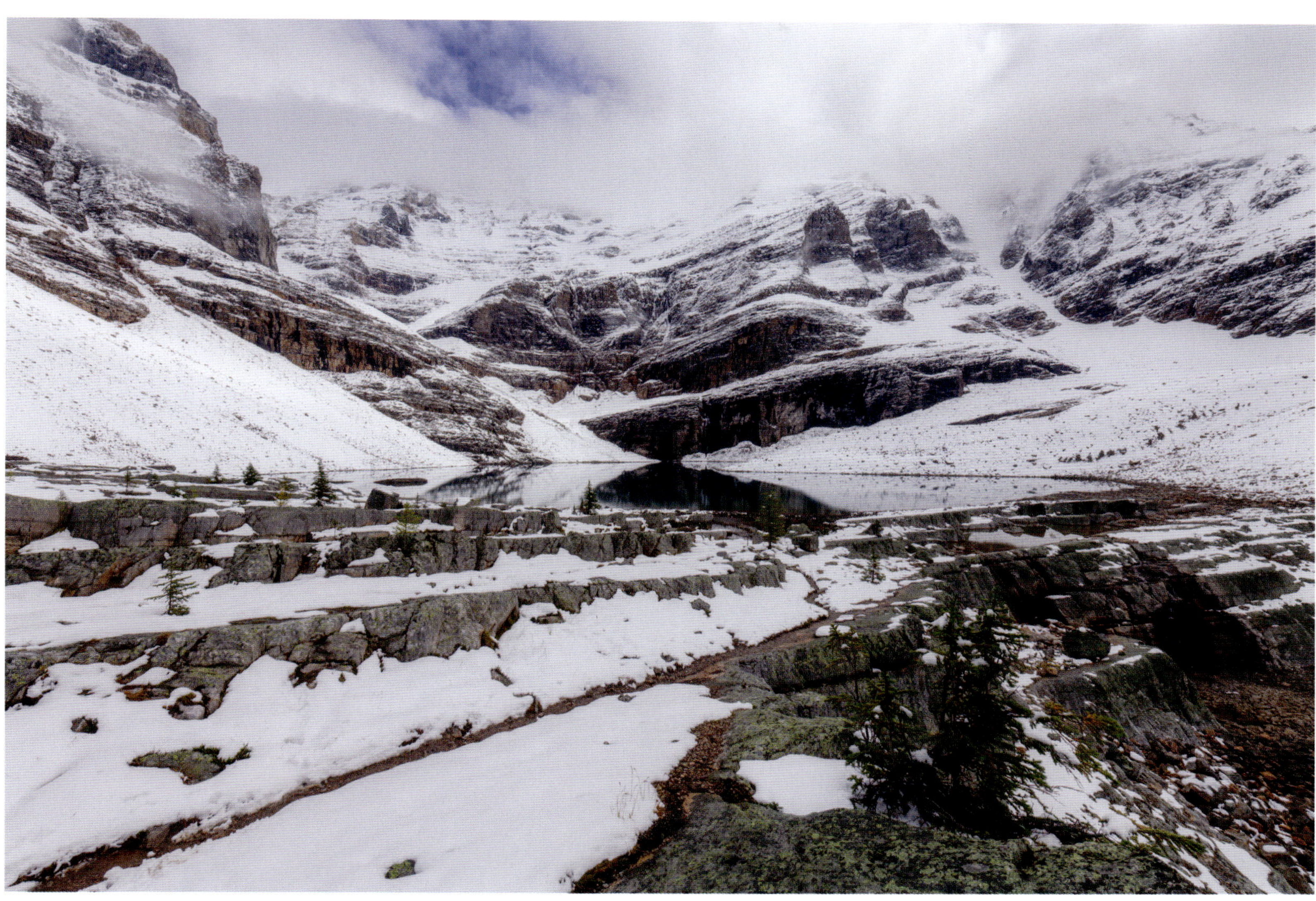

Leading Lines (2018)
The natural leading lines of the rock accentuated by the autumn snow pull our eyes toward the secluded jewel of Lake Oesa.

Autumn Snowfall (2018)
September snowfall is common at this 2270-m elevation. The contrast of the snow highlights the emerald colour of Lake Oesa.

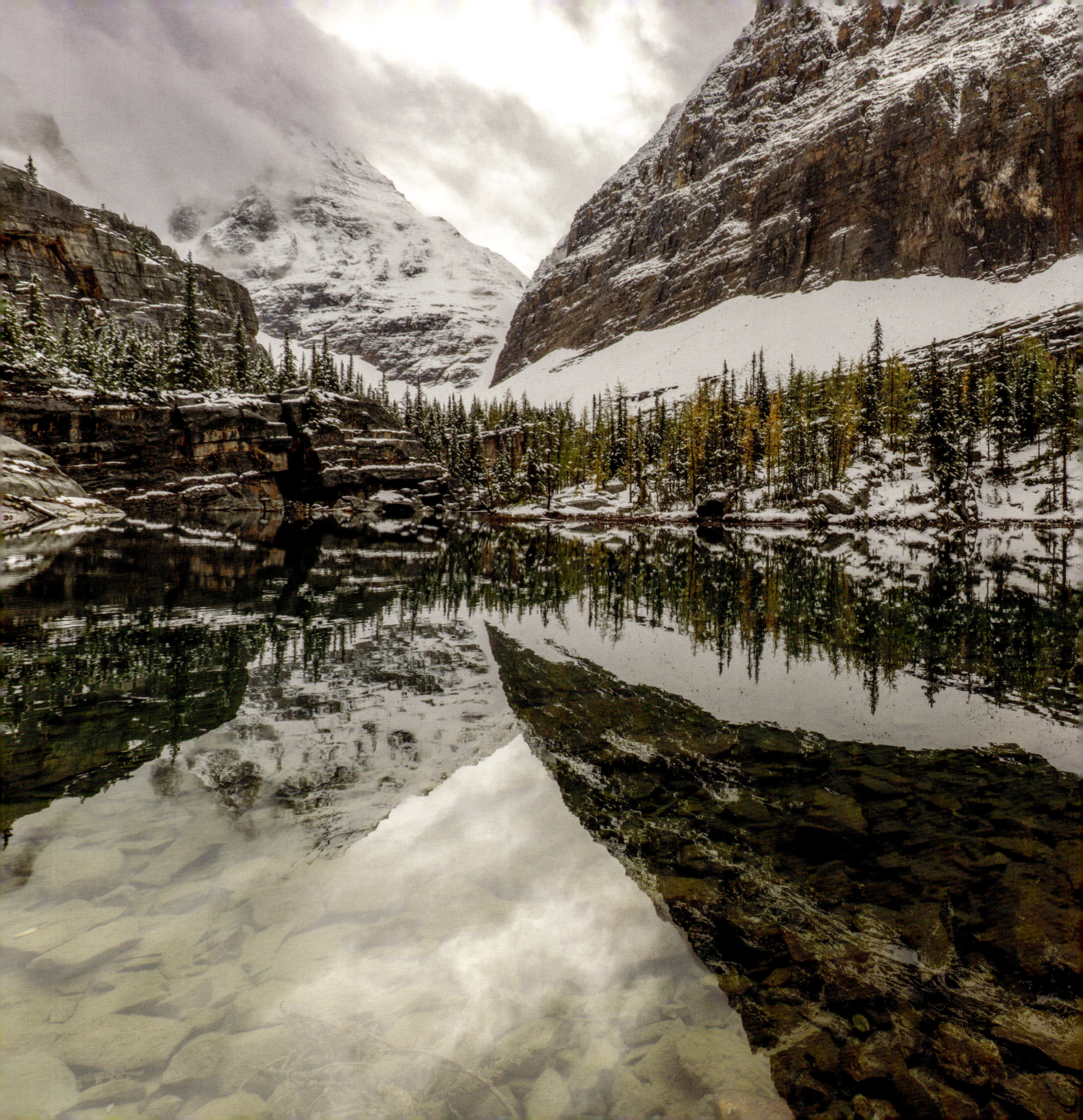

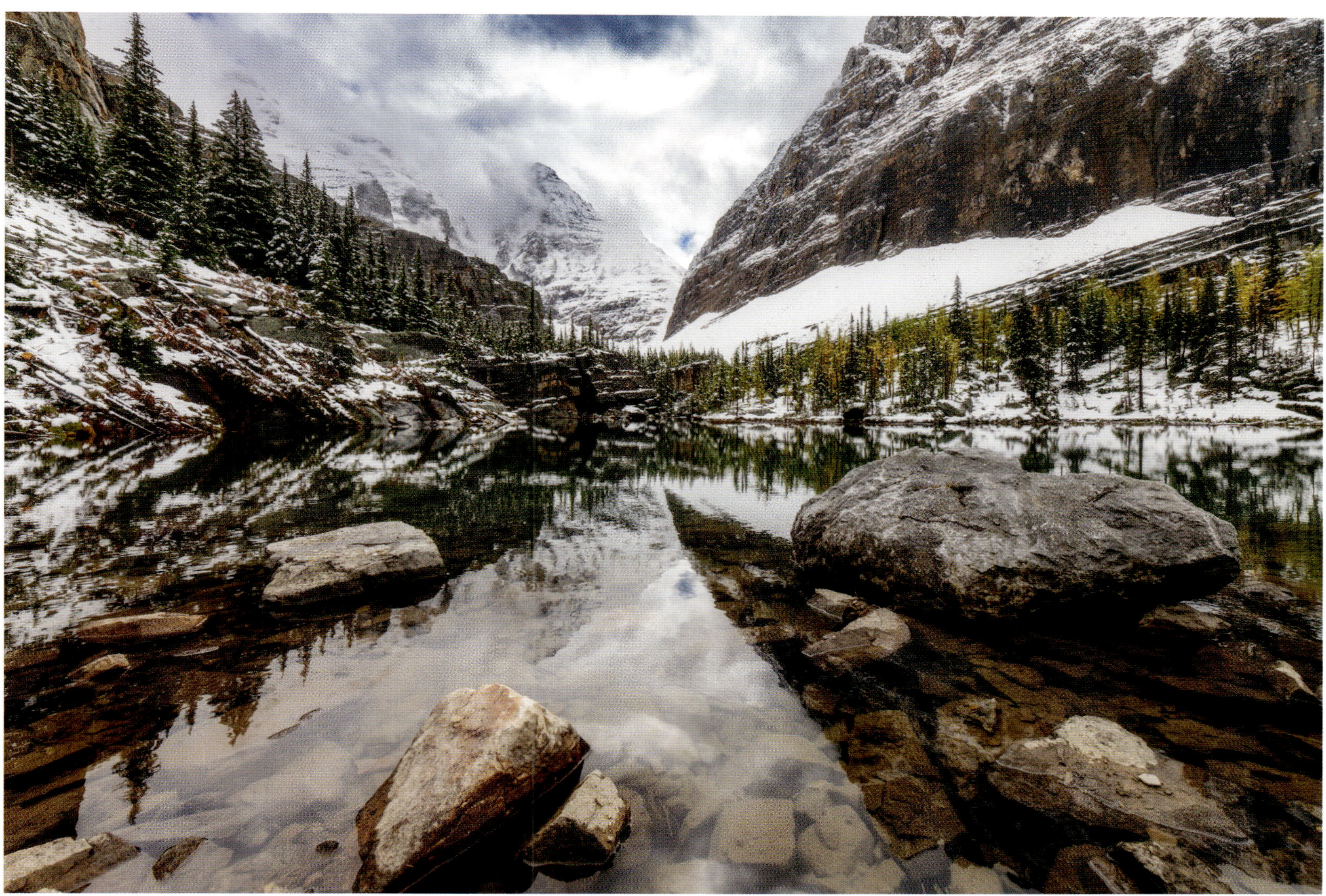

Victoria Lake Mirror (2018)
Autumn air is often less turbulent than the variance of summer temperature fluctuations, creating increased opportunities to happen upon these mirror reflections.

Shoreline Wonder (2018)
The shoreline of Victoria Lake makes a perfect place to rest out of the wind and enjoy the ever-changing composition of nature.

Overleaf **Seasons** (2018)
Open-water season nears its end for Lefroy Lake, as its saturated colour will soon be under ice until the following June.

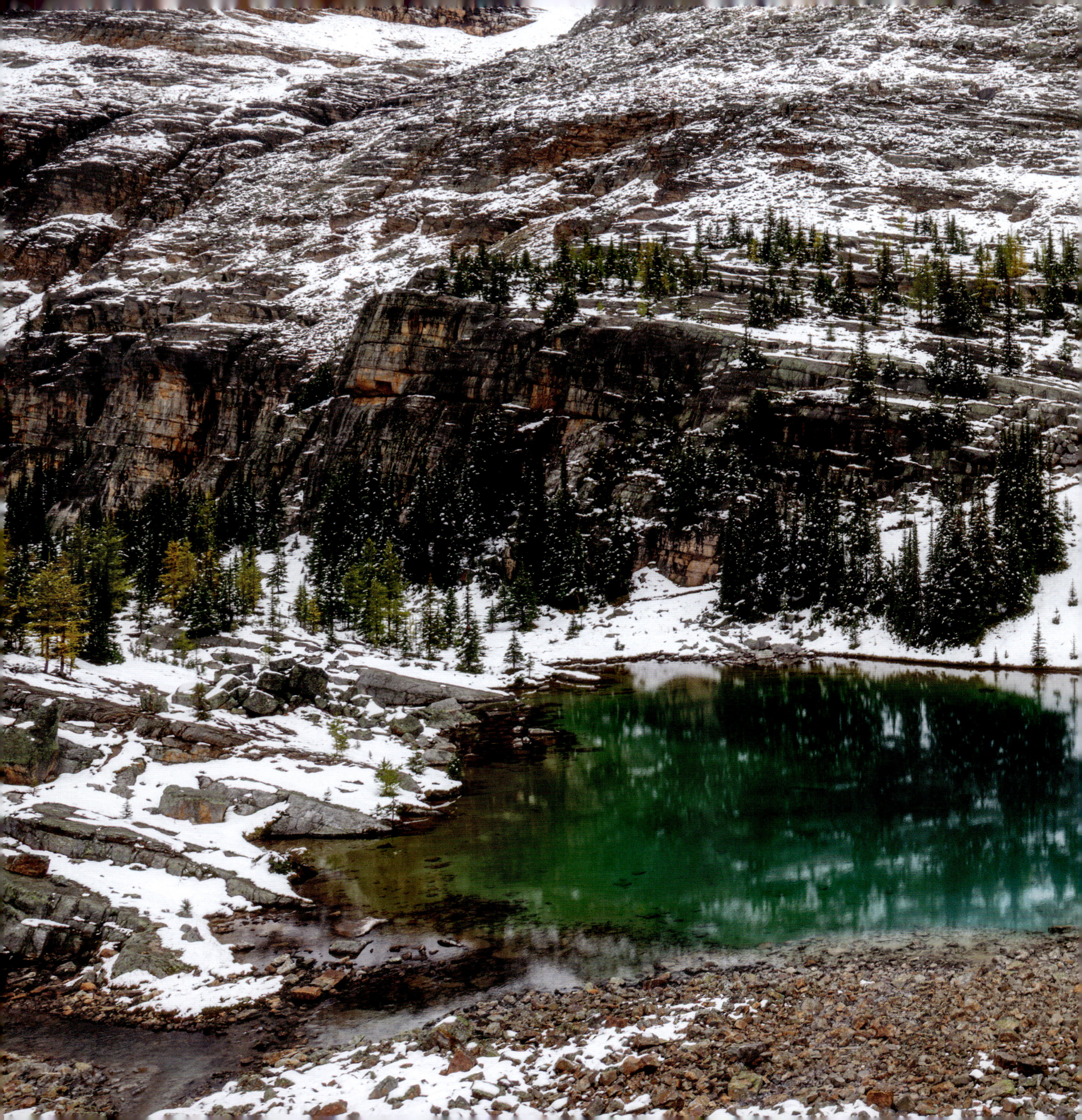

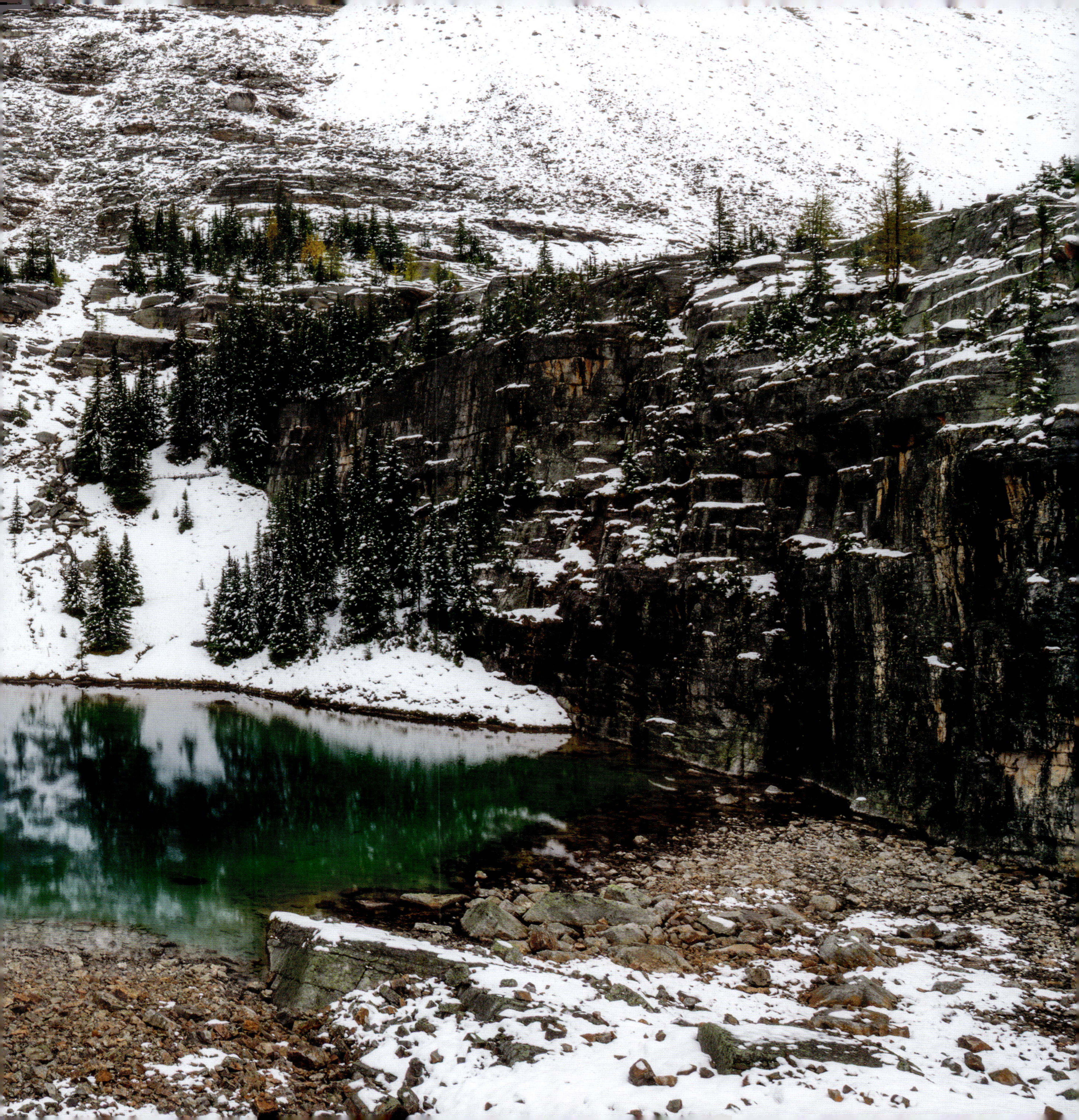

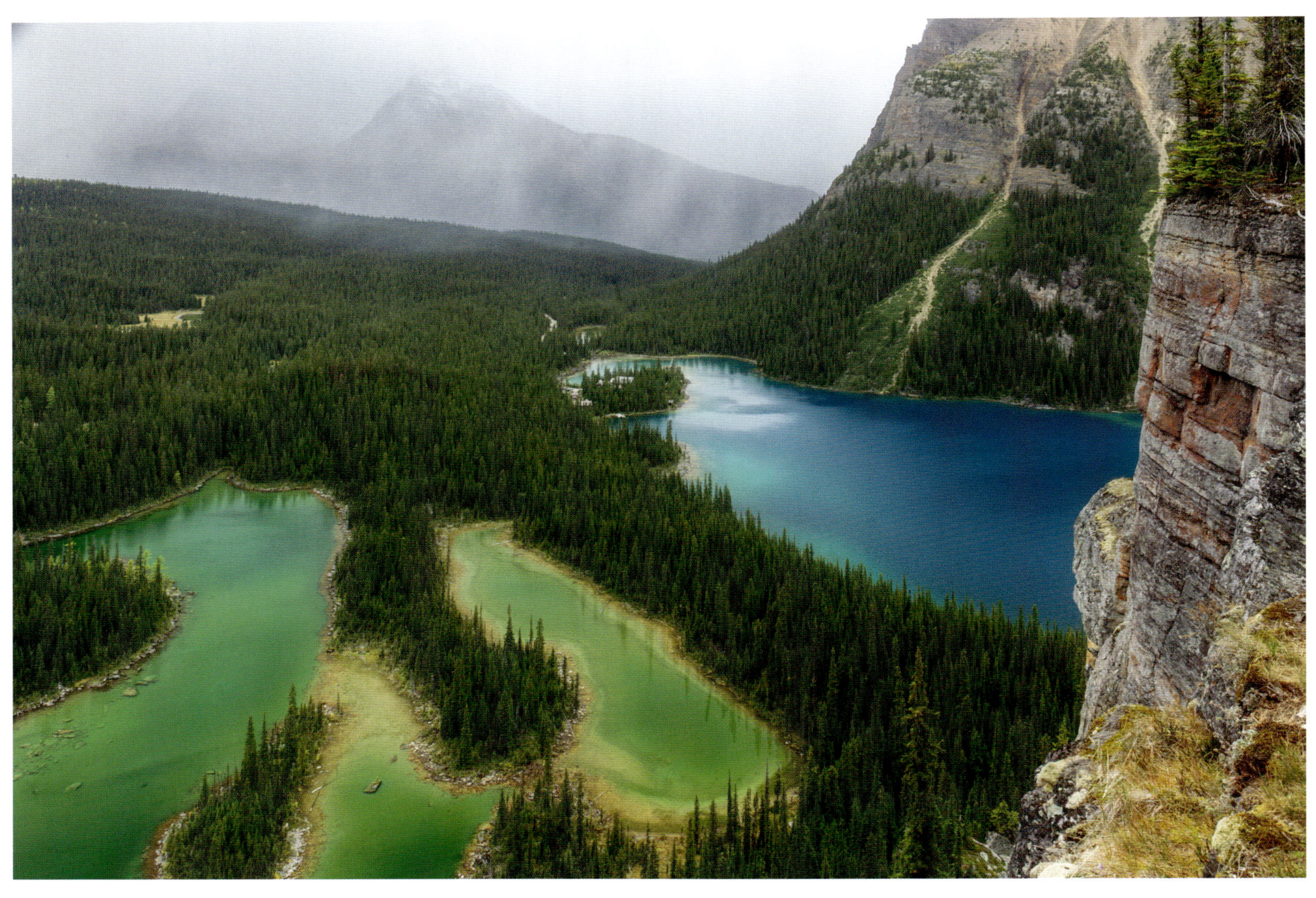

Looking Back (2011)
Looking down at Mary Lake and Lake O'Hara from West Opabin Trail on the way to Opabin Plateau.

PART THREE

Opabin Plateau Trails

Opabin Plateau is a classic hanging valley formed when a tributary glacier flows into a larger-volume glacier. The result is Opabin Prospect, a rock precipice with an unobstructed view of Lake O'Hara and the Duchesnay Basin from its 190-m perch above Lakeshore Trail. There are two trails to access Opabin Plateau: West and East Opabin, enabling a hiker to complete a 6-km round trip from Lake O'Hara to Opabin Lake and back.

Over the years, it has become my preference to ascend the 1.8-km West Opabin Trail up the 190-m rise to the plateau. Along the way, clear views of Lake O'Hara and Mary Lake emerge from a trail that passes autumn larch trees glowing in the backlit rays of sunlight. West Opabin Trail ends on the trail to Opabin Prospect, an ideal vista at which to rest and eat a well-earned lunch while overlooking the Lake O'Hara valley. The plateau is an excellent habitat for many of the local residents such as hoary marmots, pikas, weasels, ground squirrels, and the reclusive wolverine. Chipmunks often come to visit this favourite snack-eating location, so it's important not to leave food out in the open, as feeding wildlife is prohibited and harmful.

The Opabin Plateau contains an overabundance of natural beauty. There is a network of trails to choose from along the 1.4-km journey up the plateau to Opabin Lake. The Opabin Plateau is dotted with several small lakes, ponds, and rivers. This region is also covered in larch trees, making it an artist's delight in autumn as the needles transform into their golden hue. There are so many scenic places that on some of my annual trips to the Lake O'Hara region I have dedicated the entire hiking time to this plateau alone.

As you continue along the Opabin Plateau hanging valley toward Opabin Lake, a further 60 m in elevation, Hungabee Lake comes into view. Named after the nearby towering Hungabee Mountain (3492 m), and the Nakoda word for "chieftain," this shallow, fishless lake contains a high concentration of bright-red copepods called *Hesperodiaptomus arcticus*. Although each of these predatory crustaceans is the size of a pen tip, with their large population their bright-red colours are visible along the shoreline in the photographs. They are found in the Arctic but also in the Rocky Mountains with its extreme conditions due to the considerable elevation above sea level.

At 250 m in elevation above Lake O'Hara, the Opabin Plateau hike is rewarded by the destination of Opabin Lake. The Stoney Nakoda People travelled through this region, naming landmarks along the way. Early European surveyors, likely with the help of Stoney guides, recorded these names reflecting the First Nations languages and Indigenous histories in the Canadian Rockies. It is thought that "Opabin" comes from the Stoney word for "rocky" or "high rocky place," reflecting the abundant talus slopes and glacial moraine deposits surrounding the lake. The name was officially adopted by the Geological Survey of Canada in the early 20th century.

Although Opabin Lake is much smaller than Lake Oesa and Lake McArthur, its proximity to the surrounding mountainous walls creates magical geometrical shapes in its surface reflections of lingering snow and ice stretching into the month of July. Later in the season, glacial sediments transform it into a rich emerald colour. Opabin Lake is an excellent example of the importance of groundwater in alpine lakes, as there is no surface stream, yet it's the primary source of water for Opabin Creek, which flows into Lake O'Hara. The creek is quite pronounced as it falls over the hanging valley edge while running alongside East Opabin Trail. This trail, with a series of switchbacks, is my preferred route down to Lake O'Hara Lakeshore Trail, completing the round-trip tour of Opabin Plateau.

Peaceful Morning (2017)
West Opabin Trail to Opabin Plateau passes by peaceful Mary Lake. The origin of the lake's name is uncertain but thought to be in honour of Mary Schäffer Warren.

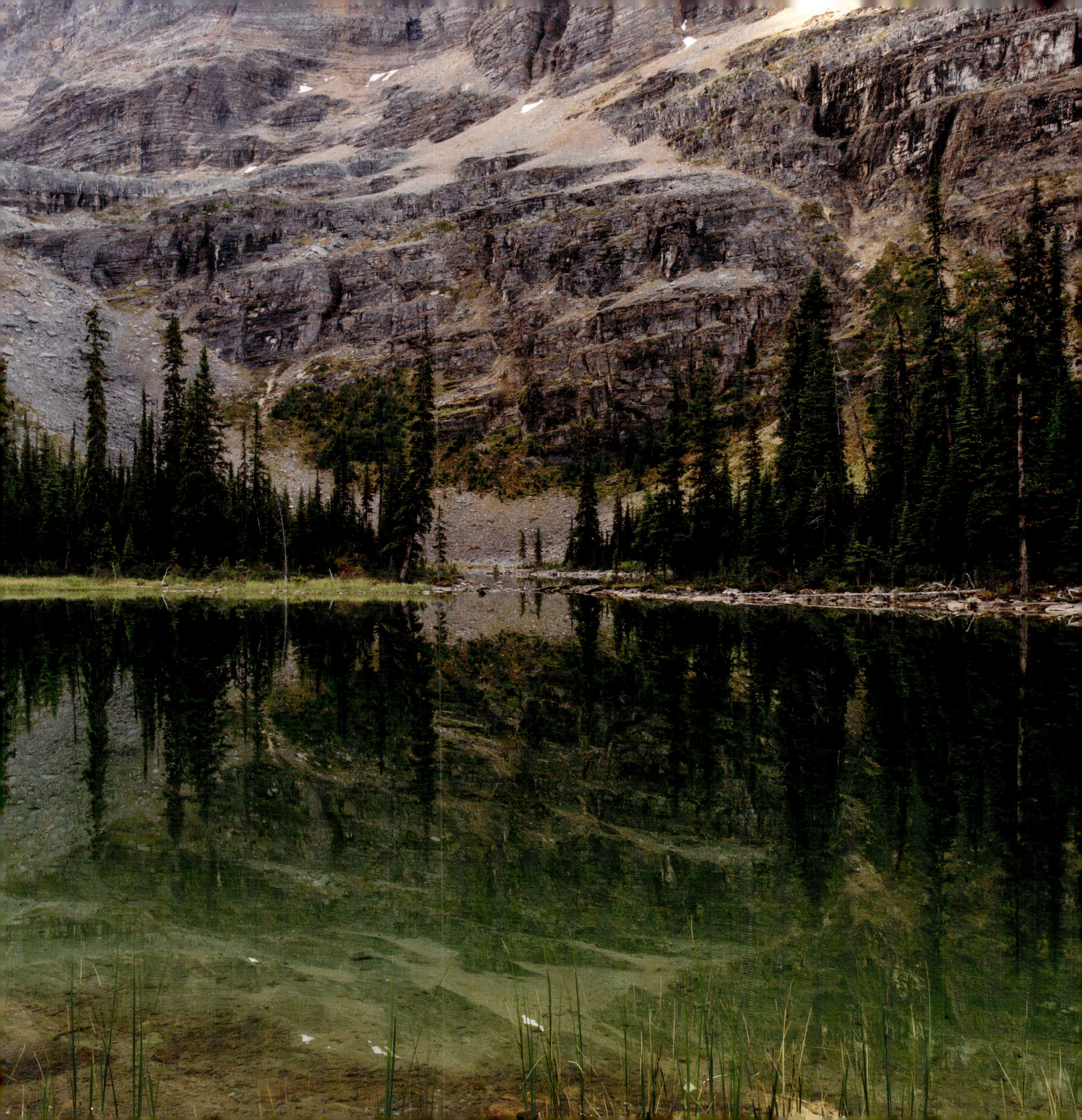

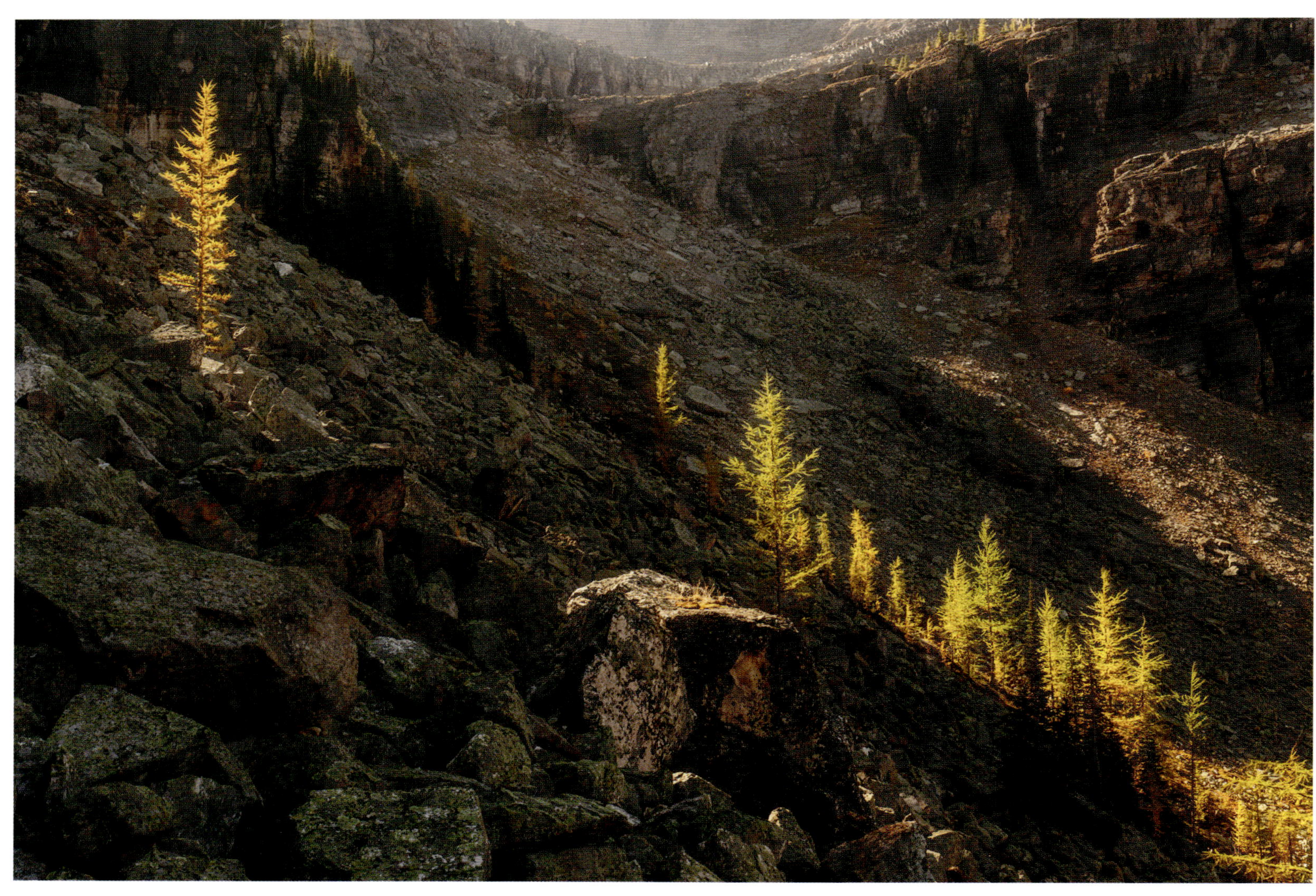

Autumn Highlight (2008)
Autumn larches glowing along West Opabin Trail to Opabin Plateau. Larch seeds are food for squirrels and birds, and even for bears preparing for hibernation.

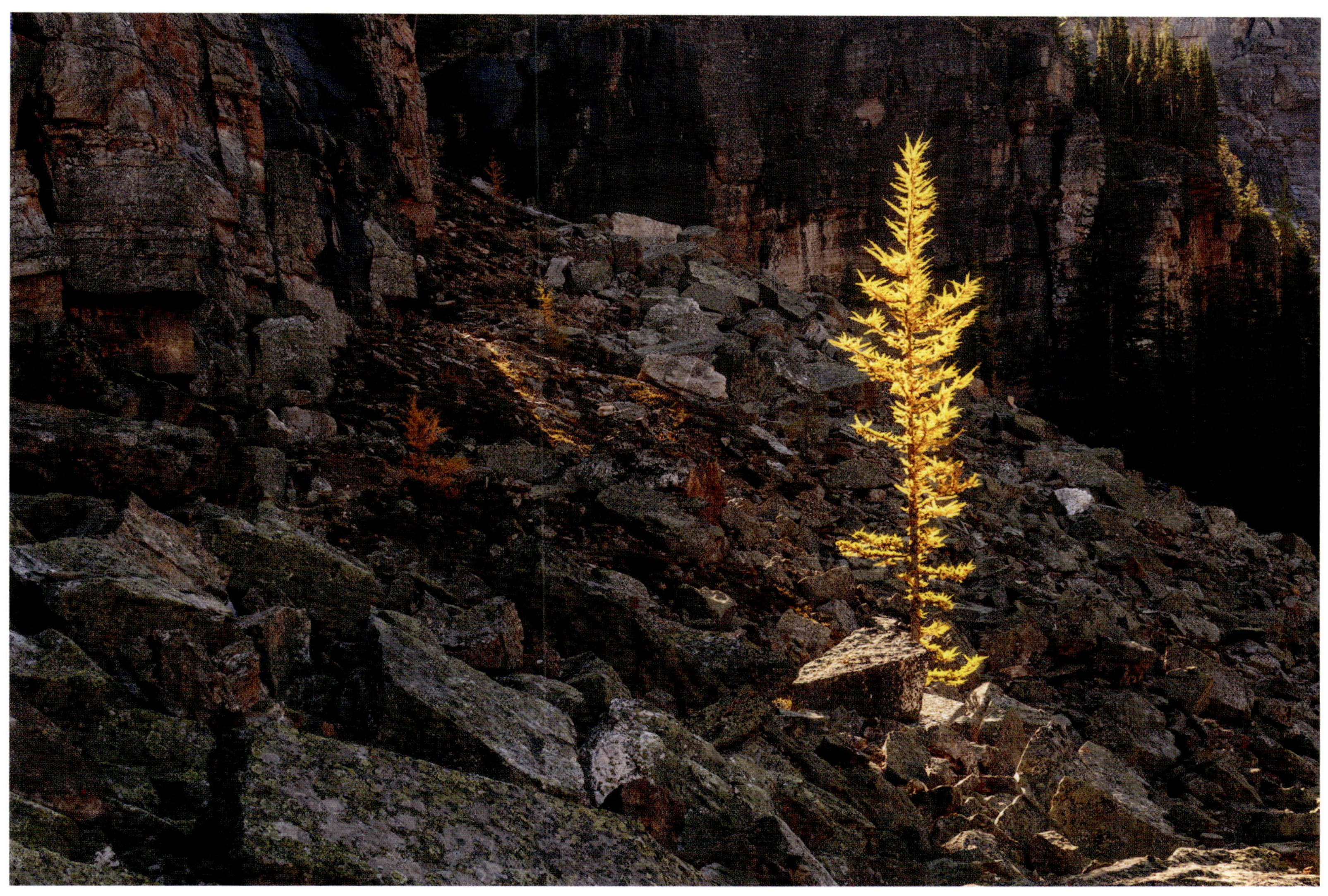

Alpine Flame (2008)
When viewing backlit autumn larch trees from a distance, it
looks as though the slopes are on fire.

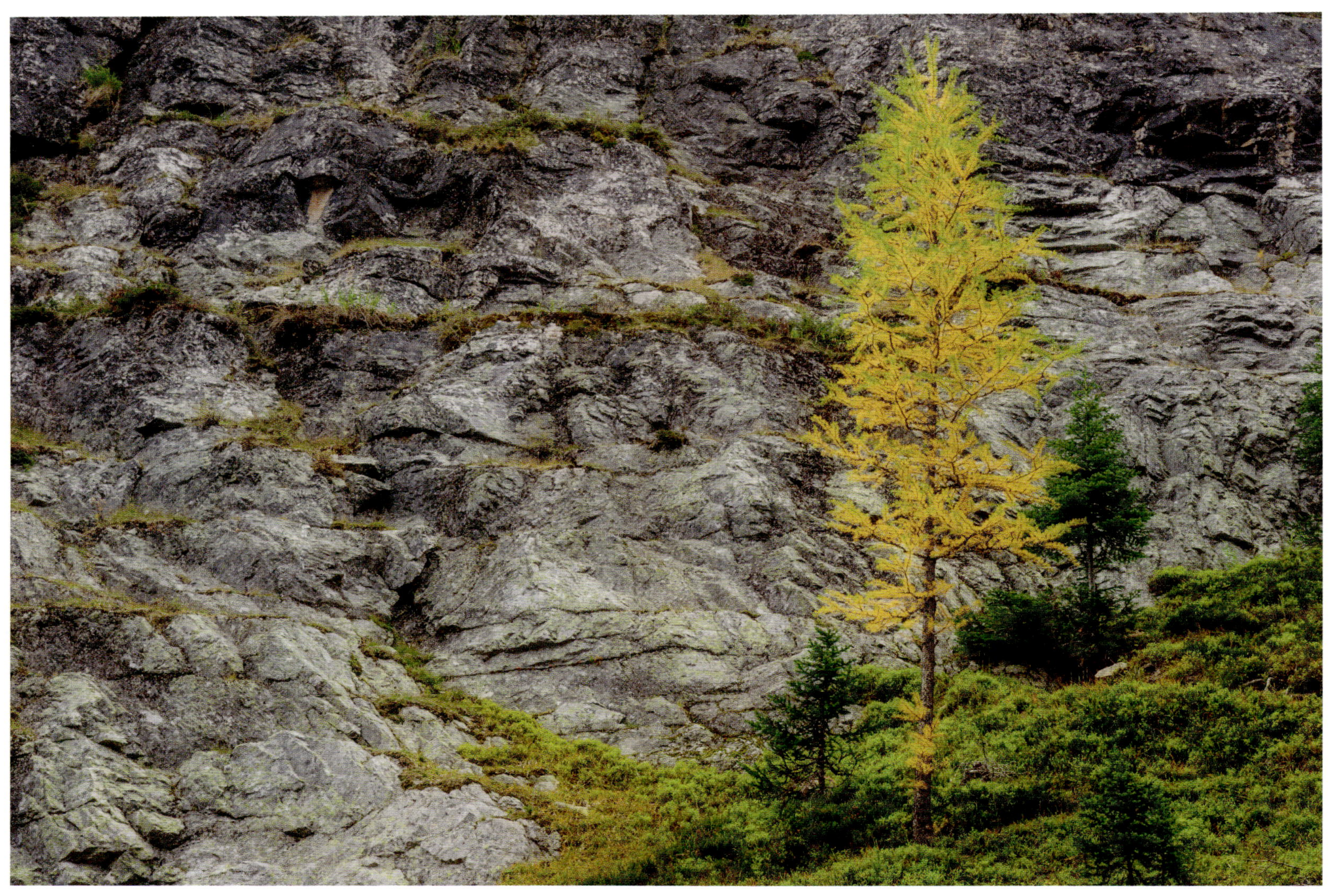

Larch Impression (2011)
A composite of one sharp image and one blurred creates a softer impression of this larch juxtaposed against the rock backdrop.

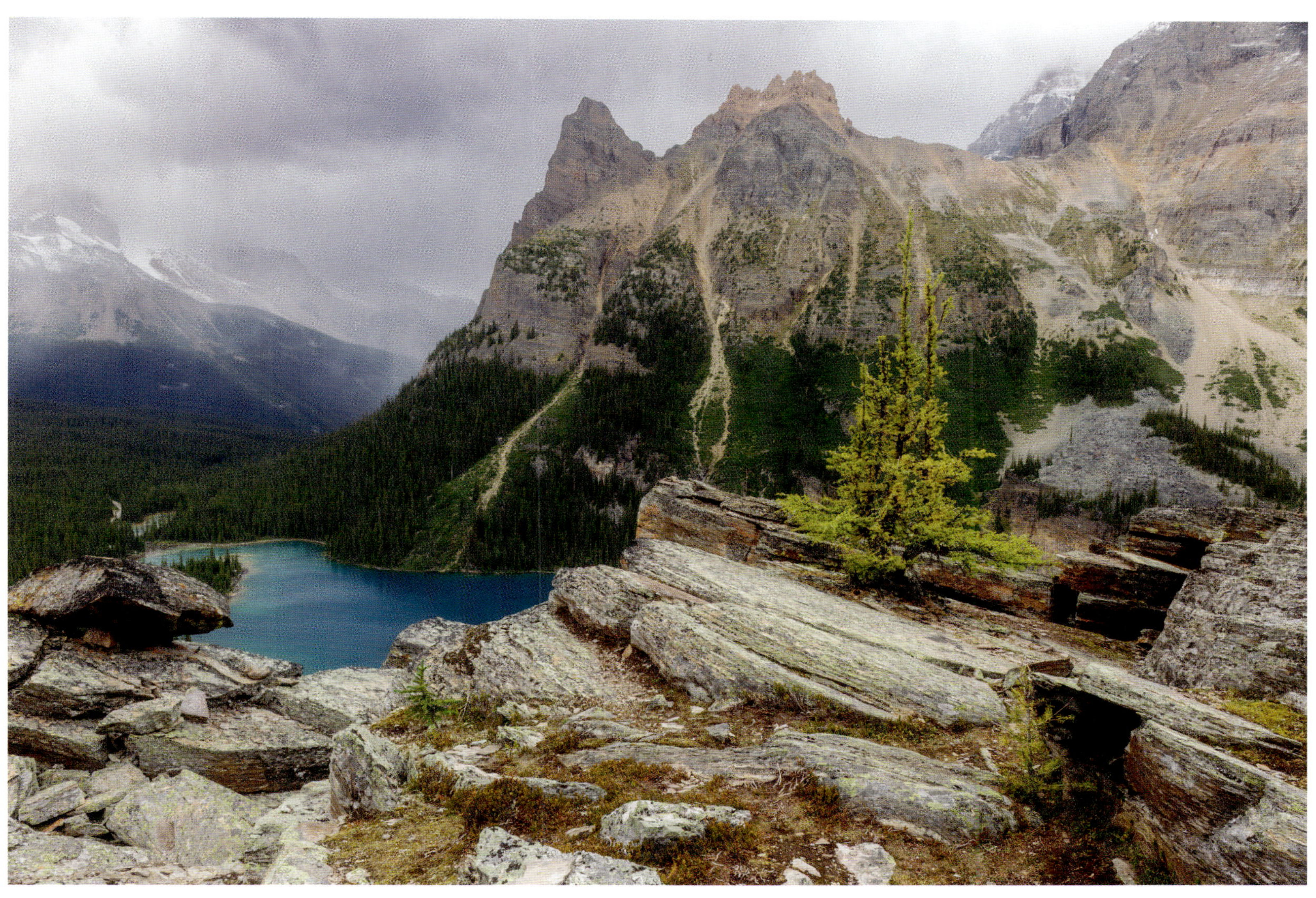

Holding Fast (2011)
A lone larch holds fast atop the windswept plateau.

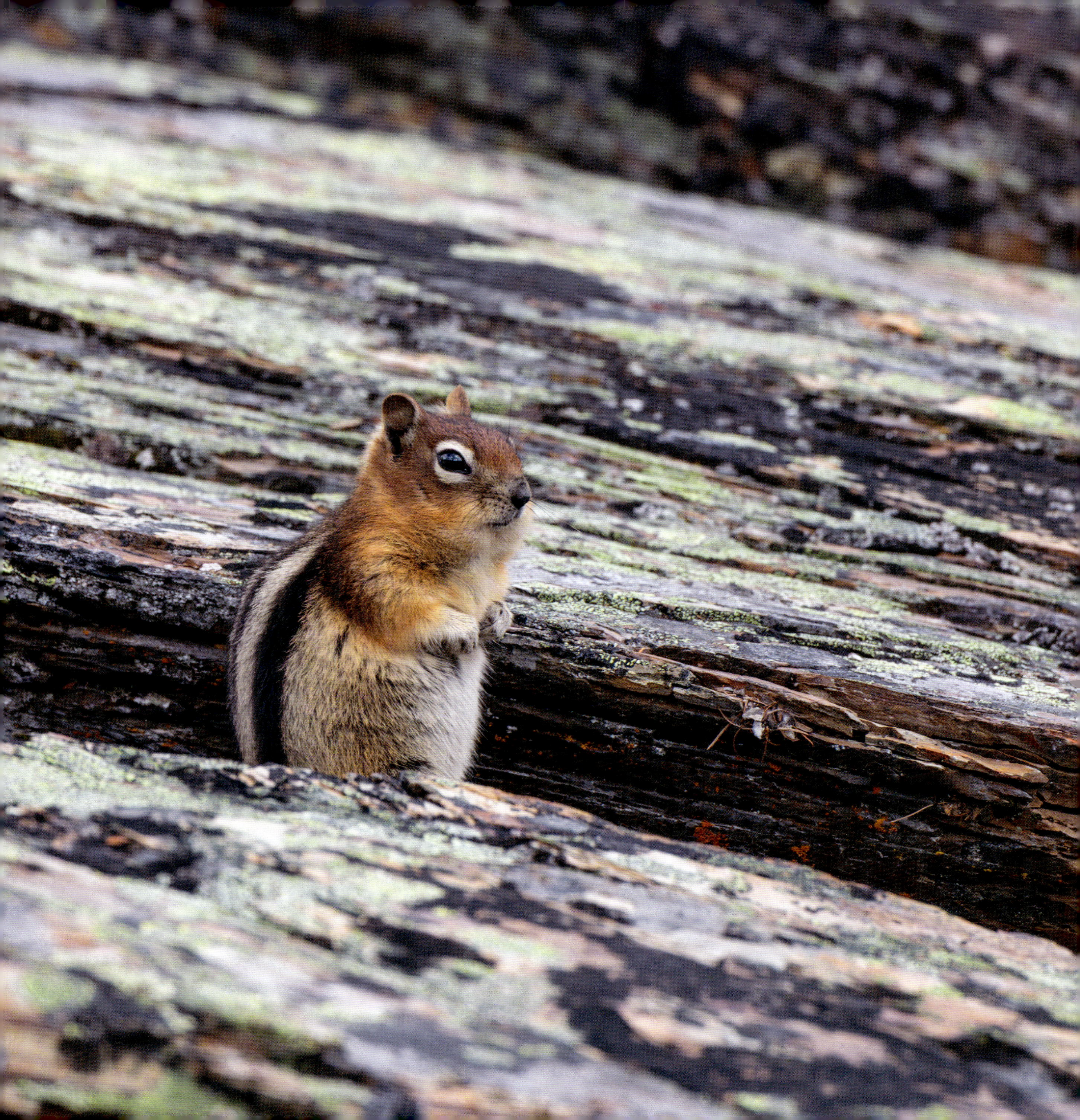

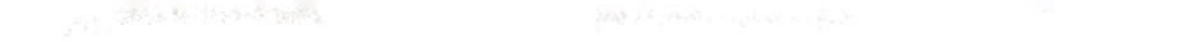

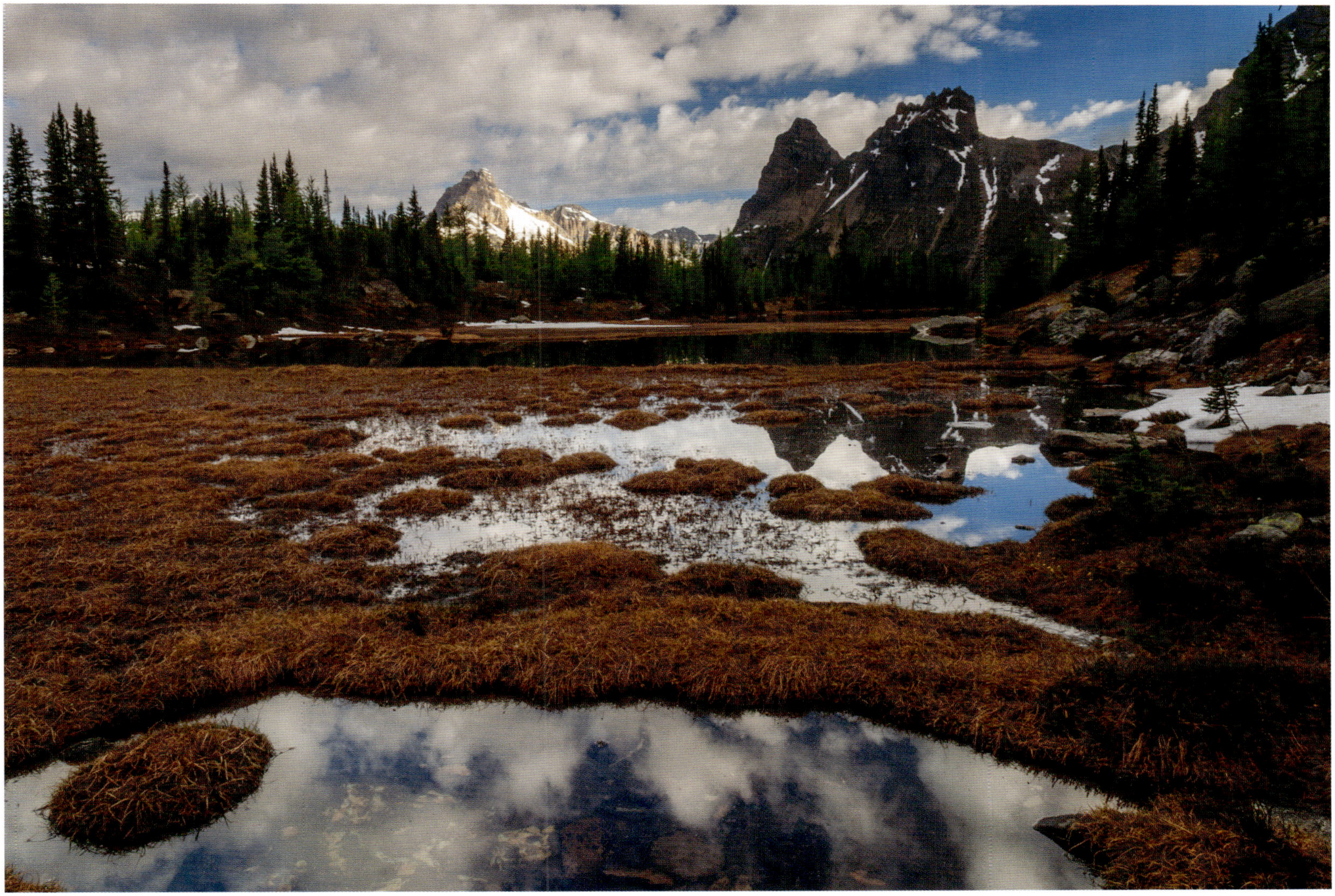

Seasonal Views (2007)
These shallow lakes vary greatly in size throughout the season, sometimes capturing reflections of the distant mountains surrounding Lake O'Hara.

Winter Preparation (2016)
Opabin Plateau chipmunk, well adapted to this rocky area, storing seeds and nuts for winter.

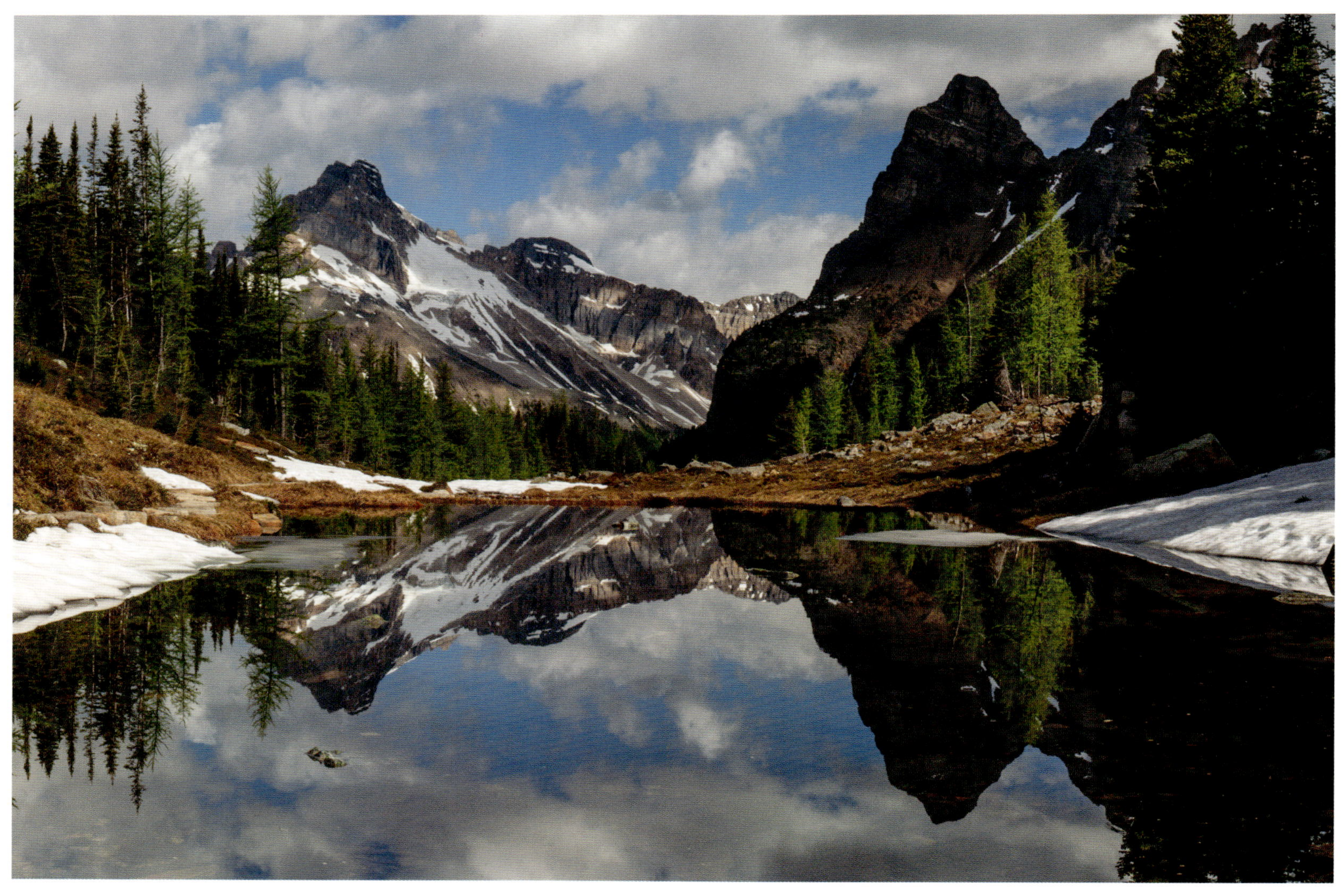

Twin Peaks (2007)
Wiwaxy and Consummation peaks reflected in the still surface
of Moor Lakes.

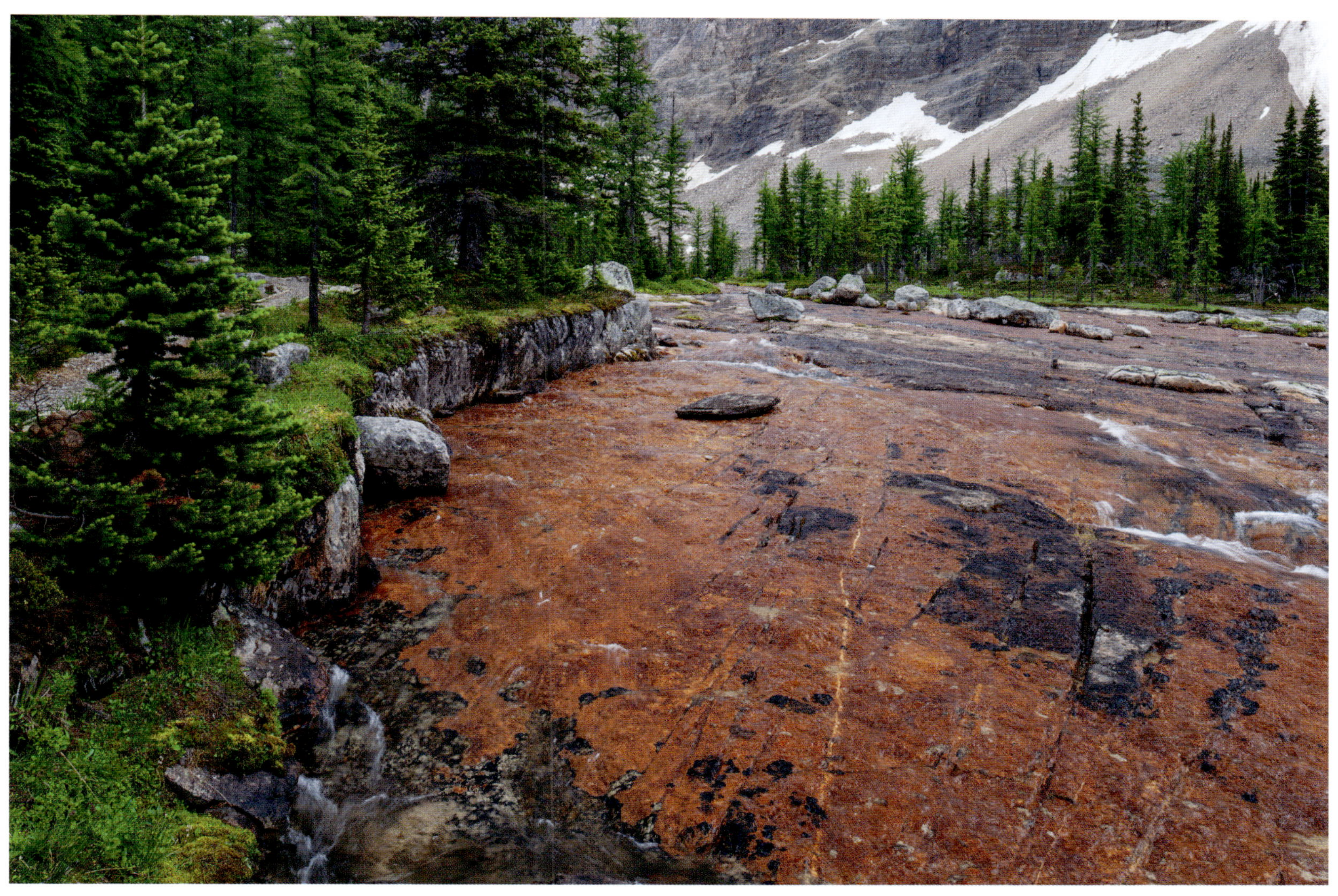

Natural Complements (2007)
Complementary colours abound in the Cascade Lakes region
of Opabin Plateau.

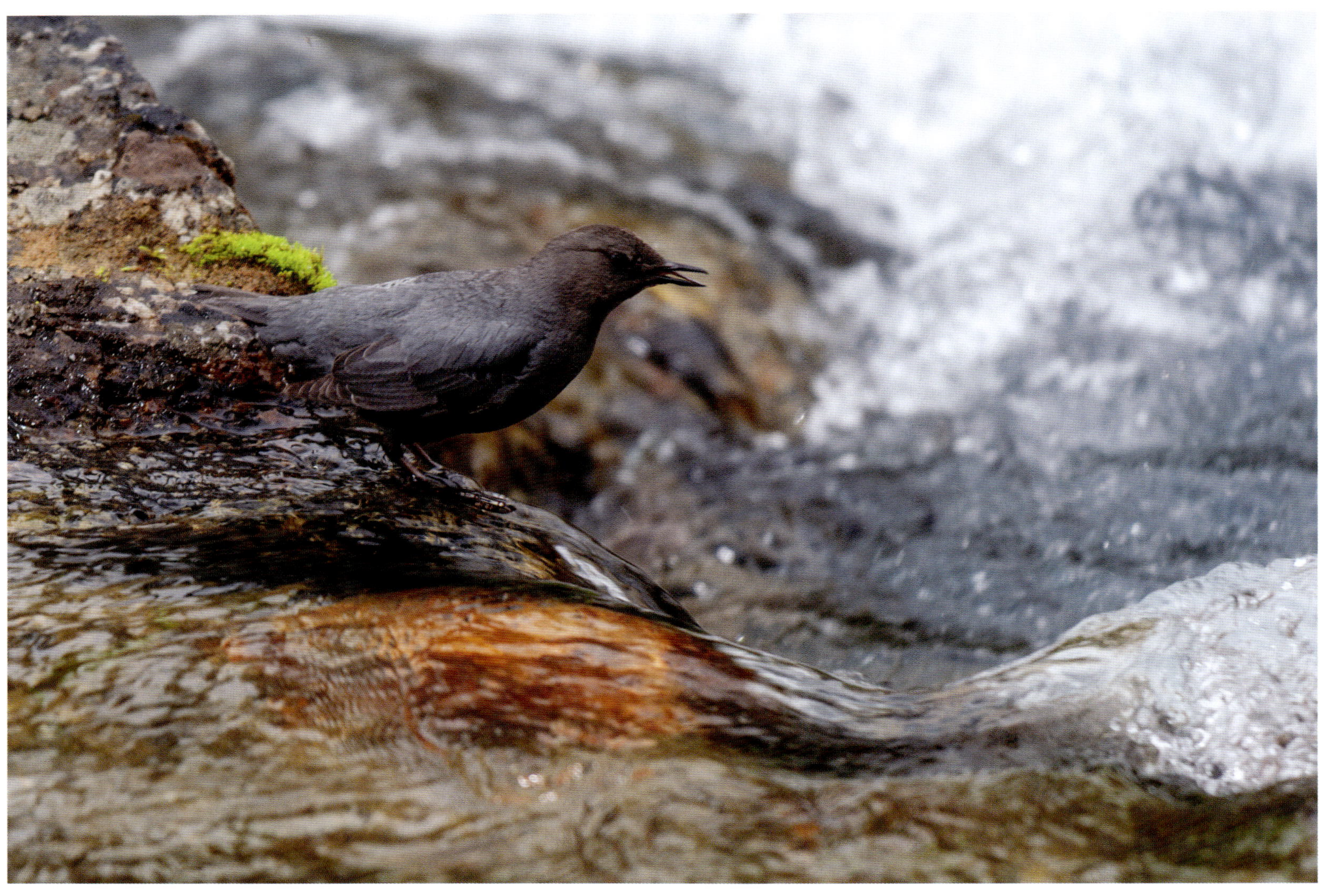

Invertebrate Hunting (2007)
An American dipper perched on a fast-moving stream along
the Cascade Lakes of Opabin Plateau.

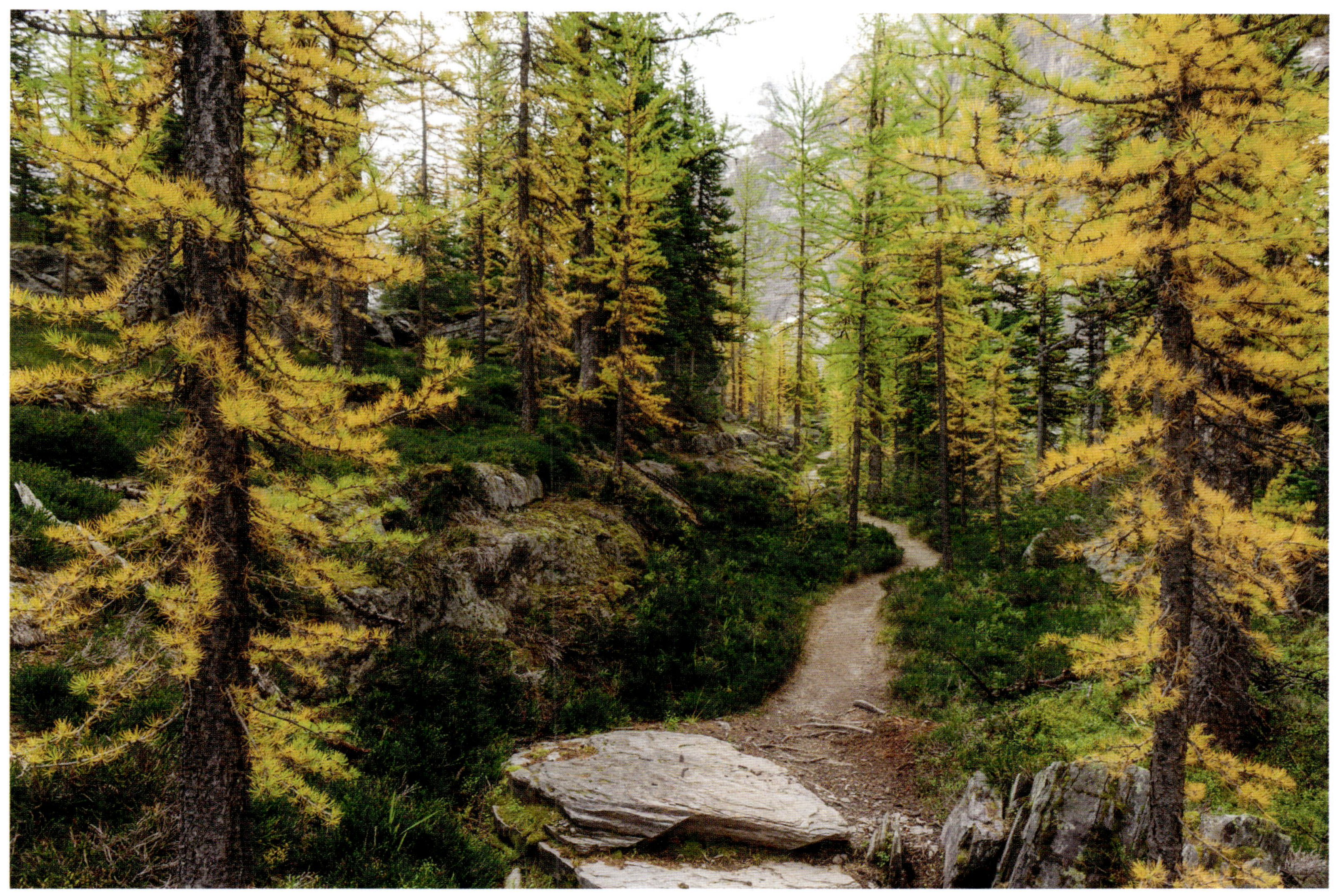

Golden Pathway (2011)
Opabin Plateau is one of the best places in the Lake O'Hara
region to experience the full effect of golden autumn larch.

Overleaf **A Giant's Playground** (2016)
Like in a giant's playground, massive rock slabs delineate the
edge of Opabin Prospect.

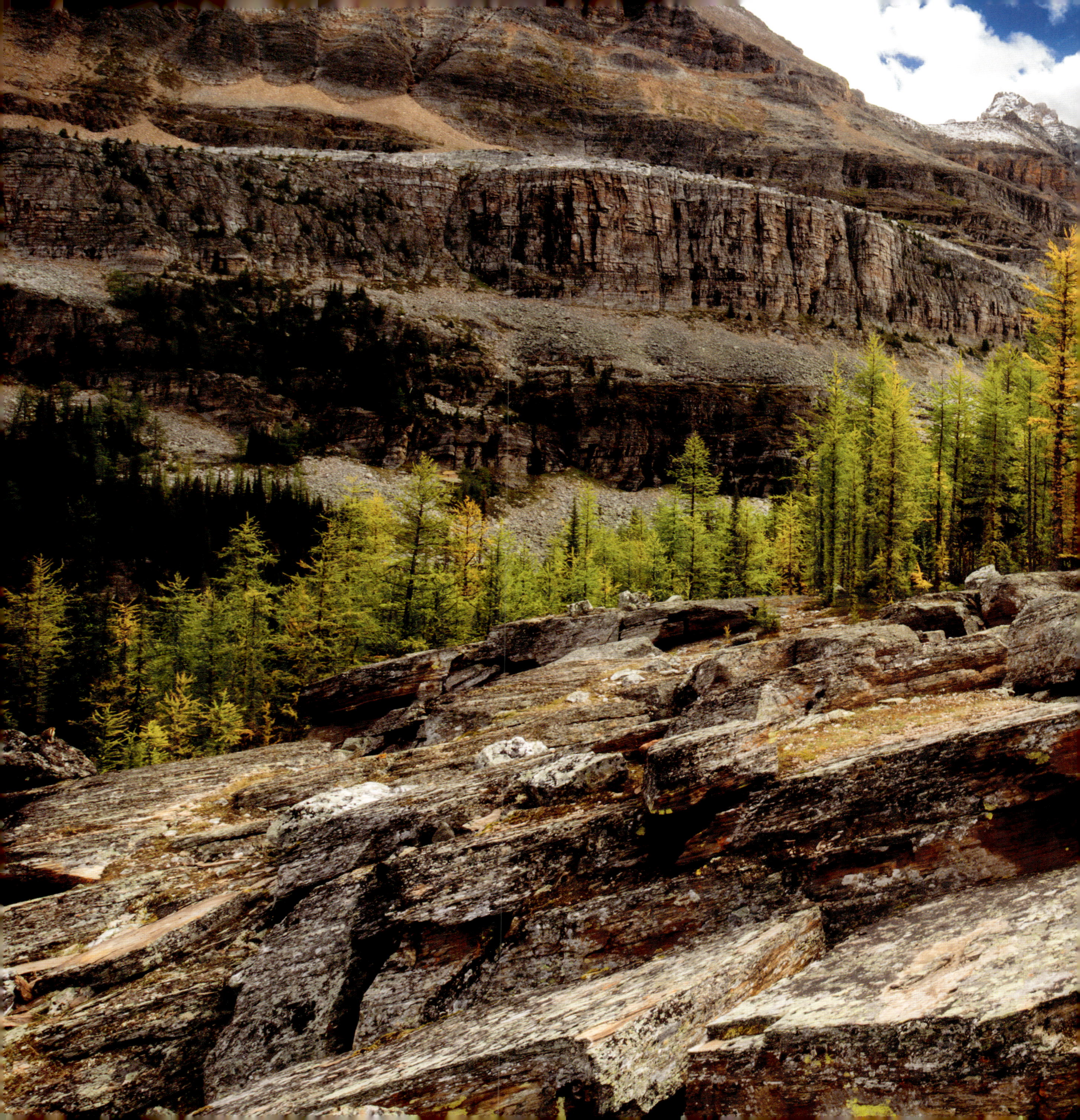

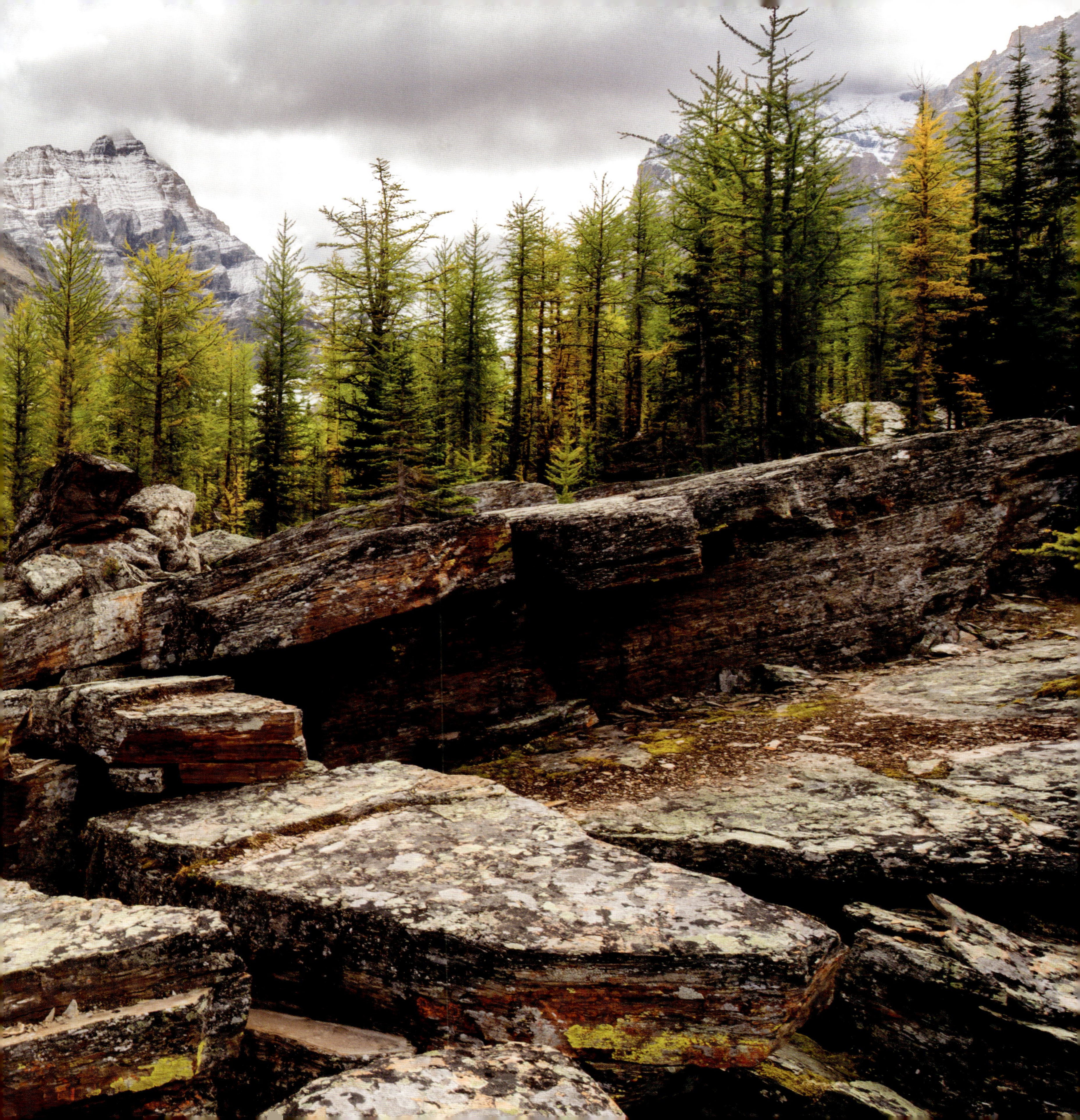

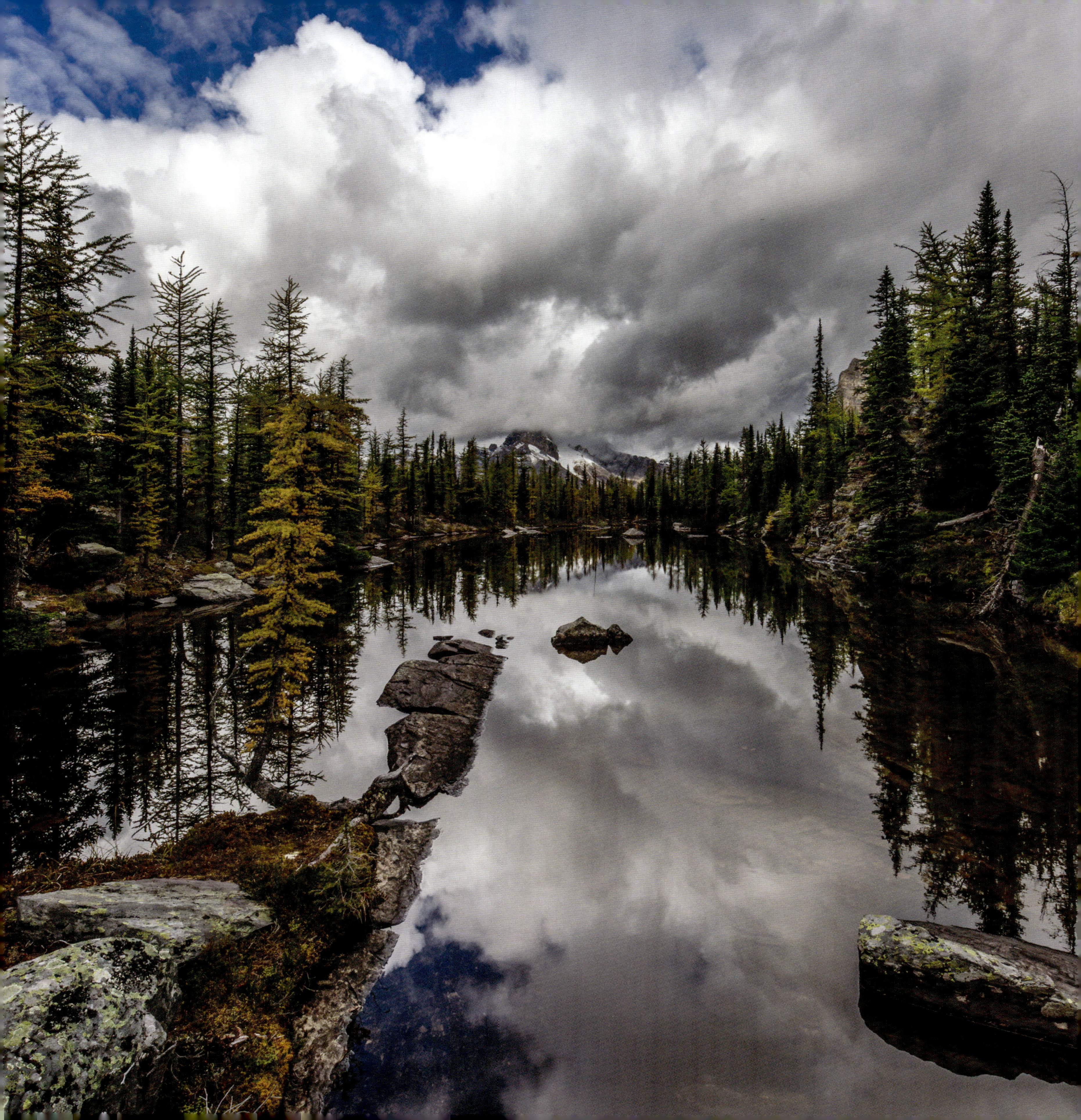

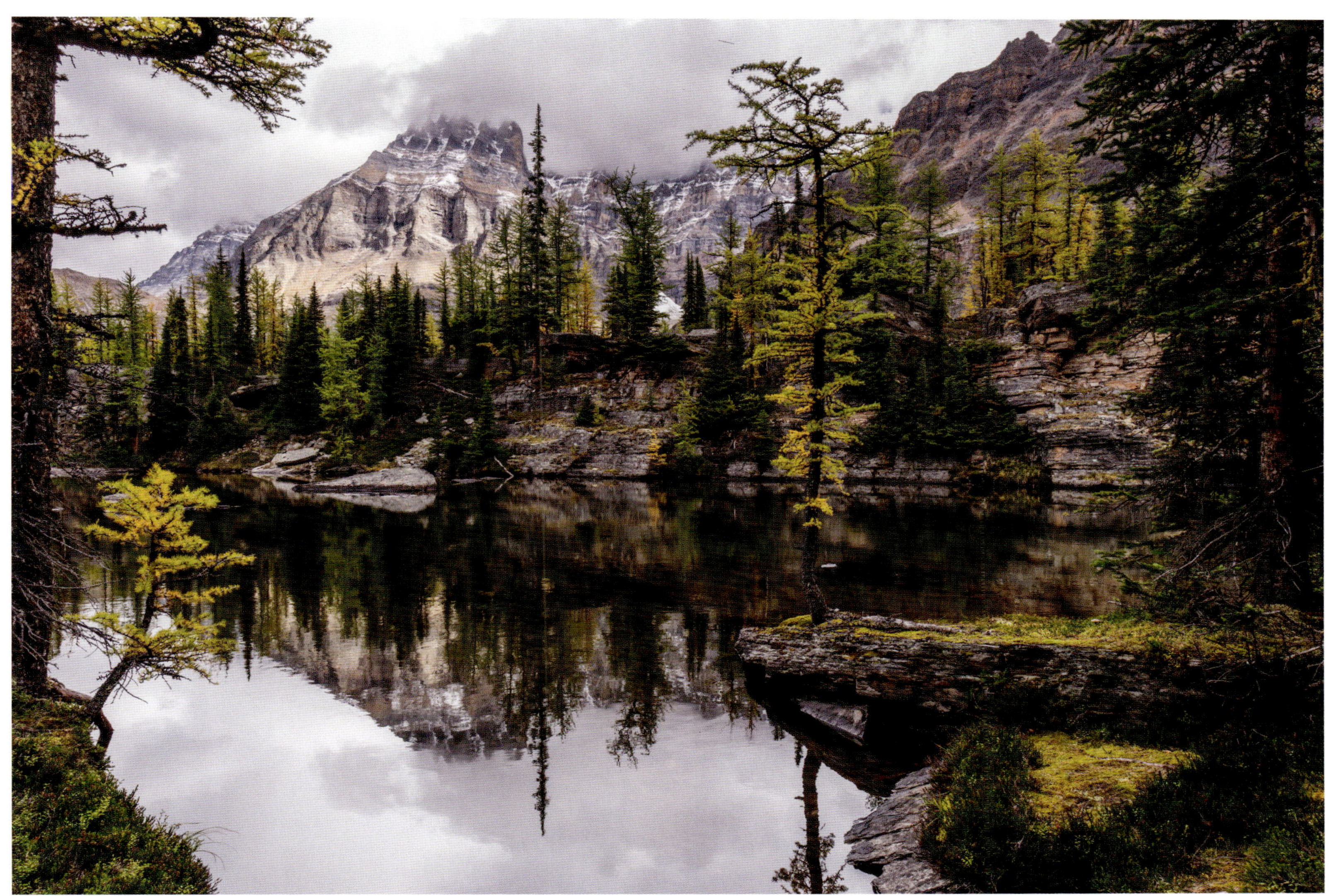

Peaceful Reflection (2016)
The weathered limestone peak of Mount Huber is reflected in a tranquil lake on Opabin Plateau.

Hidden Treasure (2016)
Intimate areas along the Opabin Prospect trail with unnamed lakes create quiet, magical spaces to simply "be present" and absorb the alpine wonder.

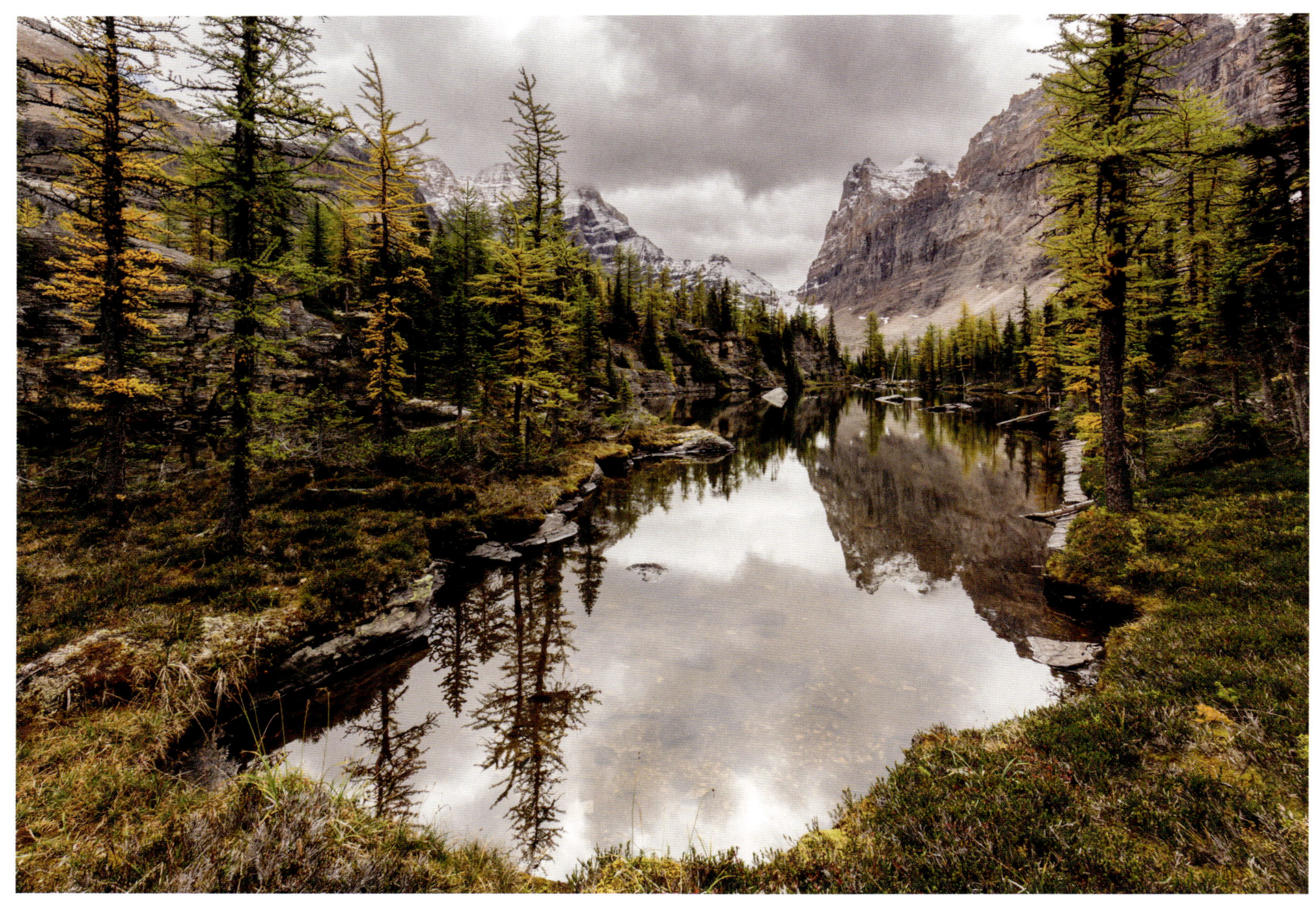

Opabin Plateau Magic (2016)
Mount Biddle is mirrored in a small lake on Opabin Plateau just
moments before an autumn snowfall.

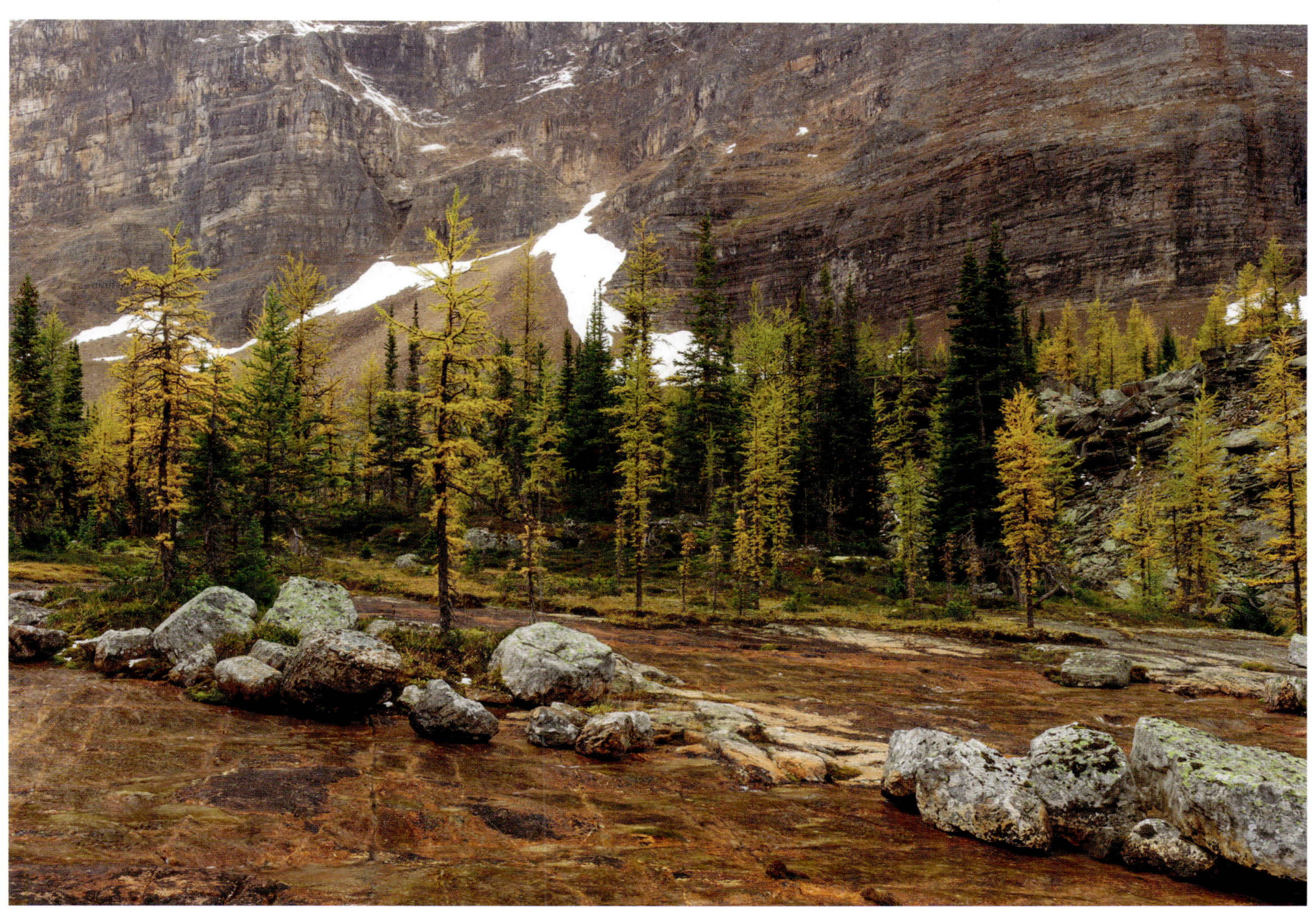

Ancient Landscape (2011)
Remnants of glacial landscaping are revealed along the Cascade Lakes of Opabin Plateau.

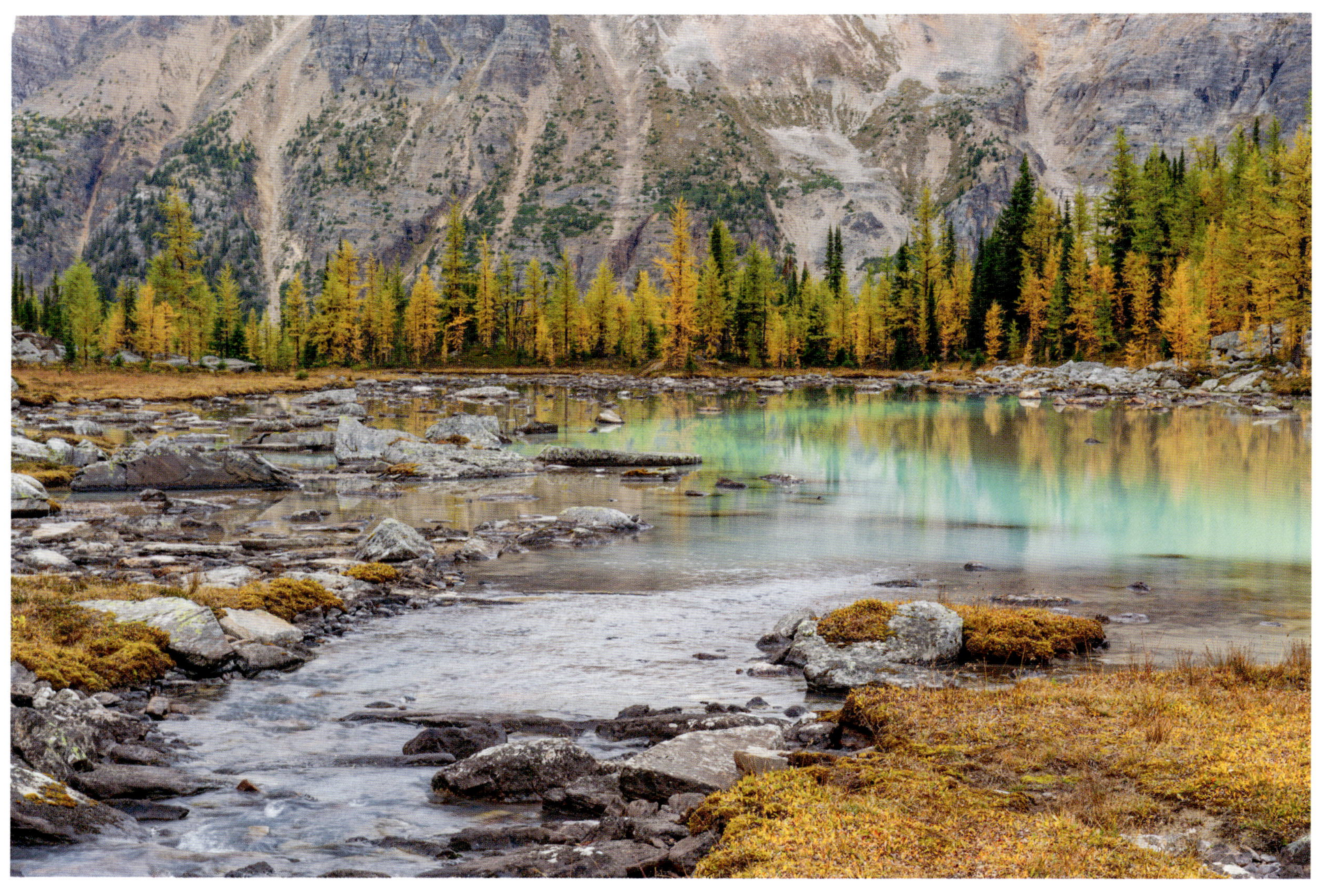

Nature's Palette (2008)
Golden larches are reflected in the shallow autumn turquoise
waters of Cascade Lakes.

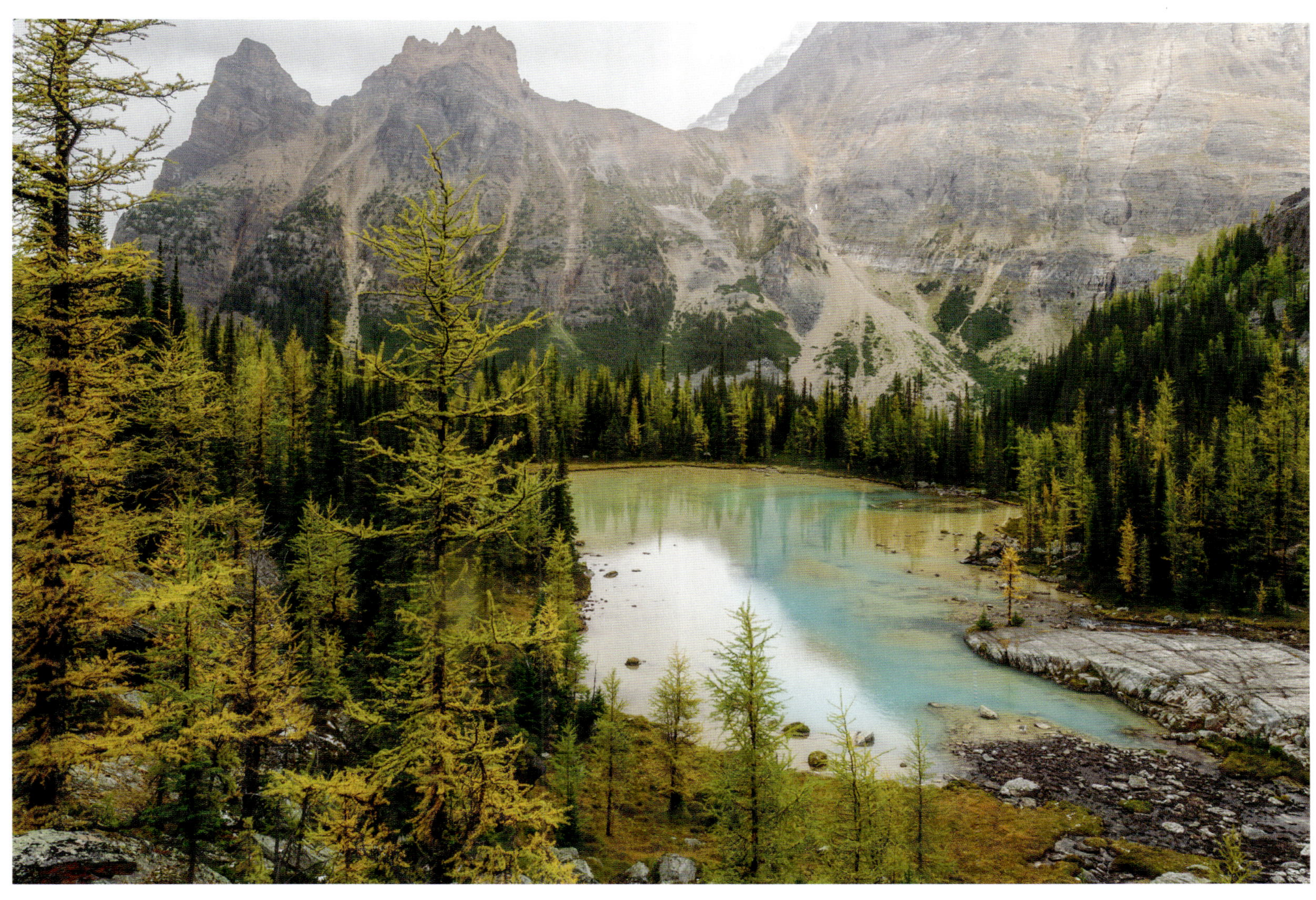

Autumn Wonder (2011)
Mount Huber and Wiwaxy Peaks rise next to the
milky-turquoise water of Cascade Lakes.

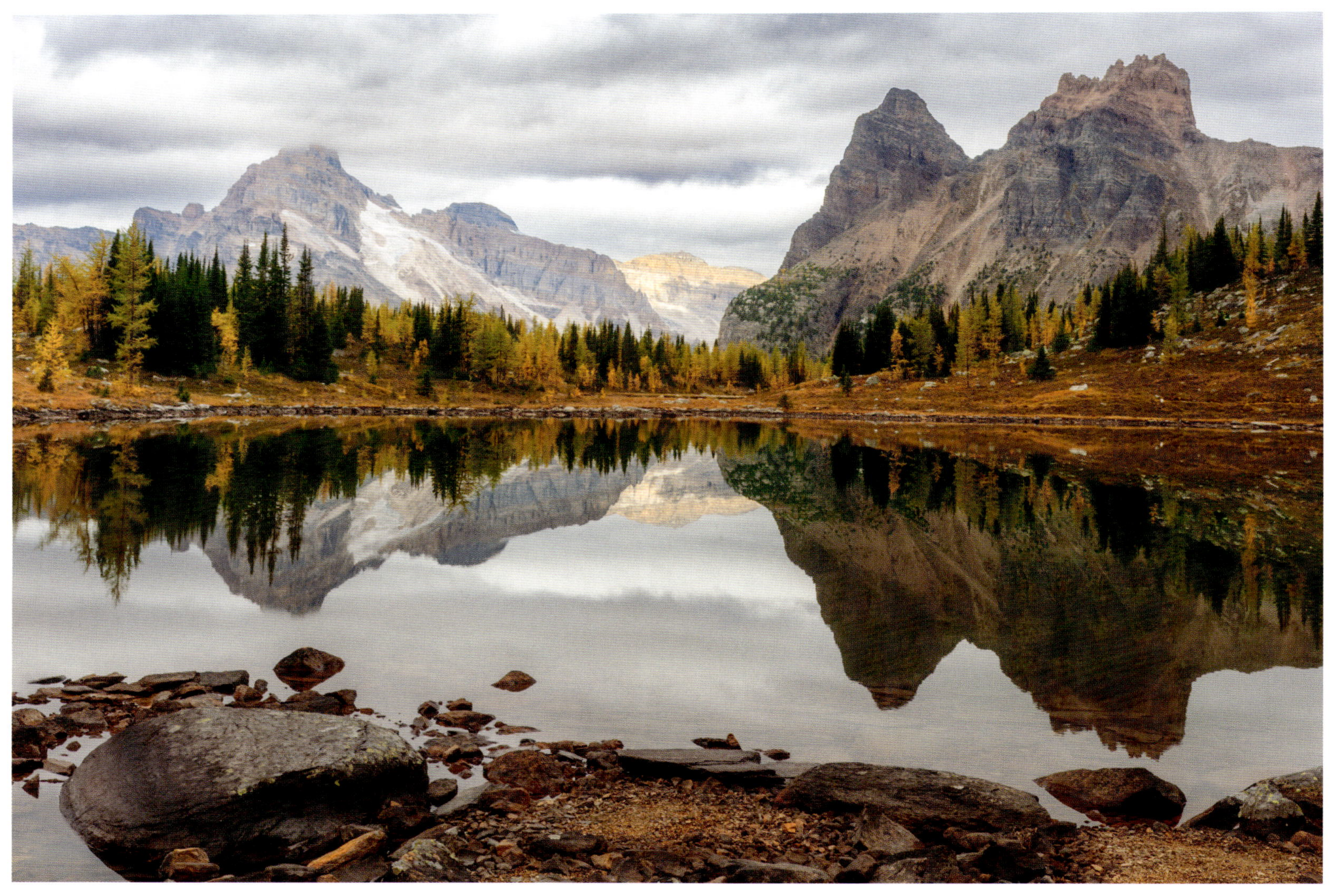

Majestic Reflection (2008)
Hungabee Lake acts as a mirror for Cathedral Mountain and
Wiwaxy Peaks.

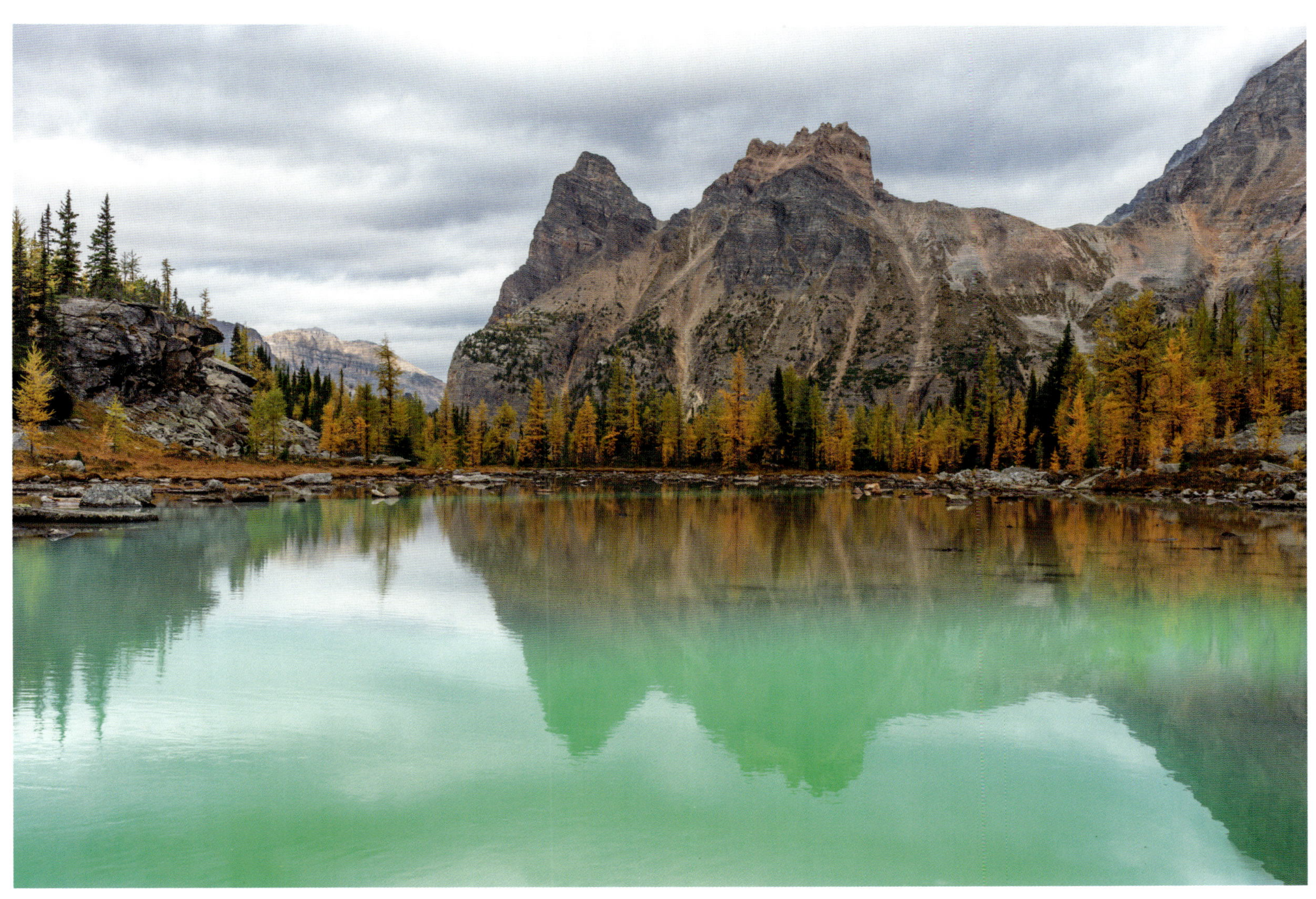

Autumn Hues (2008)
Autumn accumulation of glacier melt rock flour sediments
intensifies the turquoise hues of Cascade Lakes.

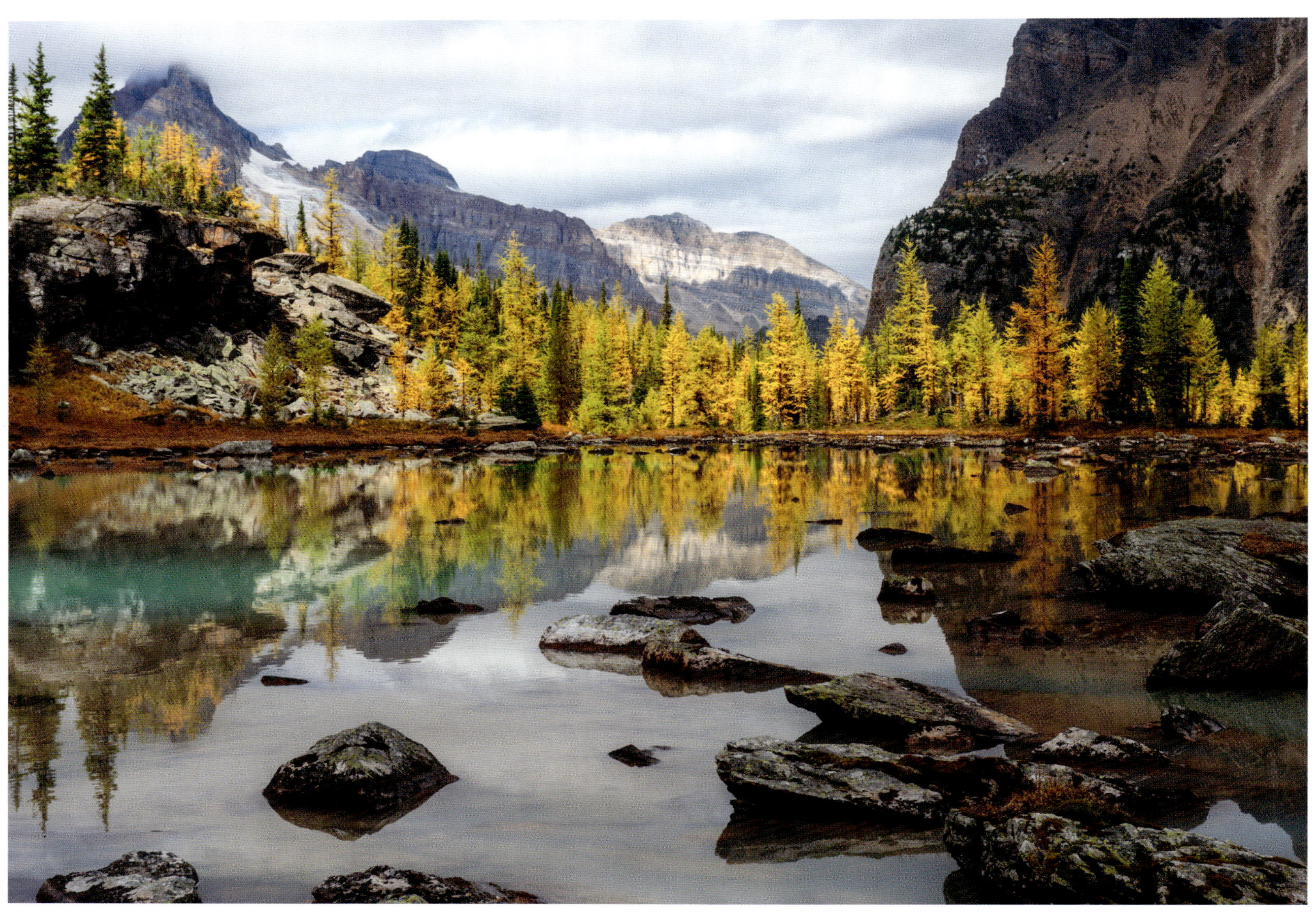

Artist's Delight (2008)
At the peak of larch season, Cascade Lakes on Opabin Plateau
are an artist's delight. Many painters and photographers are
drawn to this location in September.

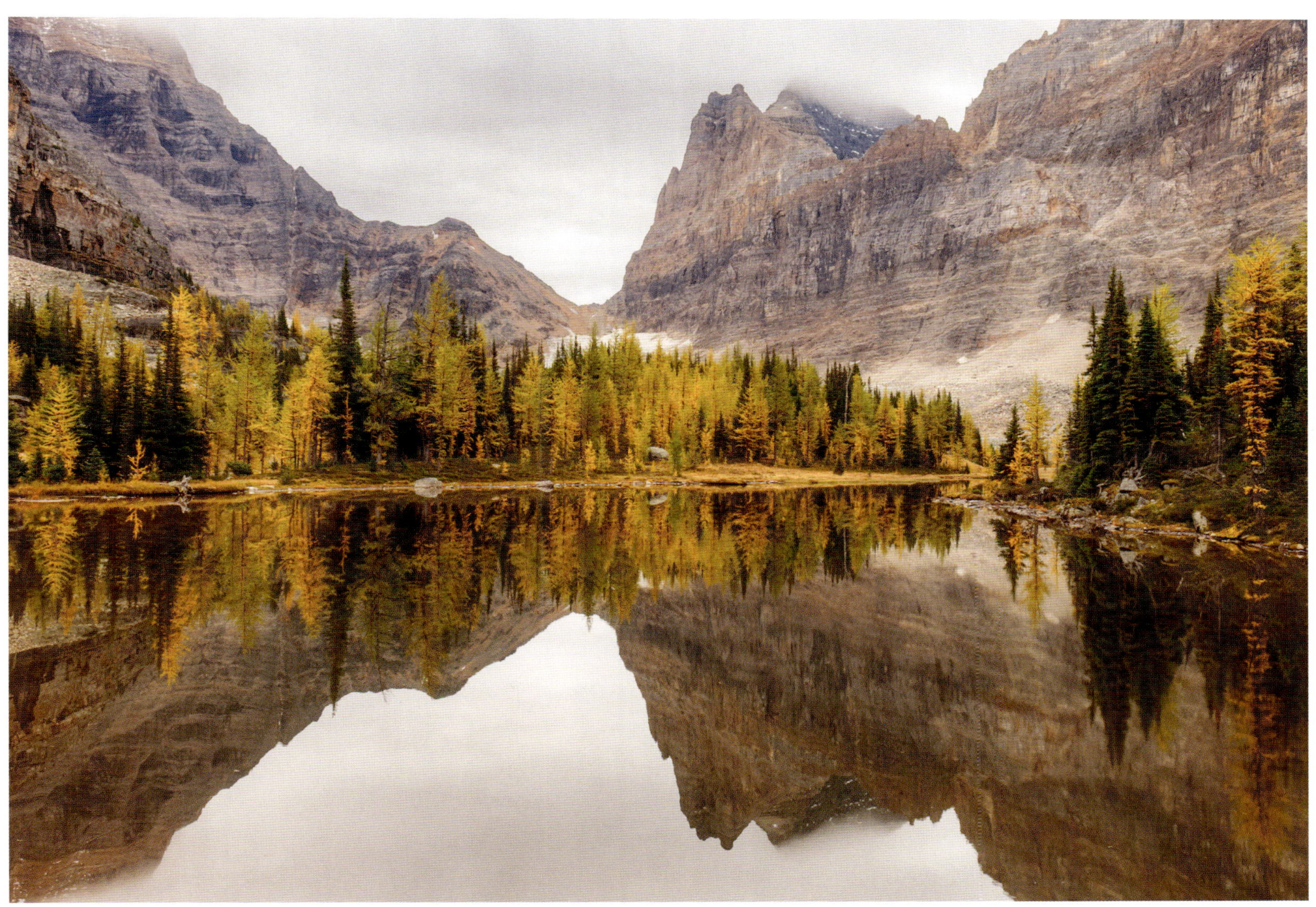

Opabin Still (2008)
Still air in an alpine cirque during daylight hours is a treasure. It often requires starting a hike in the dark to arrive at the scene before the sun's rays warming the land, which initiates the movement of air.

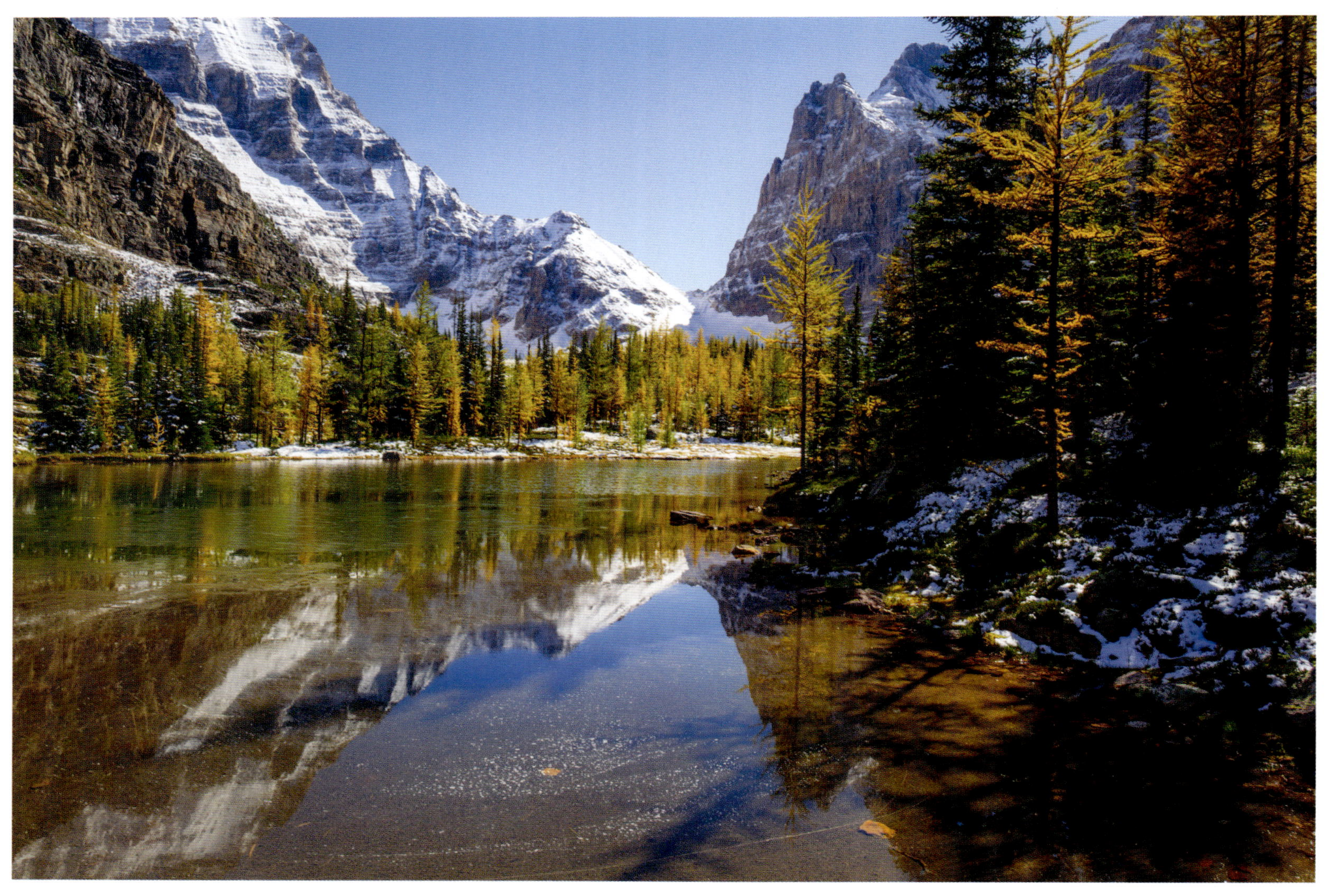

Early Ice (2011)
September snow and the first signs of ice forming on the surface of Moor Lakes.

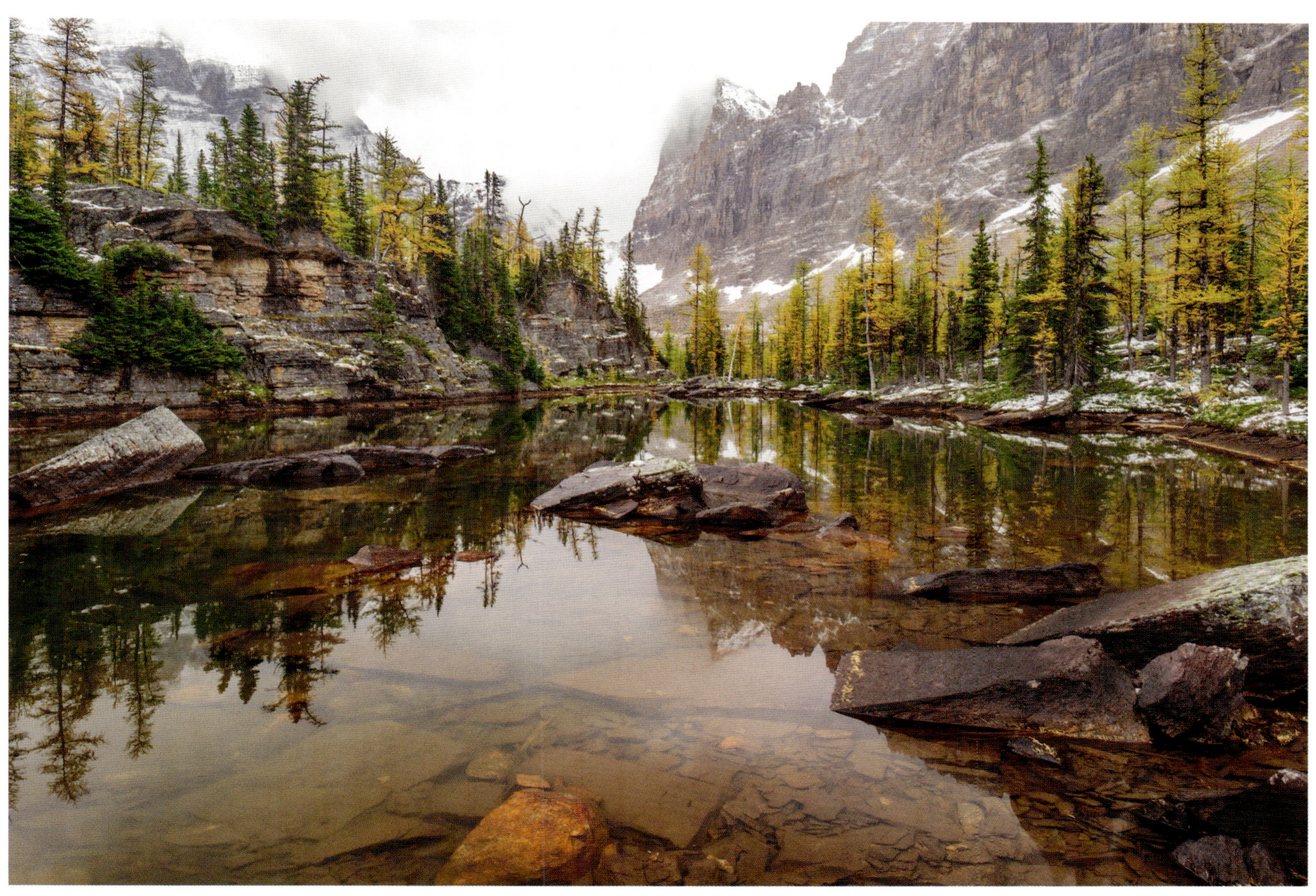

Autumn Solitude (2011)
Brief moments of solitude on Opabin Plateau become woven
into a fabric of life's most precious experiences.

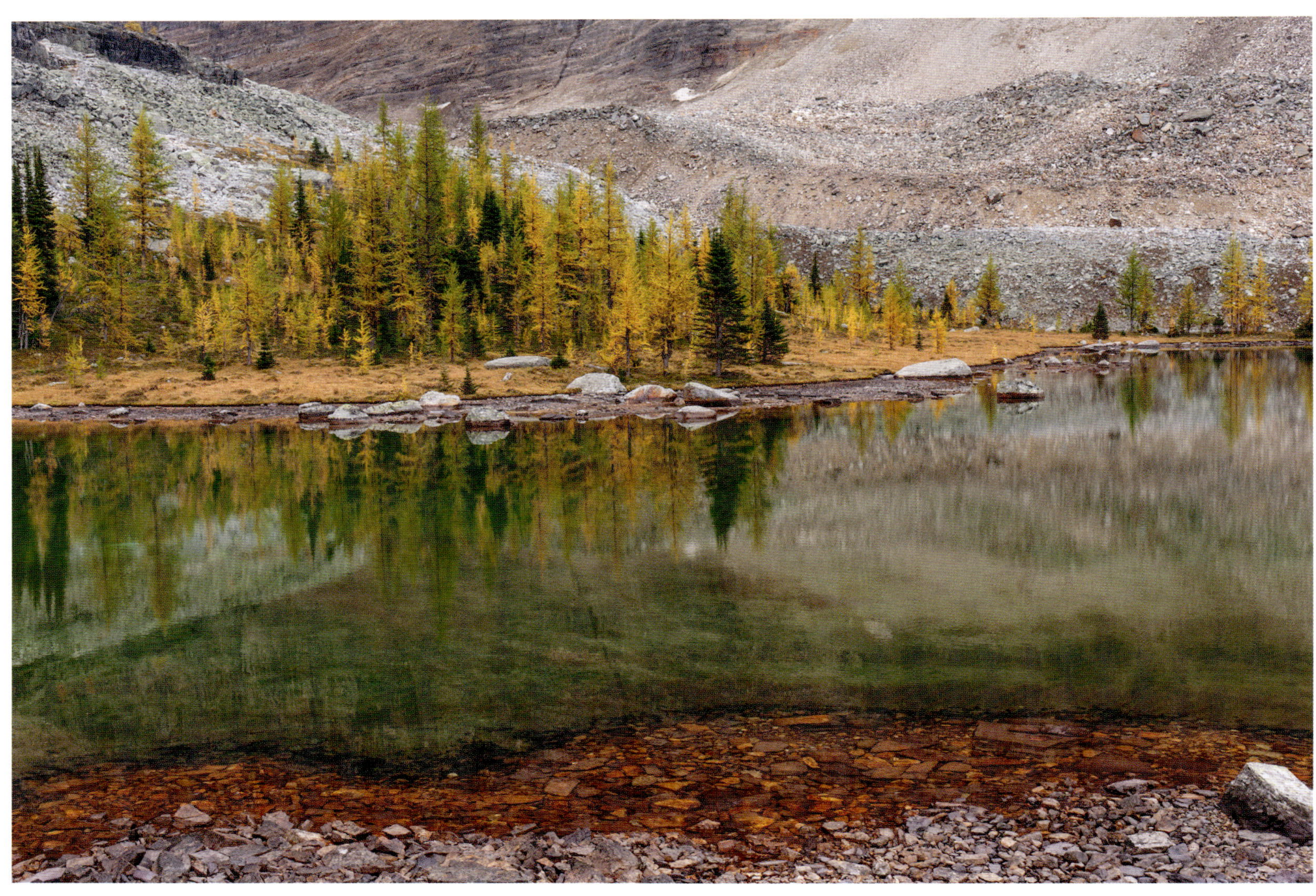

Opabin Lake Prelude (2008)
The final body of water on the way to Opabin Lake, Hunga-bee Lake is peaceful and shallow, mirroring nearby trees and mountain peaks.

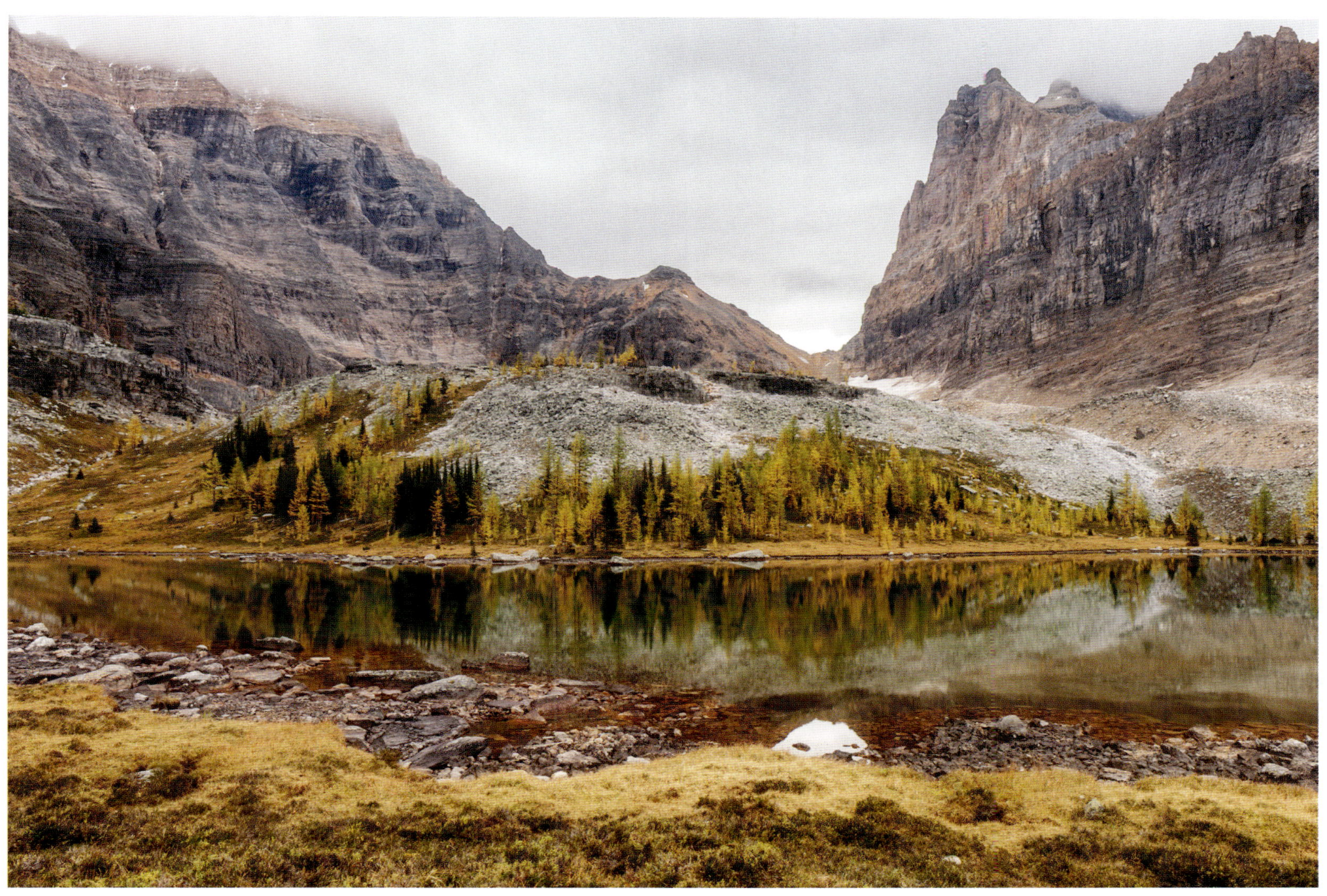

Hungabee Lake (2008)
From left to right, Yukness Mountain, the scree of Opabin
Lake's moraine, and Mount Biddle form the background to
picturesque Hungabee Lake.

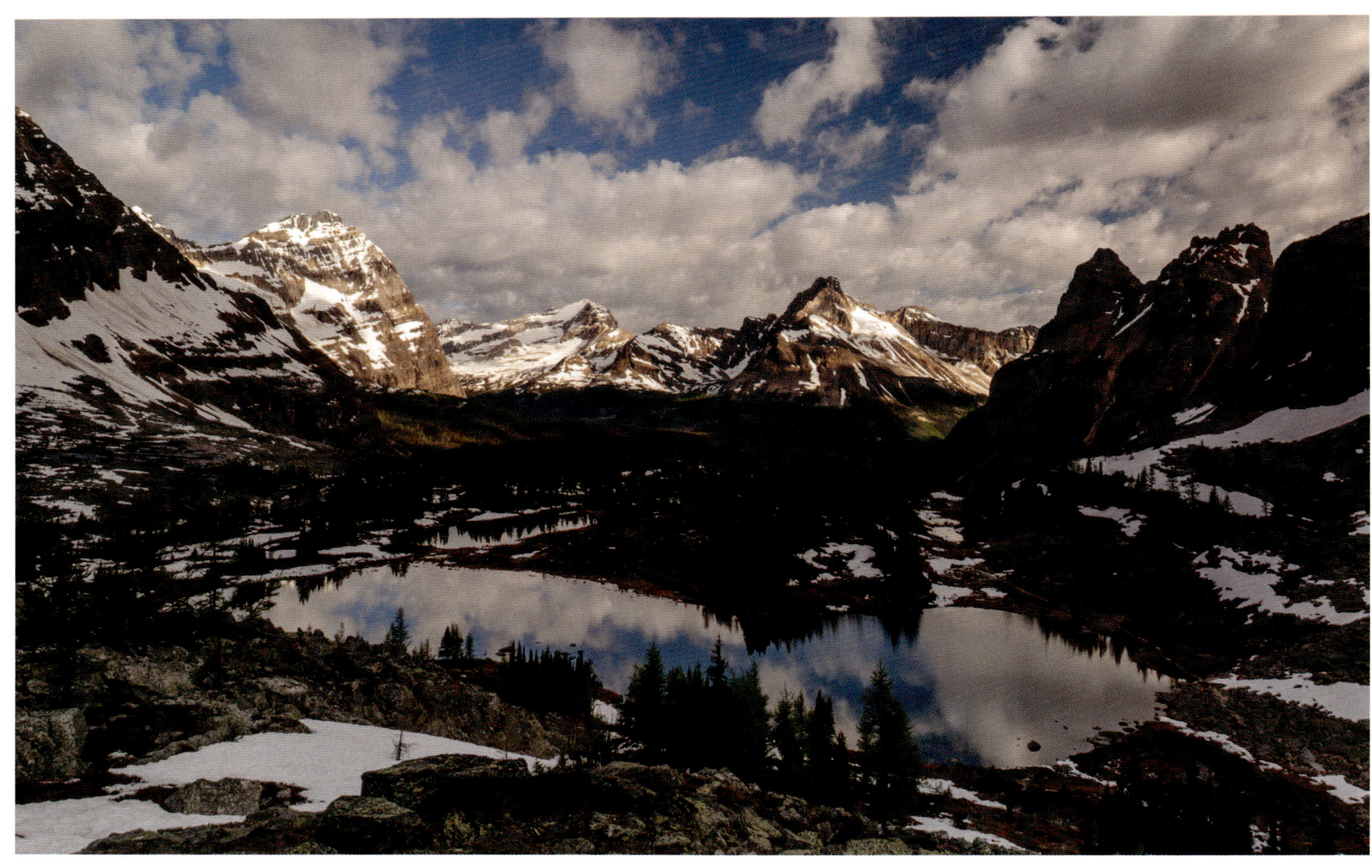

Plateau Vista (2007)
Across Hungabee Lake, the view encompasses Opabin Plateau
with the backdrop of Duchesnay Basin.

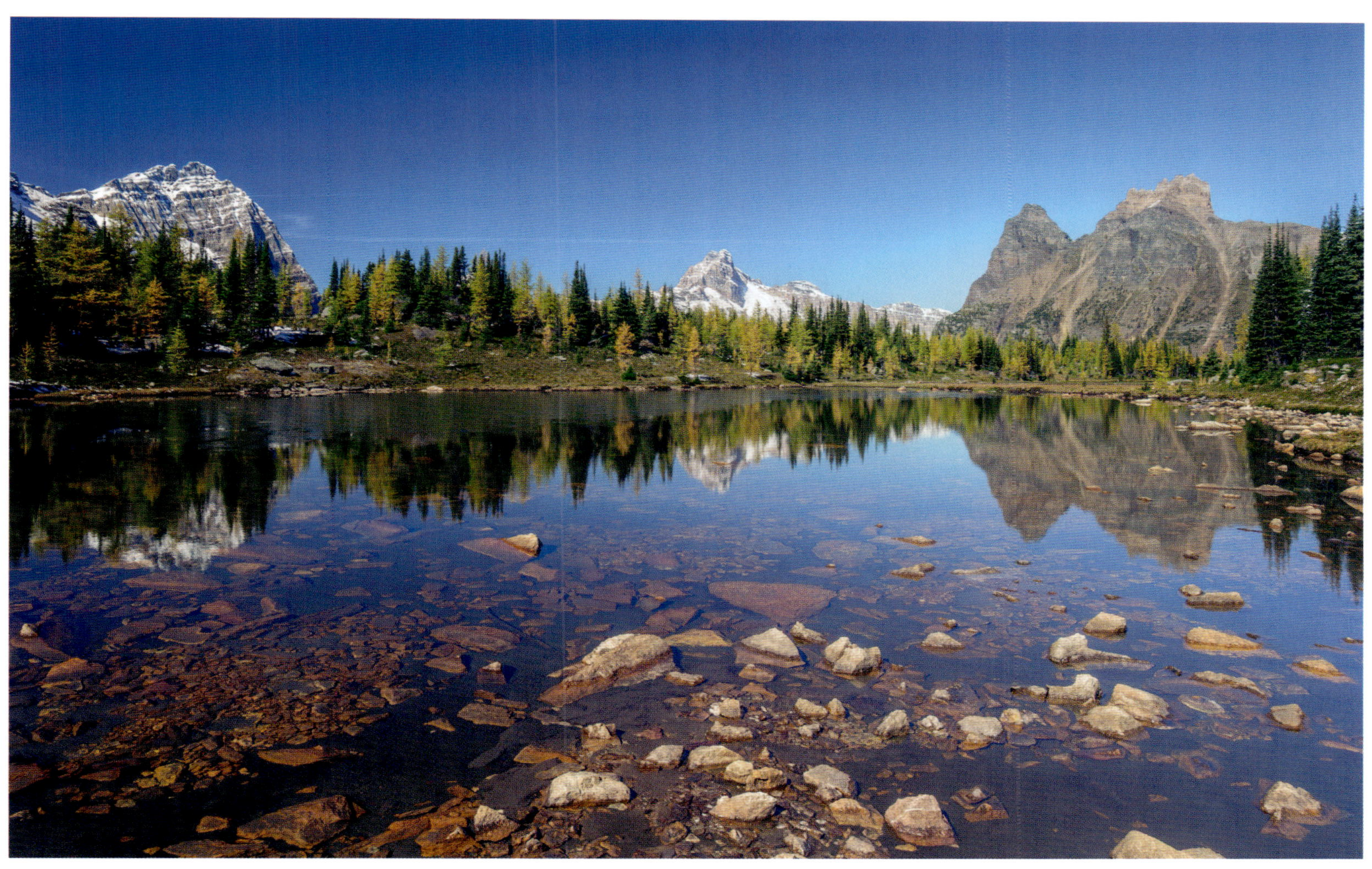

Mountain Peaks Vista (2011)
Wiwaxy Peaks, Cathedral Mountain, and Odaray Mountain
serve as a backdrop to Hungabee Lake.

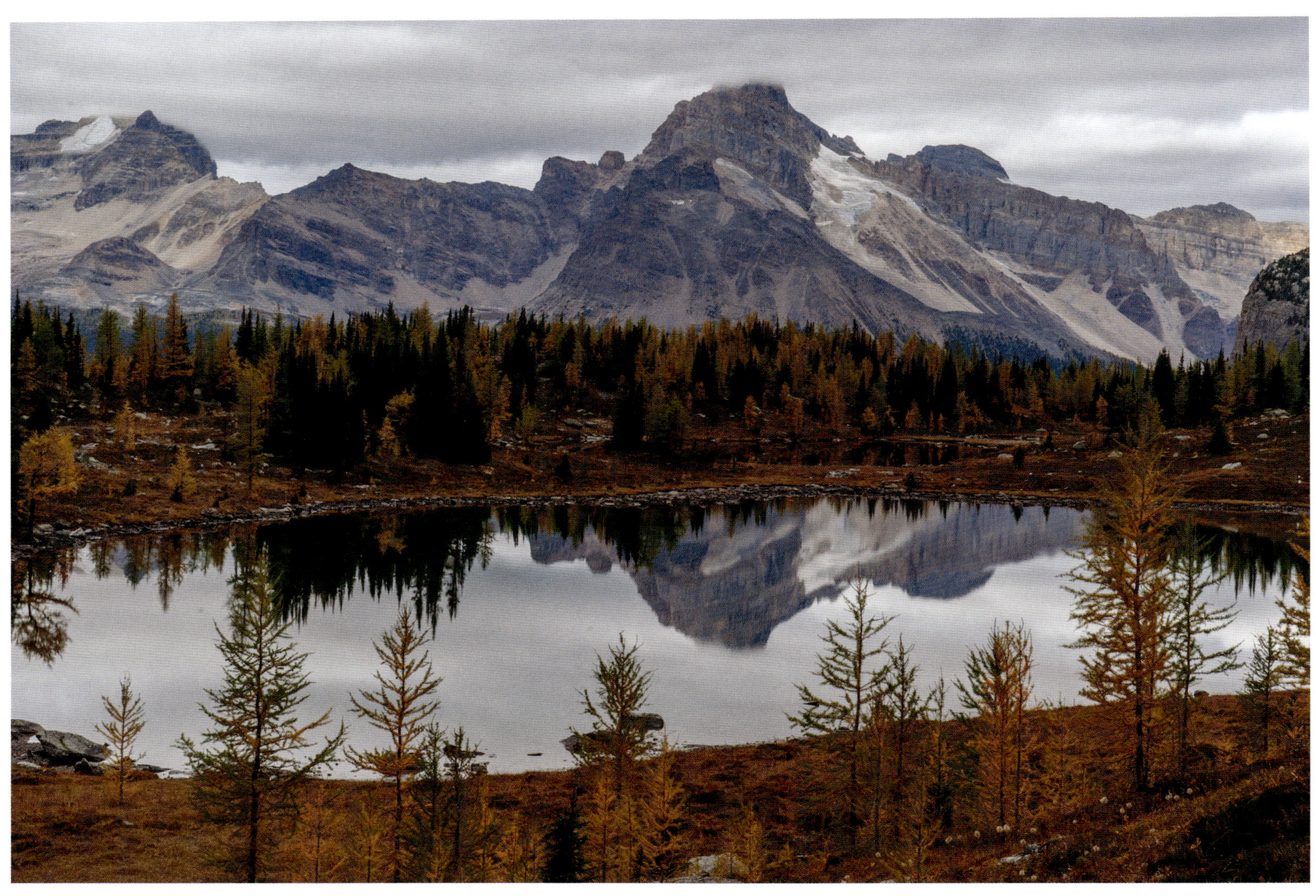

Consummation Peak Reflection (2008)
Consummation Peak and Cathedral Mountain touch the clouds
as one gains elevation on the way to Opabin Lake.

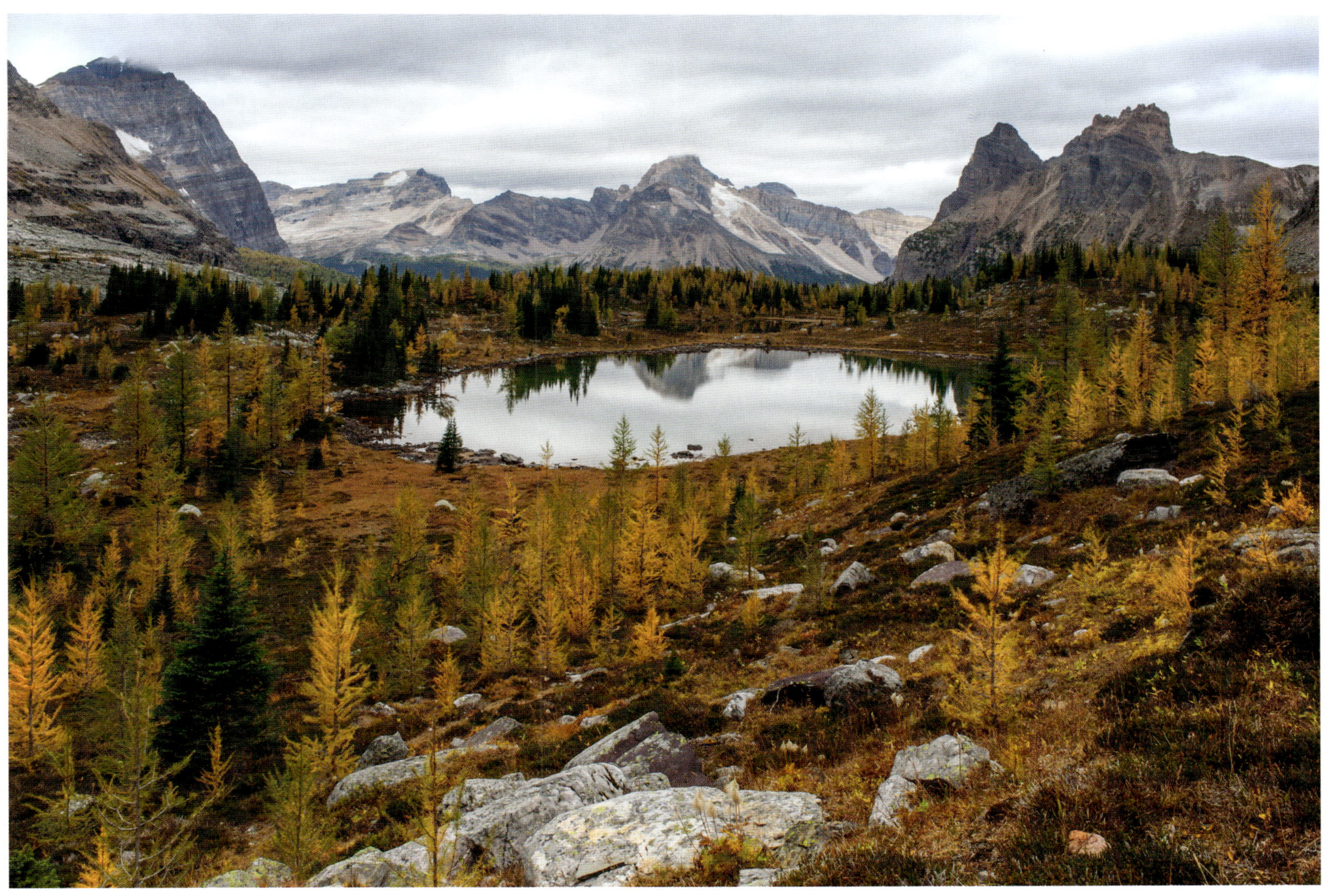

Hungabee Gold (2008)
The golden larches of autumn envelop Hungabee Lake. Indigenous Peoples used this tree's resin as medicine, and its wood
for tools and snowshoes.

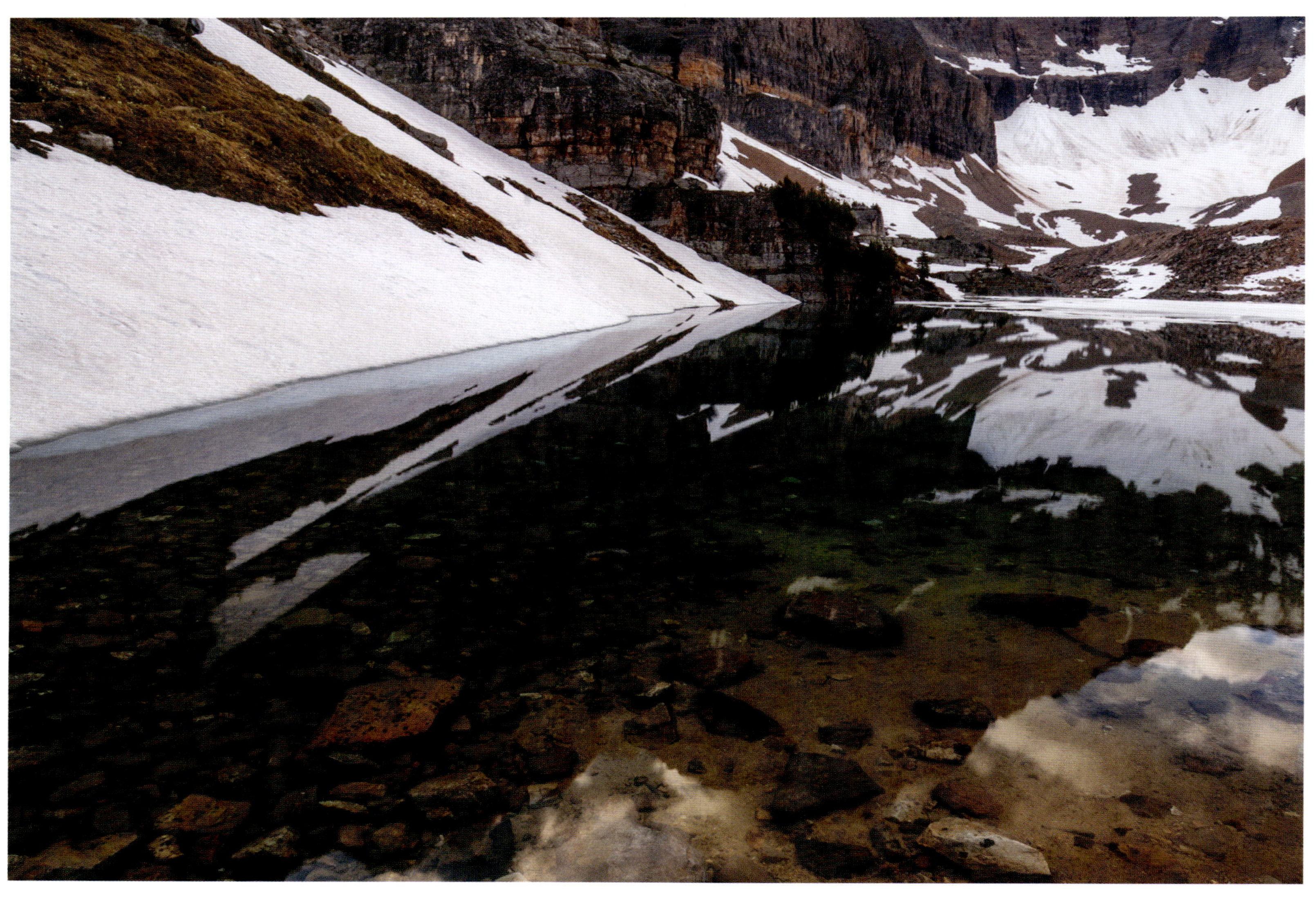

Winter Remnants (2007)
Winter's remnants linger into July on Opabin Lake at 2280 m
above sea level.

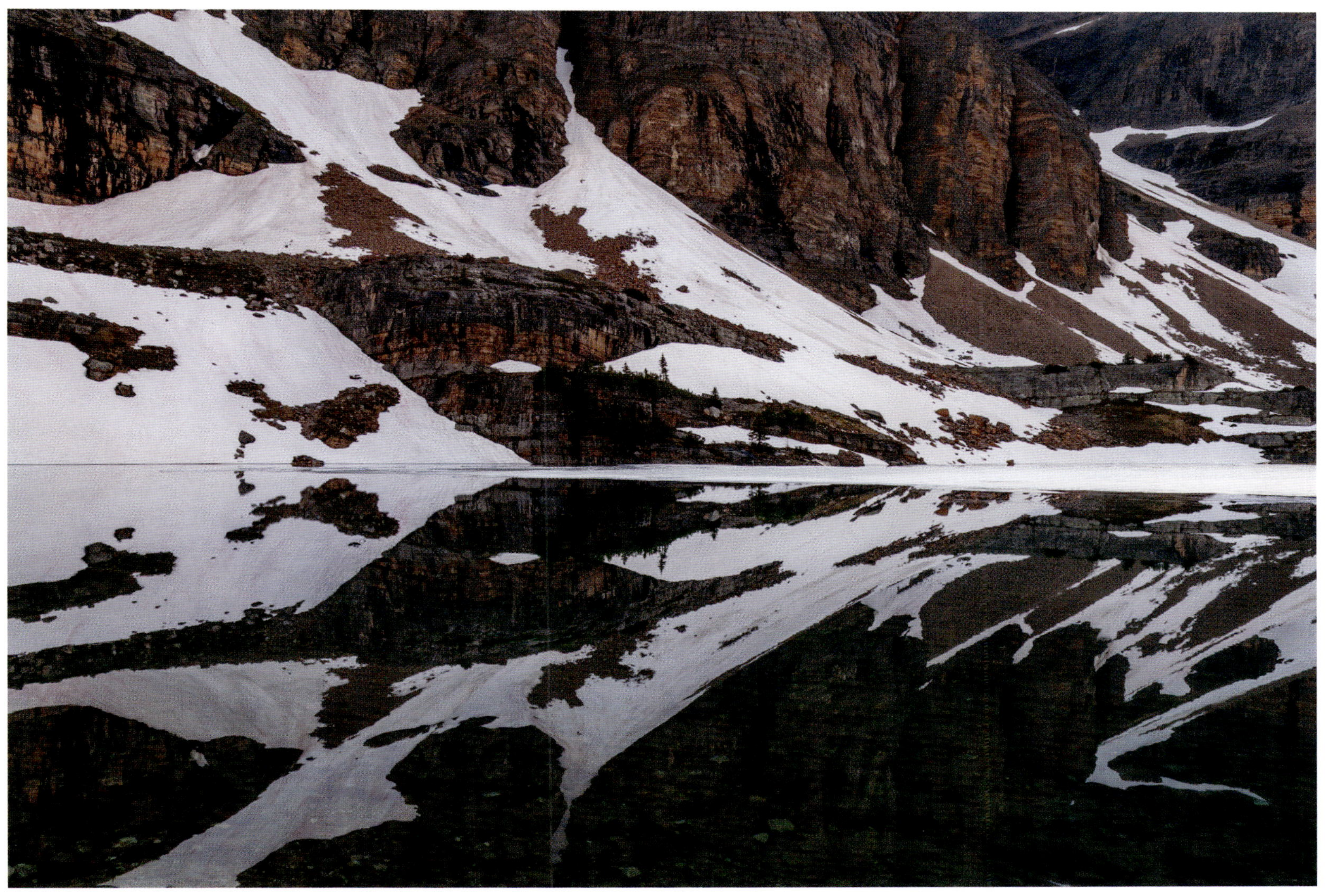

Natural Geometry (2007)
The snow of spring creates a natural geometrical design.

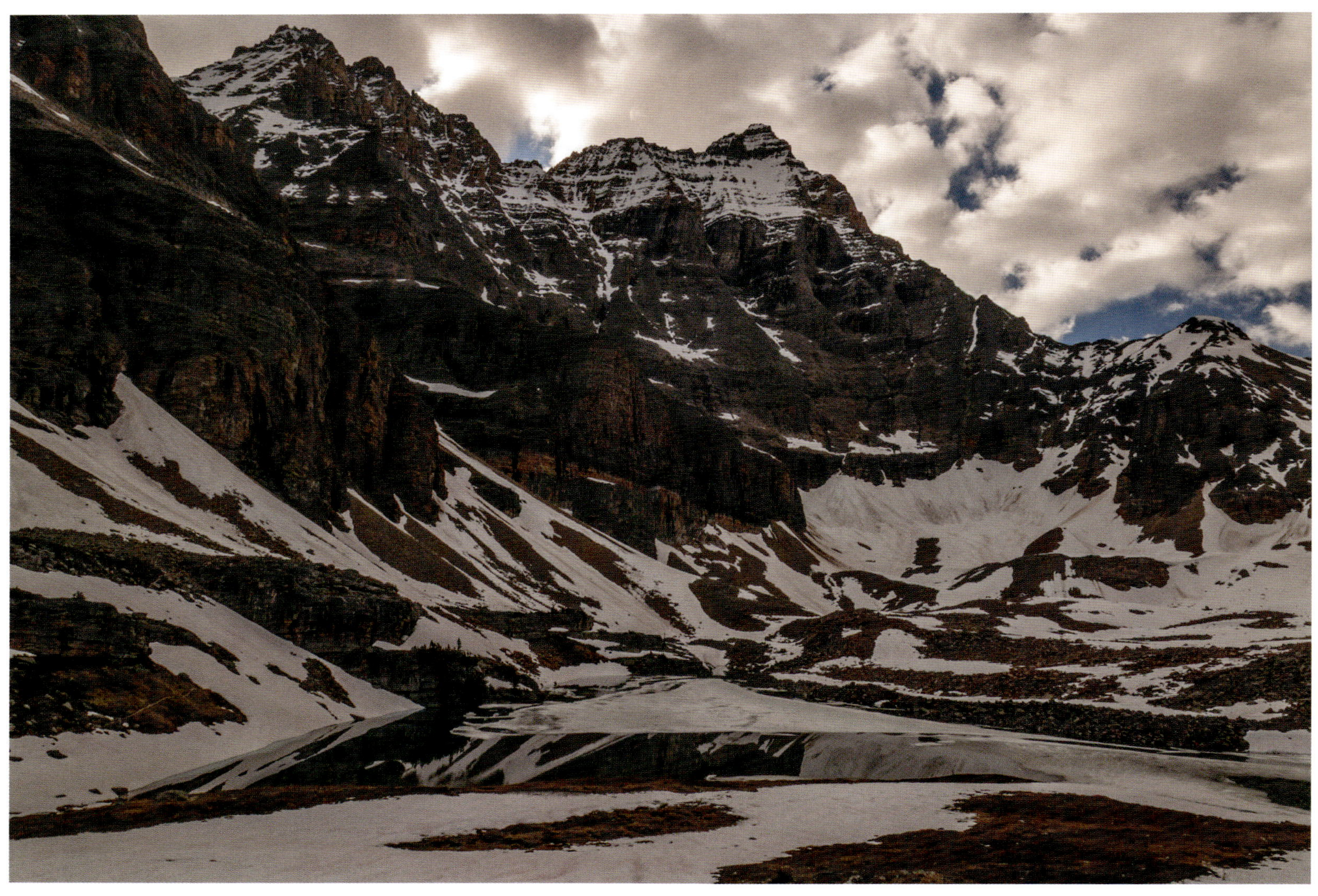

Opabin Revealed (2007)
Spring melt arrives as the emerald waters of Opabin Lake
emerge.

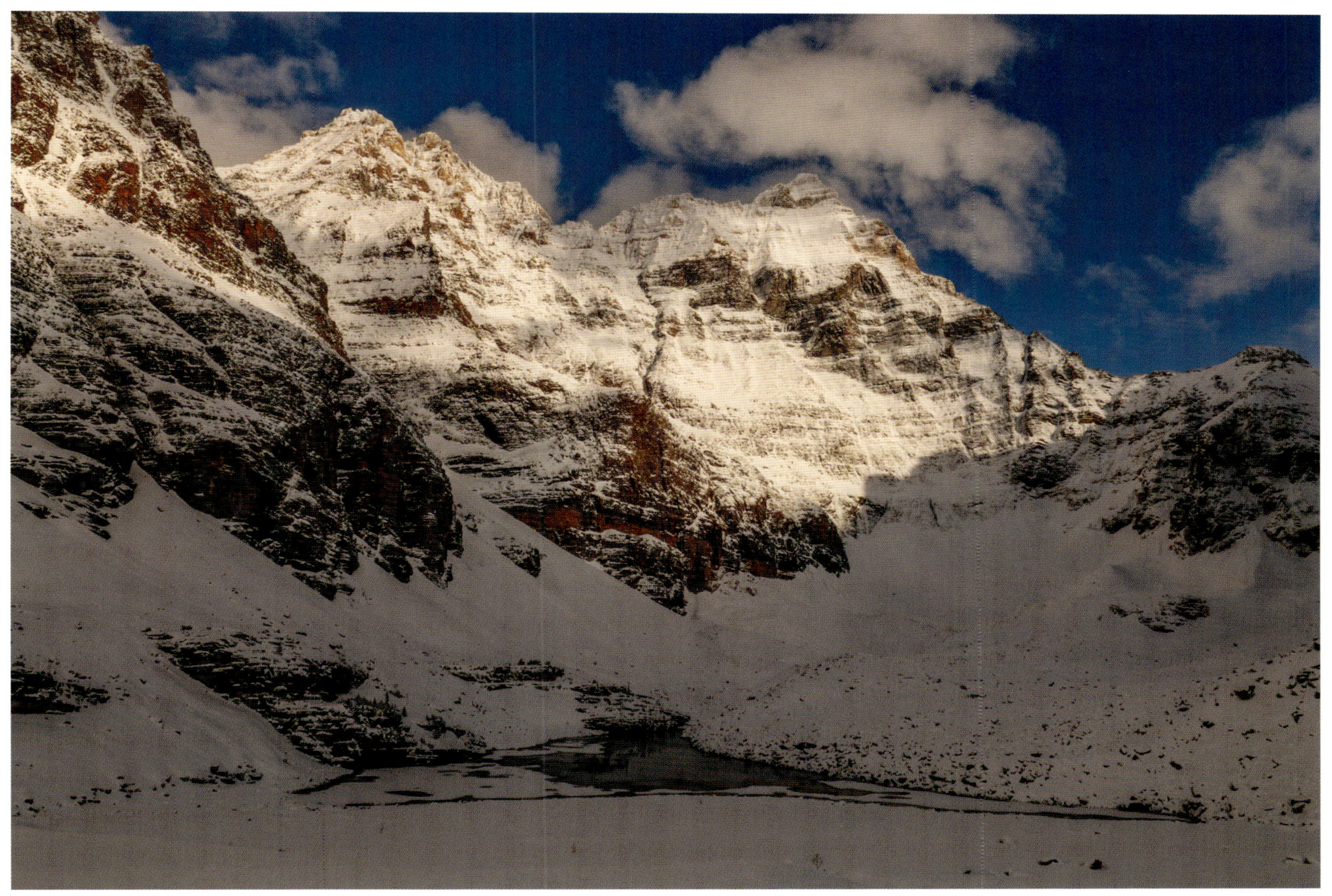

Opabin Retreat (2007)
Opabin Lake's open water appears in early July and then
freezes up again in early October.

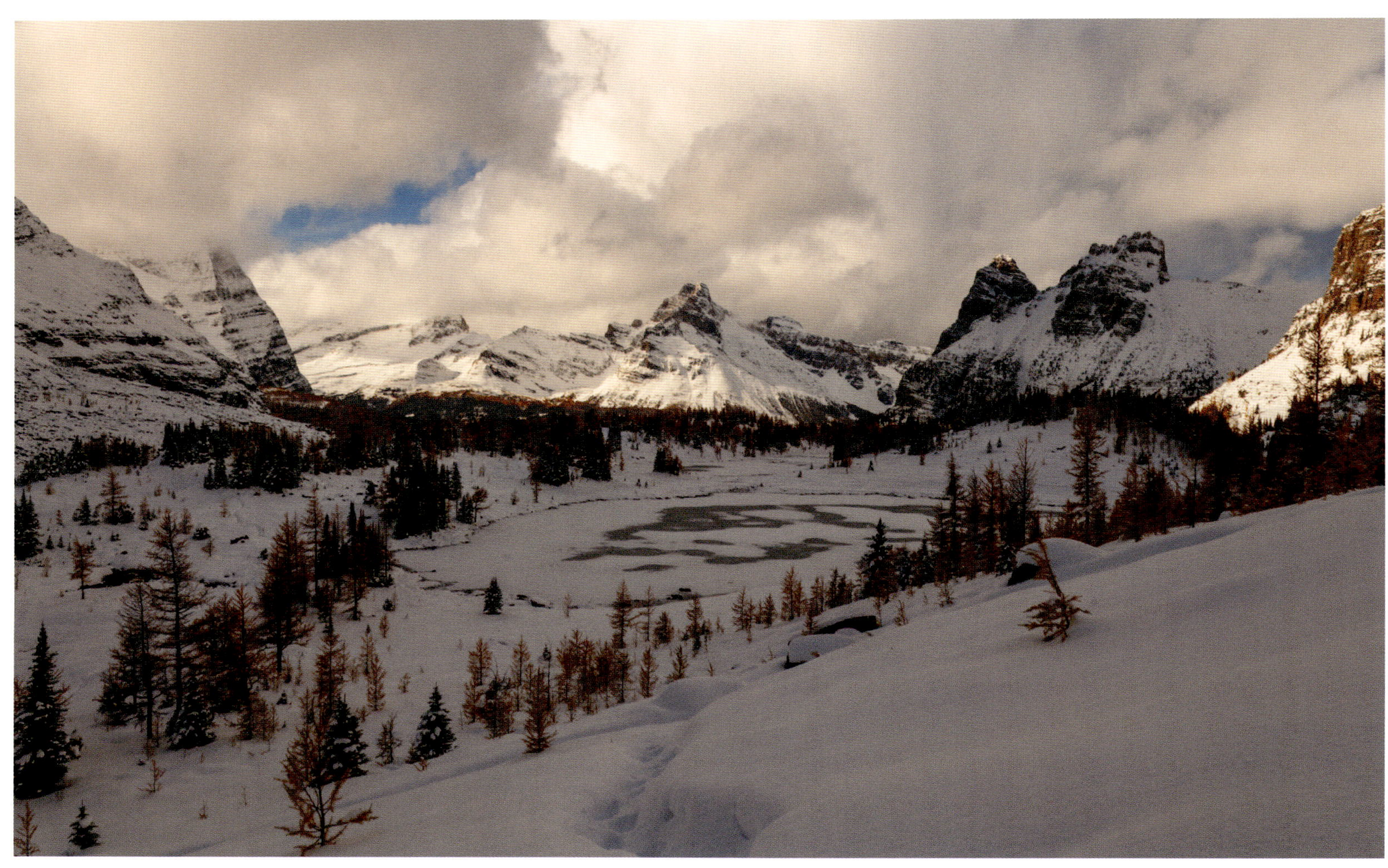

Slipping Away (2007)
The snow started getting deep in places, hiding rock crevices on the way back to the lodge. I used my folded camera tripod to test my footing as the familiar trails disappeared under the cover of snow.

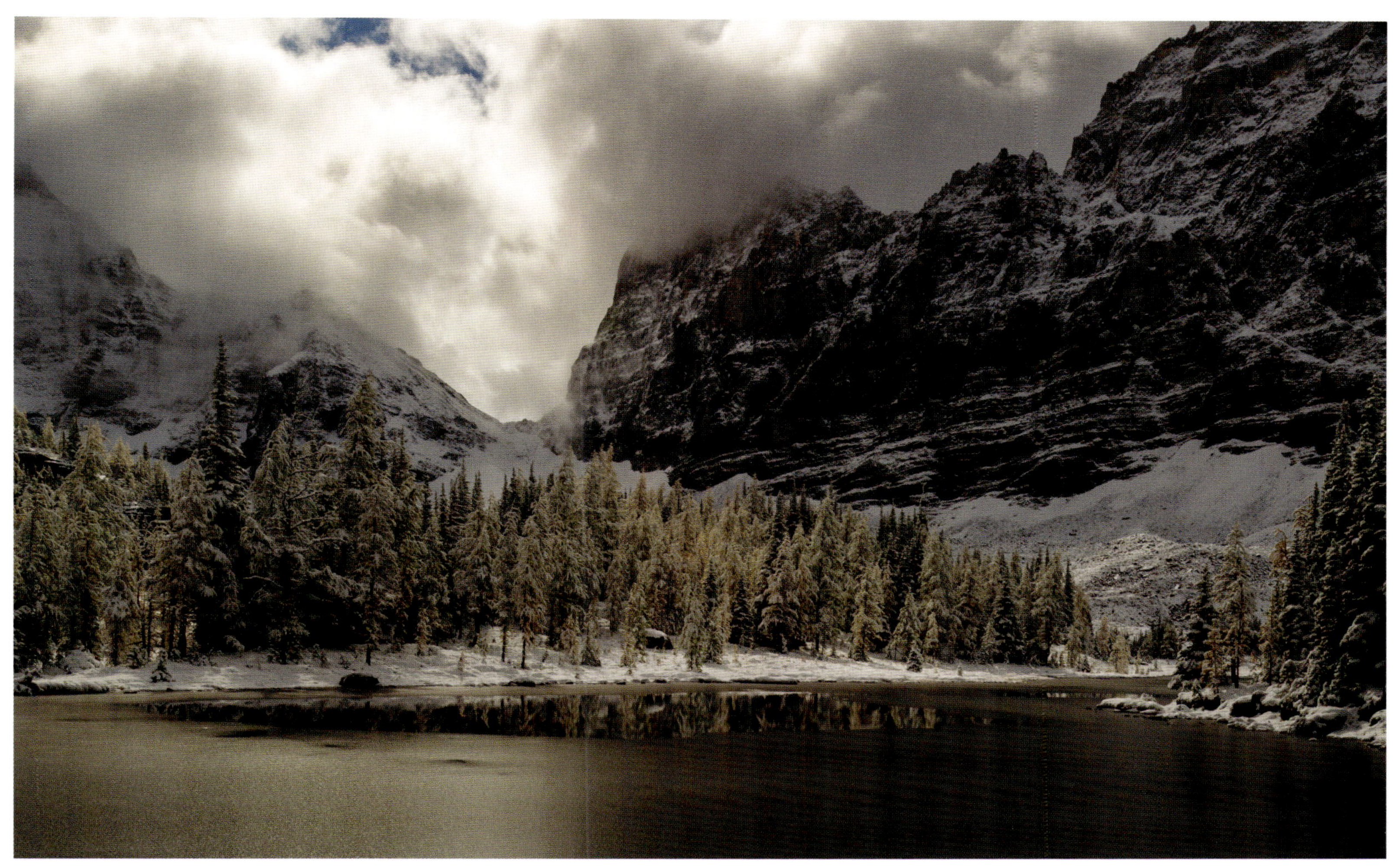

The Last Vestige (2011)
The last traces of open water linger for a few more days as
October approaches on Opabin Plateau.

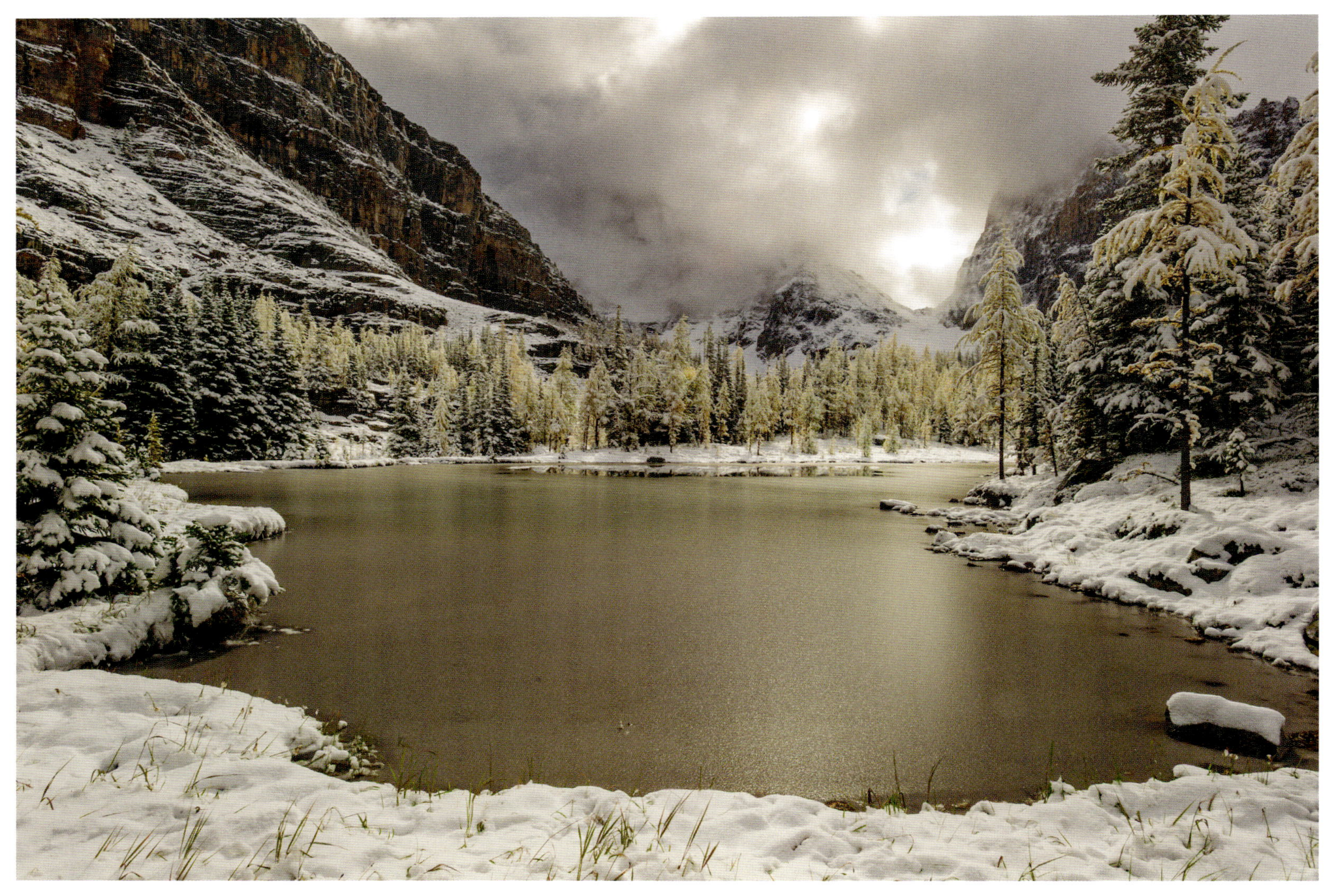

Winter Wonderland (2011)
A winter wonderland of snow, ice, and golden larches along
Moor Lakes on Opabin Plateau.

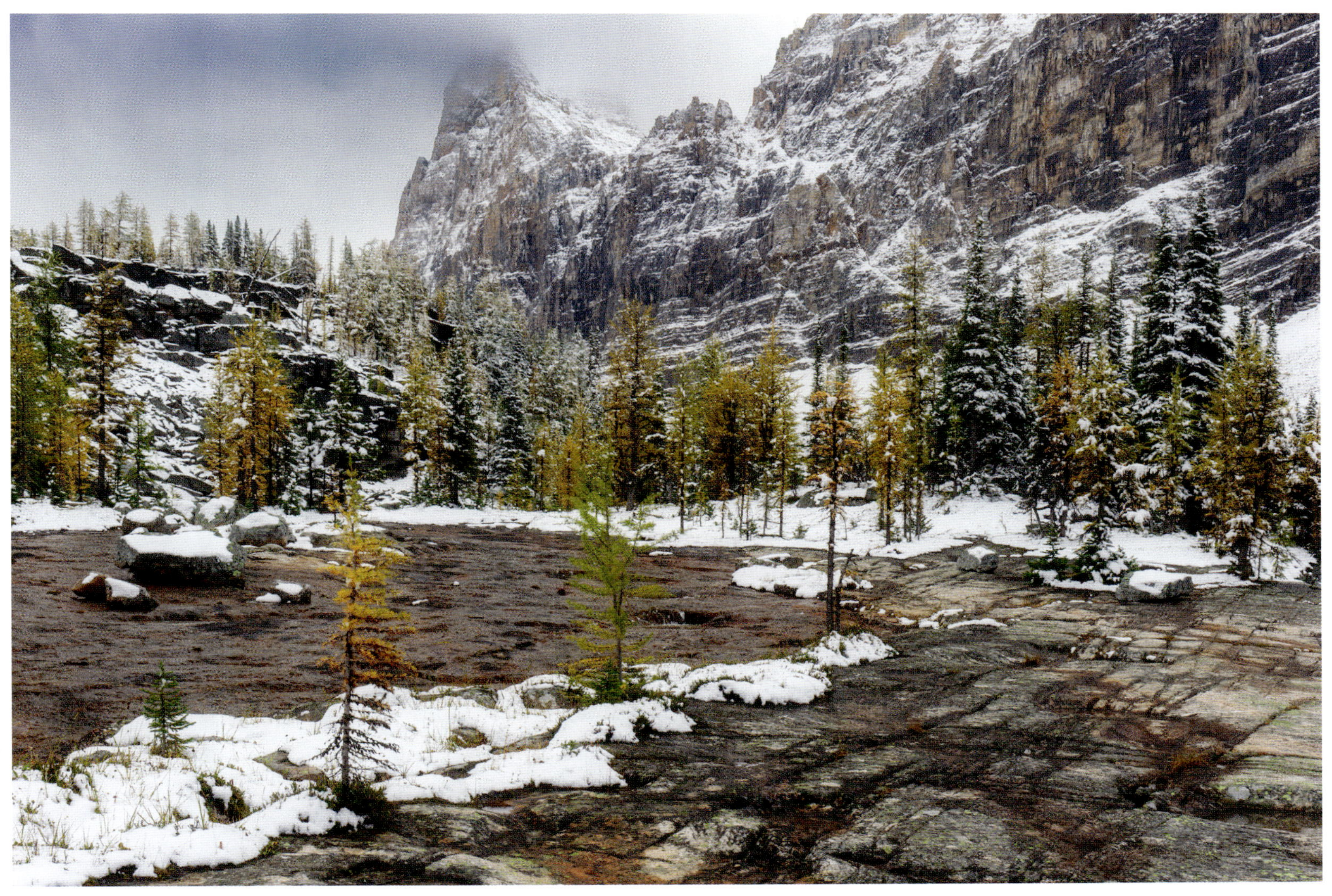

Seasons Converge (2011)
Seasons blend together on Cascade Lakes, with fresh snow on
running water lined with golden larches.

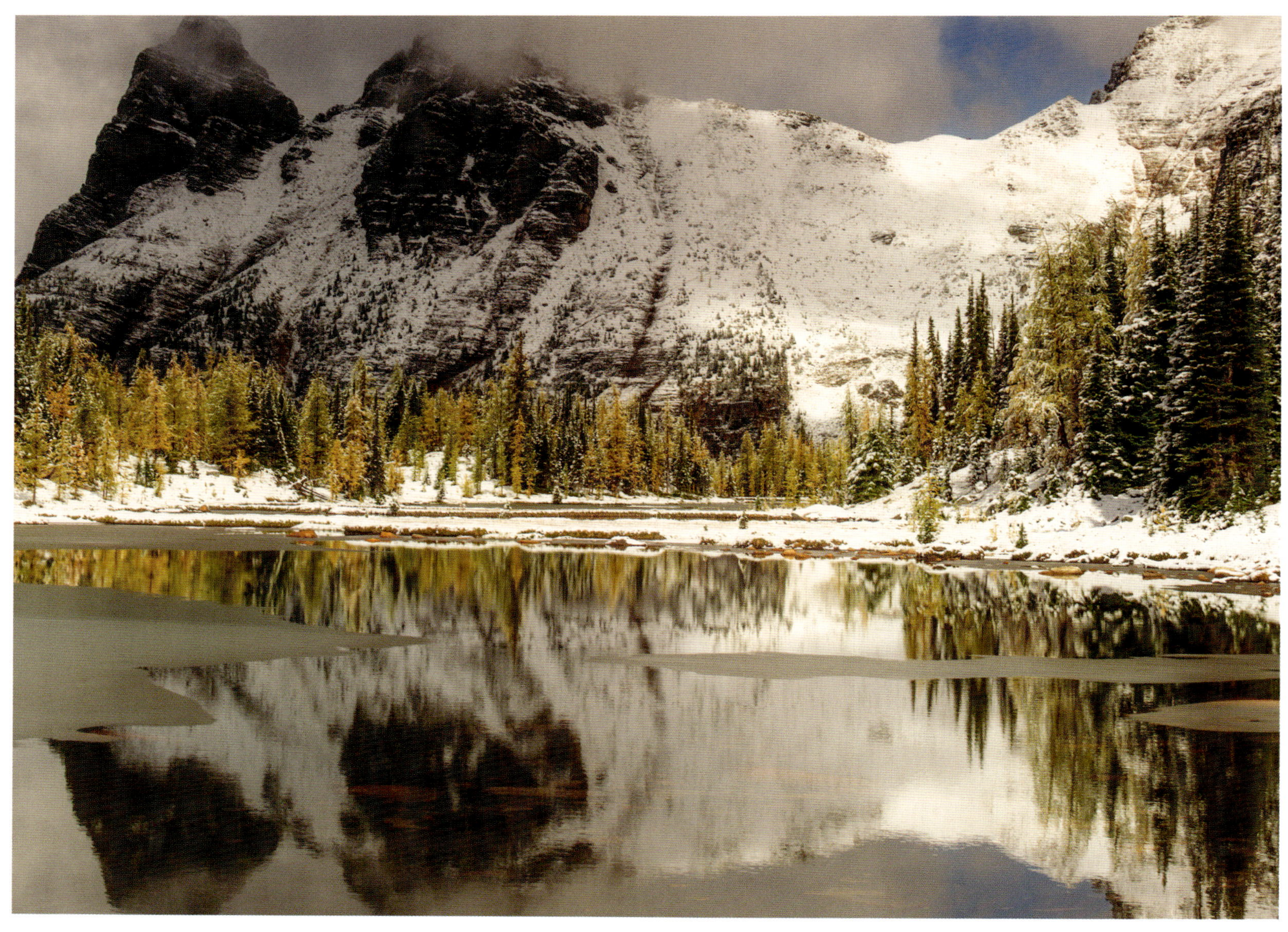

Opabin Autumn Reflections (2011)
Snow-covered Wiwaxy Peaks and Wiwaxy Gap are reflected in
Cascade Lakes.

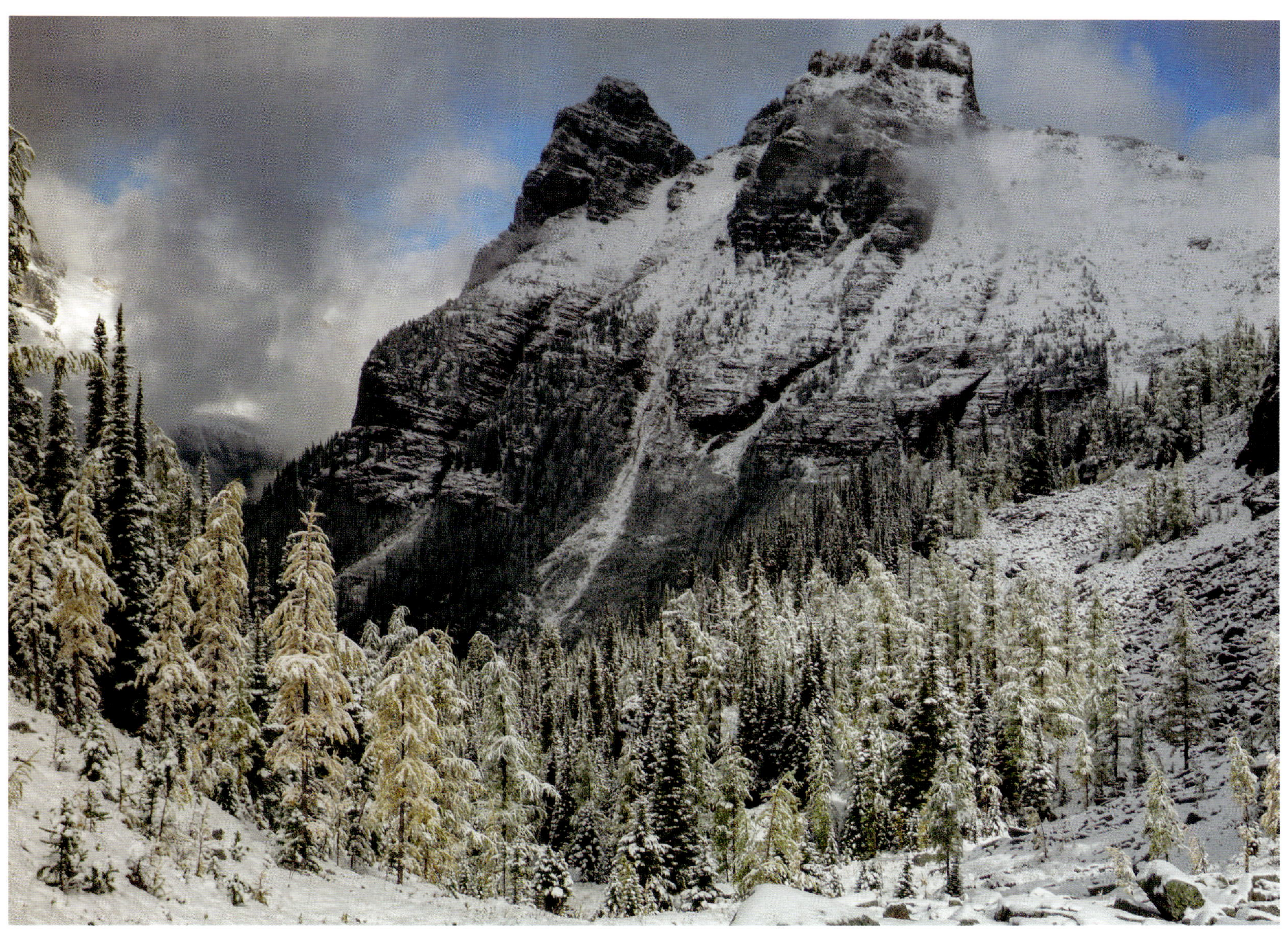

Wiwaxy Towers (2011)
Distant Wiwaxy Peaks rise high above the trail back to the
lodge on a cool autumn day.

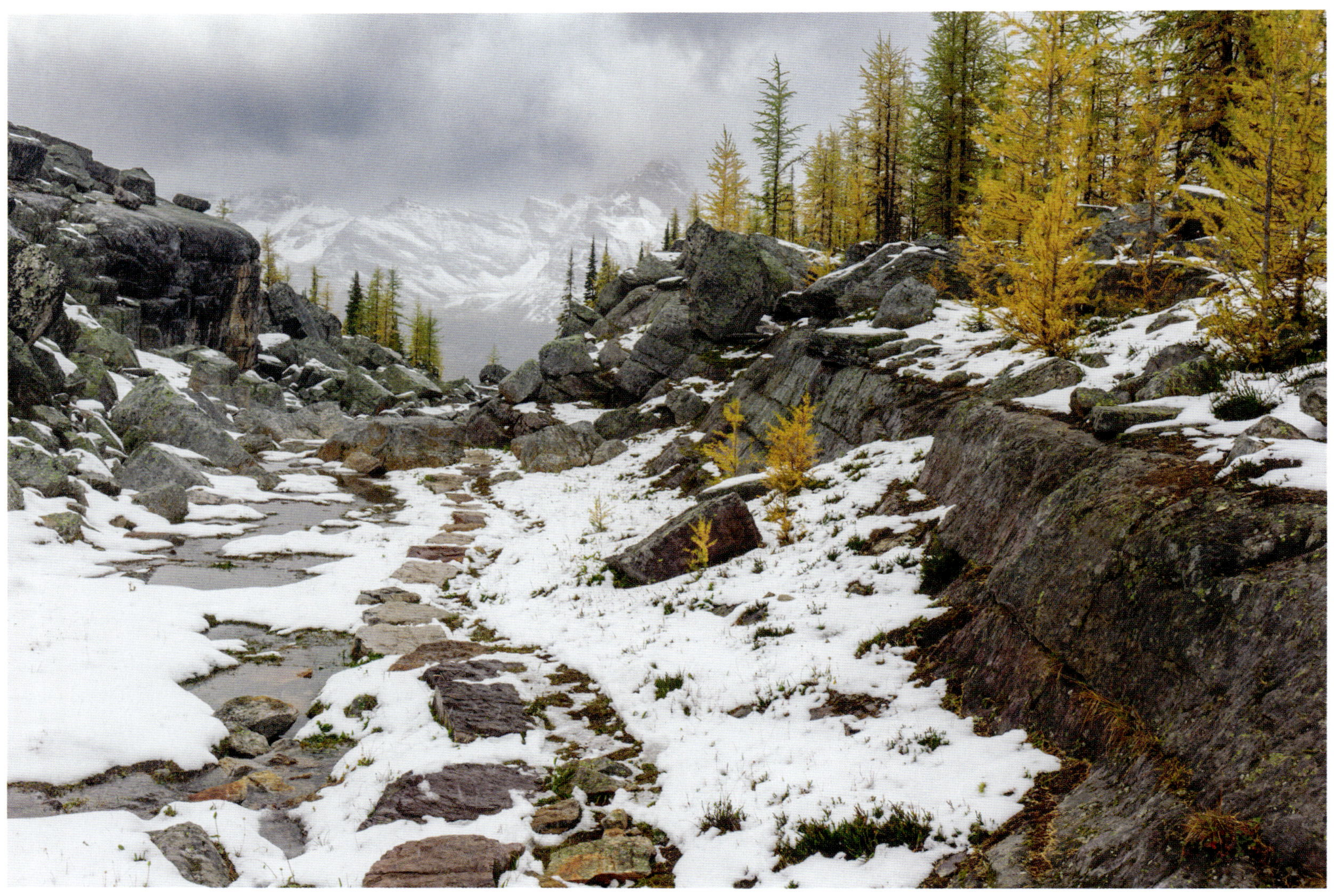

The Way Home (2011)
A stone pathway leads back to Lake O'Hara as an early snow-fall begins to cover up the route.

Grand Vista (2018)
The last grand vista of the summer hiking season as seen from Opabin Prospect.

Overleaf **Full Moon Rising** (2022)
My flight instructor, Bill Bulek, and I took an excursion over the Lake O'Hara region at sunset. The peaks of Mount Biddle and Hungabee Mountain frame the rising full moon.

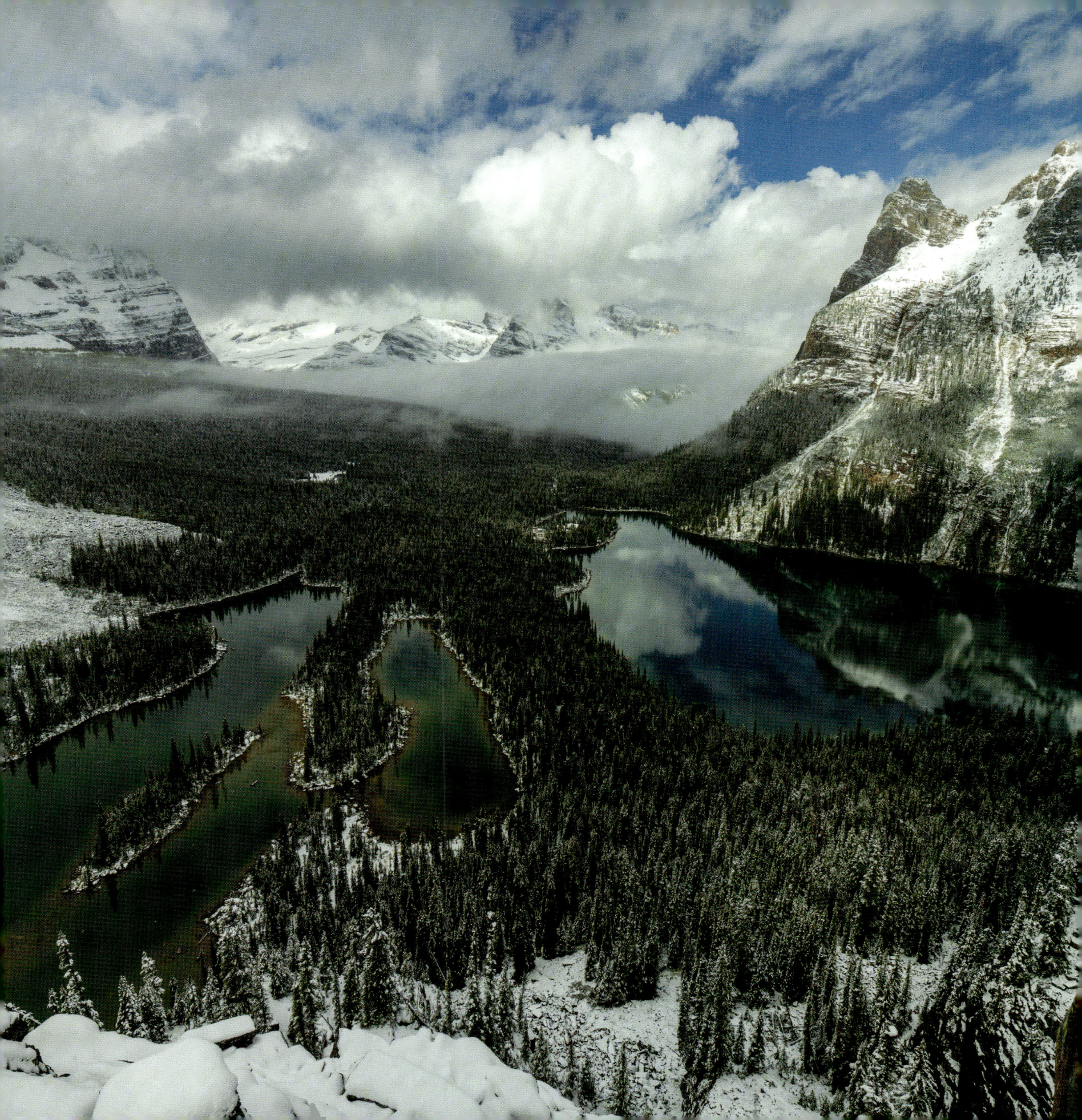

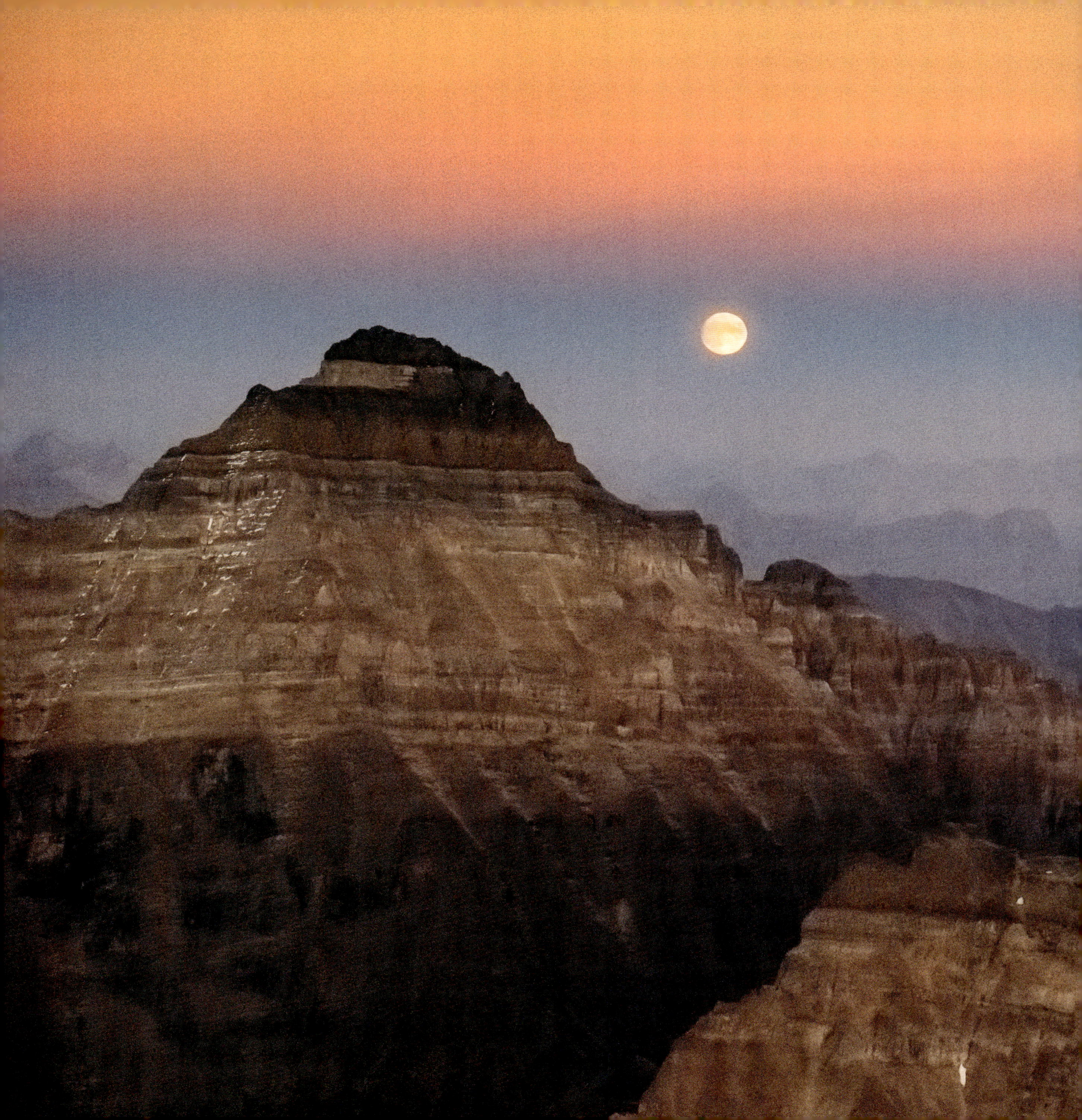

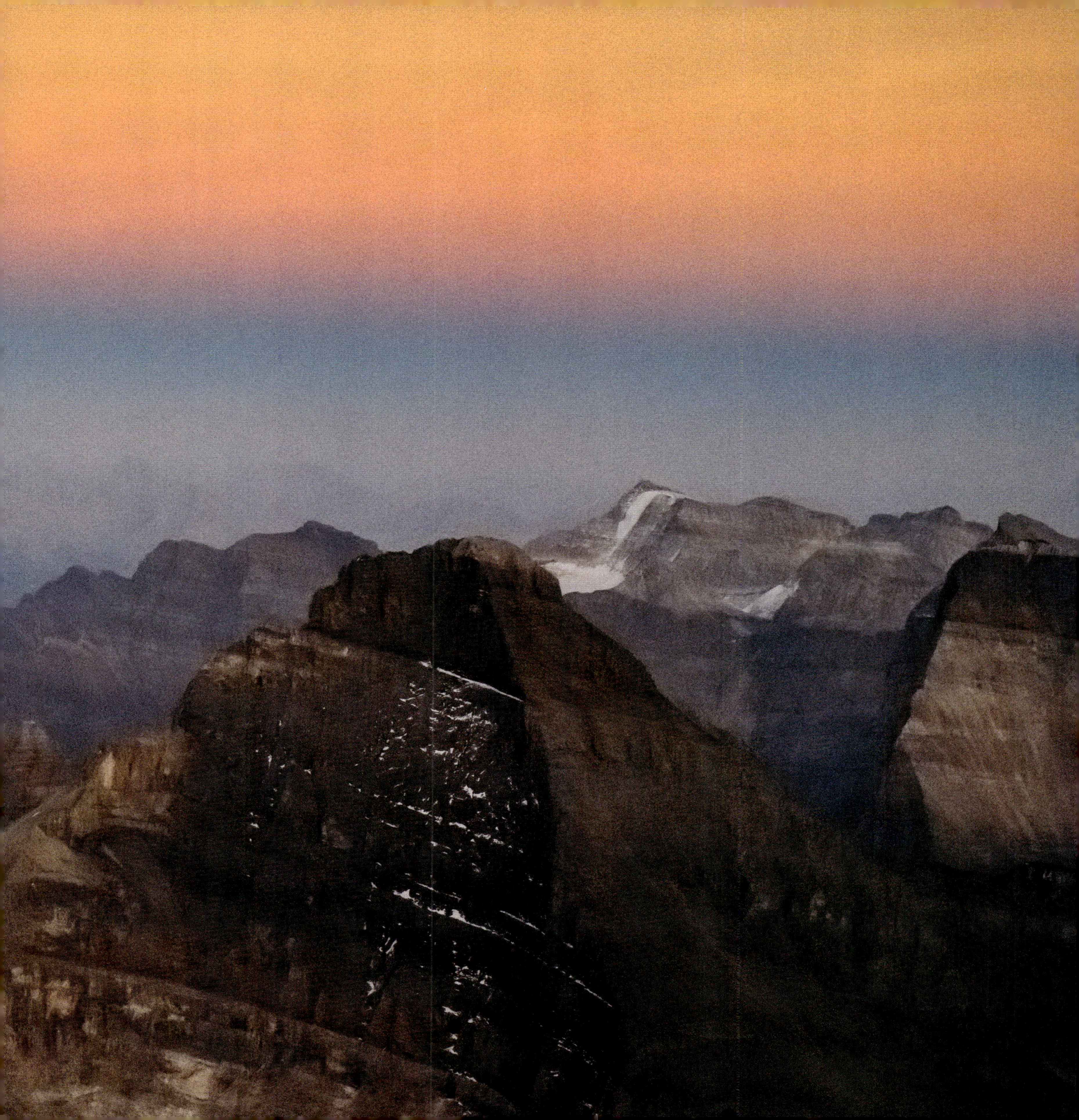

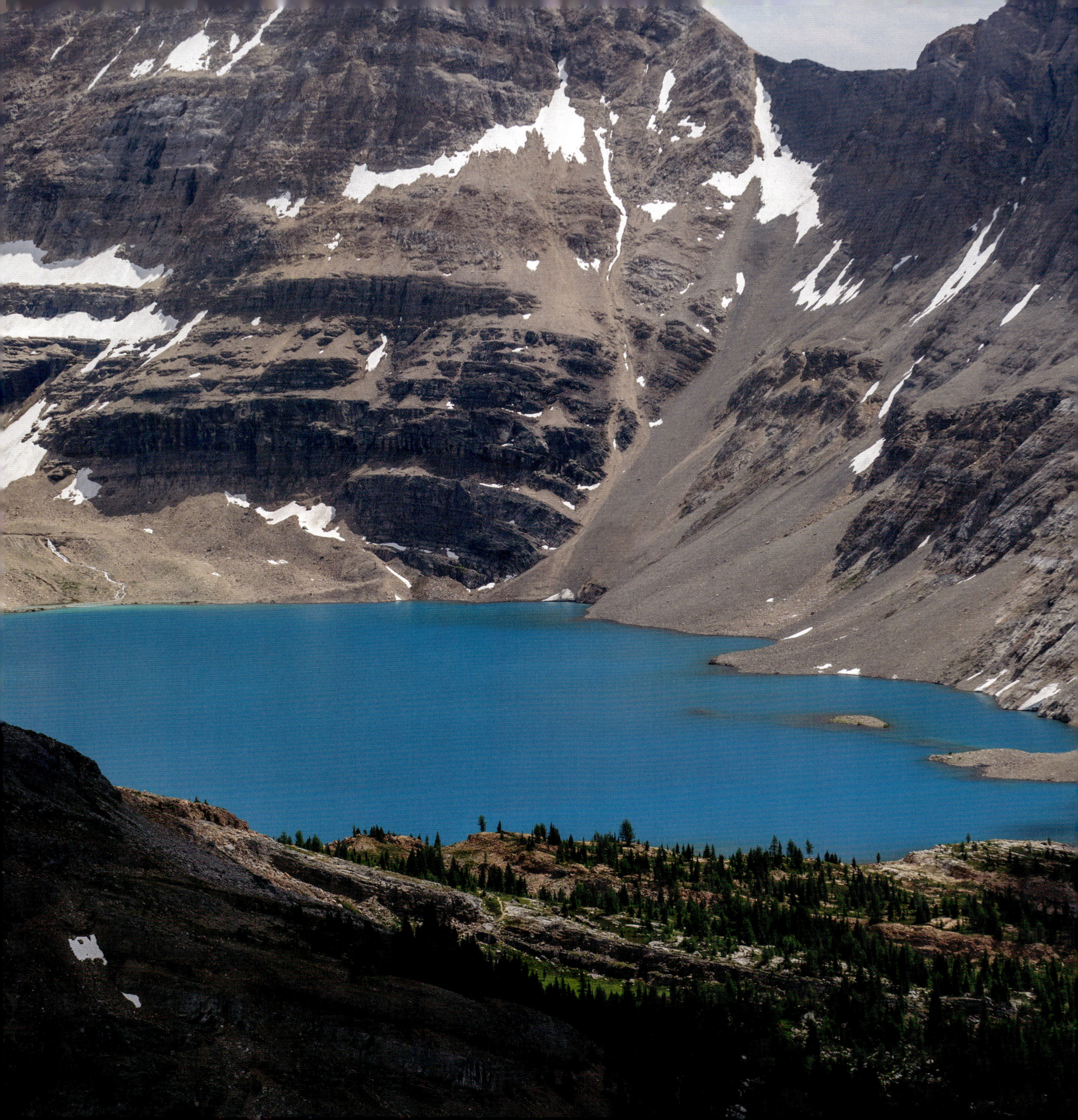

PART FOUR

Lake McArthur

The glacially sourced waters of Lake McArthur, stemming from its cirque-shaped mountainous surrounding, combined with its depth of approximately 30 m, creates a stunning sapphire-coloured lake. It is named after James Joseph McArthur of the Dominion Topographical Survey, who helped map the land route for the CPR line and is said to have been the first European to describe Lake McArthur and Lake O'Hara.

The trail access to Lake McArthur is one of the few destinations in the Lake O'Hara region that don't originate from Lakeshore Trail. Overall, it's a two-hour hike along 3 km of trail, with a 425-m elevation gain from Lake O'Hara to Lake McArthur. There are two routes available and both meet at Schäffer Lake along the way to Lake McArthur.

The first route takes hikers to Schäffer Lake via Alpine Meadow Trail. This route passes two historic structures: the EP Hut and Wiwaxy Lodge. The EP Hut is a Federal Heritage Building constructed in 1919 by the CPR. The CPR donated it to the ACC, which continues to operate it today. The original Lake O'Hara backcountry accommodations, with a central building and surrounding cabins, were located in the alpine meadows. Guests arrived by horse-drawn wagons in the early years, and supplies were carried up by strings of horses called pack trains. Once the CPR

Turquoise Delight (2021)
The contrast between turquoise Lake McArthur and white Biddle Glacier with its rust-coloured rocks creates a visually stunning composition.

constructed the current Lake O'Hara Lodge, the alpine meadows cabins were relocated the next winter to their current site along the lakeshore trail on the peninsula.

Elizabeth Parker was a journalist with a daily column in the *Manitoba Free Press* (later the *Winnipeg Free Press*) for nearly 40 years. After taking a trip to the Canadian Rockies for health reasons, as was often the case with the advertised draw of the natural Banff Hot Springs, she returned to Winnipeg 18 months later with what became a lifelong appreciation and promotion of this mountain region. In 1906, she co-founded the ACC, and served as the club's first secretary until 1910, helping to establish and contribute to the *Canadian Alpine Journal* through which her articles celebrated her affection for the mountains. Parker saw the club as an association to promote appreciation, protection, and conservation of Canadian mountain landscapes, including artistic representation and scientific study of the region. In recognition of her contribution to Canadian mountaineering, the EP Hut is named in her honour.

The second route to Lake McArthur leads to Schäffer Lake via Big Larches Trail, aptly named after the large Lyall's larch trees among which the trail passes. These are some of North America's highest-elevation living trees, thriving at 2000 to 2500 m above sea level. They grow very slowly to survive the harsh conditions of alpine winters and strong winds. A tree only a few metres tall may be older than 500 years. Their thick bark helps them survive forest fires, and their seeds are designed for best germination in post-fire soil conditions. As a result of their slow growth, larches contain centuries of climate records in their tree rings.

Both the first and second routes converge at Schäffer Lake, which is at the base of Mount Schäffer (2691 m). This picturesque meadow lake and its nearby mountain are named in honour of Mary Schäffer Warren and Charles Schäffer. Mary was a prominent early explorer, botanist, and photographer of the Canadian Rockies. She is best known for being the first non-Indigenous woman to explore Maligne Lake in what later became Jasper National Park. Thanks to her persistence, this lake is included in the park for the purpose of preservation and conservation. As a skilled botanical artist with a spirit for more rigorous forms of backcountry travel on horseback and in camps, Schäffer explored much of what is now Banff and Jasper national parks, in addition to the Lake O'Hara region. *Wildflowers*, a documentary by Trixie Pacis and Meghan J. Ward, provides wonderful insights into Mary's life.

As Schäffer Lake is a freshwater source amid McArthur Pass, it's not uncommon for wildlife to frequent the area around it. On my hike there in August 2024, I had the pleasure of watching a purposeful and unflappable porcupine gingerly pick its way across the river stones of the lake outlet.

The hike to Lake McArthur takes approximately one hour from Schäffer Lake and passes wide open valley vistas while traversing ancient sea floor geology underfoot. The pinkish beige carbonate rocks along the trail to Lake McArthur extend back in time 500 million years to a period when this was the western margin of North America.

The trails end along the lakeshore of brilliantly coloured Lake McArthur, which glimmers in an almost surreal hue under an afternoon sun. A perfect place to rest on the warm, ancient rocks and watch the cloud shadows scroll across the 1.5-km-long, cirque-shaped lake.

Alpine Meadow Huts (2021)
Built in 1919 by the Alpine Club of Canada, these are some of Canada's first backcountry huts. Today, they are well maintained, with the Elizabeth Parker Hut providing bunk beds, a wood stove, and a communal kitchen.

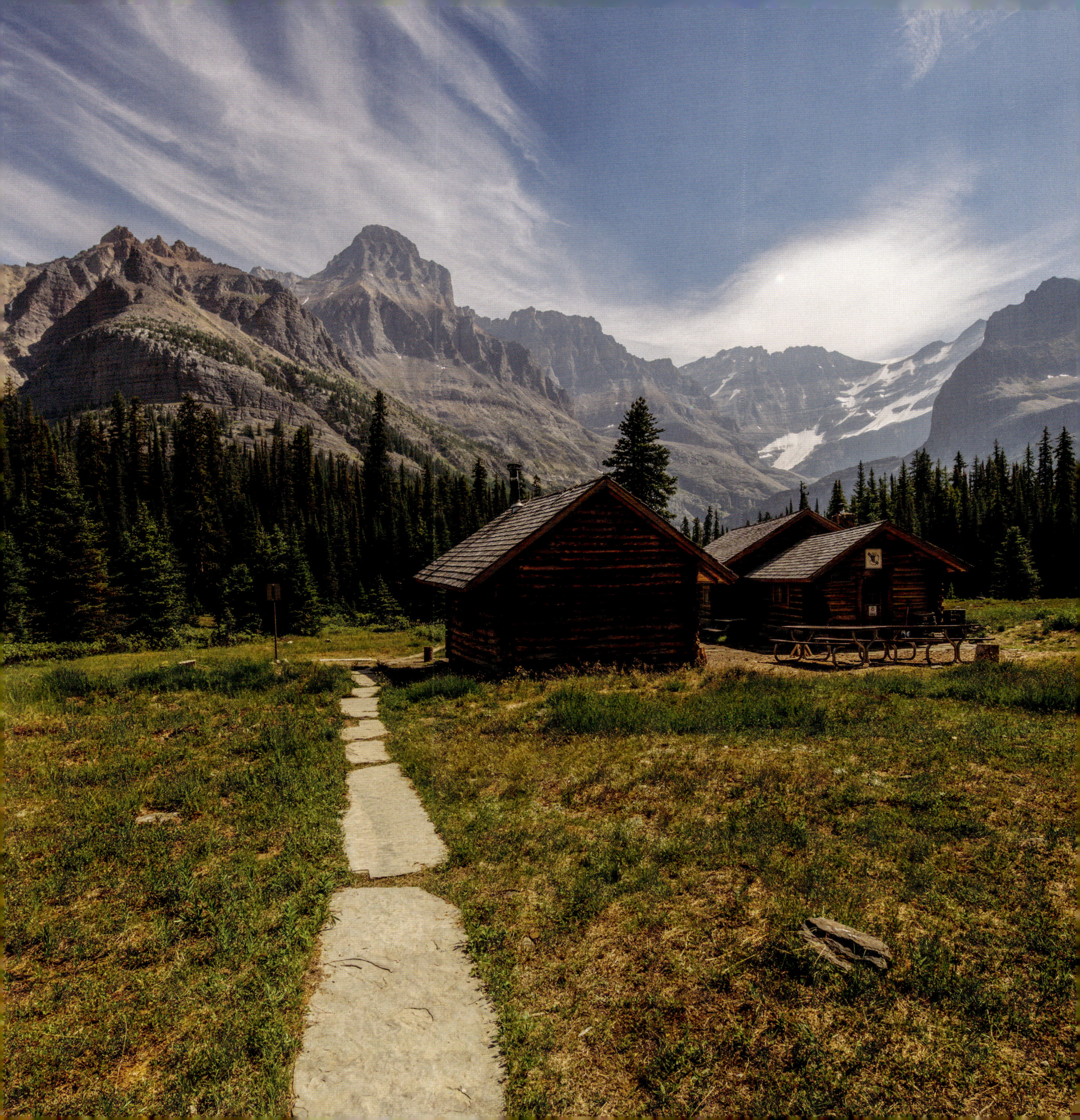

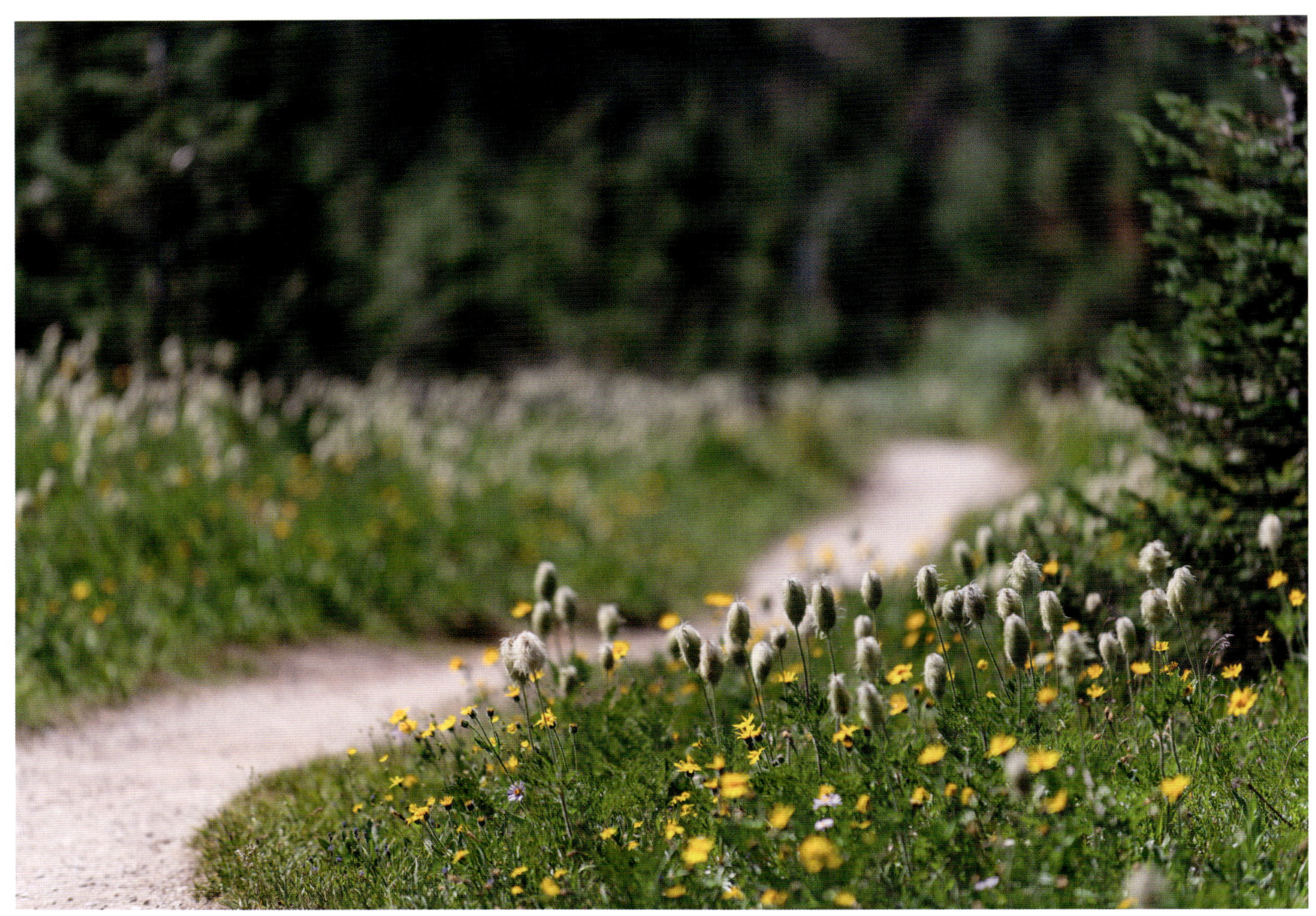

Storied Trail (2021)
There are two route options to Lake McArthur: Big Larches
Trail or the one in this photograph, Alpine Meadow Trail. It's
a storied route trod by legendary O'Hara spirits such as trail
builder Lawrence Grassi and pioneering guide Conrad Kain.

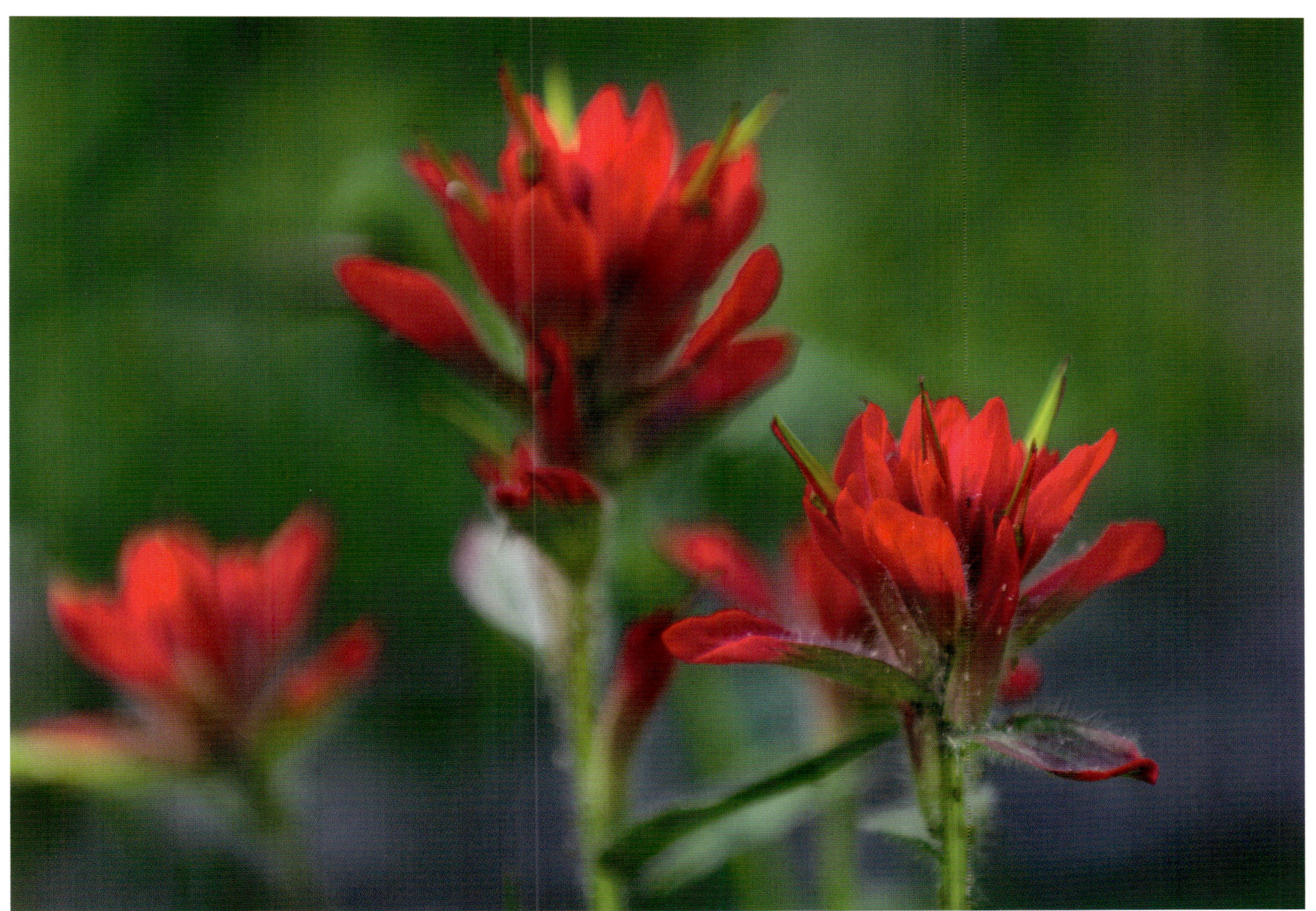

Divine Brush (2021)
Castilleja miniata, often referred to as giant Indian paintbrush, grows on slopes and in meadows and subalpine zones up to 3000 m above sea level. Folklore legend has it that the brilliant colours of its flowers come from the dipped paintbrushes left by the gods.

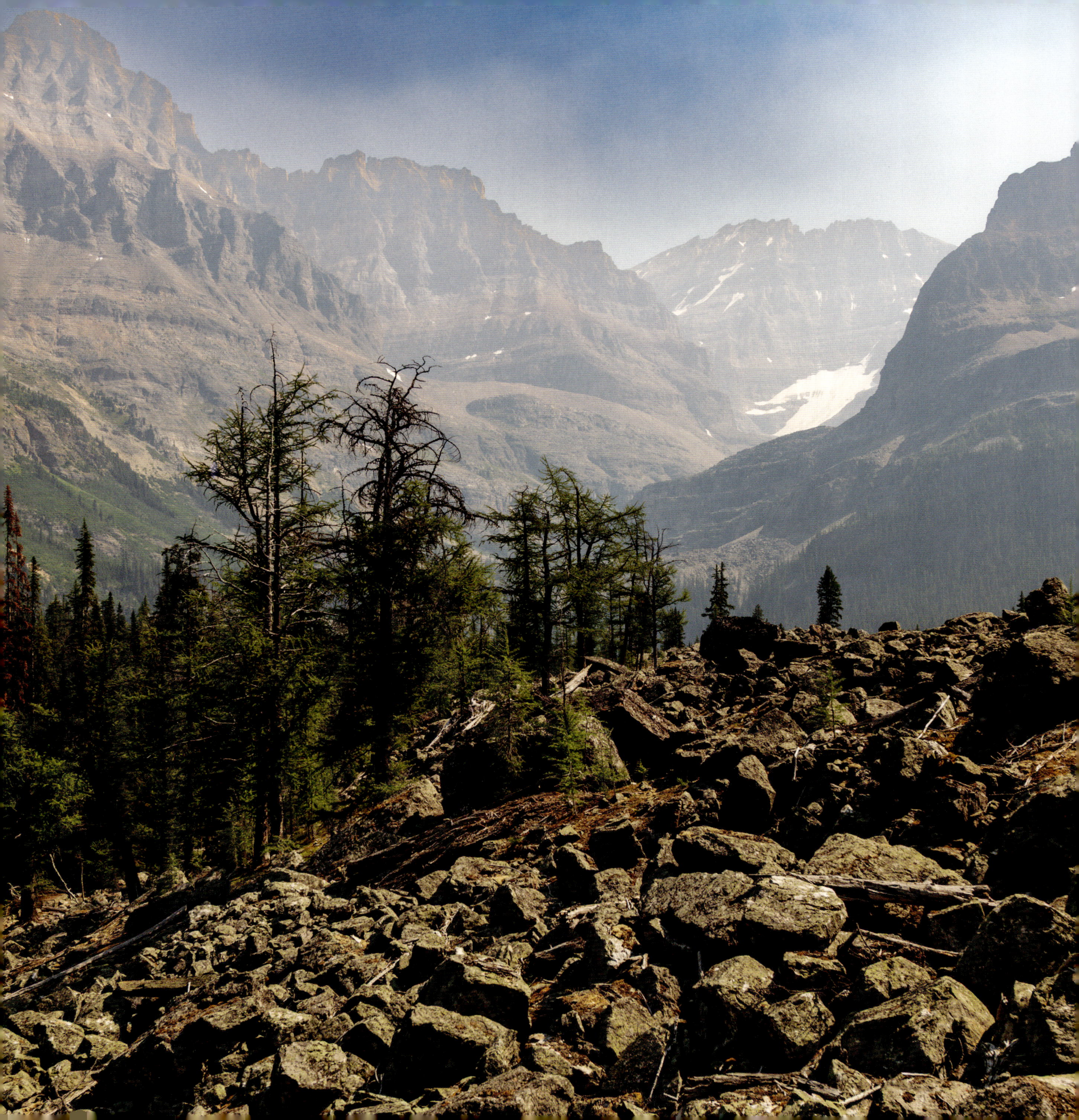

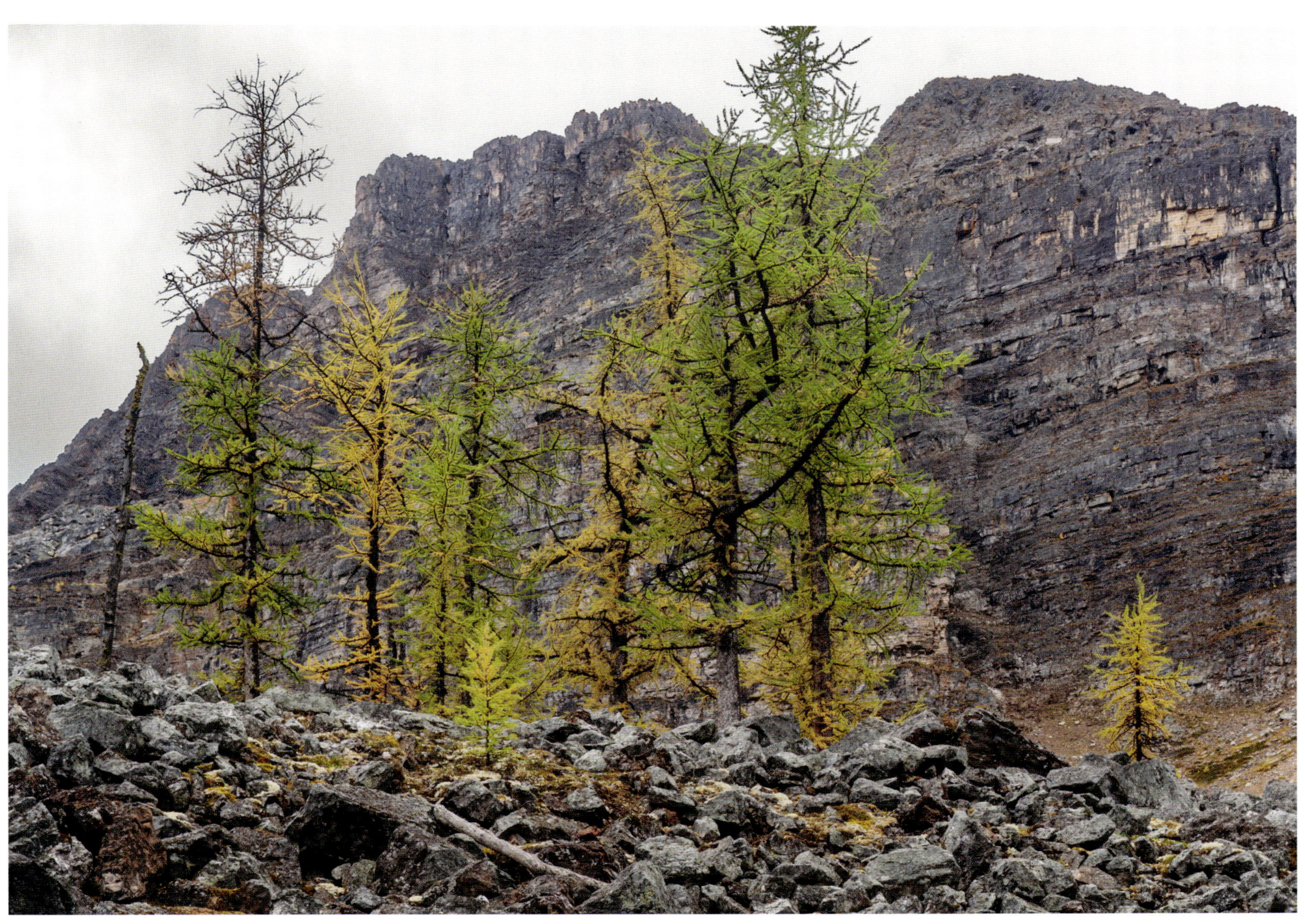

Mount Schäffer Rockfall (2021)
Big Larches Trail to Lake McArthur crosses a large rockfall from Mount Schäffer before levelling off and entering the forest.

Stature of Time (2008)
Big Larches Trail is aptly named after the large alpine larches along its path. One of the highest-elevation trees in North America, the larch survives the short growing season, strong winds, and harsh winters by growing slowly. Some of the larches in the Yoho region are the oldest in Canada, with trees over 1,000 years old.

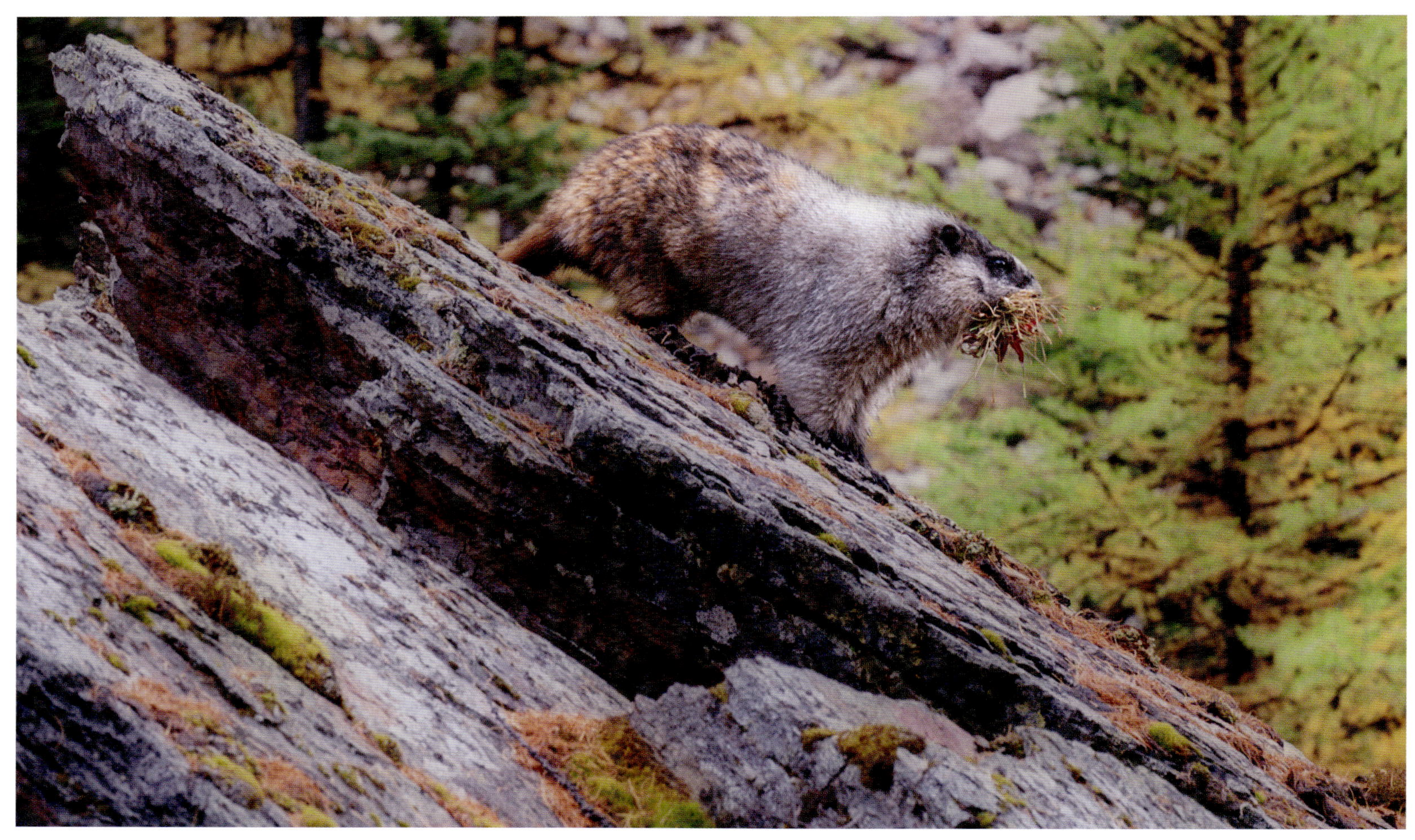

Winter Preparation (2008)
Marmots are highly social, living in colonies with complex bur-row systems. They often rest on rocks on sunny days to absorb the heat. This marmot appears to be preparing its burrow for the approaching 7–8 months of hibernation.

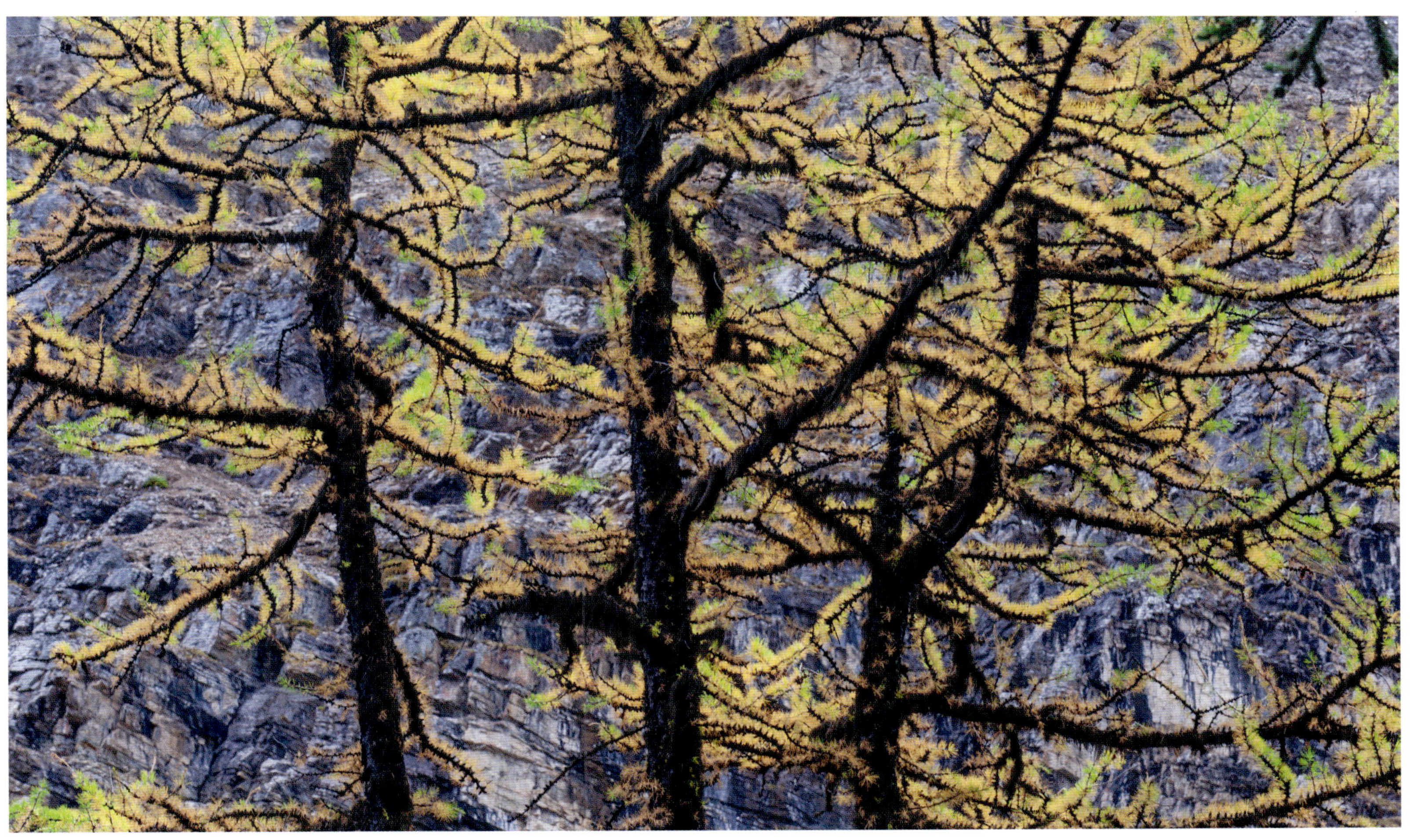

Beautiful History (2008)
The slow growth of larch trees makes their rings ideal for studying climate resilience, as the rings reveal centuries of environmental change.

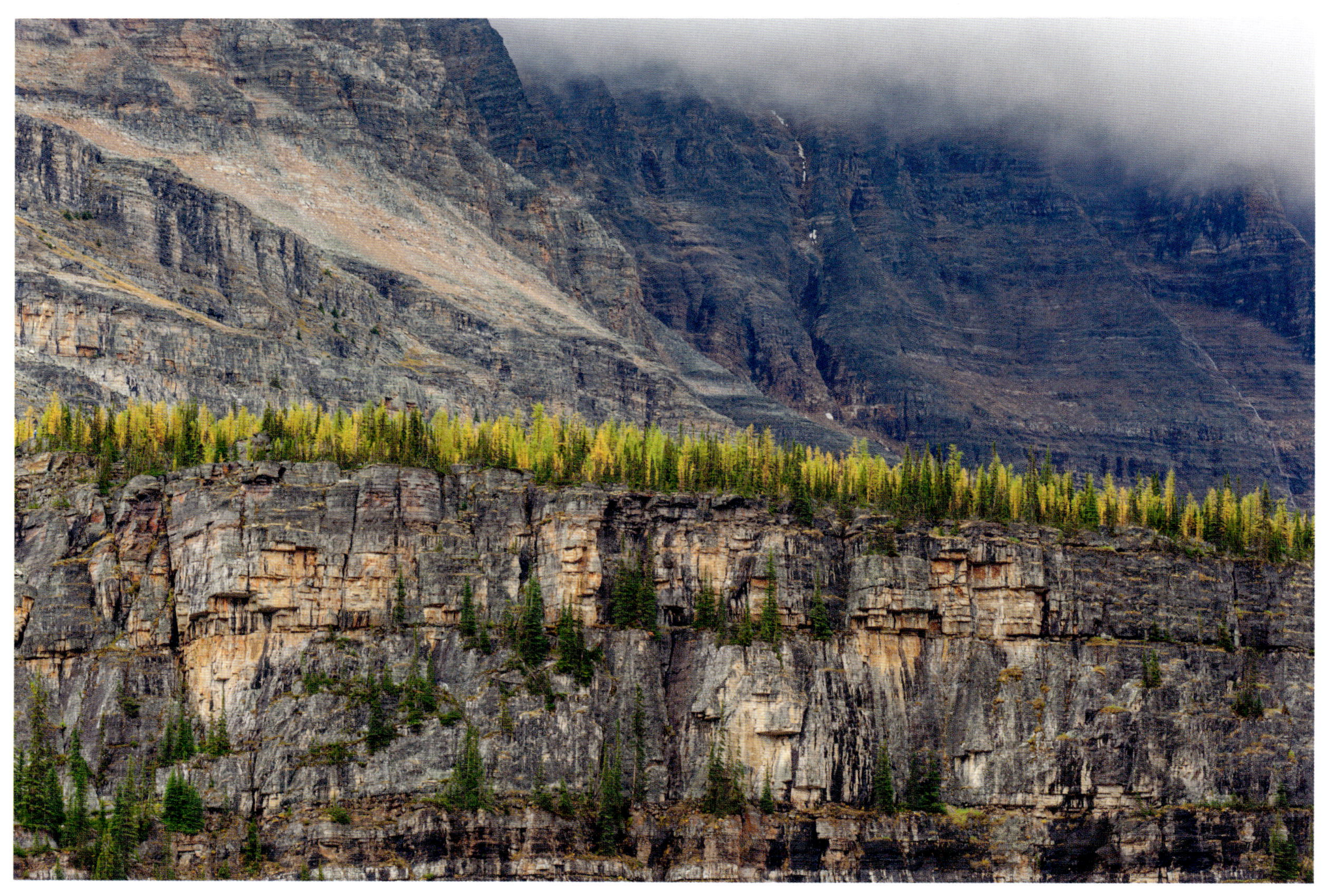

Opabin Highlight (2008)
Looking back from Big Larches Trail at the Opabin Prospect
ledge, highlighted by the autumn gold of larch needles trans-
formed into their brilliant colour before being shed for winter.

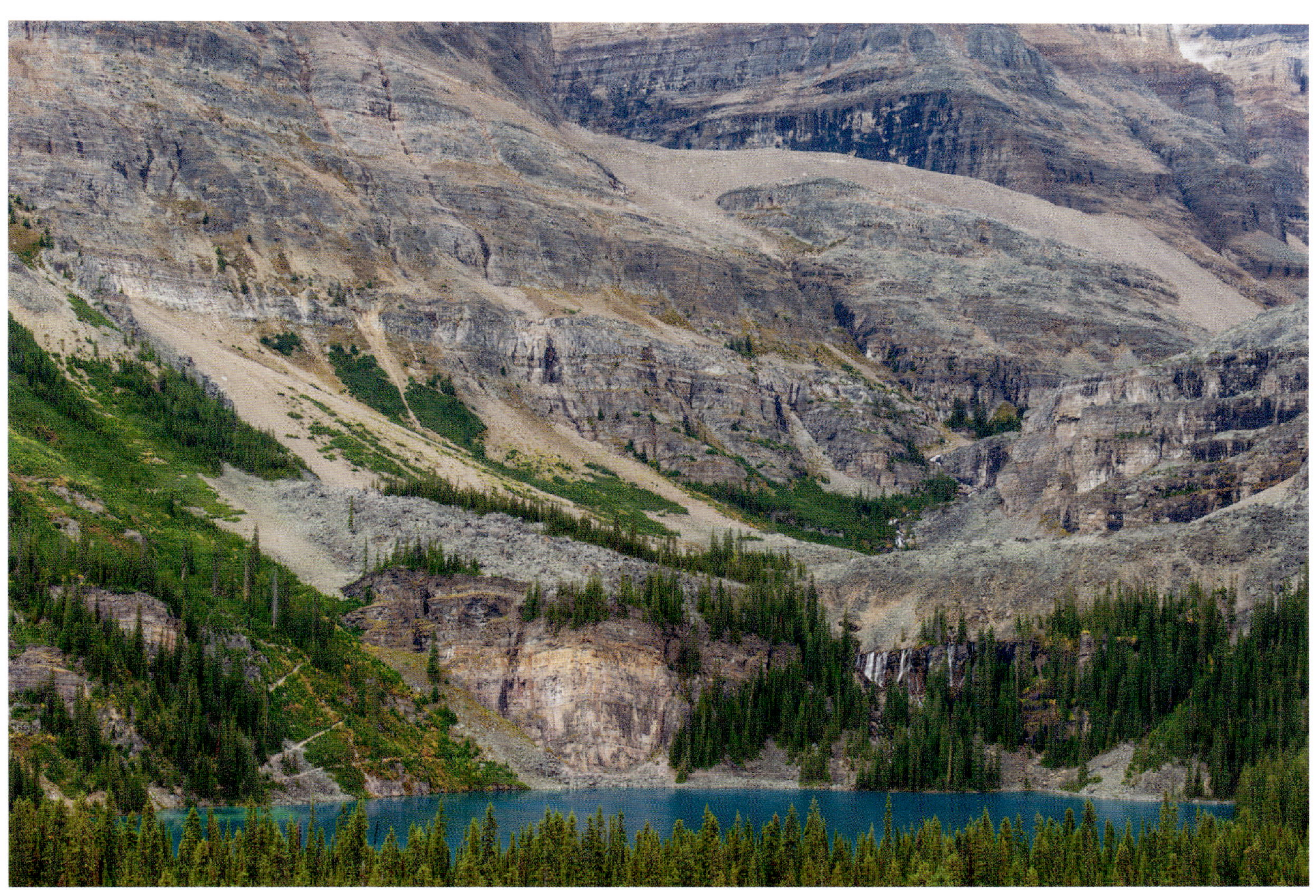

Rock Walls (2008)
Big Larches Trail provides a vantage point to see Lake O'Hara
in the full context of its towering rock walls carved by glaciers
during the last ice age.

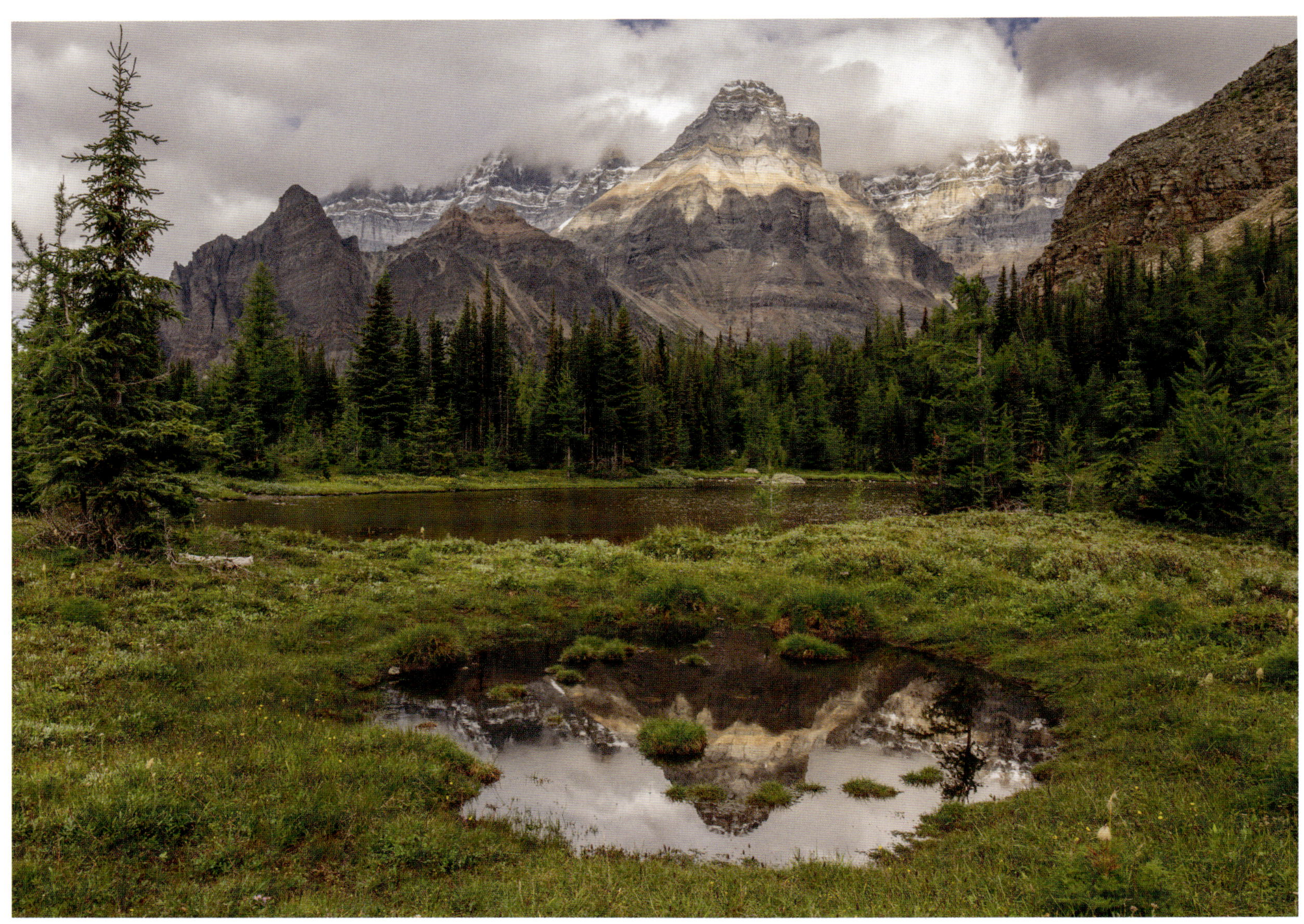

Schäffer Lake (2024)

The rugged peak of Mount Huber is reflected in a small pond in front of Schäffer Lake. The lake honours Mary Schäffer Warren, whose 1911 book *Old Indian Trails of the Canadian Rockies* is still a classic. It is said she learned about this lake's location from her Stoney Nakoda guides.

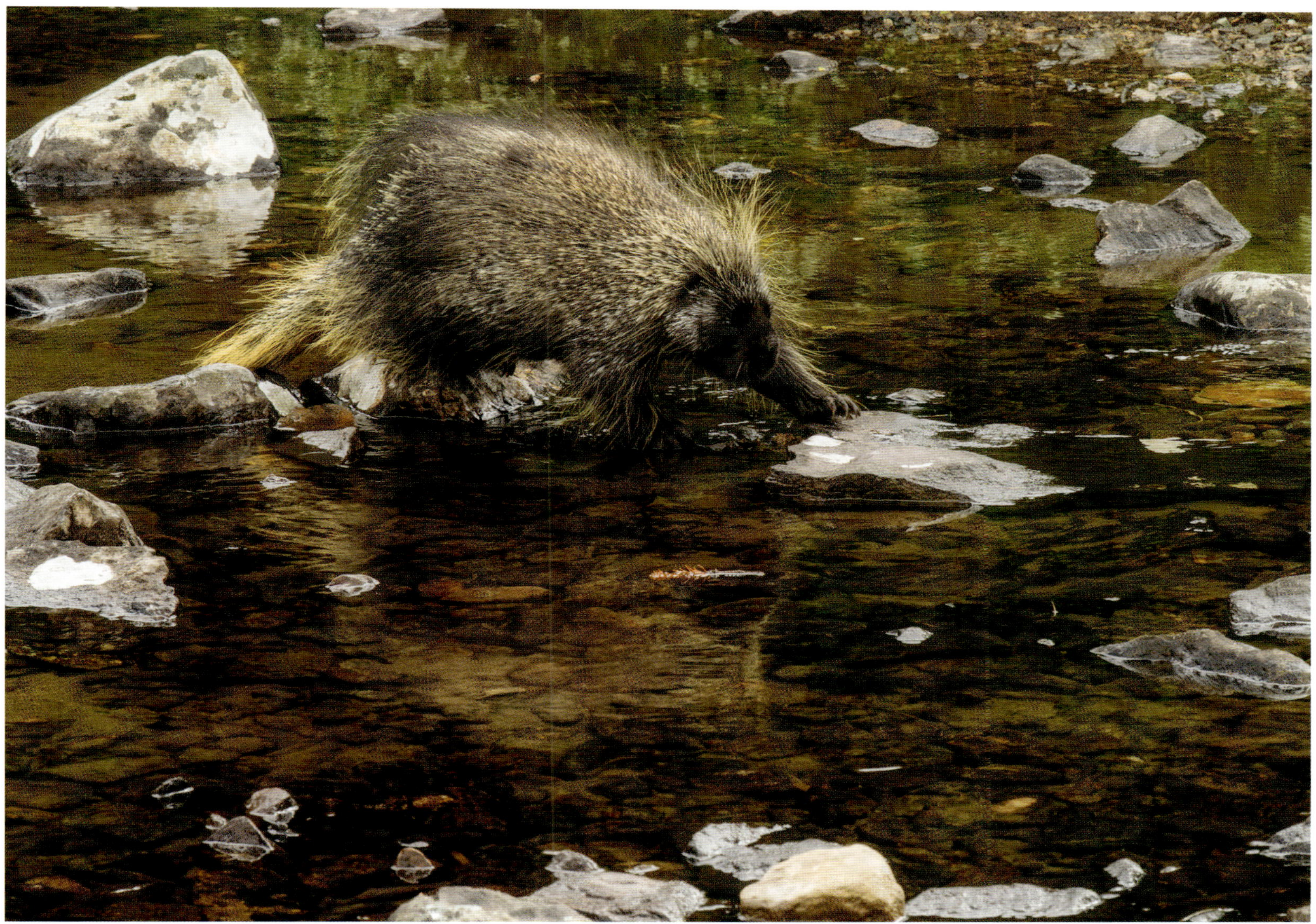

Do Not Disturb (2024)
This careful porcupine crossing the Schäffer Lake outlet stream packs upwards of 30,000 quills for defence. Unlike the local community of hoary marmots, porcupines don't hibernate. They survive the winter by eating tree bark, needles, and woody plants. Their slow movement conserves energy.

Overleaf **Almost There** (2021)
The High Level Circuit trail to Lake McArthur cozies up to the base of Mount Schäffer, with a view toward Goodsir Pass. Our daughter, Maia, adds scale to the image while she patiently waits for me to take yet another photograph.

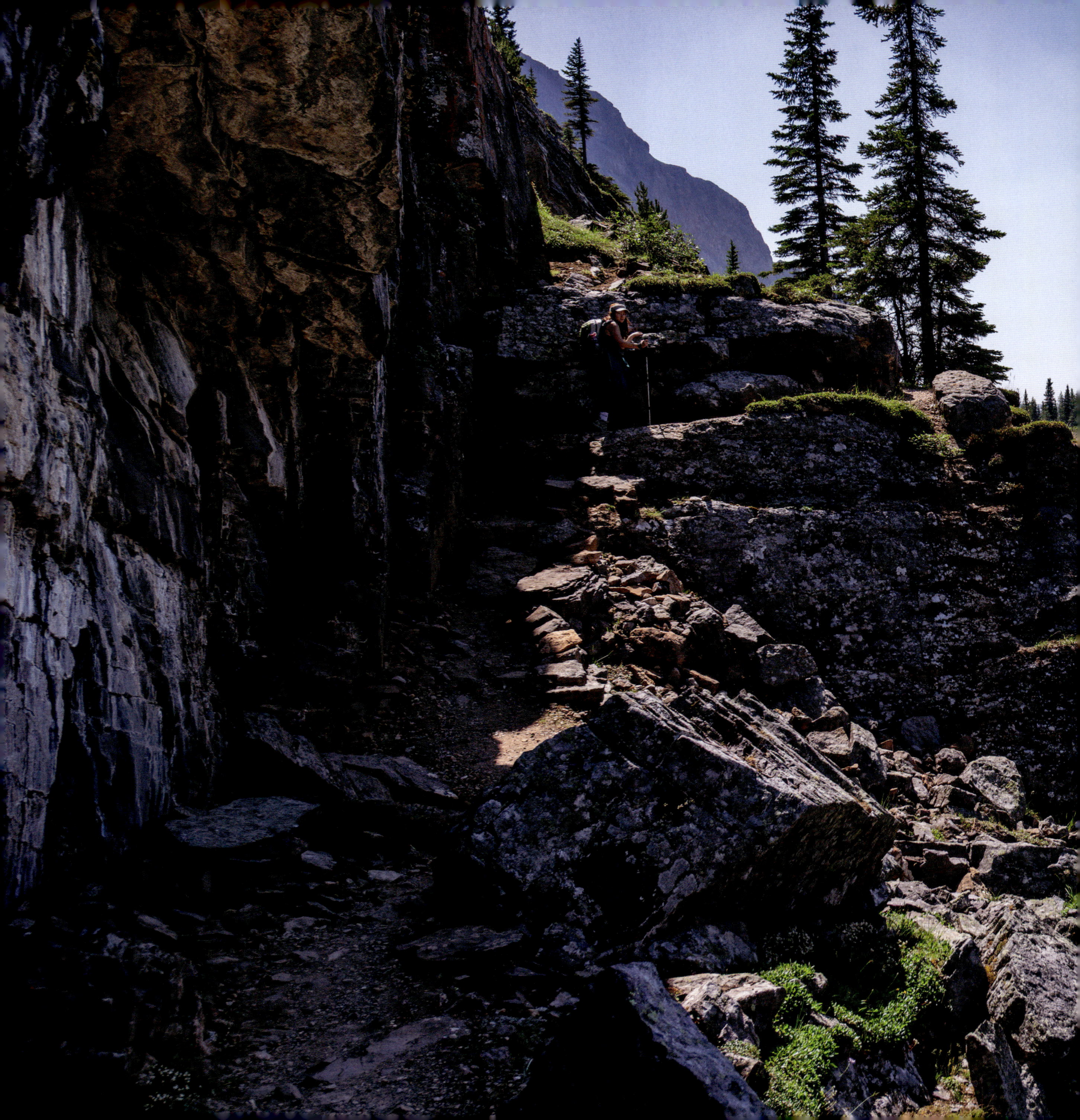

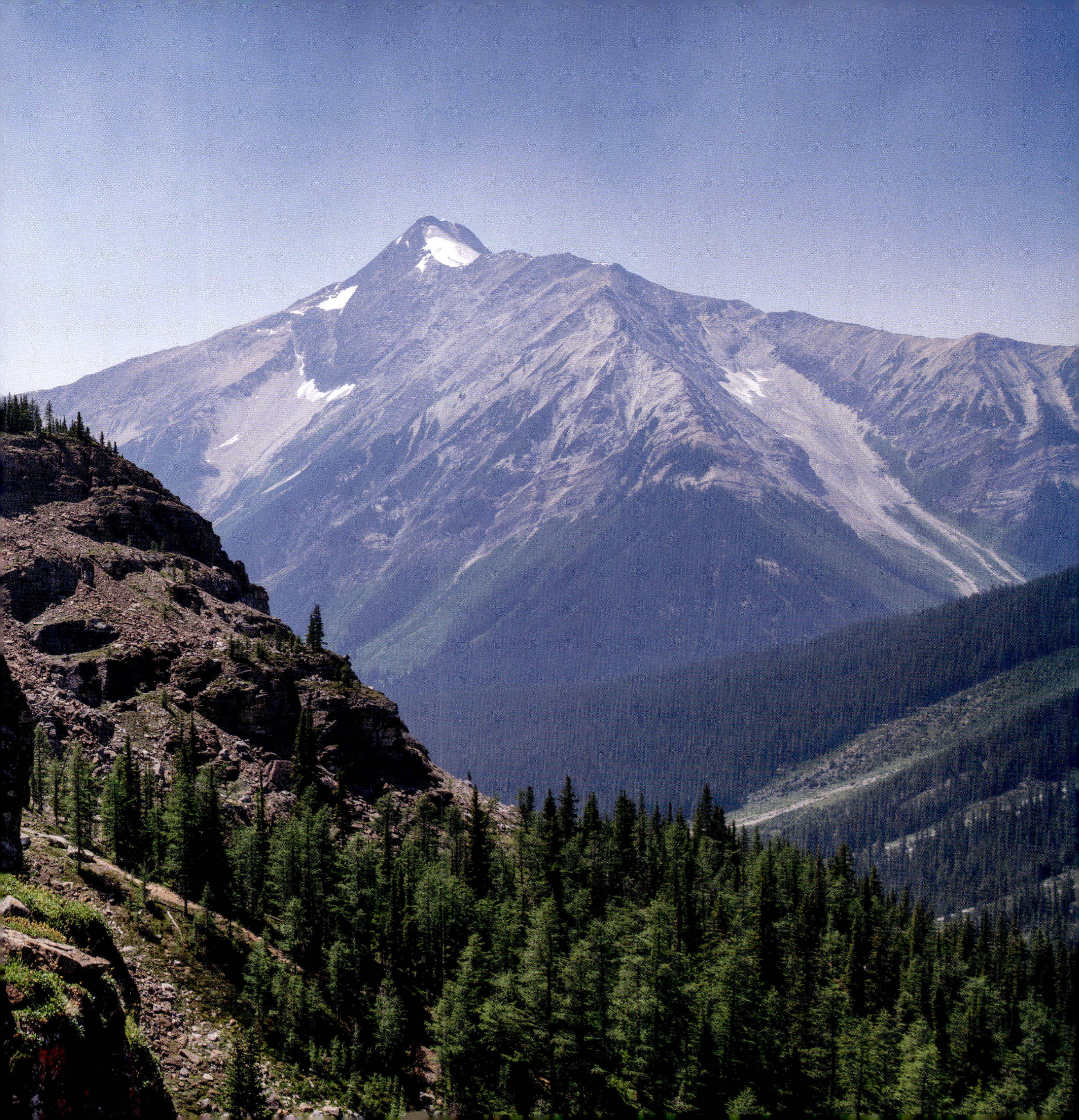

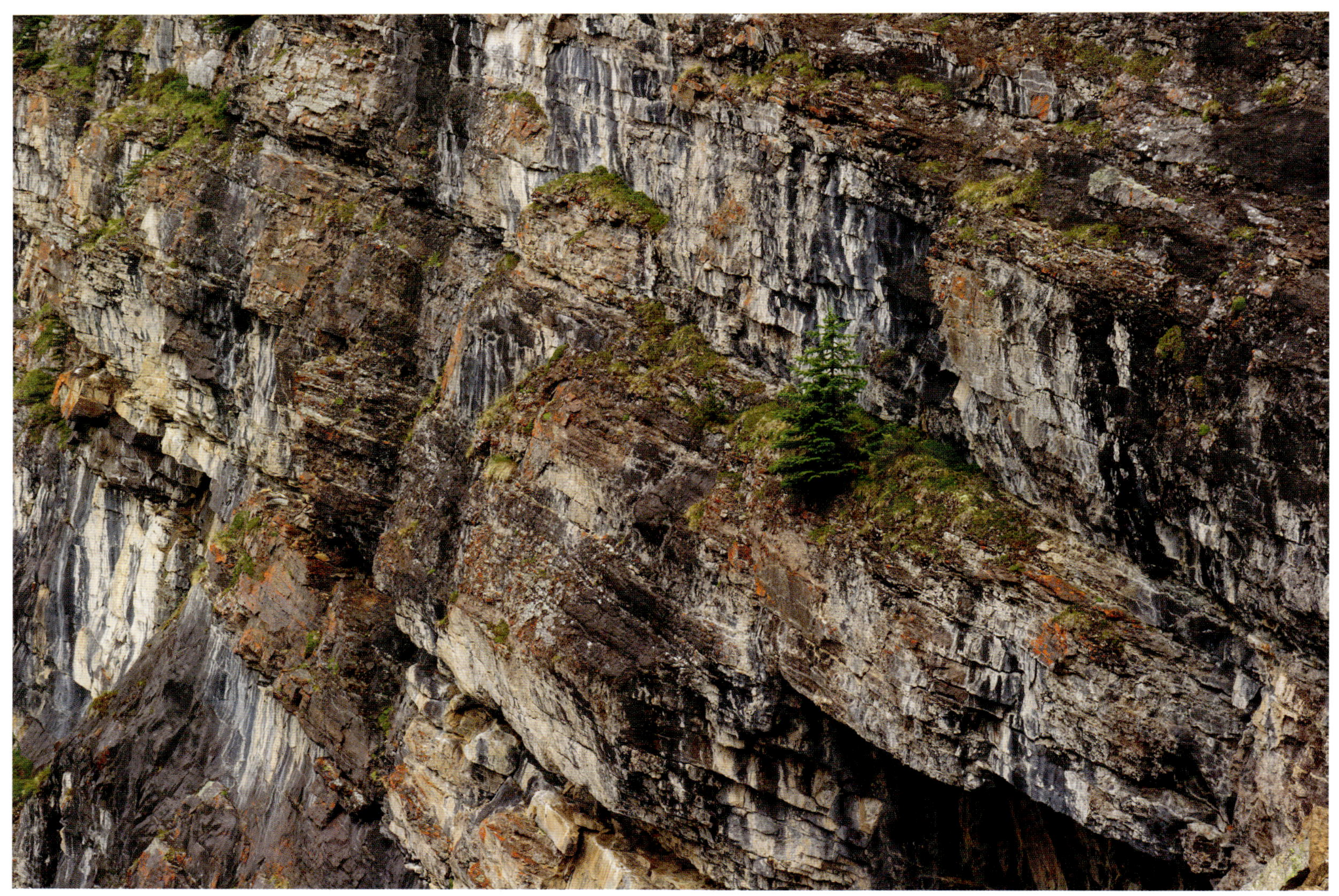

Defying Gravity (2010)
A pine tree has managed to establish a foothold on the vertical rock wall of Mount Schäffer. The adaptations of plant life never cease to amaze.

Walk through Time (2024)
The Lake McArthur circuit trail winds through ancient sea floor strata from the continental margin that are now outcropping as pinkish-beige carbonate. A geological beacon hidden in plain sight.

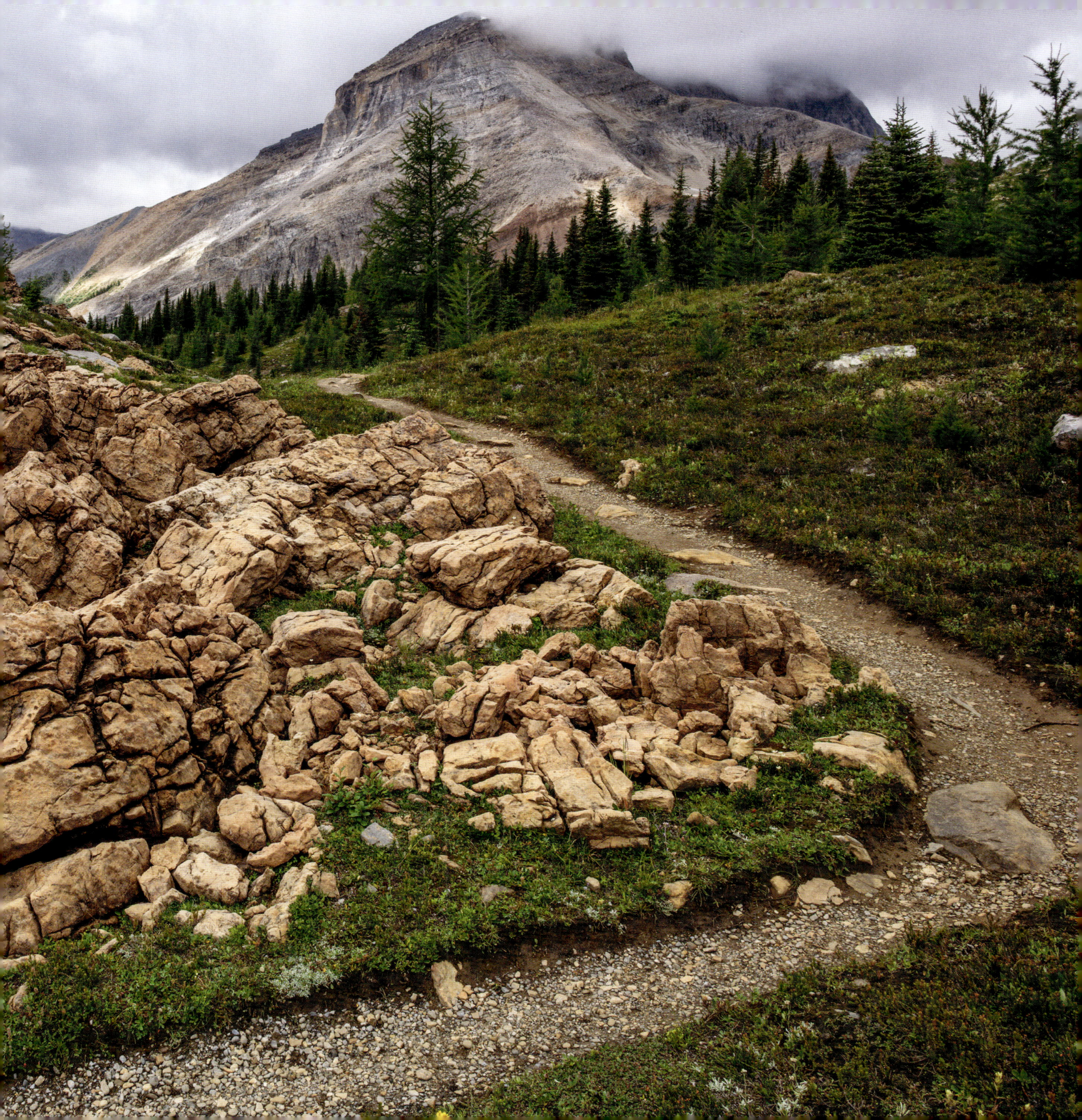

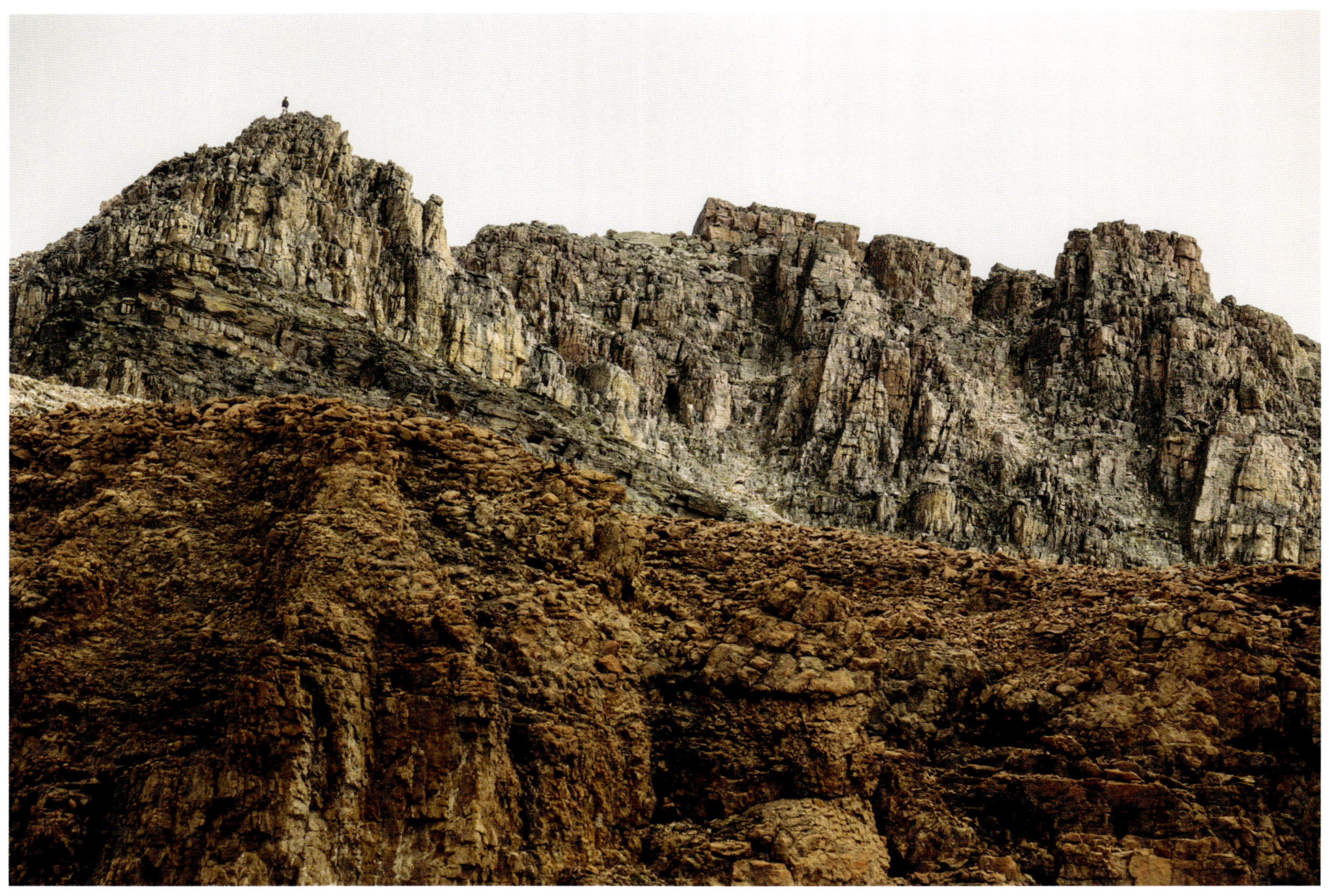

Alpine Perch (2024)
A hiker stands atop Mount Schäffer as seen from the entrance
to Lake McArthur.

Destination (2021)
A hiker (my spouse, Rossana Arcega) completes the final
stretch of the High Level Circuit to arrive at the brilliantly
coloured Lake McArthur, which at 2251 m above sea level is
one of the highest-elevation lakes in Yoho National Park.

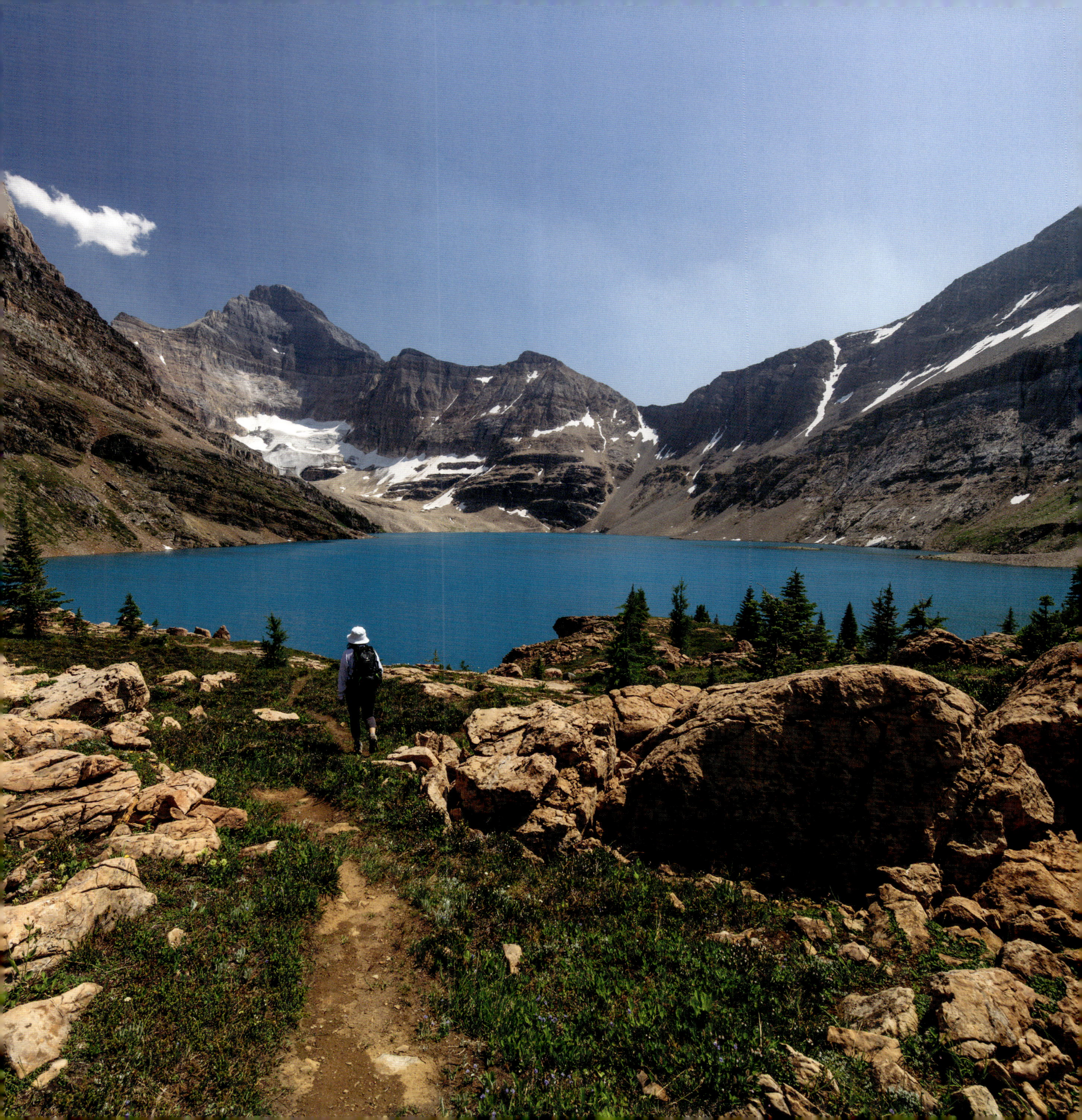

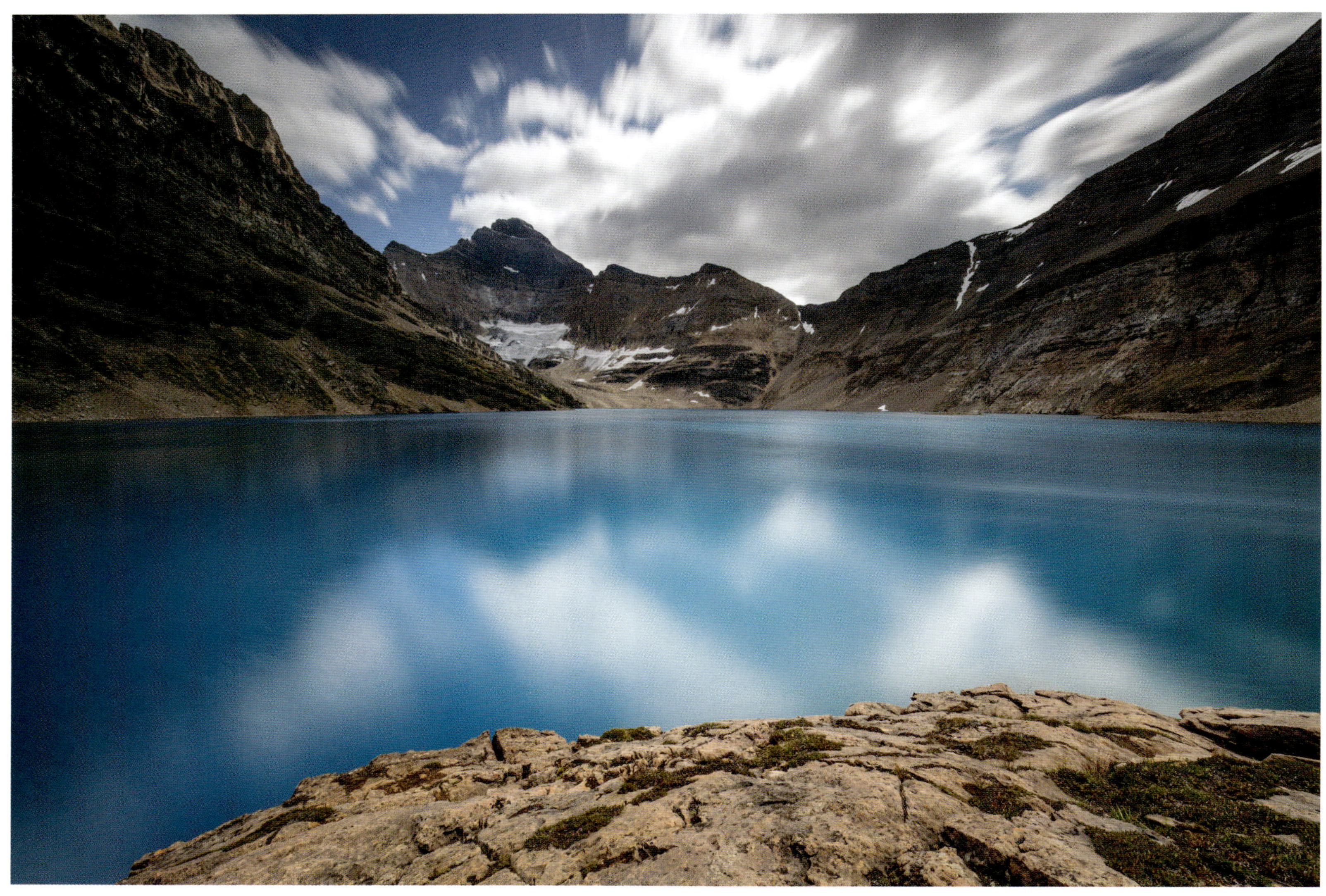

Glacial Hue (2019)
The rock flour resulting from the primary source of water, glacial melt, creates a dramatic alpine hue.

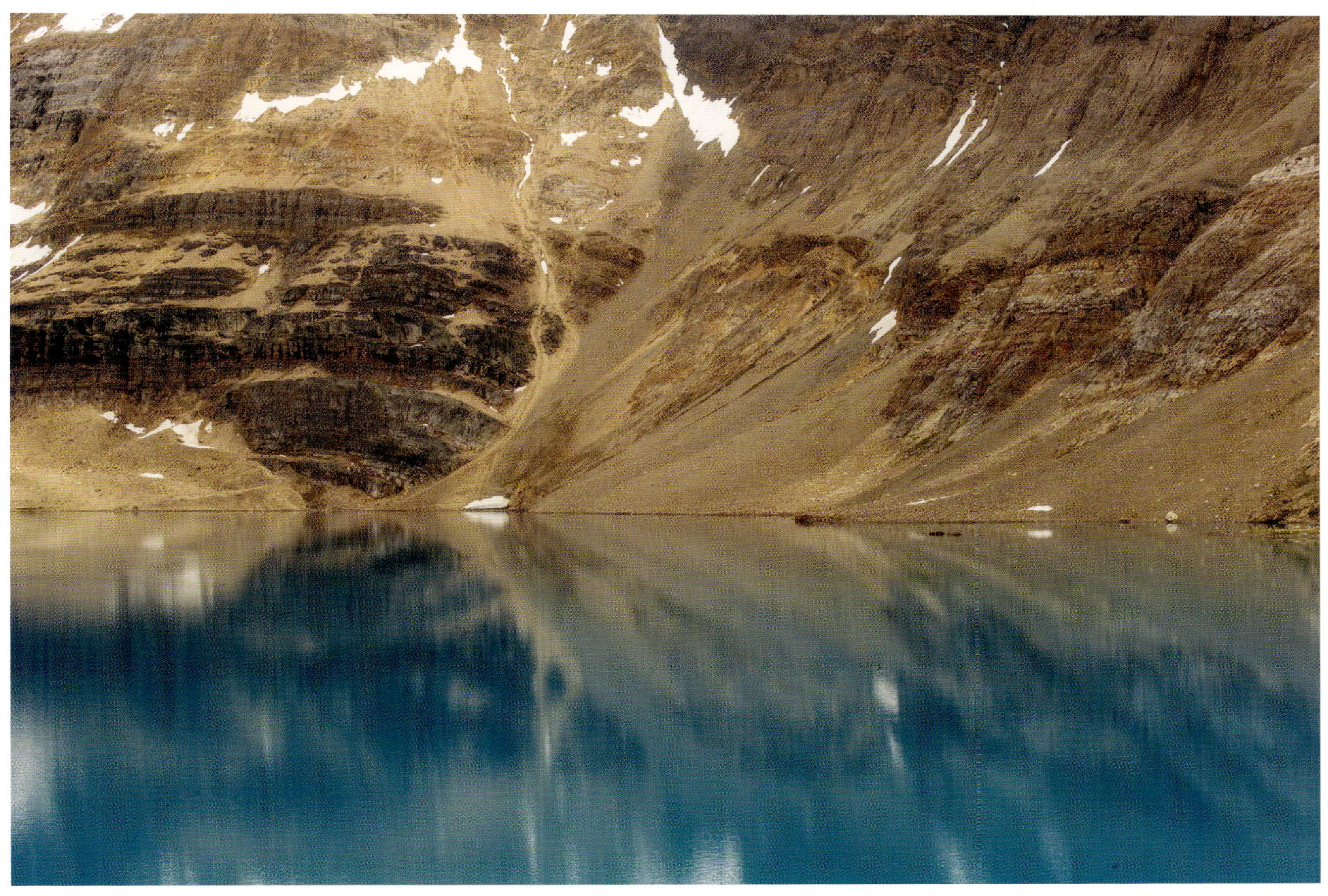

Alpine Reflection (2010)
Earth's palette of natural colours is almost beyond fiction at
times.

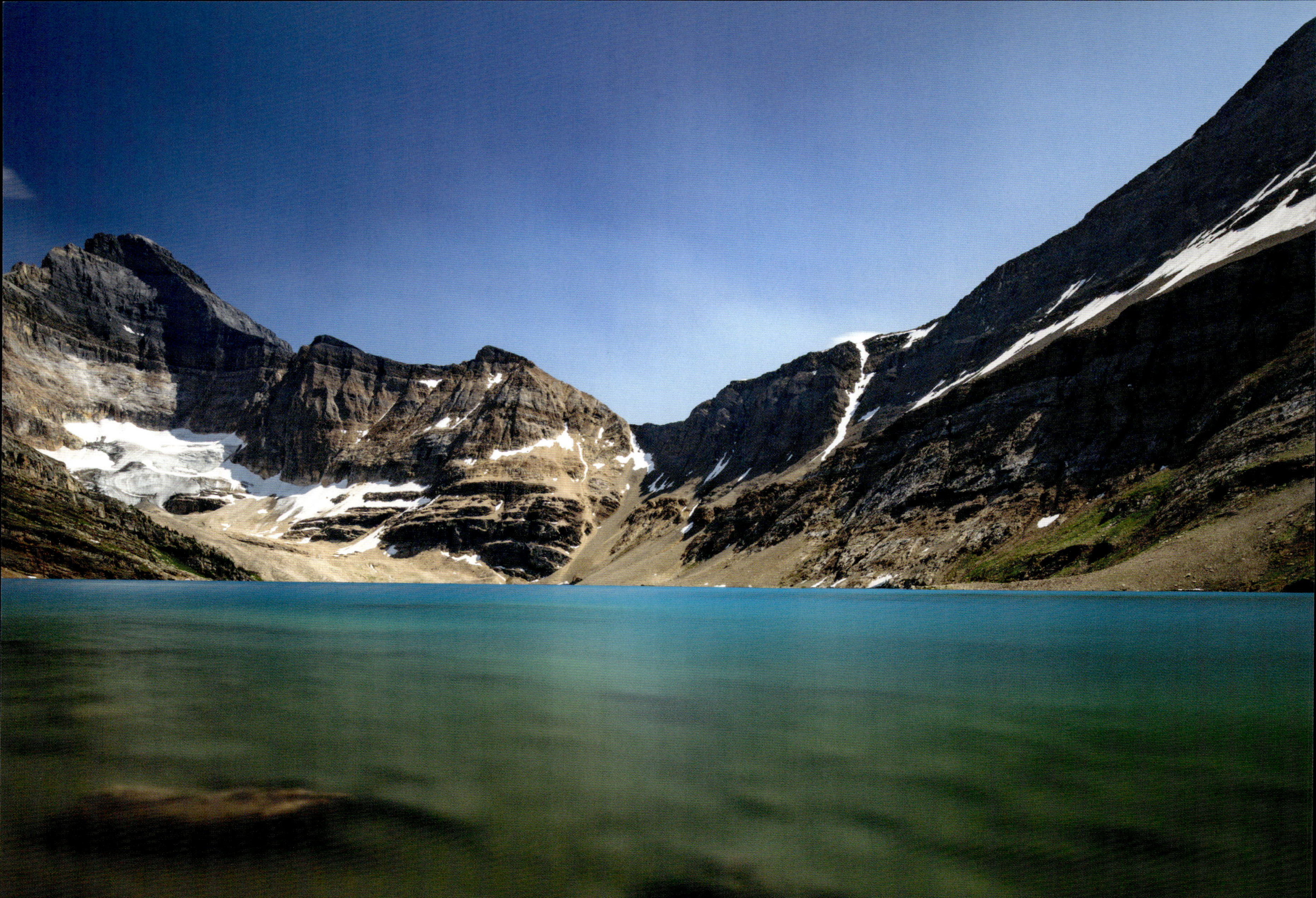

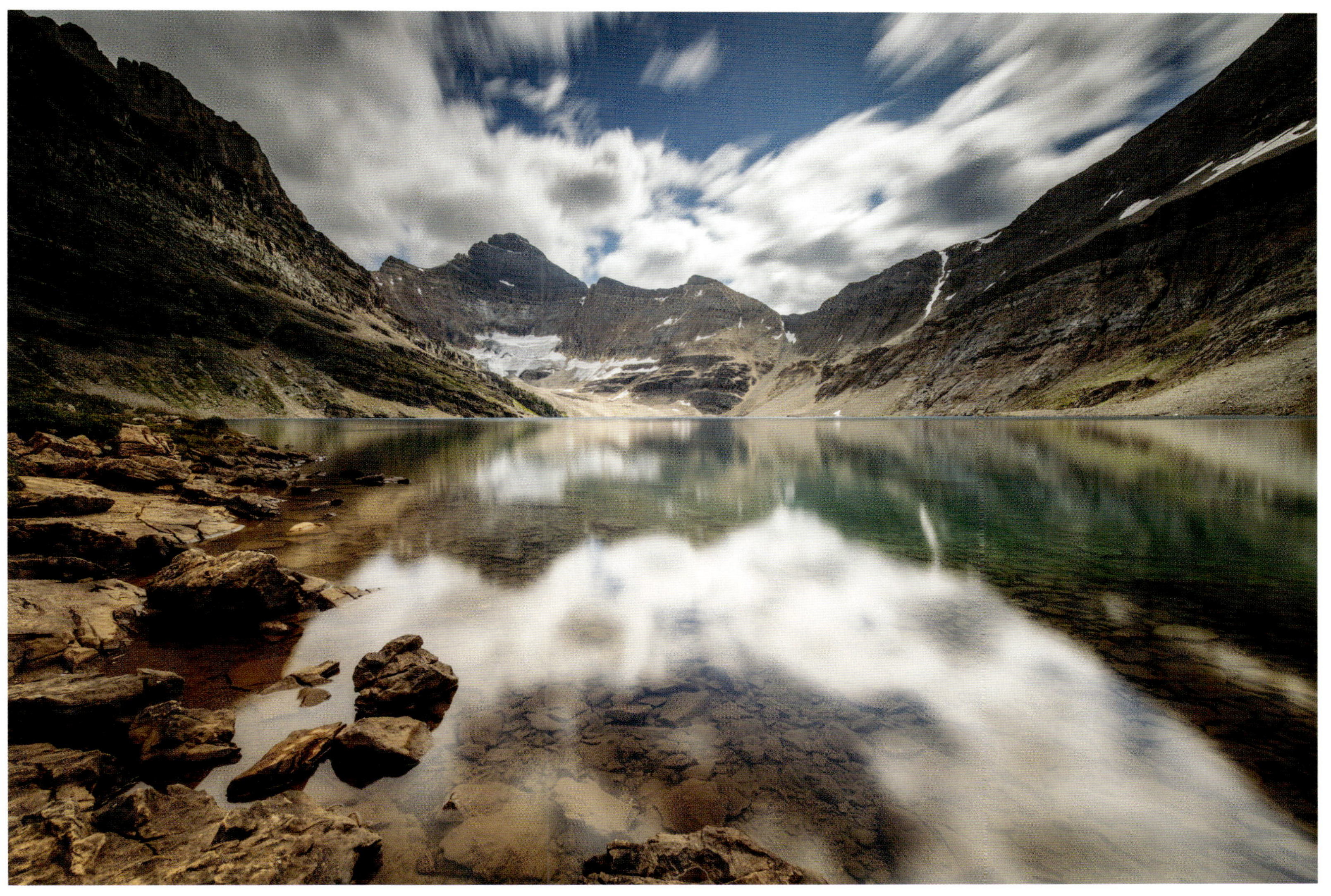

Lake Edge View (2019)
Close to the shoreline, the rock flour sediments are not as pronounced, providing a different impression of Lake McArthur.

Surface Time (2021)
A long exposure in the windy midday sun to smooth out the underlying primary colours.

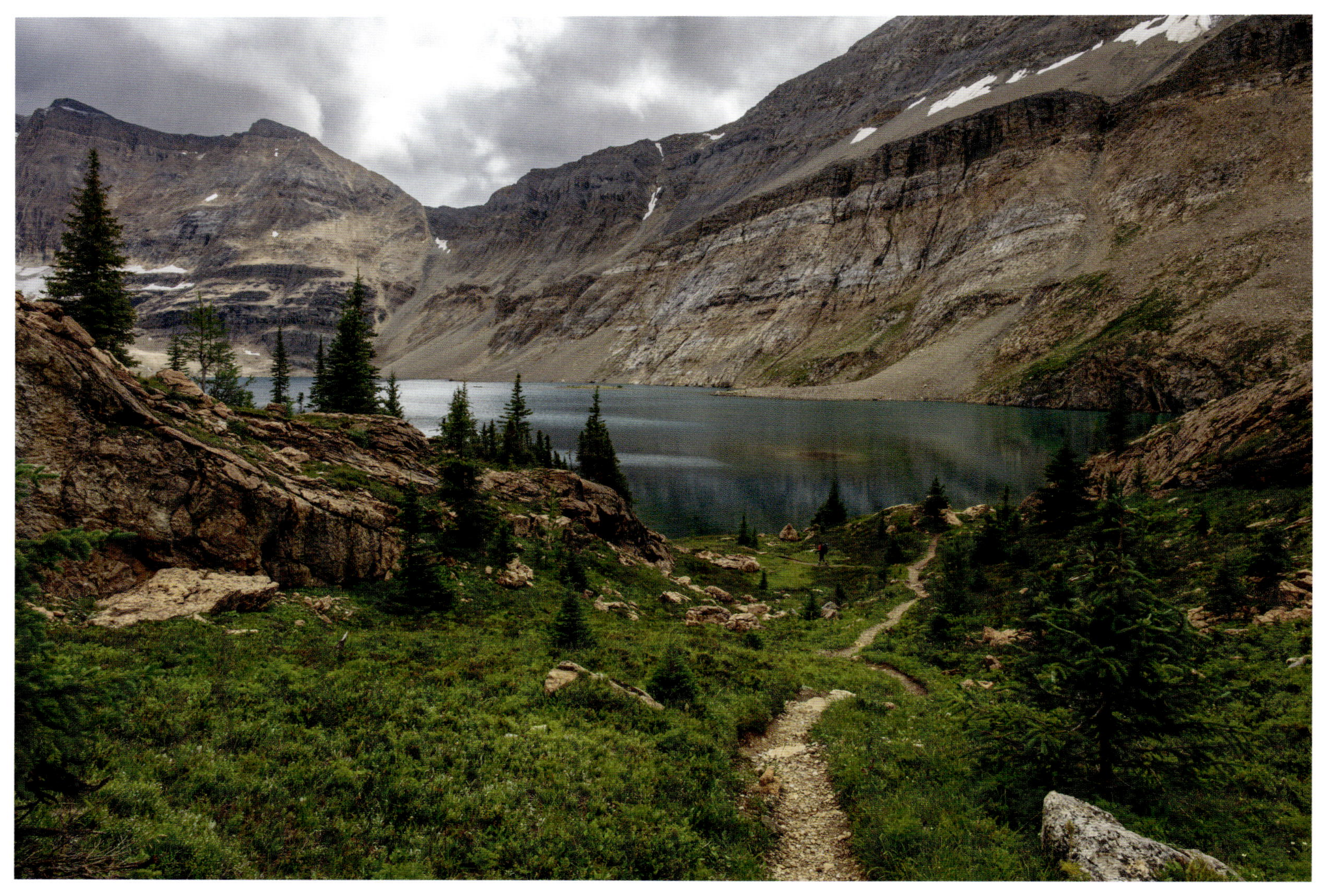

Nature's Theatre (2024)
Hiker Matthew Ferrao in the distance provides scale on the approach to Lake McArthur.

Rewarding Vista (2024)
Matthew takes in the view after a two-hour hike from Lake O'Hara, looking out over the 1.5-km-long cirque-shaped valley.

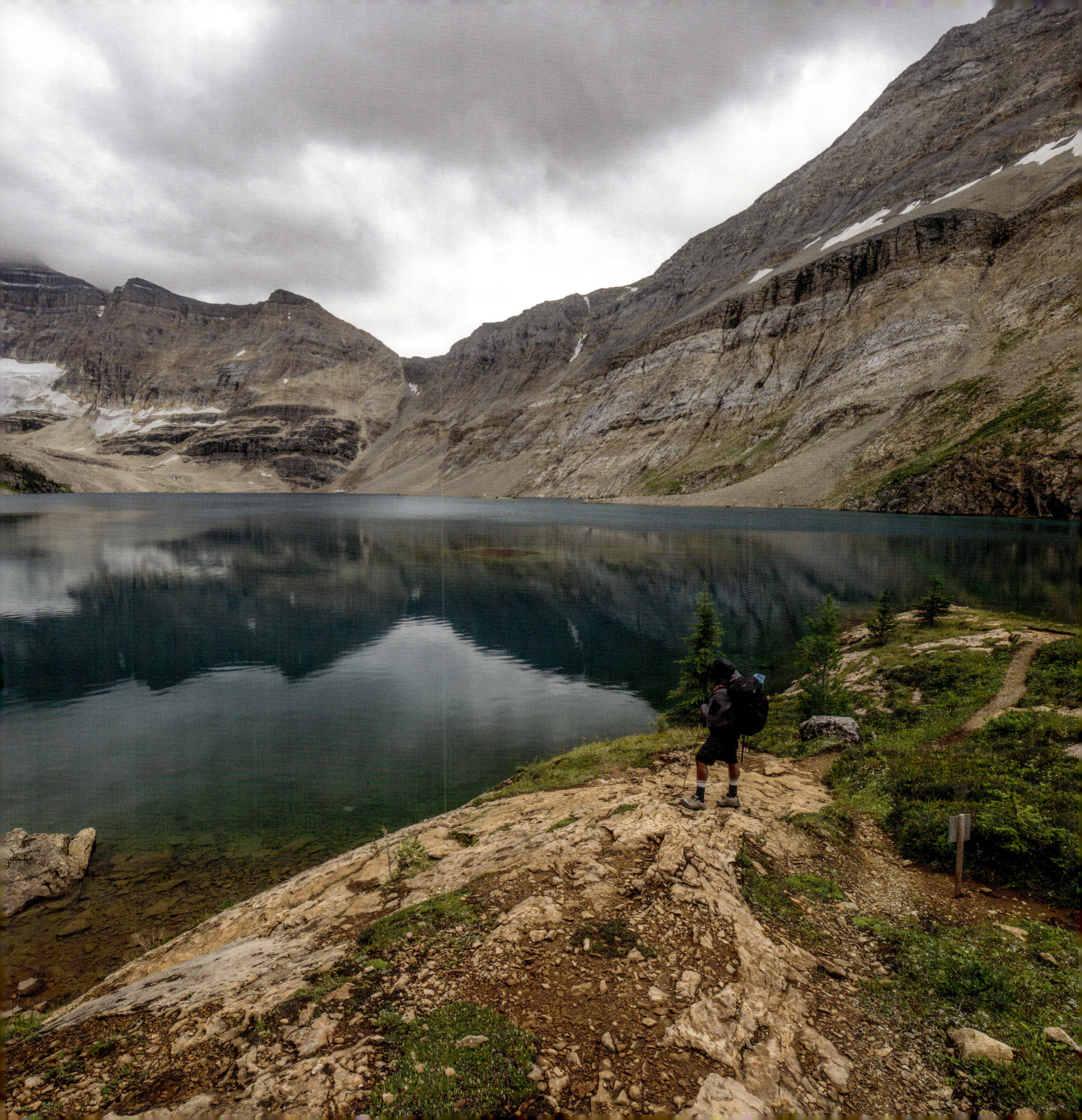

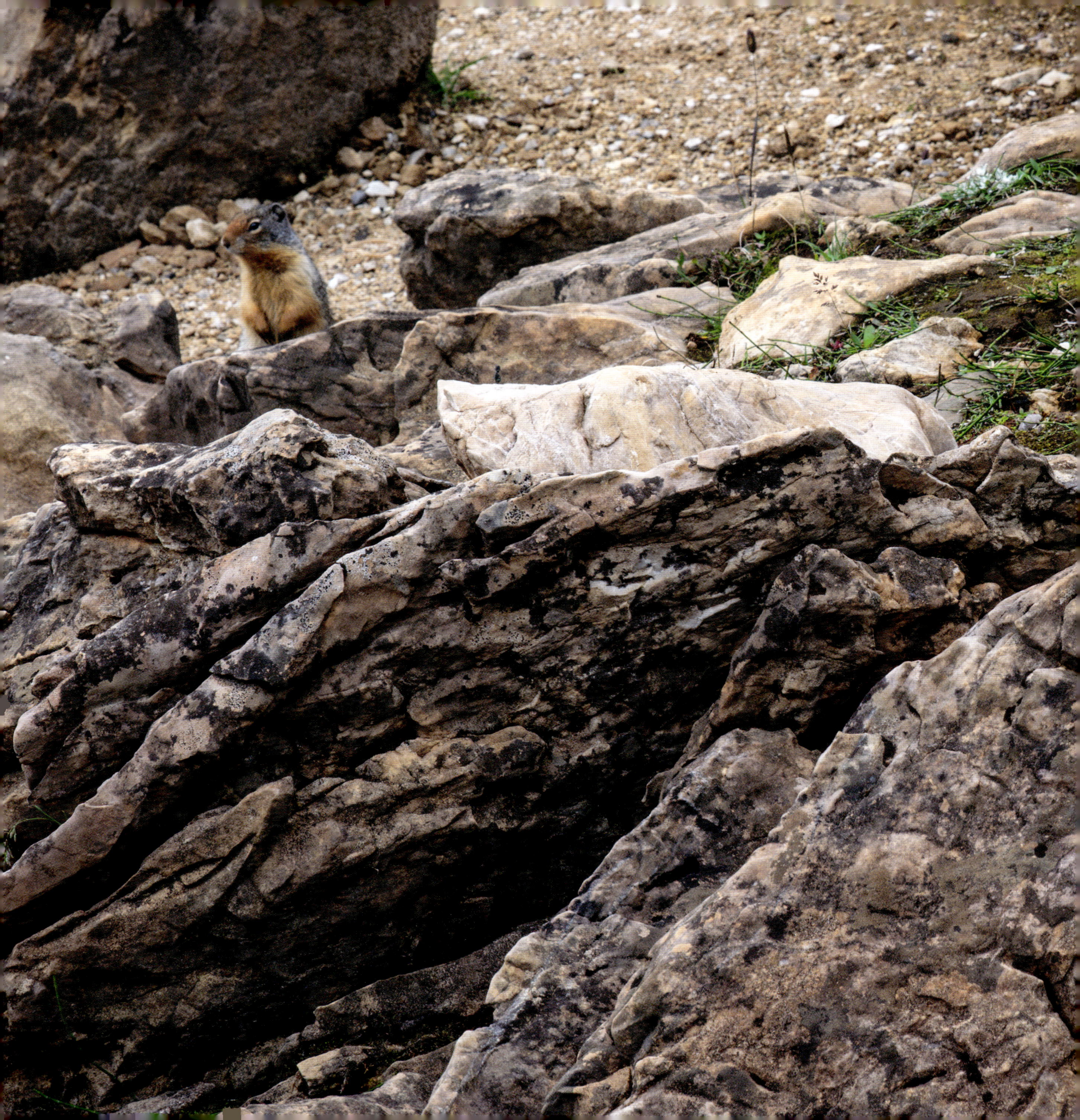

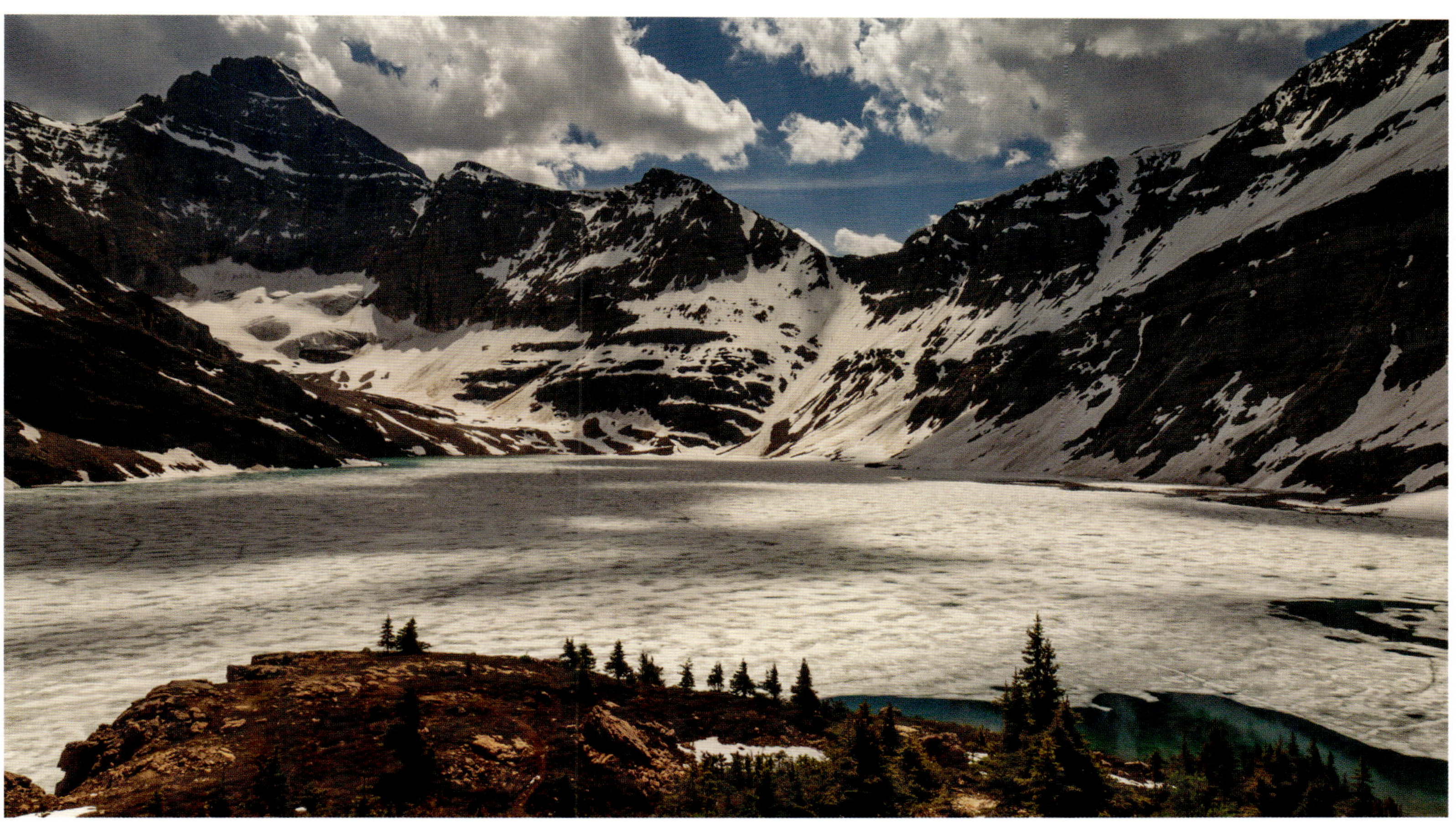

Local Resident (2024)
This Columbian ground squirrel was watching me take pictures of the lake. It hibernates for 7–8 months of the year, so each day of the summer season is precious. When threatened, it emits a sharp chirp to warm others in its colony.

Winter's Presence (2007)
At one of the Lake O'Hara region's highest-elevation lakes, the remnants of winter extend into July and return in early September, making the brief appearance of Lake McArthur's richly turquoise-coloured water even more special.

Overleaf **McArthur Colours** (2019)
This long-exposure photograph softened the effects of strong wind, drawing our attention to the range of colours on the lake from turquoise to golden-brown reflections of the mountains and clouds.

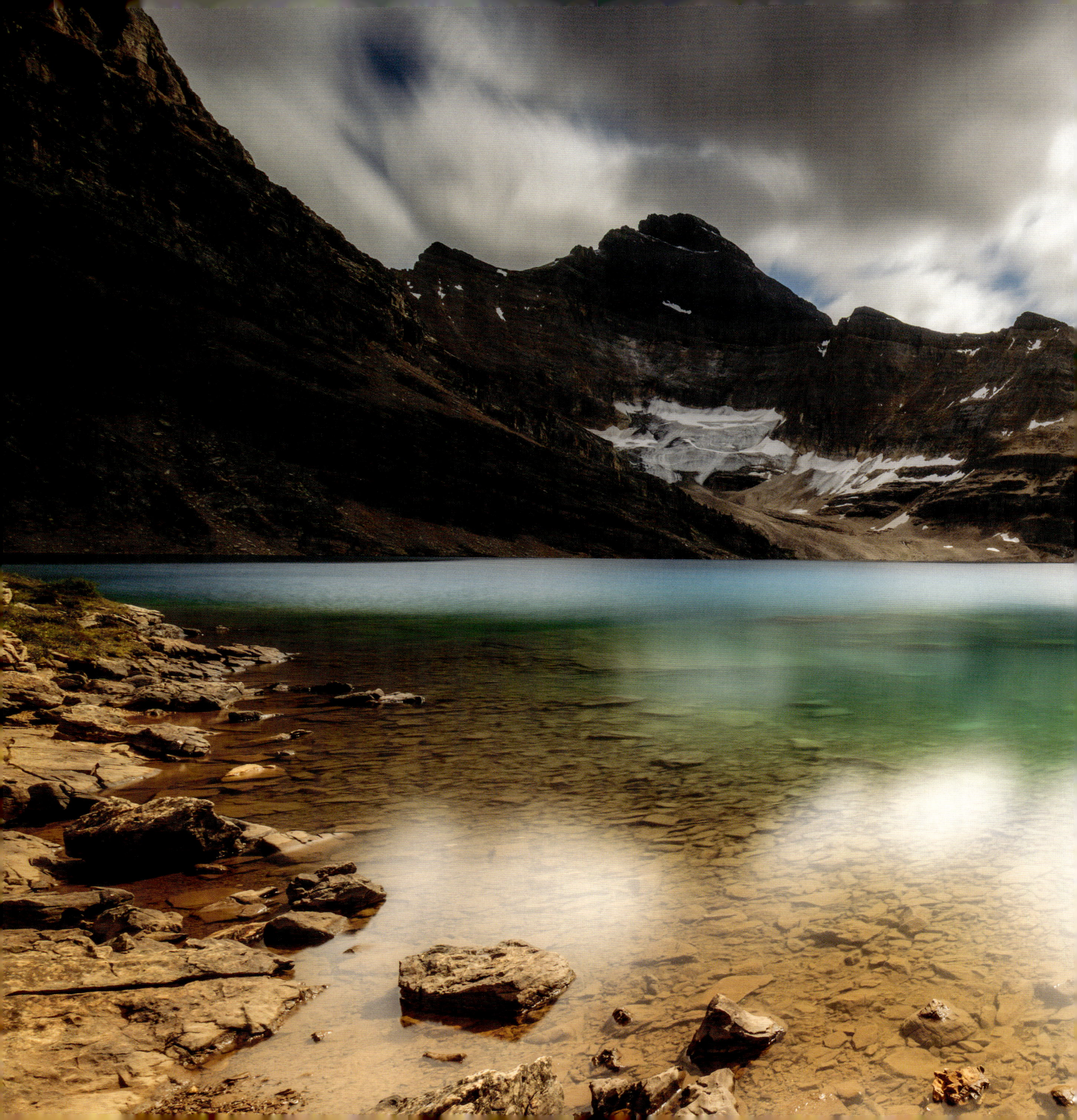

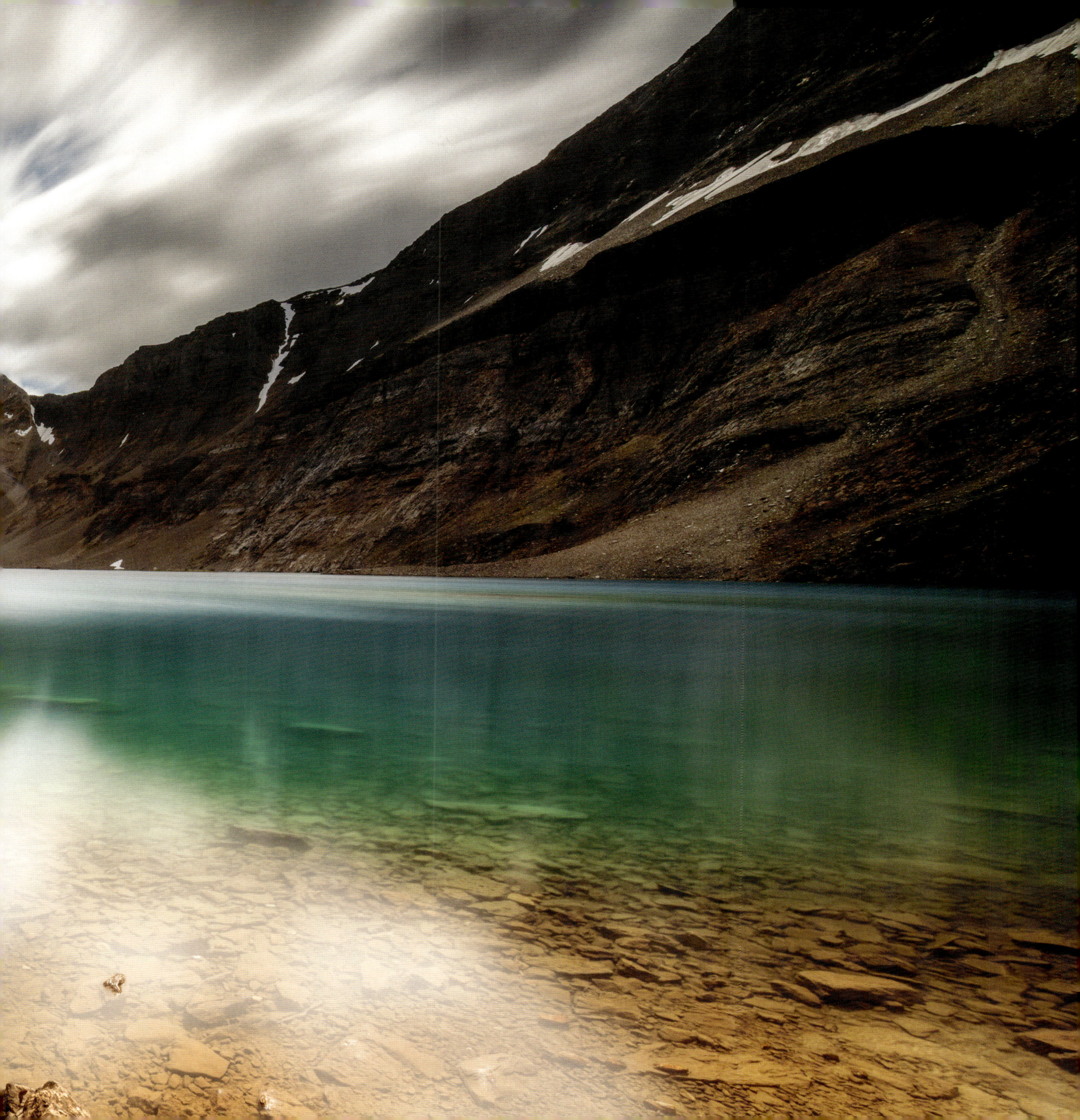

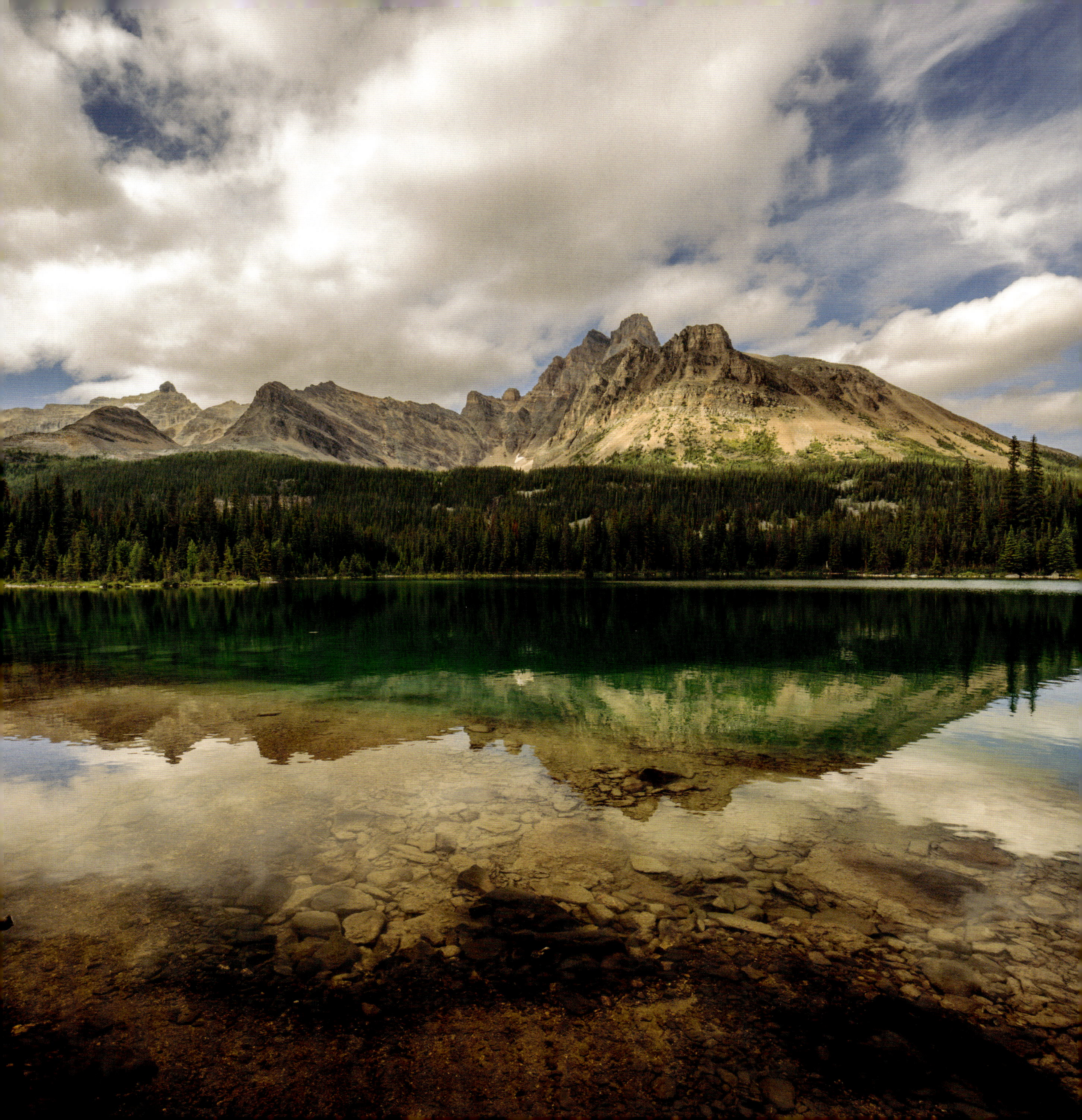

PART FIVE

Linda Lake and Cathedral Prospect

The hike from Lake O'Hara to Linda Lake and Cathedral Prospect is a six-hour round trip with 415 m of elevation gain. Hence, it's often overlooked by those visiting the region, as there are so many other, shorter trails with compelling vistas. It is perhaps telling that over my 18 years of visits to Lake O'Hara, it was only on one of my most recent trips in 2024 that I undertook this journey with a motivation to experience all of the trails in preparation for this book. Naturally, it turned out to be surprisingly rewarding! Gem Trek's *Lake O'Hara Map and Trail Guide* states this often-overlooked trail rewards the adventurous hiker with an experience of solitude unmatched in the Lake O'Hara region. Experience confirms this – over the course of my eight-hour round trip to Monica Lake, I encountered only two other hikers. The trails to Linda Lake border an area closed for a wildlife corridor, and with the distances involved, it's wise to hike with a companion while notifying others of where you are going and when you expect to return.

Le Relais Day Shelter is a good starting point for this hike. Opened in 1989 and operated by the Lake O'Hara Trails Club in cooperation with Lake O'Hara Lodge, this shelter is a convenient place to purchase light snacks and beverages. It also provides updated information on local trail conditions and any wildlife precautions. A short distance away,

Afternoon Symmetry (2024)
Light rain gives way to outbursts of sun and still waters for a mirror reflection at Linda Lake.

along the route to the beginning of Linda Lake Trail, sits the strategically situated Lake O'Hara Warden's Cabin.

The present-day Warden's Cabin was built in the 1960s, modelled on the original Parks Canada warden's cabin design. These cabins served as seasonal outposts for park wardens who patrolled the area on horseback, enforcing park regulations to protect bighorn sheep from overhunting, while also tracking grizzly bears and elk. There are some archived handwritten warden's logbooks from the 1930s to the 1950s detailing avalanches, wildlife encounters, and early ski patrols. The cabin is not open to the public and is still in use today by Parks Canada for research, monitoring ecological changes, maintenance, and emergency operations.

The 3.2-km-long Linda Lake Trail begins just after the Warden's Cabin at the outlet of Lake O'Hara and passes the Lake O'Hara Campground in a short time. Like everything in the O'Hara region, these 30 campsites are in high demand. Reservations are required, and they are fully booked early in the season. With only 140 m of elevation gain, this trail leads through a forested canopy over a carpet of moss, making it a comfortable temperature on a warm summer day. Just when it starts to feel like maybe this isn't the right trail, Linda Lake comes into view, with a mirror-image reflection of Odaray Mountain's north side. Emerald-coloured Linda Lake quickly became one of my favourite sights on the trip.

There are two independent routes to Linda Lake, the first being Linda Lake Trail just described. The other route is Morning Glory Lakes Trail. Both trails are identical in length (3.2 km), but the latter starts from the EP Hut and offers a little more elevation gain at 165 m. I decided to return via this route on my way back to Lake O'Hara from Cathedral Prospect.

From the west end of Linda Lake it's only a 20-minute hike along the 1.3-km Cathedral Lakes Trail as it gains 45 m in elevation by the time it reaches the Cathedral Lakes. This hike meanders through several meadows that during peak flower season are lit with an artist's palette of colours. Odaray Mountain (3159 m) provides the backdrop to the Cathedral Lakes, and chances are you will have this beautiful sight all to yourself.

Some weary hikers may feel satiated enough at this point to elect turning back for the long hike to Lake O'Hara. However, if you still have some residual energy, it is well worth continuing along the 1.5 km of trail, gaining an additional 230 m of elevation to reach Cathedral Prospect. From this vantage point, the entire Lake O'Hara region is visible, along with Odaray Mountain. Looking through a telephoto lens from Cathedral Prospect, the close-up view gains an aerial-like perspective of the Lake O'Hara Basin. For the sake of completeness, a short distance away is tranquil Monica Lake nestled in the Cathedral Basin.

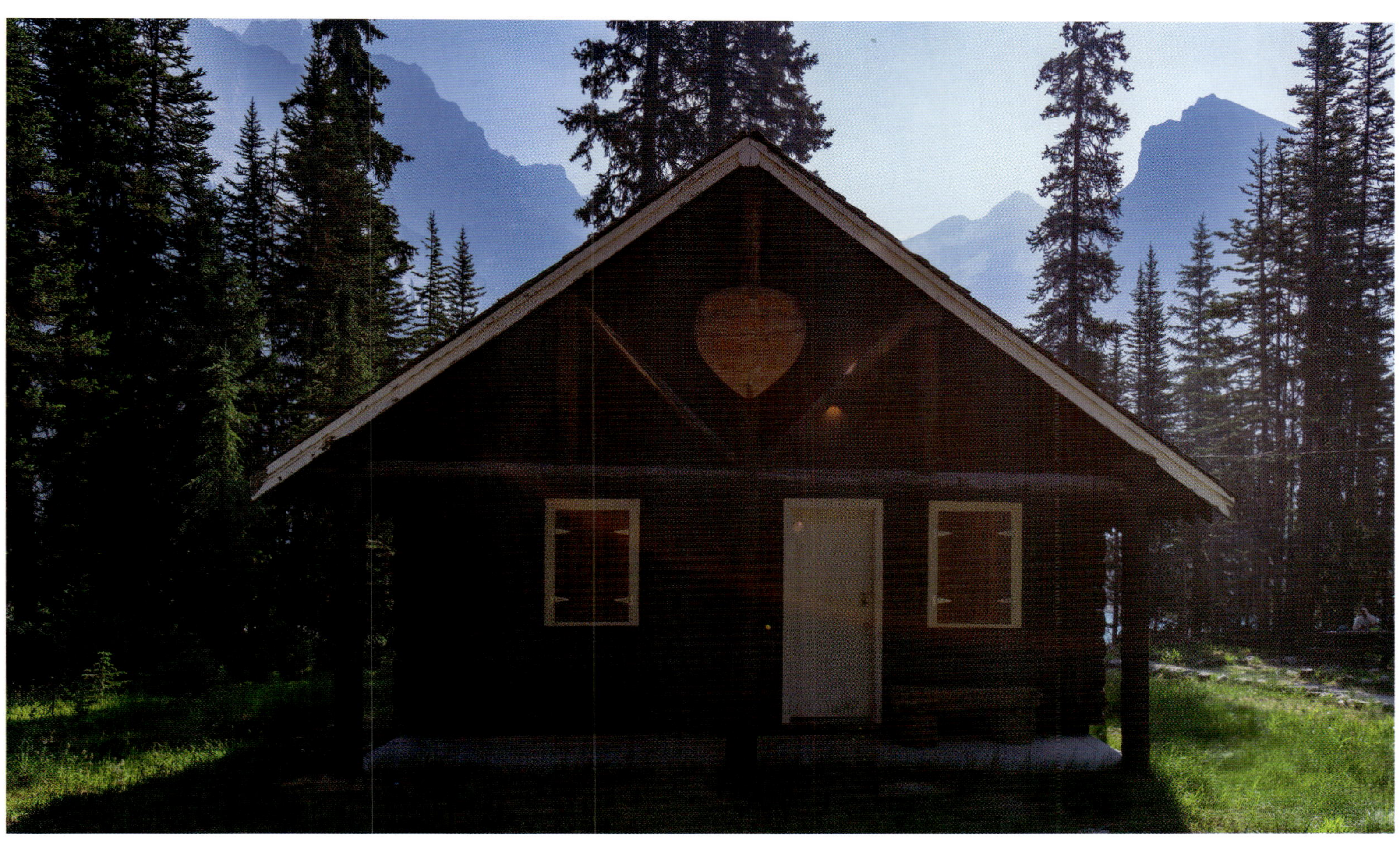

Living History (2021)

The Lake O'Hara Warden's Cabin, built in the 1960s, was based on the design formula set out for warden patrol cabins in the mountain parks by James T. Childe in 1918. Warden's cabins served as seasonal outposts for park wardens who patrolled the area on horseback, enforcing park regulations to protect bighorn sheep from overhunting, while also tracking grizzly bears and elk.

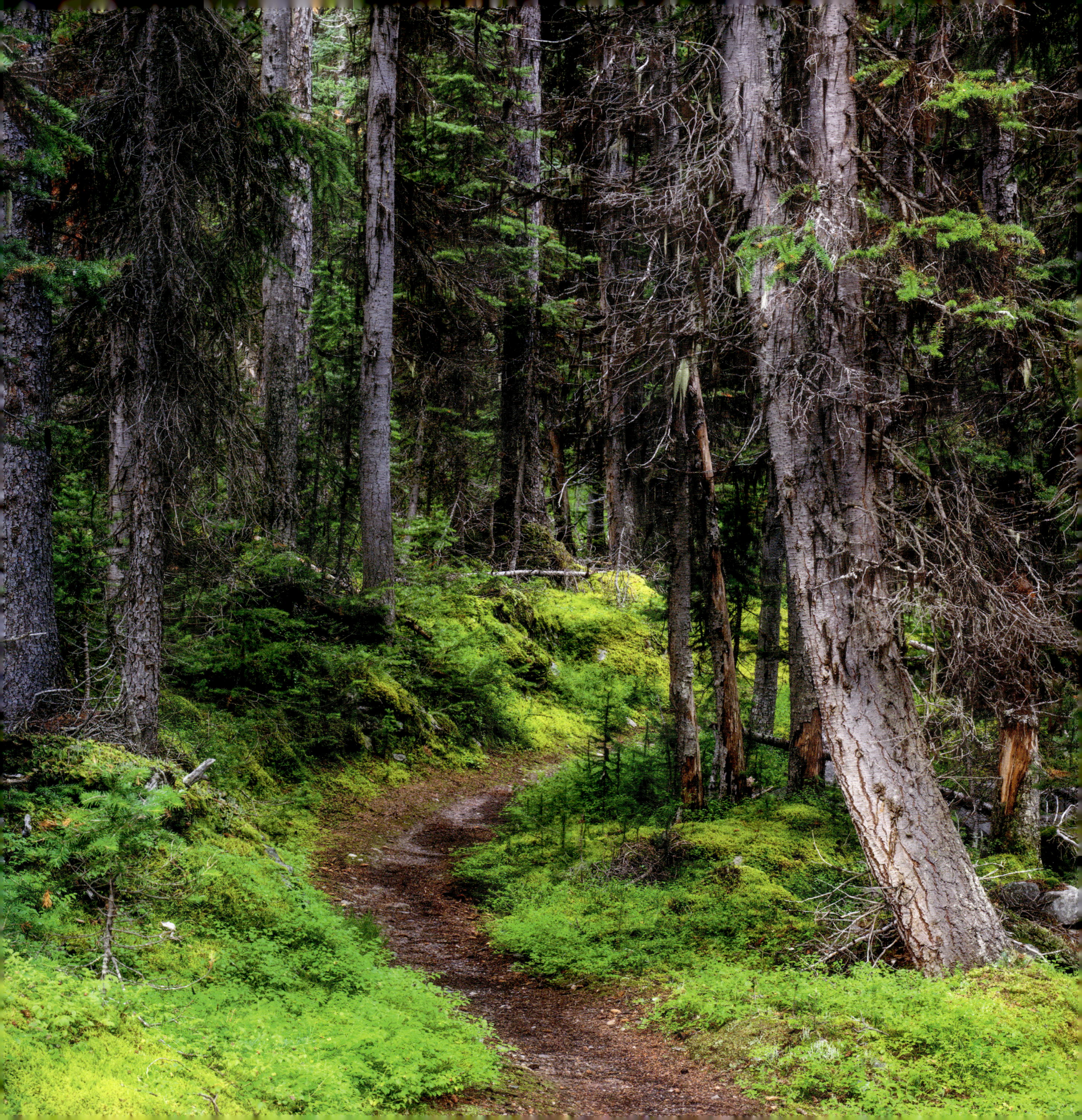

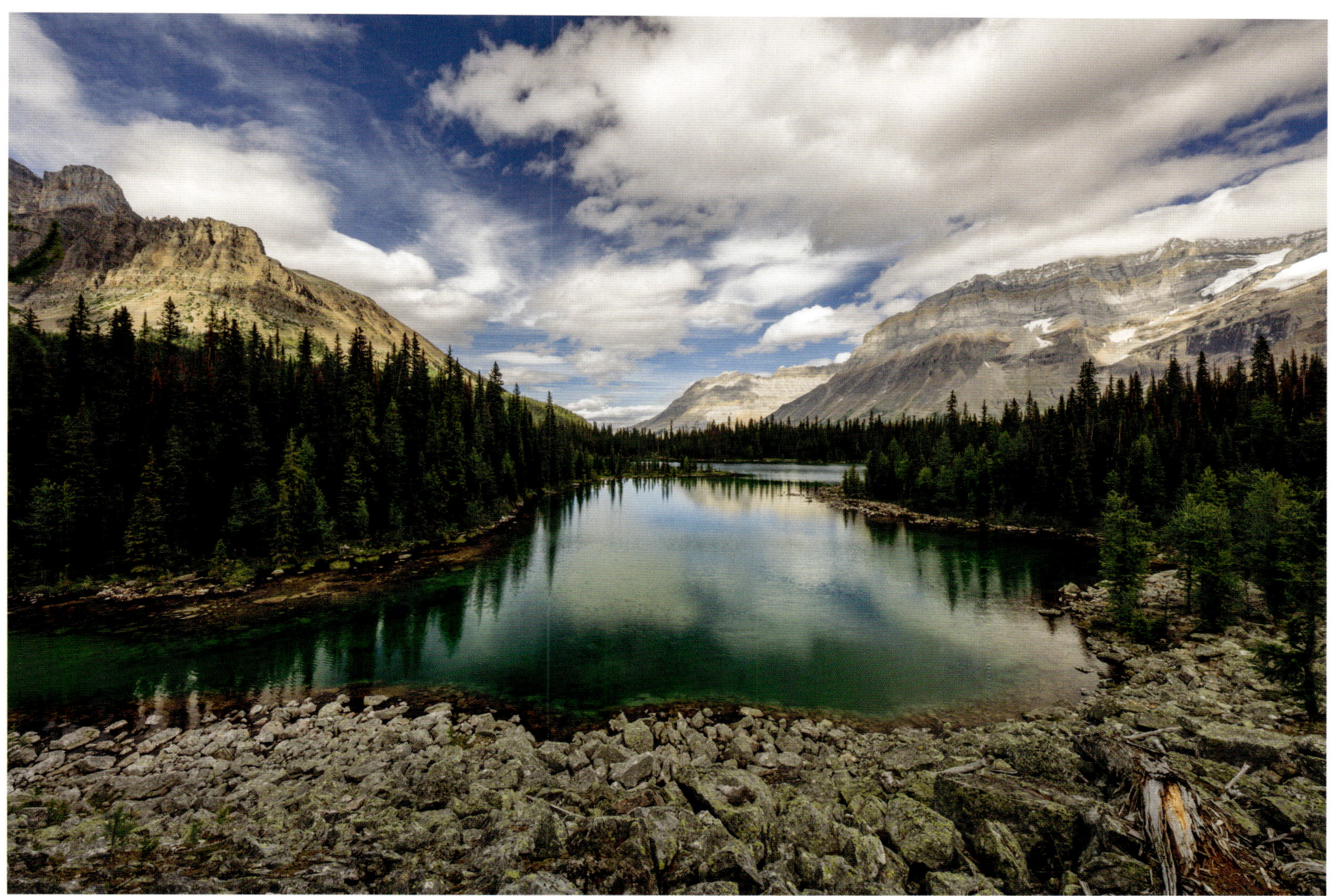

Restful Reflection (2024)
A clear view down the Duchesnay Basin at this quiet spot to rest and reflect along the south shore of Linda Lake.

Solitude (2024)
Often overlooked, this trail provides unmatched solitude on its way to the stunningly beautiful Linda Lake.

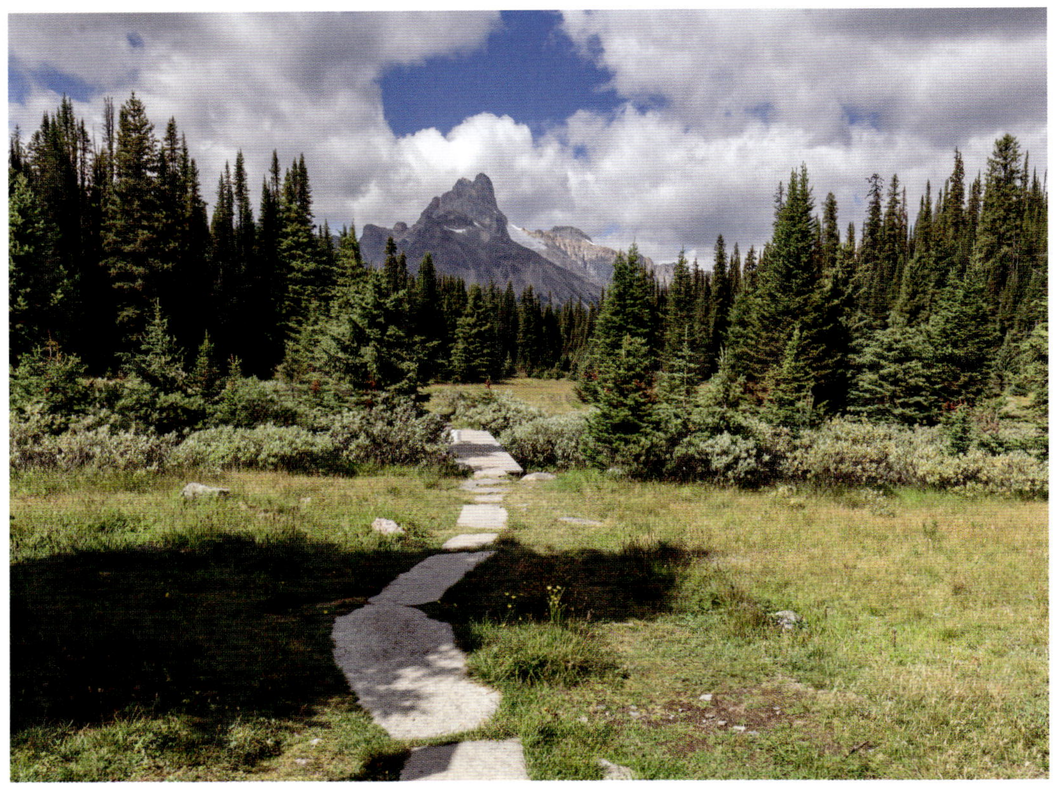

Morning Glory (2024)
An alternate route to Linda Lake is via the well-marked Morning Glory Lakes Trail facing Cathedral Mountain.

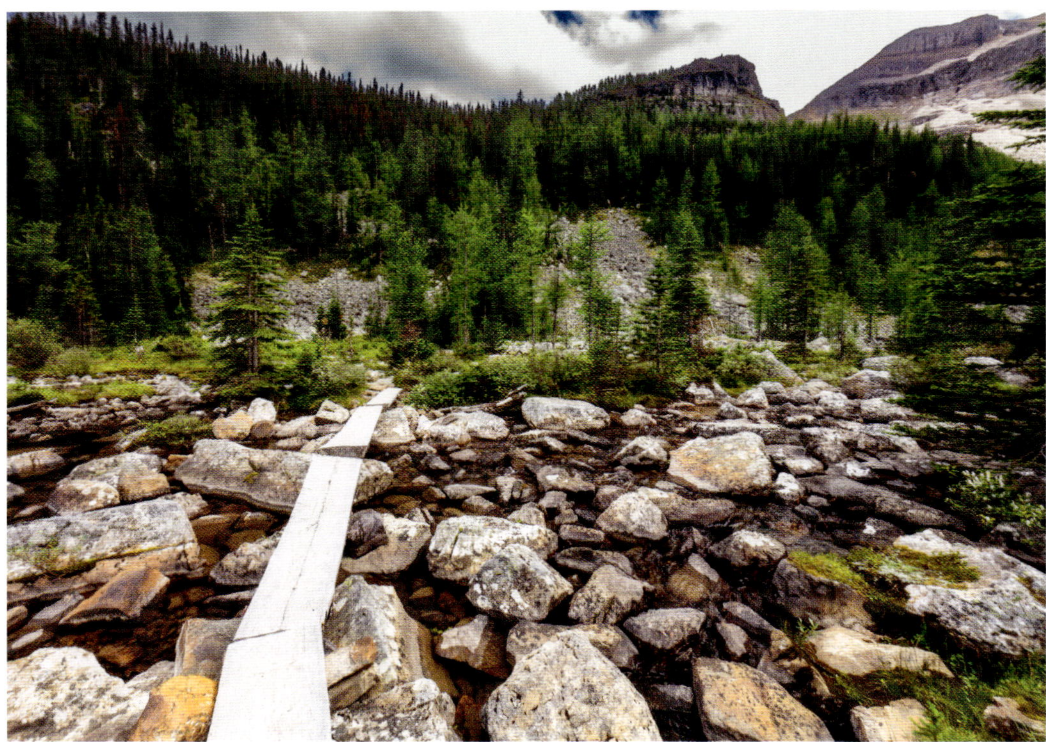

Follow the Trail (2024)
A convenient boardwalk over the inlet to the second of three lakes referred to as Morning Glory Lakes situated at the base of Odaray Mountain.

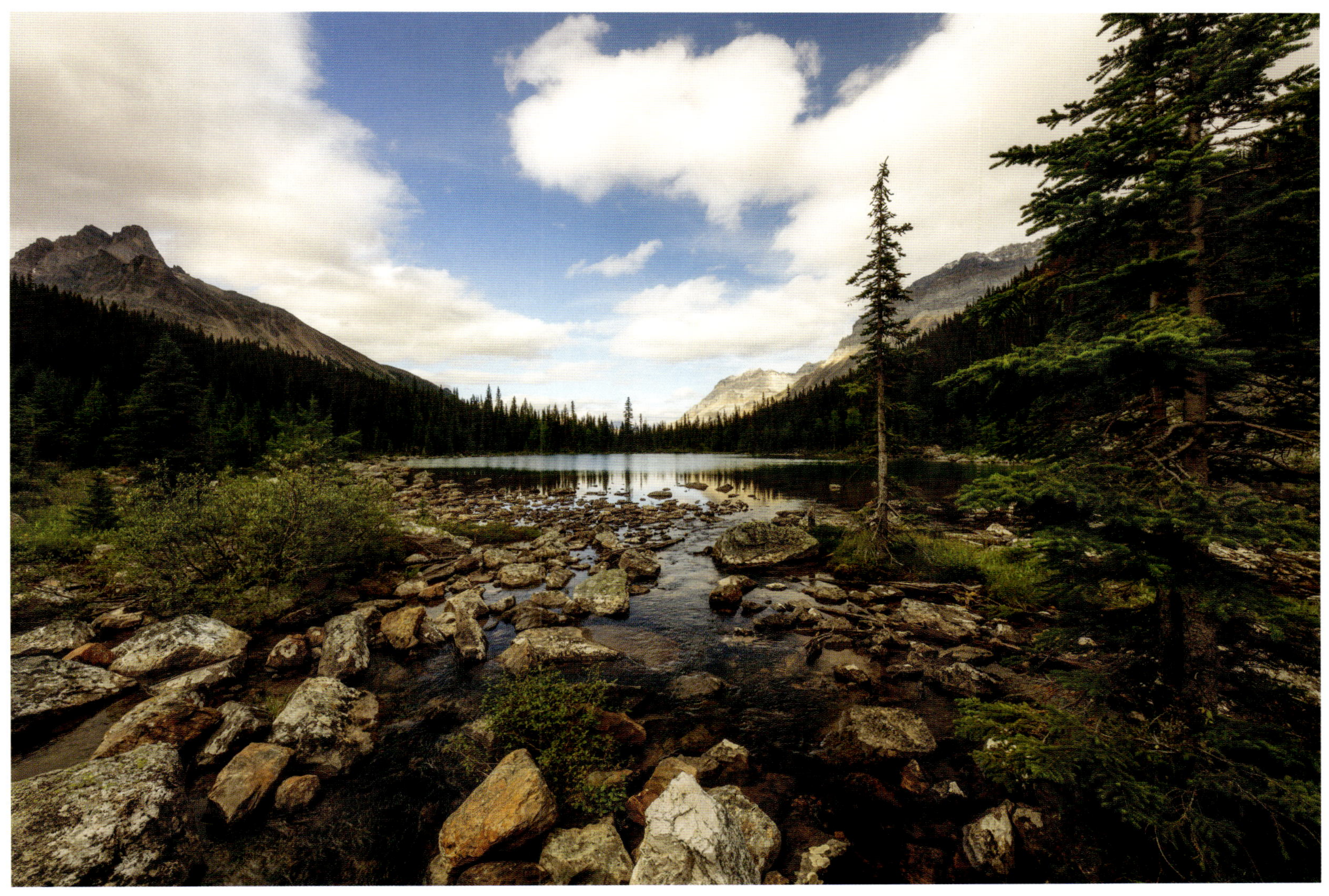

Glacier Fresh (2024)
Flanked by Cathedral Mountain on the left and Wiwaxy Peaks on the right, meltwater from Odaray Glacier feeds Morning Glory Lakes.

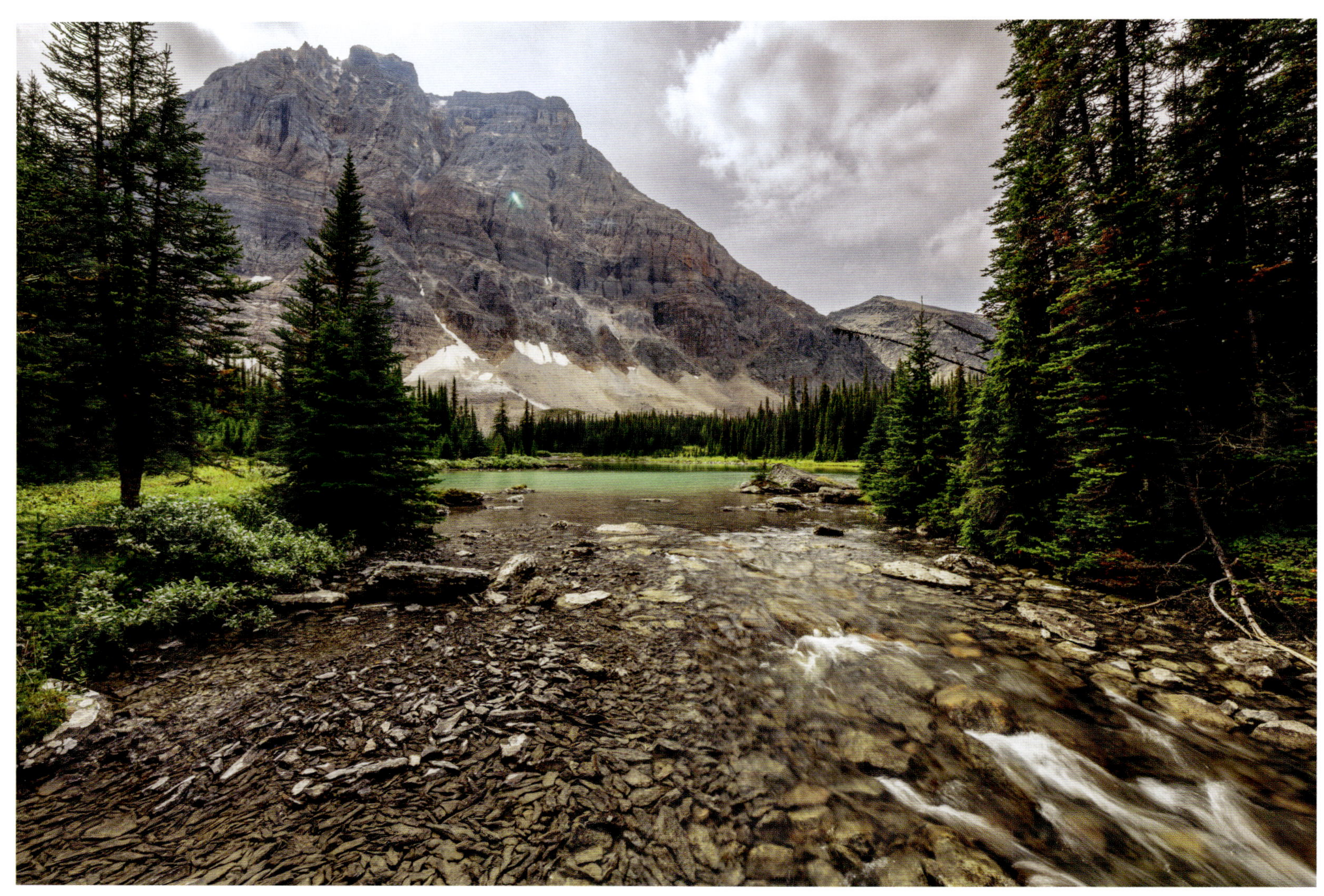

Last Rest (2024)
Cathedral Lakes outlet just before heading up the steeply elevated hike to the Cathedral Prospect trail.

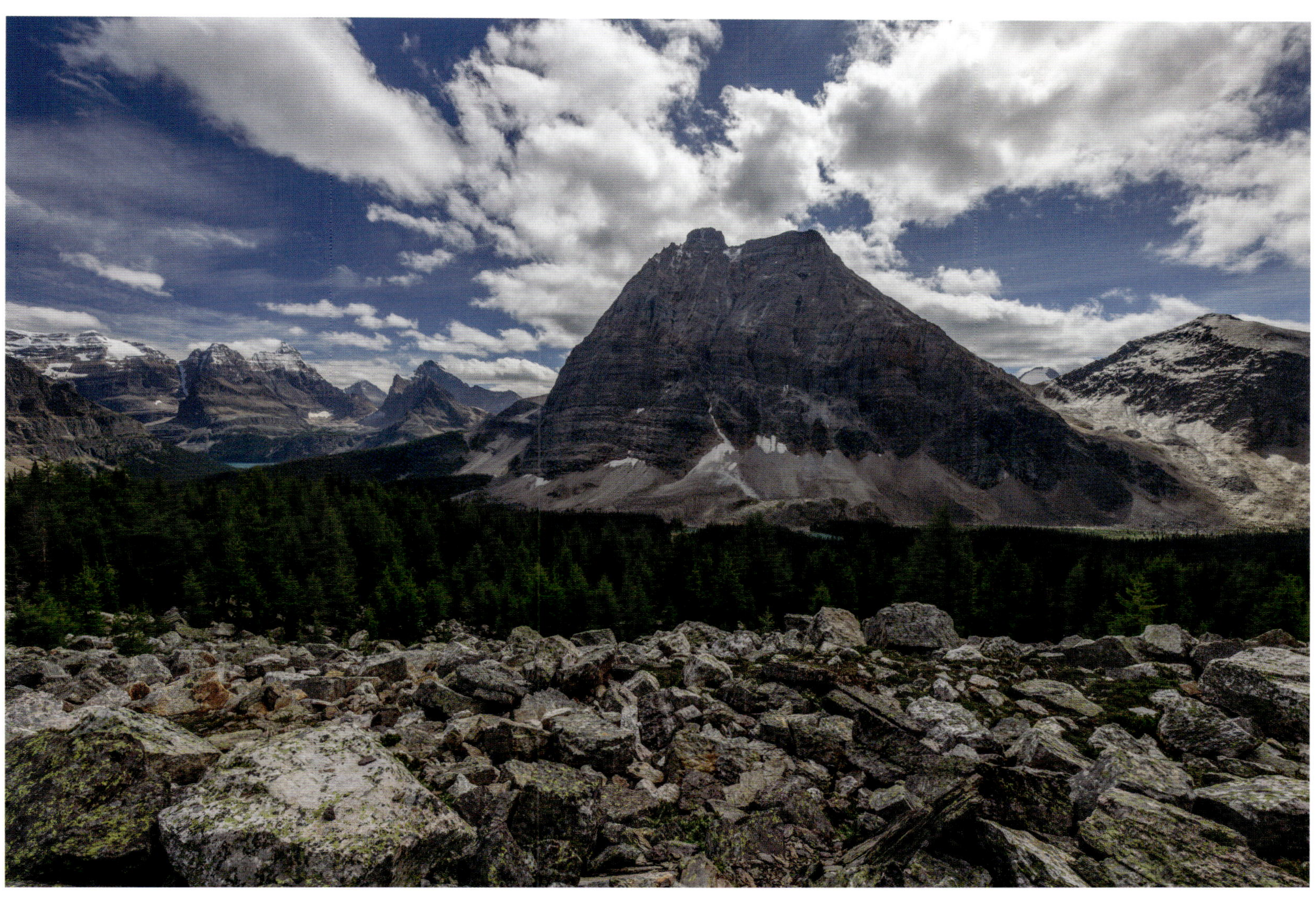

Odaray Rising (2024)
This clear view of Odaray Mountain with Lake O'Hara in the
distance is a reward for the exertion from the 230-m elevation
gain.

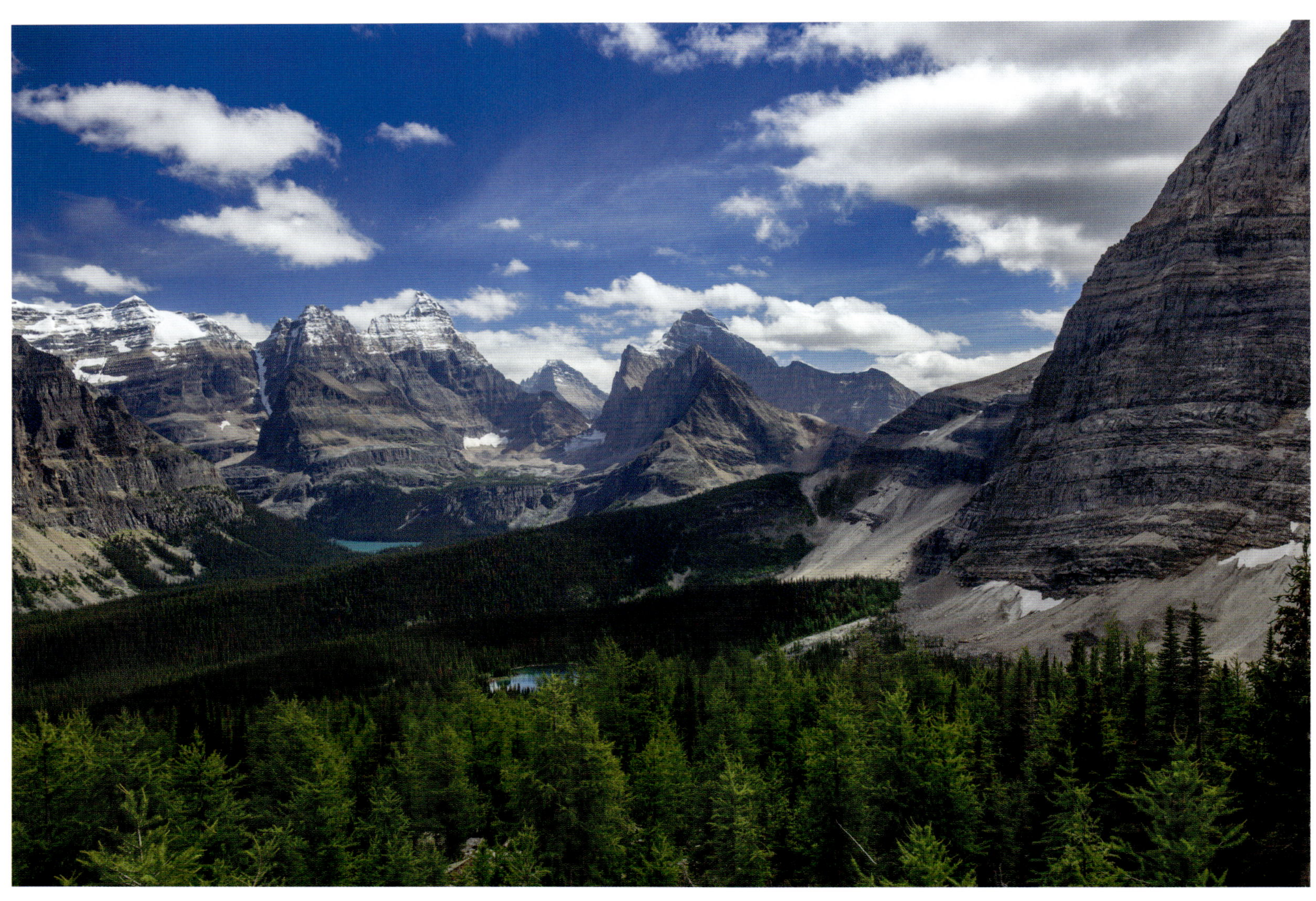

In Full View (2024)
A magnificent view from Cathedral Prospect, with Odaray Mountain in the foreground and Linda Lake and Lake O'Hara in the distance.

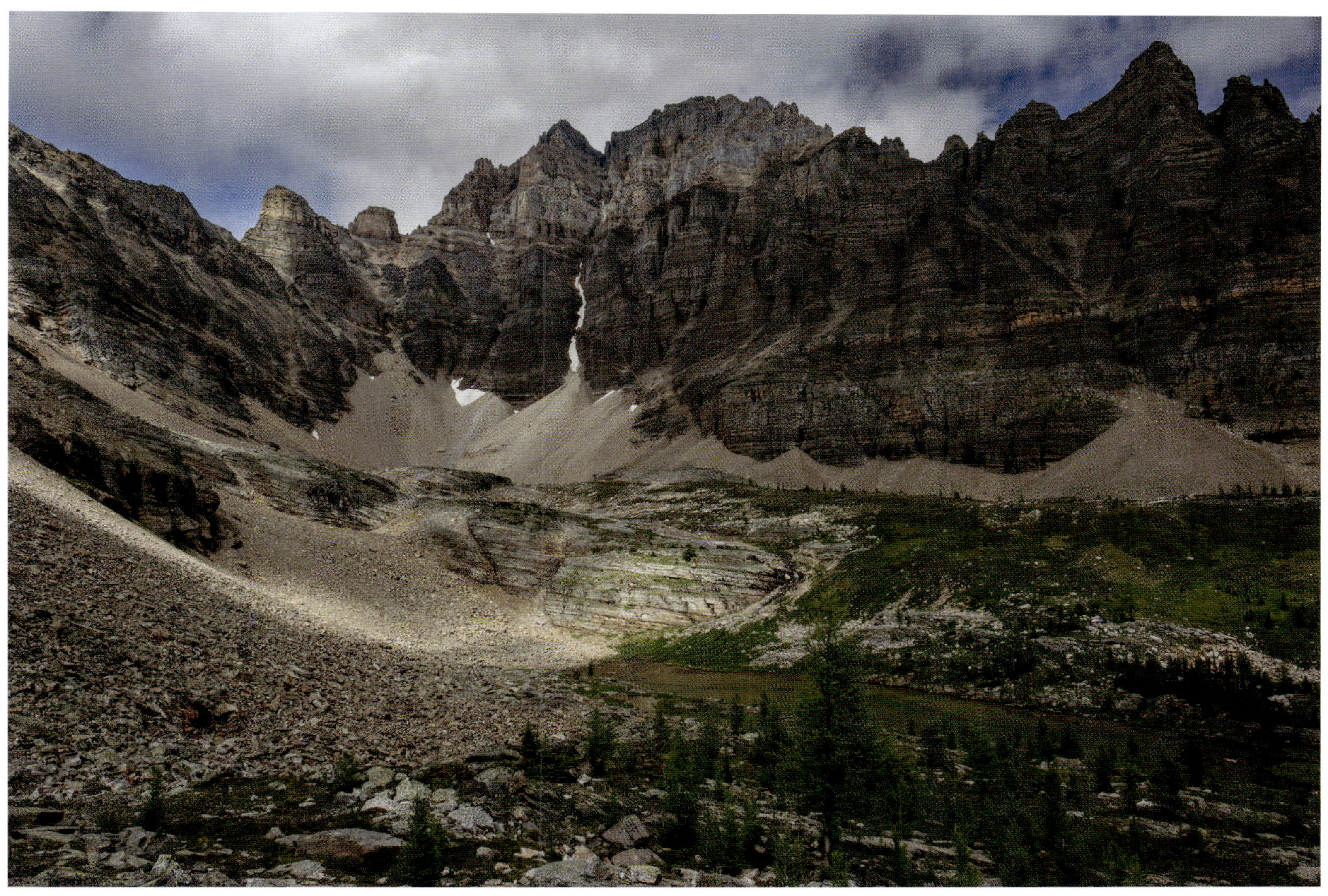

Final Destination (2024)
Nestled at the base of Cathedral Mountain is Monica Lake, the very last destination along the Linda Lake and Cathedral Prospect trail.

Overleaf **Long Way Home** (2024)
Glacier-tossed rocks foreground this expansive view all the way to Lake O'Hara in the distance.

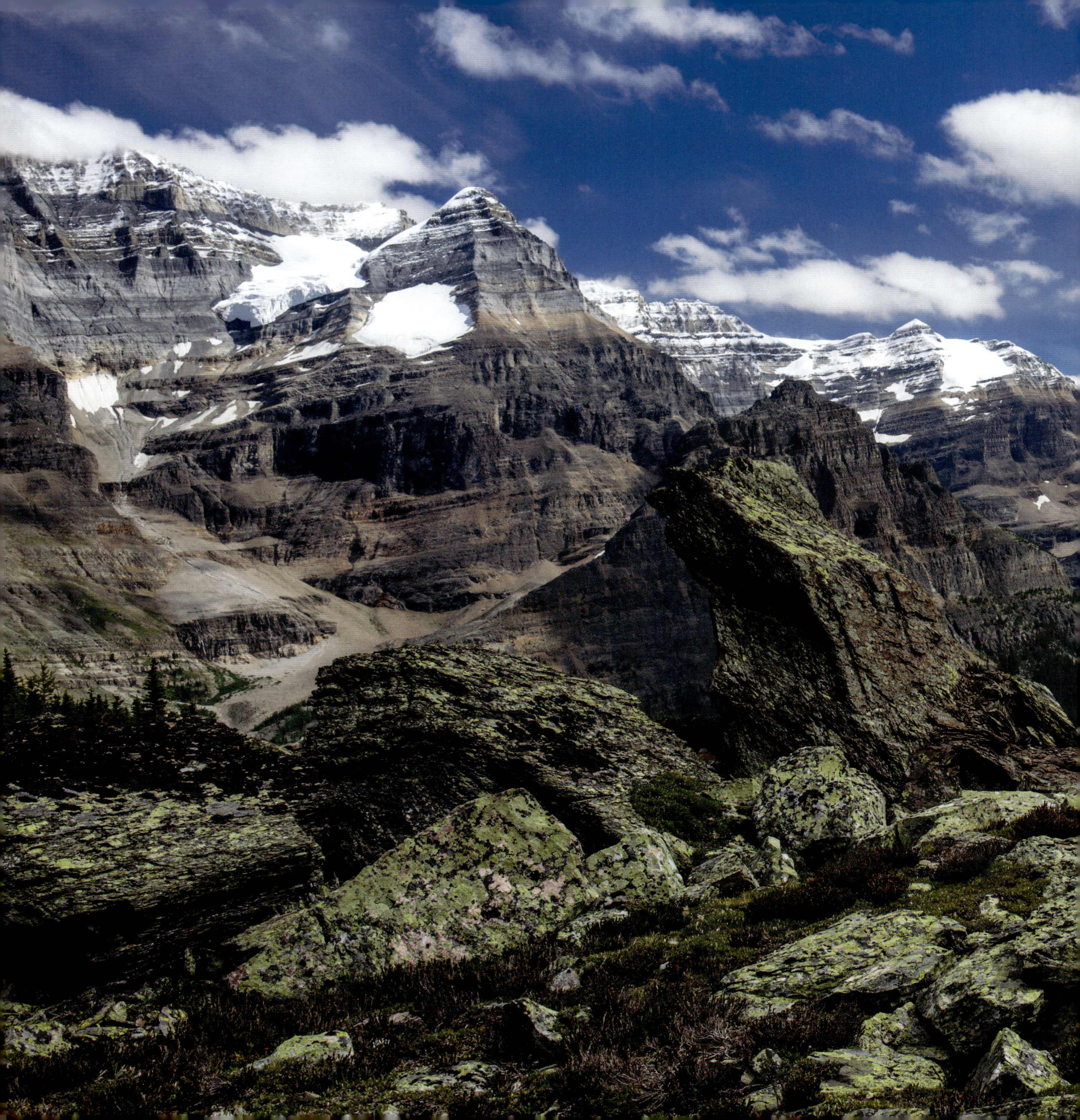

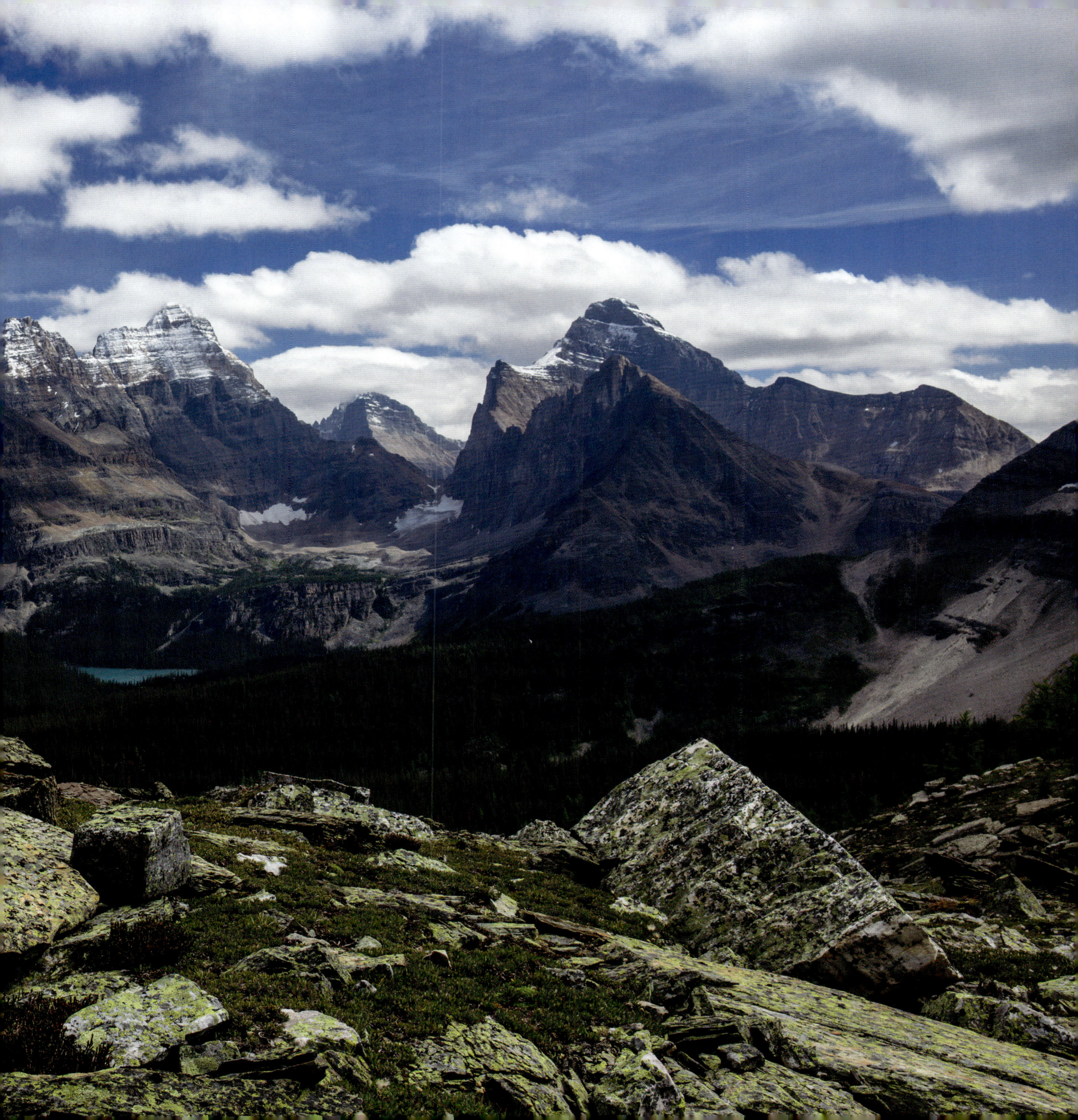

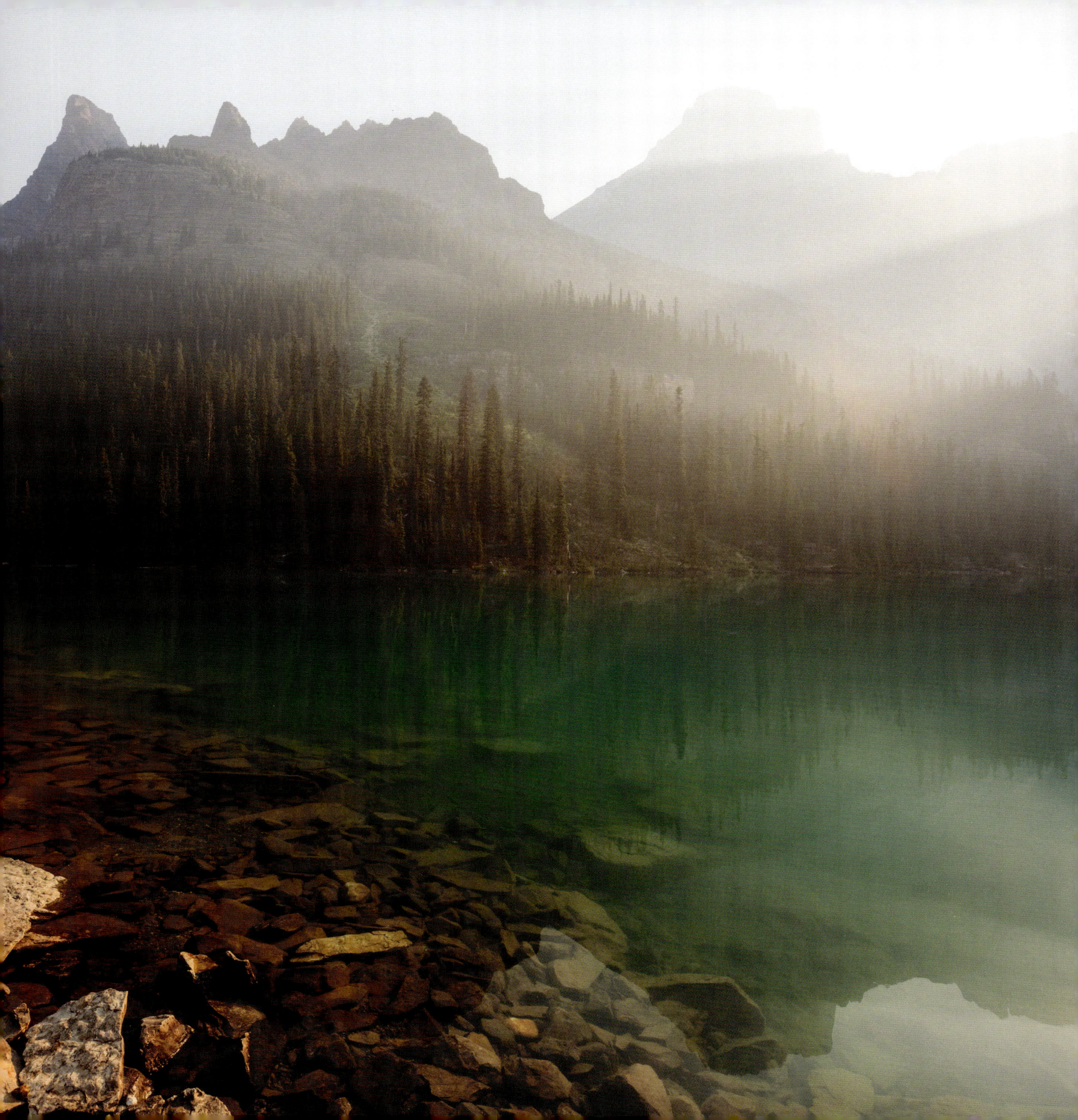

PART SIX

Lake O'Hara Alpine Circuit

Referred to by many as the most impressive day hike in the Canadian Rockies, the Lake O'Hara Alpine Circuit provides a high-elevation route around the Lake O'Hara region, connecting a series of ledges and prospect outlooks into a single spectacular hike. The route is a composite of several distinct sections that can be hiked individually or all in one day. In general terms, the entire hike will take more than six hours, as its 10 km of combined trails traverse 1105 m of vertical elevation gain throughout the route.

This unique Canadian Rockies alpine route is accessible to hikers without the need for climbing gear. However, due to the substantial elevation gains and losses, the proximity to cliffs and ledges, and the need for some route-finding skills, there is a high level of difficulty to this route in comparison to other hikes in the region. There are alpine route markers placed strategically along the way, but these require skill to identify in times of inclement weather. Early and late season hikes are especially challenging due to the frequent snow cover obscuring the trails. Since these routes cross steep gullies and avalanche areas, and are at risk of rockfall, it's always important to check the trail report posted by Parks Canada at Le Relais Day Shelter prior to embarking on the circuit hike.

The route can be hiked in either direction, but I prefer to

Wiwaxy Gap (2021)
It's easiest on the knees to start the Alpine Circuit with the steep, 495-m elevation gain on the trail to Wiwaxy Gap. The smoke of wildfires made visible the morning rays of sun.

start with the steeply inclined "grind" up to Wiwaxy Gap. It's easier on the knees to go up the steep series of switchbacks than the opposite. On the way up there are impressive views over Lake O'Hara, where it feels as though you are in an airplane looking down. In fact, at 2530 m above sea level, Wiwaxy Gap is higher than many small aircraft fly. This will be the highest elevation reached in the alpine circuit until the very last destination of Odaray Grandview Prospect (2535 m), which is 5 m higher.

Many of the mountains in this region are named after prominent surveyors who worked for the CPR. These surveyors often utilized the local place names of their Indigenous guides, incorporating this influence into what would later become the adopted terminology of the Geological Survey of Canada. Wiwaxy Gap is said to come from the Stoney Nakoda (Assiniboine) word meaning "windy" or "gusty." A very fitting name from my personal experience at this mountain pass that funnels the wind between its adjacent mountain peaks.

From the pinnacle of Wiwaxy Gap, the alpine circuit next proceeds along the Huber Ledges to Lake Oesa, in the only section of this circuit that has an elevation loss (of 260 m). The views of Lake O'Hara are expansive, with all four alpine lakes in the hanging valley visible. Huber Ledges and Mount Huber (3368 m) are named after the Swiss alpinist Emil Huber, who worked with the CPR.

The alpine circuit briefly pauses at the trail to Lake Oesa, an ideal location to take a rest and nutritional break before starting up the scree slopes of Yukness Mountain (2847 m) on Yukness Ledges Alpine Route. Although there is only 50 m of elevation gain on this route winding around the base of Yukness Mountain to Hungabee Lake on the Opabin Plateau, the route has other challenges. The trail passes among rock slabs and boulders that make it easy to get off track, and close attention needs to be paid to the sporadic alpine trail markers. However, once onto the open Yukness Ledge, there are spellbinding views across Lake O'Hara to Odaray Mountain and Duchesnay Basin. These open views mean this portion of the route is also very exposed to frequent changes in the weather. "Yukness" is another Stoney Nakoda (Assiniboine) word translating to "sharp" or "pointed," in reference to the shape of Yukness Mountain.

Once on the Opabin Plateau, the route follows tranquil paths alongside small rivers, lakes, and ponds until West Opabin Trail links up with All Soul's Alpine Route. This route traverses the lower scree of Mount Schäffer as it gains 245 m of elevation on its way to All Soul's Prospect (2435 m), where the hiker is treated to panoramic views of Lake O'Hara. The source of this route's name is not clearly documented, but it is thought to reference All Souls College at Oxford University. Several prominent British climbers and surveyors of the Canadian mountains were educated there. The name is thought to be affiliated with A.O. Wheeler, who performed surveys in this region between 1903 and 1911 for the Interprovincial Boundary Commission. From the viewpoint of All Soul's Prospect, the route leads down to Schäffer Lake to meet up with the final segment of Lake O'Hara Alpine Circuit.

The final segment of the alpine circuit to Odaray Grandview Prospect begins in McArthur Pass. This area is a wildlife corridor with seasonal restrictions. It's essential to check the sign-in book at McArthur Pass to assess whether you can proceed. Odaray Highline Trail wanders through an alpine meadow before heading into the forest and ending at the base of Odaray Mountain, where the final portion of the circuit, Odaray Grandview Prospect Route, begins. "Odaray" is another word derived from the Stoney Nakoda (Assiniboine) language and is thought to mean "many waterfalls" in reference to the numerous falls streaming down the steep mountain face. More recent linguistic studies suggest "odaray" is the Stoney word for "cone." Either translation is appropriate, as Odaray's cone shape leads to numerous waterfalls. The 315-m elevation gain from McArthur Pass to Odaray Grandview Prospect reaches the highest point along Lake O'Hara Alpine Circuit. The vantage point from this prospect provides a 270-degree view from where almost all of the Lake O'Hara region's lakes are visible. A "grand view" indeed!

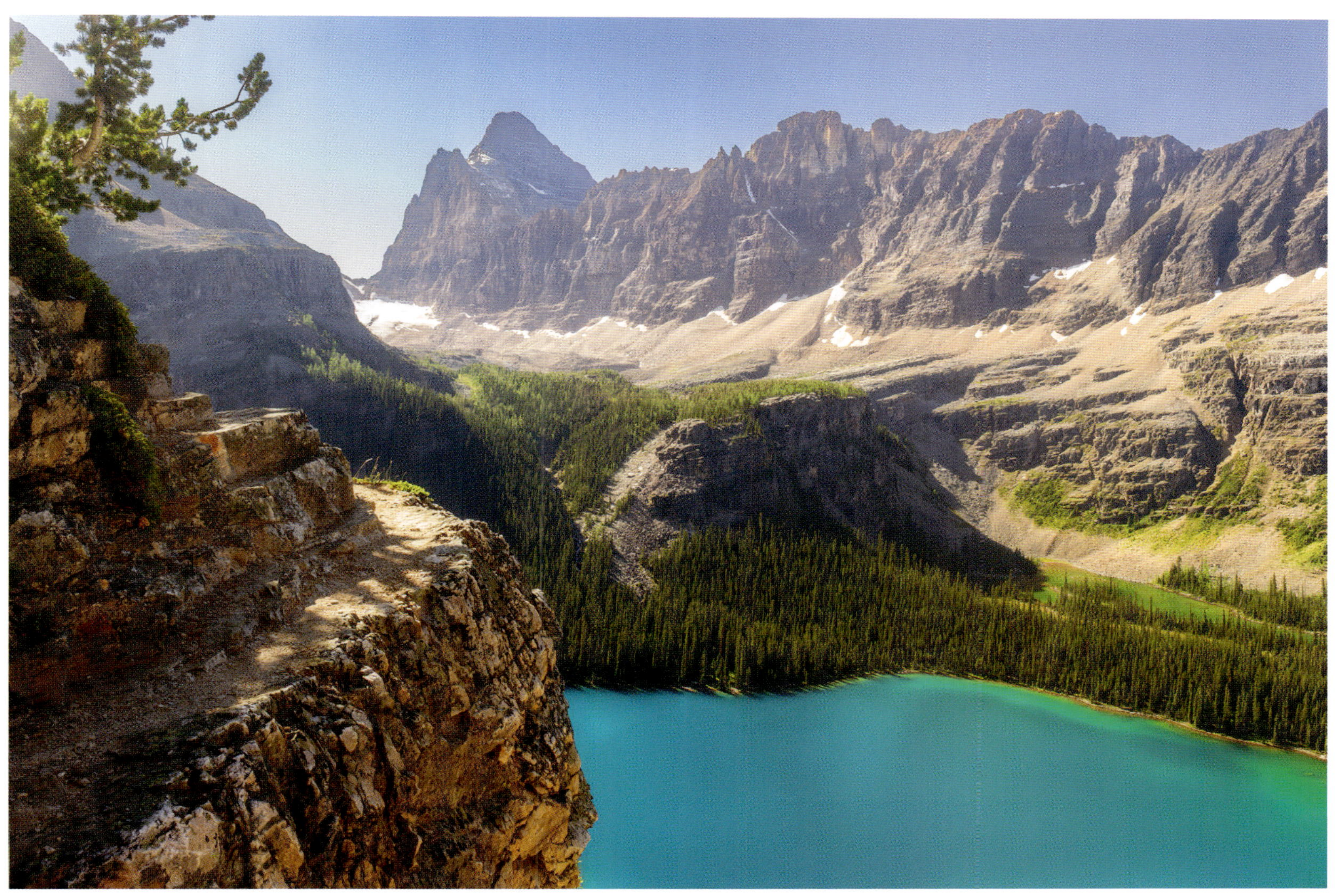

Lookout Below (2010)
The route up to Wiwaxy Gap rewards hikers with dramatic
views of Lake O'Hara below.

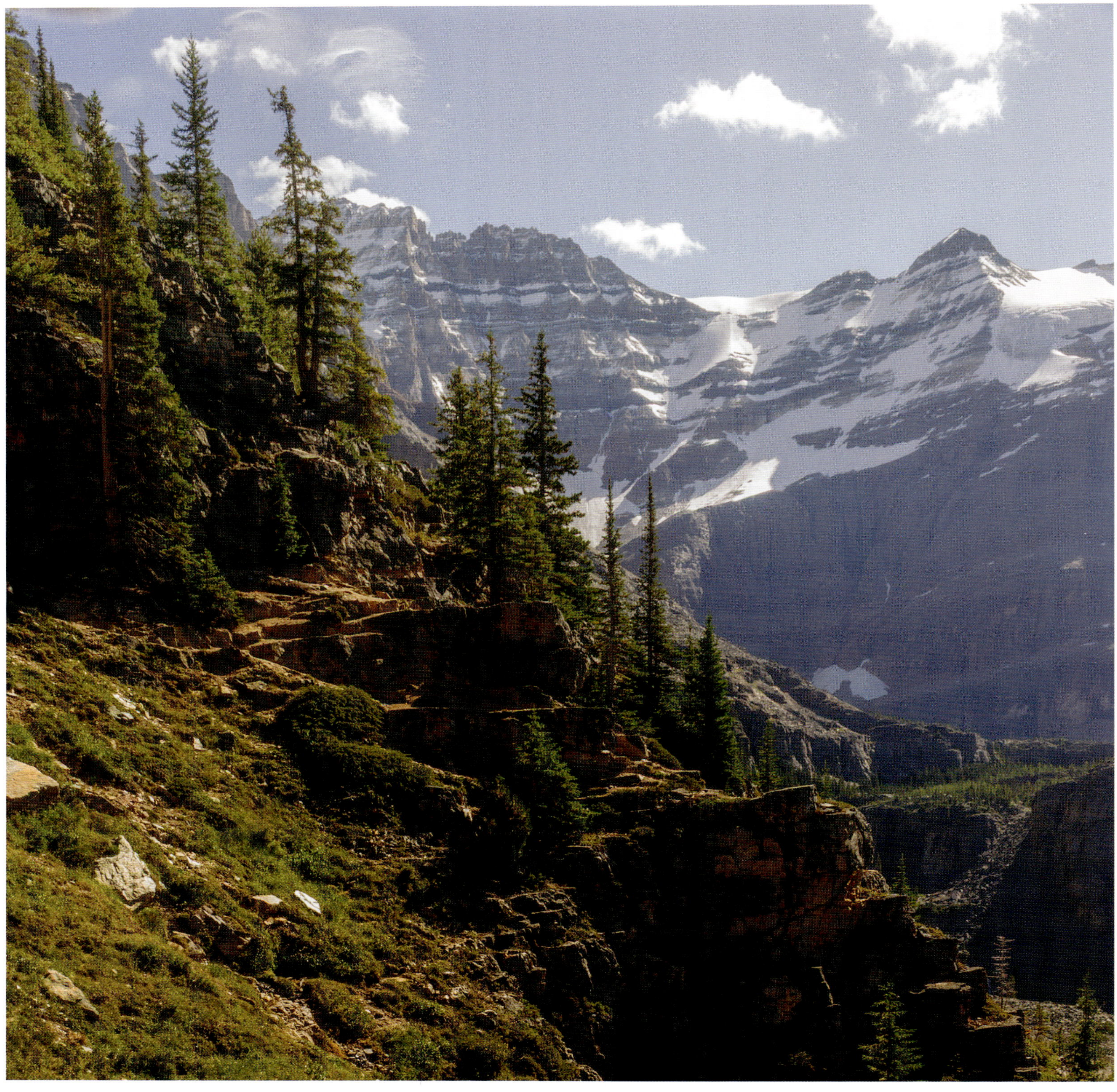

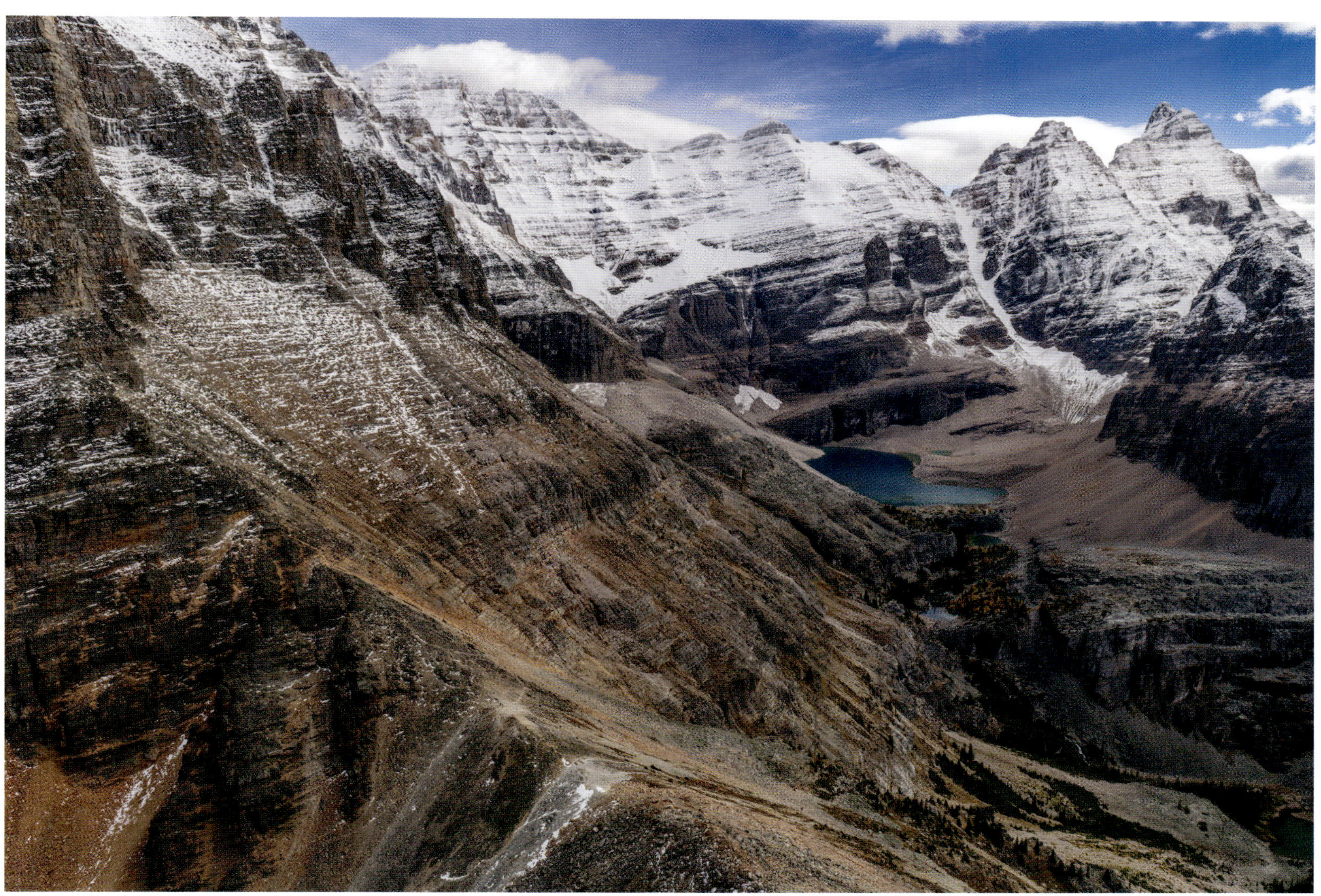

Switchback (2010)
Numerous switchbacks ease the strain from the steep elevation gain along the hike up to Wiwaxy Gap.

Huber Ledges (2021)
A view of the Huber Ledges Alpine Route as seen from a climb up Wiwaxy Peaks. The 1.7-km route from Wiwaxy Gap to Lake Oesa loses 260 m of elevation.

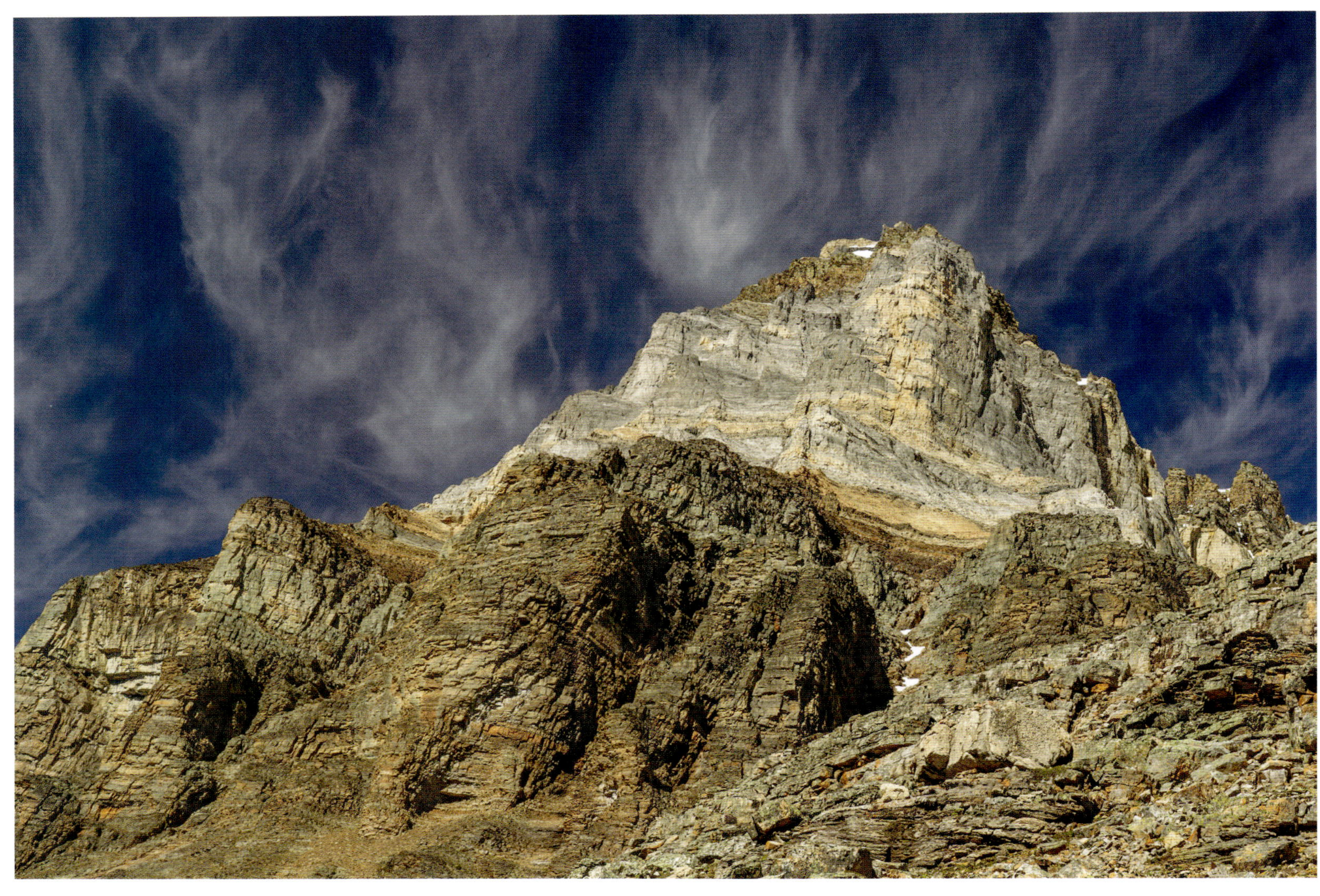

Cloud Makers (2010)
The rugged peaks of Mount Huber rise high into the sky above
the trail, creating their own effects on the forming clouds.

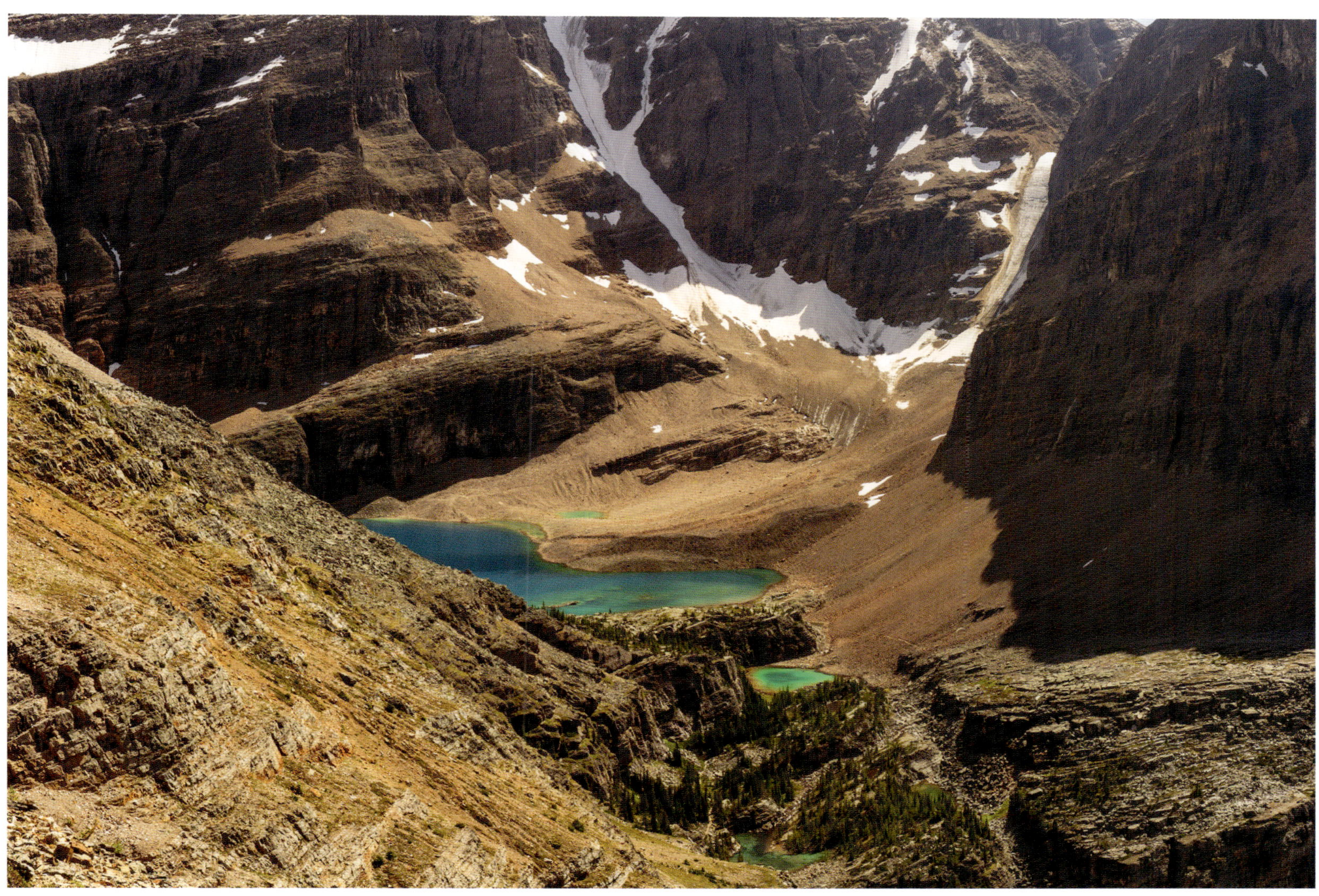

Oesa Vista (2010)
Lake Oesa, Lefroy Lake, and Victoria Lake are all visible as the
hiker approaches from Wiwaxy Gap along the Huber Ledges
Alpine Route.

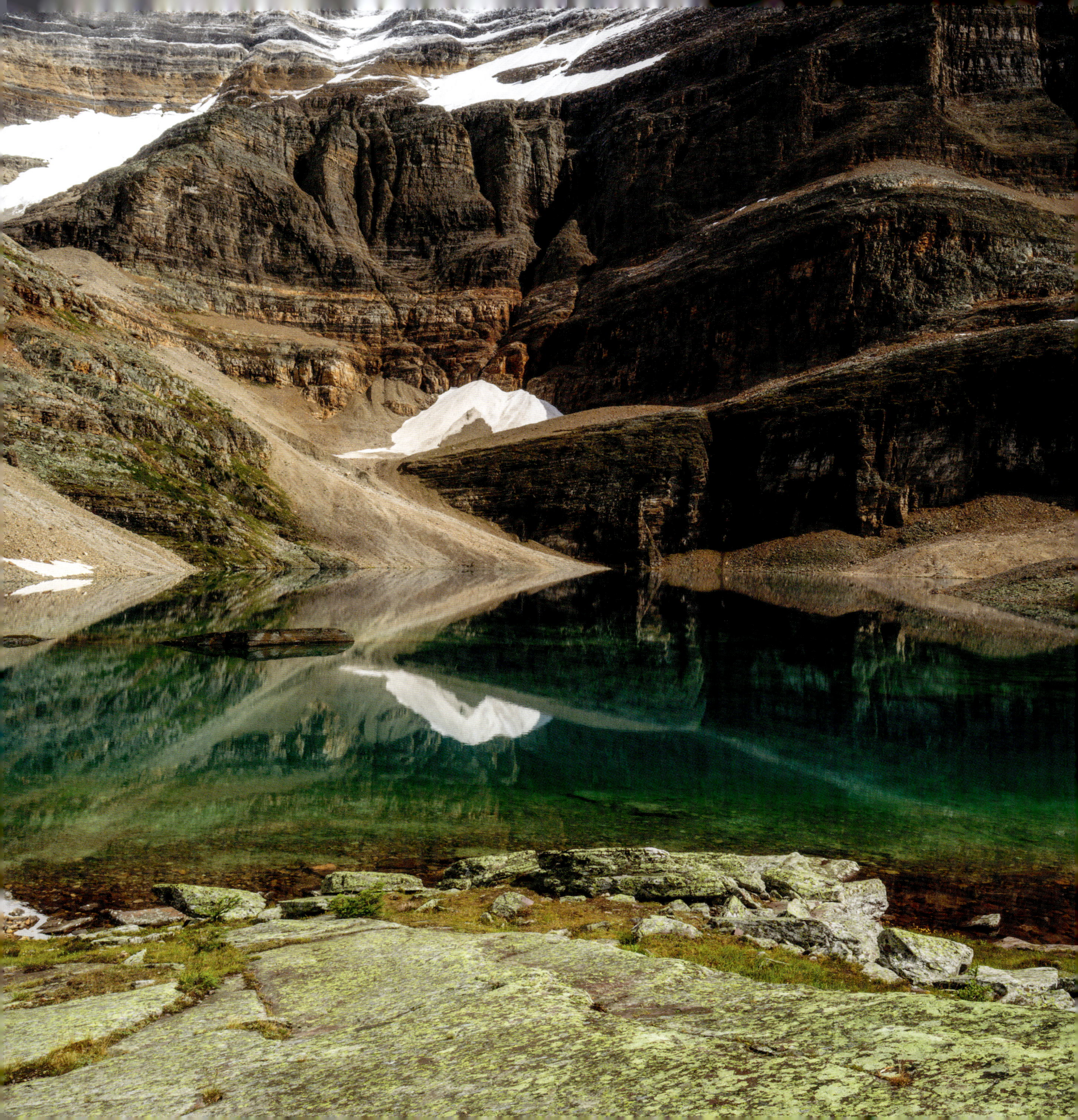

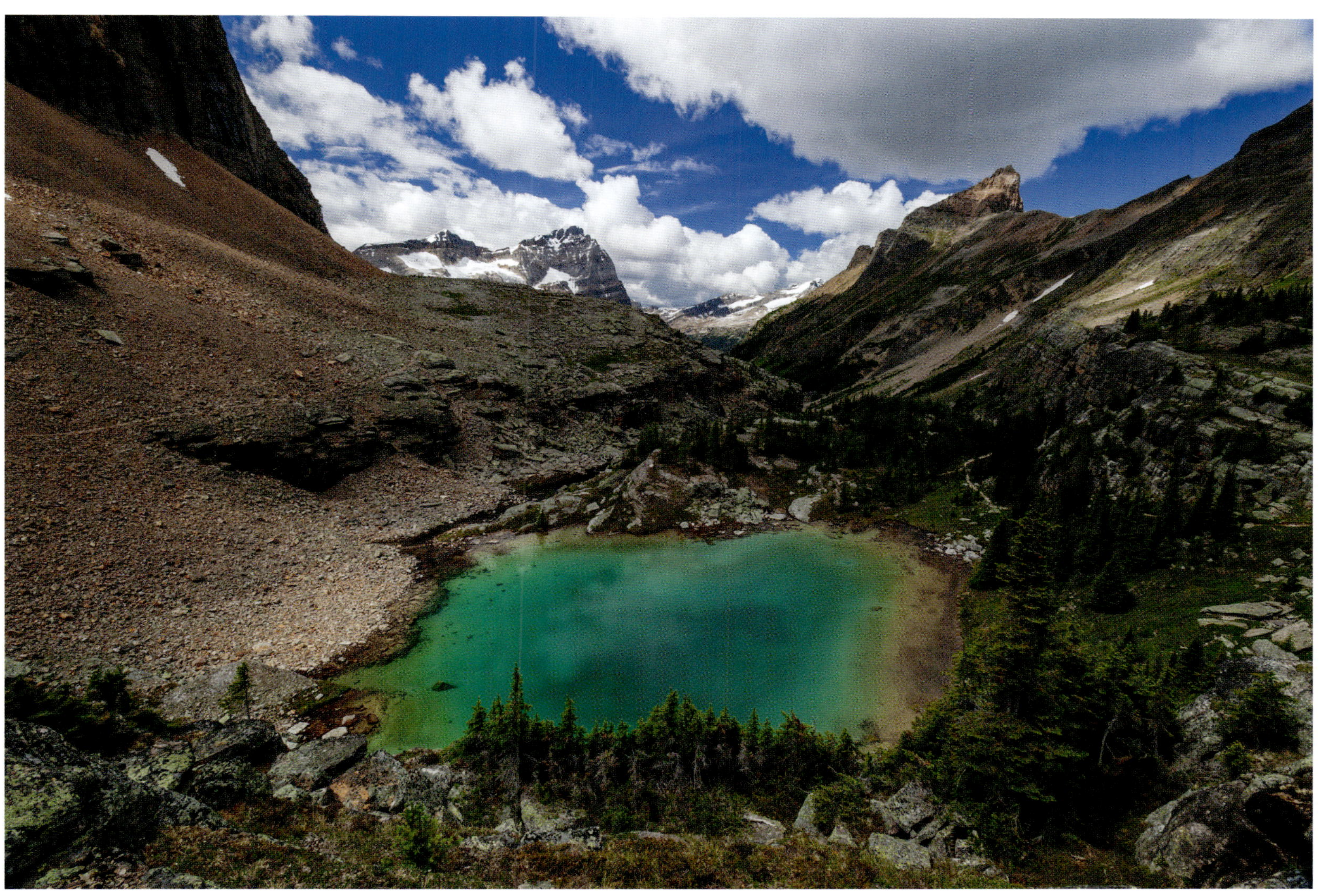

Yukness Ledges (2007)
The Lake O'Hara Alpine Circuit starts up again along the left side of this image as it winds past Lefroy Lake.

Beyond Description (2014)
Beautiful beyond measure, Lake Oesa offers a perfect lunch stop at the bottom of the Huber Ledges Alpine Route before beginning the climb toward the Yukness Mountain ledges.

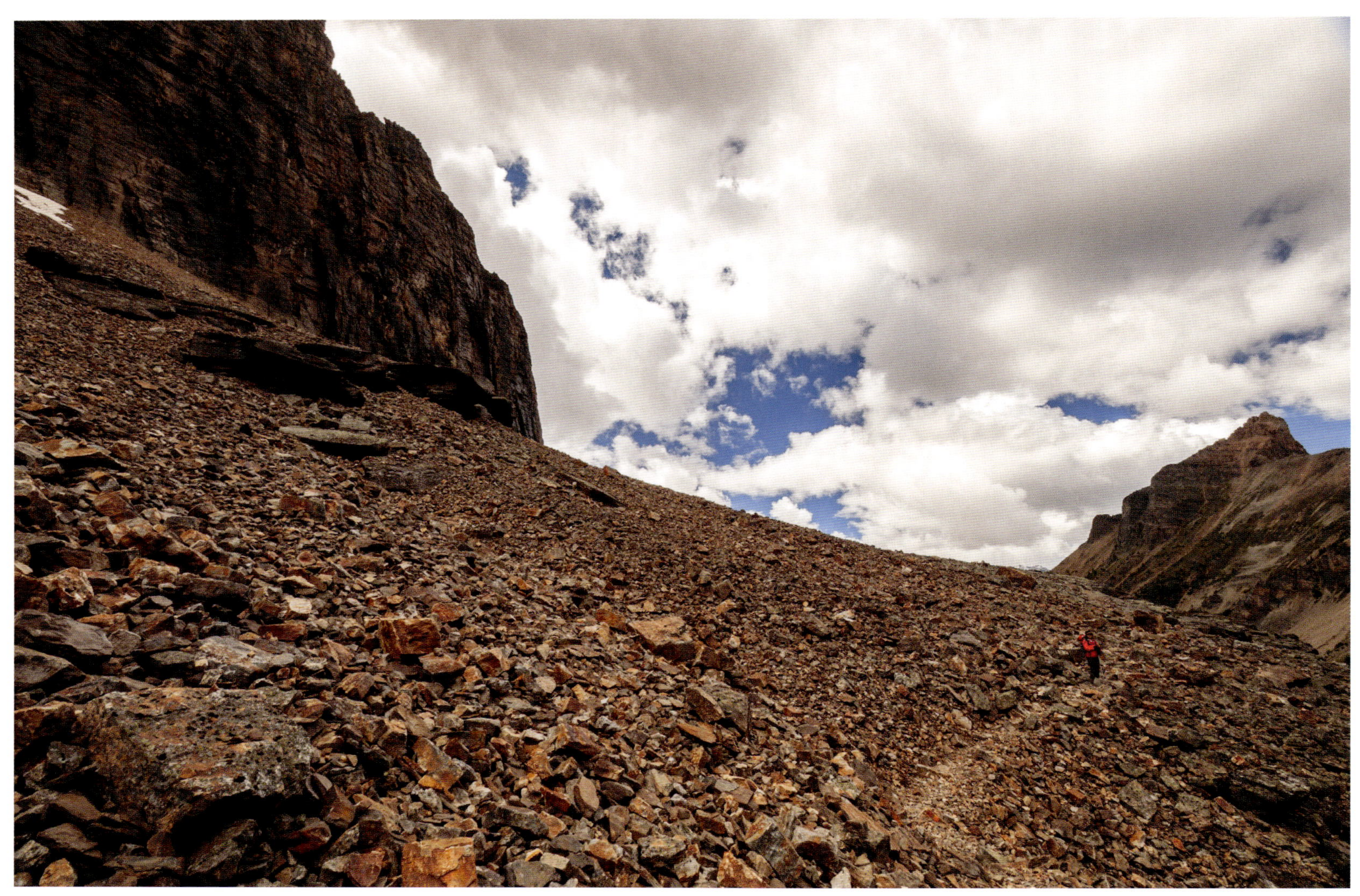

Yukness Scree (2007)
There is only a 50-m gain in elevation along this 1.5-hour hike connecting Lake Oesa to Hungabee Lake on the Opabin Plateau. A hiker (my spouse Rossana Arcega) adds scale to the beginning of this journey across the scree of Yukness Mountain.

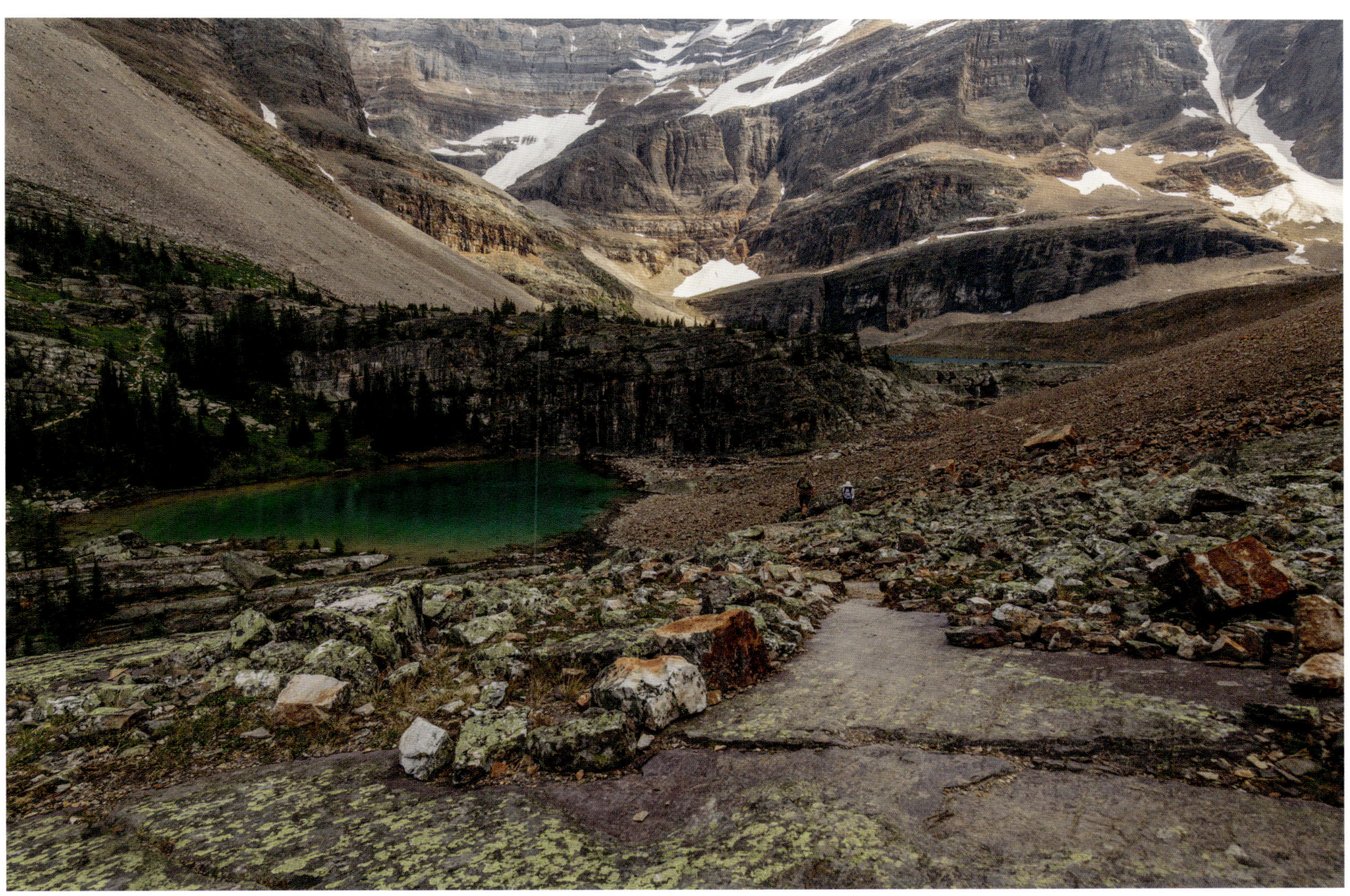

Breadth (2021)
The trail progresses from the lower scree slopes of Yukness
Mountain, crossing a series of large rock slabs before becoming punctuated by broken boulders. Hikers (Hannah Arcega
and Rob Anderson) add to a landscape clever at disguising its
scope.

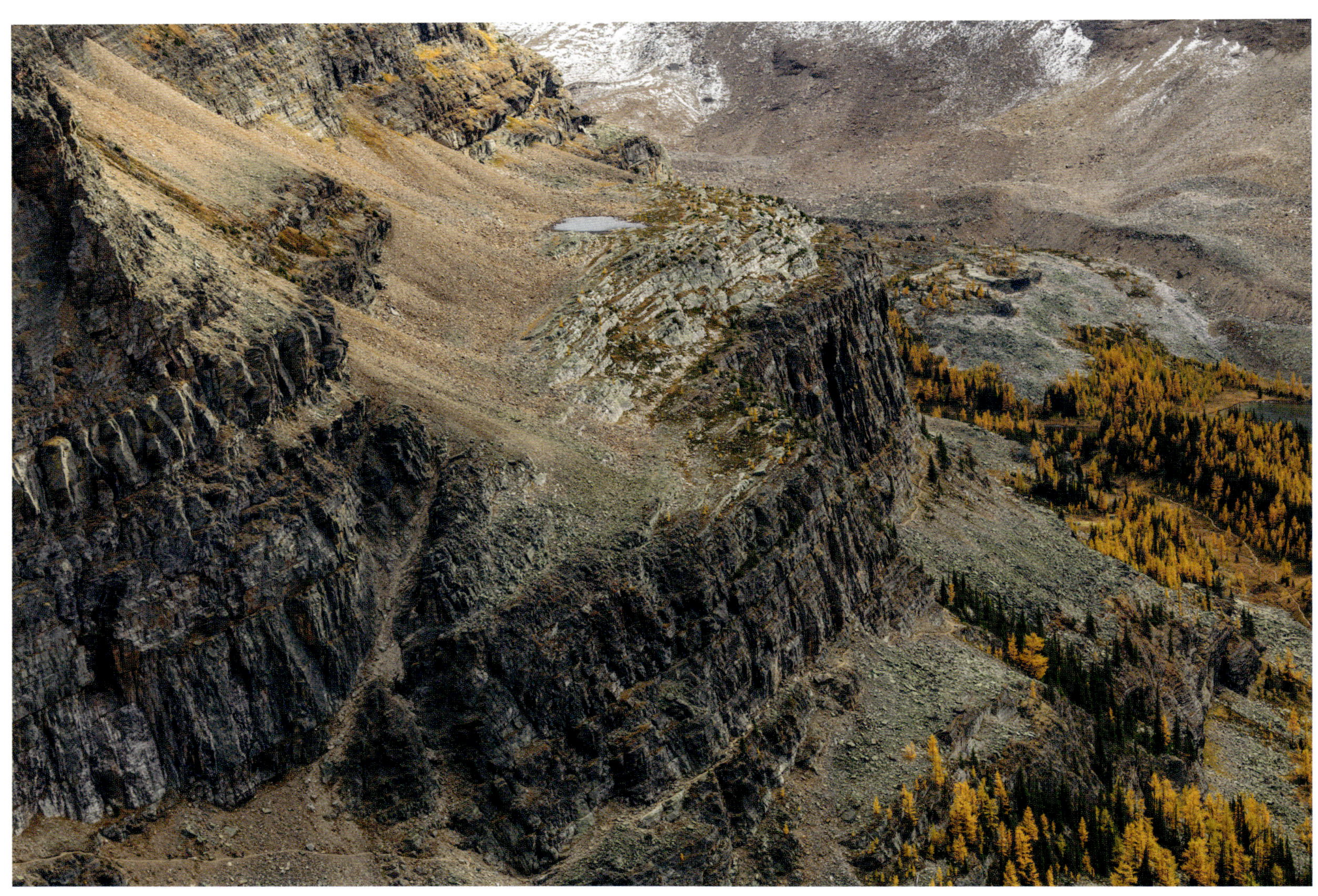

Sleeping Poet's Pool (2021)
The view from a mountain climb up Wiwaxy Peaks overlooks
a little body of water called Sleeping Poet's Pool. It's perched
high above Yukness Ledges Alpine Route, which winds its way
along the base of the cliffs.

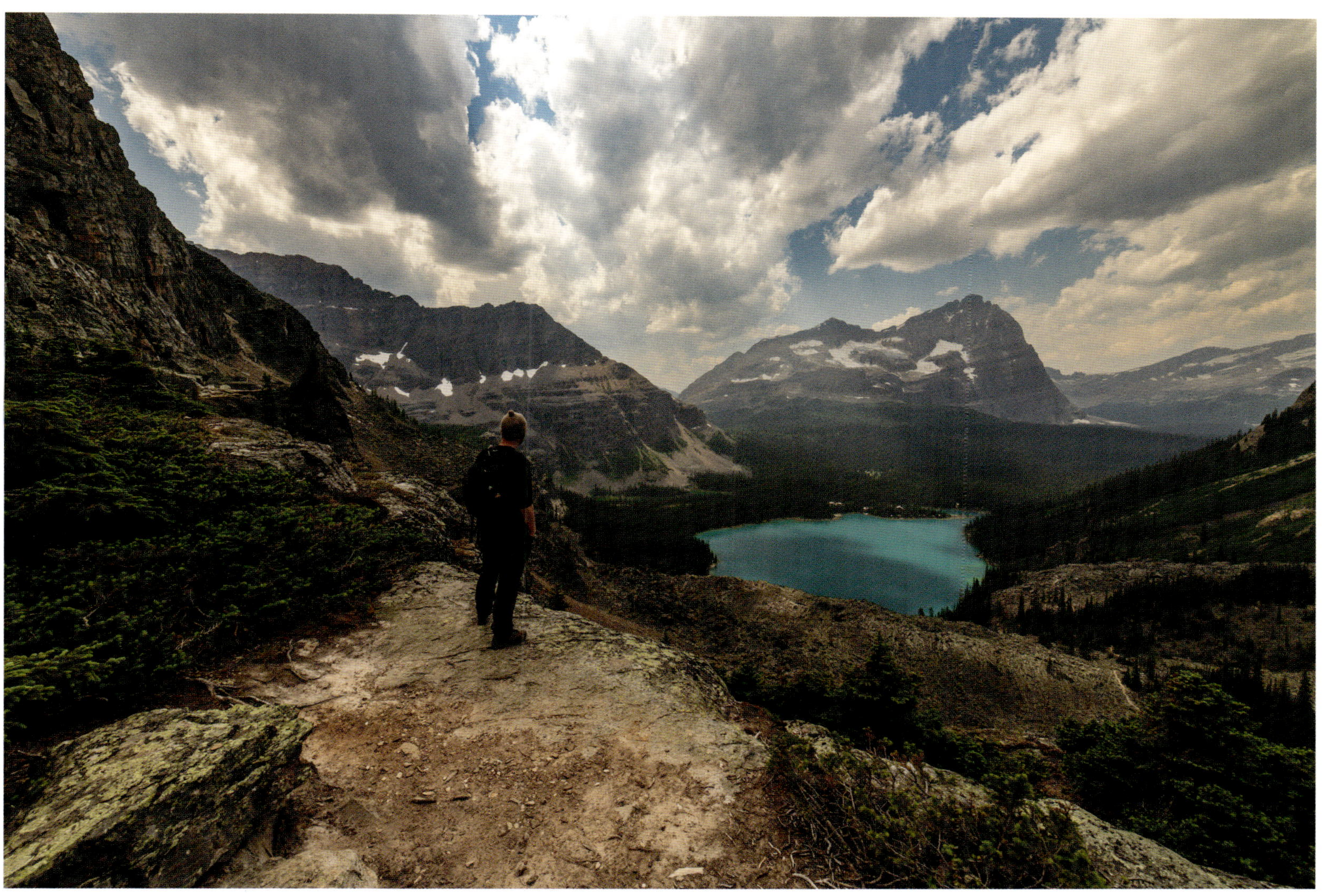

Stunning View (2021)
A hiker (Timothy Albinati) takes in the stunning view from Yukness Ledges Alpine Route overlooking Lake O'Hara Lodge and
its lakeshore cabins on the distant shoreline.

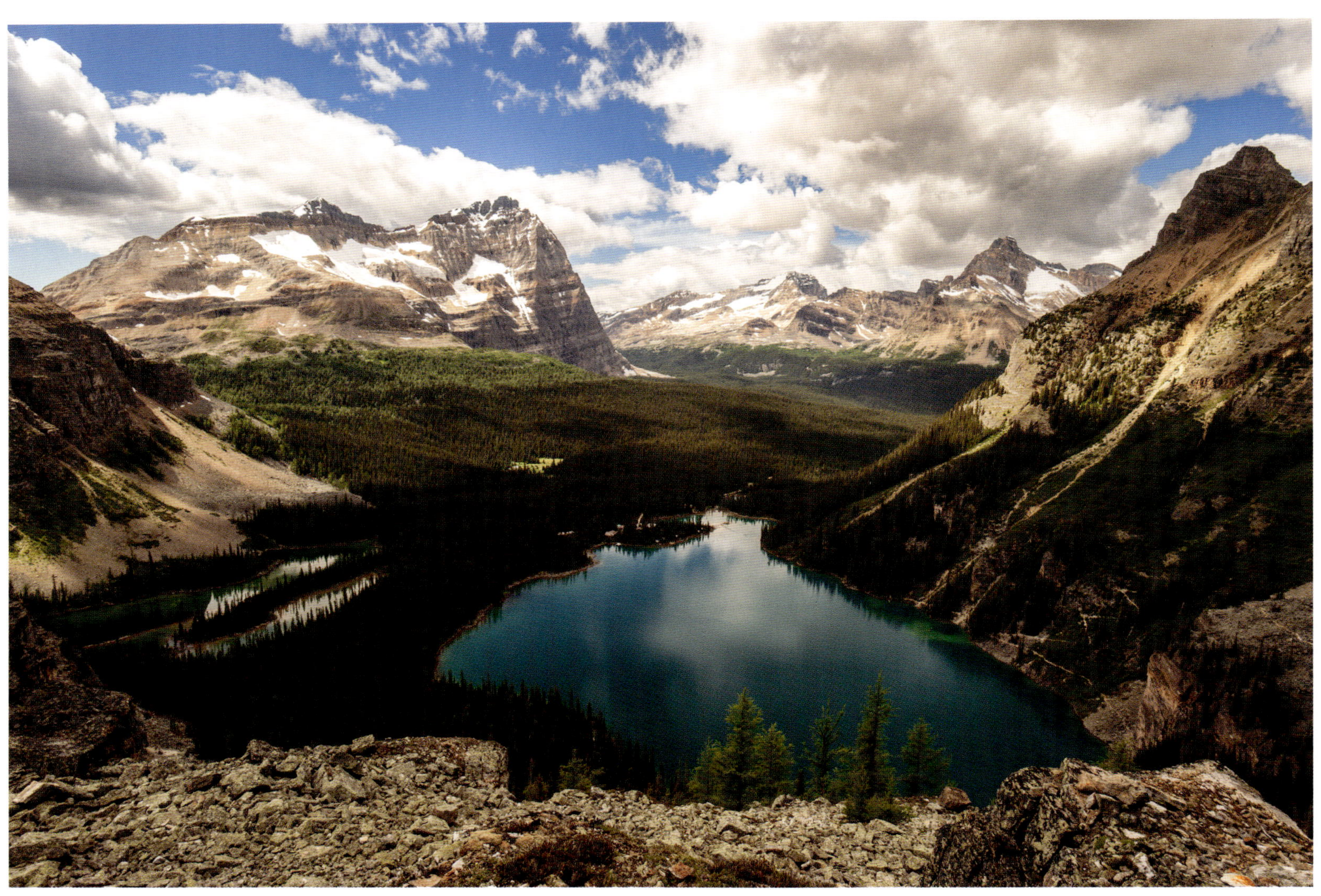

Alpine Glory (2007)
On a clear day the turquoise Lake O'Hara is in full view with the surrounding Odaray Mountain, Cathedral Mountain, and Wiwaxy Peaks in all their splendour.

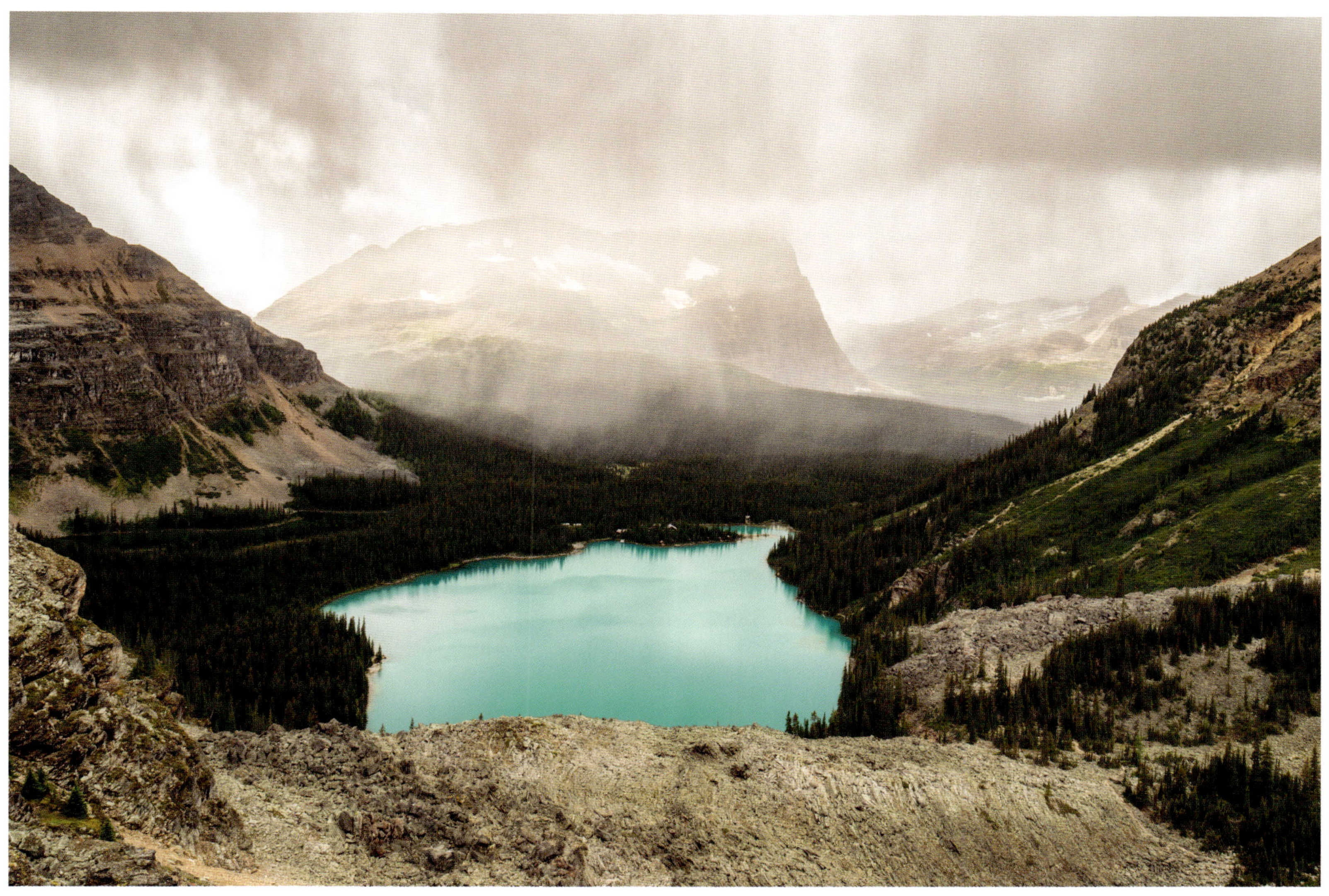

Changes (2014)
Hikers on the Lake O'Hara Alpine Circuit need to be prepared for all types of weather, dressing in layers and ready for changes such as this fast-moving front with rain.

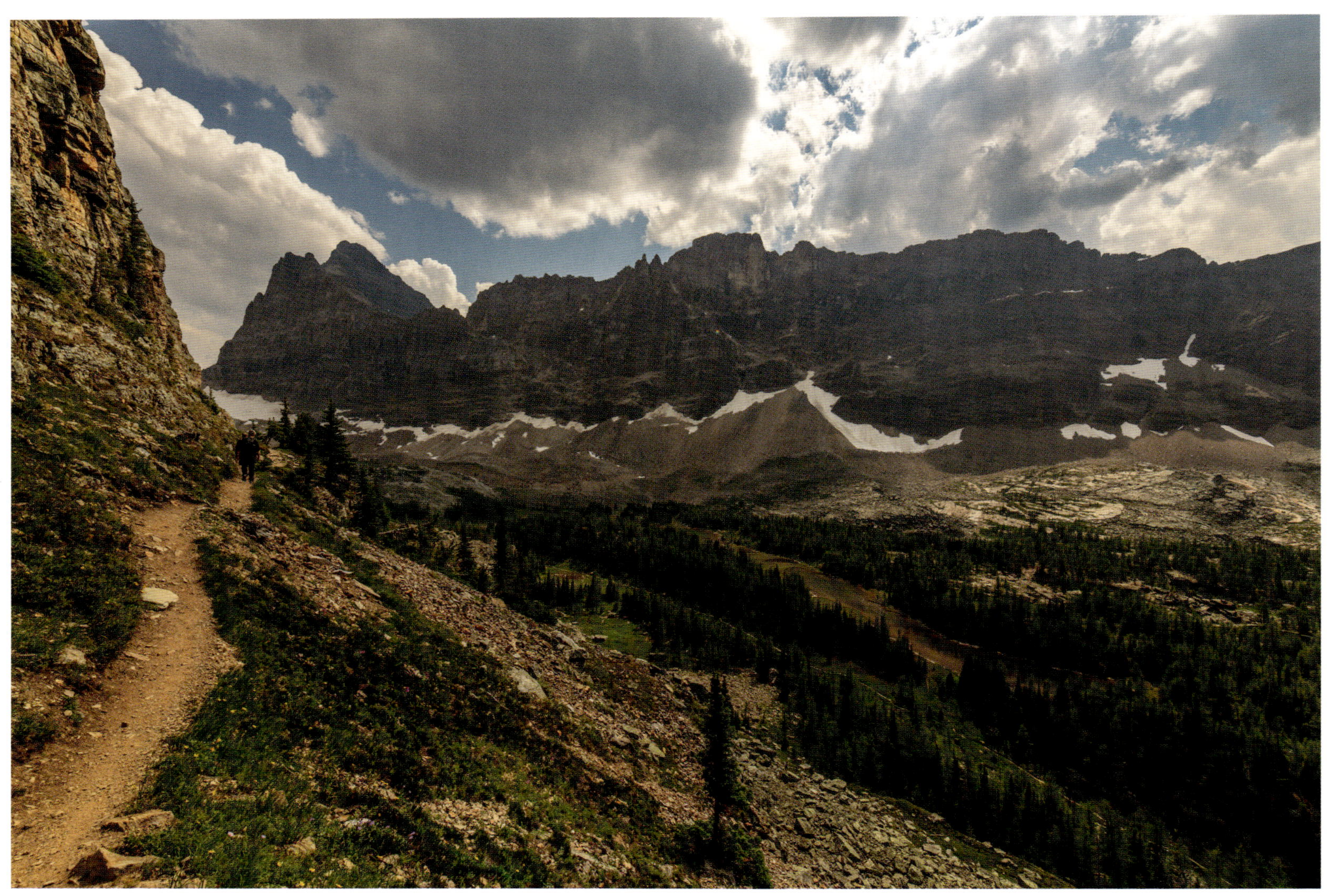

Opabin Insight (2021)
On the way toward Hungabee Lake, Opabin Plateau with its many lakes and trails comes into view. On the far side, All Soul's Prospect Alpine Route crosses the scree of Schäffer Ridge and Mount Schäffer.

Hungabee Lake Crossing (2021)
Yukness Ledges Alpine Route ends at Hungabee Lake, blending into East Opabin Trail. The hiker crosses Opabin Plateau to begin a journey toward All Soul's Prospect Alpine Route.

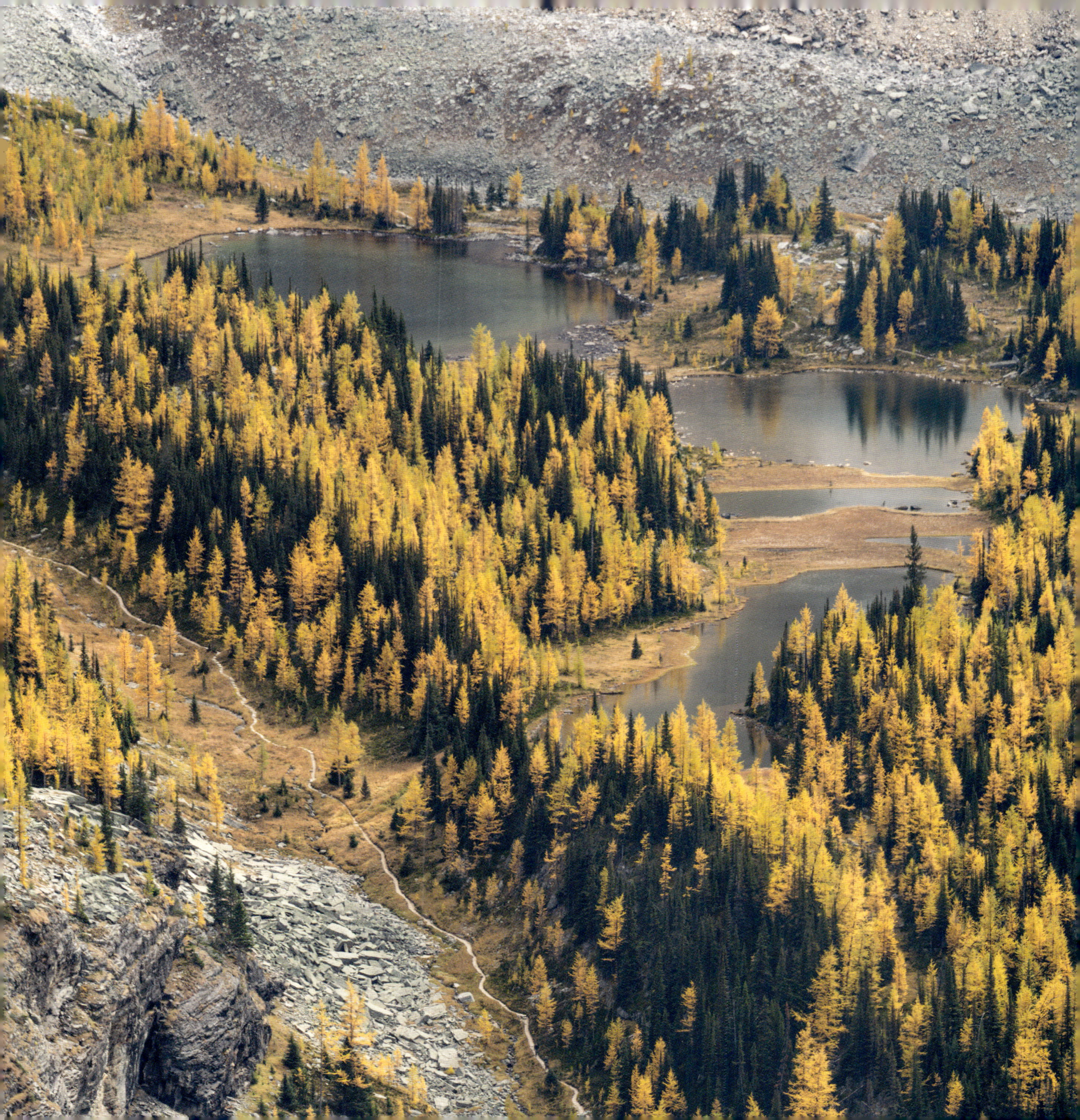

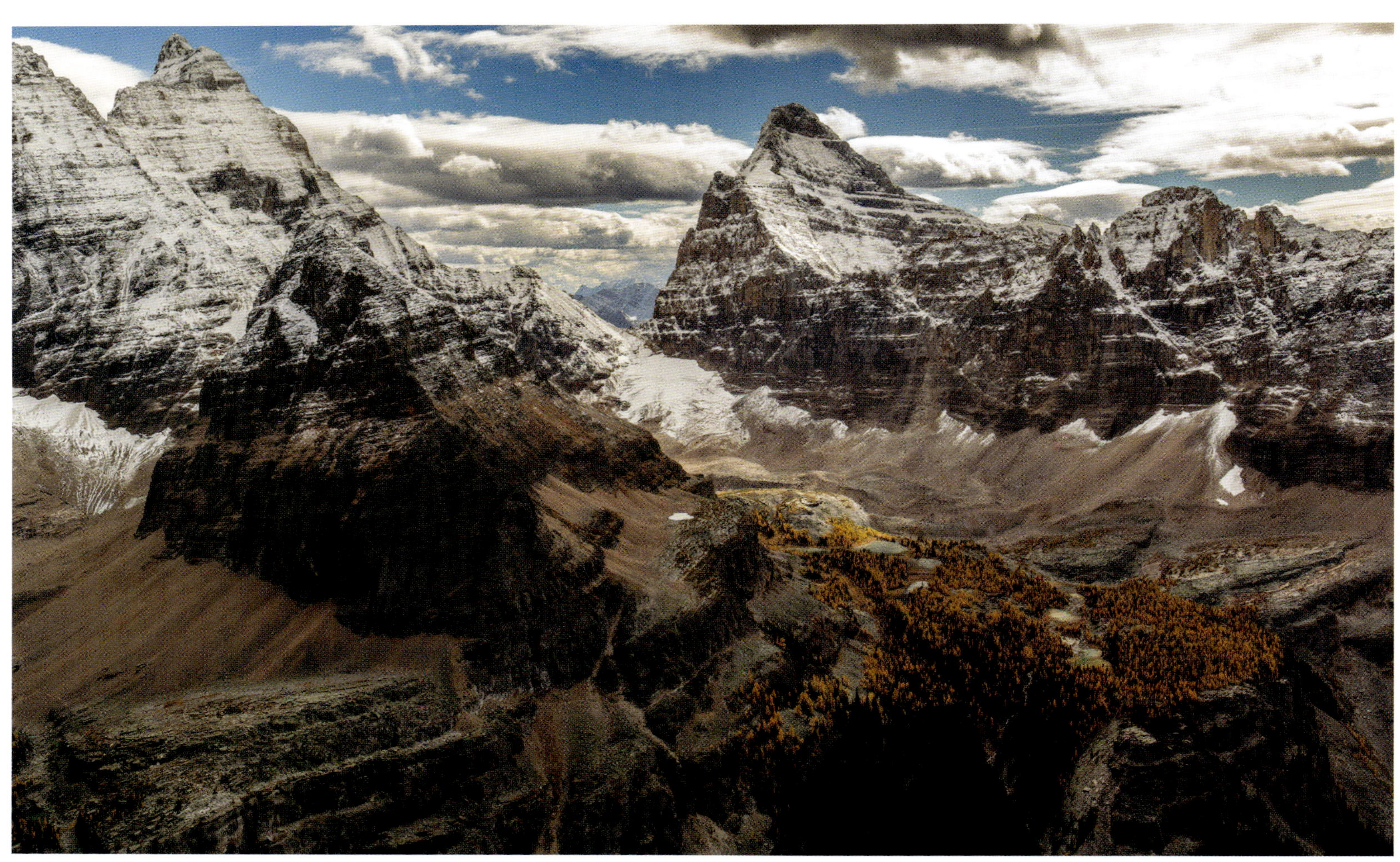

Overview (2021)
The entirety of Yukness Ledges Alpine Route from its origin
near Lake Oesa to its end near Hungabee Lake on Opabin
Plateau comes into view from the high perch of Wiwaxy Peaks.
All Soul's Prospect Alpine Route starts up along the scree of
Schäffer Ridge.

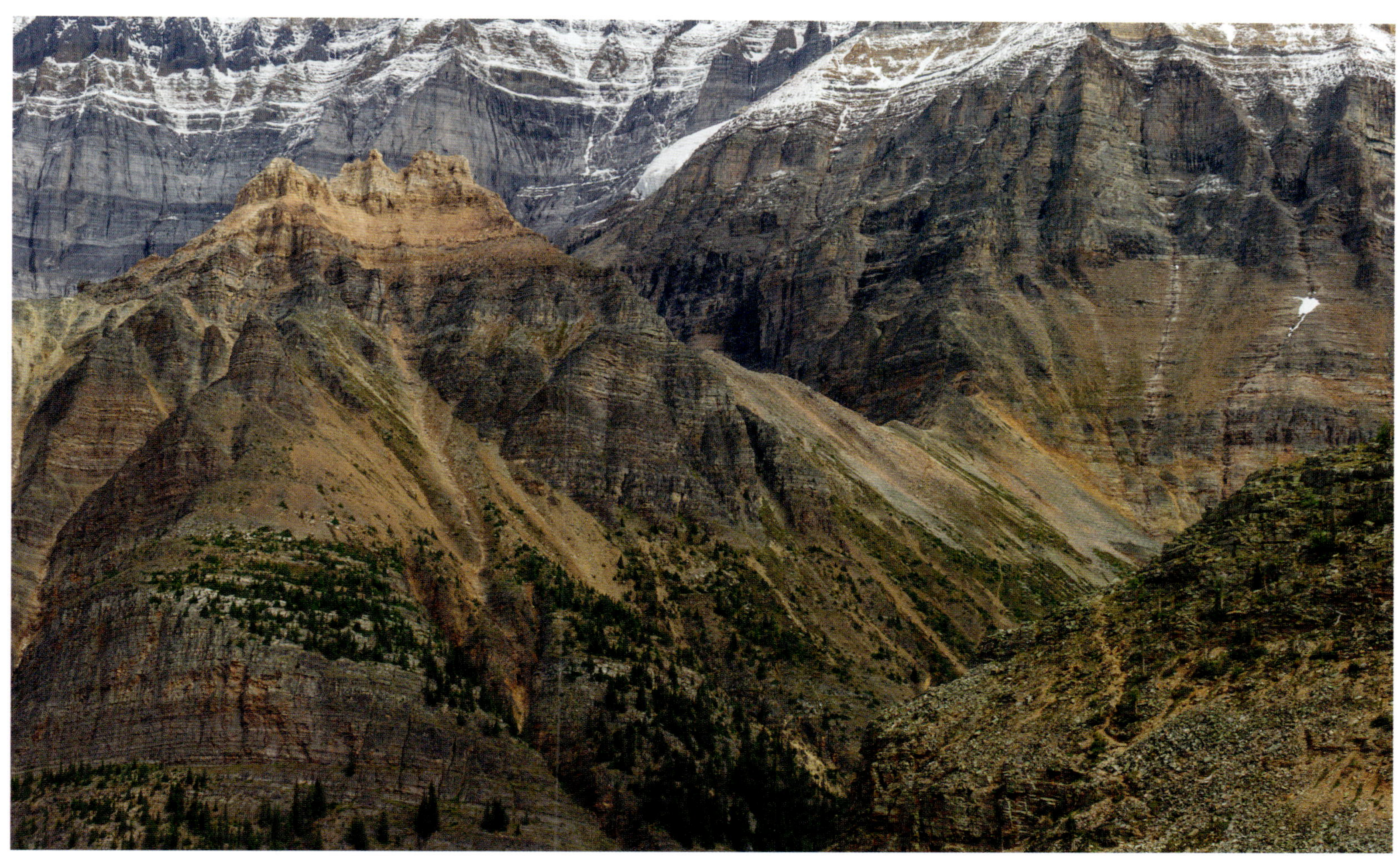

Circuit View (2010)
All Soul's Prospect is in the foreground overlooking Wiwaxy
Peaks and Huber Ledges Alpine Route.

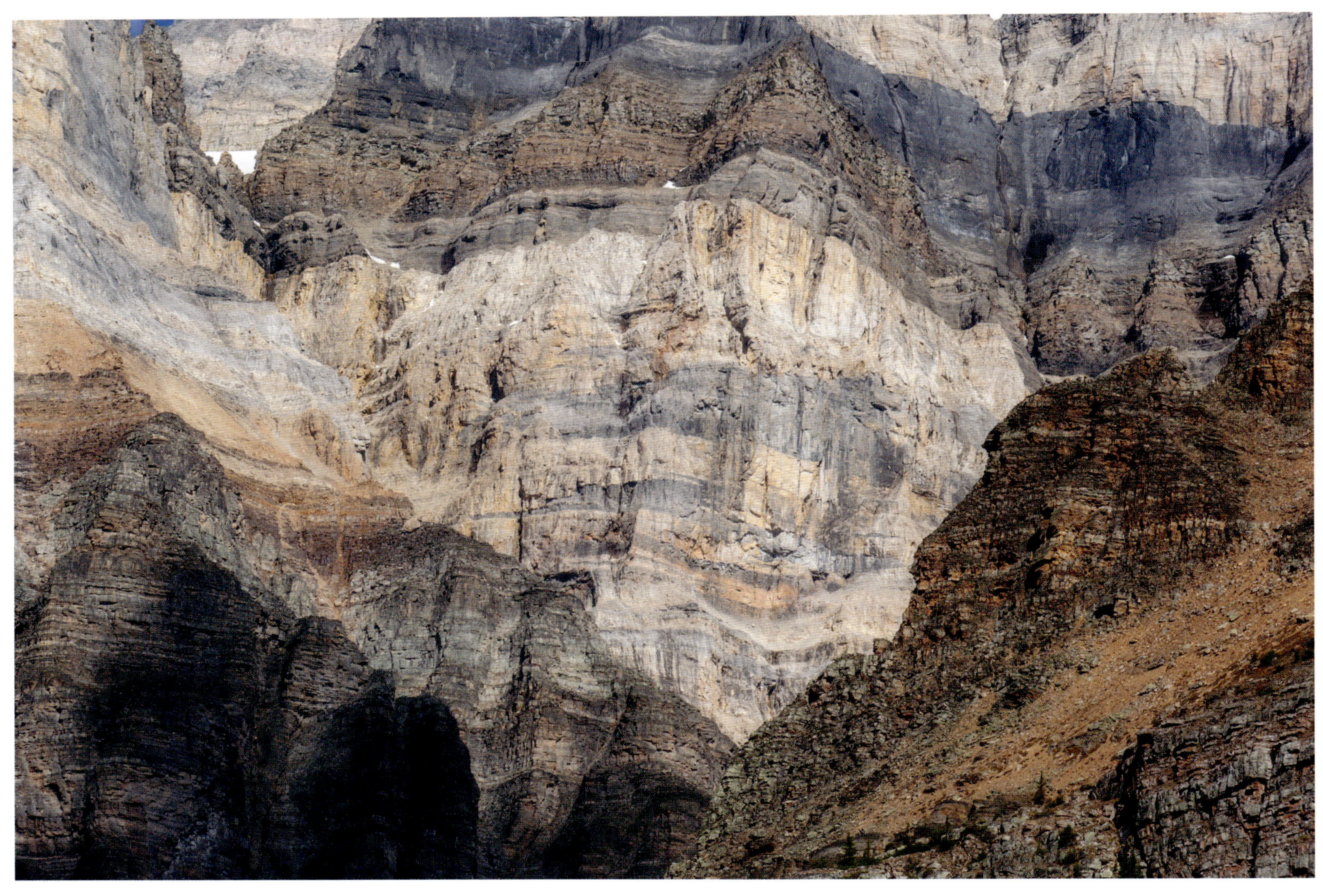

Geological Time (2008)
All Soul's Prospect juxtaposed against the geological history of
Mount Huber.

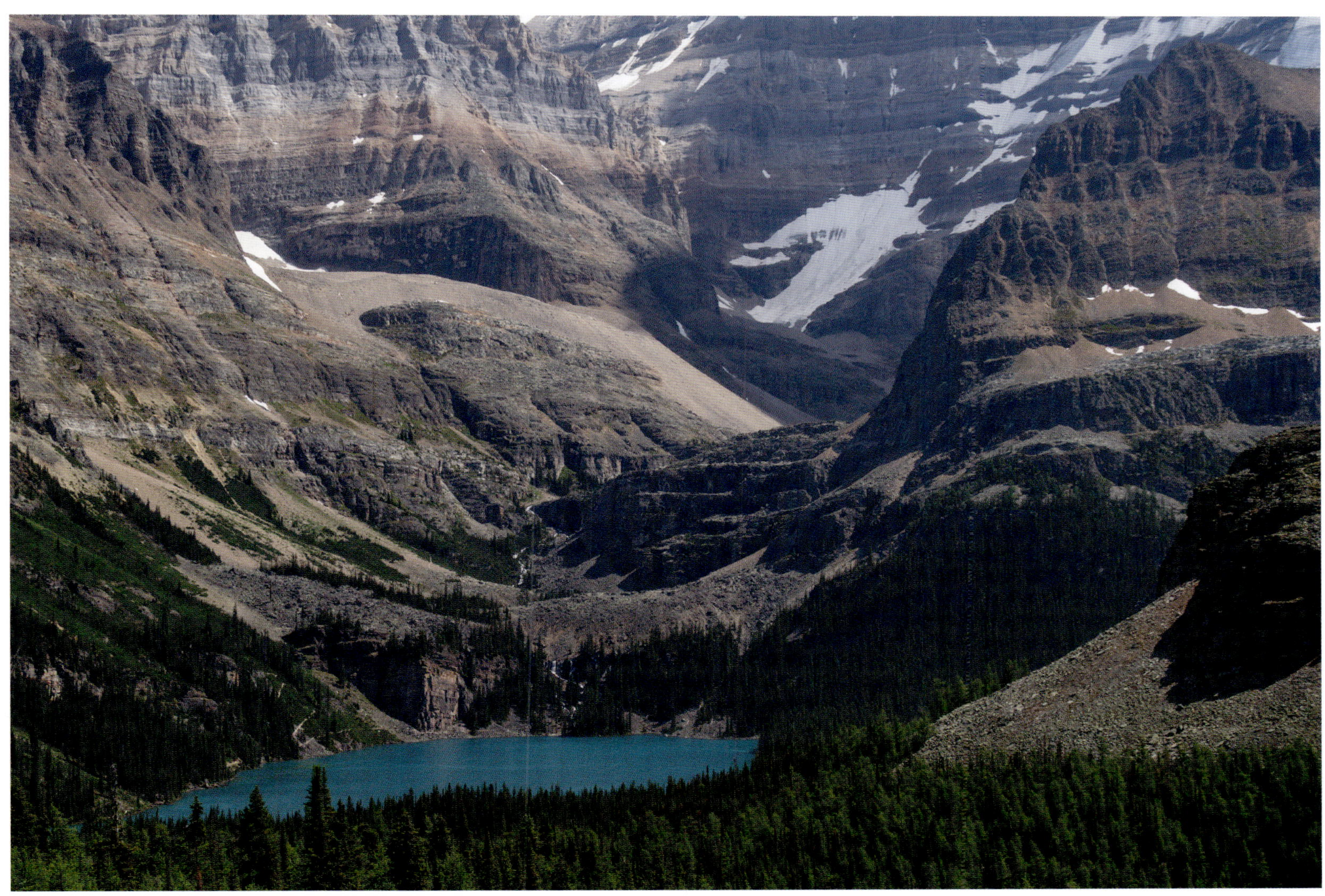

All Soul's Prospect (2021)
All Soul's Prospect in the foreground seen in relation to Lake O'Hara and a portion of the Huber Ledges Alpine Route that leads to Lake Oesa.

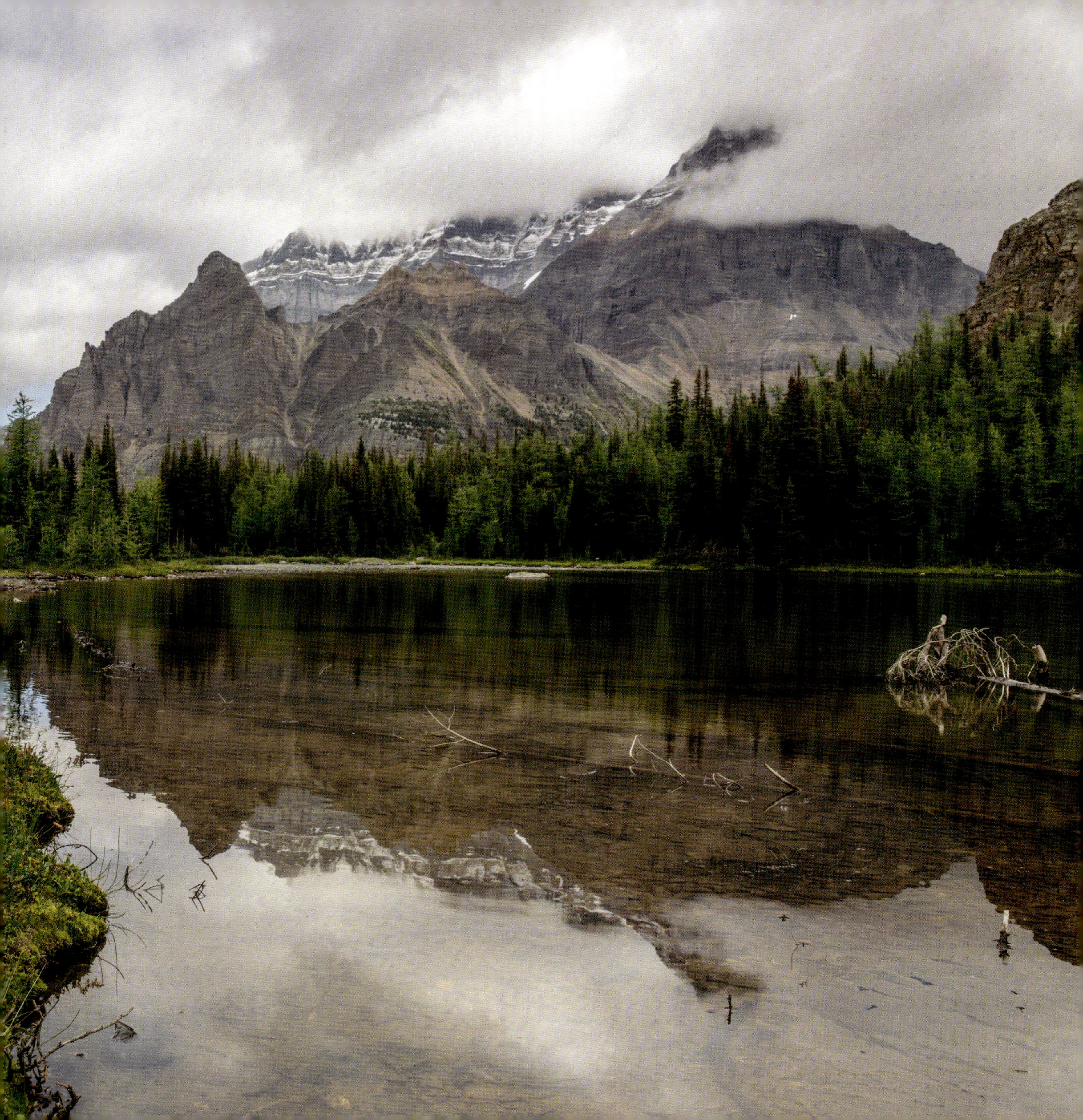

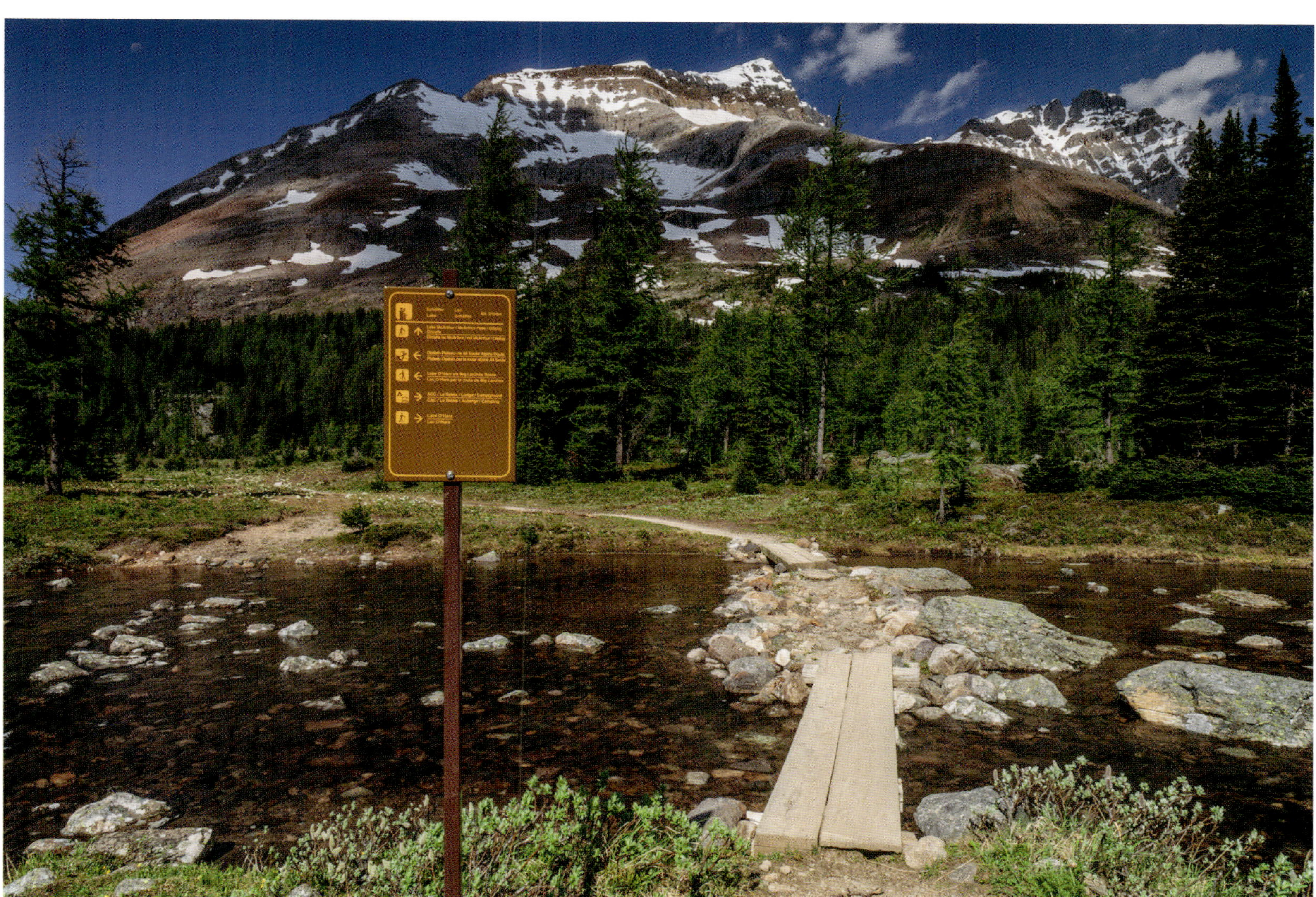

Restful Reflection (2024)
All Soul's Prospect Alpine Route ends at Big Larches Trail, which leads to Schäffer Lake. Wiwaxy Peaks, Wiwaxy Gap, and Mount Huber reflect in this shallow alpine lake at the foot of Mount Schäffer.

Follow the Signs (2007)
Signs clearly mark the direction of the extensive backcountry trail system. It's a short distance along McArthur Pass to reach the start of Odaray Highline Trail, the final link in Lake O'Hara Alpine Circuit.

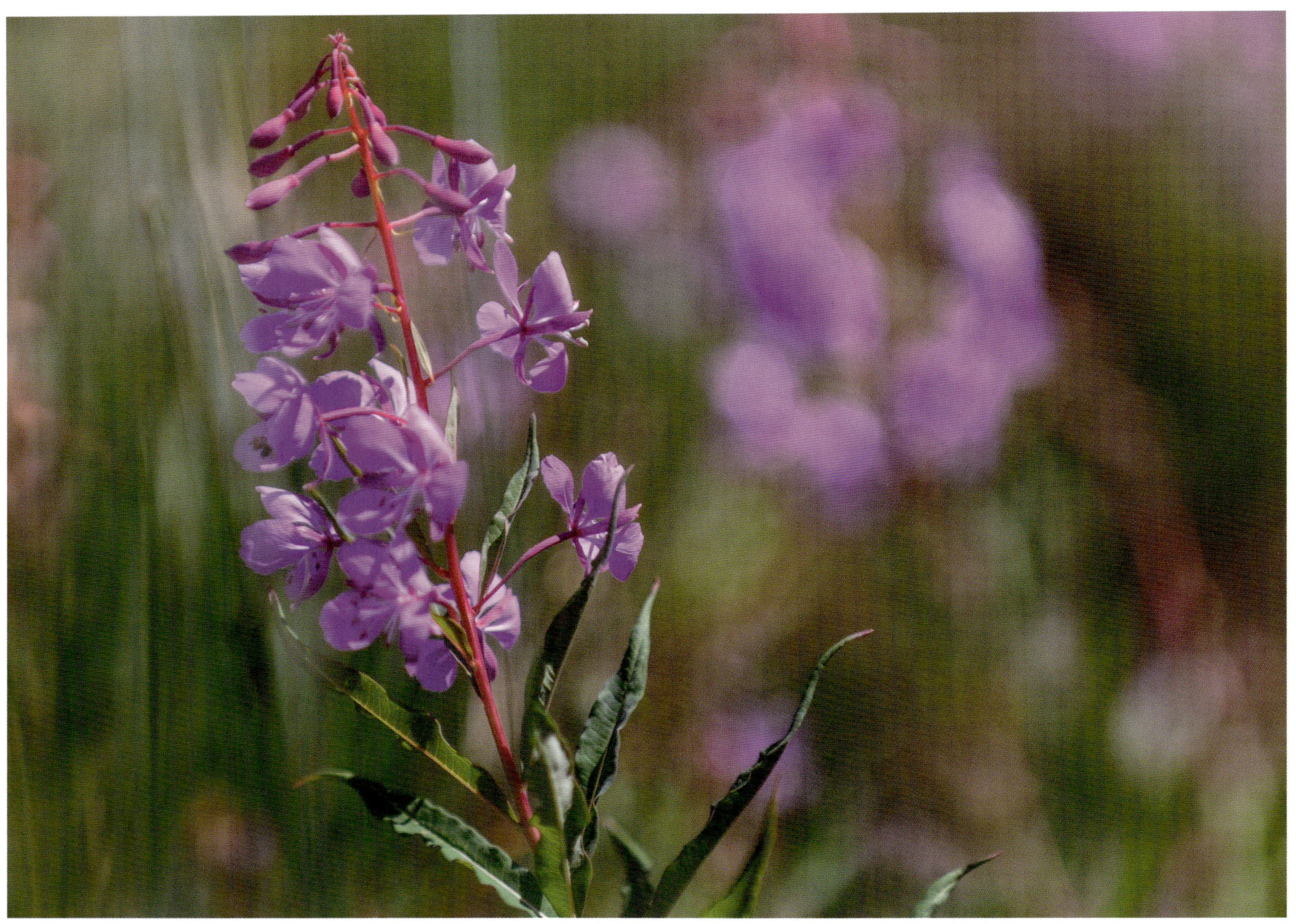

Summer Colour (2021)
Fireweed (*Epilobium angustifolium*) colours the valley meadows of McArthur Pass along the initial stretch of Odaray Highline Trail.

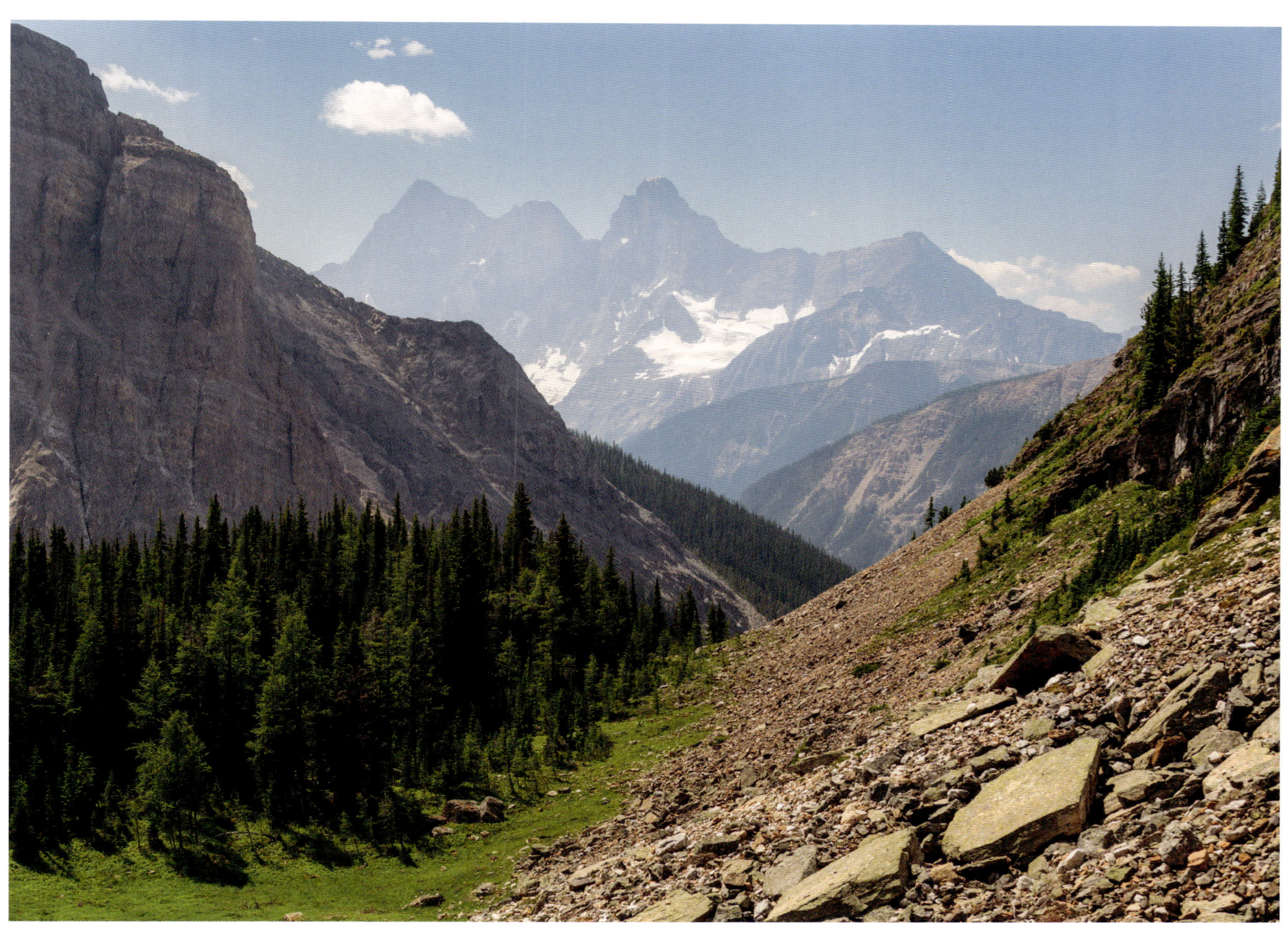

Wildlife Corridor (2021)
Access to McArthur Pass and Odaray Highline Trail is restricted
to a specific number of hiking parties allocated each day
during the open season, as this is a wildlife corridor. Hikers
must check the sign-in book at the kiosk.

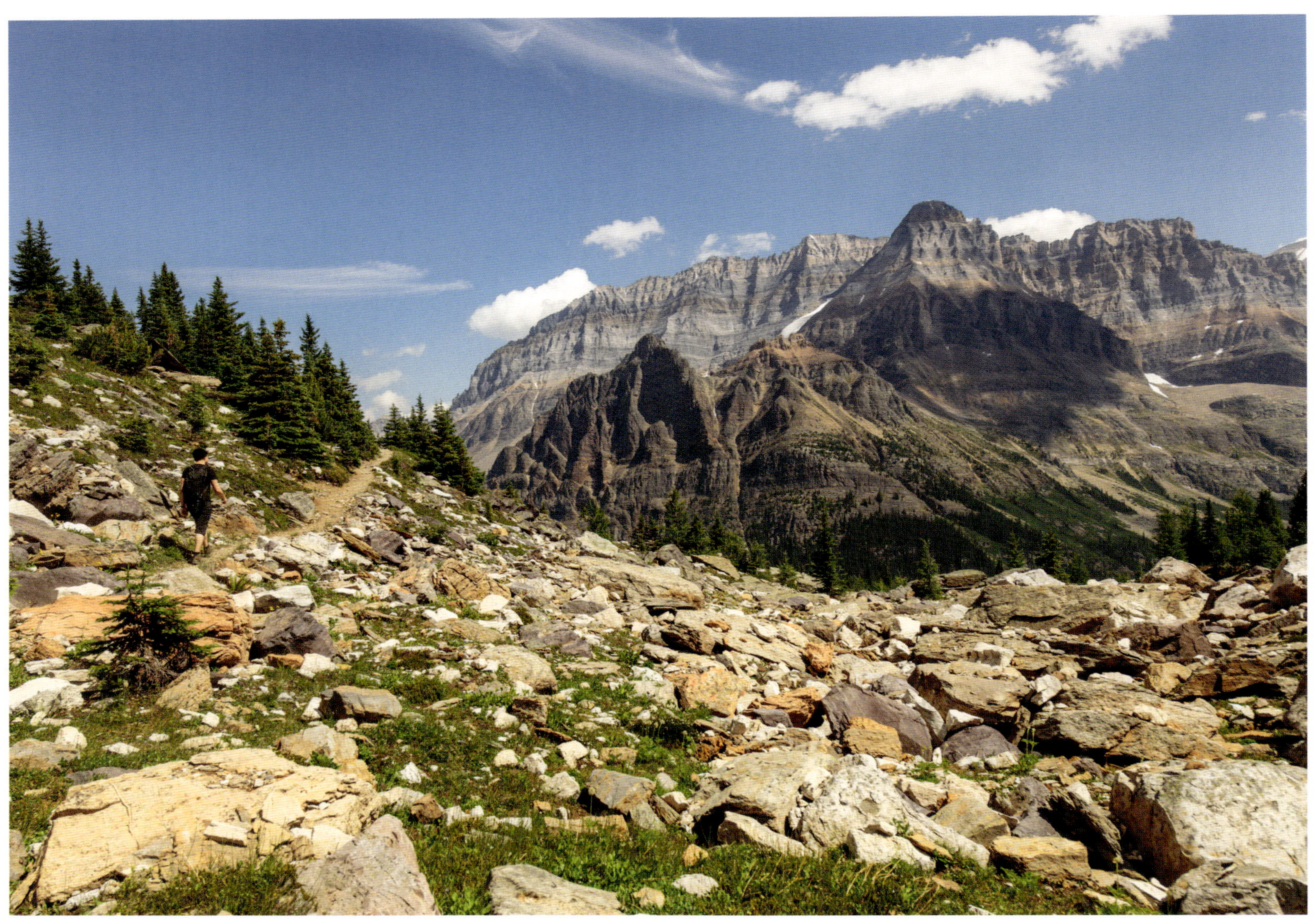

Open Views (2021)
Although the destination is Odaray Grandview Prospect, the views along the one-hour hike from McArthur Pass are rewarding in their own right.

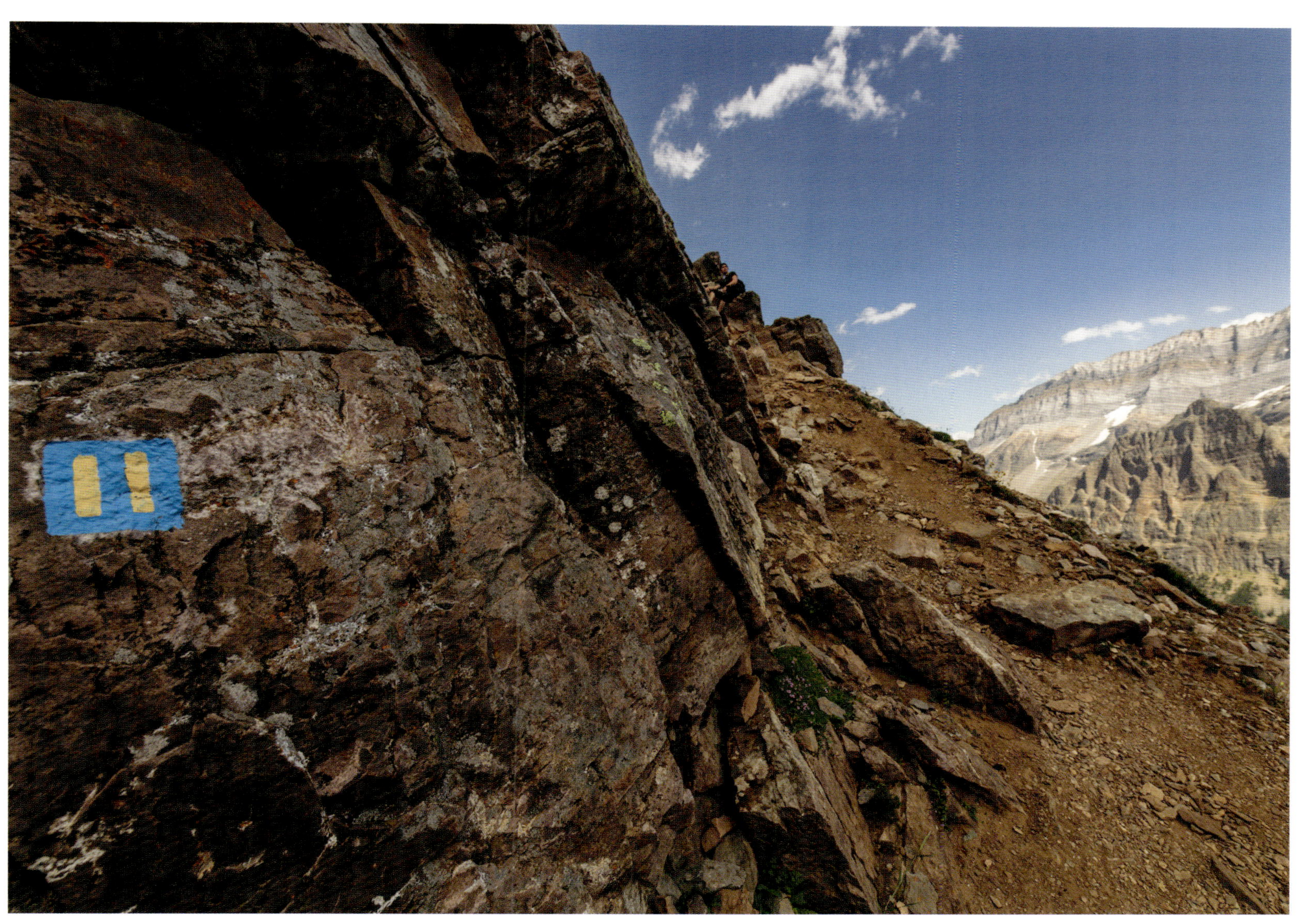

Route Marker (2021)
Alpine circuit trail markers clearly indicate the way along the
2.5-km trail from McArthur Pass, with a 315-m gain in elevation
to reach Odaray Grandview Prospect.

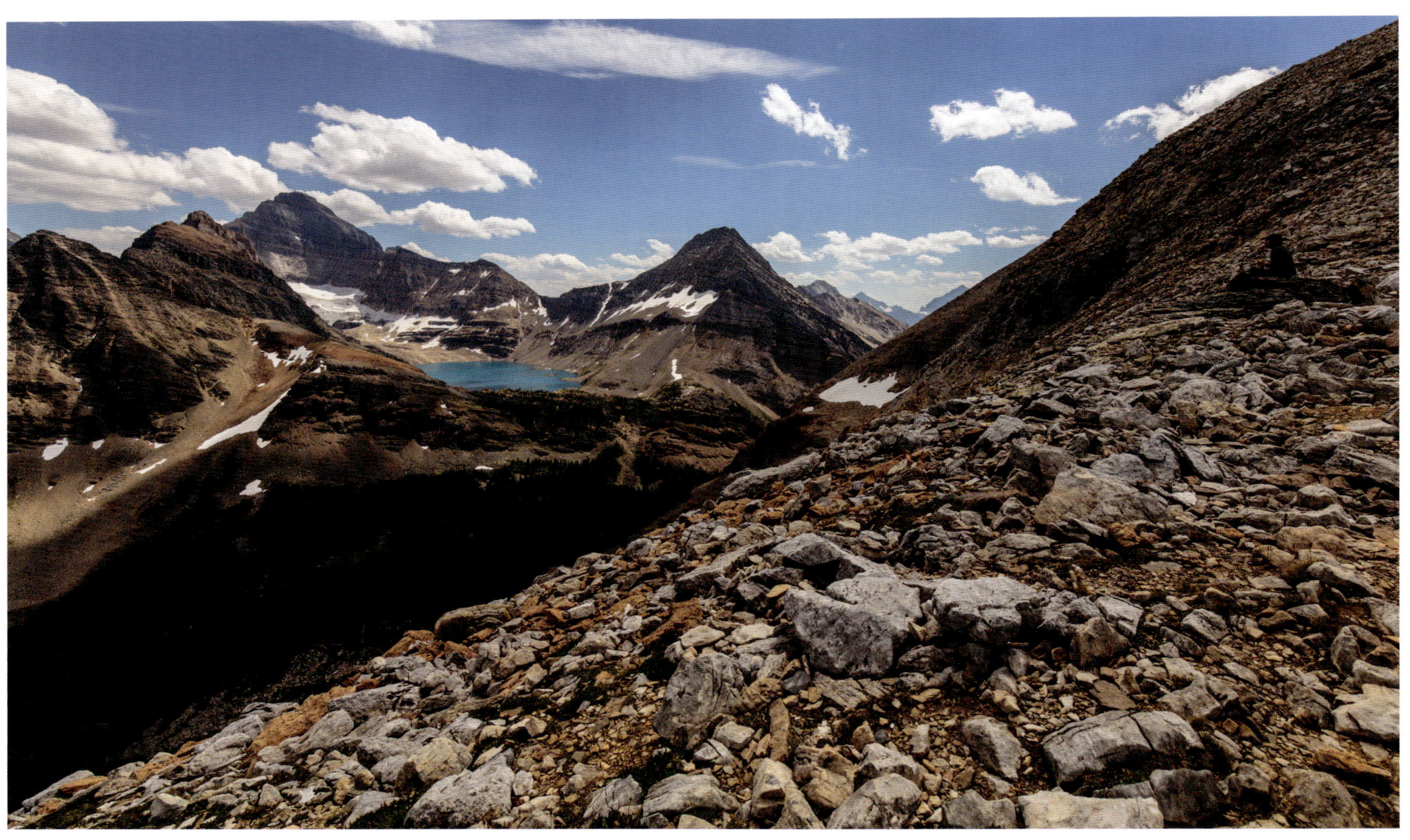

Rewarding View (2021)
Turquoise-coloured Lake McArthur shining brilliantly in the distance is a gratifying panorama after the 315-m elevation gain.

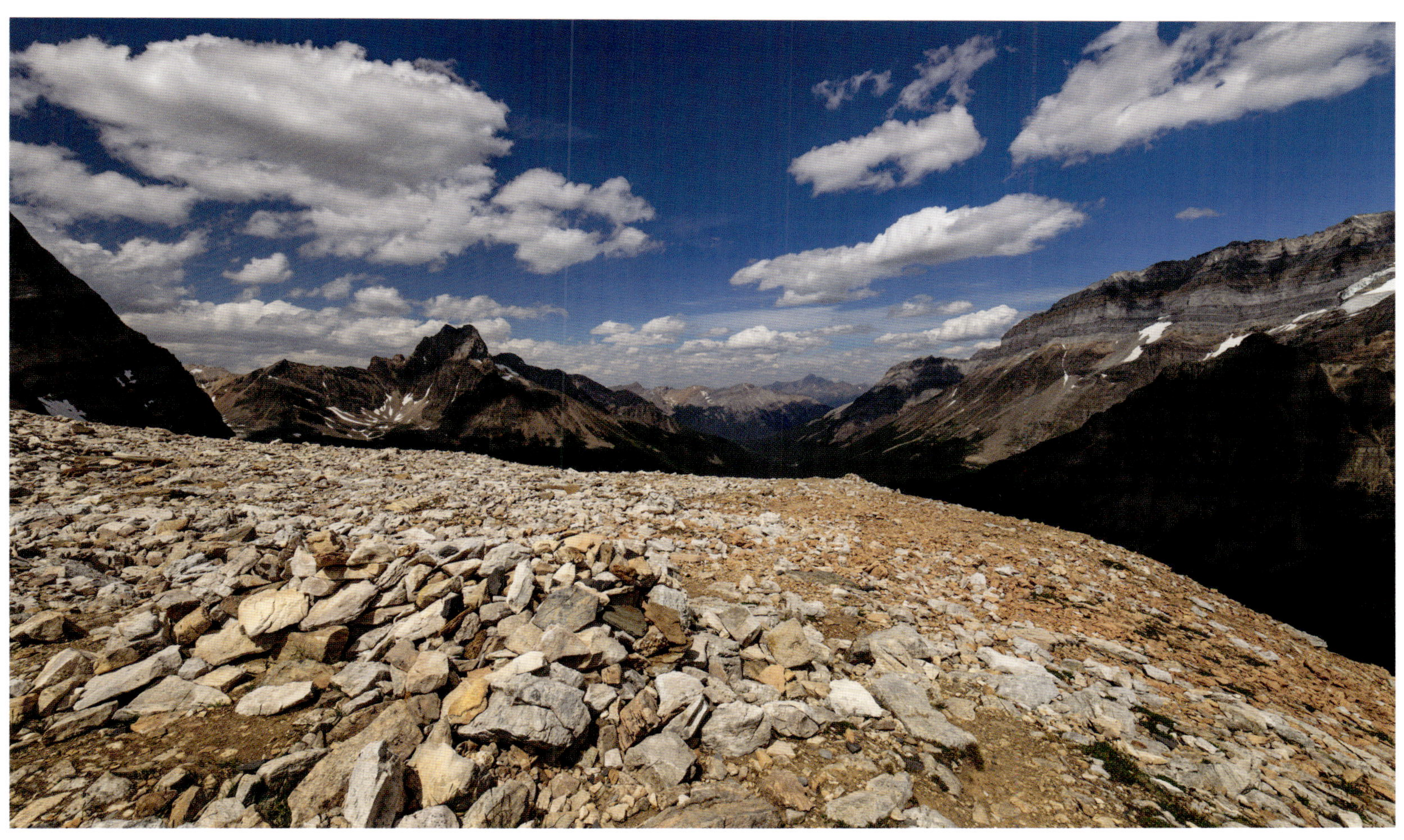

Unobstructed View (2021)
Odaray Grandview Prospect is a ledge beneath "Little Odaray"
(Feuz Peak) and Odaray Glacier. Well above the treeline, it
affords a wide-open vista of Duchesnay Basin.

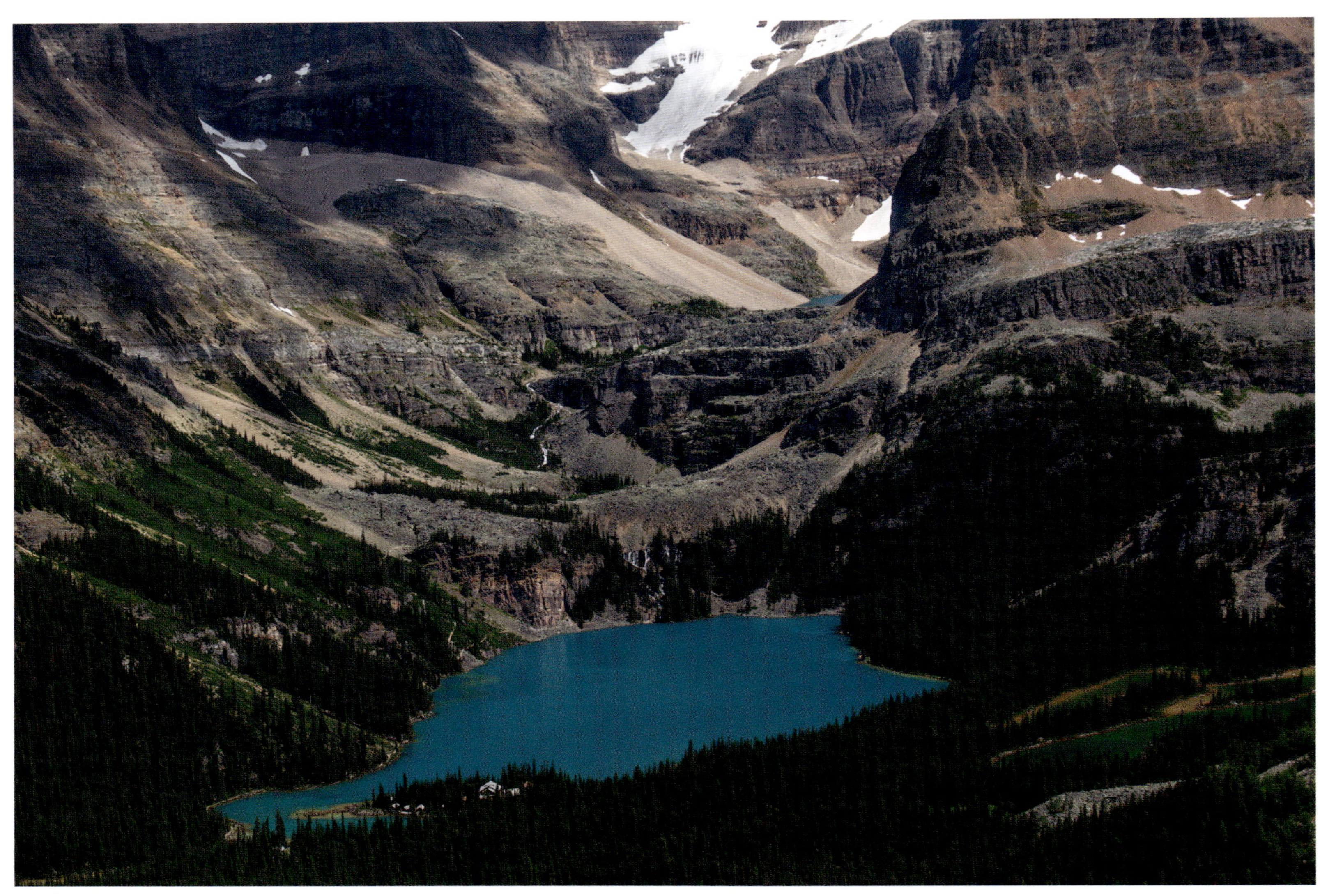

O'Hara Context (2021)
An almost aerial perspective, this telephoto view of Lake
O'Hara shows it in context with Lake O'Hara Lodge on the peninsula and nearby Mary Lake. Tucked up under Mount Lefroy, it
is possible to see a section of Lake Oesa.

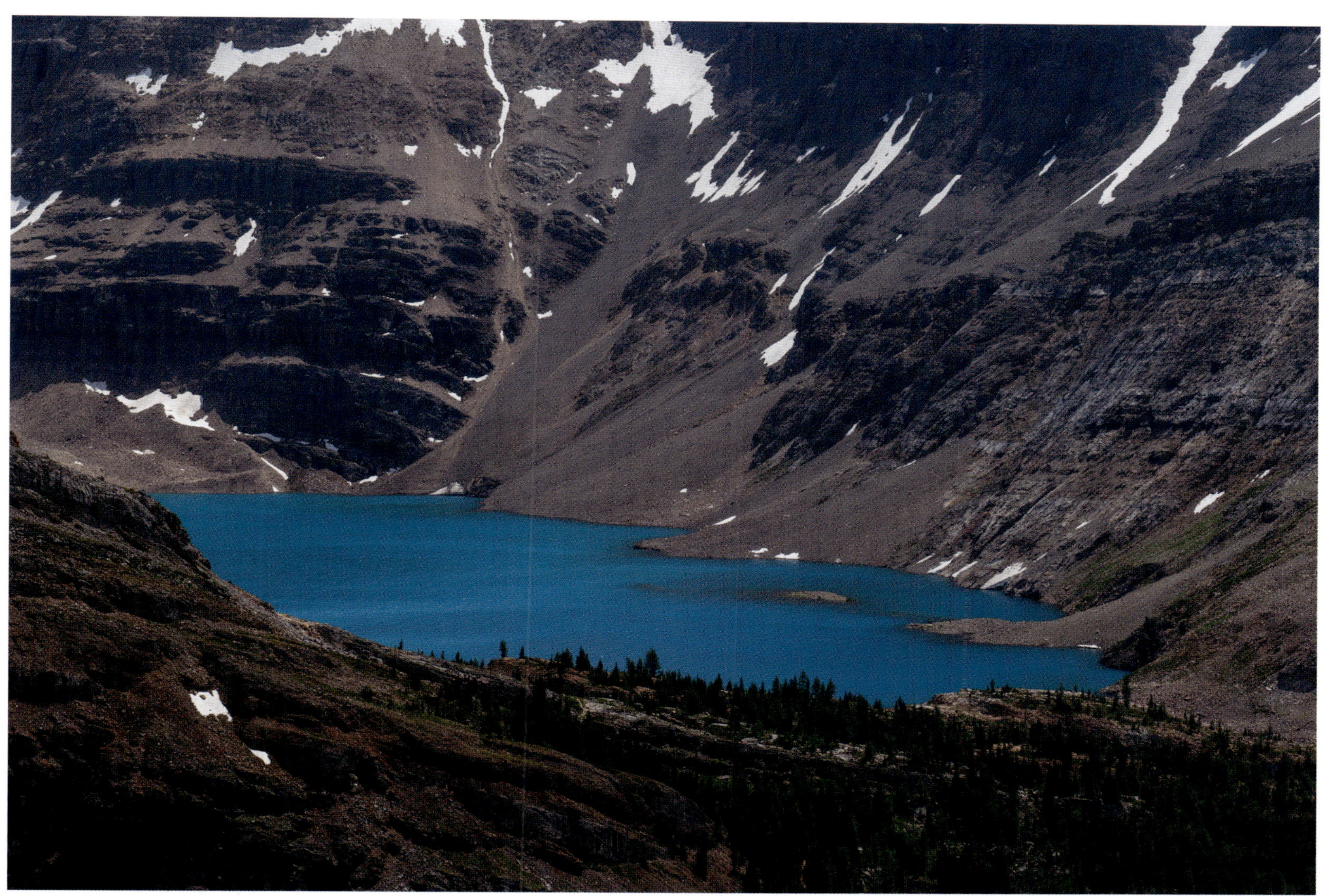

Glacial Amphitheatre (2021)

A telephoto perspective of Lake McArthur from Odaray Grandview Prospect illustrates the classic steep, amphitheatre-like structure of a valley formed by cirque glaciers.

Overleaf **Grand View** (2021)

Odaray Grandview Prospect gets its name from the 270-degree unobstructed view of the Lake O'Hara region. From this ledge it's possible to see Lake O'Hara, Lake Oesa, Opabin Plateau lakes, Mary Lake, Schäffer Lake, and Lake McArthur.

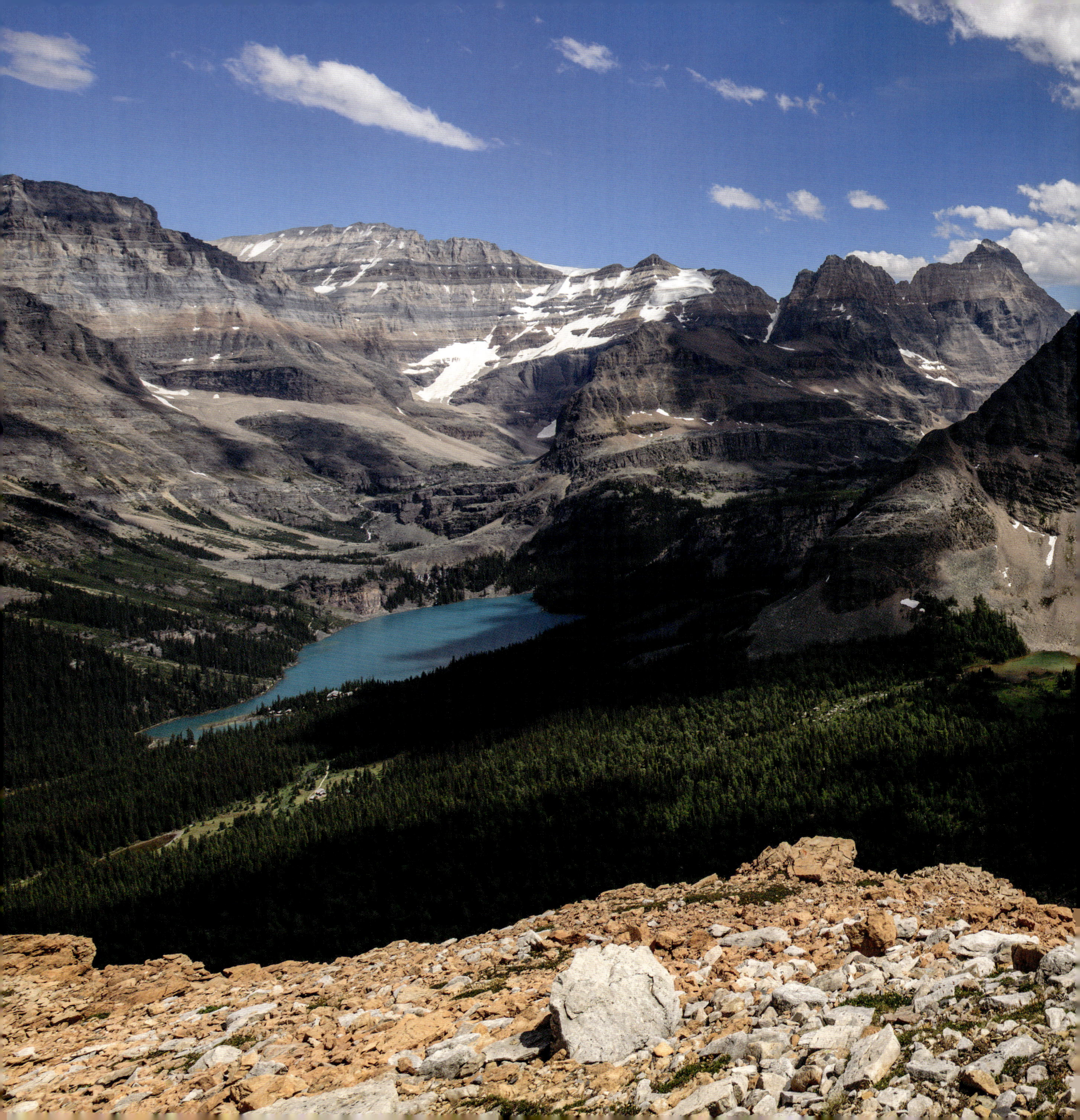

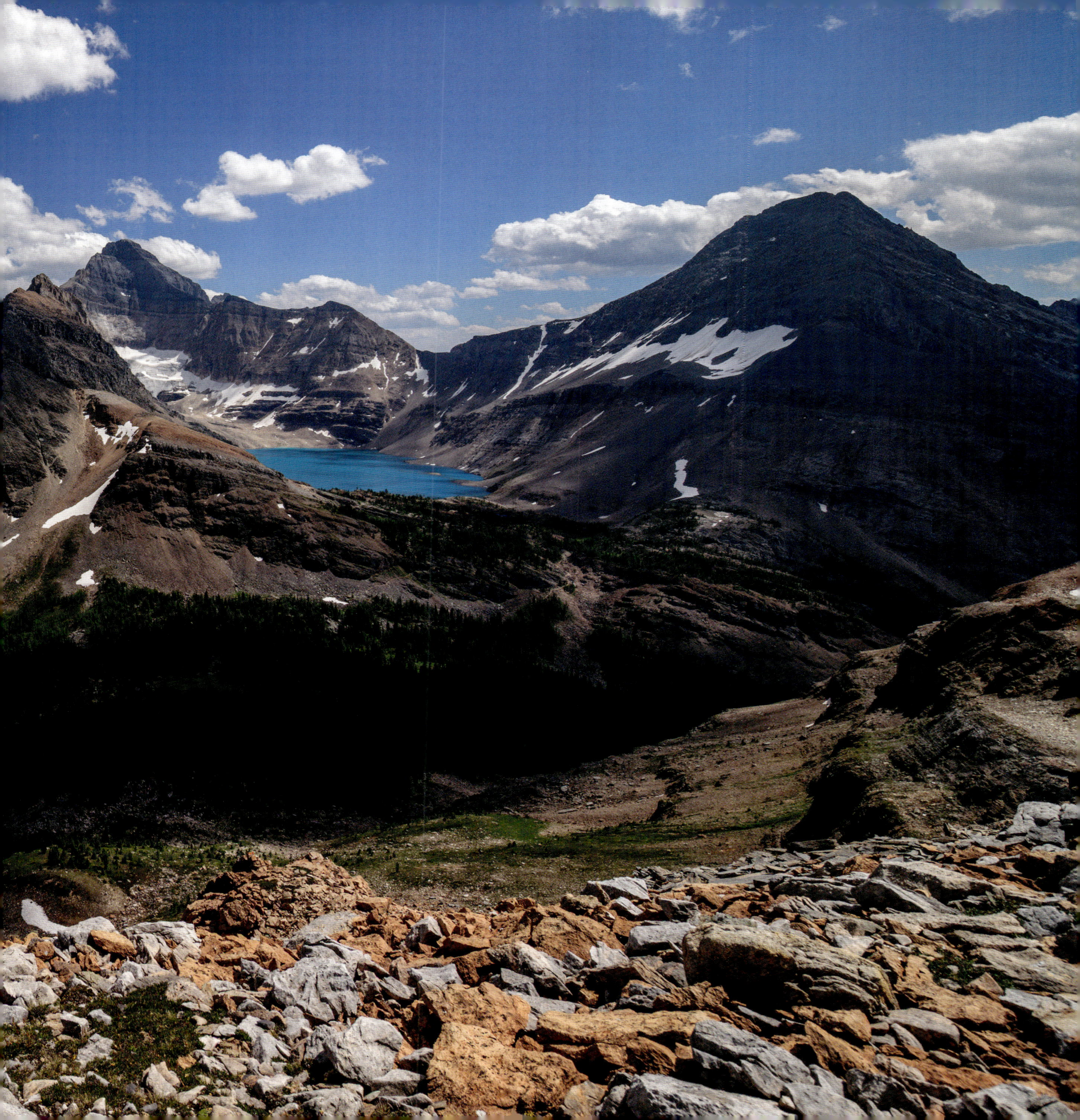

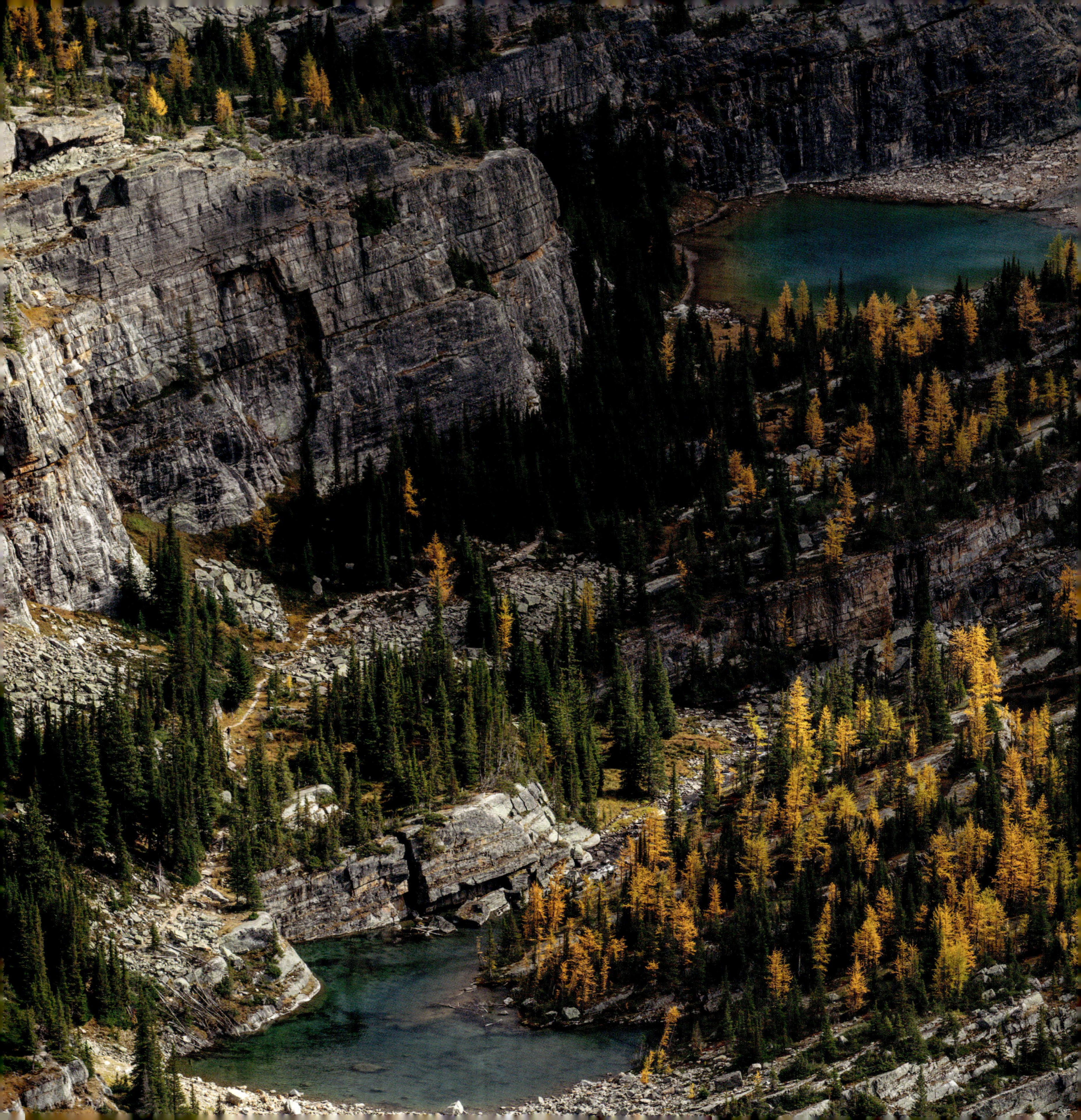

PART SEVEN

Wiwaxy Peaks Climb

This section is a slight detour from the others. Lake O'Hara's trails are accessible to all who enjoy hiking without any technical ability, and the book has focused on each of the Lake O'Hara region hiking sections. However, it is possible to go "off trail" for those who desire it. While the sedimentary rock is not ideal for rock climbing, it is possible to climb the mountains surrounding Lake O'Hara for the ultimate perspective of this geological wonder.

I had never rock climbed, yet wanted to capture this perspective for the book. So the former owner and operator of Lake O'Hara Lodge, Bruce Millar, introduced me to Canmore-based veteran mountain guide James Blench. James had been a Lake O'Hara Lodge backcountry winter guide for many years and knows the area intimately. He would be a perfect guide for my ascent of one of Wiwaxy Peaks' summits.

The first step was to learn the basics of climbing prior to our Lake O'Hara trek. James took me to a small vertical face climb near Fairmont Banff Springs Golf Course. There were a few waivers to be signed, a sombre reflection of the inherent risk of dangling by a rope from a rock face, and the sizing of gear such as a helmet and harness. Next came an introduction to some basic climbing terms and definitions – anchor, carabiner, rappelling, traversing – most important being the belay commands, involving an exchange of verbal phrases between the climber and belayer to formally establish their relationship. Belaying involves feeding out (or taking in) slack as a climber progresses along the rock face, such that if the climber slips, they will be caught by the rope to prevent a fall. The next most important item was to learn how to manage the rope, to coil it without tangles, and to learn tying in. Tying in is the act of attaching the climbing rope to your harness, and typically utilizes the figure 8 follow-through knot. It is vital to be able to attach yourself to (and of course detach yourself from) the rope when the guide isn't nearby.

A fear of heights is a healthy condition for survival, but it's hard to know where on the spectrum of that fear you are until it's put to the test. I was pleasantly surprised to discover that, in the hands of a confident belayer while tied to a rope secured in rock anchors, the thought of "heights" didn't even enter my mind. There are too many other things to focus on and so much more time to absorb the beauty all around. It was like learning to think slowly and carefully, allowing time to fade away. I can understand the appeal now. I've usually been on a self-imposed mission to get to the next destination far in the distance to photograph that elusive lake. Now our focus for the afternoon was simply to rise off the ground and reach the summit directly overhead. The very first, albeit relatively low, rock summit gave me a wonderful sense of accomplishment. We were ready to go, nearly. There was still that other skill to attempt: getting back down.

Aerial Perspective (2021)
An aerial view of Victoria Lake and Lefroy Lake from the Huber Ledges route to Wiwaxy Peaks.

A Canmore musician as well as a veteran mountaineer, James is a very thoughtful and understated person. Since he is not prone to self-aggrandizing, I've learned more about his accomplishments while researching this book than I did during my time with him. Perhaps a clue was when I was quizzing him about the strength of the permanent climbing anchors in the rock face we climbed, and I learned he was the one who installed them decades earlier. James is the recipient of the Association of Canadian Mountain Guides' highest honour, the Platinum Distinguished Service Award, for his 26 years of serving on its Technical Committee. Many of the safely secured climbing anchors around the Banff and Canmore area are the results of his handiwork.

From our modest perch, but nonetheless vertical descent, James introduced the concept of rappelling. There was a moment when the heart skips a beat as one steps over the ledge with nothing underneath but air and lowers the body to a horizontal position with respect to the ground below, as if walking on the vertical rock face in a different dimension where gravity was at right angles to itself. Again, though, the overarching impression was one of stability. It was at that moment, while hanging over the edge, that my cell phone rang. Now normally I would never take a call in a situation like this, however, I could see from my watch it was coming from Lake O'Hara Lodge. I took the call. James kept a neutral expression on his face. It was the new lodge operator Lonnie Wake, who knew James well. She was offering a coveted reservation at the lodge, which I readily accepted before completing my descent. Having mastered the basics, we were set to tackle Lake O'Hara and Wiwaxy Peaks.

As mentioned previously, access to Lake O'Hara is stringently controlled by Parks Canada to preserve the fragile ecosystem that accompanies its spectacular scenery from being overrun by visitors. An annual lottery determines who will be able to take the shuttle bus up to Lake O'Hara during its short summer season. An alternative is to hire a certified mountain guide, for whom there are a small set of designated seats available each day. James was able to secure a ride on the bus for both of us on September 23. It was several weeks after our Banff rendezvous, and we had no idea what form of weather we would encounter on that day, but it was a plan.

I arose in the dark on September 23, relieved to see a good-weather forecast for the day. I headed off in my car to meet James in Canmore, where he was waiting in the early morning light. Just over an hour later, we were parked in the Lake O'Hara Parks Canada parking lot, preparing our gear for the adventure ahead. After the shuttle bus ascended the 11-km road to Le Relais Day Shelter, we disembarked and headed off along nearby Lake O'Hara Circuit toward the route to Lake Oesa. It's possible to hike up the closer Wiwaxy Gap Alpine Route trail to the bottom of Wiwaxy Peaks, but that trail is steep and prone to wearing out the knees before the climbing even begins. It was a beautiful sunny autumn day, and our route to Lake Oesa passed stunning views of golden-larch-rimmed Victoria Lake, and Lake Oesa where we stopped briefly for a lunch rest.

The next stage, along Huber Ledges Alpine Route, doubled our vertical gain of the 245-m rise to Lake Oesa, with another 260-m gain in elevation to Wiwaxy Gap. The veteran mountaineer kept his pace slow and steady, and when occasional hikers impatiently passed us along the trail, James would tease them, saying, "You run ahead, and I'll wait for you at the top." Looking over our shoulder, there was a spectacular view of Lake Oesa and its series of cascading lakes and rivers cutting through rock on their path to Lake O'Hara. Looking ahead, a small white spot on a distant rock ledge slowly came into view. It turned out to be a lone billy mountain goat. Special adaptations to living in a vertical world, such as split hooves with rubbery hoof pads, enable the mountain goat to access alpine meadows otherwise out of reach to competitors and predators. I stopped yet again to take a photograph, and James kept his composure, but I could feel the need to continue moving, as there was still a lot of work ahead of us.

We reached the base of Wiwaxy Peaks and shed our hiking shoes for climbing footwear, slimming down our packs to the basics of ropes and camera gear while donning our harnesses and helmets. Everything had come down to this moment: the training climb, the bus reservations, the beautiful weather. It was time to climb.

James is such an experienced climber that I really didn't have any idea how much work it was. Everything seemed to go very easily as we wound ourselves around the rock tower and eventually hoisted ourselves onto the precipice.

I've heard about the "Rocky Mountain High" – where the release of adrenaline and dopamine is combined with mild oxygen deprivation from the exertion at altitude – and this was my first time experiencing it. I felt as though I could stay up here on this precarious peak forever. Looking out at the expanse of mountain peaks, the greater forces that created them became discernible. The vastness of the mountain range seemed somehow less alienating. Standing on top of hundreds of millions of years of Earth's history, looking out at the curvature of the horizon, for a moment the connectedness of everything, including ourselves, was much clearer.

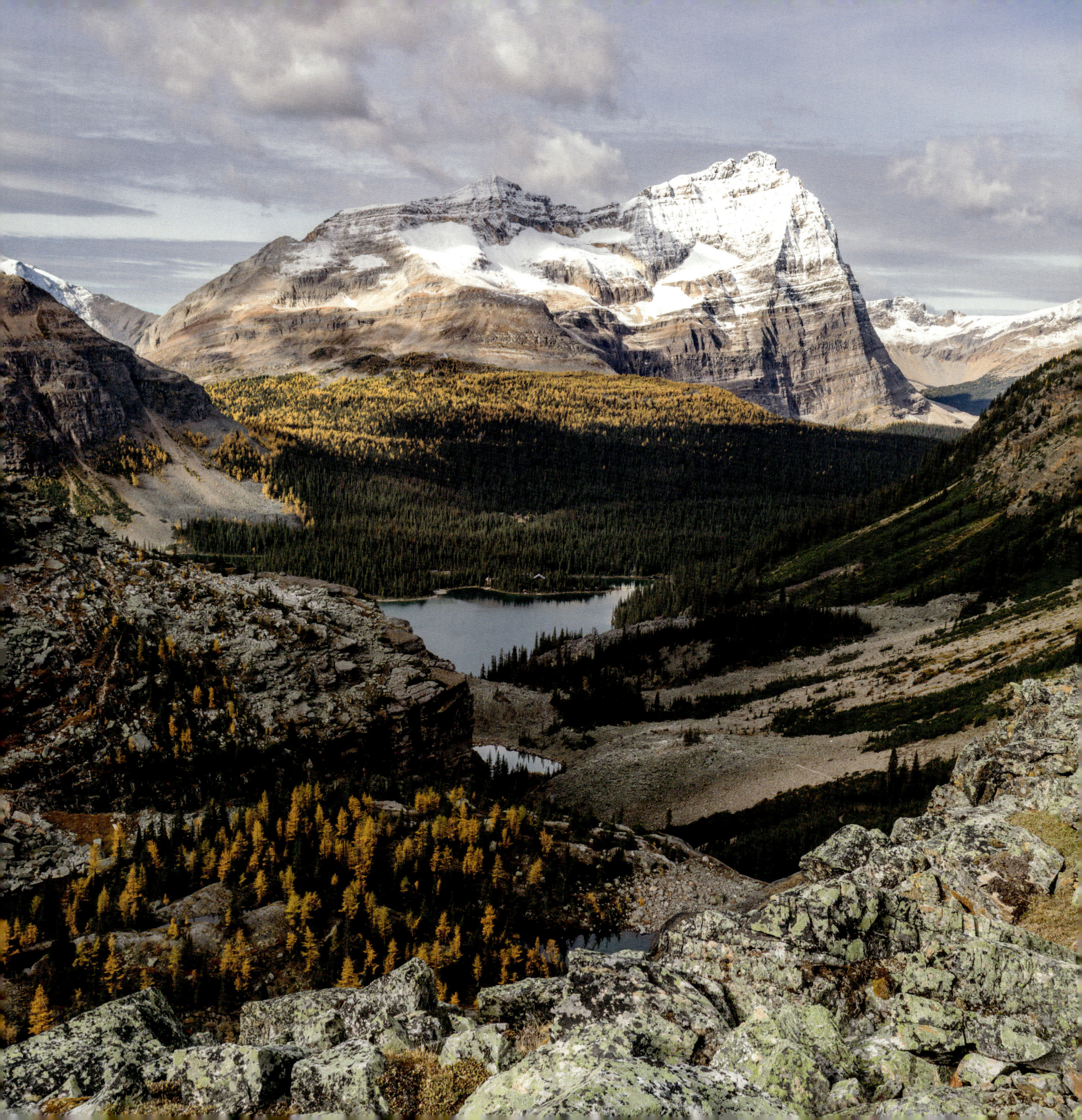

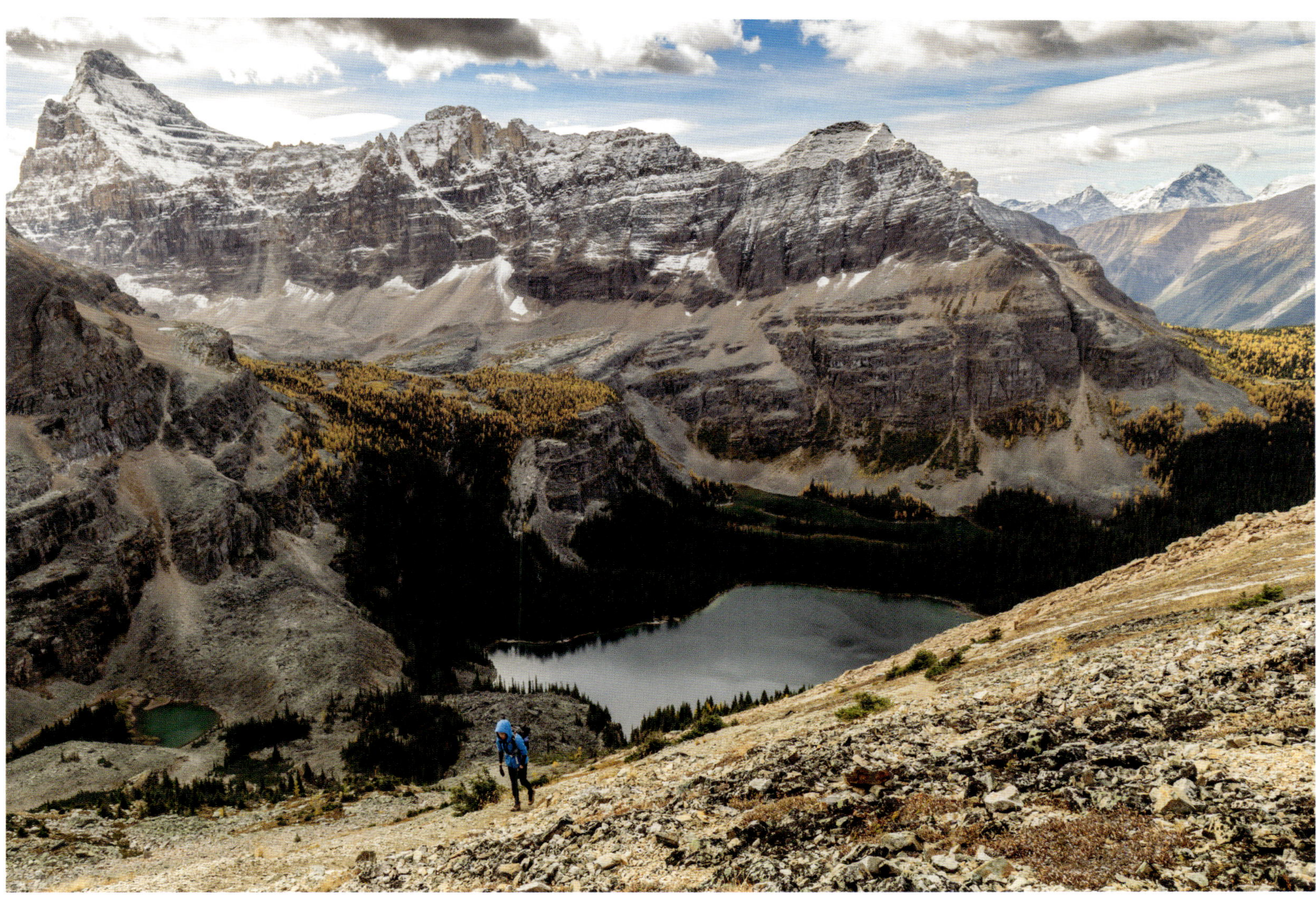

To the Climb (2021)
In order to preserve our knees, we chose to hike up to the beginning of our Wiwaxy Peaks climb from the Huber Ledges route. This route has a gentle 260-m gain in elevation compared to the steep 495-m gain of the Wiwaxy Gap Alpine Route.

Above the Trees (2021)
Leaving the trees behind as we made our way upward to the base of Wiwaxy Peaks. The roof of Lake O'Hara Lodge and some of its lakeside cabins are in view on the distant shoreline.

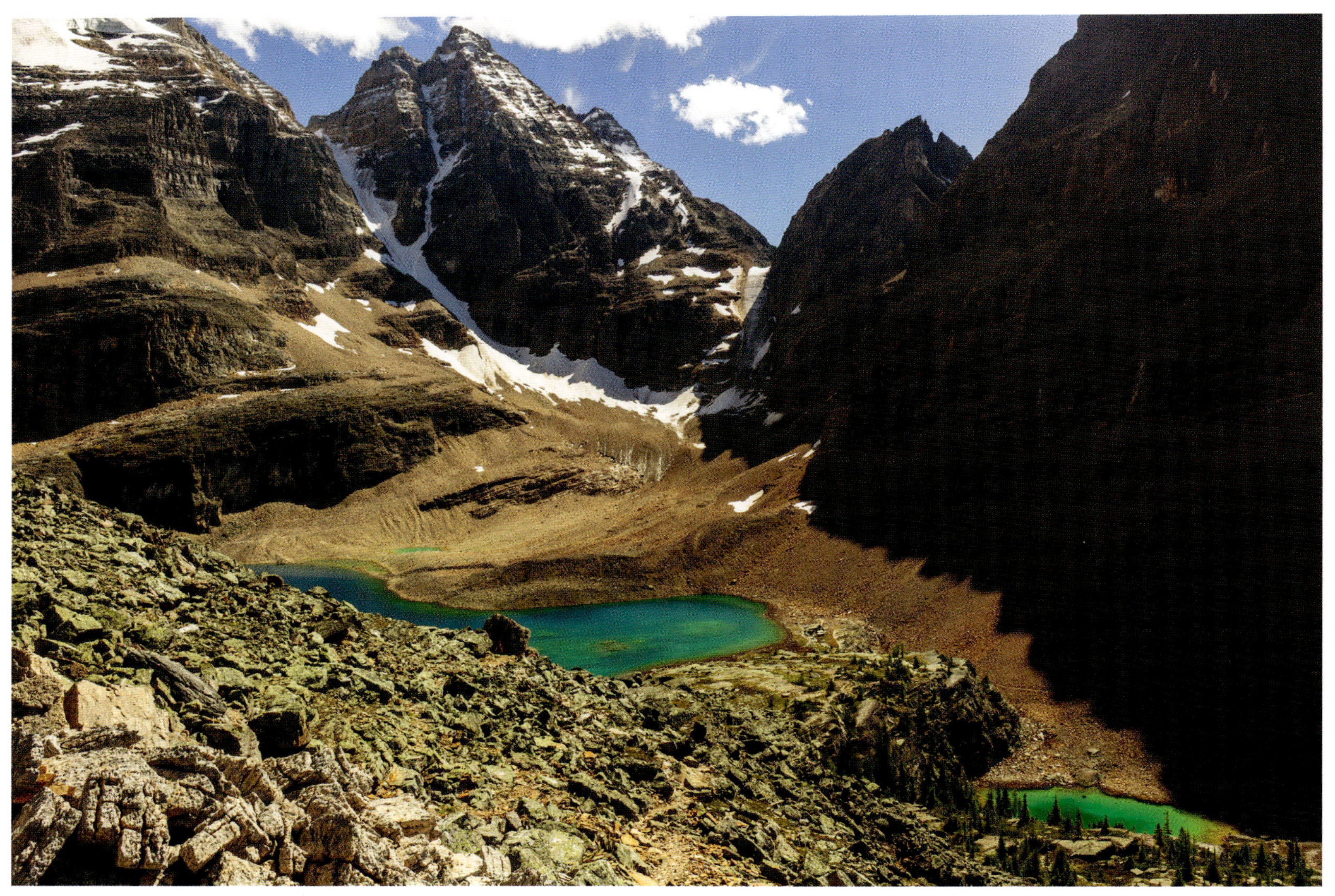

Glacial Lake Hues (2010)
The turquoise and emerald hues of Lake Oesa and Lefroy Lake
are seen in full display from the Huber Ledges route.

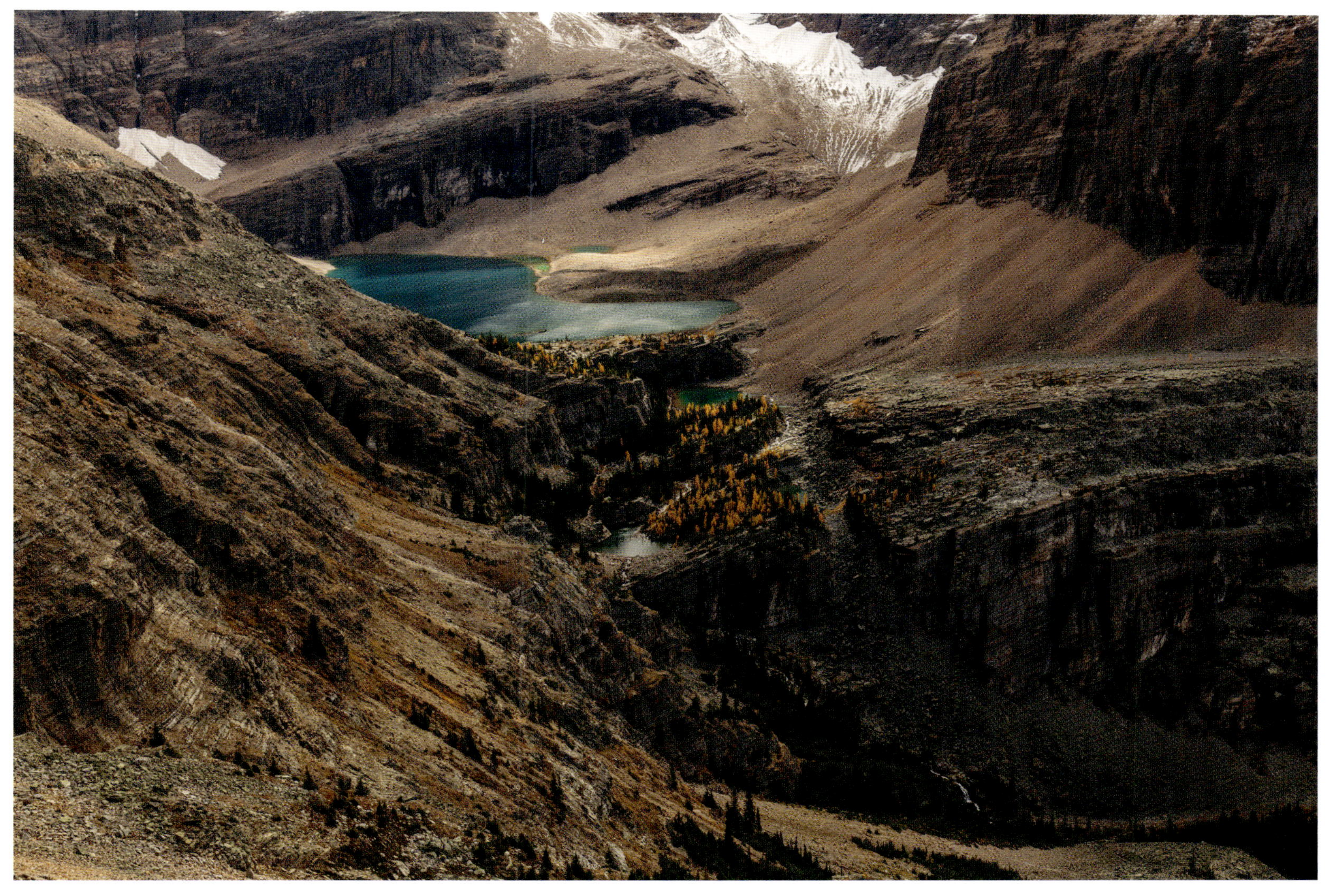

Oesa Trinity (2021)
The trio of Lake Oesa, Lefroy Lake, and Victoria Lake are all
within view along the hike up to Wiwaxy Peaks.

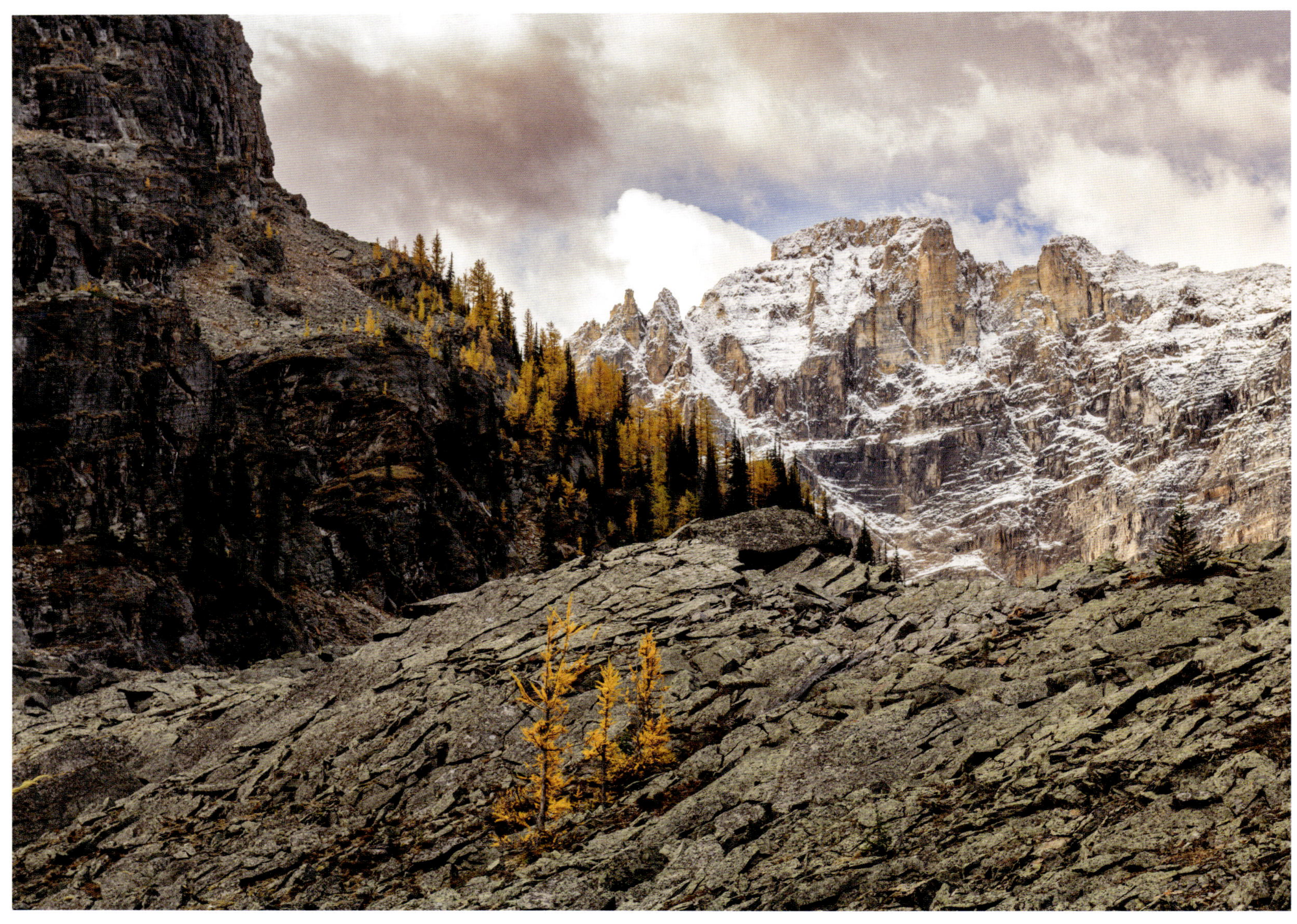

Golden Accent (2021)
A telephoto perspective of Yukness Mountain juxtaposed against Schäffer Ridge, accentuated by the brilliant golden larches of autumn.

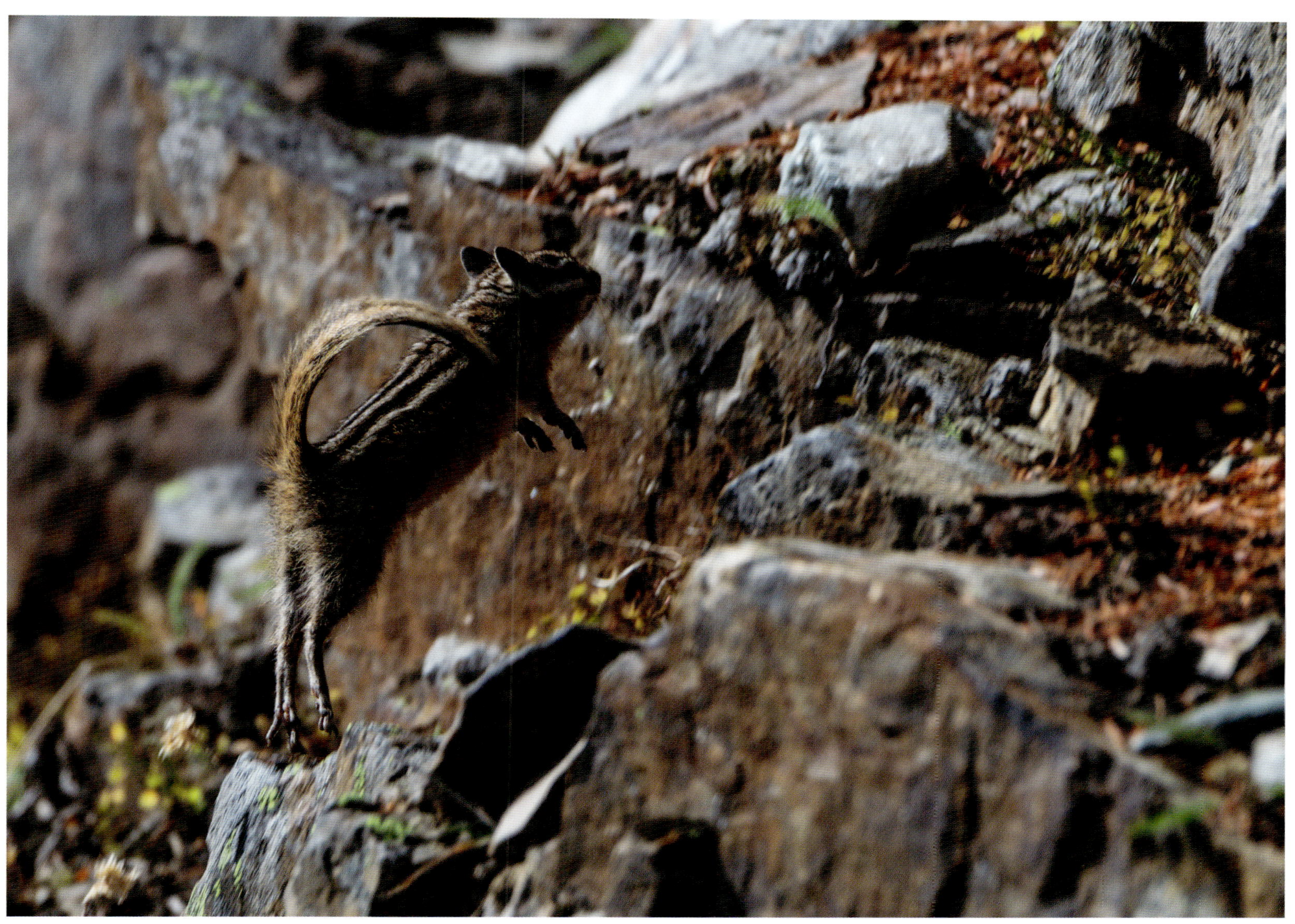

Alpine Stewards (2021)
Chipmunks help steward the landscape by collecting and dis-
persing seeds.

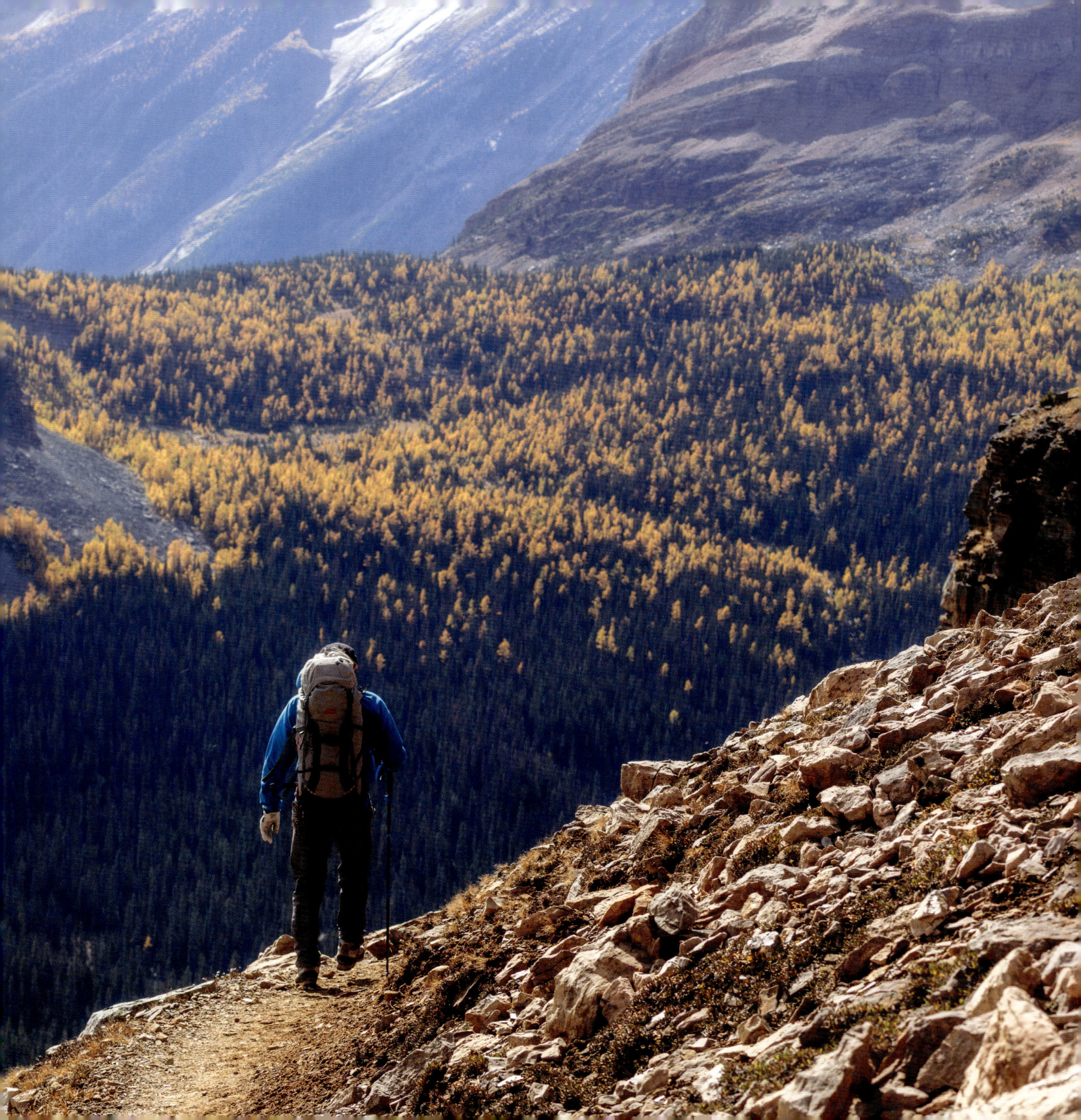

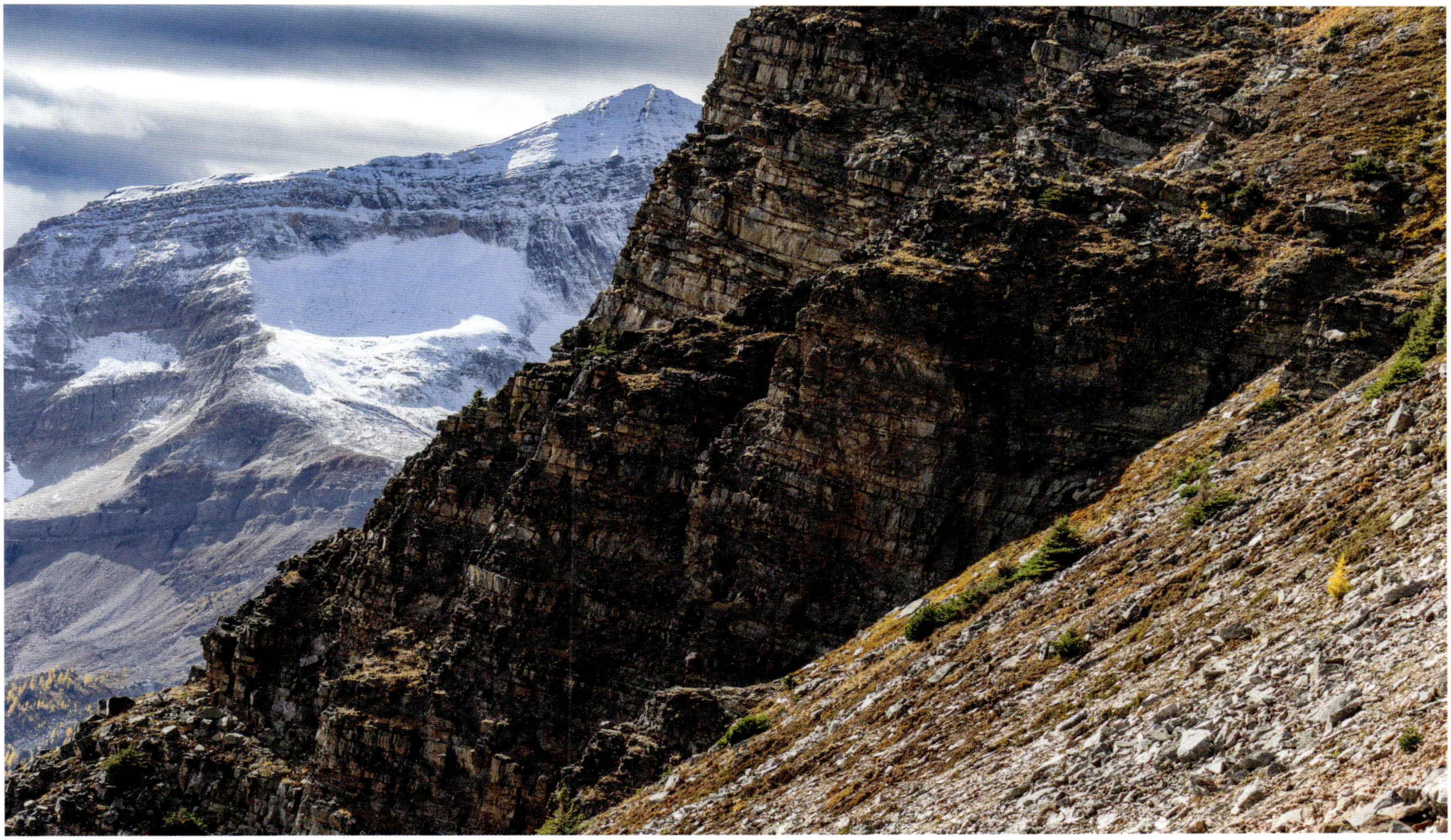

Billy View (2021)
Look carefully and you will see a billy goat resting on a rock ledge in the upper-right portion of this photograph. This male mountain goat spends its time alone, foraging for food at these high elevations.

Expert Guidance (2021)
A veteran mountain guide and Lake O'Hara backcountry guide for decades, mountaineer James Blench offers sage climbing advice matched to wisdom from incomparable experience.

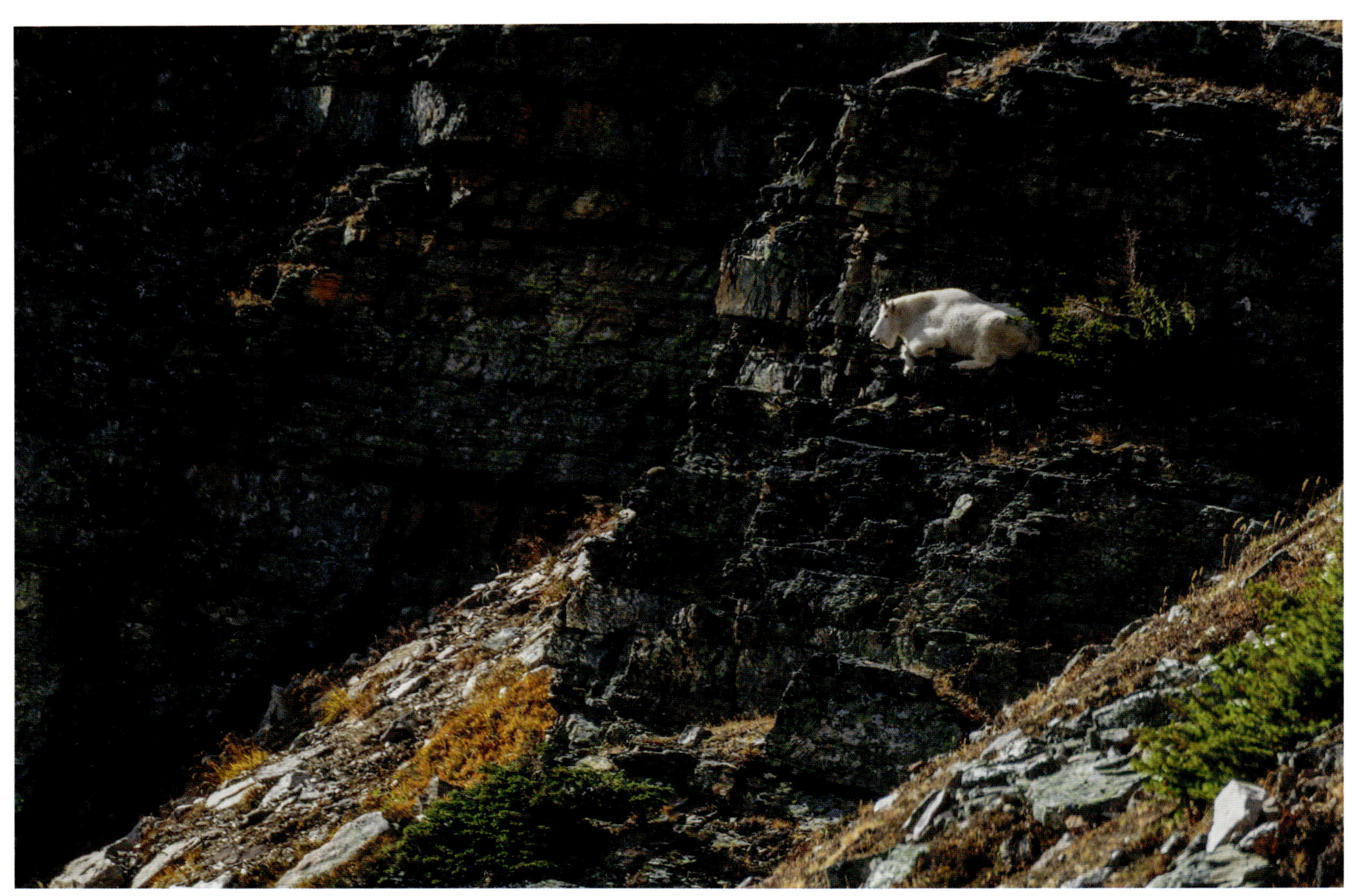

Out of Reach (2021)
Perhaps the "best mountain climbers in the world" designation goes to the mountain goat. Their specialized split hooves,
rough, rubbery hoof pads, low centre of gravity, and fearless
instincts enable them to use vertical terrain to avoid predators
and access grassy alpine meadows unattainable to others.

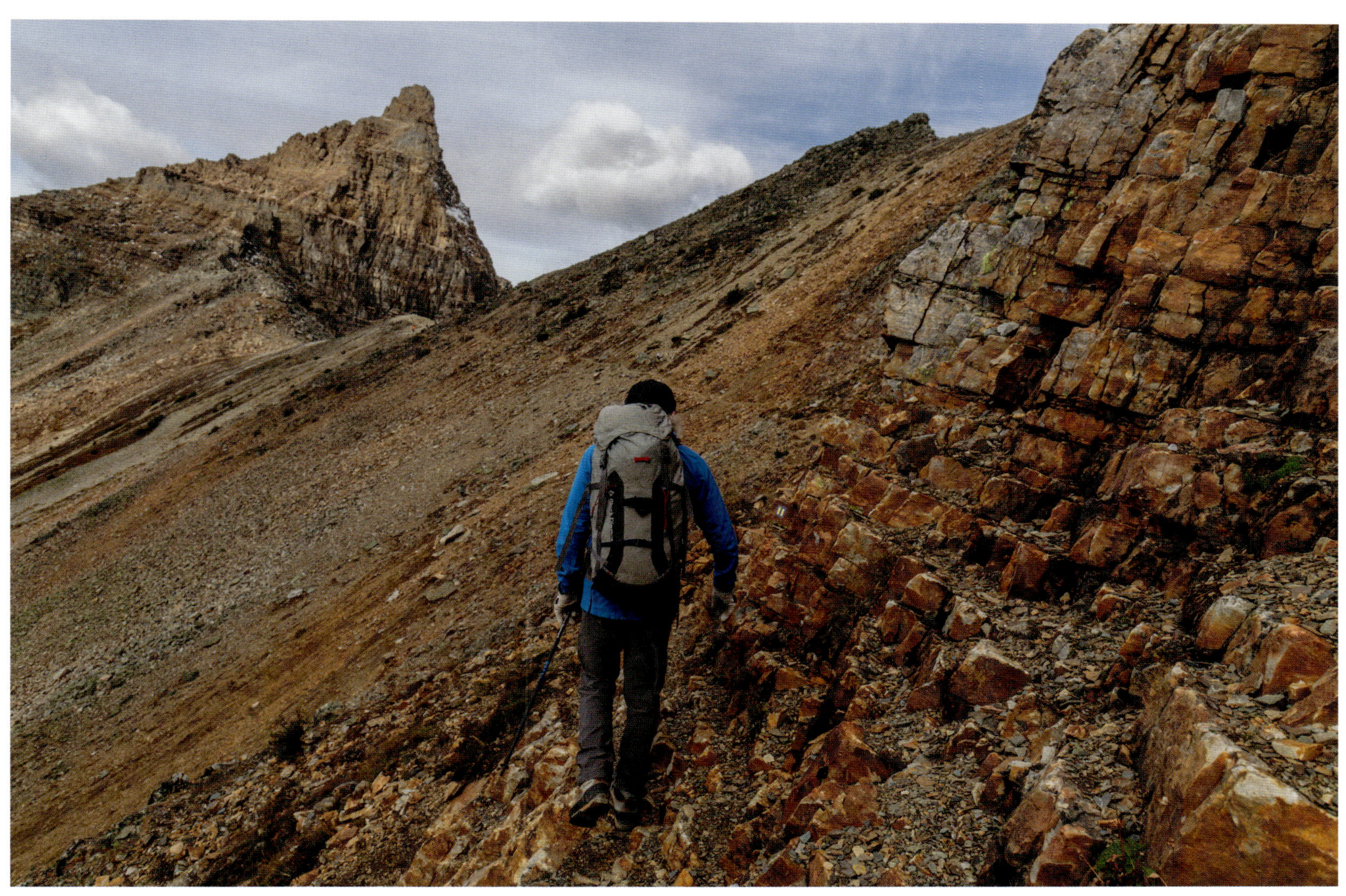

Alpine Pace (2021)
A master climber, James Blench regulates his even pace up the slopes one step at a time without any rest stops required. To hikers eager to rush pass, he steps aside and quips, "You run ahead, and I'll wait for you at the top."

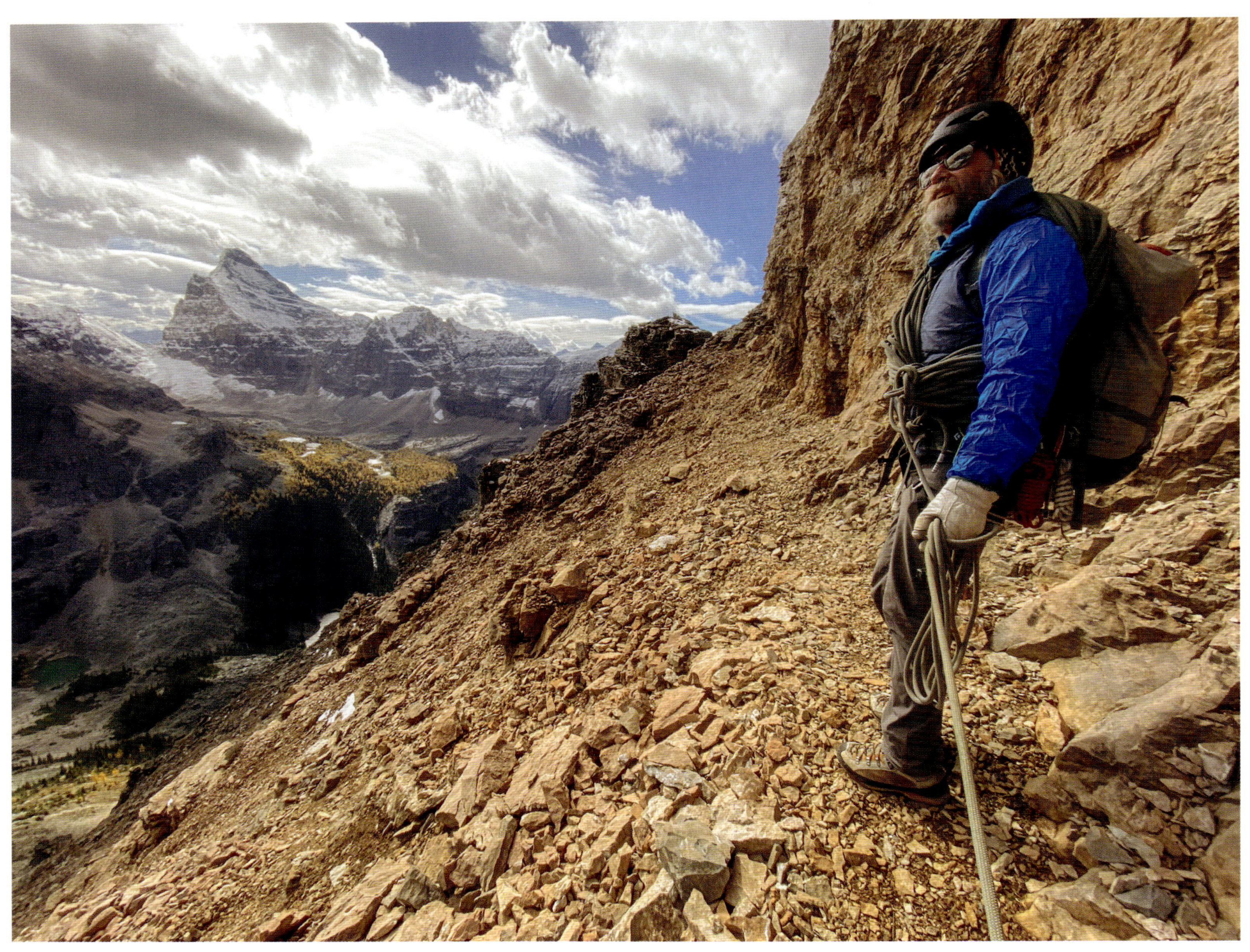

Distinguished Service (2021)
It was a privilege to be guided by James Blench, recipient of
the Association of Canadian Mountain Guides' highest honour,
the Platinum Distinguished Service Award.

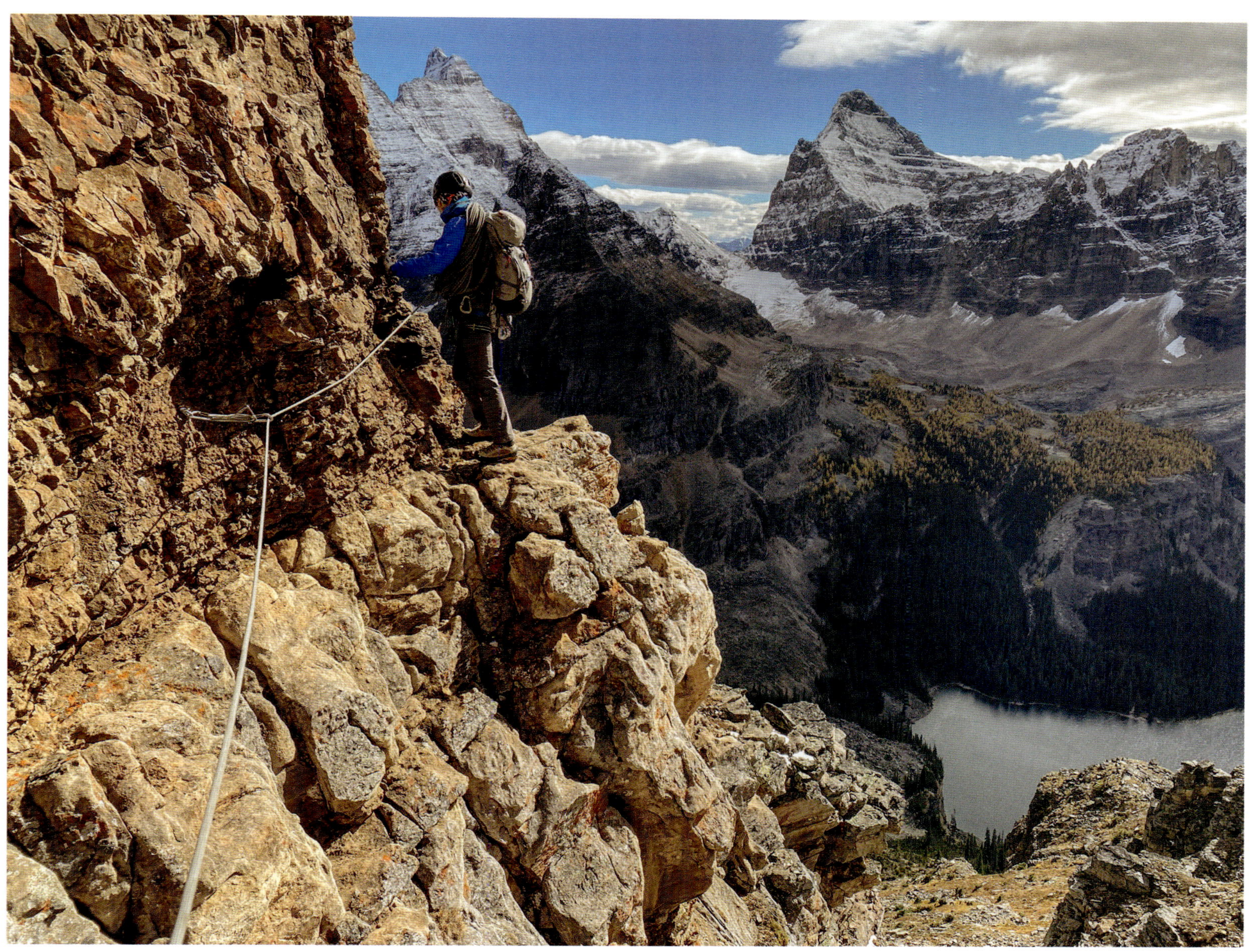

The Way Up (2021)
Many of the fixed anchors for climbing routes around the Banff
and Canmore region were put in place by James Blench over
the past three decades. Nicely in view, Opabin Plateau is blan-
keted in golden larch.

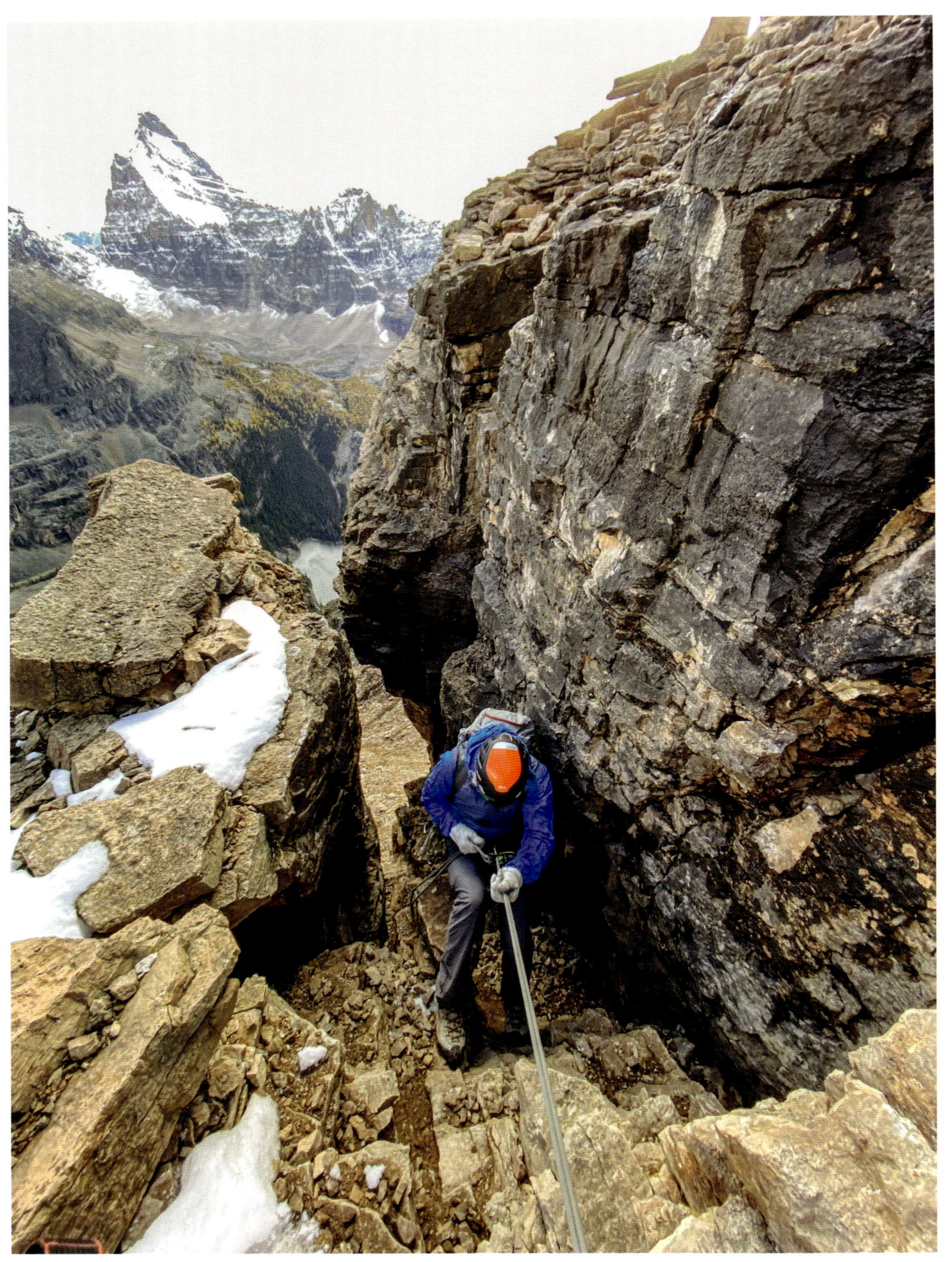

Life Rope (2021)
James Blench introduced me to the basics of harness climbing on a low-elevation rock near Banff. I learned to tie the figure 8 follow-through knot, and to lean back over the edge with my full commitment, my life entirely in the hands of my trusted belayer. I felt surprisingly secure. Weeks later, we met on location and put the lesson successfully to task.

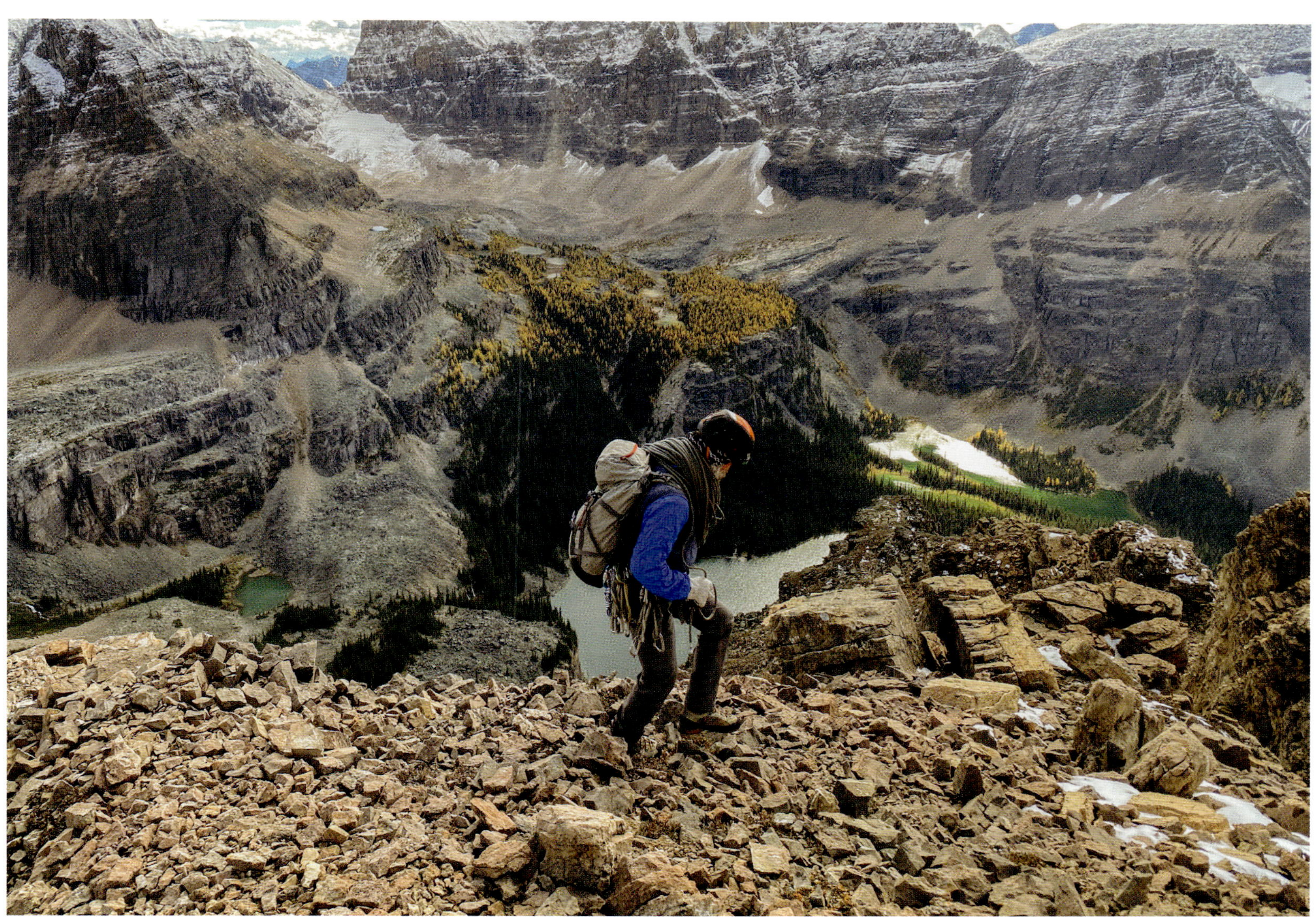

Unravelled (2021)
The more risk there is in an activity, the more important it is to adhere to protocol. James Blench always keeps his ropes and clips untangled and organized as he meticulously plans the next move.

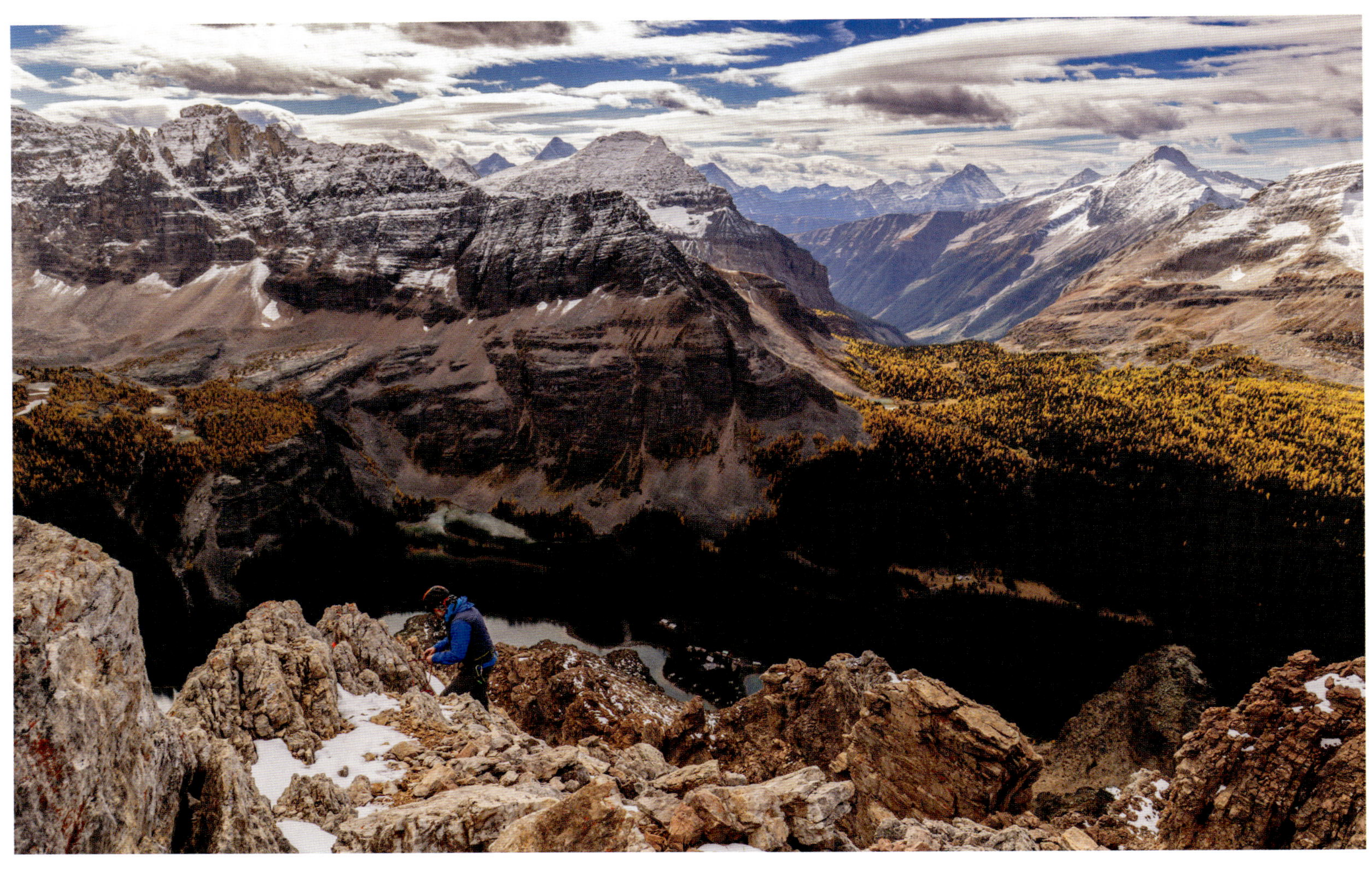

Summit View (2021)
Lake O'Hara Lodge and its ring of lakeside cabins are all visible
from this perch atop Wiwaxy Peaks.

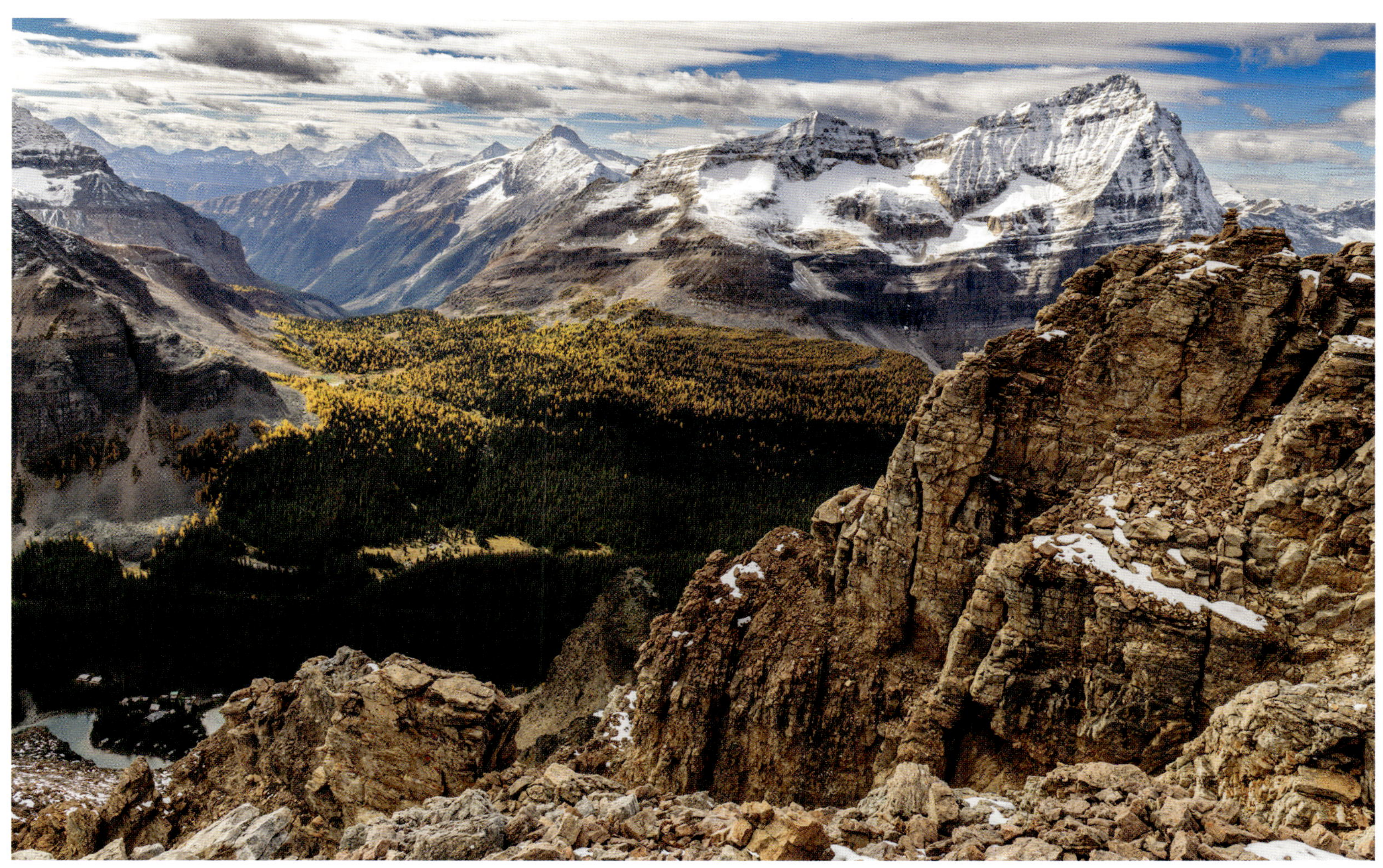

Peak View (2021)
A climber's eye view of the Wiwaxy Peaks foreground set against distant Lake O'Hara Lodge and the Elizabeth Parker Hut. Mount Schäffer on the left and Odaray Mountain on the right frame the view, with McArthur Pass draped in golden larch.

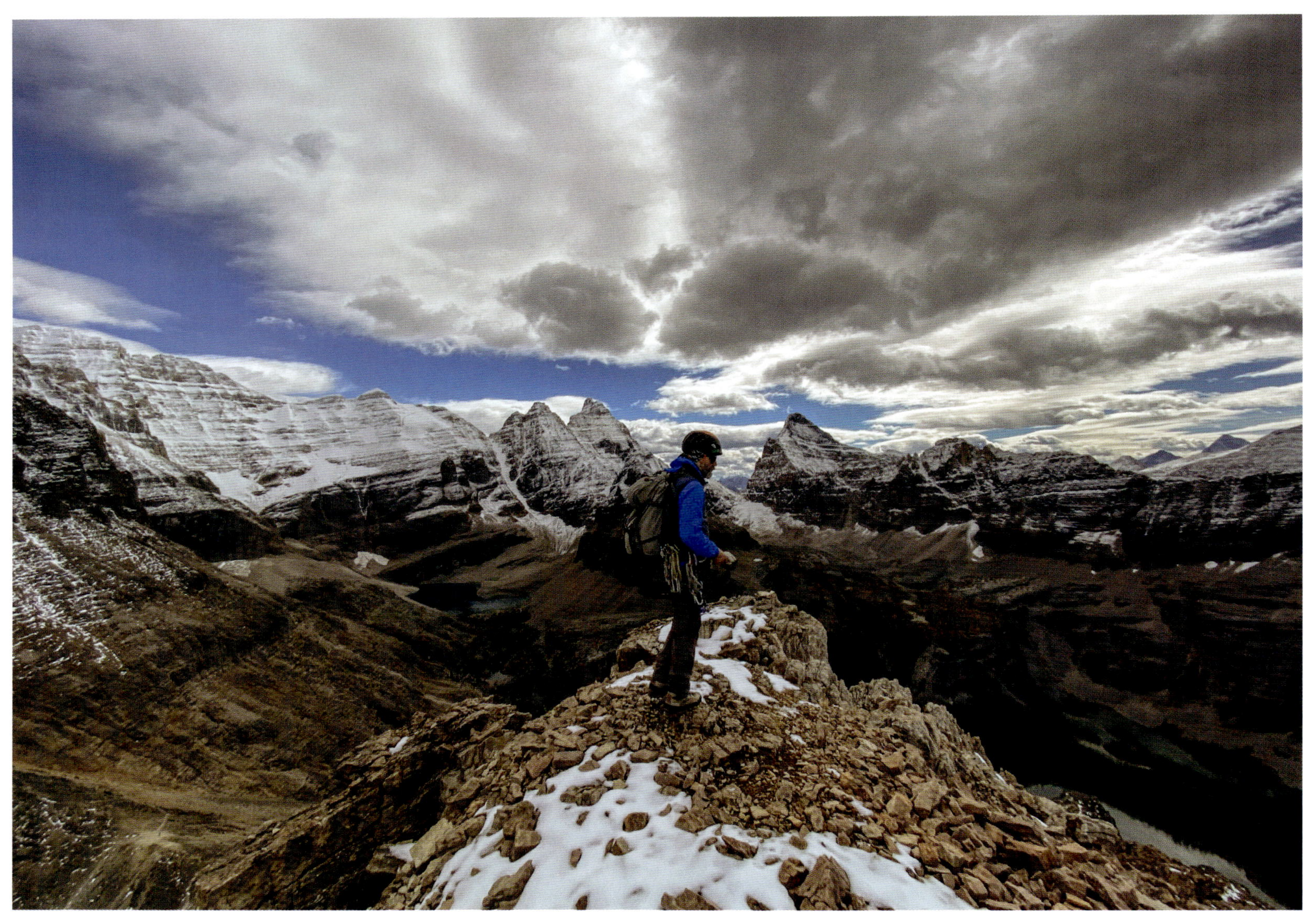

Summit High (2021)
A triumphant moment of dopamine and adrenaline release in
the context of mild oxygen deprivation for that undeniable
"Rocky Mountain High."

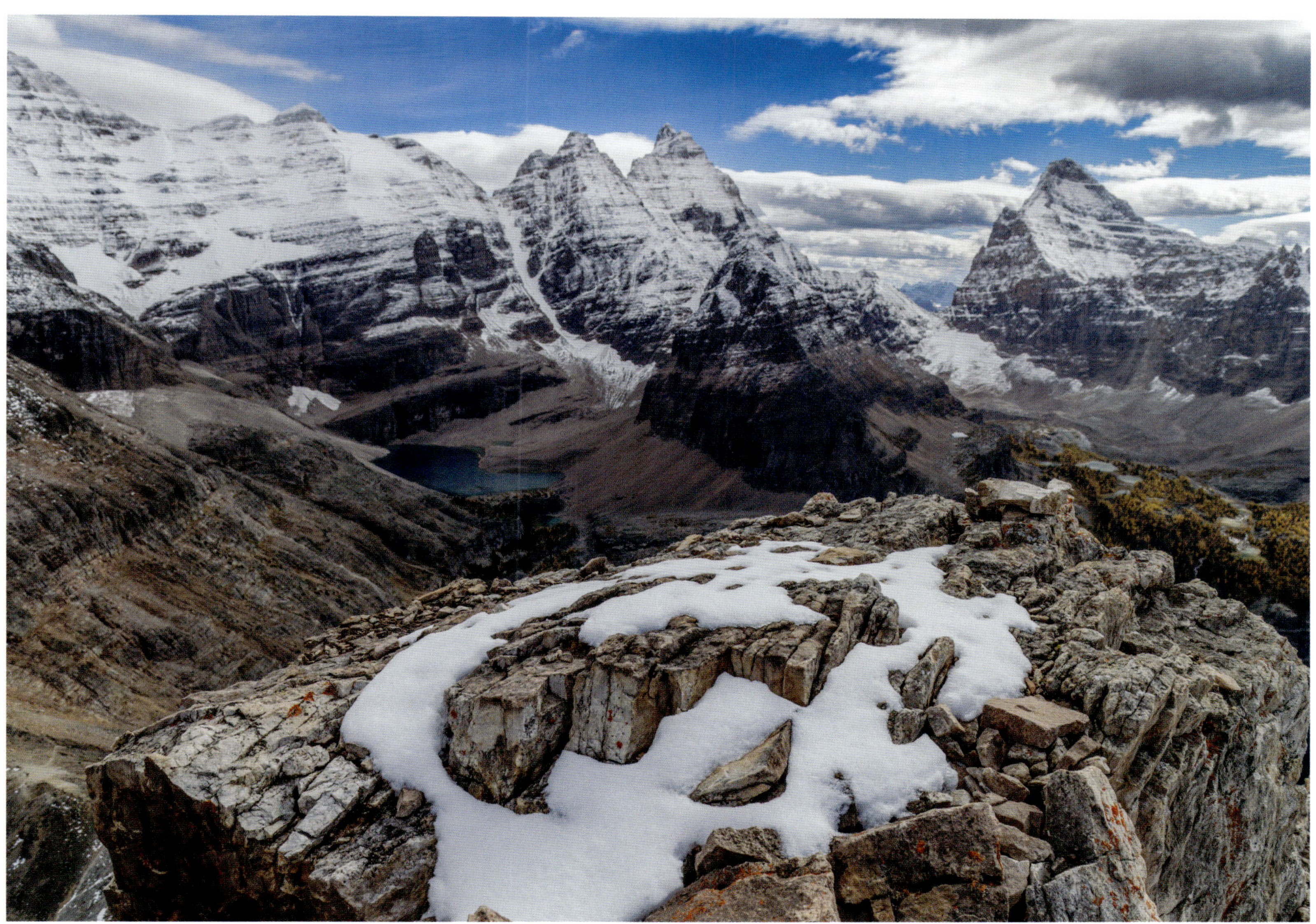

Connected (2021)

Imagine yourself standing right here. The trails connecting
Opabin Plateau to Lake Oesa appear so small they look like
threads weaving between the trees and rock. Distant lakes
look like small ponds, and clouds are just above your eye level.
Known as the "overview effect," this shift in awareness helps us
see the connectedness of everything, including ourselves.

Overleaf **Standing on Time** (2021)

The farther out we look in space, the farther back in time we
see. It's not dissimilar to geology. From this vantage point,
we stand upon hundreds of millions of years of time past, our
planet's creation story in plain view waiting to be understood
and still unfolding.

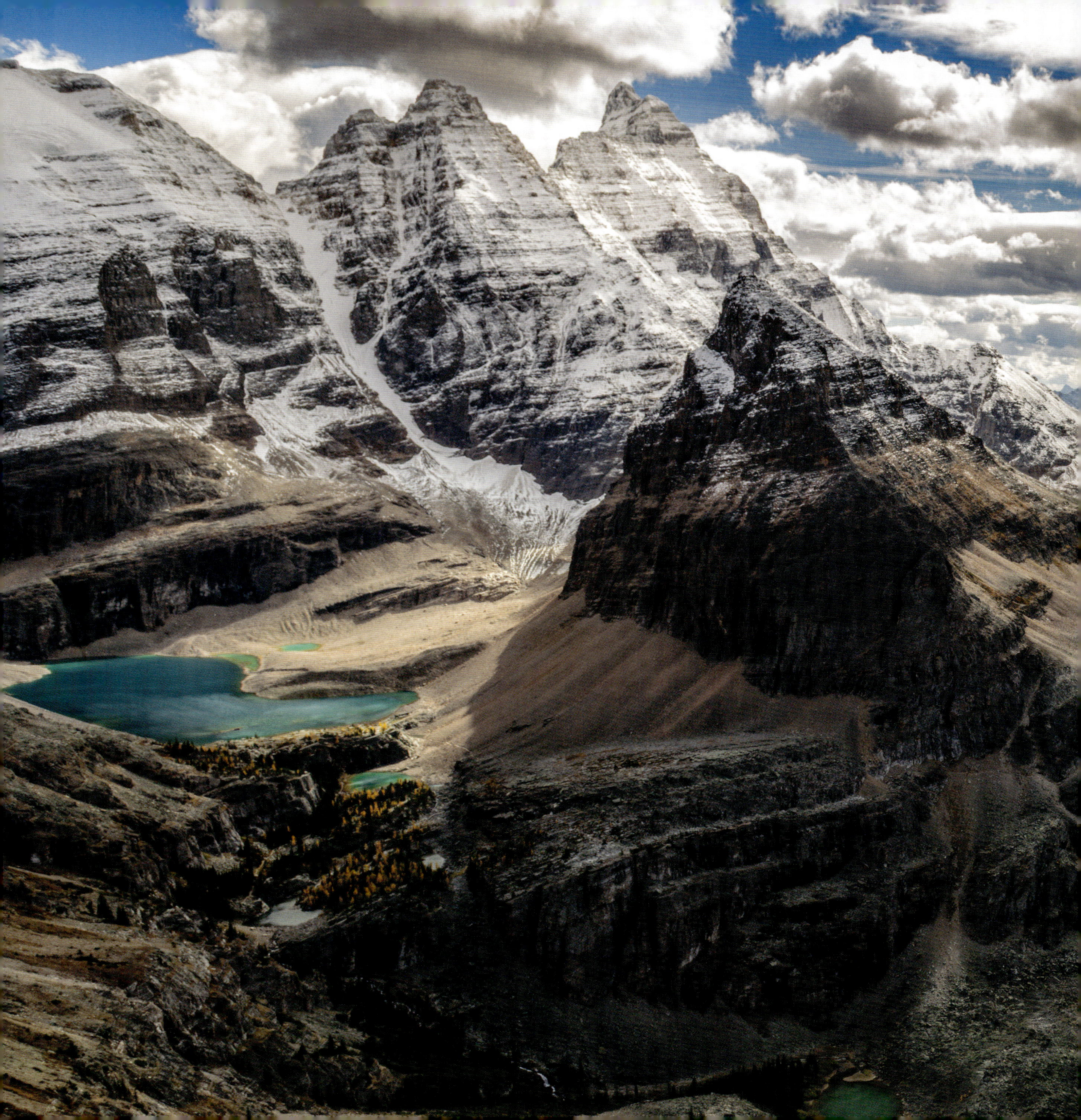

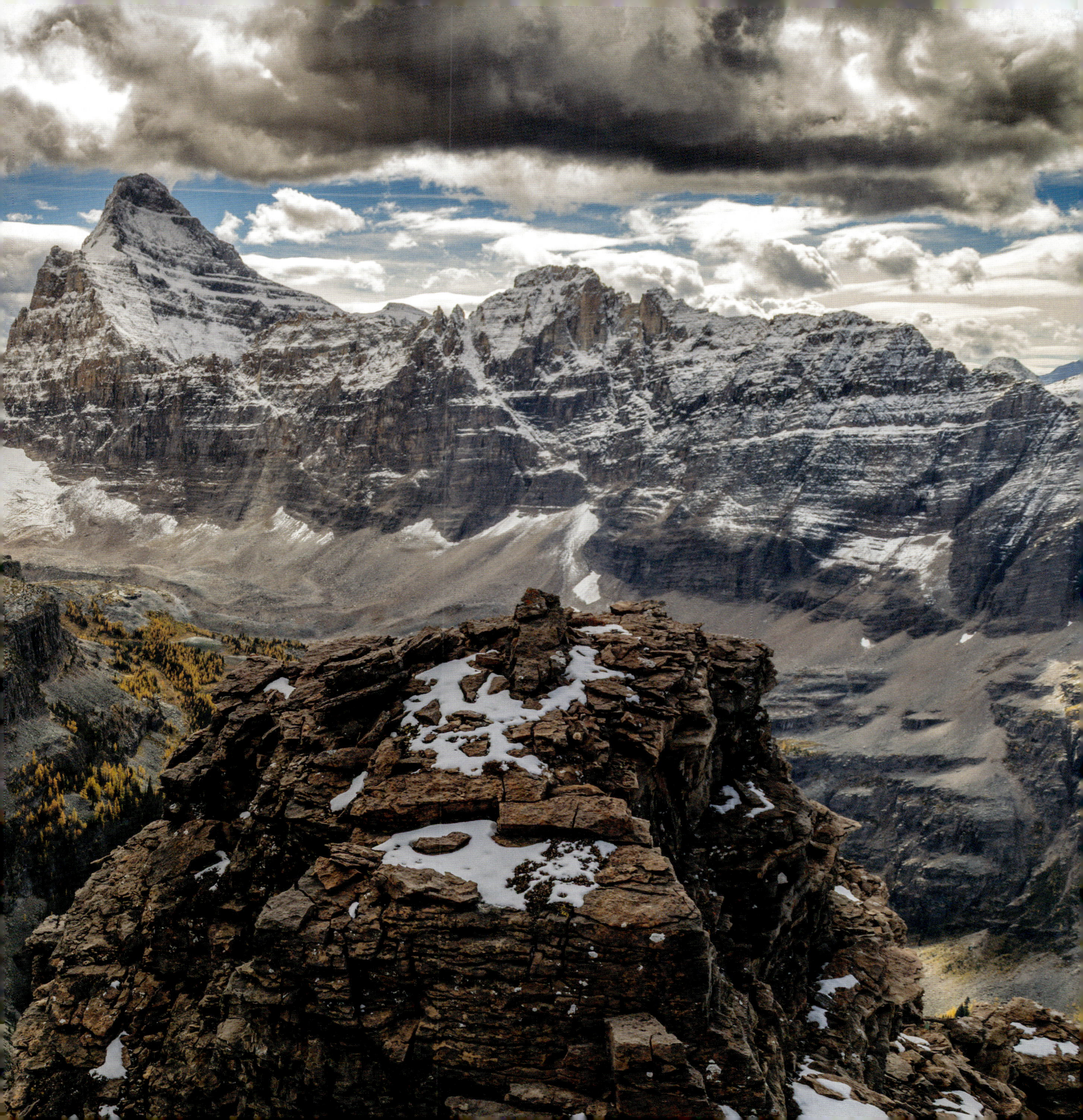

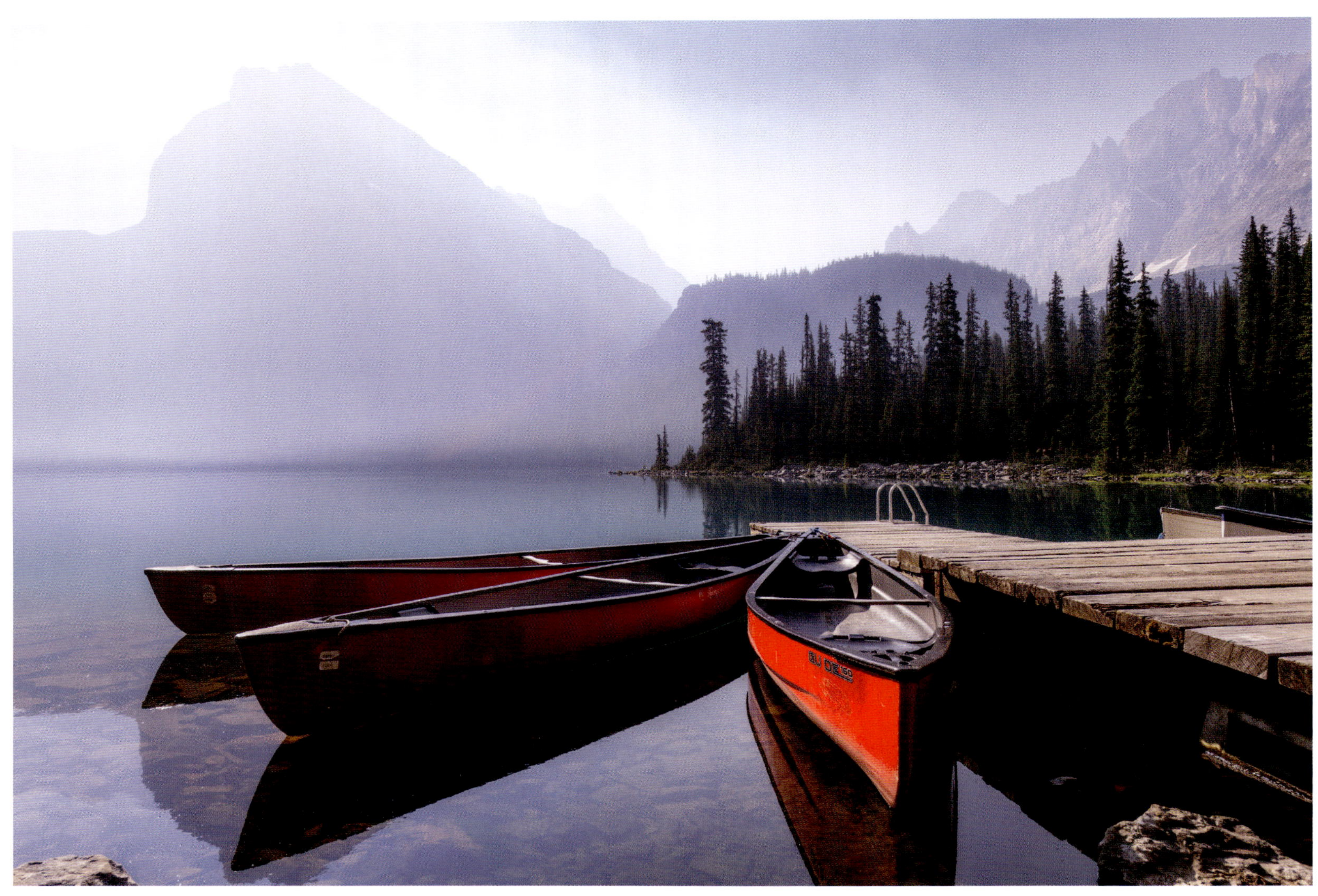

Adventures Await (2021)
Classic red Rocky Mountain canoes calling for a morning pad-
dler. These boats are free for use by Lake O'Hara Lodge guests.

About the Area

The spectacular scenery of the Lake O'Hara region, with its unparalleled vistas and extensive trail network maintained by the Lake O'Hara Trails Club and Parks Canada, places it at risk of being overrun by visitors due to popular demand. In order to preserve this fragile and sensitive alpine ecosystem, with its unique varieties of wildlife and plants, for generations to come, access to the region is carefully limited. Parks Canada's website offers information on how best to access the Lake O'Hara region for day use, overnight camping, ACC Hut accommodations, or stays at Lake O'Hara Lodge.

DAY USE

Day-Use Shuttle Bus

Parks Canada operates a day-use shuttle bus from the Lake O'Hara parking lot (12 km west of Lake Louise, AB, or 13 km east of Field, BC) between late June and early October. The bus transports visitors up the 11-km access road to Le Relais Day Shelter near Lake O'Hara. Reservations are required and are allocated through a randomized draw in the month of March. It is best to check the Parks Canada website for up-to-date reservation information. Without a bus reservation, visitors have to hike the 22-km round trip along the access road to the base of Lake O'Hara and back to the parking lot by nightfall, and be prepared with food, water, and bear spray. Cycling and pets are not permitted on either the bus or the access road.

Le Relais Day Shelter

The Lake O'Hara Trails Club was established in 1949 as a nonprofit organization with the mission, as stated on its

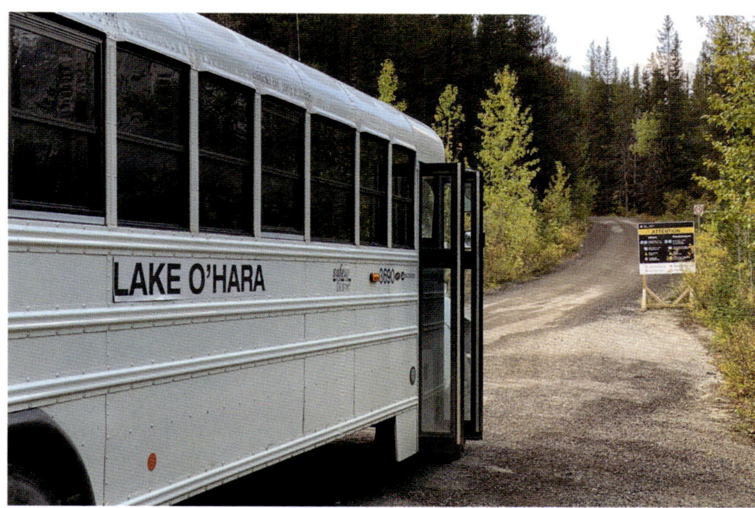

Coveted Transport (2025)
The Parks Canada day-use shuttle bus awaits passengers fortunate enough to be allotted a seat through the annual spring lottery.

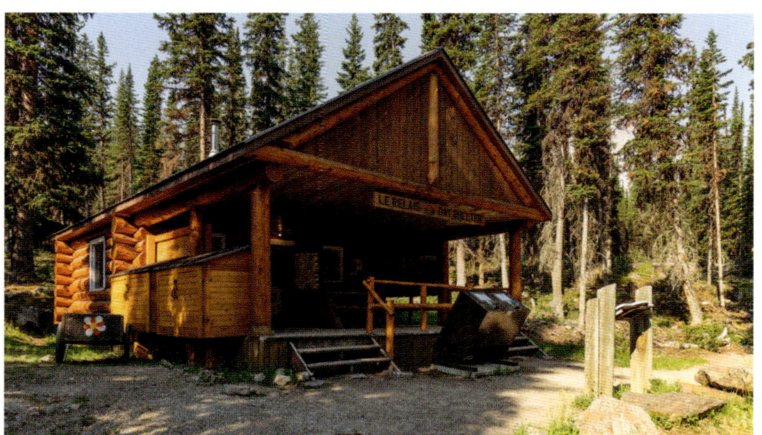

Day Tripper (2021)
Located near the Parks Canada Lake O'Hara shuttle bus drop-off, Le Relais Day Shelter provides some food, along with park interpretation and notifications. It also serves as a meeting space for scheduled presentations on local interests.

website, to "inspire and facilitate the stewardship of the Lake O'Hara area's trail system, as well as the appreciation of the area's cultural and natural history." As part of its duties, the club, in cooperation with Lake O'Hara Lodge, operates Le Relais Day Shelter near Lake O'Hara. The shelter first opened in 1989 and is open daily from mid-June to early October. It's an excellent first stop where welcoming and knowledgeable staff are available with up-to-date information on local conditions and hiking suggestions. Trail maps, beverages, and light snacks are also available for purchase (cash only).

To learn more about the Lake O'Hara Trails Club, visit its website to sign up for its newsletter and to learn how to volunteer.

OVERNIGHT USE

Lake O'Hara Campground

Visitors can camp up to three nights at Lake O'Hara Campground, a popular campsite open from mid-June to early October. There are only 30 campsites available and reservations are required for overnight guests. Facilities include two cooking shelters, one firepit, food and garbage storage and gray water disposal, outhouses, firewood, and treated well water (the latter is not always available early or late in the season).

Elizabeth Parker Hut

The Elizabeth Parker Hut was built in 1919 by the CPR and was later taken over by Parks Canada. The EP Hut has been designated a Federal Heritage Building and stands as an example of the rustic aesthetic of traditional log cabins built in the Canadian national parks during the 1900s. The EP Hut offers rustic accommodation that includes propane-sourced heat and light, a stove, and an oven. Mattresses are provided, but guests are required to bring their own bedding.

The EP Hut is currently operated by the Alpine Club of Canada, a nonprofit organization that is over 100 years old

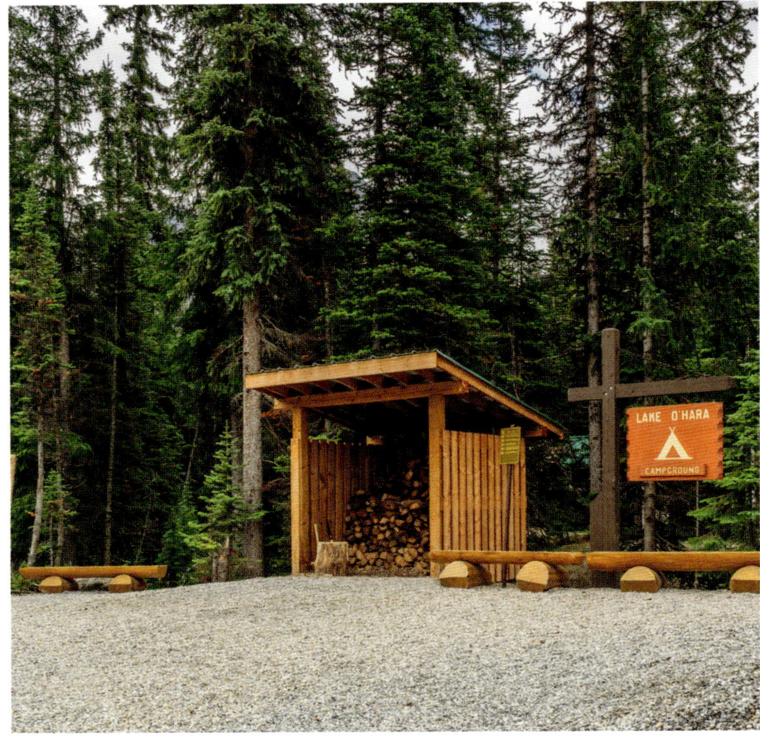

Camp Lottery (2024)
With only 30 tent sites, the annual April lottery by Parks Canada fills up within minutes for this coveted campsite.

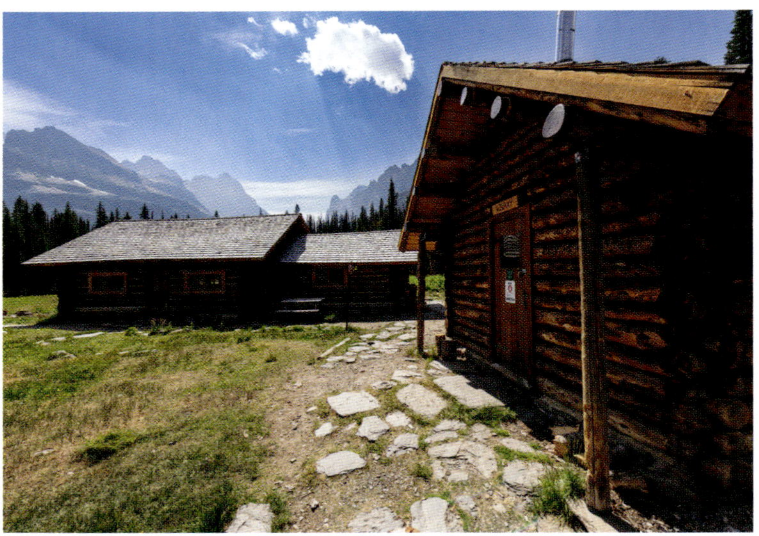

Elizabeth Parker Hut (2021)
The Elizabeth Parker Hut is named after a trail-blazing journalist prominent in promoting mountain recreation and conservation in the 1900s. She was also a co-founder of the Alpine Club of Canada.

and whose mission, as stated on its website, is to "encourage and facilitate access to wild places while ensuring their long-term preservation for future generations." The EP Hut is open to guests all year round, however reservations are required. Access during the popular summer months (June–October) is granted through a reservation lottery system available on the ACC's website.

In addition to the EP Hut, the ACC operates huts all across Canada. For more information, visit its website.

Lake O'Hara Lodge

Completed in 1926, Lake O'Hara Lodge has provided 100 years of hospitality. Reservations are required to stay at the lodge. Parks Canada's policy to limit access to this region in order to preserve it for future generations, combined with the limited spaces available in the lodge and lakeside cabins, results in a significant wait list for accommodation availability. It is not uncommon for prospective guests to wait years for an opening.

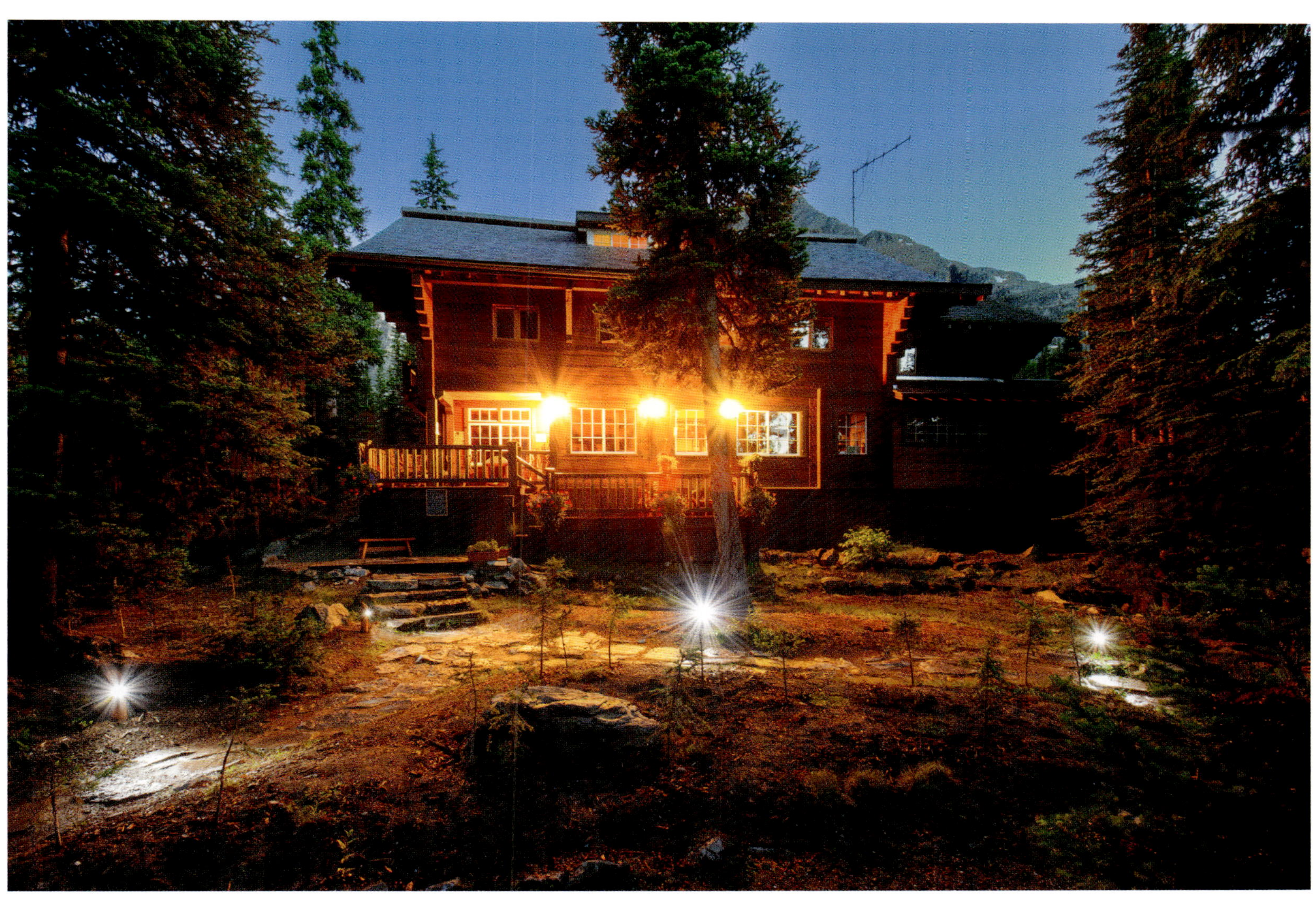

Historic CPR Lodge (2007)
The CPR constructed Lake O'Hara Lodge in 1926 using local stone and timber.

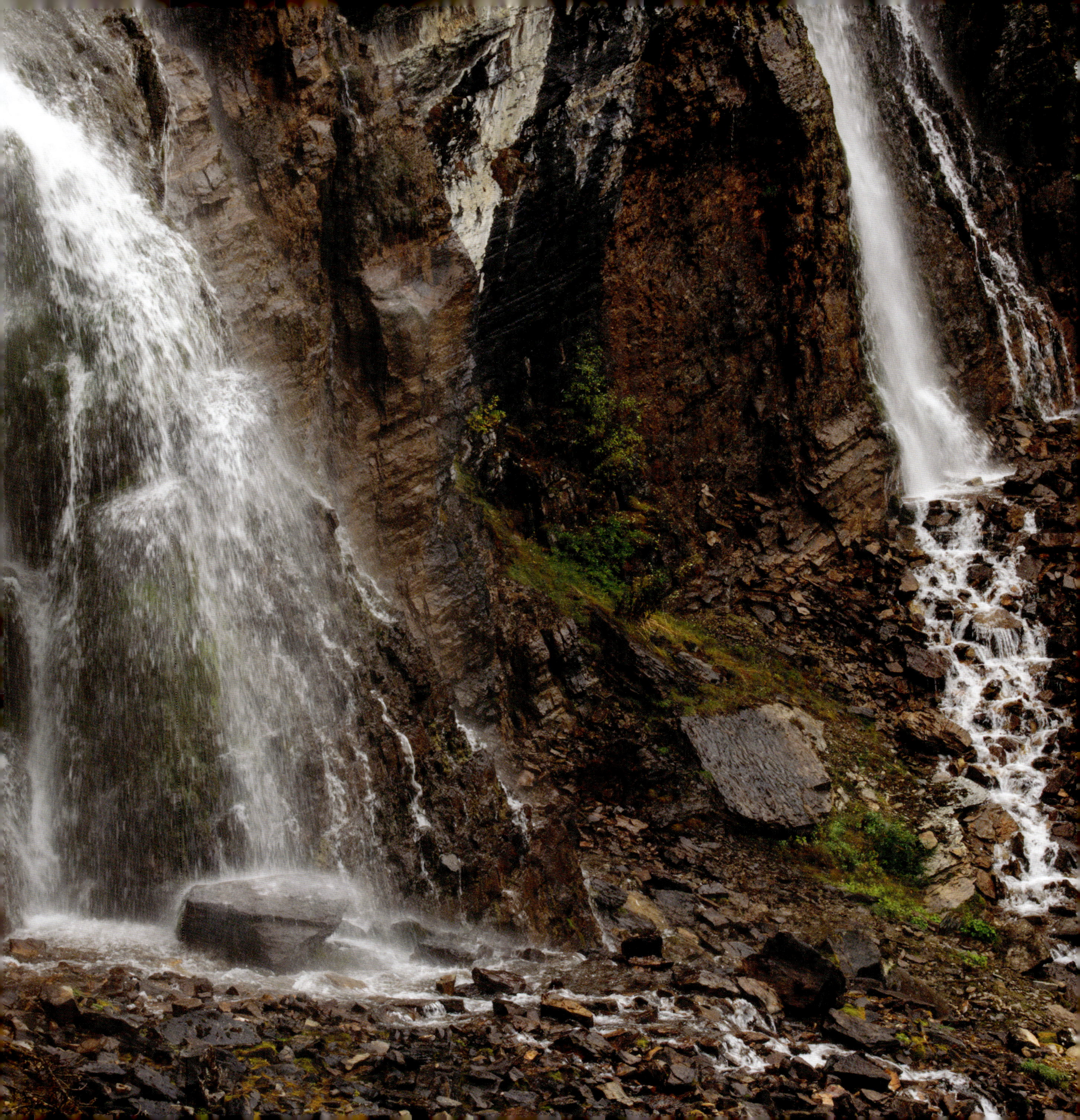

A Story Written in Stone

BY MARC ST-ONGE

A DYNAMIC PAST: THE PACIFIC'S INFLUENCE

The breathtaking landscapes of western Canada, including the stunning Lake O'Hara area, owe their existence to an incredible geological journey shaped by the Pacific Ocean.

Geologically, the modern Pacific Ocean is the successor to the original ocean that formed when Laurentia – our continent's Precambrian[1] core – rifted and drifted apart from other continental land masses to the west (Australia, Australia/Antarctica, and/or North China being top contenders) that were all initially part of the supercontinent Rodinia, with the western ocean opening and widening until it became Panthalassa, the World Ocean. Unlike the eastern side of the North American continent, which experienced the closing and reopening of several ocean basins over time, western North America has faced the same vast ocean for more than 700 million years. During this long period of Earth history, the region's geological story was one of constant change, starting with continental rifting leading to the quiet formation of a passive continental shelf, followed by the transition to an active and deforming margin characterized by dramatic episodes of faulting, mountain building, and volcanic activity. As a result, changing geological environments have created the complex and varied geology and physiography of western Canada: its mountain belts, volcanoes, and granite canyons; its scarps, plateaus, and soaring vistas.

The history of the western margin of North America in Canada (Figure 1) can be viewed as comprising five phases of geological evolution. From oldest to youngest, these include:

1. **Rifted Margin (~700–540 million years ago)**: This phase began with the breakup of the ancient supercontinent Rodinia. As the land masses drifted apart, a vast new ocean formed, laying the foundation for what would become the Pacific coastline of North America.

2. **Passive Margin (~540–400 million years ago)**: Over time, sediments accumulated along the new continental margin, creating a thick westward-thickening wedge of rock. These deposits, now beautifully exposed in the Rocky Mountains, include both carbonate and sandy siliciclastic layers.

Gentle Roar (2018)
Lake Oesa finishes its journey to Lake O'Hara through Seven Veils Falls, the gentle roar of which echoes throughout the mountainous basin as the waters cascade over the sandstone strata of the lower Gog Group.

1 The reader is referred to the International Chronostratigraphic Chart (Figure 9) for the time periods (in millions of years) encapsulated by Earth history terms such as Precambrian, Neoproterozoic, Paleozoic, Cambrian, etc.

3. **Oceans and Islands (beginning ~400 million years ago)**: Subduction, where older oceanic crust sinks beneath the edge of a continental or oceanic margin, led to the formation of offshore volcanic island chains and intervening marginal oceans from which the continent retreated, creating a scenario much like the modern southeastern Pacific Ocean. A large portion of British Columbia west of the Rocky Mountains is made up of rocks of volcanic island to oceanic affinity that occur in relatively coherent packages separated from each other by faults (Intermontane, Insular, and Outboard belts, see Figure 1). These packages, famously termed collages of "suspect terranes" by geologists Peter Coney and Jim Monger, have had uncertain relationships to the North American continent during at least part of their history. Eventually, most of them were shown to either contain fossil assemblages of eastern Pacific affinity or to exhibit sedimentological, geochemical, and/or historical aspects that link them, however distally, to the North American continent. Some, however, are more convincingly exotic imports: parts of the Intermontane belt (Figure 1) with the occurrence of Japanese/Chinese fossils; parts of the Insular belt (Figure 1), with the preservation of fossils with a Scandinavian affinity; and fragments of continental crust in Alaska with Precambrian ages that are unknown in the rest of North America.

4. **Terrane Accretion/Orogeny (beginning ~180 million years ago)**: At present, the Pacific Ocean is highly asymmetric, its west side festooned with volcanic island chains, its east side bare, bordering a North American continental margin made up of fragments of just such volcanic chains and marginal oceans. As is the case for most oceanic basins, it is reasonable to suppose that both sides of the Pacific were once mirror images. However, opening of the northern Atlantic Ocean to the east destroyed that symmetry. Although earlier compressional events affected some of the suspect terranes, their tectonic emplacement (thrusting) on top of the western continental margin dates from the early Jurassic epoch, roughly 180 million years ago – the same age as the basalt flows related to the opening of the Atlantic Ocean on the eastern seaboard. The period approximately 180–66 million years ago saw intense mountain building along the western margin of the continent, with both suspect terranes and the sedimentary strata of the continental margin (Figure 1) stacked into a complex but overall easterly tapering (thinning) thrust fault-laden orogenic wedge, forming the rugged peaks we see today.

5. **Post-Accretion (since ~66 million years ago)**: With the Pacific plate moving (and subducting) toward the northeast with respect to North America, massive horizontal faults – like the Rocky Mountain Trench, the Pinchi, and the Fraser River faults in British Columbia (Figure 1) – developed, shifting the landscape further. The story continues even now, with earthquakes and volcanic activity occasionally shaking and further reshaping Canada's rugged west coast.

THE SANDIEST SEAS

The well-exposed rock formations of Lake O'Hara provide a unique window into Earth's past, including the transition from the older Rifted Margin to the Passive Margin phases of continental evolution as introduced above. It should be noted that, as is the case for all sedimentary rock sequences worldwide, this rock record is best understood if it is "read" starting with the older chapters of Earth history, or rock formations, exposed at the bottom through to the younger, overlying rock formations sitting on top (Figures 2 and 3).

The oldest rocks exposed in the Lake O'Hara area belong to the late Precambrian – early Cambrian, shallow-marine, Gog Group (Figures 2 and 3), part of a vast apron of sandy siliciclastic strata deposited along the ancient continental margins of western Canada and much of Laurentia at that time. The group records the transition from late continental

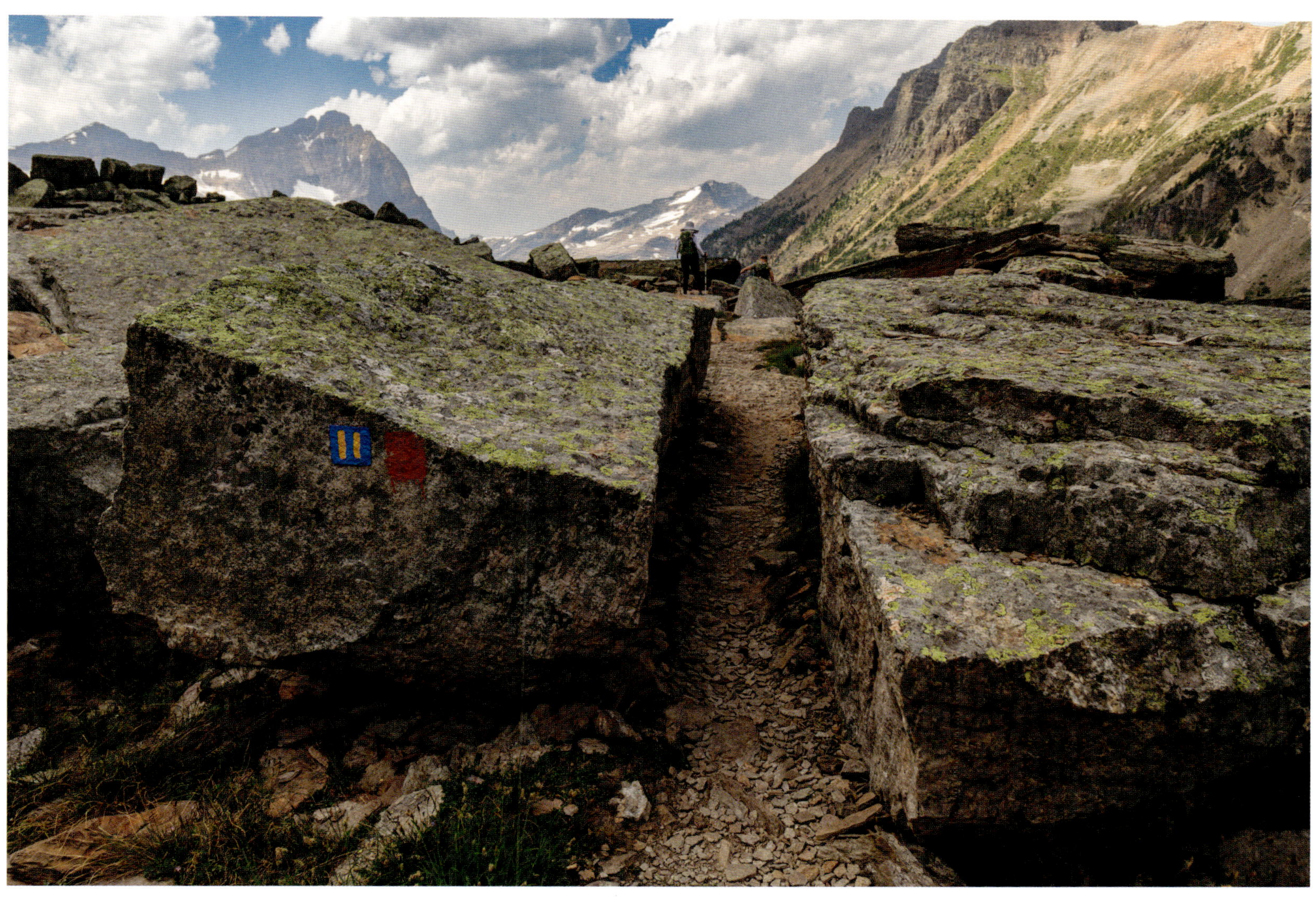

Trail Marker (2021)
The fluorescent blue and yellow alpine route markers help hikers stay on course. The Lake O'Hara Alpine Circuit passes through steep gullies and avalanche areas with risk of falling rocks, including from overlying coarse-grained sandstone beds of the lower Gog Group, and therefore hikers need to be mindful of the prevailing weather conditions and follow appropriate protocols.

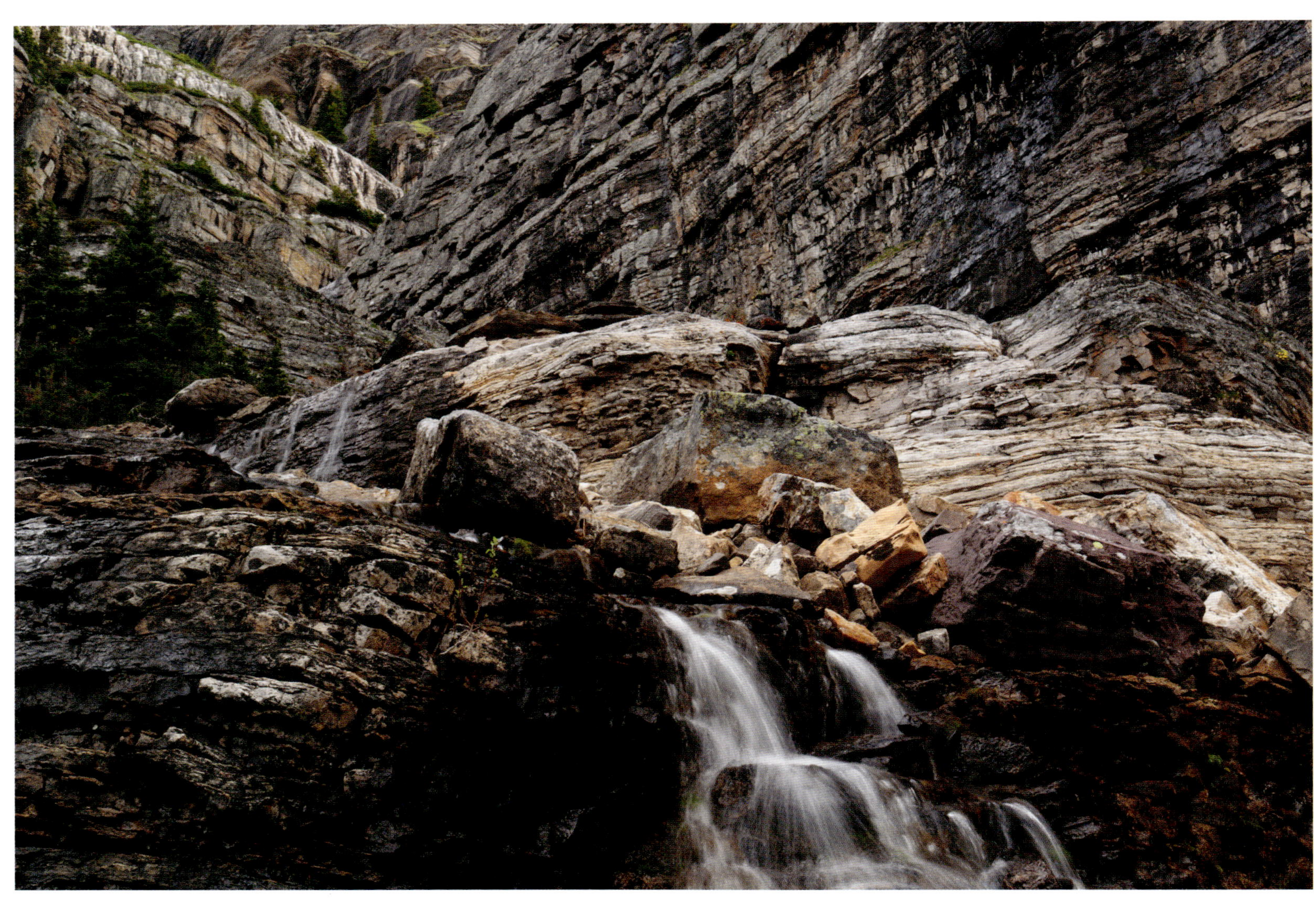

Least Resistance (2021)
The glacier meltwater of Lake Oesa pours over Victoria Falls, which is underlain by thin to thick sandstone beds of the middle Gog Group, carving a route alongside Lake Oesa Trail, following the path of least resistance on its journey to Lake O'Hara.

rifting (Figure 4A) to early marine transgression (rising sea levels) (Figure 4B) with the accumulation of a continental shelf sedimentary sequence. Dominant rivers flowed toward the west, carrying sandy material derived from the weathering and erosion of the Canadian Shield and its extension beneath the Canadian Prairies. Because land plants were virtually absent at this time, extensive sandy dune fields and braided river systems were dominant features on land, generating large amounts of sediment that were transported unimpeded from the continent to the continental margin. These sediments created some of the sandiest seas in Earth's history!

Overall, the lower Gog Group is characterized by pink to red, very well sorted, medium- to fine-grained sandstone. Beds are commonly tabular to lenticular, with sharp bases and planar to wavy tops. Individual beds range from 7 to 20 cm to 1 m thick. Mudstone laminae and clasts of partially lithified sandstone (intraclasts) are rare. The unit forms a coarsening upward succession. This part of the Gog Group records progressively rising sea levels over an area of low relief (Figure 4B). A basal lag of scattered pebbles in a coarse-grained sandstone matrix was formed by waves and tidal currents during the initial marine transgression and rising sea levels. Later, sand was deposited in a shallow-subtidal environment punctuated by low energy periods that allowed the deposition of rose-brown, thin-bedded siltstone.

The top of the lower Gog Group is a recessive-weathering unit with a characteristic dull green weathering colour. With a maximum thickness of 25 m, it consists of intercalated, very well sorted, fine- to very fine-grained sandstone and shale, with abundant lenticular and wavy sandstone beds. Intraclasts are common in medium- to coarse-grained sandstone beds. This part of the Gog Group records inner- to outer-continental shelf sedimentation characterized by low rates of sand transport to the shelf. The base of this unit marks a change from a shallow-subtidal to deeper

inner-shelf environment during peak marine transgression (Figure 4C). The fine-grained facies herald dominantly deeper, less turbulent conditions, in contrast to the older underlying strata described above.

The middle Gog Group is characterized by the presence of light gray, thick- to very-thick-bedded Skolithos pipe rock intercalated with minor thin- to very-thin-bedded, lenticular- to wavy-bedded sandstone. The pipe rock is a clean sandstone (quartzite) containing what are thought to be traces of vertical burrows originally made by a worm-like animal (Skolithos). The famous Pipe Rock of northwest Scotland is a well-known example of Skolithos. Shrinkage cracks are sporadically present. Individual Skolithos pipe rock intervals are overlain by recessive red- to purple-weathering, mudstone-dominated units containing fining-upwards successions with sandstone packages at their bases. The mudstone reaches a maximum thickness of slightly more than 9 m in the Lake O'Hara area and represents a tidal-flat complex established after shoreline progradation (re-advance toward the sea) (Figure 4D), with polygonal mud cracks recording subaerial exposure and desiccation of the sandstone/mudstone shoreline. At least three major progradation events are recorded in the middle Gog Group in the Lake O'Hara area (Figure 4E).

The transition from quartz sand-dominated to carbonate-dominated sedimentation is recorded by the uppermost Gog Group, and it is one of the most important shifts in sedimentation styles within the rock record of not only the Lake O'Hara area but the whole of the western margin of North America. The depletion of siliciclastic sediment input is related to the eastward migration of the shoreline, with continuing rising sea levels as the marine transgression took hold and progressed toward the interior of the continent (Figure 4E).

The Mount Whyte Formation (Figures 2 and 3) was deposited on top of the Gog Group in warm, shallow marine waters along the western margin of North America

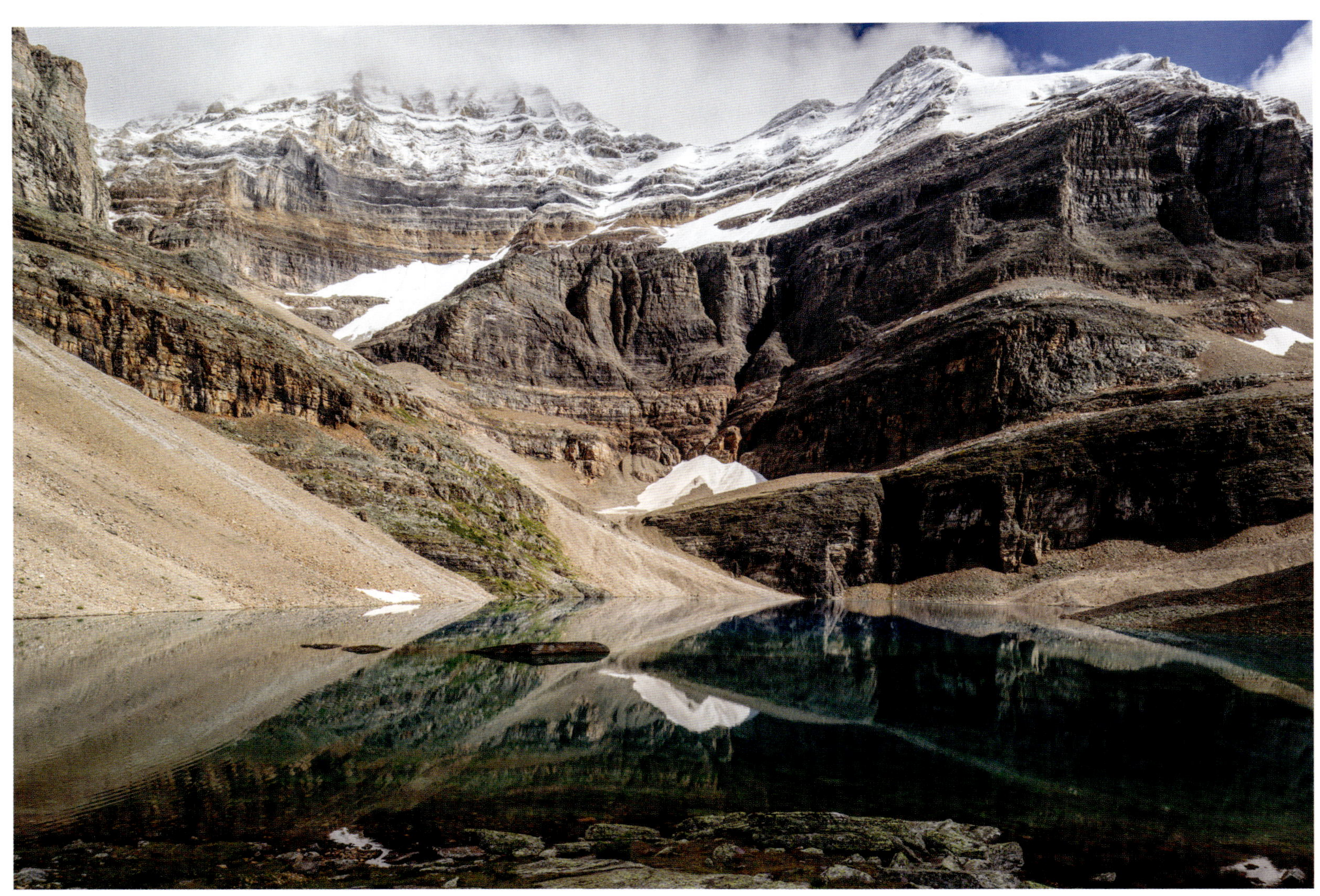

Historic Inspiration (2014)
Mount Lefroy towers over Lake Oesa and records in the bedrock landscape the change from sand-dominated to carbonate-dominated sedimentary strata. The mountain was inspiration for the Group of Seven painter Lawren Harris in his transition toward his distinctly stylistic and eventually abstract portrayal of Canadian landscapes.

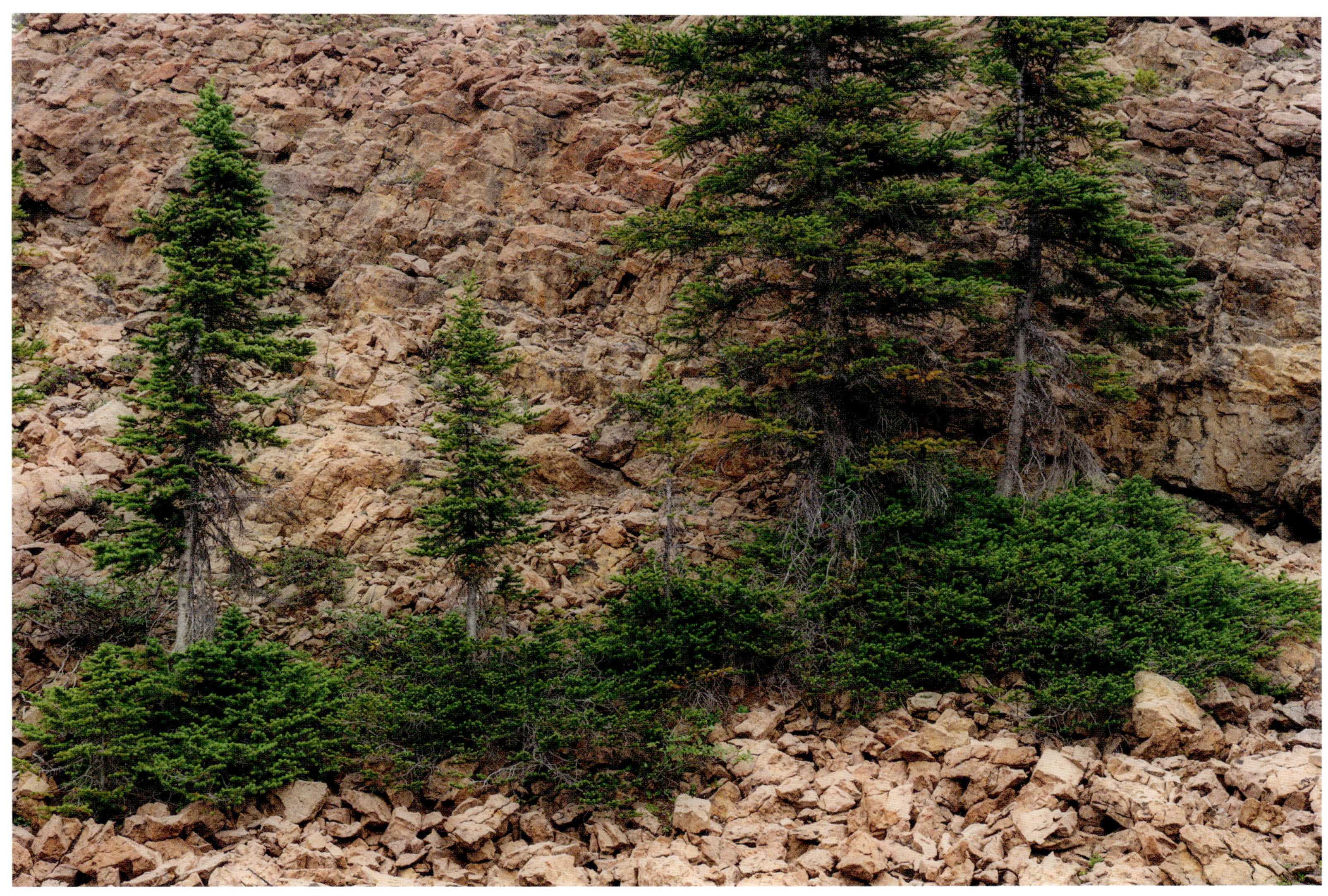

Nature's Complement (2010)
Pinkish-beige marine carbonate strata of the Cathedral Formation provide a valuable source of protection and warmth for
these trees cleverly tucked alongside.

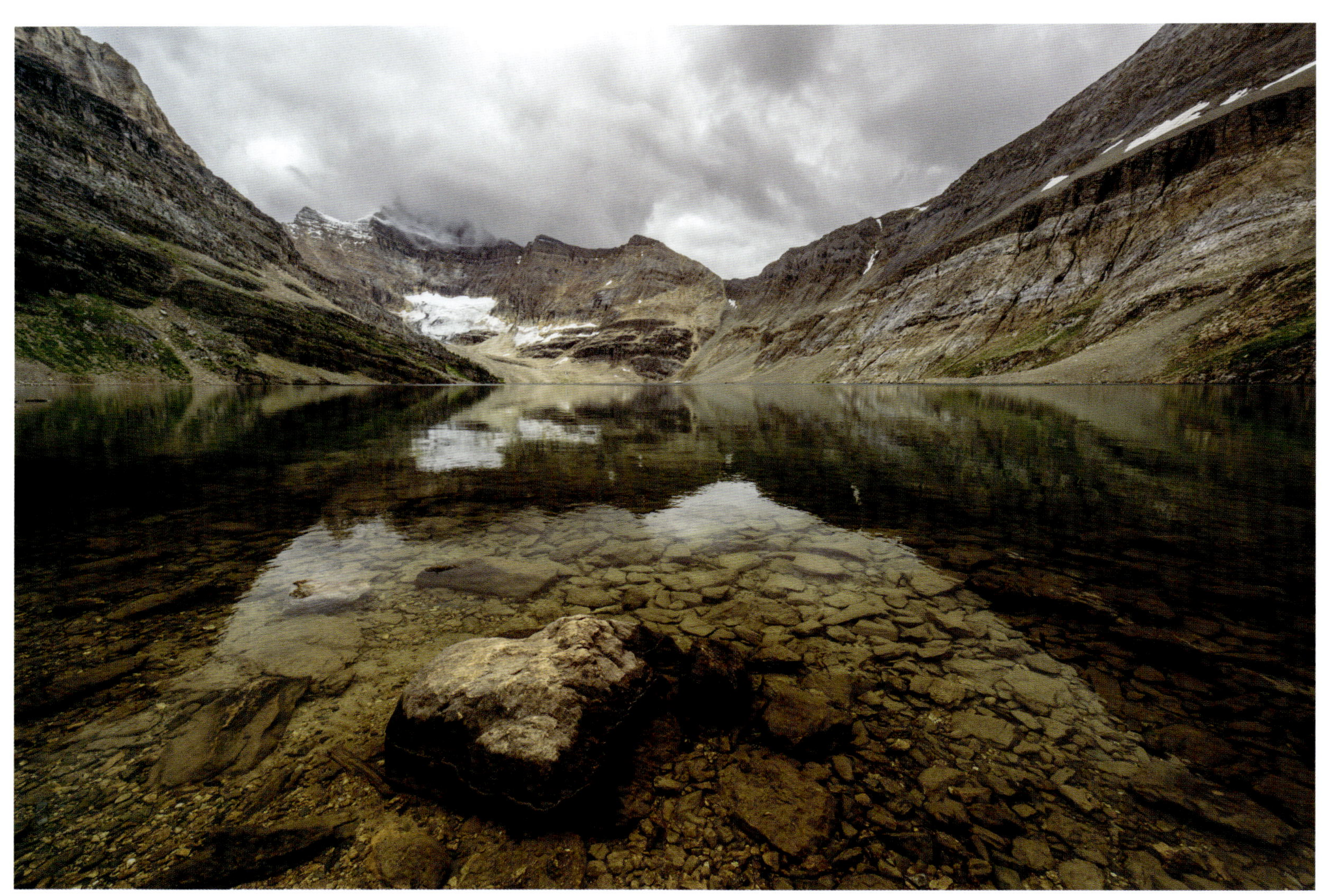

Momentary Still (2024)
Given the elevation and cirque shape of Lake McArthur, flanked by the Stephen Formation (dark) overlying the Cathedral Formation (light), the air often moves swiftly through it during daylight hours. Moments of stillness take patience; every now and then a calmness would settle in for a few moments.

during the middle Cambrian epoch. It consists mainly of dark gray shale interbedded with thin beds of sandstone, sandy gray limestone, and limestone containing oolites (from the ancient Greek word for "egg stone" – spherical grains of carbonate up to 2 mm in diameter). The formation provides the sedimentological record of the continuing change from deposition of sand to accumulation of carbonate strata on the continental shelf.

The overlying Cathedral Formation (Figures 2 and 3) consists primarily of massive, cliff-forming, light to dark pinkish beige carbonate rocks. It was originally deposited as limestone, much of which may have been secreted by marine algae. Deposition took place in shallow water on an extensive carbonate shelf that had developed along the western margin of North America during the middle Cambrian. The Cathedral Formation includes fossil stromatolites, oncolites, and other algal remains, as well as a few dark gray shale beds with trilobites. The westernmost edge of the Cathedral Formation is the aptly named Cathedral Escarpment (a major submarine cliff about 160 m tall), now exposed on the western slopes of Mount Field and Mount Stephen to the northwest of Lake O'Hara. The Cathedral Escarpment is thought to have played a major role in the deposition and subsequent preservation of the world-famous Burgess Shale fossils in a buttressed continental slope setting (see below).

The Stephen Formation (Figures 2 and 3) overlies the Cathedral Formation, and it consists of dark shale, thin-bedded limestone, and siltstone that was deposited during middle Cambrian time. It is famous for the exceptional preservation of soft-bodied fossils: the Burgess Shale biota mentioned above. Detrital sediments of the Stephen Formation were washed in by rivers from the continent on top of and beyond the carbonate shelf (and bounding submarine cliff) that formed the shallow sea floor of the underlying Cathedral Formation.

The stratigraphically highest, and therefore one of the youngest, bedrock formations in the Lake O'Hara area is the Eldon Formation (Figures 2 and 3). The formation comprises a thick sequence of massive, cliff-forming, light to dark gray limestones and dolomites that was named for the Eldon Switch on the CPR near Castle Mountain in Banff National Park by Charles Doolittle Walcott, who discovered the Burgess Shale fossils. The Eldon Formation was also deposited during middle Cambrian time, and it includes fossil stromatolites. It forms the towering cliffs at the top of Castle Mountain (formerly Mount Eisenhower) in Banff National Park, as well as those of Mount Victoria, Mount Huber, Mount Lefroy, Hungabee Mountain, and Odaray Mountain in the Lake O'Hara region.

WHENCE THE MOUNTAINS?

Lake O'Hara's dramatic landscapes result from a combination of rock type, geological structure, and erosion. Local relief is considerable, with elevation gains of 1300 m within 2 km of Lake O'Hara itself (Figure 3). The sandstone-rich Gog Group underlies Lake O'Hara, as well as Lake Oesa, Lake McArthur, and Duchesnay Basin, while the overlying carbonate formations outcrop at elevations generally above 2700 m, creating the towering peaks.

The dramatic changes in bed thickness (thin versus massive) and rock type (sandstone versus carbonate) that occur with increasing elevation and stratigraphic level in the Lake O'Hara area involve important changes in the mechanical rock properties that have exerted a profound influence on the nature of the resulting landscape. A first-order correlation can be made between the sandstone-dominated Gog Group with lower elevations and valley floors (Figure 3). Conversely, the more resistant, cliff-forming, carbonate strata of the overlying Cathedral, Stephen, and Eldon rock formations can be equated with the higher peaks surrounding Lake O'Hara, as well as those forming the spine of the Continental Divide and the eastern boundary of Yoho National Park (Figures 2 and 3).

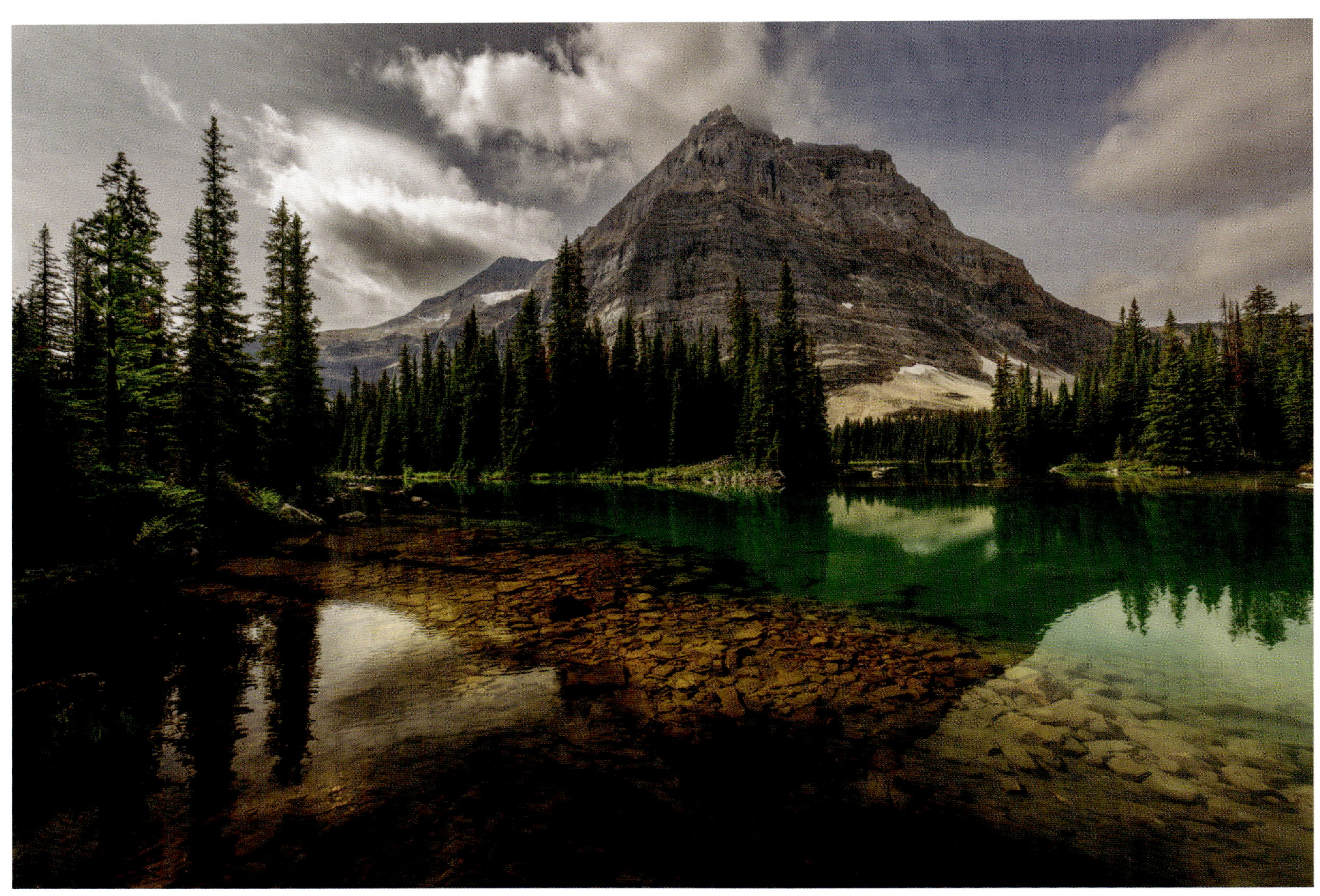

Odaray Reflection (2024)
Breathtakingly beautiful and relatively unfrequented Linda
Lake makes a perfect lunch stop after a long hike through
the trees from Lake O'Hara. In the background are cliff-form-
ing carbonate strata of the Eldon Formation capping Odaray
Mountain tower.

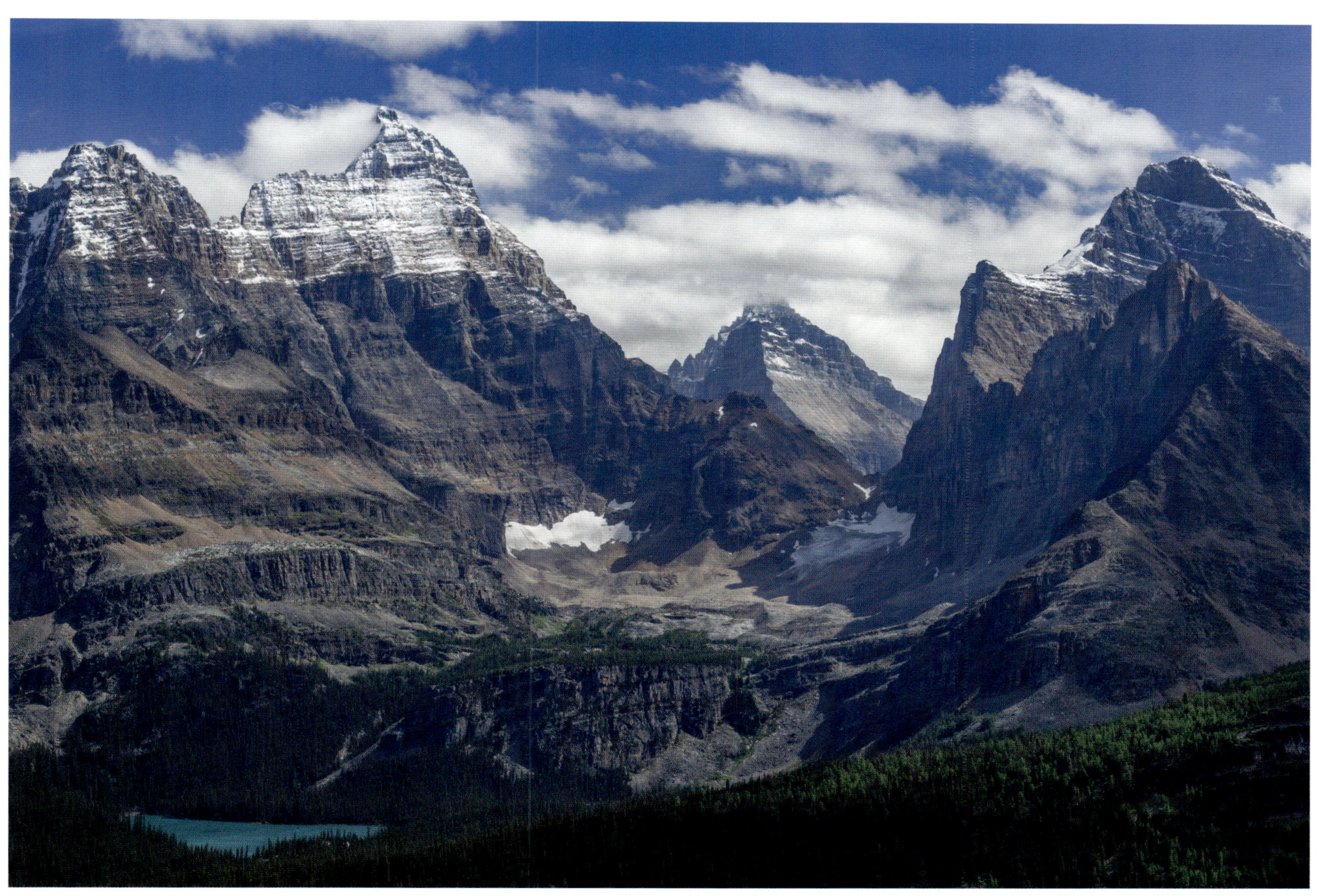

Distant Perspective (2024)
A telephoto lens view from Cathedral Prospect displays
Lake O'Hara with a clear view of Opabin Plateau. The sand-
stone-dominated Gog Group floors the Lake O'Hara and Lake
Oesa valleys, and is overlain by the cliff-forming carbonate
strata of the Cathedral, Stephen, and Eldon formations.

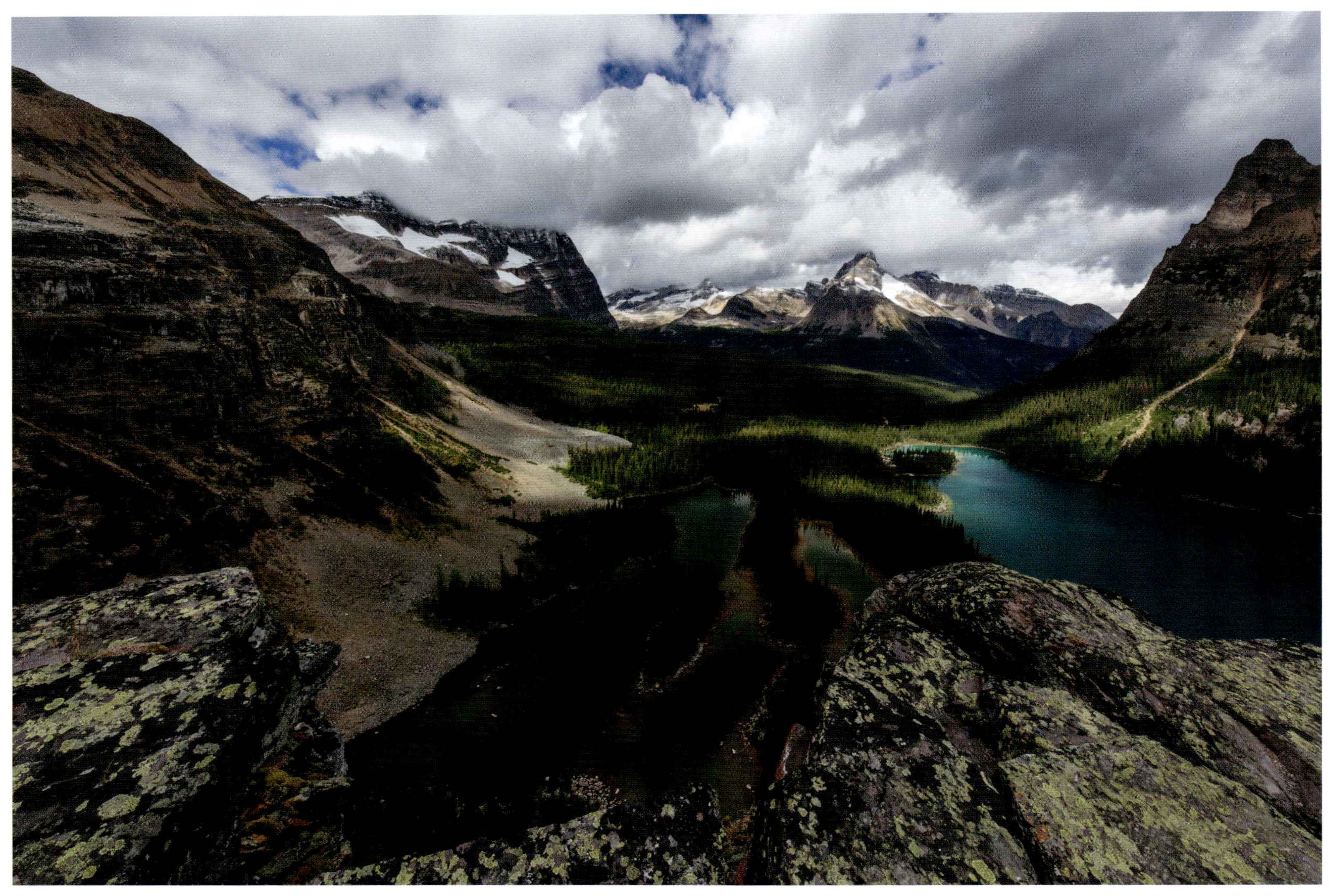

Opabin's Reward (2016)
Looking out over Duchesnay Basin is a magnificent view of the
gently dipping fold limbs of the Cathedral Crags anticline as
seen from Opabin Prospect.

At the scale of the Rocky Mountains, primary stratigraphic features including bed thicknesses and rock types exert a dominant control on how sedimentary rocks subsequently deform. Ultimately, they account for the development of a series of distinct linear deformation belts that include, from east to west: the Foothills, the Front Ranges, the eastern Main Ranges, and the western Main Ranges. Each of these belts displays distinctive characteristics of structural style and physiography as well as stratigraphy.

In the Foothills belt, where the sedimentary sequence consists of a very thin continental shelf succession overlain by a thicker foreland (mountain belt-derived) sedimentary succession, the structure is dominated by closely spaced, steeply dipping, imbricate thrust faults, which give rise to relatively subdued topography dominated by ridges that are held up by sandstone and valleys that are eroded in shale.

In the Front Ranges of the Rocky Mountains, where the continental shelf succession is thicker, thrust fault displacements are greater and the structure is dominated by three to six major thrust fault panels and related folding. The steeply inclined resistant carbonate rocks, which are etched into relief by erosion of overlying younger shaly rocks, form conspicuous linear mountain ranges, including the mountain front that can be admired from Calgary on clear days year-round.

In the eastern Main Ranges (including Lake O'Hara), the thick, competent, carbonate-dominated strata of the outer shelf succession form massive coherent thrust sheets in which bedding is generally gently dipping (Figure 5). The widely spaced thrust faults and open folds yield distinctive castellated carbonate peaks. The broad Cathedral Crags anticline that crosses the Lake O'Hara area (Figures 2 and 3) and the gently dipping sandstone beds in its core, which give way at higher elevation to the middle Cambrian carbonate rock formations, typify the structural and physiographic style that is characteristic of the eastern Main Ranges.

An additional structural complexity in the eastern Main Ranges involves a network of north-northwest-striking normal faults (the result of apparent crustal extension). The normal faults include Cataract Brook and its splays in the Lake O'Hara area (Figures 2 and 3). The origin, timing, and nature of the normal faults remain unresolved. A widely accepted explanation is that the normal faults developed because of trans-tension that occurred west of the Rocky Mountain Trench during the Post-Accretion phase (since ~66 million years ago). An alternate explanation is that the network of normal faults developed because of a period of renewed rifting that separated the terranes of the Intermontane belt from the continental margin of North America during the late Phanerozoic.

To the west of Lake O'Hara, Kicking Horse River separates the thick, shallow-water, carbonate strata of the outer continental shelf that are characteristic of the eastern Main Ranges from an equivalently thick, deeper-water, shale and limestone continental slope sequence that is characteristic of the western Main Ranges. A conspicuous change in style of deformation is associated with the stratigraphic change. In the thicker, incompetent, shale and argillaceous limestone facies of the western Main Ranges, penetrative deformation and cleavage formation are pervasive, complex folds are common, and the influence of structure on topography is much less obvious than in the Lake O'Hara area of the eastern Main Ranges.

The geometry of the faulted, folded, and detached sedimentary rocks within the Cordilleran thrust-and-fold belt of western Canada (Figure 1) provides evidence for major tectonic thickening resulting in mountain building, and for significant eastward-directed transport of rock sequences. Estimates of the horizontal convergence (shortening) between the ancestral North American continent and the accreted suspect terranes that underlay the interior of British Columbia (Figure 1) vary from place to place between 100 to 300 km.

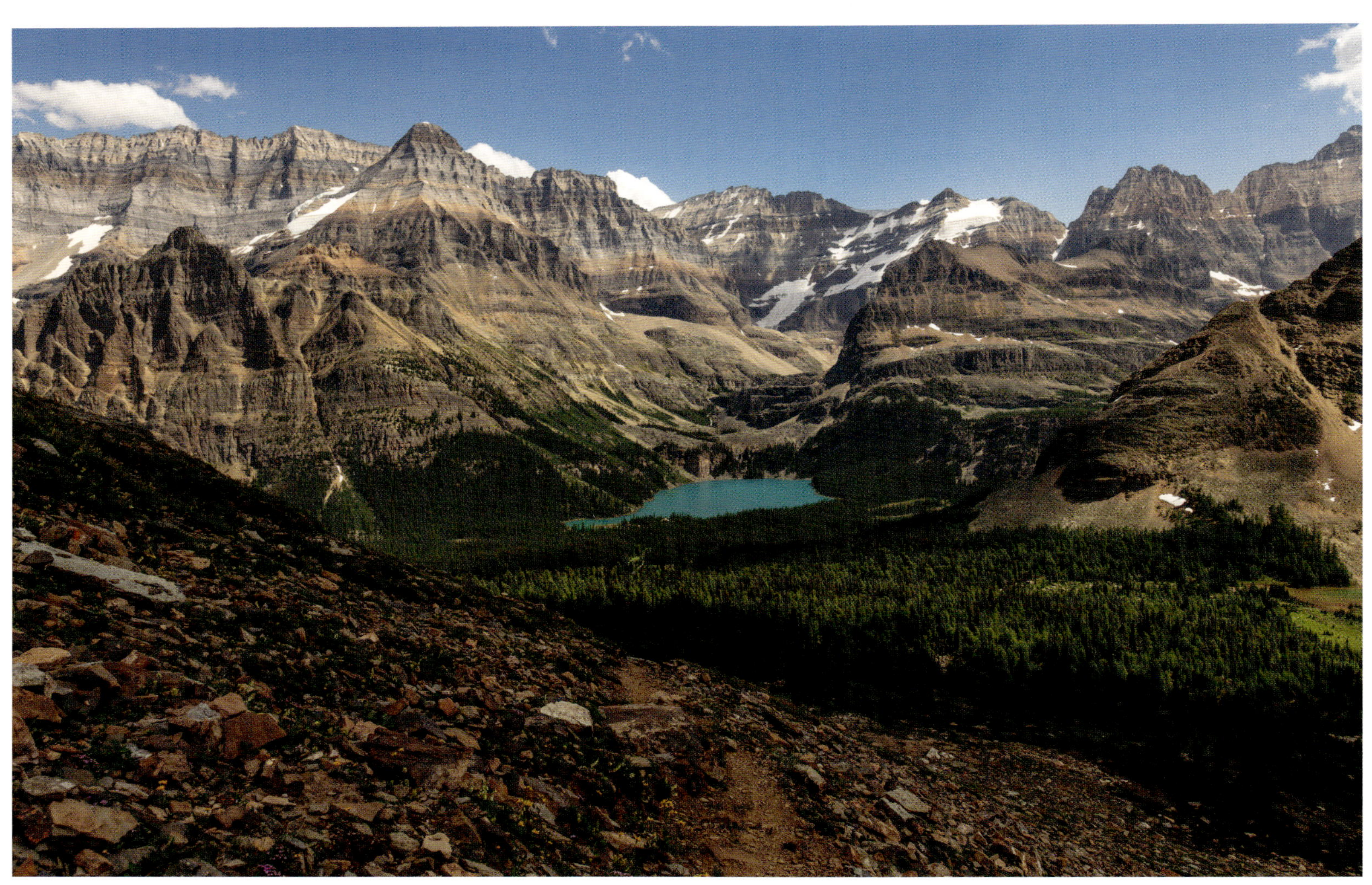

Alpine Circuit View (2021)
As the hiker gains elevation, Lake O'Hara comes into full view along with nearly all of the mountain slopes upon which Lake O'Hara Alpine Circuit navigates. This includes Wiwaxy Peaks north of Lake O'Hara (left middle ground), which is separated from mounts Victoria, Huber, and Lefroy (background) by the Cataract Brook normal fault.

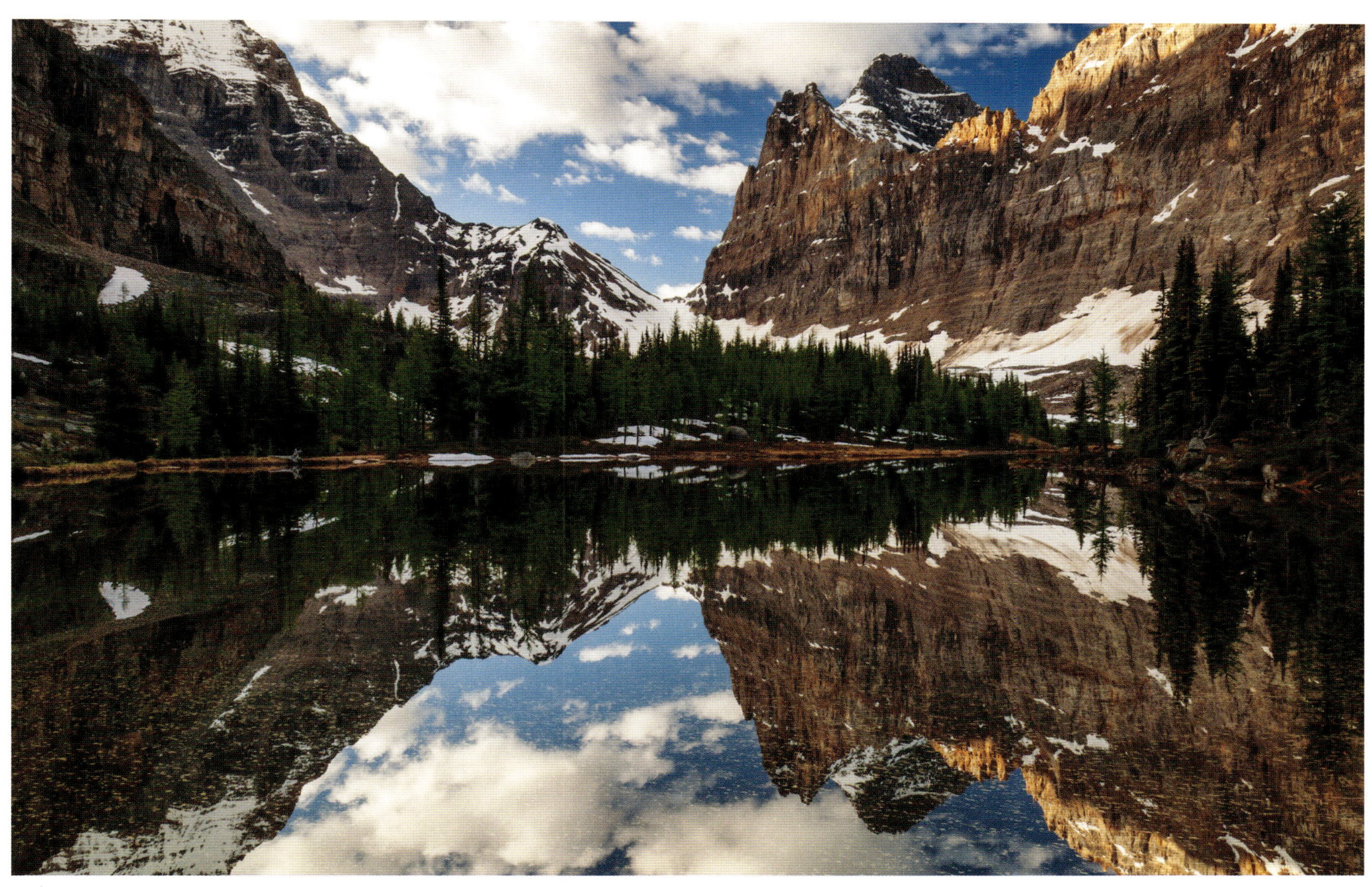

Opabin Daybreak (2007)
Mount Biddle and Hungabee Mountain reflected in the Moor Lakes of Opabin Plateau. The trace of the western splay of the Cataract Brook normal fault forms steep cliffs south of Moor Lakes (right side of photograph).

The mountain-building deformation was "thin-skinned." The top surface of ancestral (Precambrian) North America slopes under the thrust-and-fold belt without disruption from beneath the western Alberta plains at least as far southwest as the Rocky Mountain Trench (Figure 1). Individual faults cut upsection through the stratigraphic layering northeastward, but en route they commonly follow layering over large areas. The mechanical anisotropy and heterogeneity associated with the stratigraphic layering have clearly exerted a fundamental control on the style of the thrusting and folding and consequent physiography and landscape at the surface.

ICE, GLACIERS, AND A CHANGING LANDSCAPE

British Columbia lies within the mid-latitudes of the northern hemisphere adjacent to the Pacific Ocean, which is the moisture source for present and past glaciers in the region. The high mountains of British Columbia presently support valley and cirque glaciers and several ice caps. The total current ice cover in British Columbia is about 26,000 km², which is probably close to the minimum value for the entire Quaternary period.

The Cordillera of western Canada was repeatedly enveloped by a continental ice sheet, known as the Cordilleran ice sheet, during the Pleistocene and latest Pliocene. At its maximum extent, the Cordilleran ice sheet and its satellite glaciers covered almost all of British Columbia, as well as southern Yukon and southern Alaska. It extended south into the northwestern conterminous United States (Figure 6). The ice sheet, to a considerable extent, was confined between the high mountain ranges bordering the Canadian Cordillera on its western and eastern flanks, but in addition areas beyond the east flank of the Rocky Mountains and the west flank of the Coast Mountains were also covered by ice.

The last Cordilleran ice sheet attained its maximum size in British Columbia, where it was up to 900 km wide and reached to 2000–3000 m of elevation over the plateaus of the interior. When fully formed, the ice sheet probably had the shape of an elongate dish, with gentle slopes in the interior region and steeper slopes at the periphery. It likely resembled the present-day Greenland Inland Ice at such times.

On the eastern flank of the mountains in Alberta, ice flowed from the British Columbia interior and the Rocky Mountains and locally coalesced with ice sourced from the Keewatin (now primarily the Kivalliq) region in Nunavut to the east. The latter was part of the Laurentide ice sheet that covered much of Canada during the Pleistocene and the Last Ice Age. However, it should be noted that these ice masses coalesced only rarely, at times of maximum glaciation, most recently about 17,000 years ago. At other times, an ice-free zone (the ice-free corridor) existed between the Cordilleran and Laurentide ice sheets.

The Cordilleran ice sheet nucleated in the high mountains of British Columbia (Figure 7A). Small mountain ice fields grew, and valley glaciers advanced when the climate deteriorated early during each glaciation (Figure 7B). With continued cooling and an increase in precipitation, glaciers expanded and merged to form a more extensive cover of ice in the mountains. The glaciers then advanced out of the mountains and across plateaus and lowlands, eventually coalescing to form an ice sheet that covered most of British Columbia and adjacent areas (Figure 7C). During this period, which spanned thousands of years, the major mountain ranges remained the principal sources of ice, and ice flow was controlled by topography. Eventually, the ice thickened to such an extent during the final phase of glaciation that one or more domes became established over the interior of British Columbia, with surface ice flow becoming radial away from their centres.

Most glacial cycles terminated with rapid climate warming, which characterized the Holocene, with deglaciation

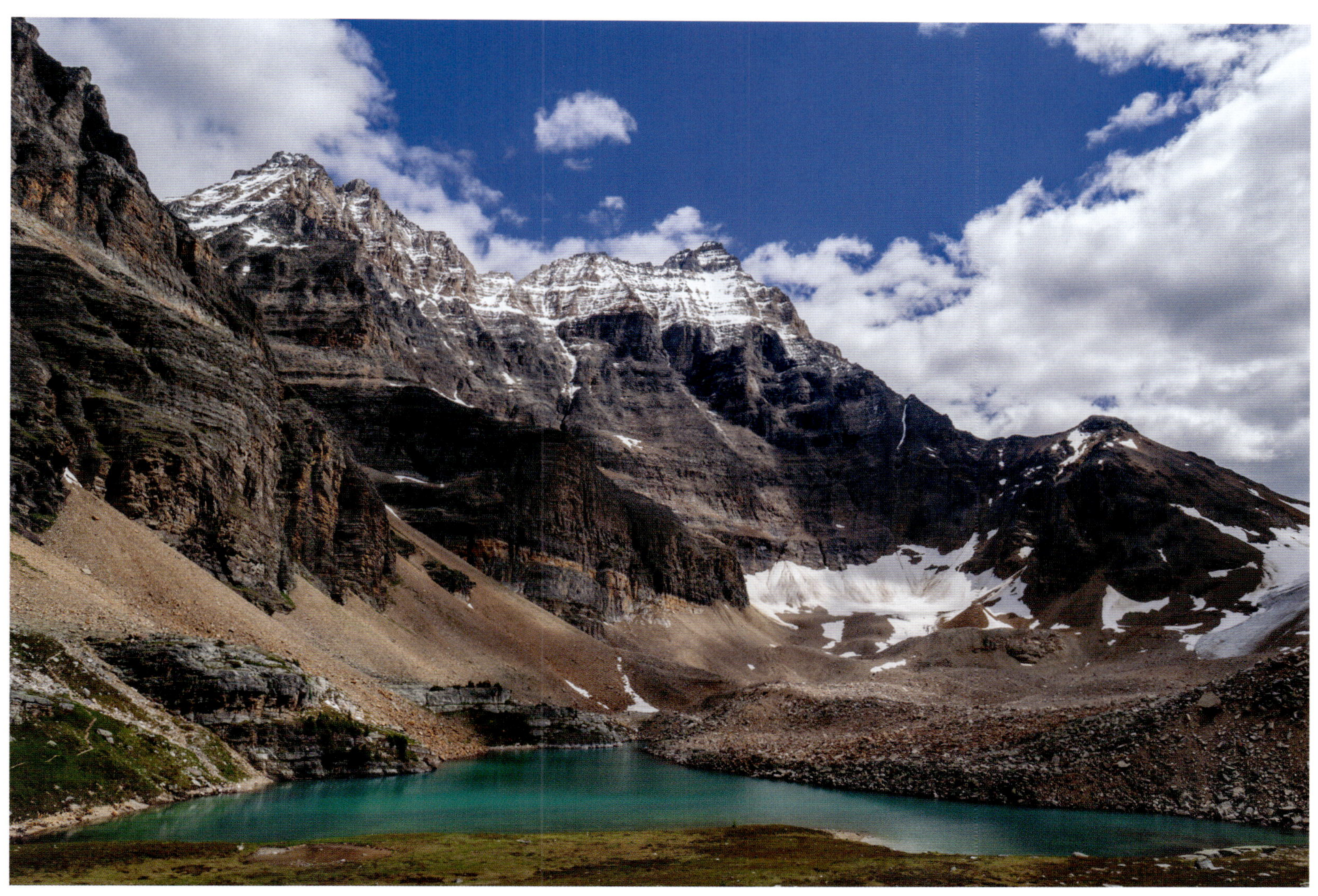

Opabin's Jewel (2007)
At the end of East Opabin Trail lies Opabin Lake. The name "Opabin" is derived from the Stoney Nakoda (Assiniboine) language translating as "rocky" or "rock-covered," in reference to the abundant moraines and boulders that surround the glacial cirque.

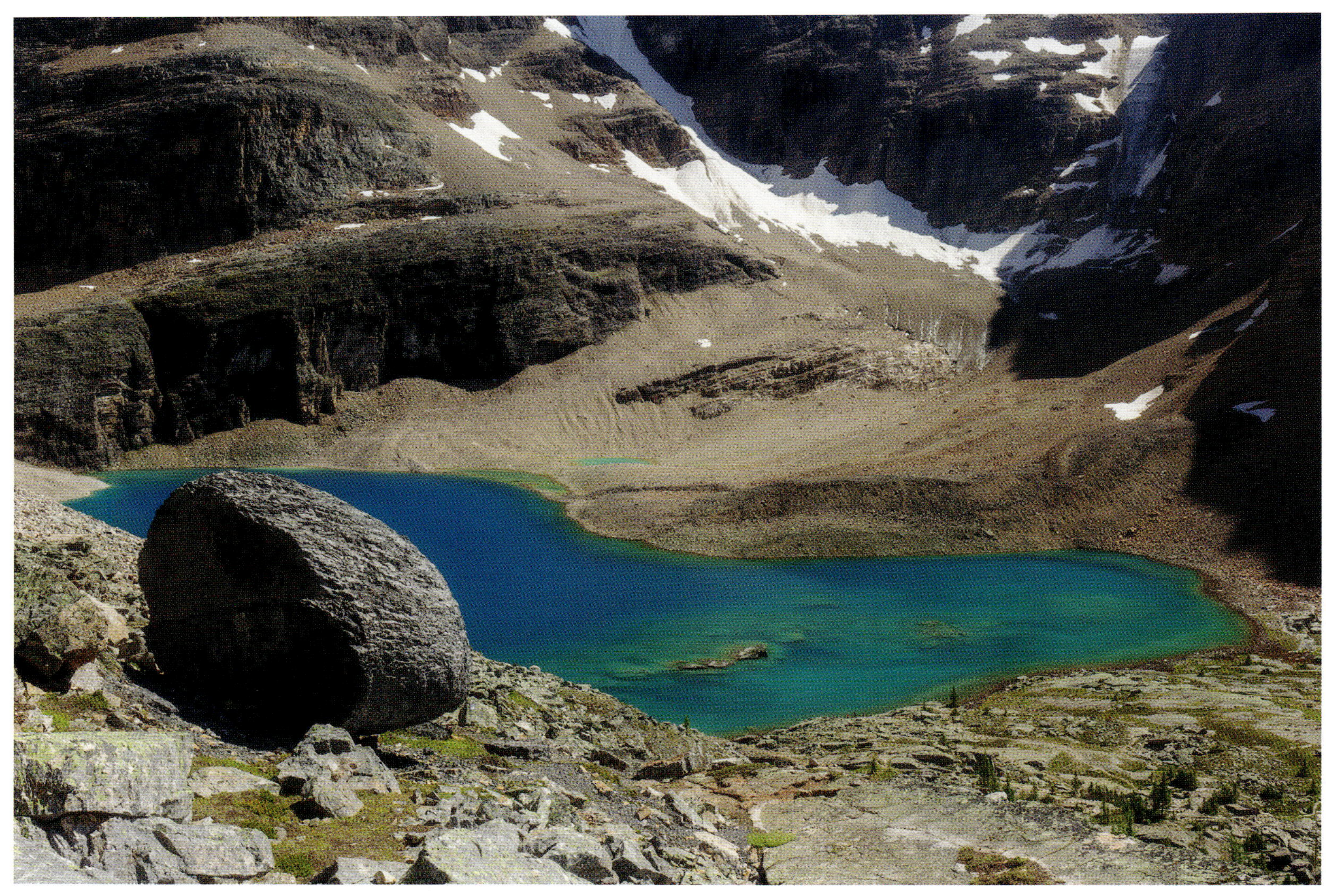

Precarious Perch (2010)
A seemingly precarious perch for this boulder overlooking the brilliant turquoise water of Lake Oesa and its glacial moraine ridge.

involving complex glacier retreat in peripheral glaciated areas such as the Canadian Rockies.

The ice sheet, and the alpine glaciers from which it formed, dramatically modified the bedrock landscape of British Columbia. As a result, mountainous areas such as the environs of Lake O'Hara are dominated by erosional glacial landforms. In high mountains such as the eastern Main Ranges, classic alpine features include cirques (e.g., Oesa, Opabin, McArthur), over-deepened valley heads (e.g., Duchesnay Basin), horns, and comb ridges. Most mountain valleys, including Cataract Brook Valley, are classic glacial troughs (U-shaped valleys). Valley floors and sides are typically festooned with lateral and terminal moraine ridges.

Lake O'Hara is situated approximately midway between younger, vegetation-free, Holocene (Little Ice Age) moraines and older, vegetation-covered, moraines attributed to the Last Ice Age. Just to the east, Opabin Lake is specifically bound on its southern shore by Holocence moraines. In general, the most extensive Holocene ice advances occurred in the Rocky Mountains during the early 18th and mid-late 19th centuries.

Postglacial palaeoenvironmental reconstructions for the upper Cataract Brook Valley are derived from radiocarbon dating of organic material, as well as the dating of volcanic ash in lake-bottom sediment cores recovered from subalpine Lake O'Hara, situated at an elevation of 2015 m above mean sea level (maximum depth of 42 m), and alpine Opabin Lake, situated at an elevation of 2280 m above mean sea level (maximum depth of 5 m). Dating of conifer needles extracted from a sediment core at Lake O'Hara indicates that Holocene deglaciation had proceeded up valley from the O'Hara basin prior to approximately 10,000 years ago, and preliminary palaeobotanical and macrofossil data suggest that a pine and fir forest with lesser spruce was established in the vicinity of the lake by this time.

The postglacial colonizing vegetation prior to approximately 10,000 years ago at Lake O'Hara, and before approximately 8,500 years ago at Opabin Lake, was a shrub-herb community not unlike that found in many parts of the Canadian Arctic today (Figures 8A and 8B). As per above, pioneering forests at both sites were pine and fir with lesser abundances of spruce. The timberline remained above the elevation of Opabin Lake, at least 90 m above modern timberline elevation, during the period between approximately 8,500 years ago to approximately 3,000 years ago (Figures 8C and 8D) in response to warmer climatic conditions associated with restricted glacial activity. Forest compositions resembling the modern subalpine spruce-fir forest of Europe had developed by the end of this period. The period from approximately 3,000 years ago to the present was marked by deteriorating climatic conditions associated with renewed glacial activity in the Opabin Cirque and declining timberlines to below the elevation of Opabin Lake (Figure 8E).

The present alpine timberline belt is situated between Lake O'Hara and Opabin Lake, spanning elevations between approximately 2100 and 2300 m above mean sea level. The upper elevation of continuous forest, or the timberline, occurs slightly above the lower lip of the Opabin Cirque at an elevation of approximately 2130 m above mean sea level. The position of the timberline in the region is probably associated with the location of the July 10°C isotherm, as is the case for the treeline in much of the circumpolar Arctic region.

A STORY STILL UNFOLDING

Lake O'Hara is more than just a stunning mountain getaway – it's a living record of Earth's dynamic history. From ancient oceans to towering peaks, from ice sheets to alpine lakes, the area's geology tells a fascinating story of transformation that continues today. The next time you visit, take a moment to appreciate the rocks beneath your feet – they hold the secrets of a world millions of years in the making!

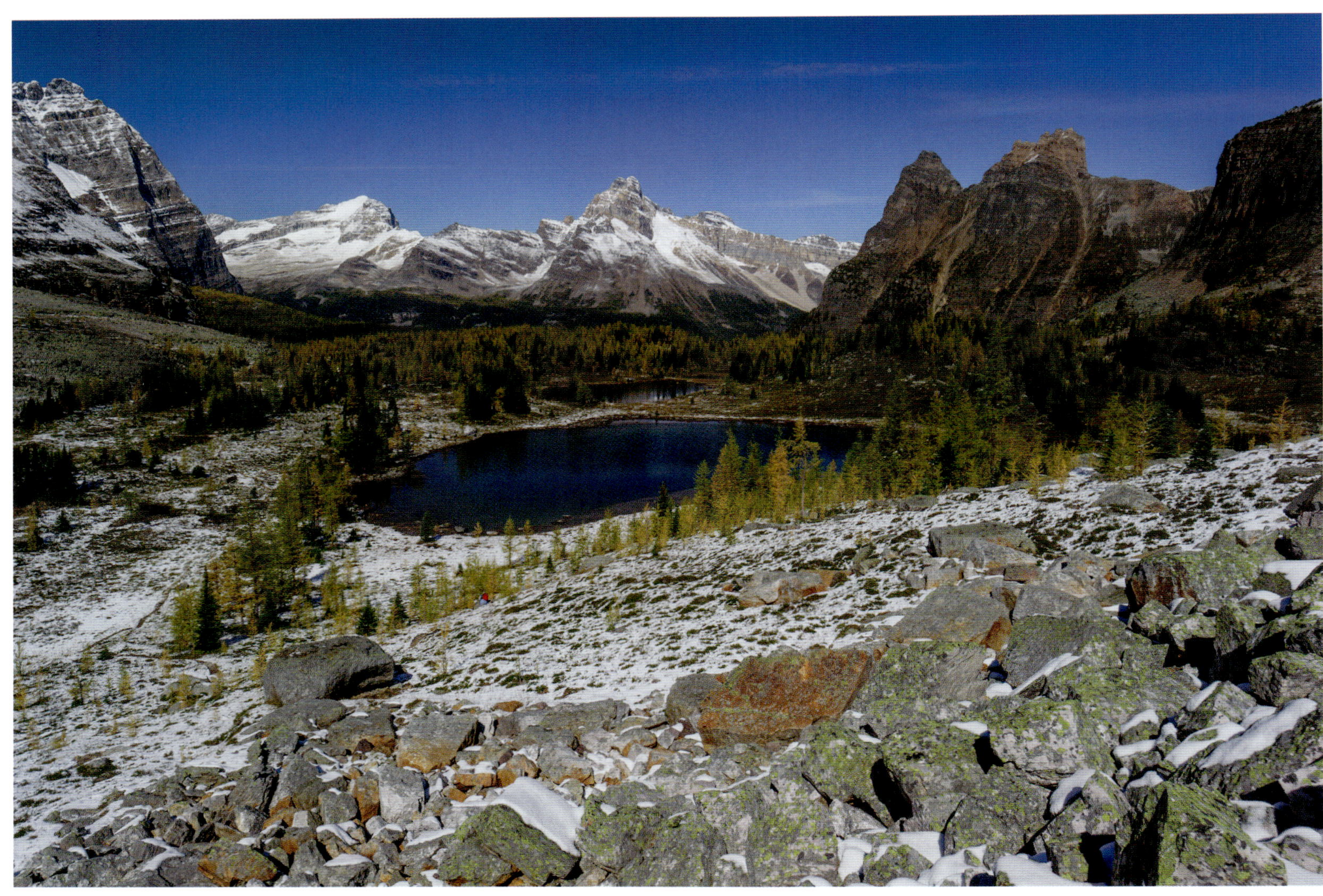

Autumn's Nod (2011)
In the final open-water days on Hungabee Lake, snow falls
on the surrounding golden larch trees that define the present
timberline.

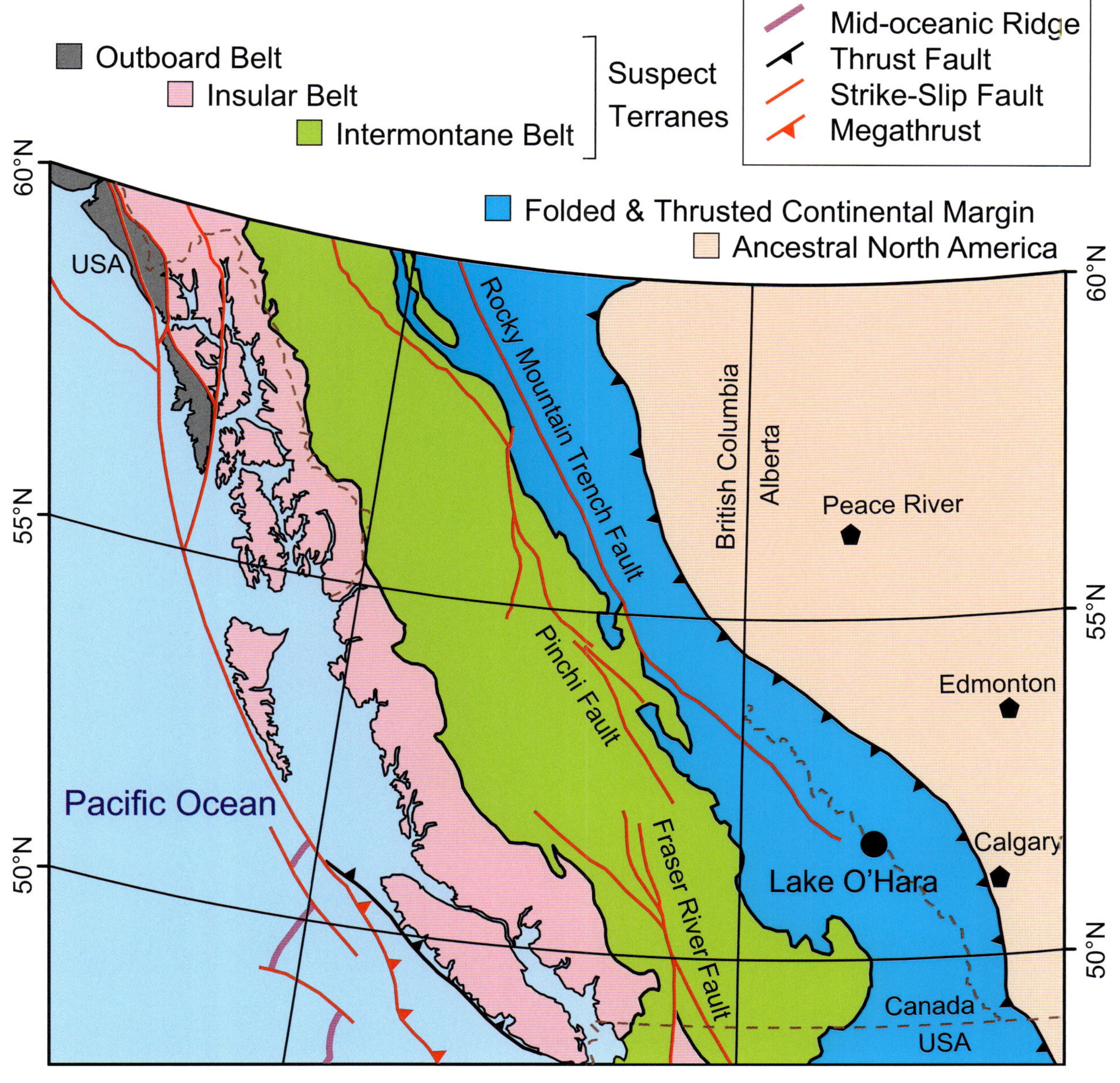

Figure 1: Geological map of the western margin of North America in British Columbia and Alberta showing the location of the ancestral North American continent, the folded and thrusted continental margin strata of the Rocky Mountains, and the accreted terranes of the Intermontane, Insular, and Outboard belts. Modified from Colpron and Nelson (2011). Location of the Lake O'Hara area shown with black dot.

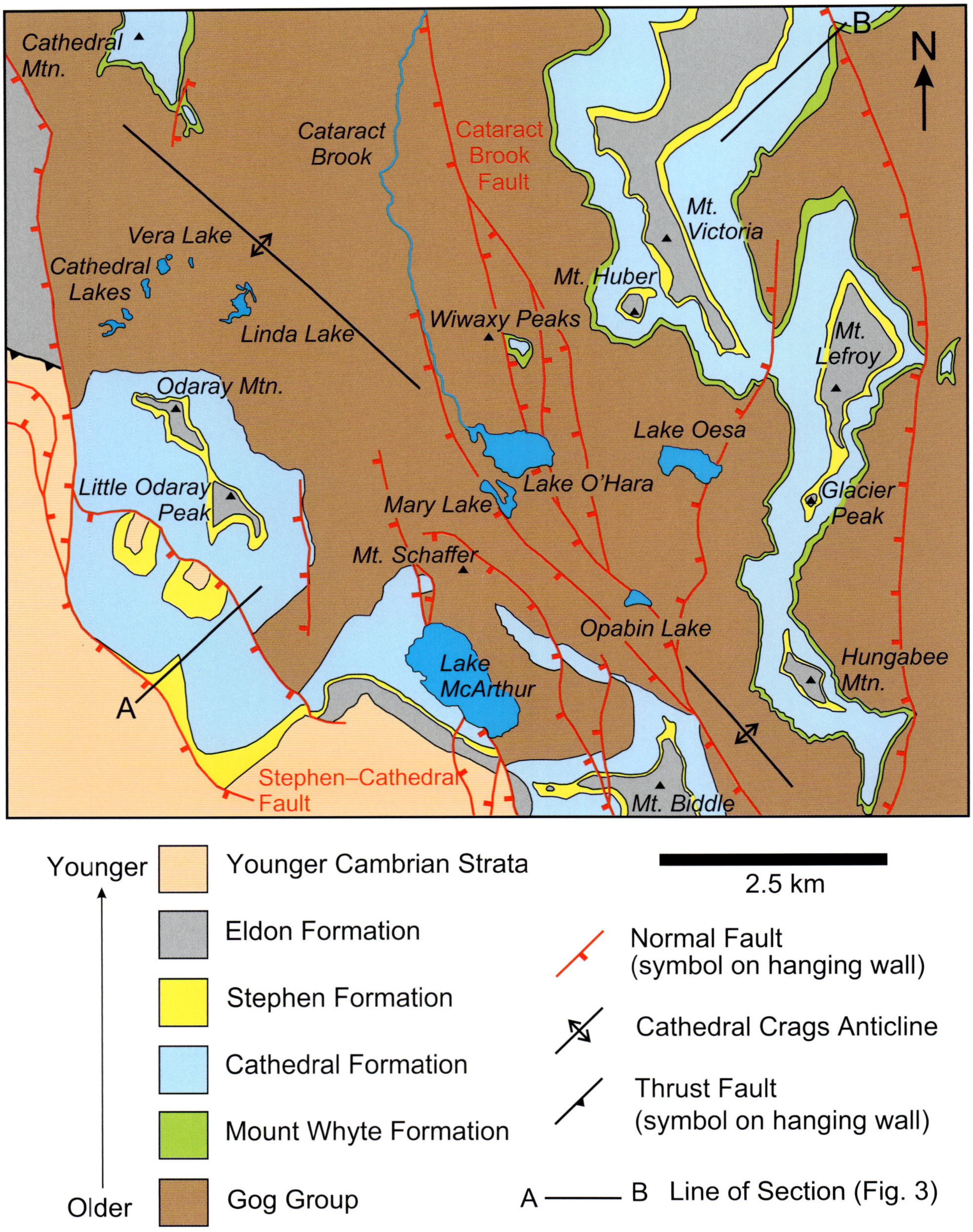

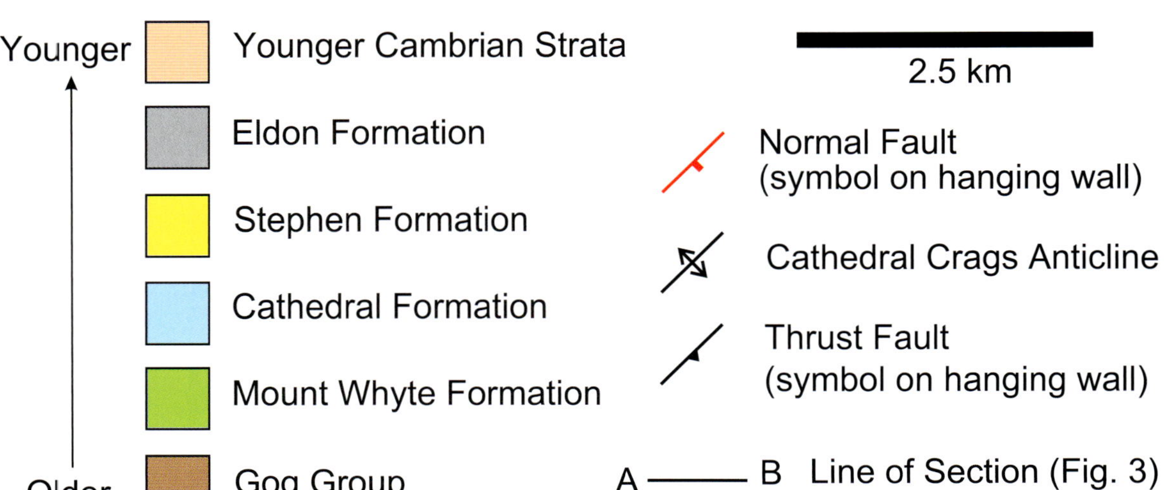

Figure 2: Bedrock geological map of the Lake O'Hara area. Modified from Price et al. (1980) and Taerum (2022).

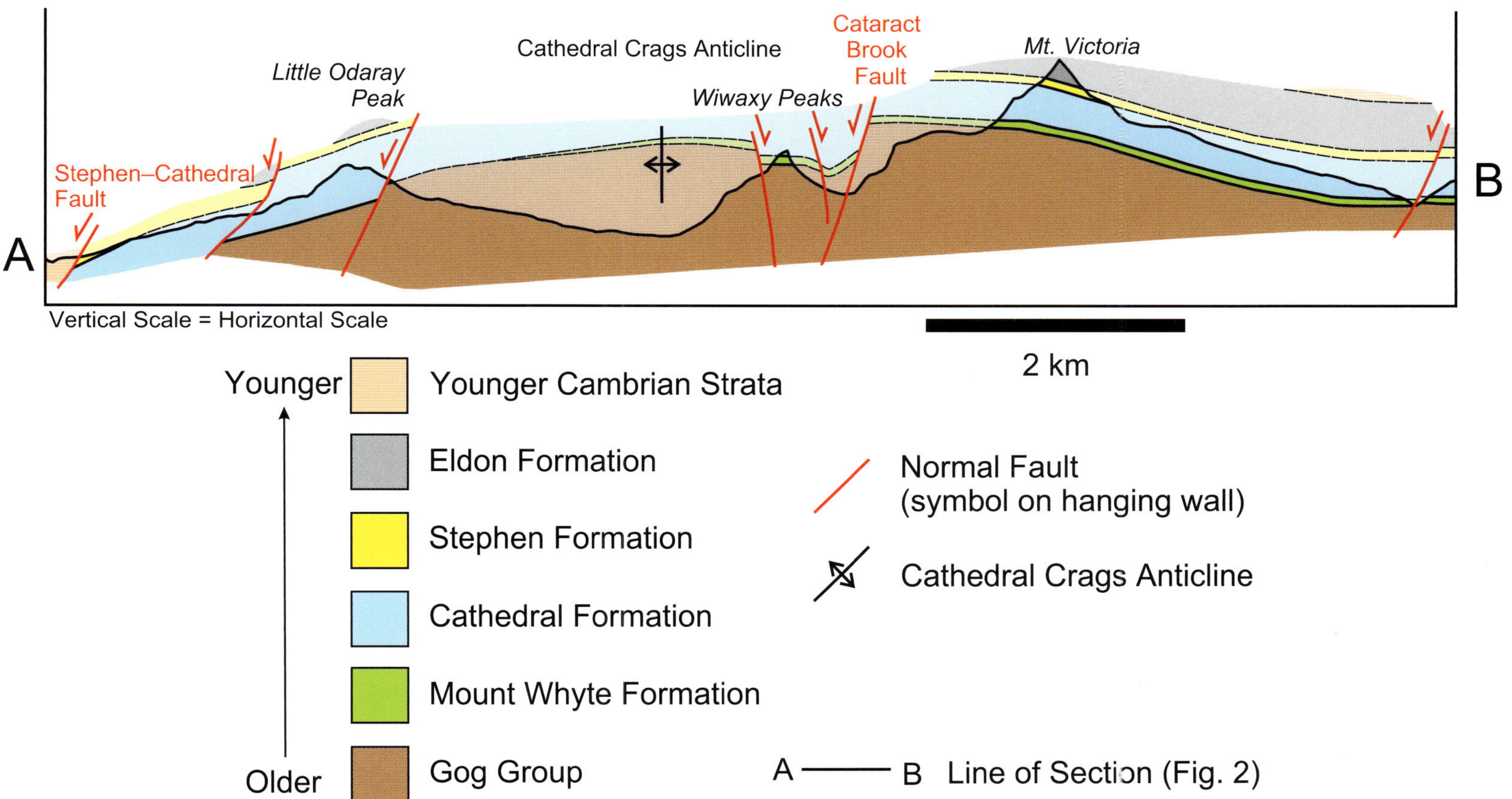

Figure 3: Diagrammatic bedrock geological cross-section of the Lake O'Hara area. The line of section crosses Little Odaray Peak, Wiwaxy Peaks, and Mount Victoria, and is drawn from the southwest (left) to the northeast (right). Modified from Taerum (2022).

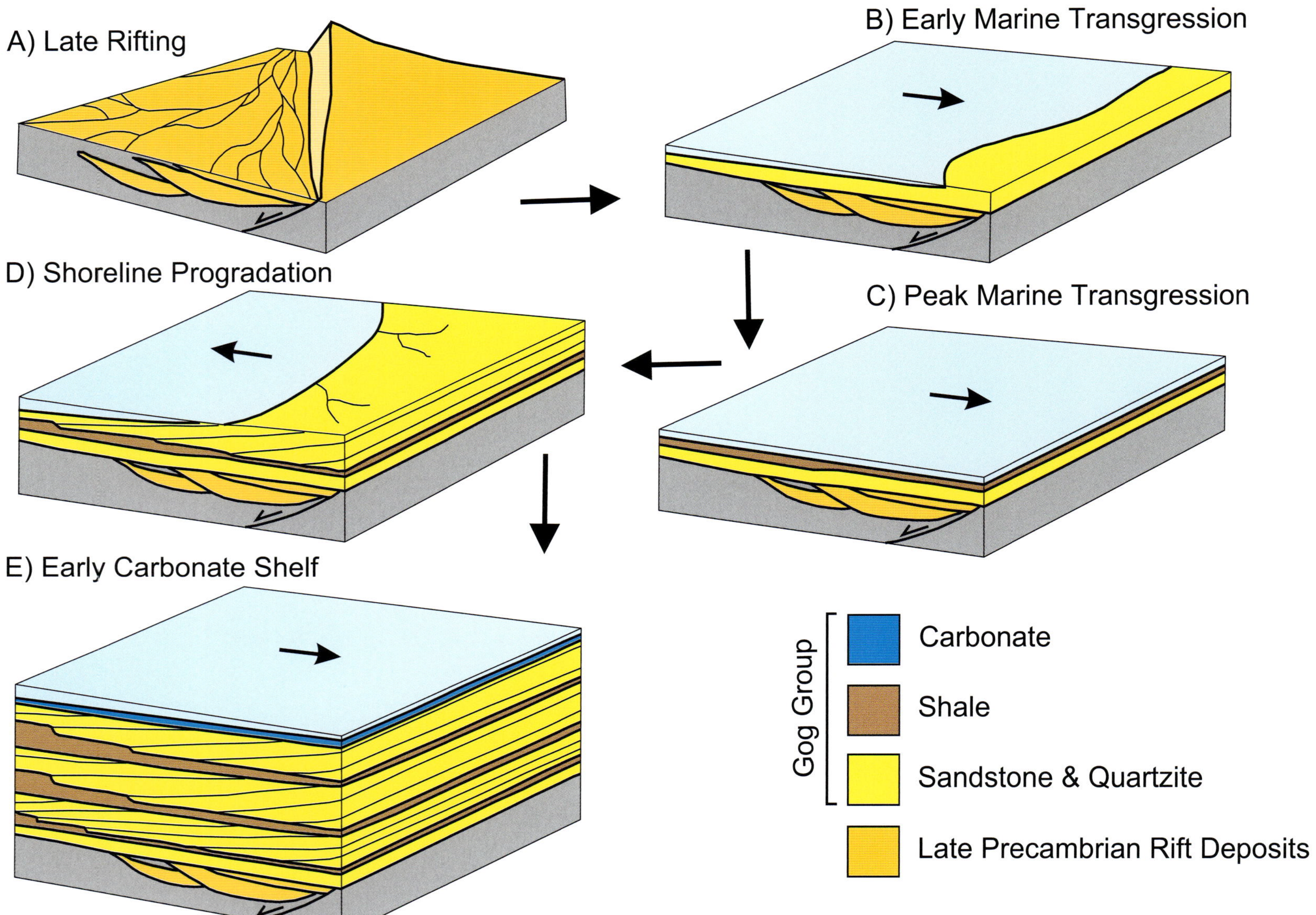

Figure 4: Palaeoenvironmental evolution of the inner part of the continental shelf recorded by the sedimentary rocks in the Bow Valley and Lake O'Hara region. Continental rifting along the western margin of North America (A) was followed by a change from an early braided fluvial setting to a shallow marine shelf environment (B). The inner continental margin experienced a marine transgression (C) and a series of progradational events (D) until clastic sediment supply ceased and the setting became dominated by deposition of carbonate sediment (E). Modified from Desjardins et al. (2010).

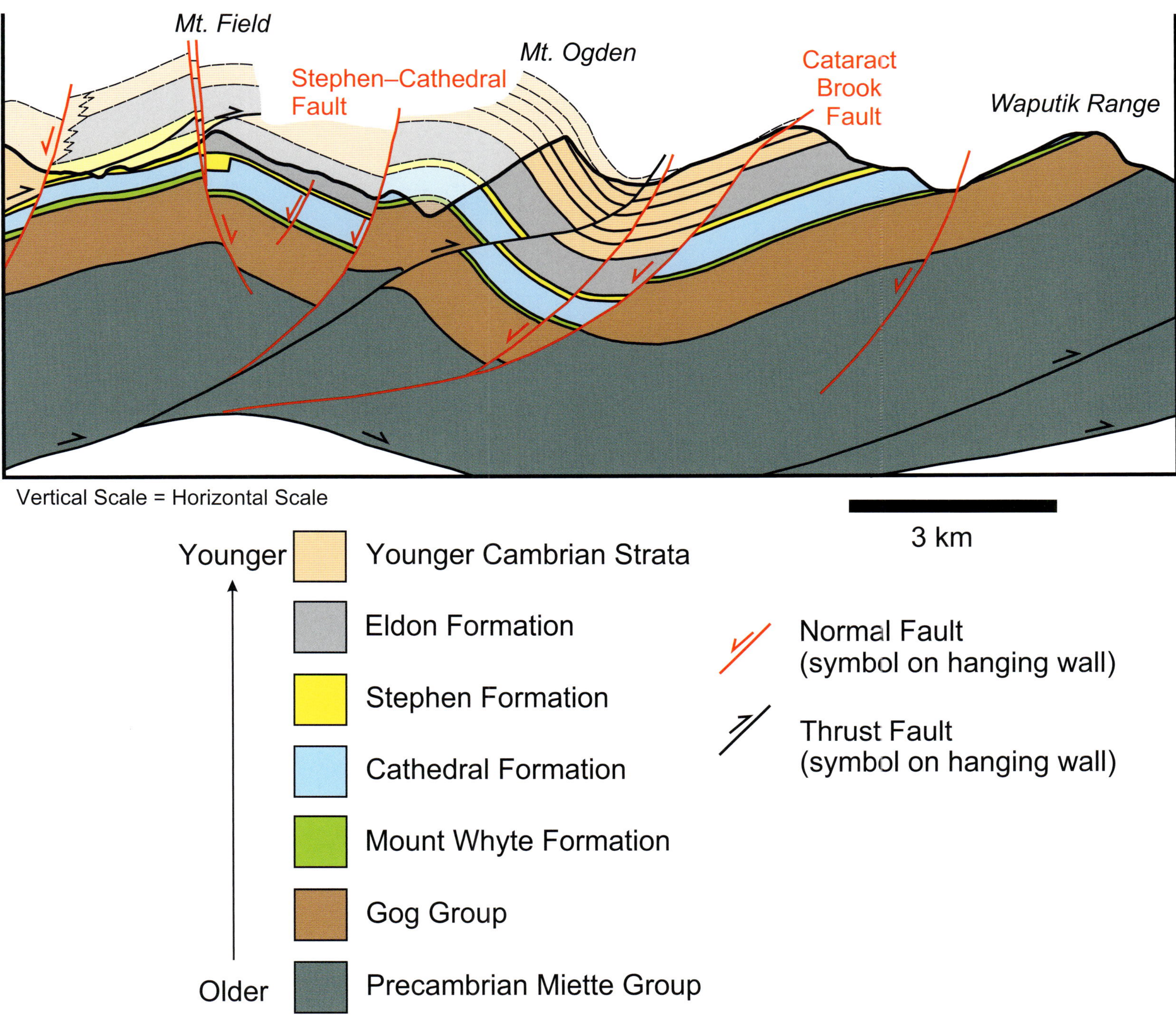

Figure 5: Diagrammatic bedrock geological cross-section across the eastern Main Ranges on the north side of the Trans-Canada Highway, drawn from the southwest (left) to the northeast (right). From Price and Monger (2003).

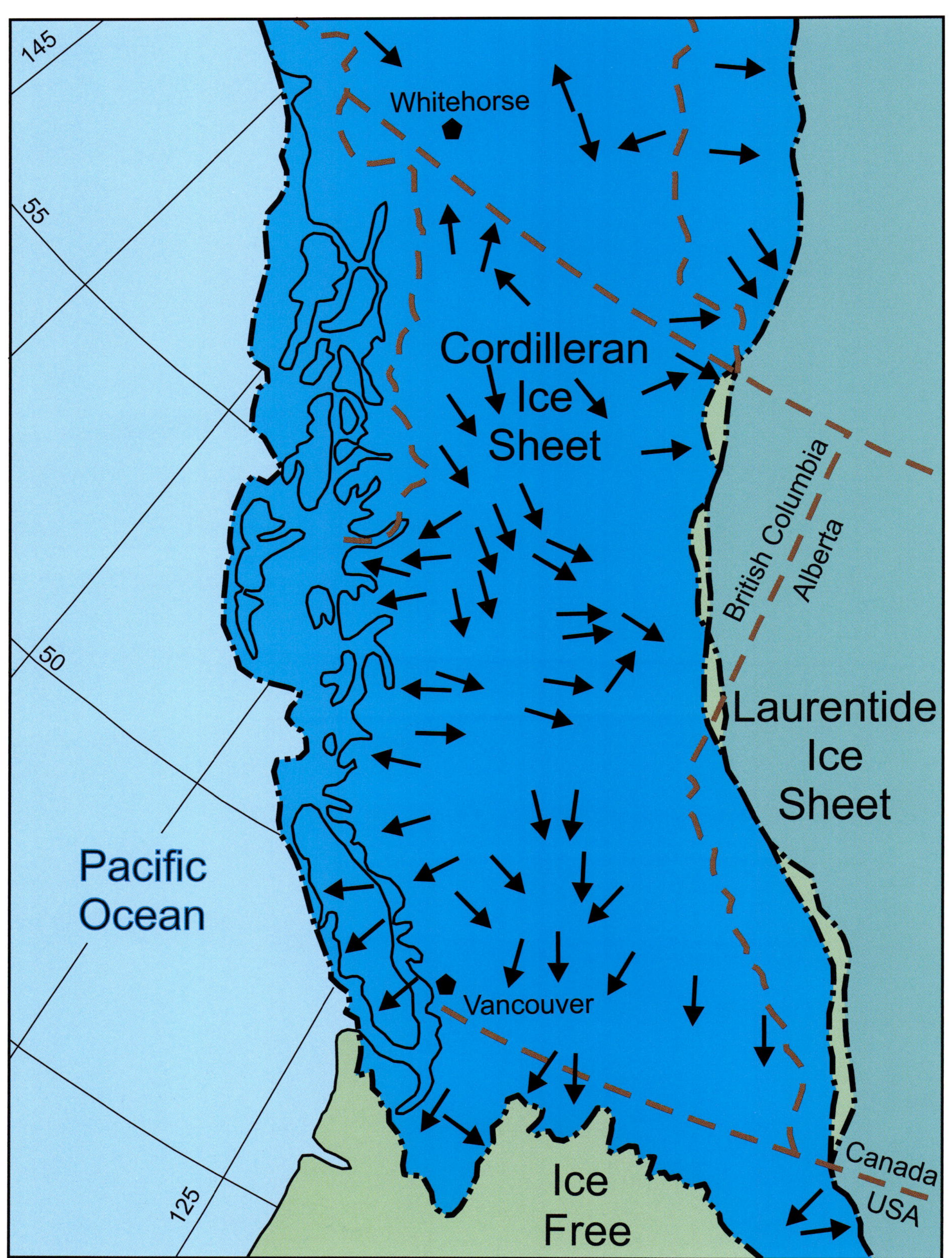

Figure 6: The Cordilleran ice sheet about 17,000 years ago at the peak of the Last Ice Age. The upper surface of the ice sheet reached up to 2000–3000 m above mean sea levels. Arrows indicate directions of ice flow. From Clague and Ward (2011).

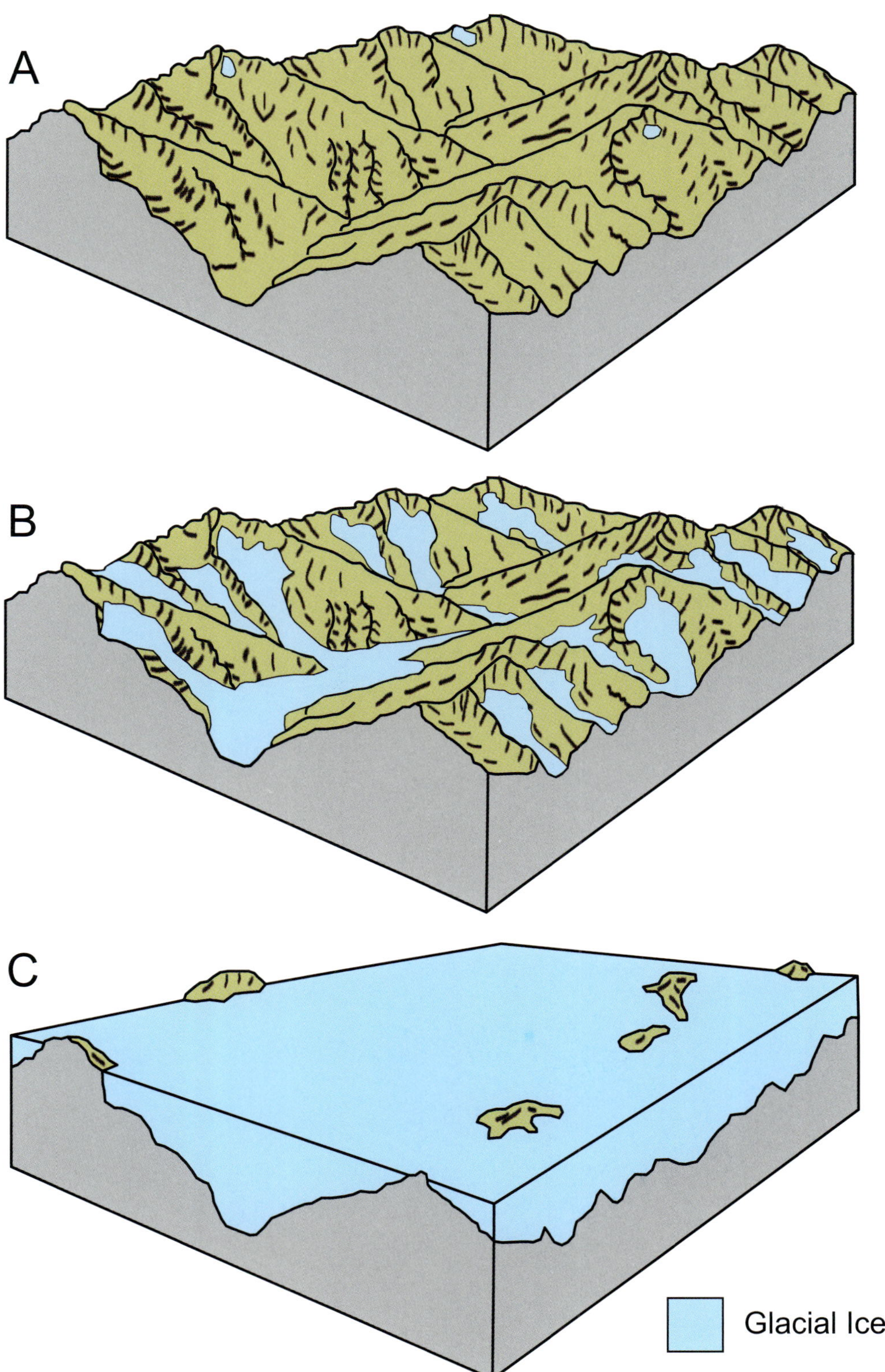

Figure 7: Schematic diagram showing the growth of the Cordilleran ice sheet: (A) mountain area at the beginning of a glaciation; (B) development of a network of valley glaciers; (C) coalescence of va ley and piedmont lobes to form an ice sheet. Modified from Clague and Ward (2011).

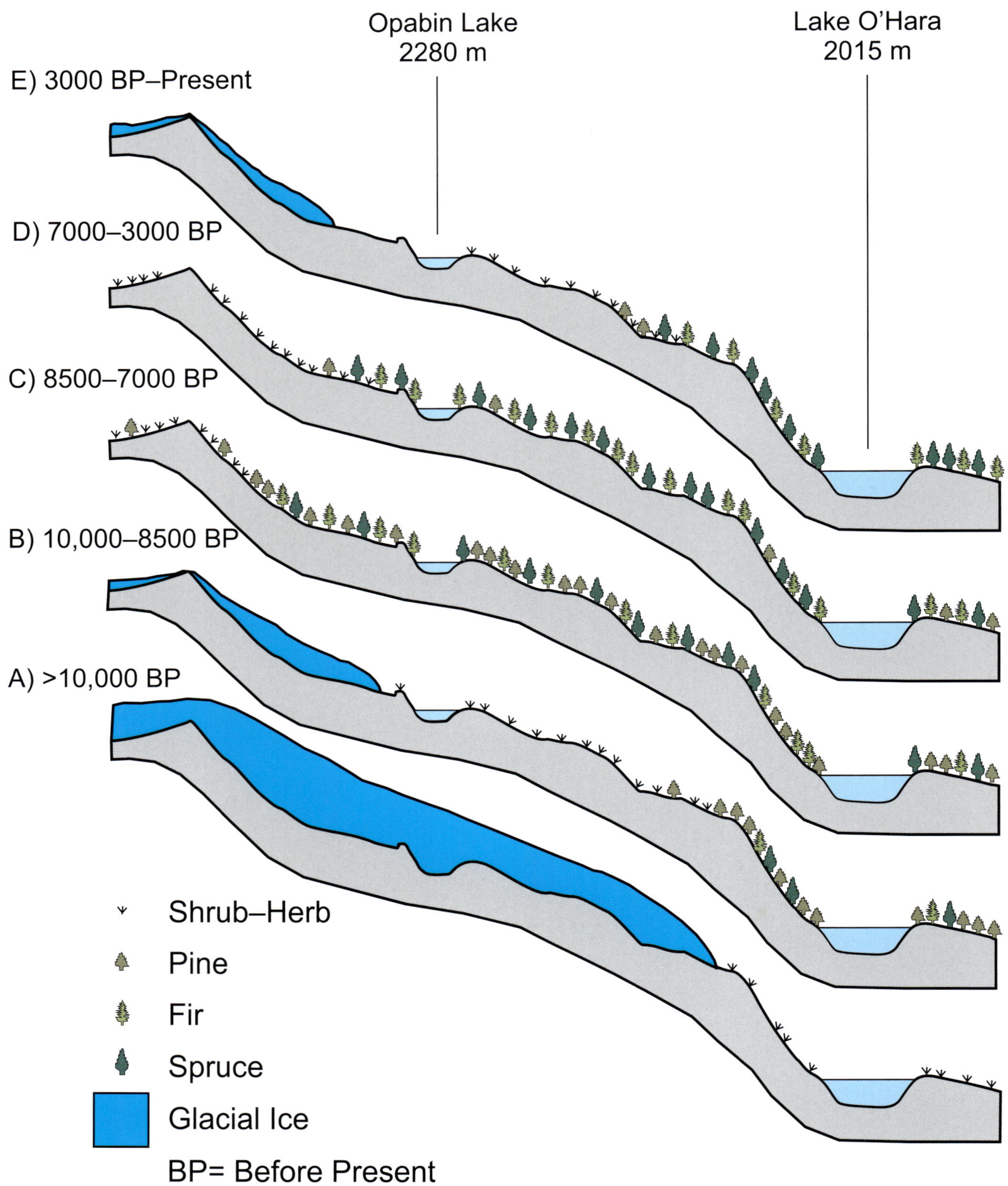

Figure 8: Schematic transect across the upper Cataract Brook Valley from Opabin Pass (left) and Lake Opabin to Lake O'Hara (right), showing dominant vegetation and ice distribution for the periods: (A) >10,000 years ago; (B) 10,000–8,500 years ago; (C) 8,500–7,000 years ago; (D) 7,000–3,000 years ago; and (E) 3,000 years ago to the present. Modified from Reasoner and Hickman (1989).

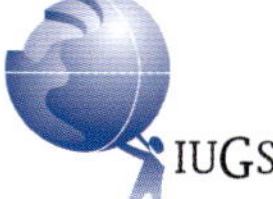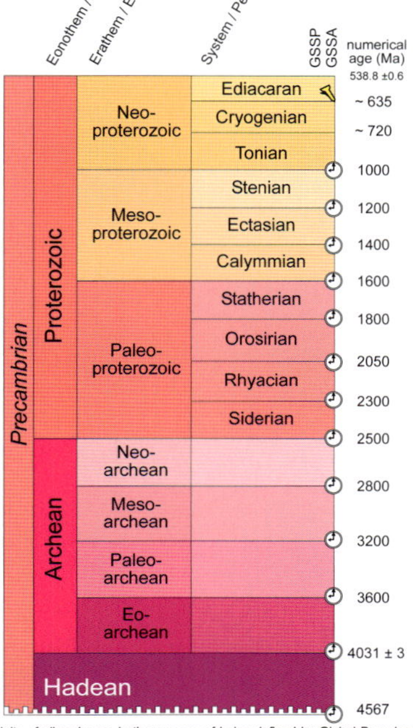

Figure 9: International Chronostratigraphic Chart document-ing the periods of Earth history from youngest to oldest over 4.567 billion years, with the numerical age of intervening boundaries specified in millions of years. From Cohen et al. (2013, updated 2024).

REFERENCES AND ADDITIONAL READING

Clague, J.J., and B. Ward. 2011. "Pleistocene Glaciation of British Columbia." *Developments in Quaternary Science* 15. https://doi.org/10.1016/B978-0-444-53447-7.00044-1.

Cohen, K.M., S.C. Finney, P.L. Gibbard, and J.-X. Fan. 2013 (updated 2024). "The ICS International Chronostratigraphic Chart." *Episodes* 36: 199–204.

Colpron, M., and Nelson, J.L. 2011. "A Digital Atlas of Terranes for the Northern Cordillera." Yukon Geological Survey. https://data.geology.gov.yk.ca/Reference/95879#InfoTab.

Desjardins, P.R., B.R. Pratt, L.A. Buatois, and M.G. Mangano. 2010. "Stratigraphy and sedimentary environments of the Lower Cambrian Gog Group in the southern Rocky Mountains of western Canada: Transgressive sandstones on a broad continental margin." *Bulletin of Canadian Petroleum Geology* 58 (4): 1–37.

Price, R.A. 1981. "The Cordilleran foreland thrust and fold belt in the southern Canadian Rocky Mountains." *Thrust and Nappe Tectonics: Geological Society, London, Special Publication* 9: 427–48. https://doi.org/10.1144/GSL.SP.1981.009.01.39.

Price, R.A. 2000. "The southern Canadian Rockies: Evolution of a foreland thrust and fold belt." In *GeoCanada 2000 Field Trip Guidebook*, Vol. 13. Geological Association of Canada.

Price, R.A., D.G. Cook, J.D. Aitken, and E.W. Mountjoy. 1980. "Geology, Lake Louise, West Half (82 N/8 W/2), British Columbia." *Geological Survey of Canada Map 1483A, scale 1:50,000.* https://doi.org/10.4095/108873.

Price, R.A., and J.W.H. Monger. 2003. "A transect of the southern Canadian Cordillera from Calgary to Vancouver." In *Cordilleran Section 2003 Field Trip Guidebook*. Geological Association of Canada.

Reasoner, M.A., and M. Hickman. 1989. "Late Quaternary environmental change in the Lake O'Hara region, Yoho National Park, British Columbia." *Palaeogeography, Palaeoclimatology, Palaeoecology* 72: 291–316.

Reasoner, M.A., and N.W. Rutter. 1988. "Deglaciation of the Lake O'Hara region, Yoho National Park, British Columbia; an evaluation of sedimentation rates and bulk amino acid ratios in lacustrine records." *Canadian Journal of Earth Sciences* 25: 1037–48.

Taerum, R.L. 2022. "Evidence for pre-Cenozoic extension in the eastern Main Ranges of the southern Canadian Rockies." *Geosphere* 18 (3): 1152–76. https://doi.org/10.1130/GES02347.1.

SCOTT FORSYTH

Author and photographer Scott Forsyth is a Fellow of both the Royal Canadian Geographical Society and the Explorers Club. In 2019, *Canadian Geographic* awarded him the designation of Photographer-in-Residence, and as its Travel Ambassador he has photographed excursions near and far, from backcountry horseback riding in the Canadian Rockies to balloon flying over the plains of the Masai Mara in Kenya.

A winner of the 2020 Banff Centre Mountain Film and Book Festival's Mountain Book Competition, his RMB book *The Wild Coasts of Canada* depicts Canada's epic scenery across the longest coastline in the world. Interested in storytelling, natural history, and photographic beauty, he enjoys sharing sights and facts relating to the subjects of his camera lens.

When not on photographic assignment, he works as an aviation medical examiner for Transport Canada and the Federal Aviation Administration at his YBW Aeromedical Clinic at Springbank Airport in Alberta. Visit his website at www.scottforsyth.ca.

MARC ST-ONGE

Marc St-Onge graduated in 1981 from Queen's University with a PhD in geology. For 37 years, he was an Officer of the Geological Survey of Canada (GSC), leading science expeditions to the Canadian Arctic, Greenland, the Himalaya of Pakistan, India, Nepal, and the Tibetan Plateau in China. His contributions are evidenced by the publication of 135 scientific papers and 120 geological maps. He was appointed a Fellow of the Royal Canadian Geographical Society (RCGS) in 2010, Vice-President of the Commission for the Geological Map of the World in 2012, Senior Scholar at the University of Cambridge in 2019, and Visiting Professor at the University of Oxford in 2019. The RCGS named him one of Canada's 90 Greatest Explorers of All Time in 2020. He received the Florence Bascom Geologic Mapping Award from the Geological Society of America in 2016 and the Stefansson Medal from the Explorers Club (Canada) in 2022. He is presently Senior Emeritus Scientist at the GSC.